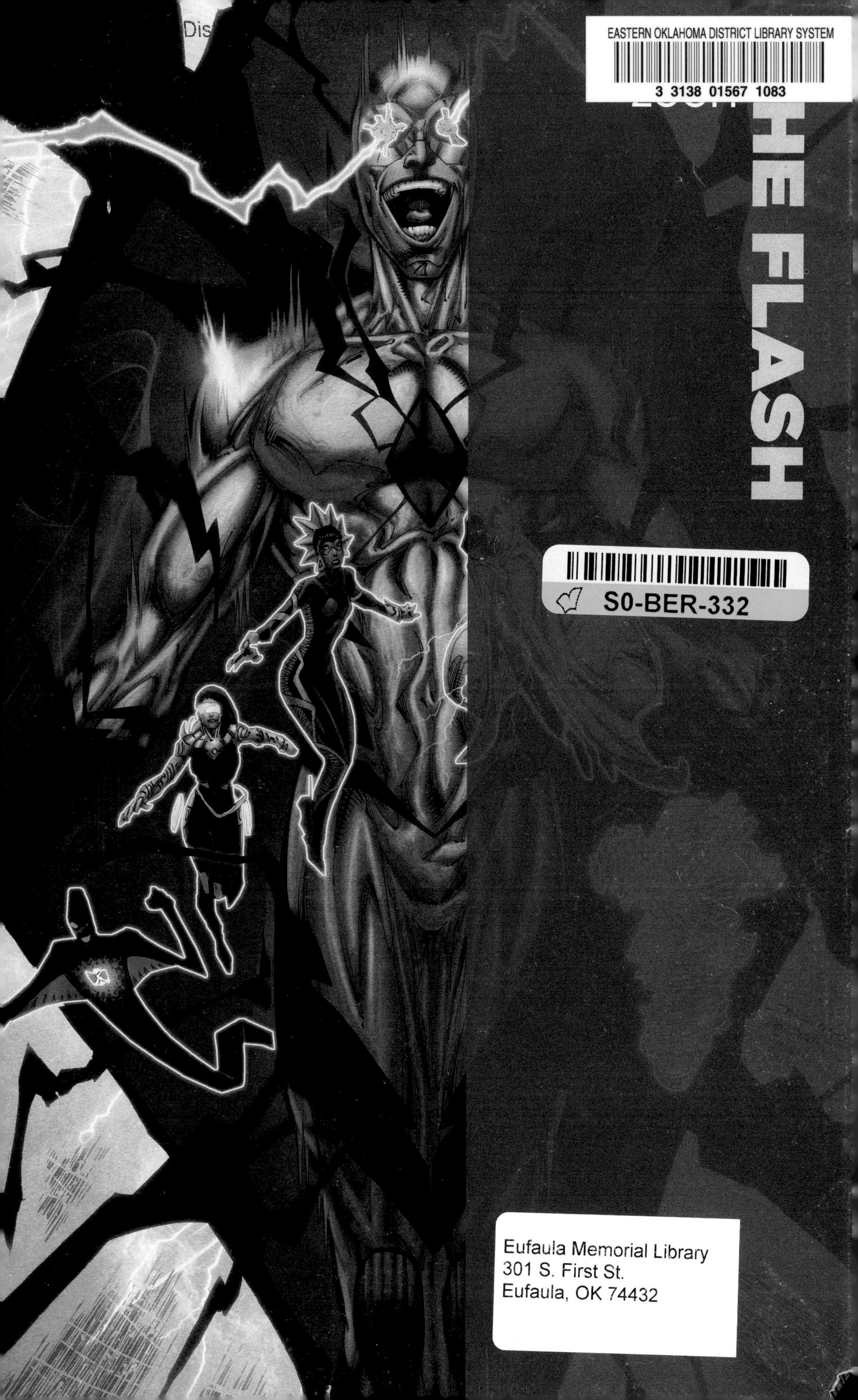
HE FLASH

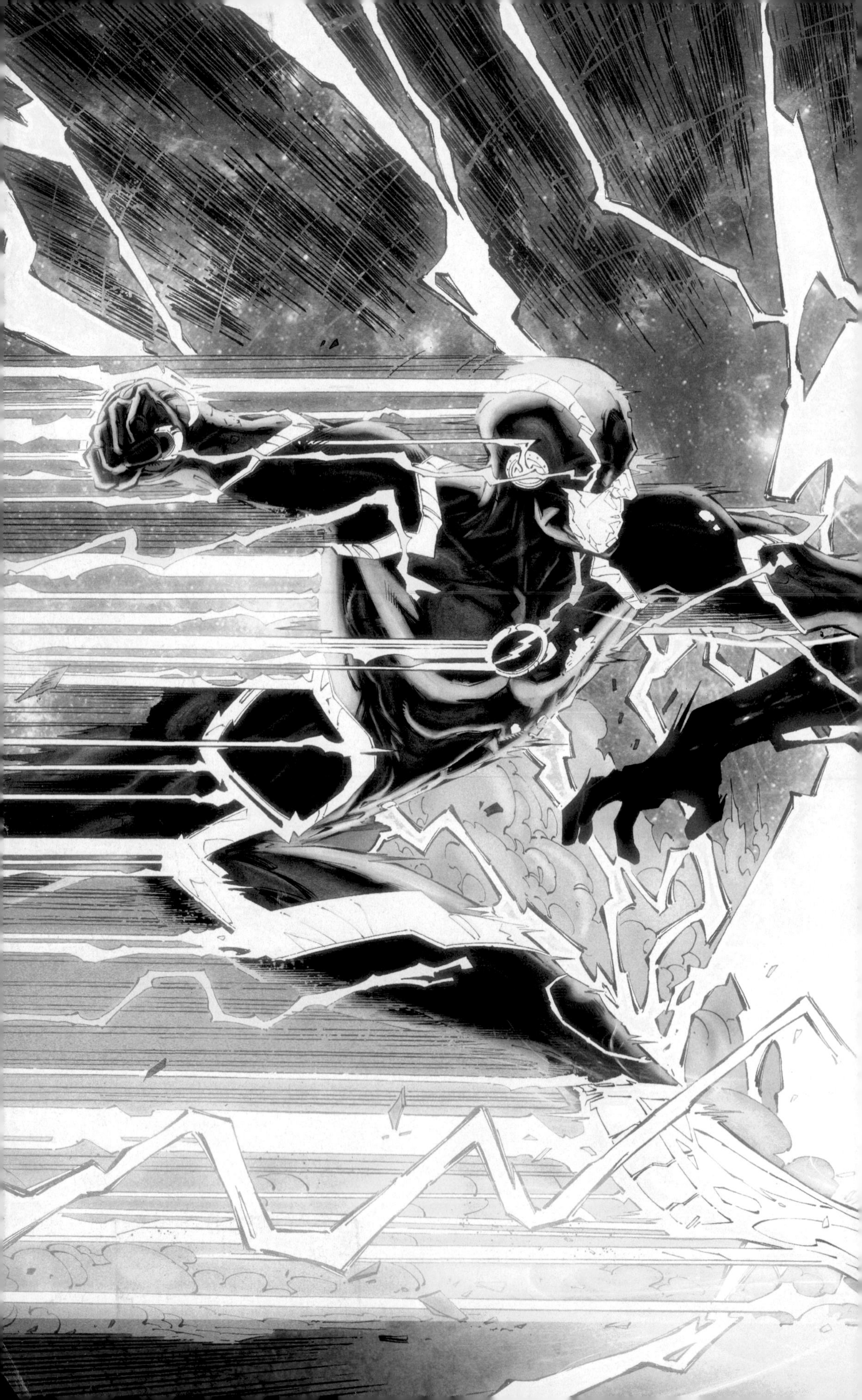

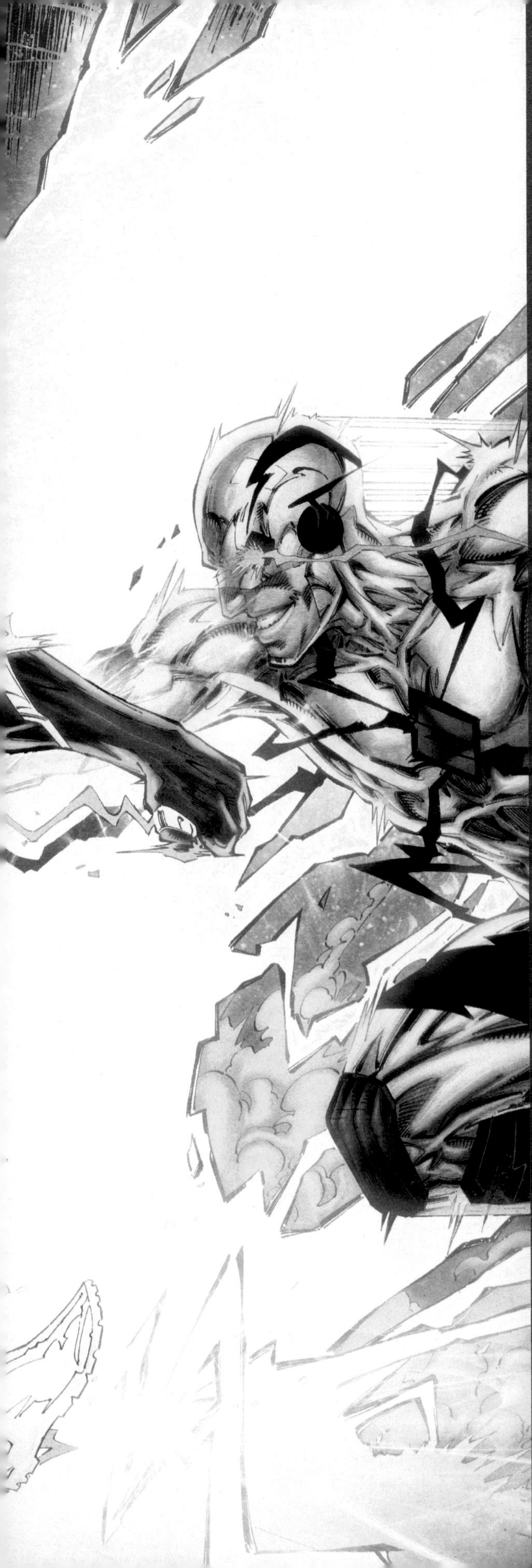

THE FLASH

VOLUME 8
ZOOM

WRITTEN BY
ROBERT VENDITTI
VAN JENSEN

PENCILS BY
BRETT BOOTH
BONG DAZO
VICENTE CIFUENTES
ALÉ GARZA

INKS BY
NORM RAPMUND

COLOR BY
ANDREW DALHOUSE
WENDY BROOME
JEROMY COX

LETTERS BY
PAT BROSSEAU
CARLOS M. MANGUAL

COLLECTION COVER ART BY
BRETT BOOTH,
NORM RAPMUND
& ANDREW DALHOUSE

THE FLASH VOLUME 8: ZOOM

Published by DC Comics. Compilation and all new material Copyright © 2016 DC Comics. All Rights Reserved.

Originally published online as DC SNEAK PEEK: THE FLASH 1 and in single magazine form as THE FLASH 42-47 and
THE FLASH ANNUAL 4 Copyright © 2015, 2016 DC Comics. All Rights Reserved. All characters, their distinctive likenesses and related
elements featured in this publication are trademarks of DC Comics. The stories, characters and incidents featured in this publication
are entirely fictional. DC Comics does not read or accept unsolicited ideas, stories or artwork.

DC Comics, 2900 West Alameda Ave., Burbank, CA 91505
Printed by LSC Communications, Salem, VA, USA. 10/14/16. First Printing.
ISBN: 978-1-4012-6926-5

Library of Congress Cataloging-in-Publication Data

Names: Venditti, Robert, author. | Jensen, Van, author. | Booth, Brett,
illustrator. | Rapmund, Norm, illustrator.
Title: The Flash. Volume 8, Zoom / Robert Venditti, Van Jensen, writers ;
Brett Booth, Norm Rapmund, artists.
Other titles: Zoom
Description: Burbank, CA : DC Comics, [2016]
Identifiers: LCCN 2016017016 | ISBN 9781401263669 (hardback)
Subjects: LCSH: Comic books, strips, etc. | BISAC: COMICS & GRAPHIC NOVELS /
Superheroes.
Classification: LCC PN6728.F53 V47 2016 | DDC 741.5/973—dc23
LC record available at https://lccn.loc.gov/2016017016

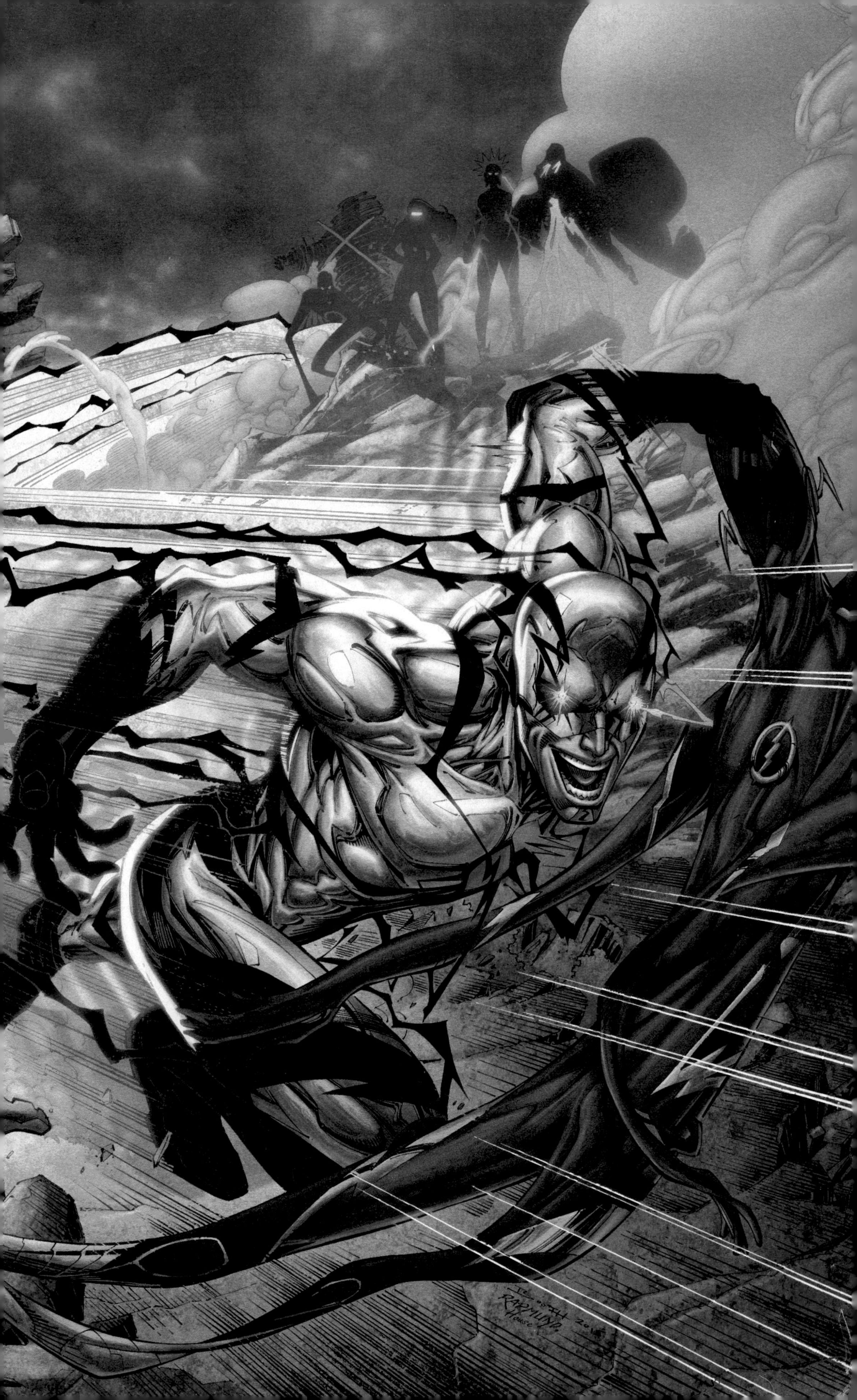

YELLOW

ROBERT VENDITTI, VAN JENSEN writers BRETT BOOTH penciller NORM RAPMUND inker ANDREW DALHOUSE colorist PAT BROSSEAU letterer
cover by BRETT BOOTH, NORM RAPMUND, ANDREW DALHOUSE

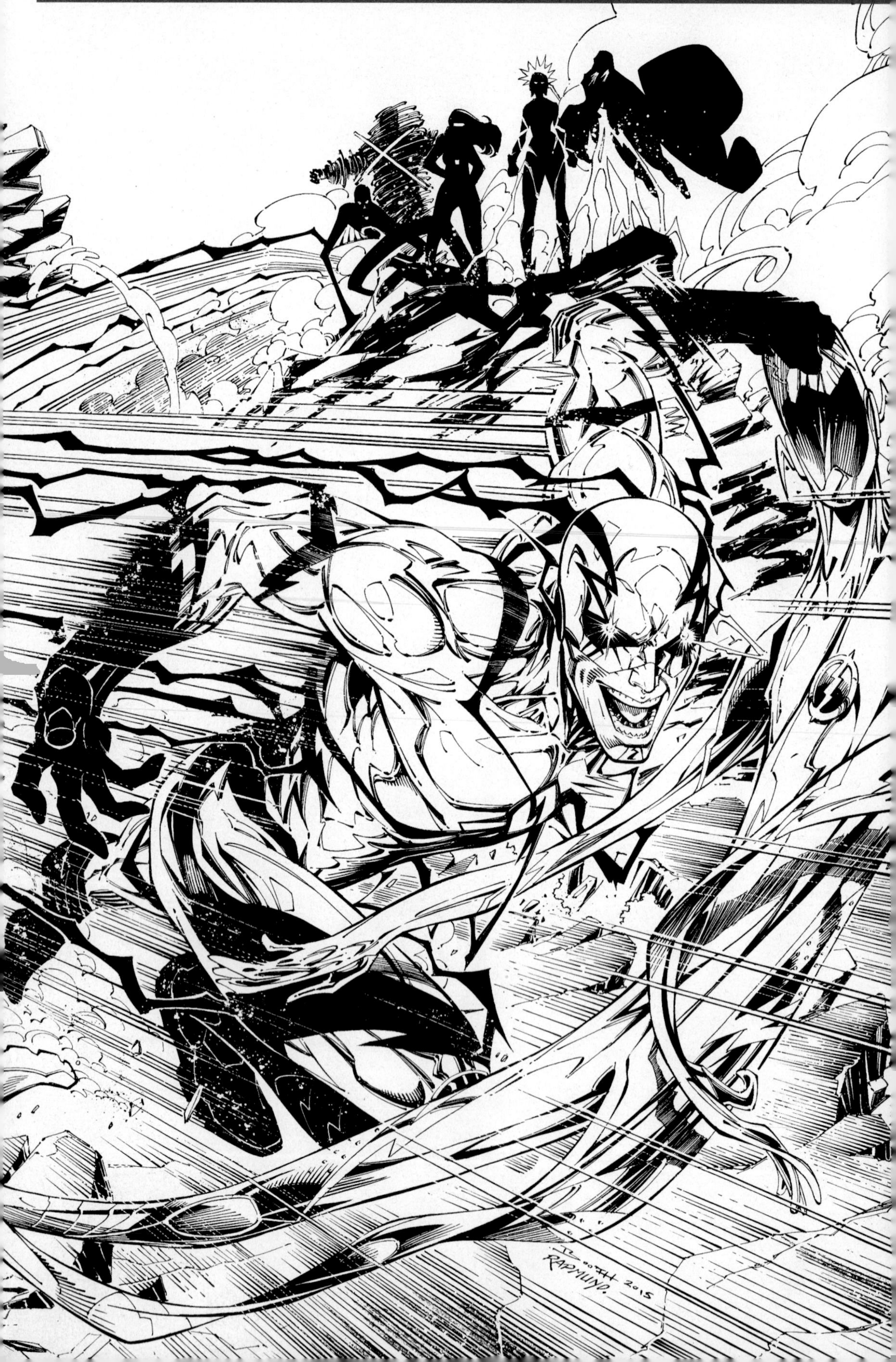
BOOTH 2015
RAPMUND

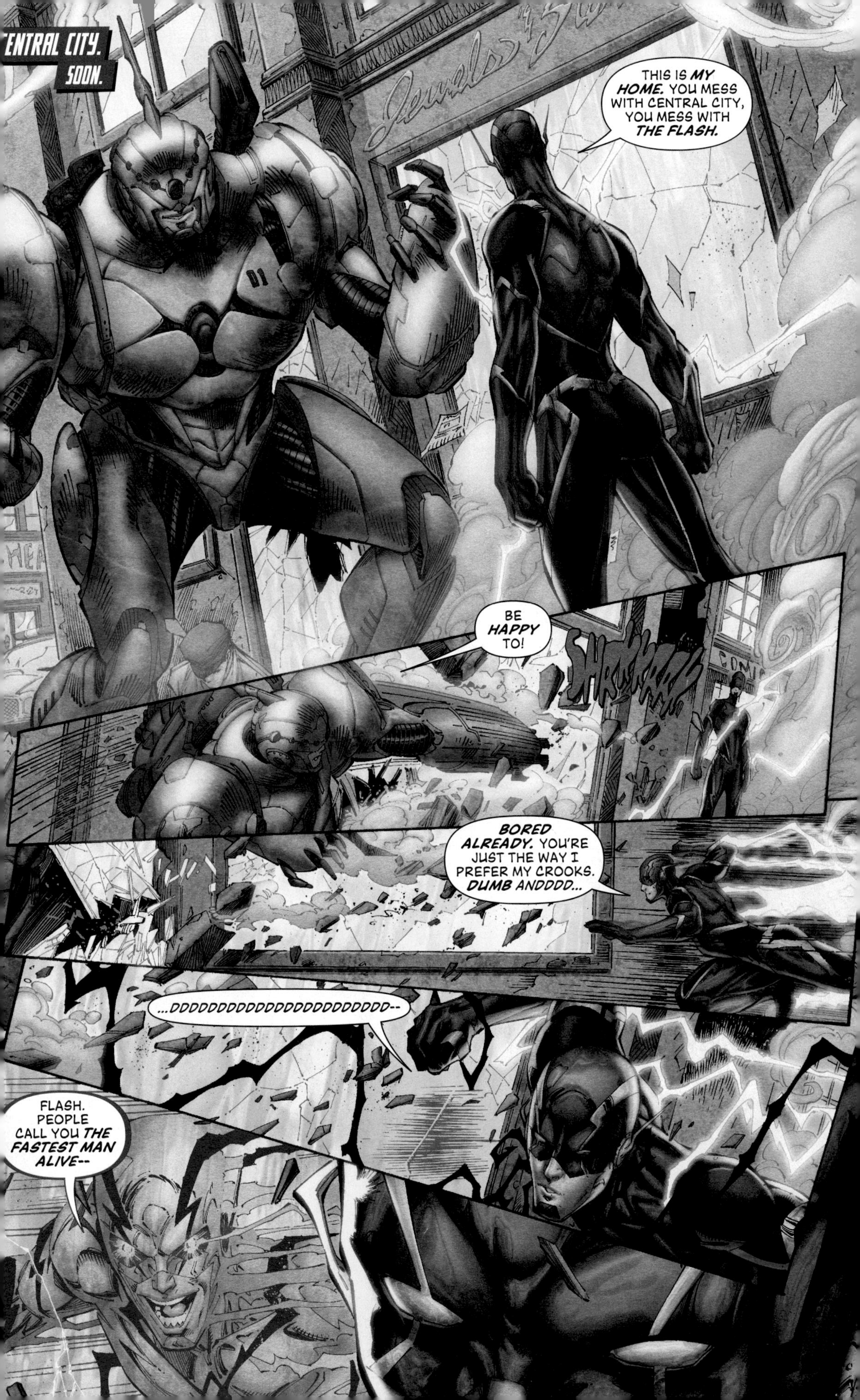
ENTRAL CITY. SOON.
THIS IS MY HOME. YOU MESS WITH CENTRAL CITY, YOU MESS WITH THE FLASH.
BE HAPPY TO!
BORED ALREADY. YOU'RE JUST THE WAY I PREFER MY CROOKS. DUMB ANDDDD...
...DDDDDDDDDDDDDDDDDDDDDDD--
FLASH. PEOPLE CALL YOU THE FASTEST MAN ALIVE--

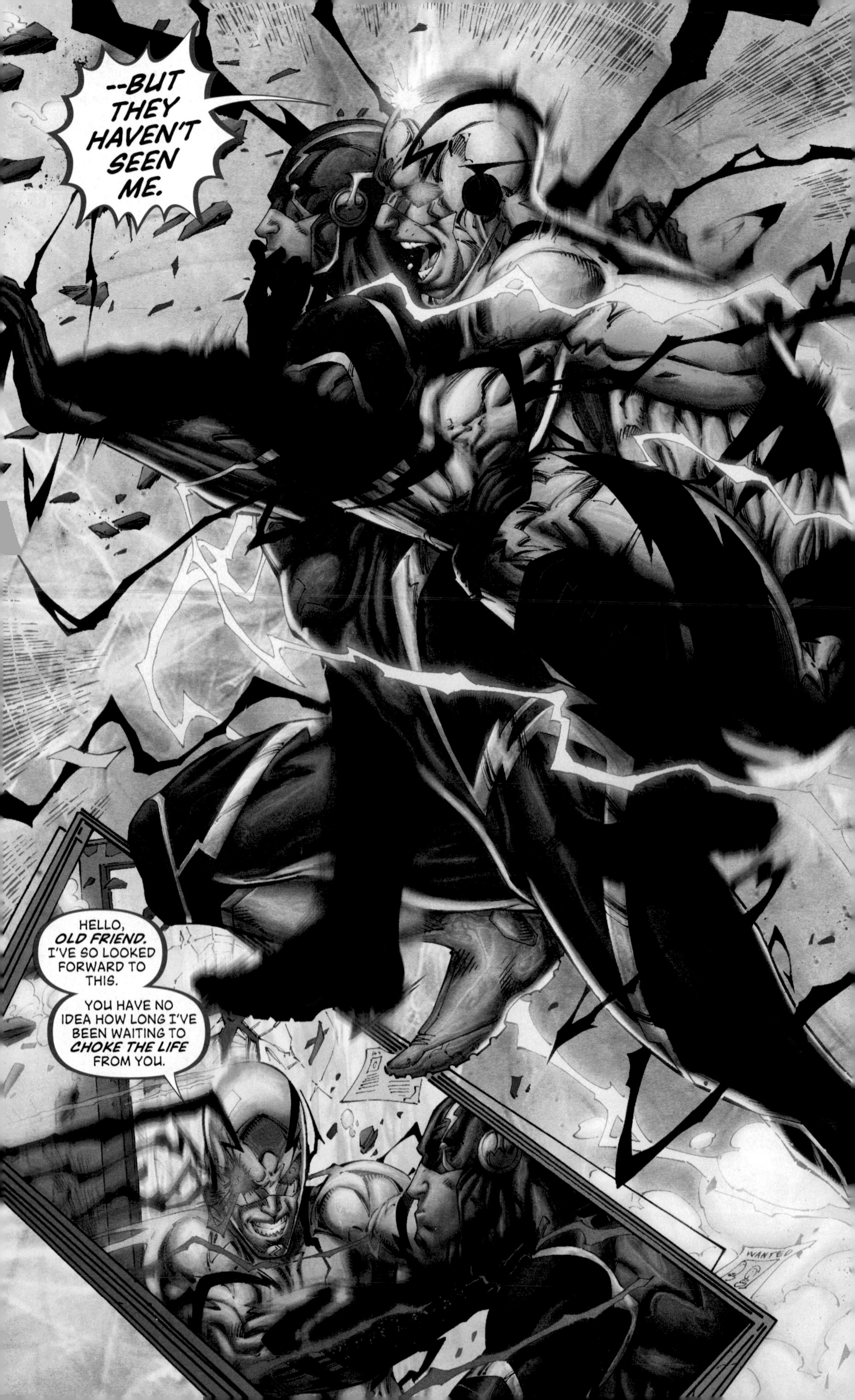

--BUT THEY HAVEN'T SEEN ME.
HELLO, OLD FRIEND. I'VE SO LOOKED FORWARD TO THIS.
YOU HAVE NO IDEA HOW LONG I'VE BEEN WAITING TO CHOKE THE LIFE FROM YOU.
WANTED

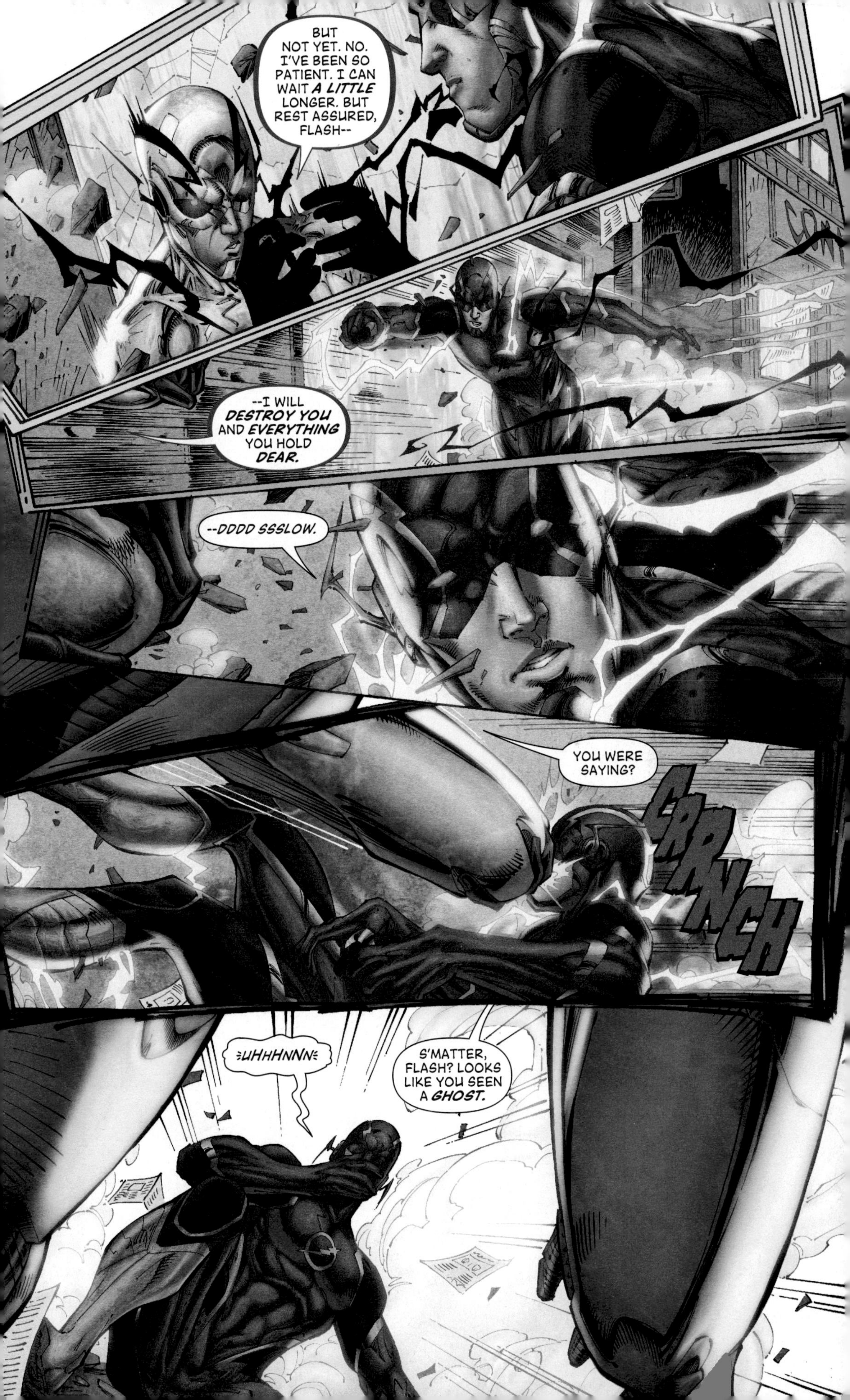
BUT NOT YET. NO. I'VE BEEN SO PATIENT. I CAN WAIT A LITTLE LONGER. BUT REST ASSURED, FLASH--
--I WILL DESTROY YOU AND EVERYTHING YOU HOLD DEAR.
--DDDD SSSLOW.
YOU WERE SAYING?
CRRNCH
UHHHNNN
S'MATTER, FLASH? LOOKS LIKE YOU SEEN A GHOST.

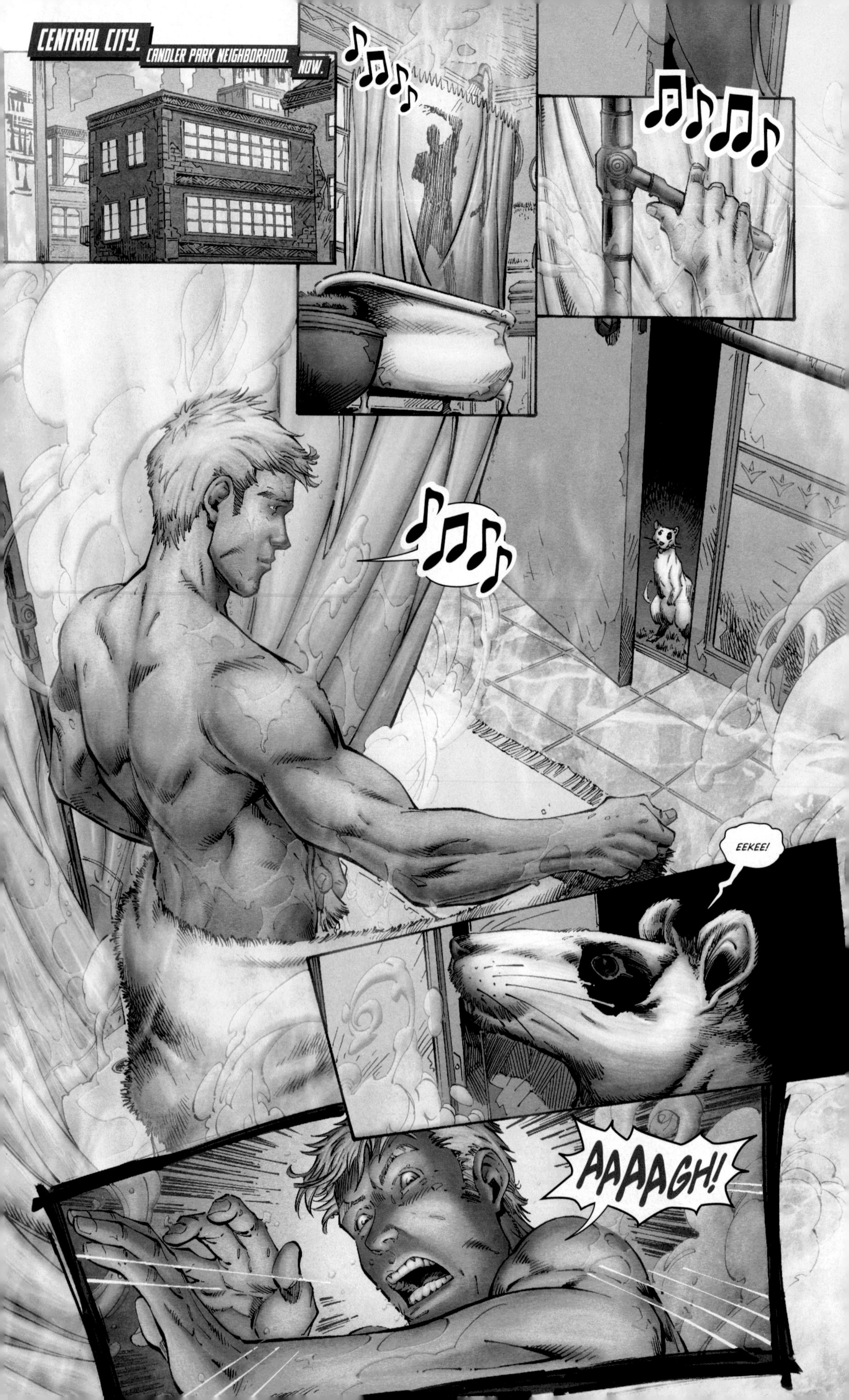
CENTRAL CITY.
CANDLER PARK NEIGHBORHOOD.
NOW.
EEKEE!
AAAAGH!

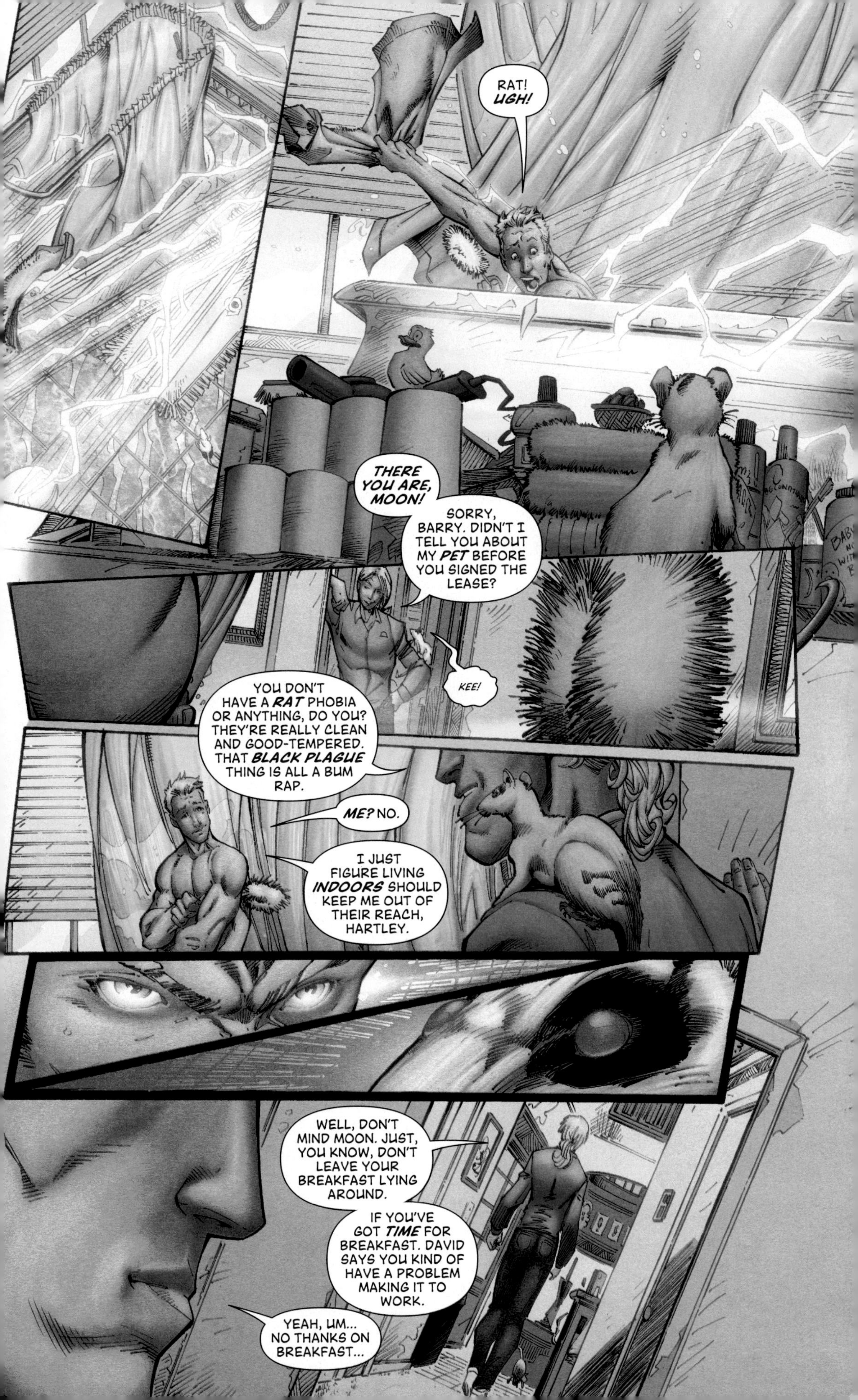
RAT! UGH!
THERE YOU ARE, MOON!
SORRY, BARRY. DIDN'T I TELL YOU ABOUT MY PET BEFORE YOU SIGNED THE LEASE?
KEE!
YOU DON'T HAVE A RAT PHOBIA OR ANYTHING, DO YOU? THEY'RE REALLY CLEAN AND GOOD-TEMPERED. THAT BLACK PLAGUE THING IS ALL A BUM RAP.
ME? NO.
I JUST FIGURE LIVING INDOORS SHOULD KEEP ME OUT OF THEIR REACH, HARTLEY.
WELL, DON'T MIND MOON. JUST, YOU KNOW, DON'T LEAVE YOUR BREAKFAST LYING AROUND.
IF YOU'VE GOT TIME FOR BREAKFAST. DAVID SAYS YOU KIND OF HAVE A PROBLEM MAKING IT TO WORK.
YEAH, UM... NO THANKS ON BREAKFAST...

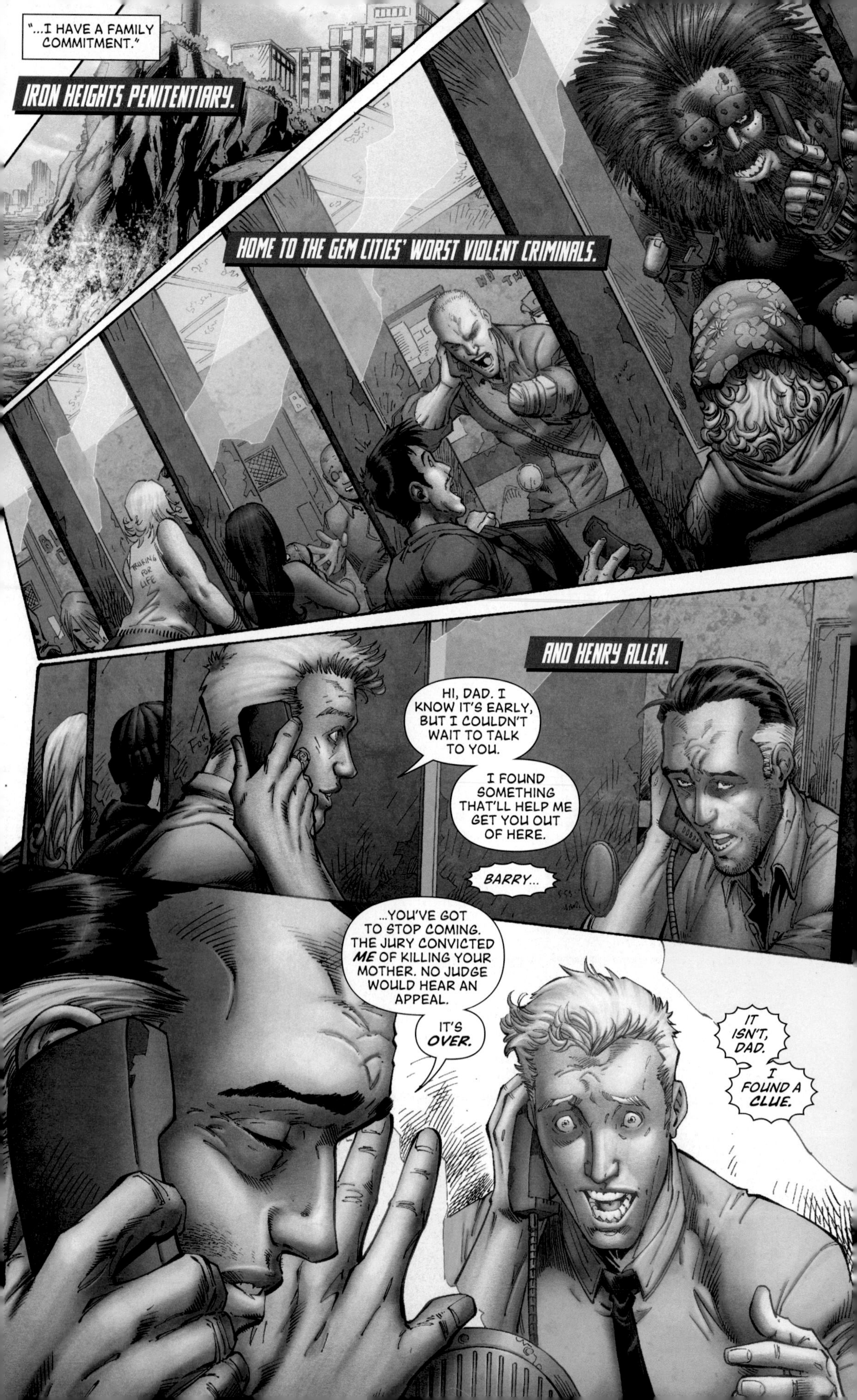

"...I HAVE A FAMILY COMMITMENT."
IRON HEIGHTS PENITENTIARY.
HOME TO THE GEM CITIES' WORST VIOLENT CRIMINALS.
AND HENRY ALLEN.
HI, DAD. I KNOW IT'S EARLY, BUT I COULDN'T WAIT TO TALK TO YOU.
I FOUND SOMETHING THAT'LL HELP ME GET YOU OUT OF HERE.
BARRY...
...YOU'VE GOT TO STOP COMING. THE JURY CONVICTED ME OF KILLING YOUR MOTHER. NO JUDGE WOULD HEAR AN APPEAL.
IT'S OVER.
IT ISN'T, DAD.
I FOUND A CLUE.

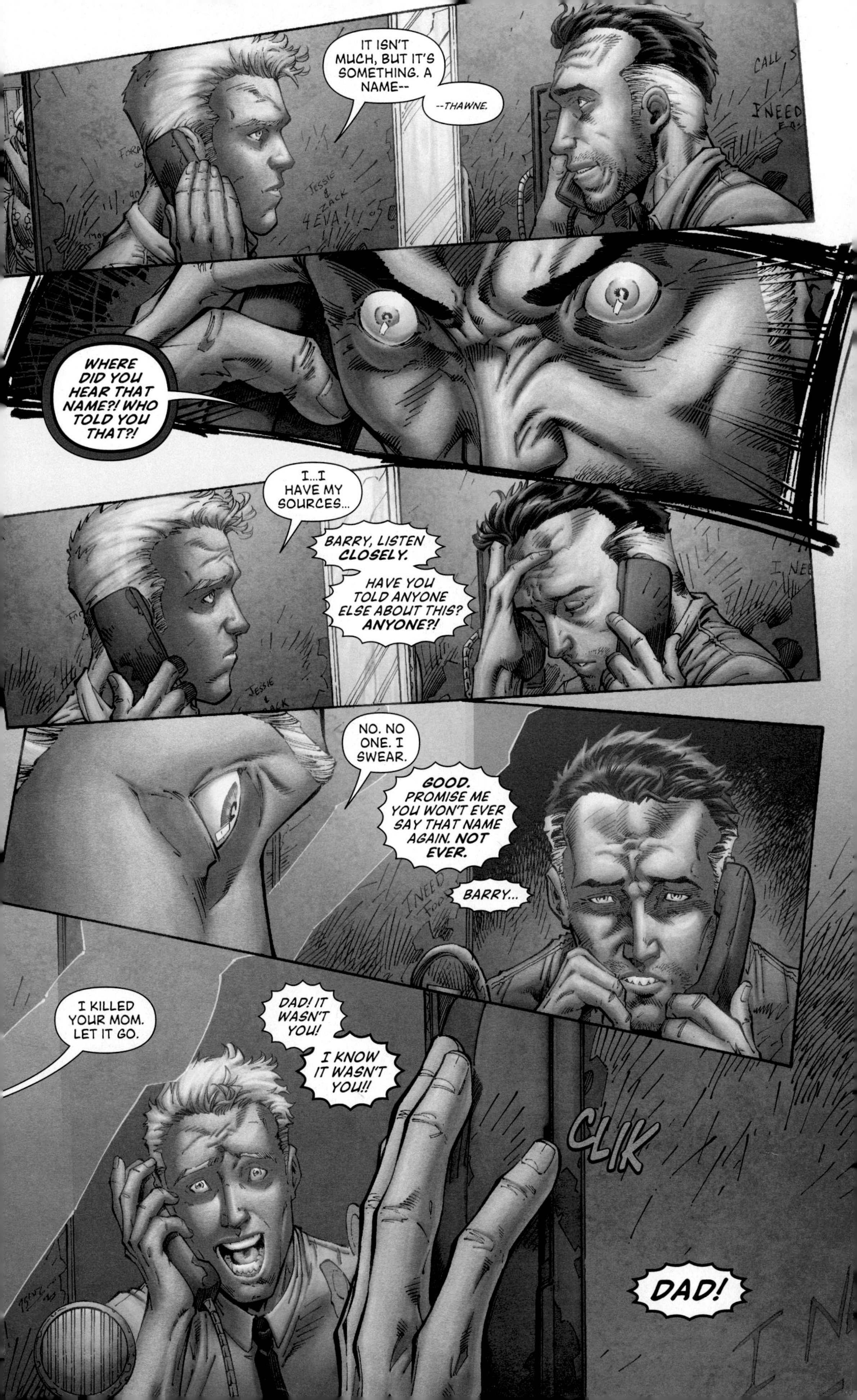
IT ISN'T MUCH, BUT IT'S SOMETHING. A NAME--
--THAWNE.
WHERE DID YOU HEAR THAT NAME?! WHO TOLD YOU THAT?!
I...I HAVE MY SOURCES...
BARRY, LISTEN CLOSELY.
HAVE YOU TOLD ANYONE ELSE ABOUT THIS? ANYONE?!
NO. NO ONE. I SWEAR.
GOOD. PROMISE ME YOU WON'T EVER SAY THAT NAME AGAIN. NOT EVER.
BARRY...
I KILLED YOUR MOM. LET IT GO.
DAD! IT WASN'T YOU!
I KNOW IT WASN'T YOU!!
CLIK
DAD!

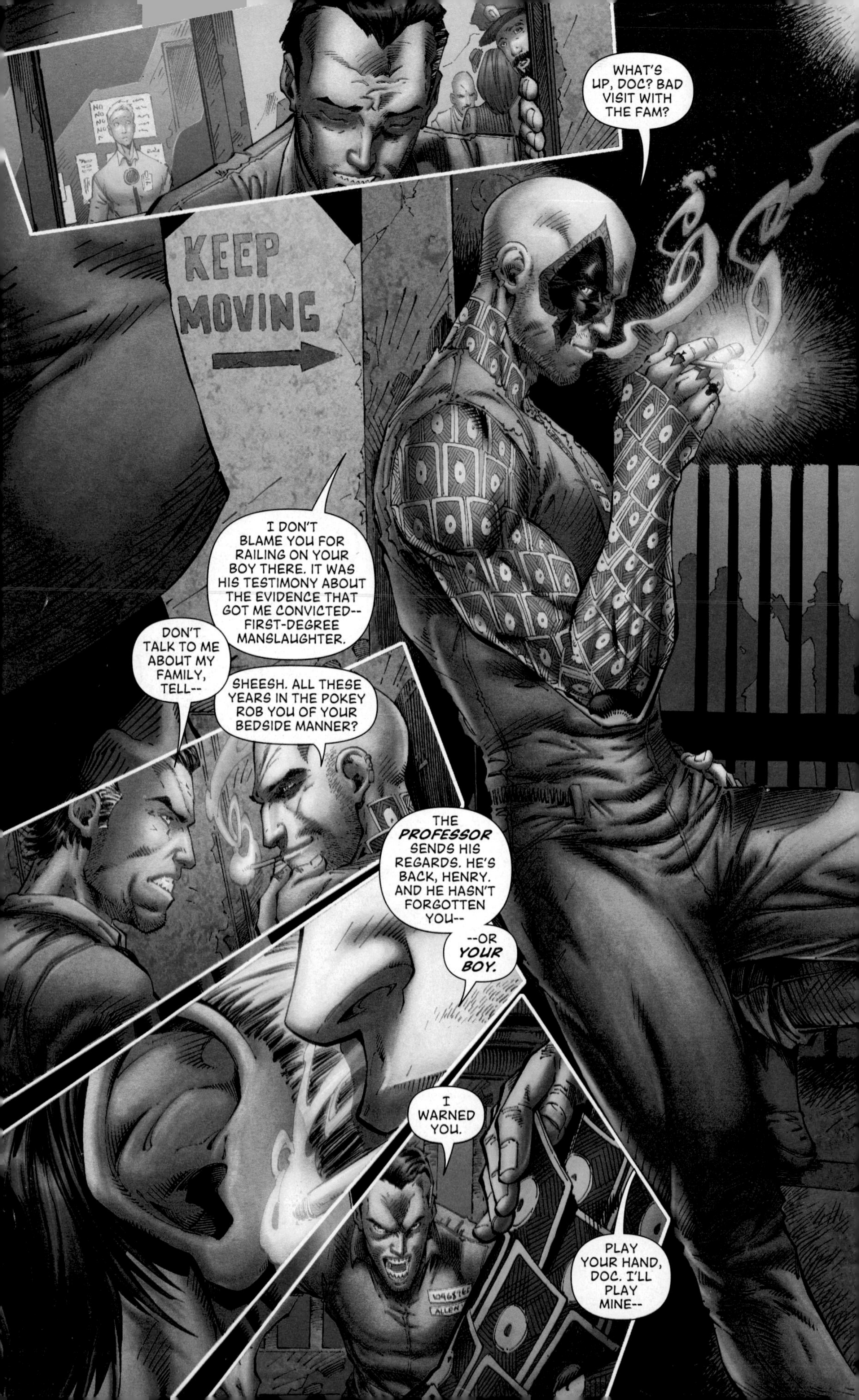
WHAT'S UP, DOC? BAD VISIT WITH THE FAM?
KEEP MOVING
I DON'T BLAME YOU FOR RAILING ON YOUR BOY THERE. IT WAS HIS TESTIMONY ABOUT THE EVIDENCE THAT GOT ME CONVICTED-- FIRST-DEGREE MANSLAUGHTER.
DON'T TALK TO ME ABOUT MY FAMILY, TELL--
SHEESH. ALL THESE YEARS IN THE POKEY ROB YOU OF YOUR BEDSIDE MANNER?
THE *PROFESSOR* SENDS HIS REGARDS. HE'S BACK, HENRY. AND HE HASN'T FORGOTTEN YOU--
--OR *YOUR BOY.*
I WARNED YOU.
PLAY YOUR HAND, DOC. I'LL PLAY MINE--

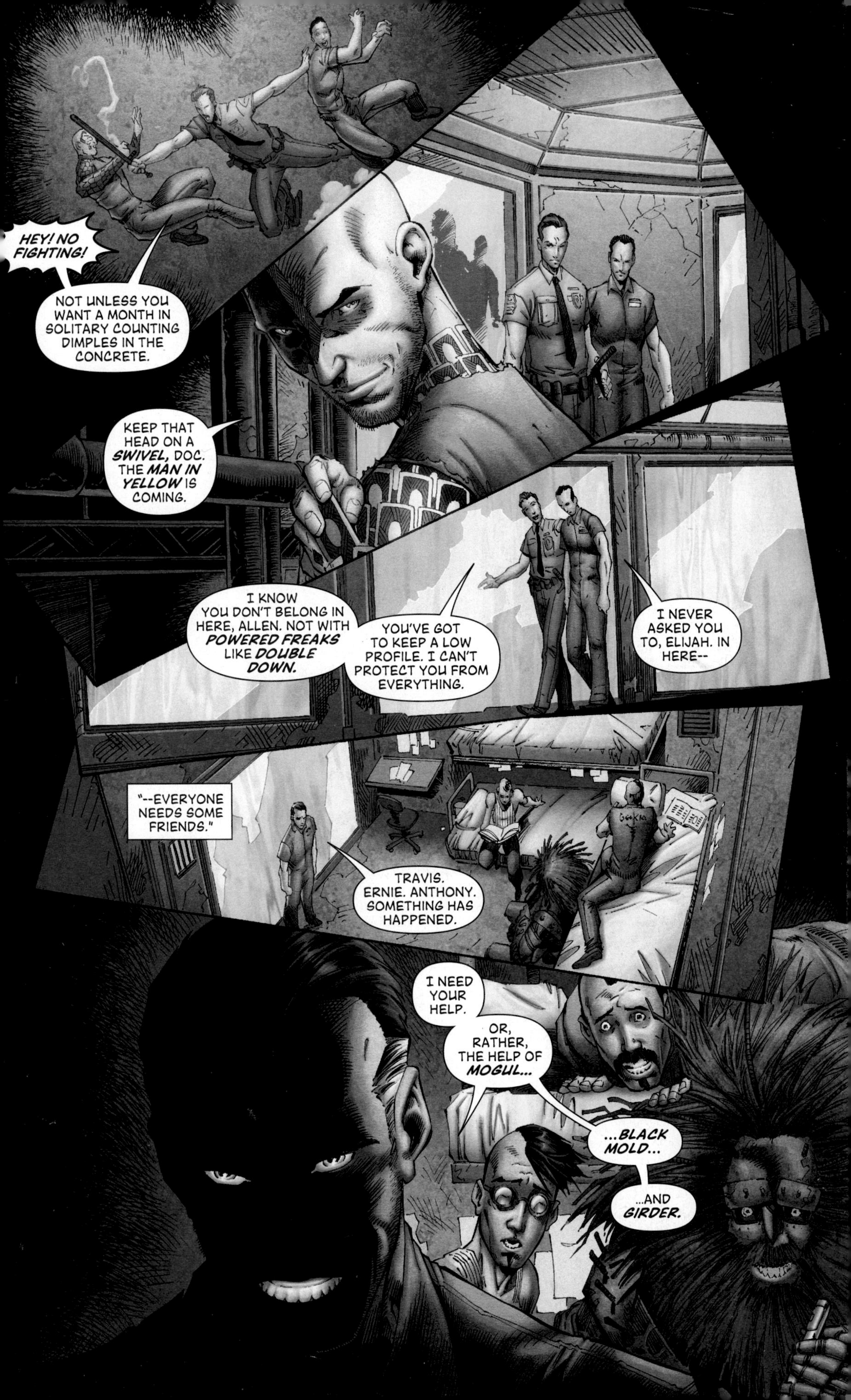
HEY! NO FIGHTING!
NOT UNLESS YOU WANT A MONTH IN SOLITARY COUNTING DIMPLES IN THE CONCRETE.
KEEP THAT HEAD ON A SWIVEL, DOC. THE MAN IN YELLOW IS COMING.
I KNOW YOU DON'T BELONG IN HERE, ALLEN. NOT WITH POWERED FREAKS LIKE DOUBLE DOWN.
YOU'VE GOT TO KEEP A LOW PROFILE. I CAN'T PROTECT YOU FROM EVERYTHING.
I NEVER ASKED YOU TO, ELIJAH. IN HERE--
"--EVERYONE NEEDS SOME FRIENDS."
TRAVIS. ERNIE. ANTHONY. SOMETHING HAS HAPPENED.
I NEED YOUR HELP.
OR, RATHER, THE HELP OF MOGUL...
...BLACK MOLD...
...AND GIRDER.

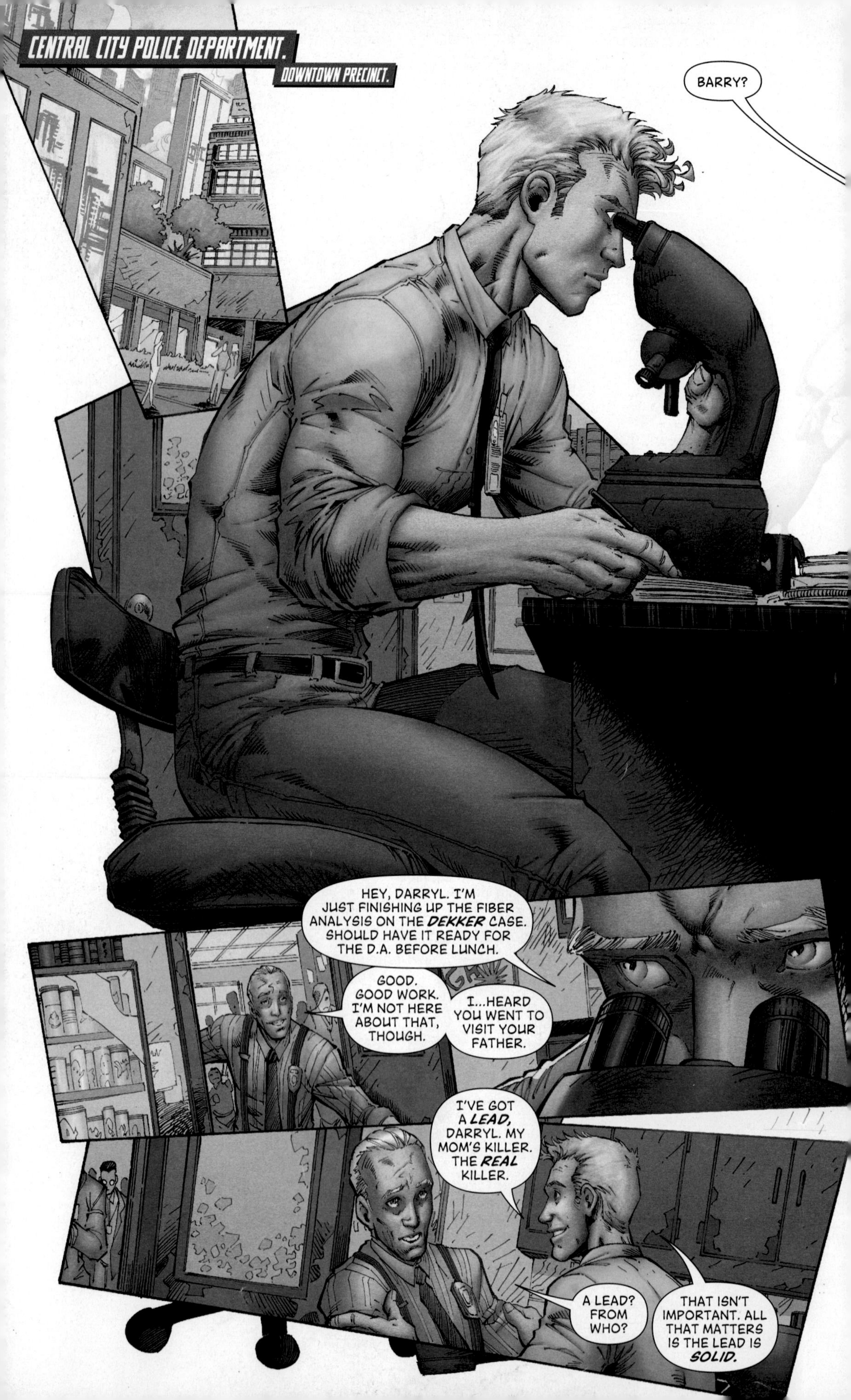

CENTRAL CITY POLICE DEPARTMENT.
DOWNTOWN PRECINCT.
BARRY?
HEY, DARRYL. I'M JUST FINISHING UP THE FIBER ANALYSIS ON THE DEKKER CASE. SHOULD HAVE IT READY FOR THE D.A. BEFORE LUNCH.
GOOD. GOOD WORK. I'M NOT HERE ABOUT THAT, THOUGH.
I...HEARD YOU WENT TO VISIT YOUR FATHER.
I'VE GOT A LEAD, DARRYL. MY MOM'S KILLER. THE REAL KILLER.
A LEAD? FROM WHO?
THAT ISN'T IMPORTANT. ALL THAT MATTERS IS THE LEAD IS SOLID.

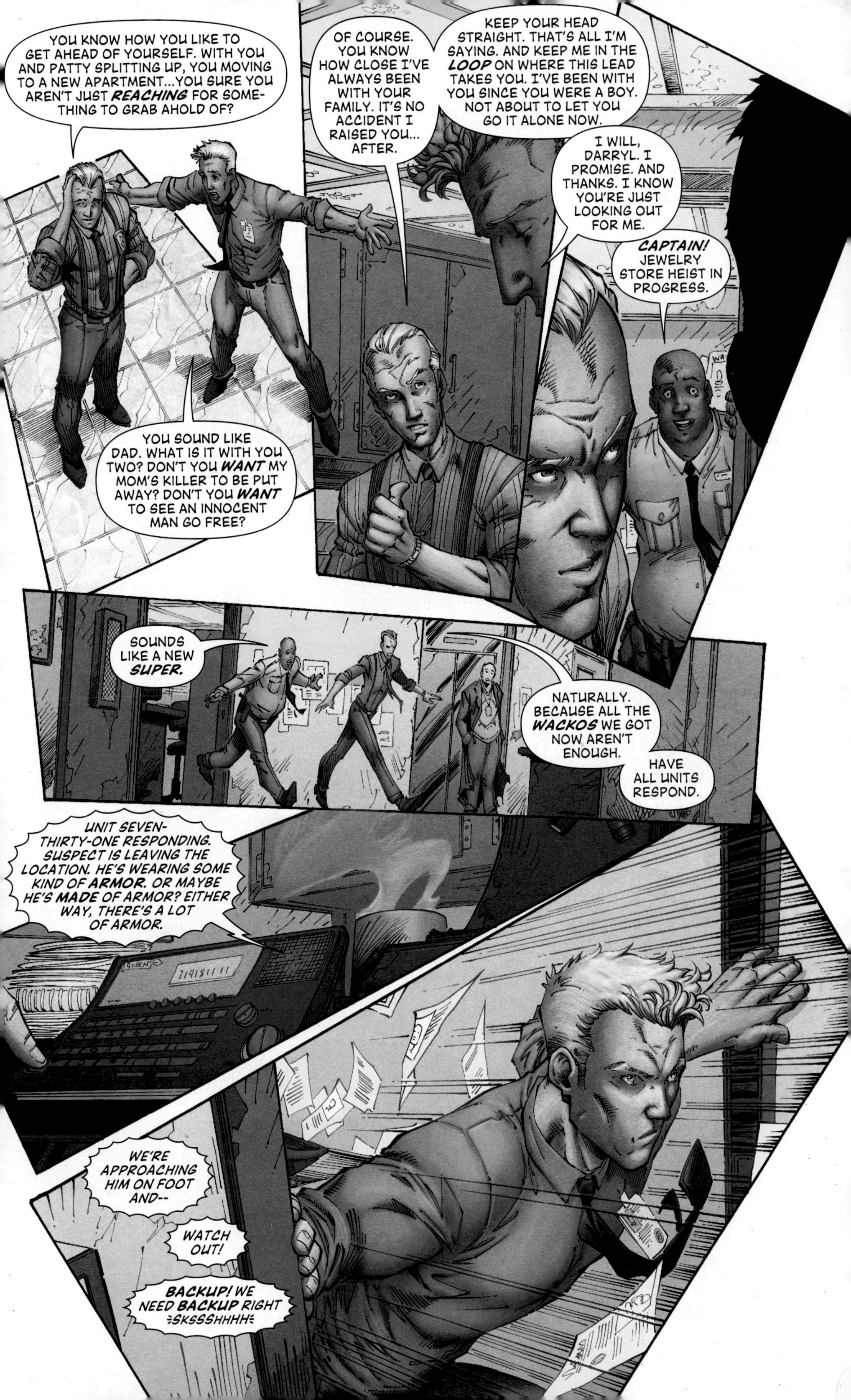
YOU KNOW HOW YOU LIKE TO GET AHEAD OF YOURSELF. WITH YOU AND PATTY SPLITTING UP, YOU MOVING TO A NEW APARTMENT...YOU SURE YOU AREN'T JUST REACHING FOR SOMETHING TO GRAB AHOLD OF?
YOU SOUND LIKE DAD. WHAT IS IT WITH YOU TWO? DON'T YOU WANT MY MOM'S KILLER TO BE PUT AWAY? DON'T YOU WANT TO SEE AN INNOCENT MAN GO FREE?
OF COURSE. YOU KNOW HOW CLOSE I'VE ALWAYS BEEN WITH YOUR FAMILY. IT'S NO ACCIDENT I RAISED YOU... AFTER.
KEEP YOUR HEAD STRAIGHT. THAT'S ALL I'M SAYING. AND KEEP ME IN THE LOOP ON WHERE THIS LEAD TAKES YOU. I'VE BEEN WITH YOU SINCE YOU WERE A BOY. NOT ABOUT TO LET YOU GO IT ALONE NOW.
I WILL, DARRYL. I PROMISE. AND THANKS. I KNOW YOU'RE JUST LOOKING OUT FOR ME.
CAPTAIN! JEWELRY STORE HEIST IN PROGRESS.
SOUNDS LIKE A NEW SUPER.
NATURALLY. BECAUSE ALL THE WACKOS WE GOT NOW AREN'T ENOUGH.
HAVE ALL UNITS RESPOND.
UNIT SEVEN-THIRTY-ONE RESPONDING. SUSPECT IS LEAVING THE LOCATION. HE'S WEARING SOME KIND OF ARMOR. OR MAYBE HE'S MADE OF ARMOR? EITHER WAY, THERE'S A LOT OF ARMOR.
WE'RE APPROACHING HIM ON FOOT AND--
WATCH OUT!
BACKUP! WE NEED BACKUP RIGHT
SKSSSHHHH

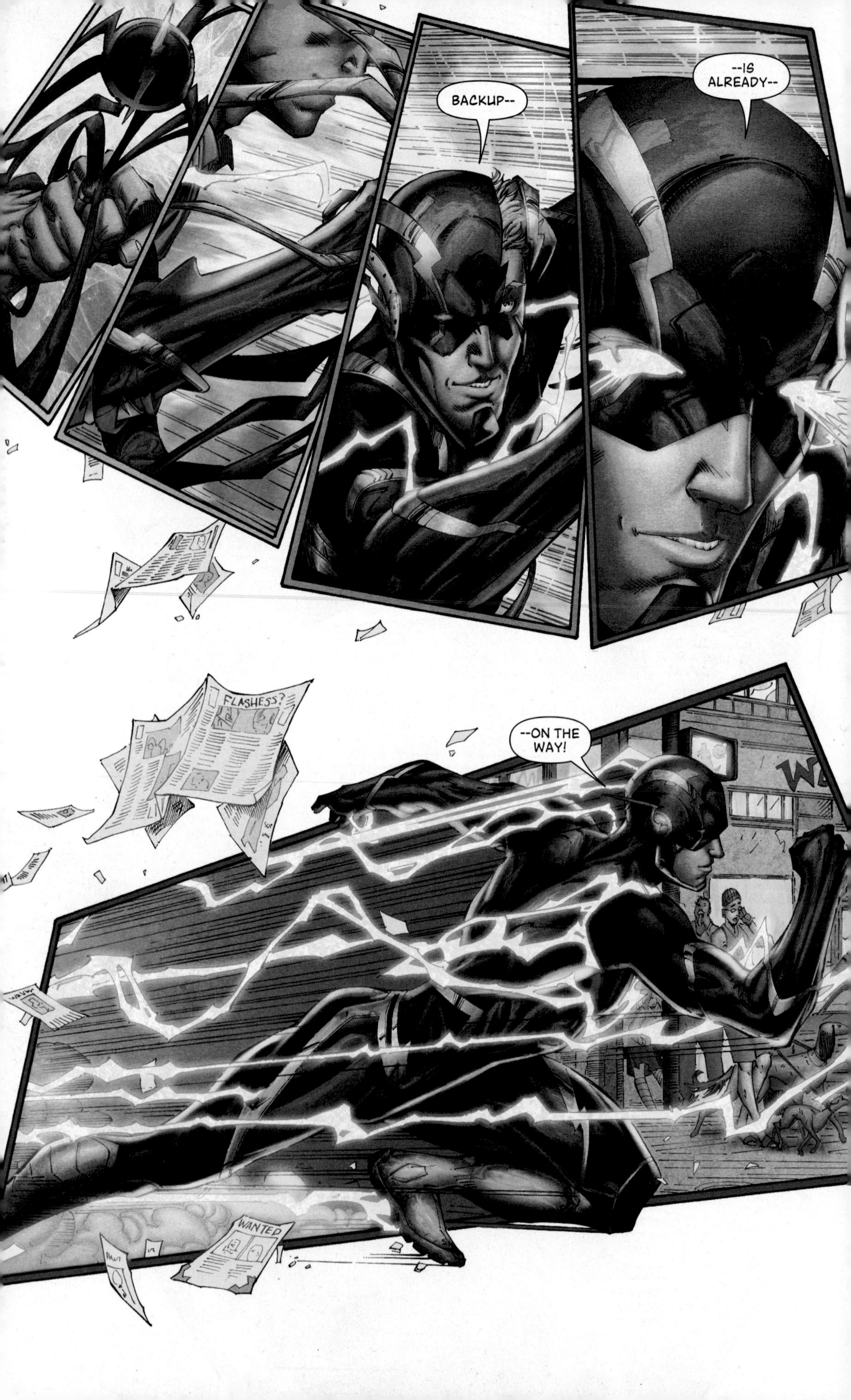
BACKUP--
--IS ALREADY--
FLASHESS?
--ON THE WAY!
WANTED

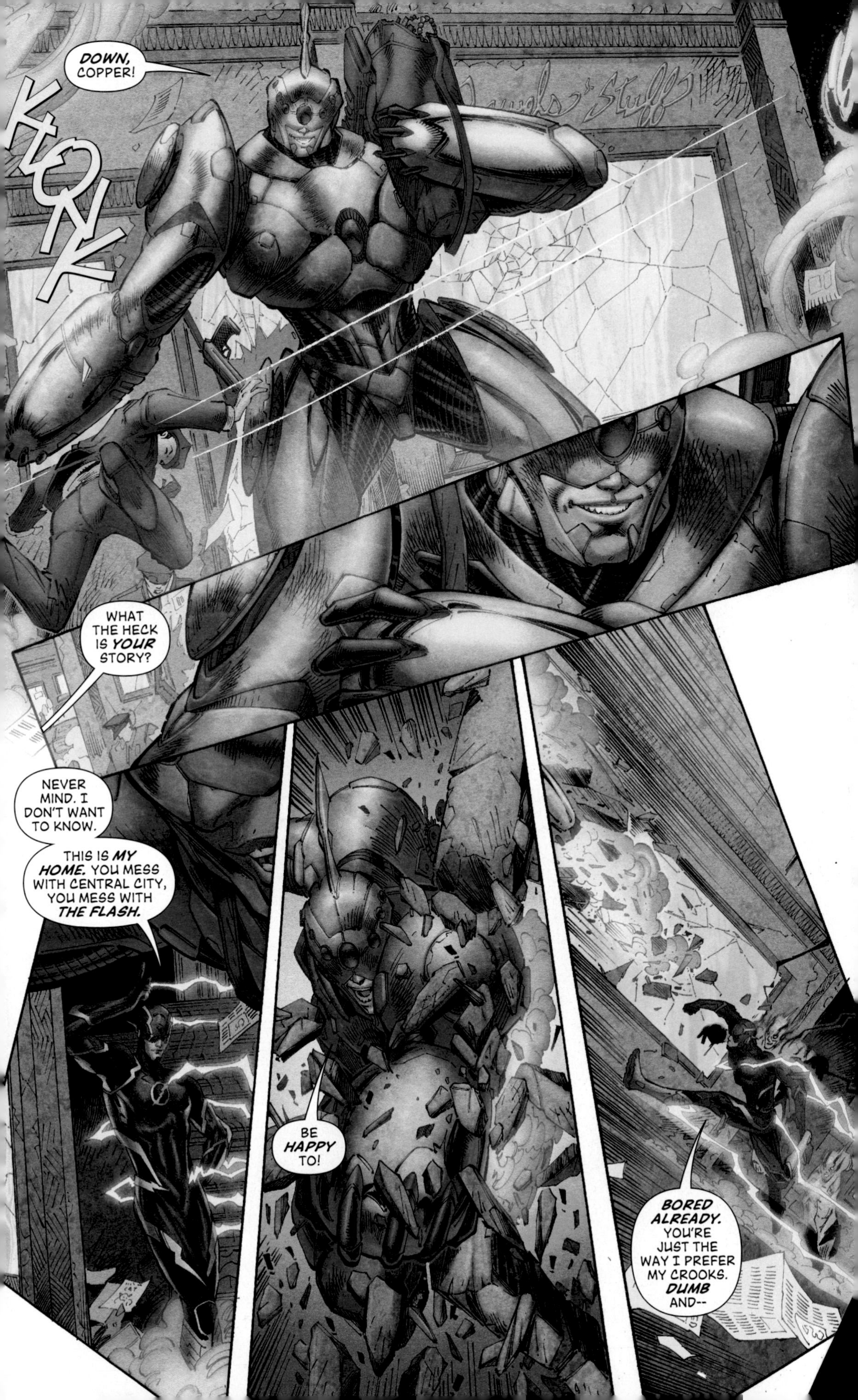
DOWN, COPPER!
KLONK
WHAT THE HECK IS YOUR STORY?
NEVER MIND. I DON'T WANT TO KNOW.
THIS IS MY HOME. YOU MESS WITH CENTRAL CITY, YOU MESS WITH THE FLASH.
BE HAPPY TO!
BORED ALREADY. YOU'RE JUST THE WAY I PREFER MY CROOKS. DUMB AND--

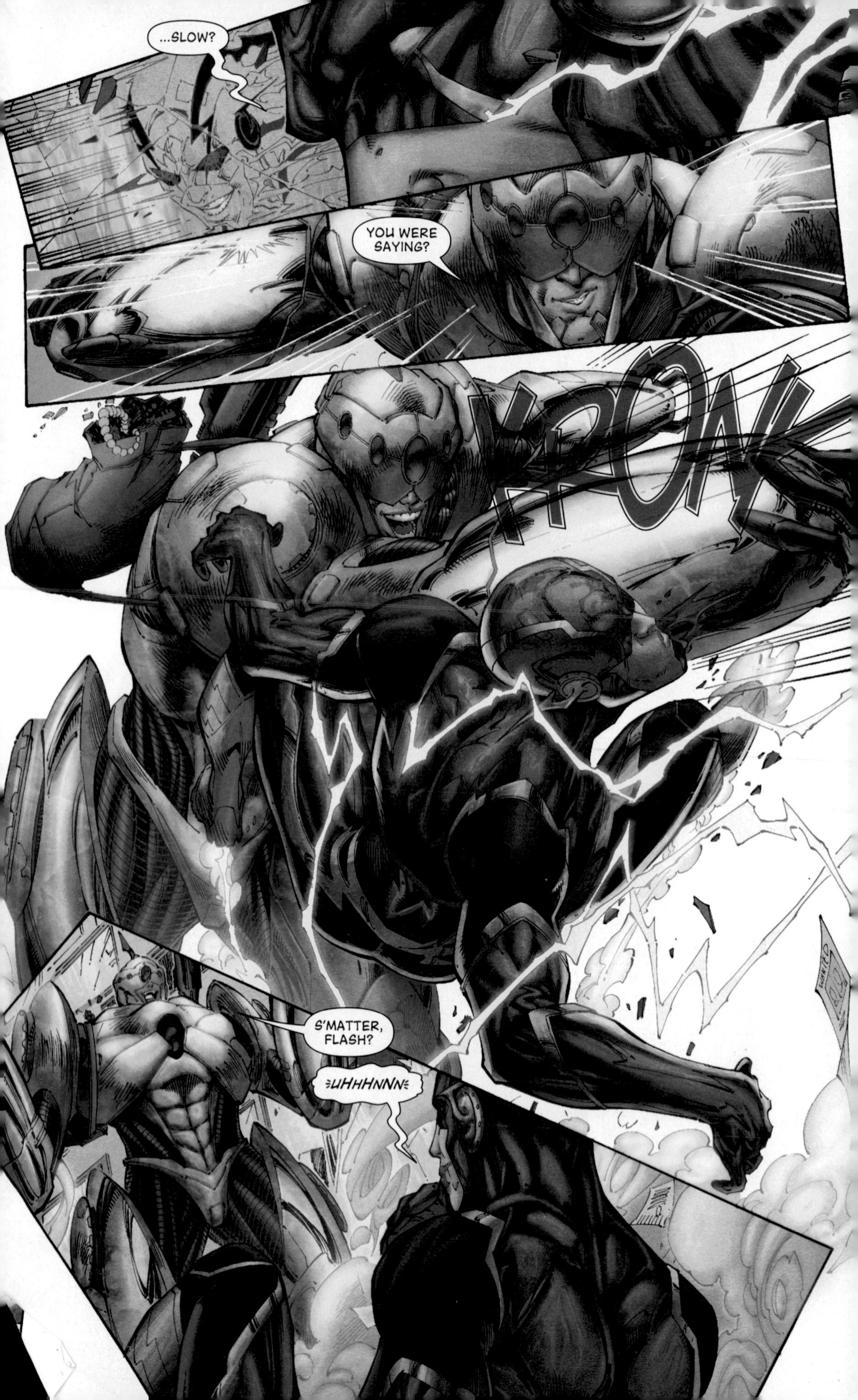
...SLOW?
YOU WERE SAYING?
KRAK!
S'MATTER, FLASH?
UHHHNNN

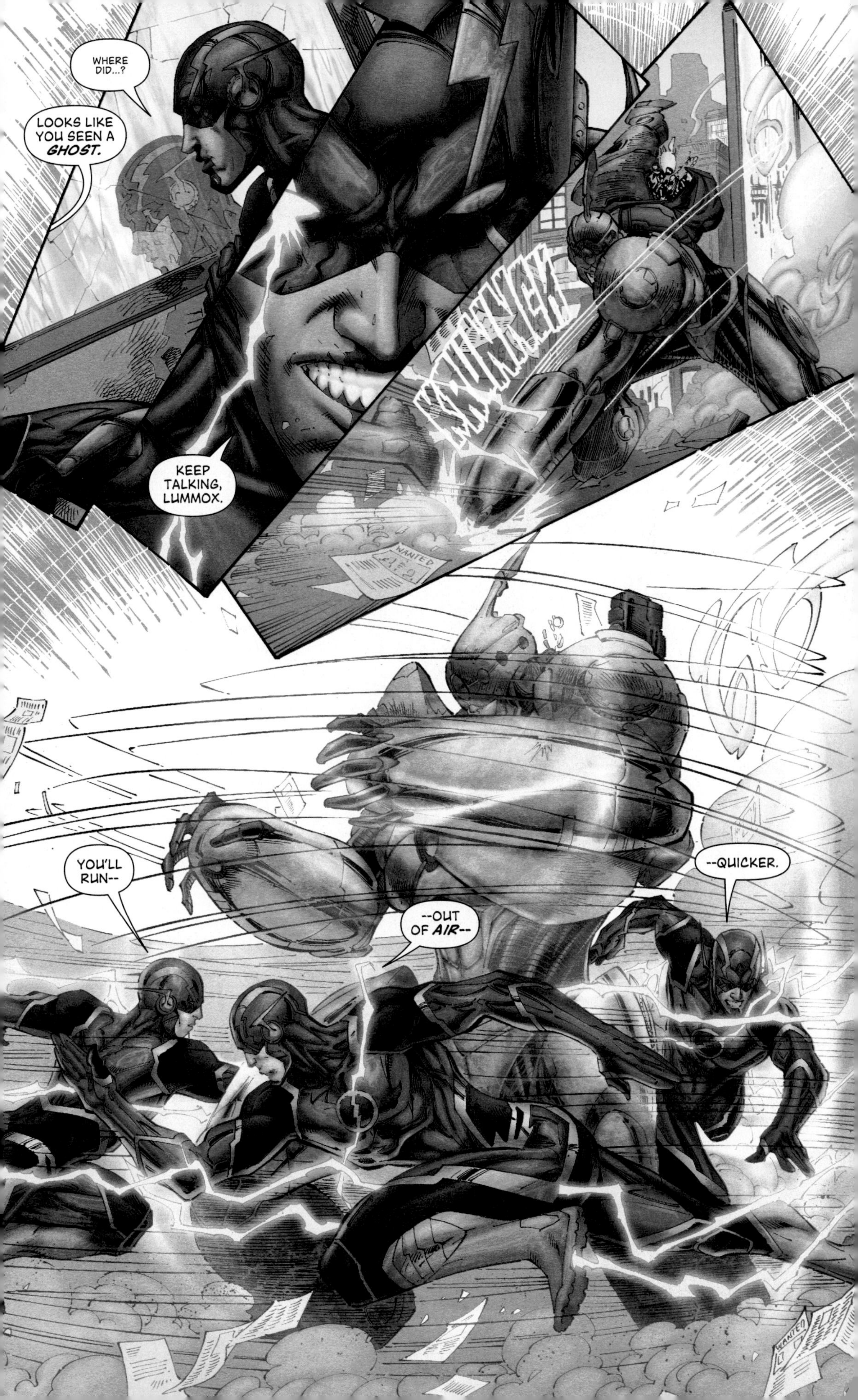
WHERE DID...?
LOOKS LIKE YOU SEEN A *GHOST.*
KEEP TALKING, LUMMOX.
YOU'LL RUN--
--OUT OF *AIR*--
--QUICKER.

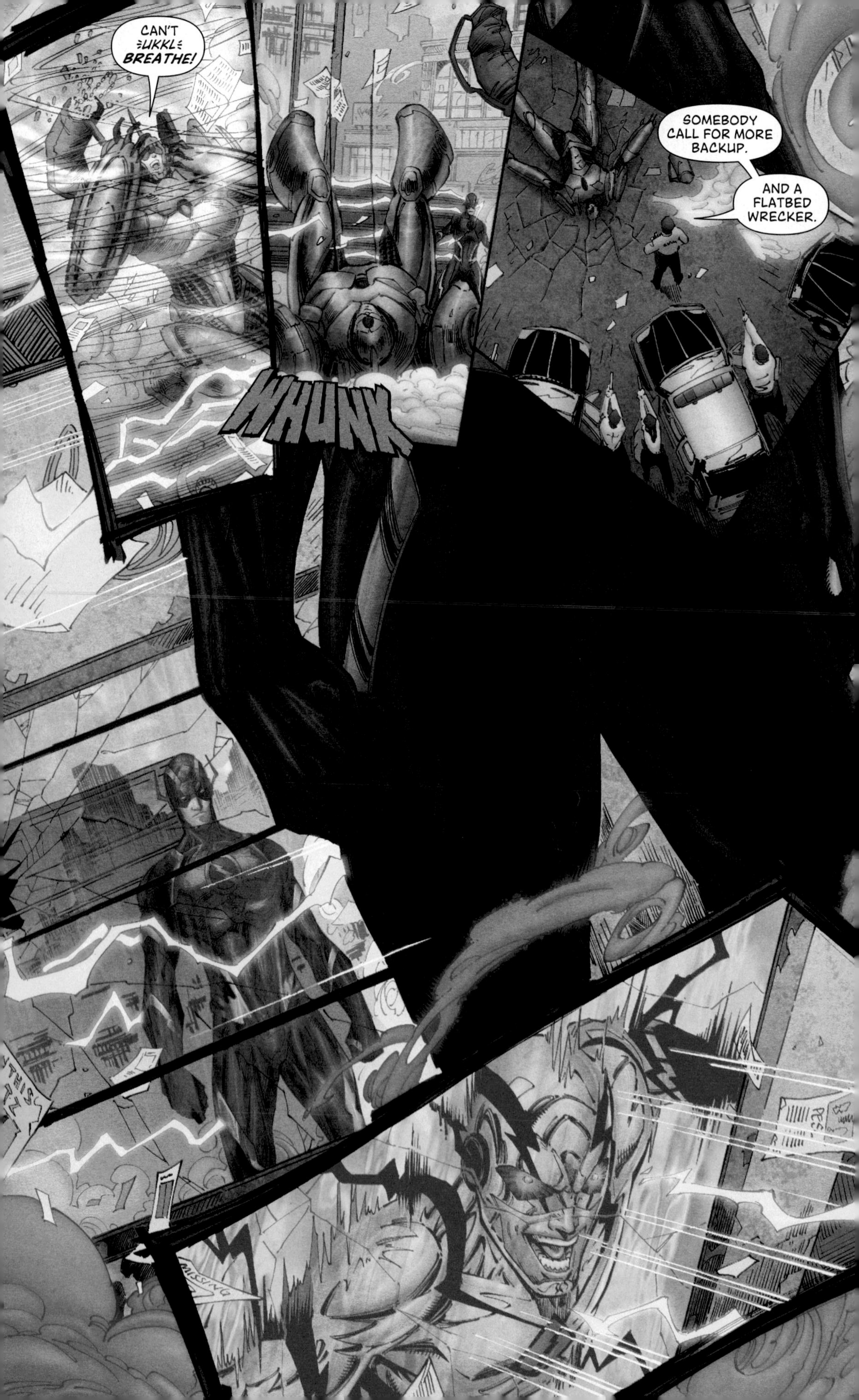
CAN'T ≈UKKL≈ BREATHE!
WHUNK
SOMEBODY CALL FOR MORE BACKUP.
AND A FLATBED WRECKER.

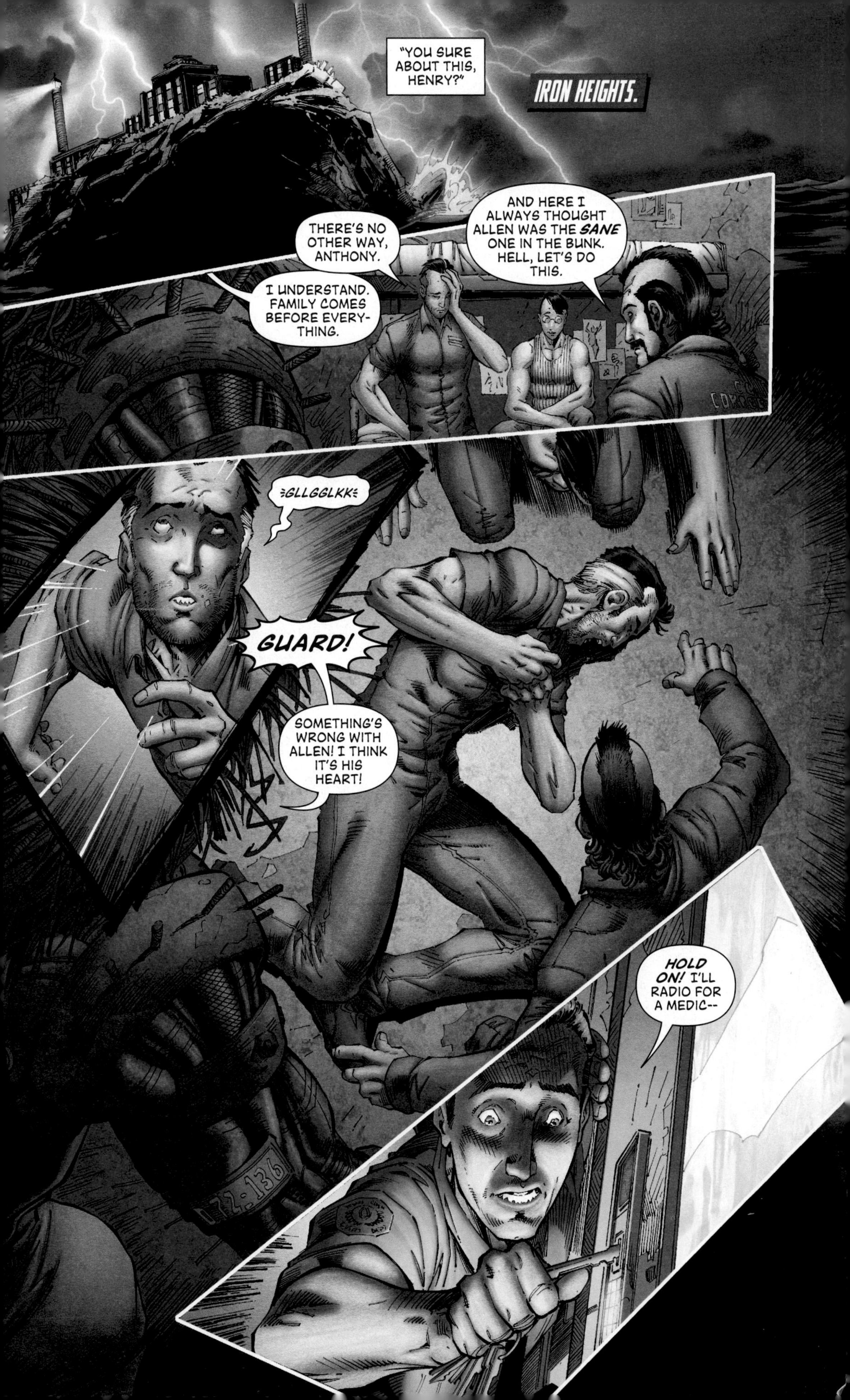
"YOU SURE ABOUT THIS, HENRY?"
IRON HEIGHTS.
THERE'S NO OTHER WAY, ANTHONY.
AND HERE I ALWAYS THOUGHT ALLEN WAS THE SANE ONE IN THE BUNK. HELL, LET'S DO THIS.
I UNDERSTAND. FAMILY COMES BEFORE EVERY-THING.
GLLGGLKK
GUARD!
SOMETHING'S WRONG WITH ALLEN! I THINK IT'S HIS HEART!
HOLD ON! I'LL RADIO FOR A MEDIC--
22-136

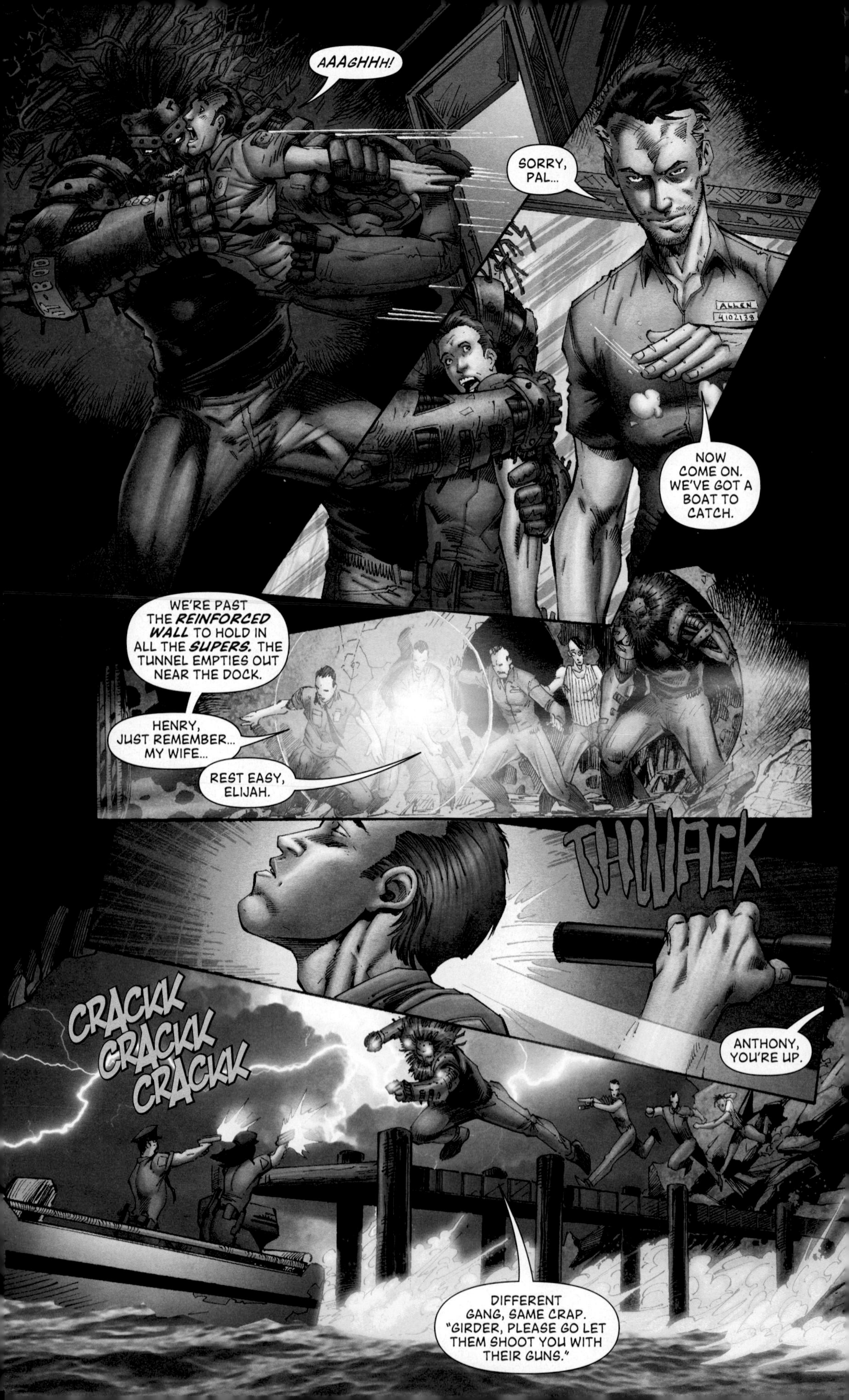
AAAGHHH!
SORRY, PAL...
ALLEN 4102138
NOW COME ON. WE'VE GOT A BOAT TO CATCH.
WE'RE PAST THE **REINFORCED WALL** TO HOLD IN ALL THE **SUPERS.** THE TUNNEL EMPTIES OUT NEAR THE DOCK.
HENRY, JUST REMEMBER... MY WIFE...
REST EASY, ELIJAH.
THWACK
CRACKK CRACKK CRACKK
ANTHONY, YOU'RE UP.
DIFFERENT GANG, SAME CRAP. "GIRDER, PLEASE GO LET THEM SHOOT YOU WITH THEIR GUNS."

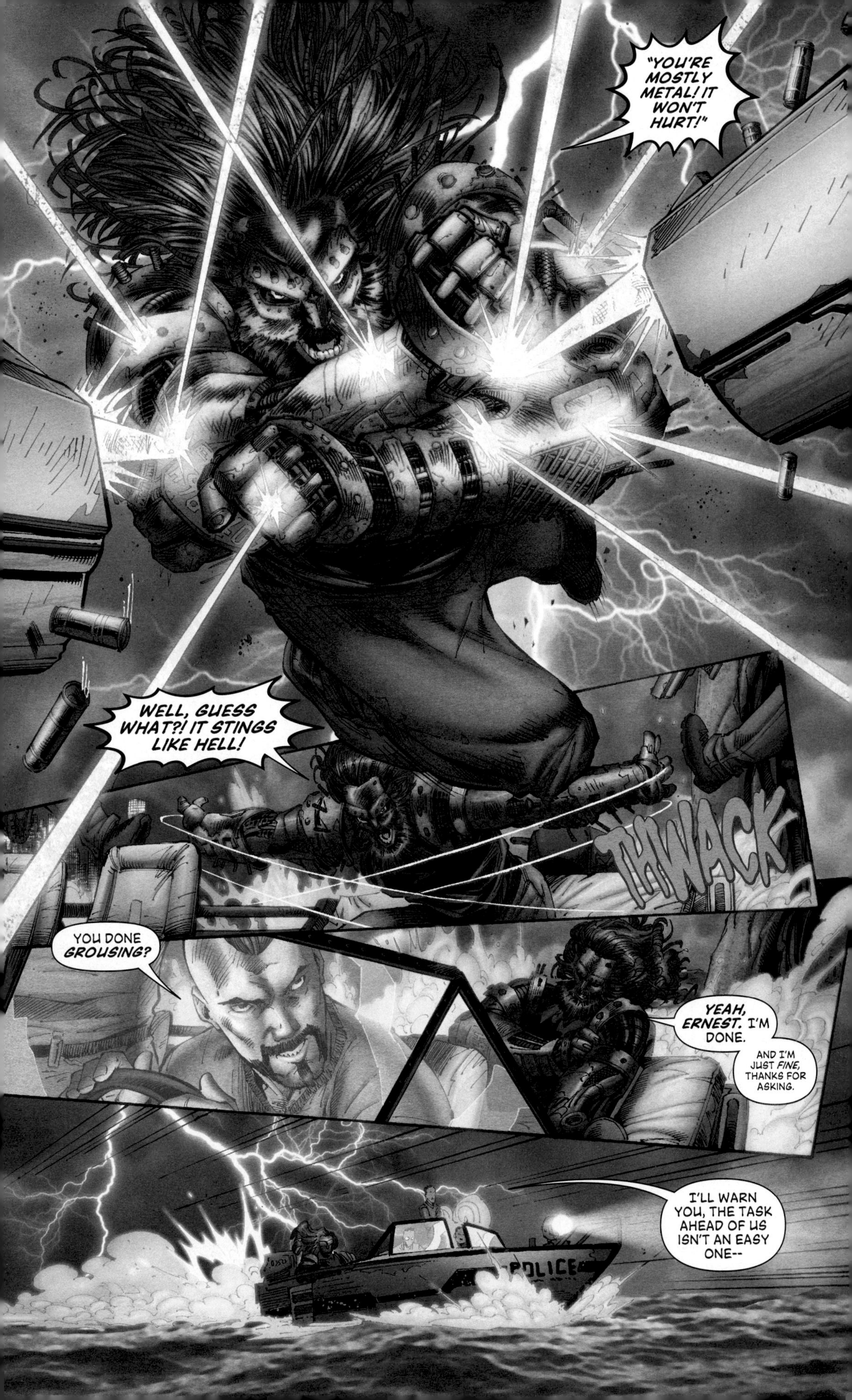
"YOU'RE MOSTLY METAL! IT WON'T HURT!"
WELL, GUESS WHAT?! IT STINGS LIKE HELL!
THWACK
YOU DONE GROUSING?
YEAH, ERNEST. I'M DONE.
AND I'M JUST FINE, THANKS FOR ASKING.
I'LL WARN YOU, THE TASK AHEAD OF US ISN'T AN EASY ONE--
POLICE

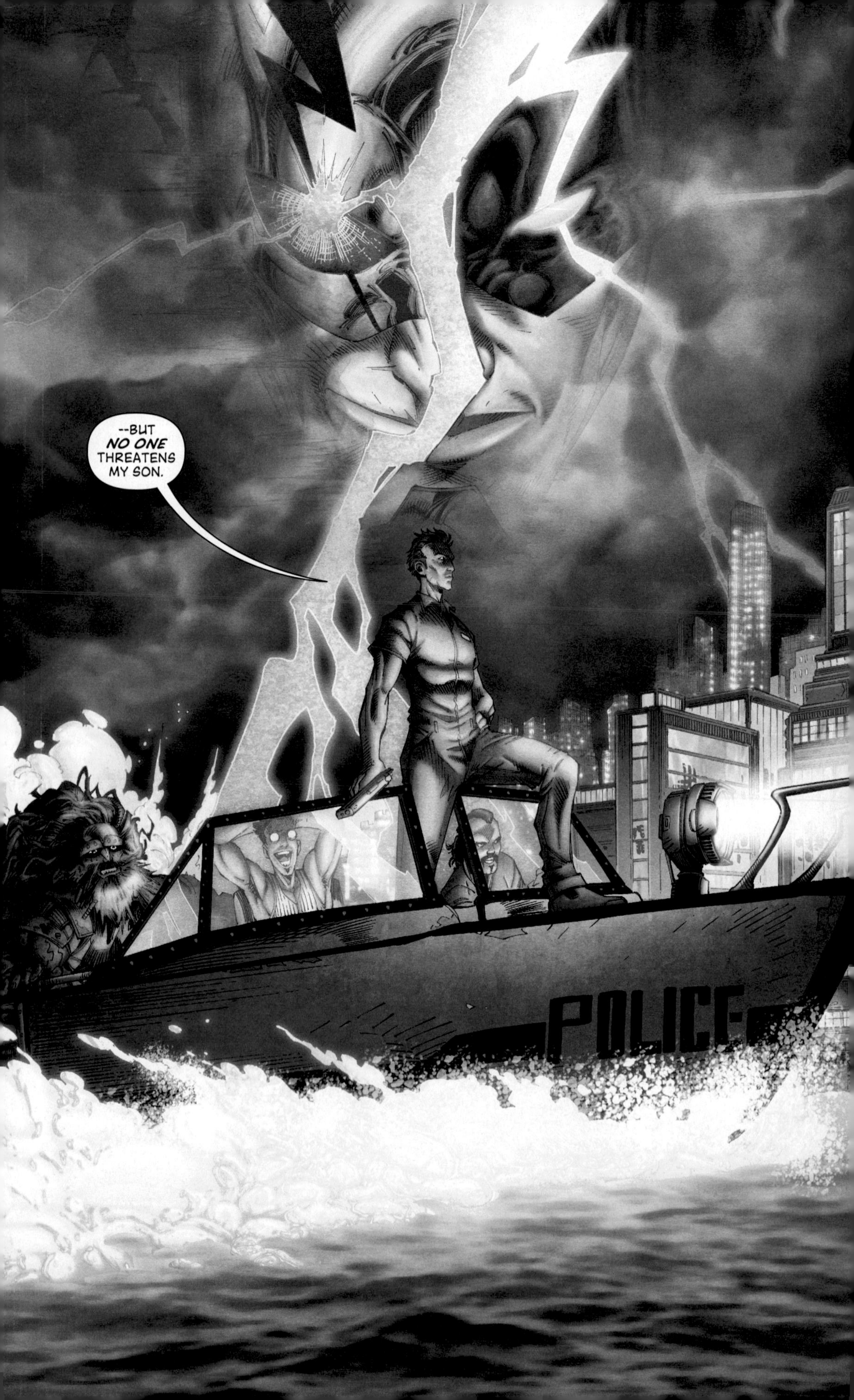
--BUT NO ONE THREATENS MY SON.
POLICE

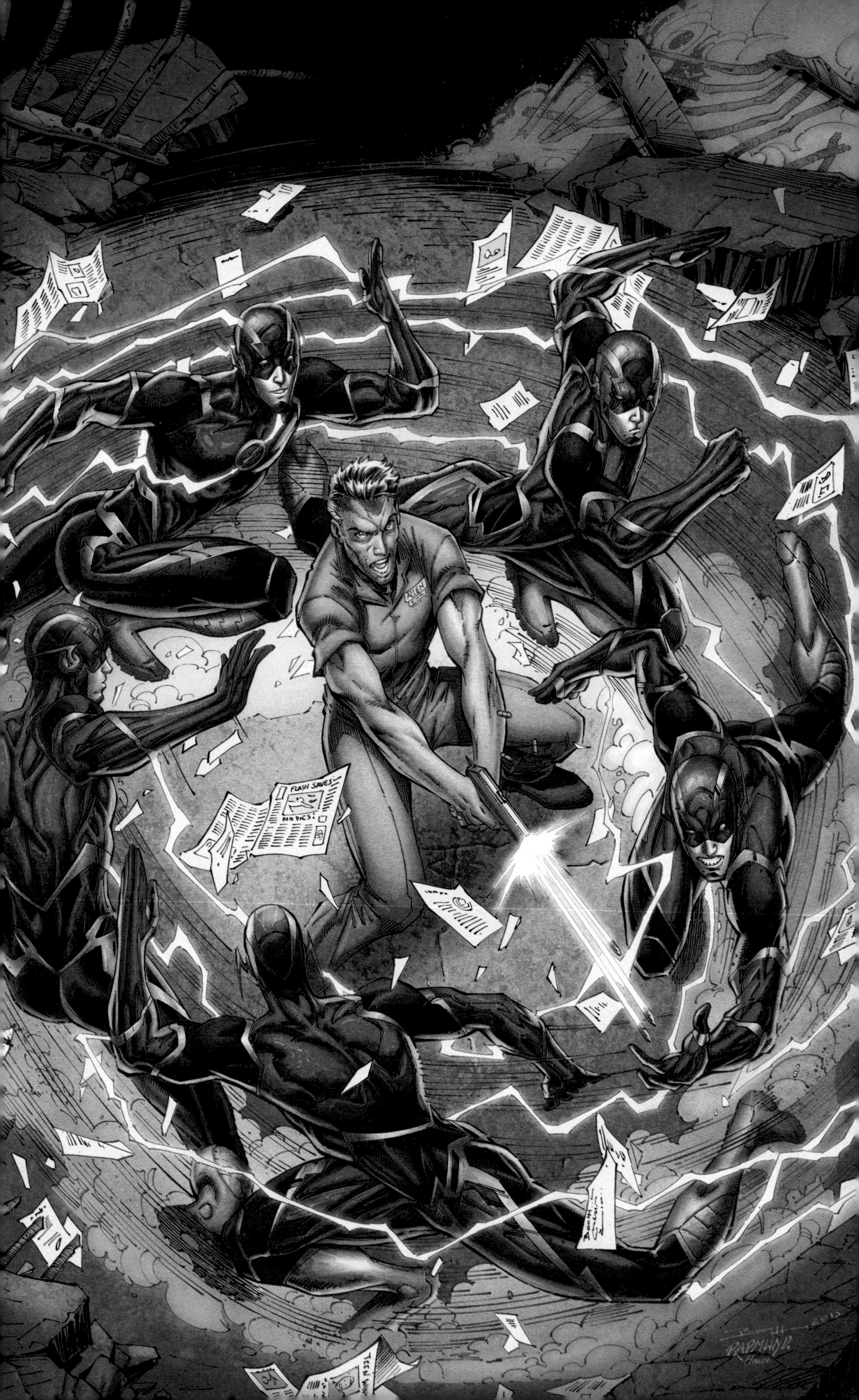
FLASH SAVES
NO PICS!

ROBERT VENDITTI, VAN JENSEN writers BRETT BOOTH penciller NORM RAPMUND inker ANDREW DALHOUSE colorist PAT BROSS letterer
cover by BRETT BOOTH, NORM RAPMUND, ANDREW DALHOUSE

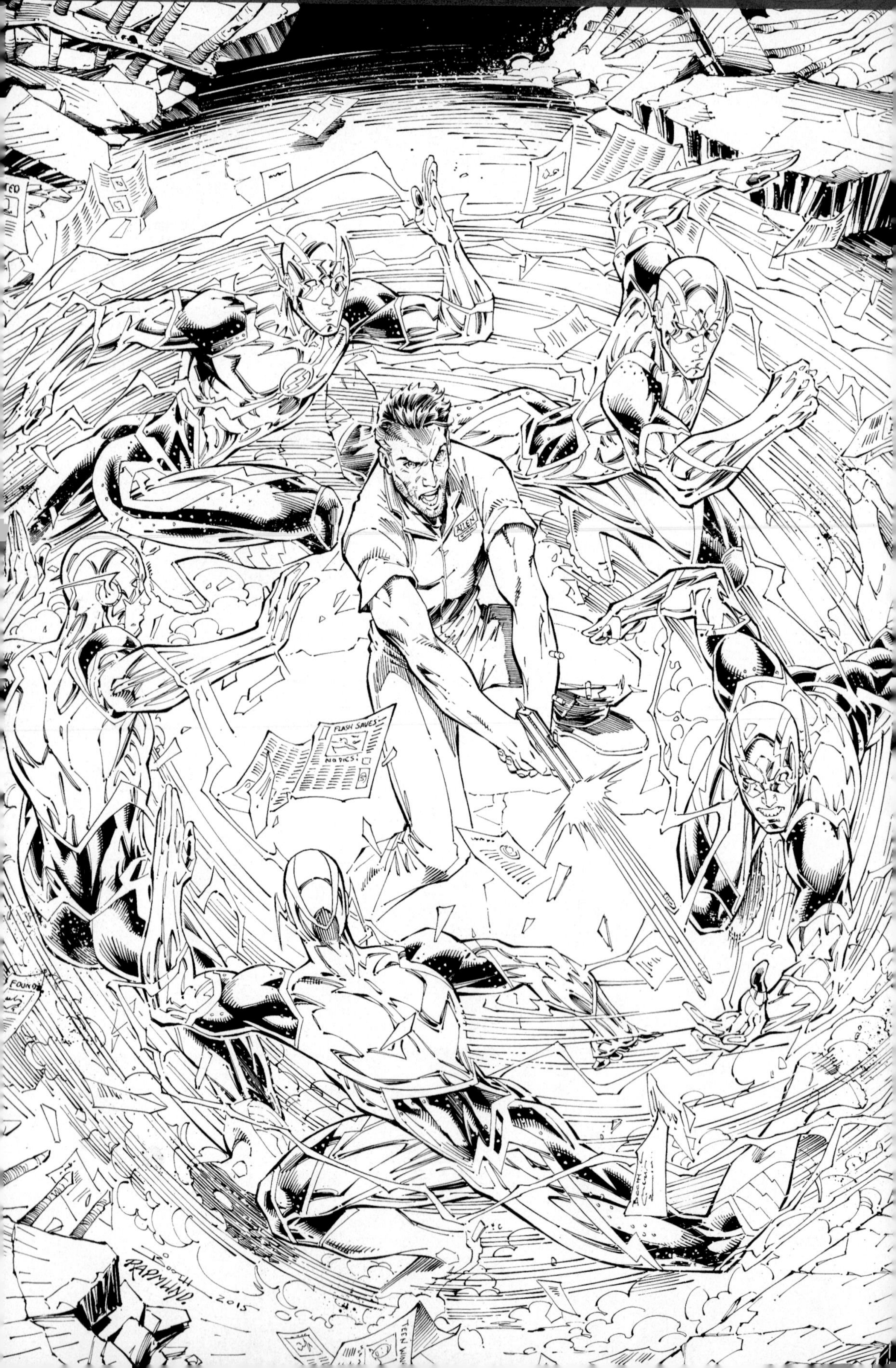
FLASH SAVES
ALLEN
RAPMUND
2015

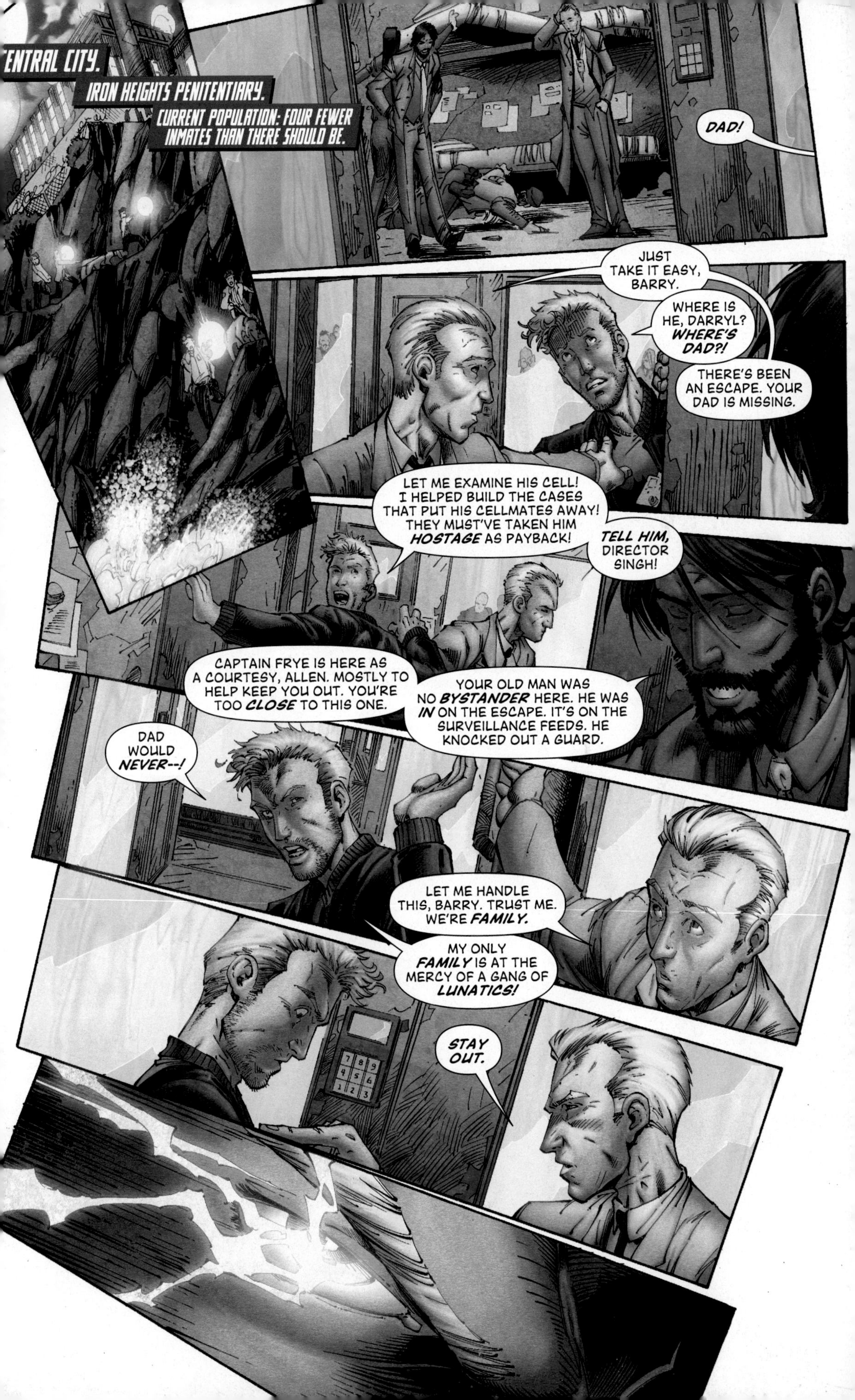
ENTRAL CITY.
IRON HEIGHTS PENITENTIARY.
CURRENT POPULATION: FOUR FEWER INMATES THAN THERE SHOULD BE.
DAD!
JUST TAKE IT EASY, BARRY.
WHERE IS HE, DARRYL? WHERE'S DAD?!
THERE'S BEEN AN ESCAPE. YOUR DAD IS MISSING.
LET ME EXAMINE HIS CELL! I HELPED BUILD THE CASES THAT PUT HIS CELLMATES AWAY! THEY MUST'VE TAKEN HIM HOSTAGE AS PAYBACK!
TELL HIM, DIRECTOR SINGH!
CAPTAIN FRYE IS HERE AS A COURTESY, ALLEN. MOSTLY TO HELP KEEP YOU OUT. YOU'RE TOO CLOSE TO THIS ONE.
YOUR OLD MAN WAS NO BYSTANDER HERE. HE WAS IN ON THE ESCAPE. IT'S ON THE SURVEILLANCE FEEDS. HE KNOCKED OUT A GUARD.
DAD WOULD NEVER--!
LET ME HANDLE THIS, BARRY. TRUST ME. WE'RE FAMILY.
MY ONLY FAMILY IS AT THE MERCY OF A GANG OF LUNATICS!
STAY OUT.

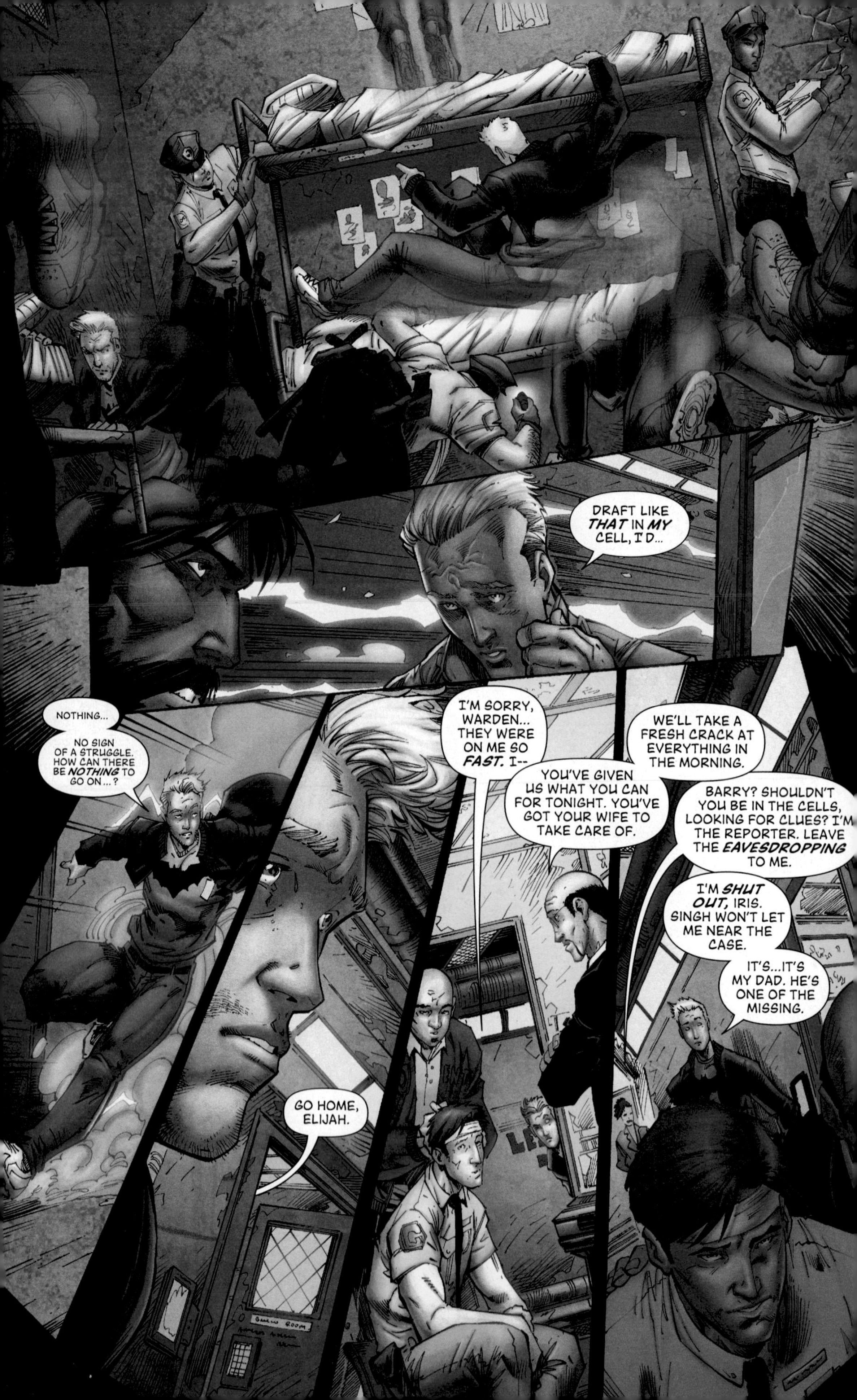
DRAFT LIKE THAT IN MY CELL, I'D...
NOTHING...
NO SIGN OF A STRUGGLE. HOW CAN THERE BE NOTHING TO GO ON...?
I'M SORRY, WARDEN... THEY WERE ON ME SO FAST. I--
YOU'VE GIVEN US WHAT YOU CAN FOR TONIGHT. YOU'VE GOT YOUR WIFE TO TAKE CARE OF.
GO HOME, ELIJAH.
WE'LL TAKE A FRESH CRACK AT EVERYTHING IN THE MORNING.
BARRY? SHOULDN'T YOU BE IN THE CELLS, LOOKING FOR CLUES? I'M THE REPORTER. LEAVE THE EAVESDROPPING TO ME.
I'M SHUT OUT, IRIS. SINGH WON'T LET ME NEAR THE CASE.
IT'S...IT'S MY DAD. HE'S ONE OF THE MISSING.

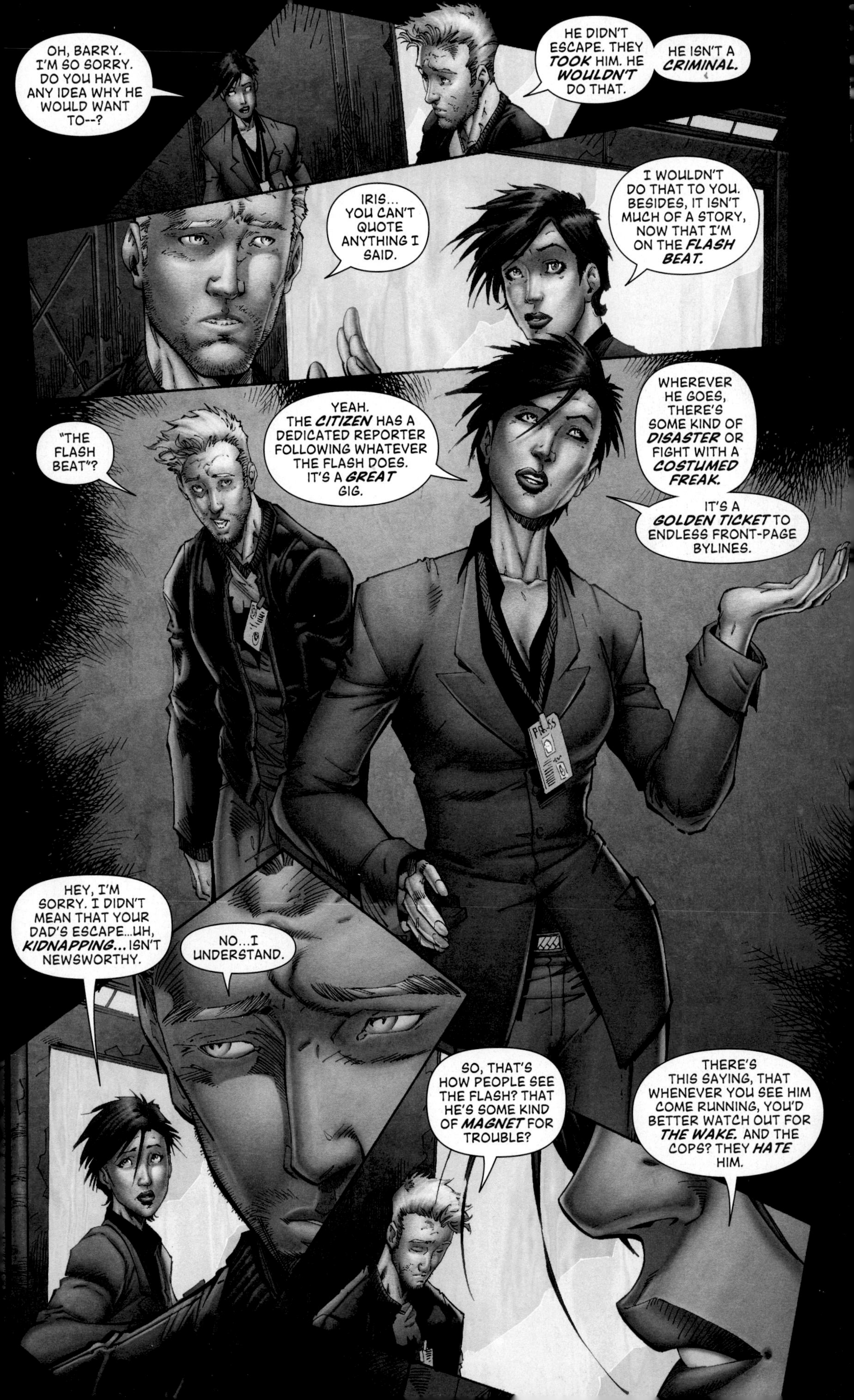

OH, BARRY. I'M SO SORRY. DO YOU HAVE ANY IDEA WHY HE WOULD WANT TO--?
HE DIDN'T ESCAPE. THEY *TOOK* HIM. HE *WOULDN'T* DO THAT.
HE ISN'T A *CRIMINAL.*
IRIS... YOU CAN'T QUOTE ANYTHING I SAID.
I WOULDN'T DO THAT TO YOU. BESIDES, IT ISN'T MUCH OF A STORY, NOW THAT I'M ON THE *FLASH BEAT.*
"THE FLASH BEAT"?
YEAH. THE *CITIZEN* HAS A DEDICATED REPORTER FOLLOWING WHATEVER THE FLASH DOES. IT'S A *GREAT* GIG.
WHEREVER HE GOES, THERE'S SOME KIND OF *DISASTER* OR FIGHT WITH A *COSTUMED FREAK.*
IT'S A *GOLDEN TICKET* TO ENDLESS FRONT-PAGE BYLINES.
HEY, I'M SORRY. I DIDN'T MEAN THAT YOUR DAD'S ESCAPE...UH, *KIDNAPPING...* ISN'T NEWSWORTHY.
NO...I UNDERSTAND.
SO, THAT'S HOW PEOPLE SEE THE FLASH? THAT HE'S SOME KIND OF *MAGNET* FOR TROUBLE?
THERE'S THIS SAYING, THAT WHENEVER YOU SEE HIM COME RUNNING, YOU'D BETTER WATCH OUT FOR *THE WAKE.* AND THE COPS? THEY *HATE* HIM.

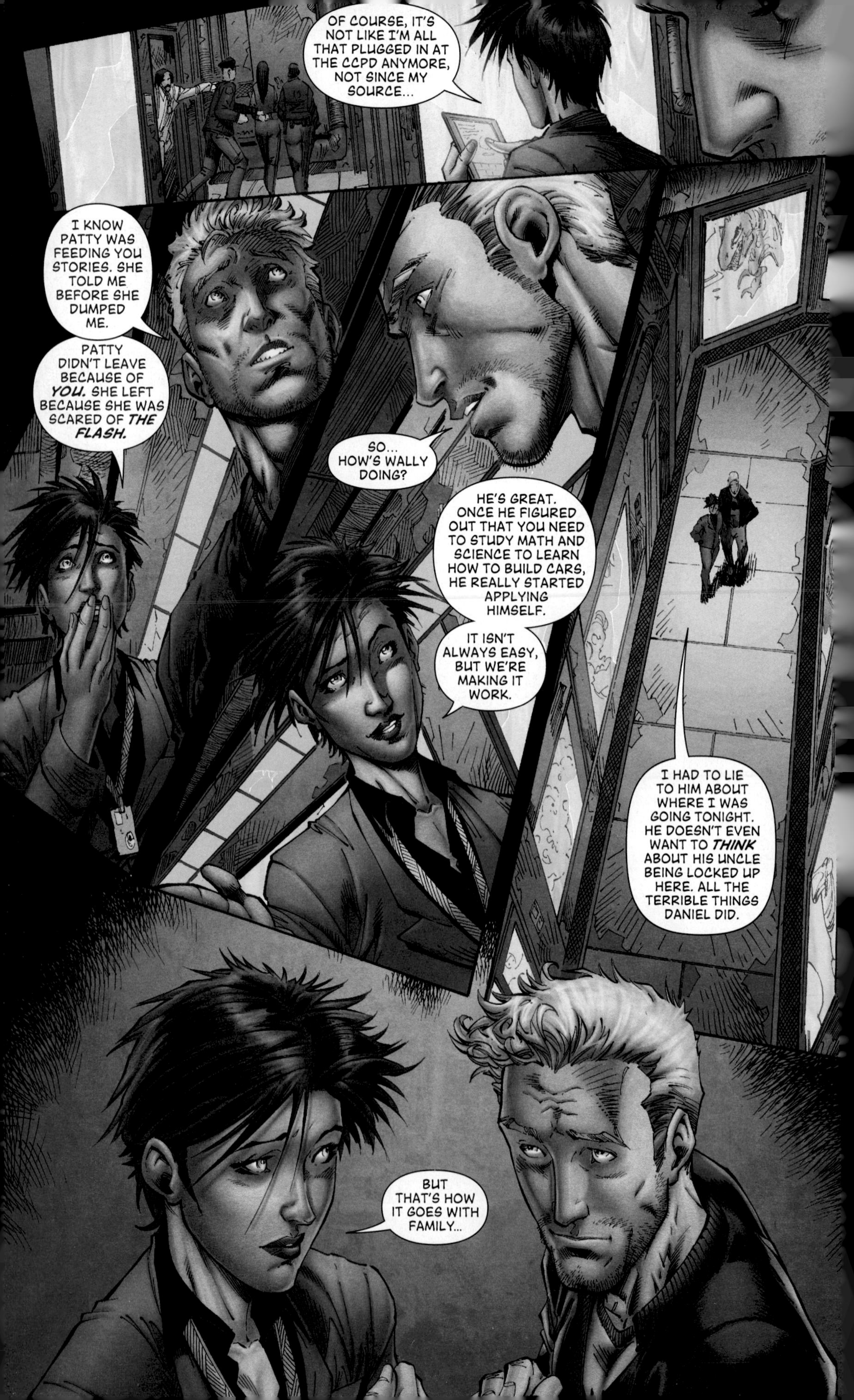
OF COURSE, IT'S NOT LIKE I'M ALL THAT PLUGGED IN AT THE CCPD ANYMORE, NOT SINCE MY SOURCE...
I KNOW PATTY WAS FEEDING YOU STORIES. SHE TOLD ME BEFORE SHE DUMPED ME.
PATTY DIDN'T LEAVE BECAUSE OF *YOU.* SHE LEFT BECAUSE SHE WAS SCARED OF *THE FLASH.*
SO... HOW'S WALLY DOING?
HE'S GREAT. ONCE HE FIGURED OUT THAT YOU NEED TO STUDY MATH AND SCIENCE TO LEARN HOW TO BUILD CARS, HE REALLY STARTED APPLYING HIMSELF.
IT ISN'T ALWAYS EASY, BUT WE'RE MAKING IT WORK.
I HAD TO LIE TO HIM ABOUT WHERE I WAS GOING TONIGHT. HE DOESN'T EVEN WANT TO *THINK* ABOUT HIS UNCLE BEING LOCKED UP HERE. ALL THE TERRIBLE THINGS DANIEL DID.
BUT THAT'S HOW IT GOES WITH FAMILY...

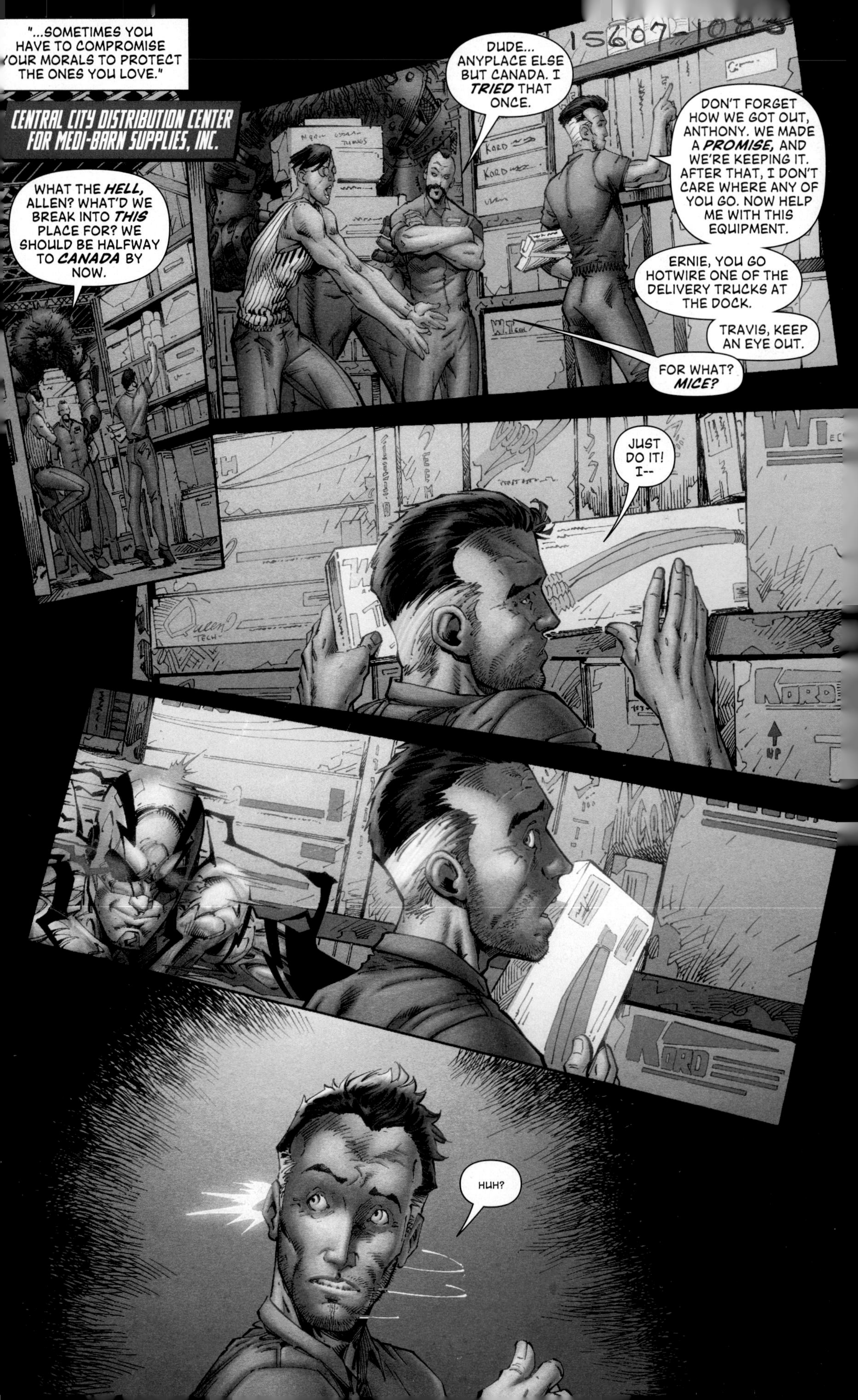
"...SOMETIMES YOU HAVE TO COMPROMISE YOUR MORALS TO PROTECT THE ONES YOU LOVE."
CENTRAL CITY DISTRIBUTION CENTER FOR MEDI-BARN SUPPLIES, INC.
WHAT THE HELL, ALLEN? WHAT'D WE BREAK INTO THIS PLACE FOR? WE SHOULD BE HALFWAY TO CANADA BY NOW.
DUDE... ANYPLACE ELSE BUT CANADA. I TRIED THAT ONCE.
DON'T FORGET HOW WE GOT OUT, ANTHONY. WE MADE A PROMISE, AND WE'RE KEEPING IT. AFTER THAT, I DON'T CARE WHERE ANY OF YOU GO. NOW HELP ME WITH THIS EQUIPMENT.
ERNIE, YOU GO HOTWIRE ONE OF THE DELIVERY TRUCKS AT THE DOCK.
TRAVIS, KEEP AN EYE OUT.
FOR WHAT? MICE?
JUST DO IT! I--
HUH?

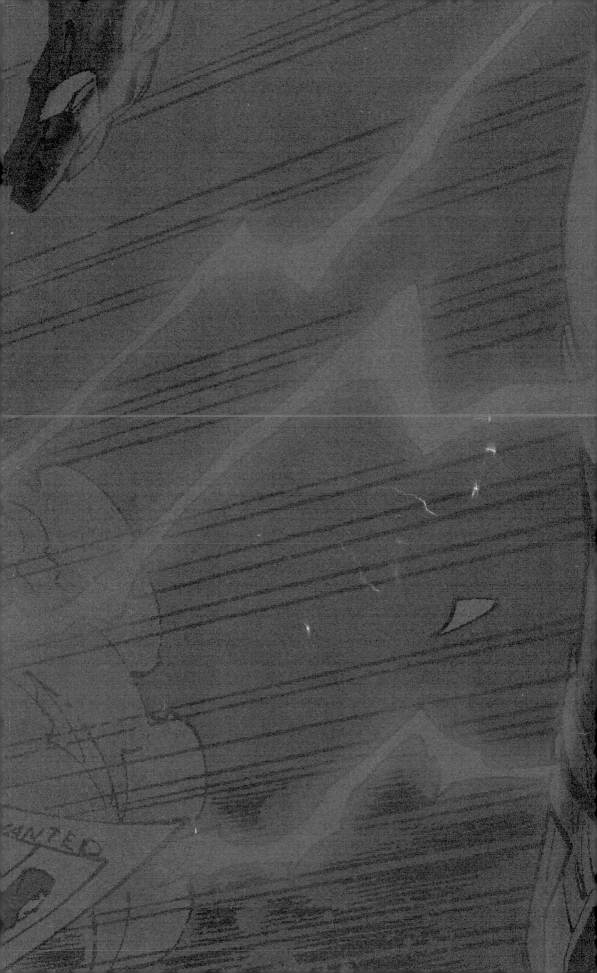

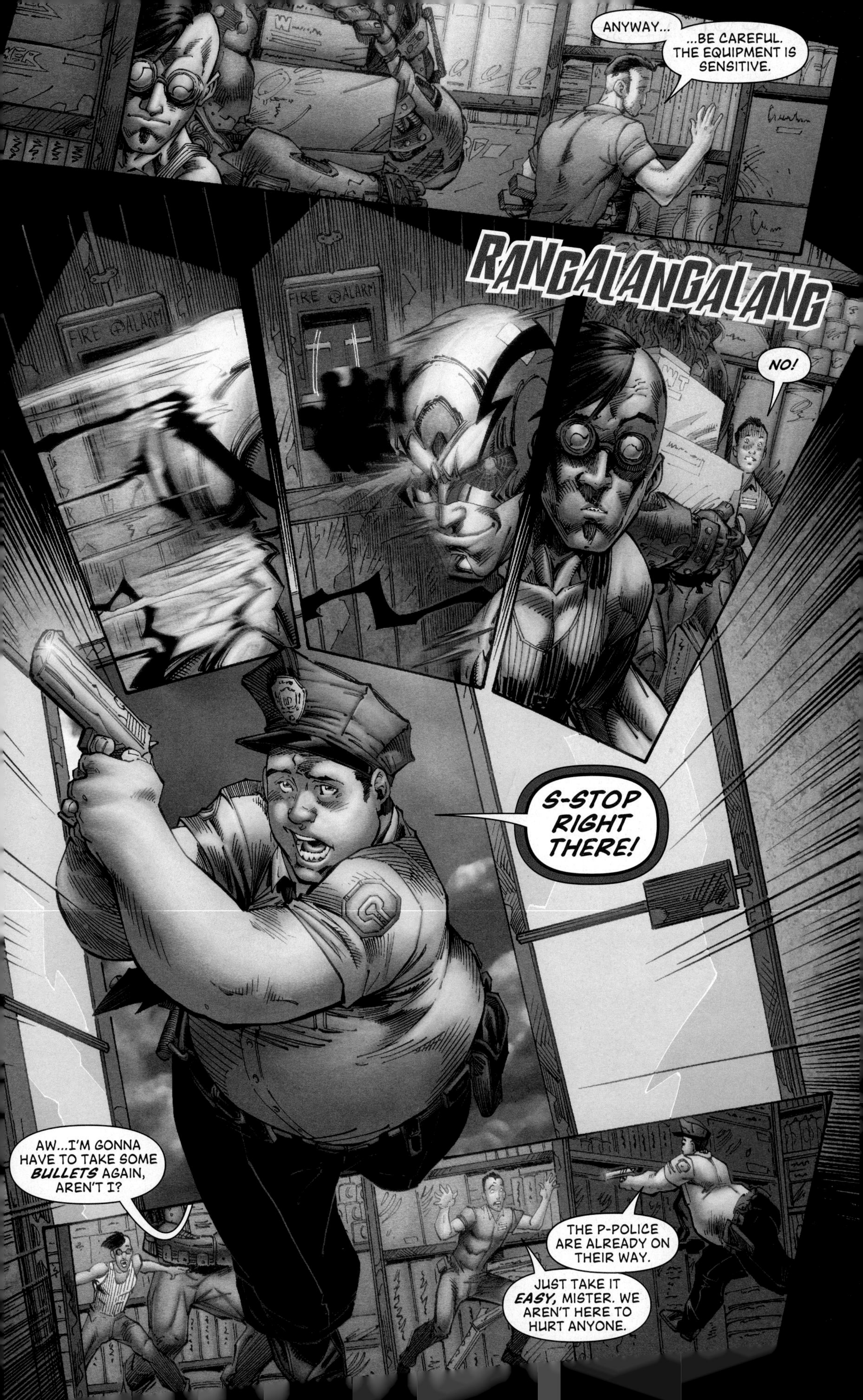
ANYWAY...
...BE CAREFUL. THE EQUIPMENT IS SENSITIVE.
RANGALANGALANG
NO!
FIRE ALARM
S-STOP RIGHT THERE!
AW...I'M GONNA HAVE TO TAKE SOME *BULLETS* AGAIN, AREN'T I?
THE P-POLICE ARE ALREADY ON THEIR WAY.
JUST TAKE IT *EASY,* MISTER. WE AREN'T HERE TO HURT ANYONE.

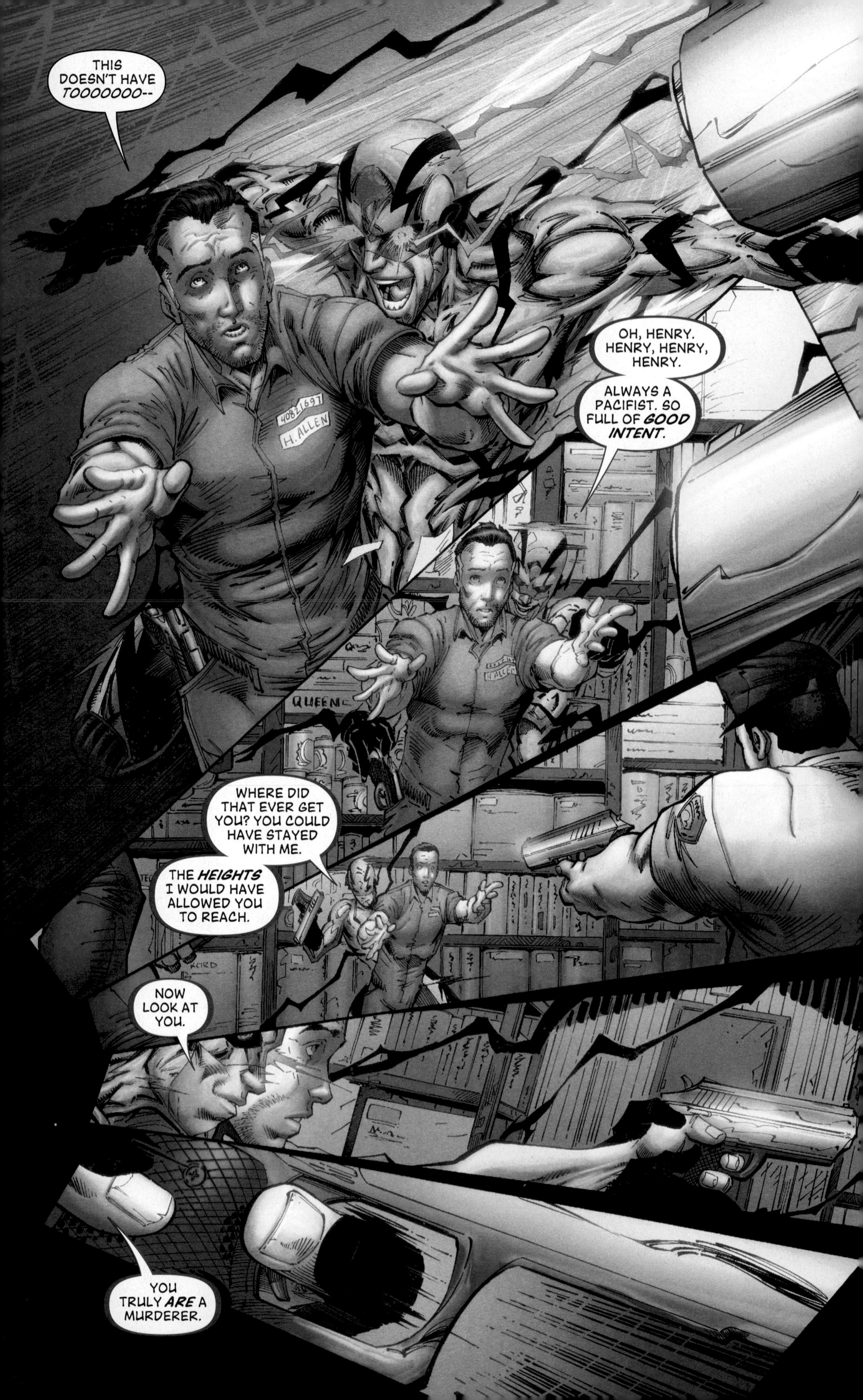
THIS DOESN'T HAVE *TOOOOOOO*--
OH, HENRY. HENRY, HENRY, HENRY.
ALWAYS A PACIFIST. SO FULL OF ***GOOD INTENT***.
4082 1697
H. ALLEN
WHERE DID THAT EVER GET YOU? YOU COULD HAVE STAYED WITH ME.
THE ***HEIGHTS*** I WOULD HAVE ALLOWED YOU TO REACH.
NOW LOOK AT YOU.
YOU TRULY ***ARE*** A MURDERER.

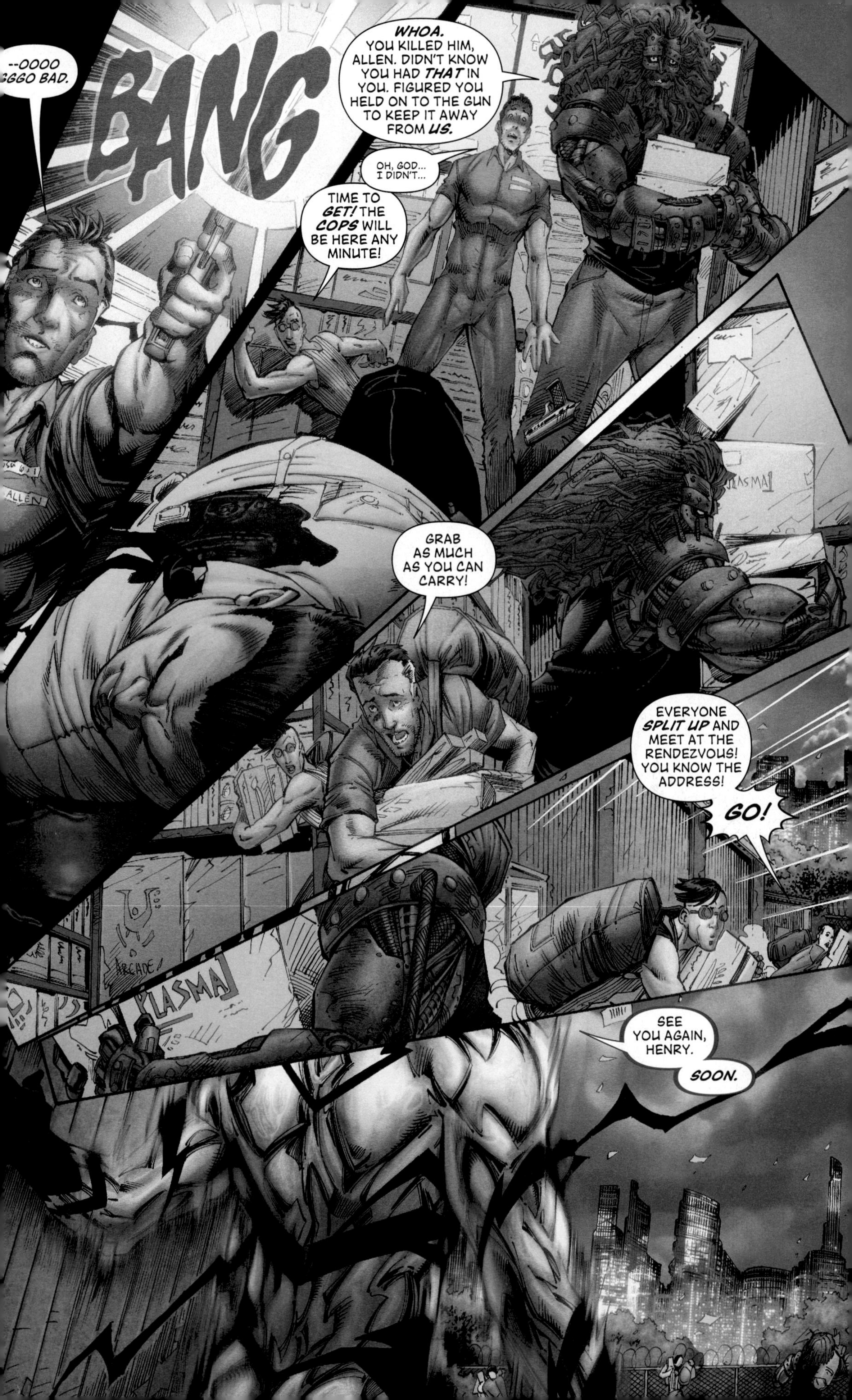
--OOOO
GGGO BAD.
BANG
WHOA. YOU KILLED HIM, ALLEN. DIDN'T KNOW YOU HAD THAT IN YOU. FIGURED YOU HELD ON TO THE GUN TO KEEP IT AWAY FROM US.
OH, GOD... I DIDN'T...
TIME TO GET! THE COPS WILL BE HERE ANY MINUTE!
ALLEN
PLASMA
GRAB AS MUCH AS YOU CAN CARRY!
EVERYONE SPLIT UP AND MEET AT THE RENDEZVOUS! YOU KNOW THE ADDRESS!
GO!
PLASMA
SEE YOU AGAIN, HENRY.
SOON.

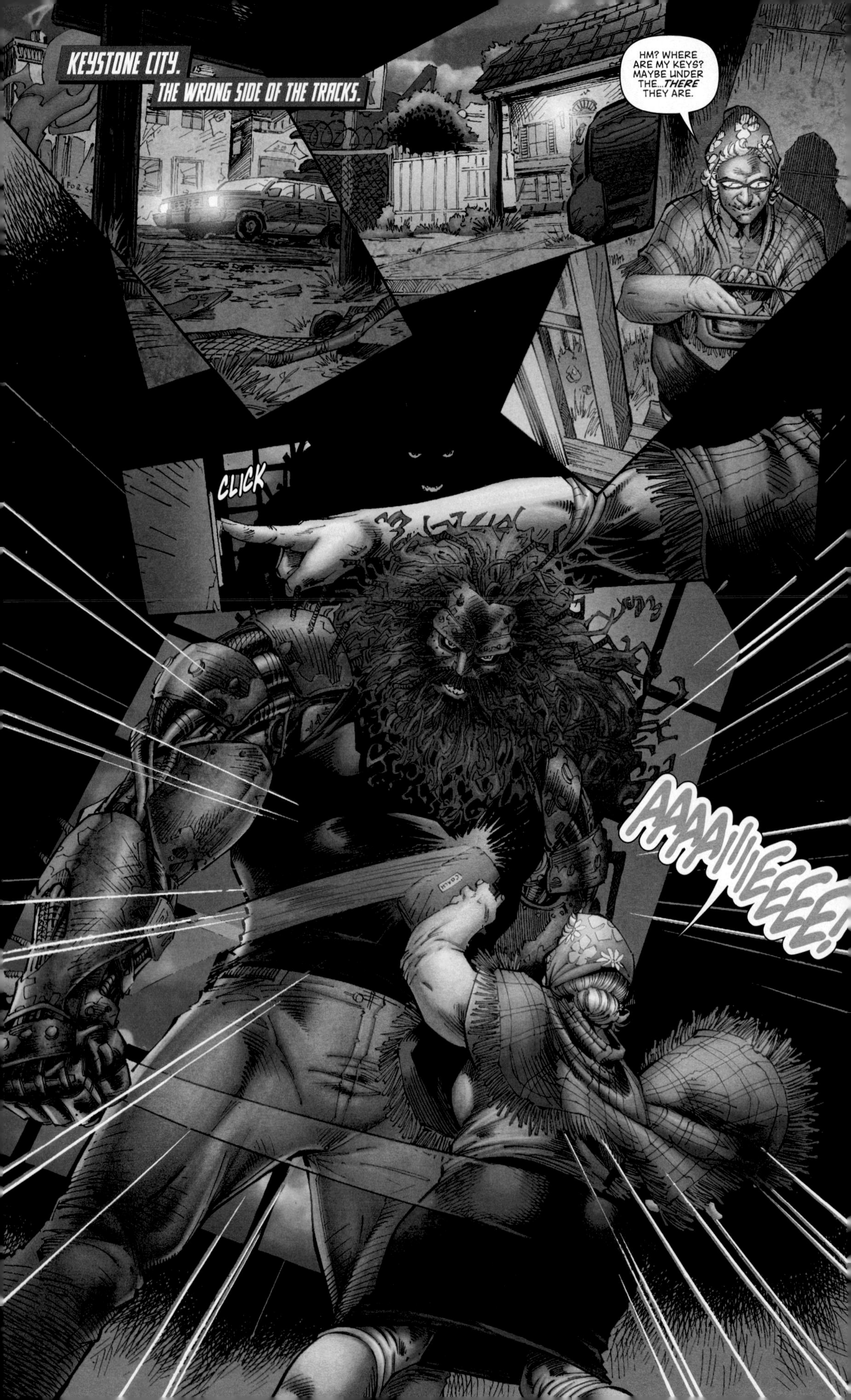
KEYSTONE CITY.
THE WRONG SIDE OF THE TRACKS.
HM? WHERE ARE MY KEYS? MAYBE UNDER THE...THERE THEY ARE.
CLICK
AAAAIIIEEEE!

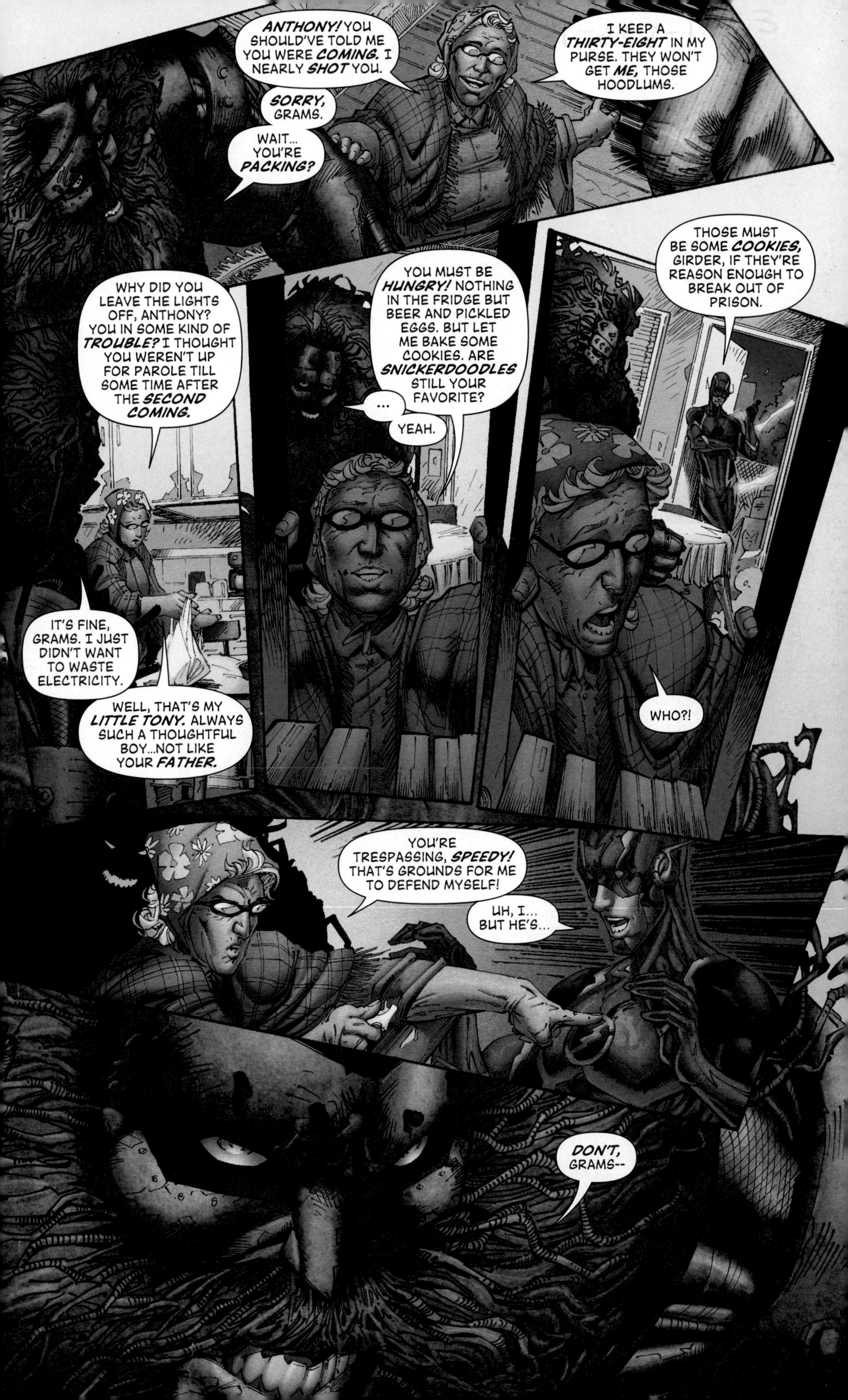
ANTHONY! YOU SHOULD'VE TOLD ME YOU WERE COMING. I NEARLY SHOT YOU.
SORRY, GRAMS.
WAIT... YOU'RE PACKING?
I KEEP A THIRTY-EIGHT IN MY PURSE. THEY WON'T GET ME, THOSE HOODLUMS.
WHY DID YOU LEAVE THE LIGHTS OFF, ANTHONY? YOU IN SOME KIND OF TROUBLE? I THOUGHT YOU WEREN'T UP FOR PAROLE TILL SOME TIME AFTER THE SECOND COMING.
IT'S FINE, GRAMS. I JUST DIDN'T WANT TO WASTE ELECTRICITY.
WELL, THAT'S MY LITTLE TONY. ALWAYS SUCH A THOUGHTFUL BOY...NOT LIKE YOUR FATHER.
YOU MUST BE HUNGRY! NOTHING IN THE FRIDGE BUT BEER AND PICKLED EGGS. BUT LET ME BAKE SOME COOKIES. ARE SNICKERDOODLES STILL YOUR FAVORITE?
...
YEAH.
THOSE MUST BE SOME COOKIES, GIRDER, IF THEY'RE REASON ENOUGH TO BREAK OUT OF PRISON.
WHO?!
YOU'RE TRESPASSING, SPEEDY! THAT'S GROUNDS FOR ME TO DEFEND MYSELF!
UH, I... BUT HE'S...
DON'T, GRAMS--

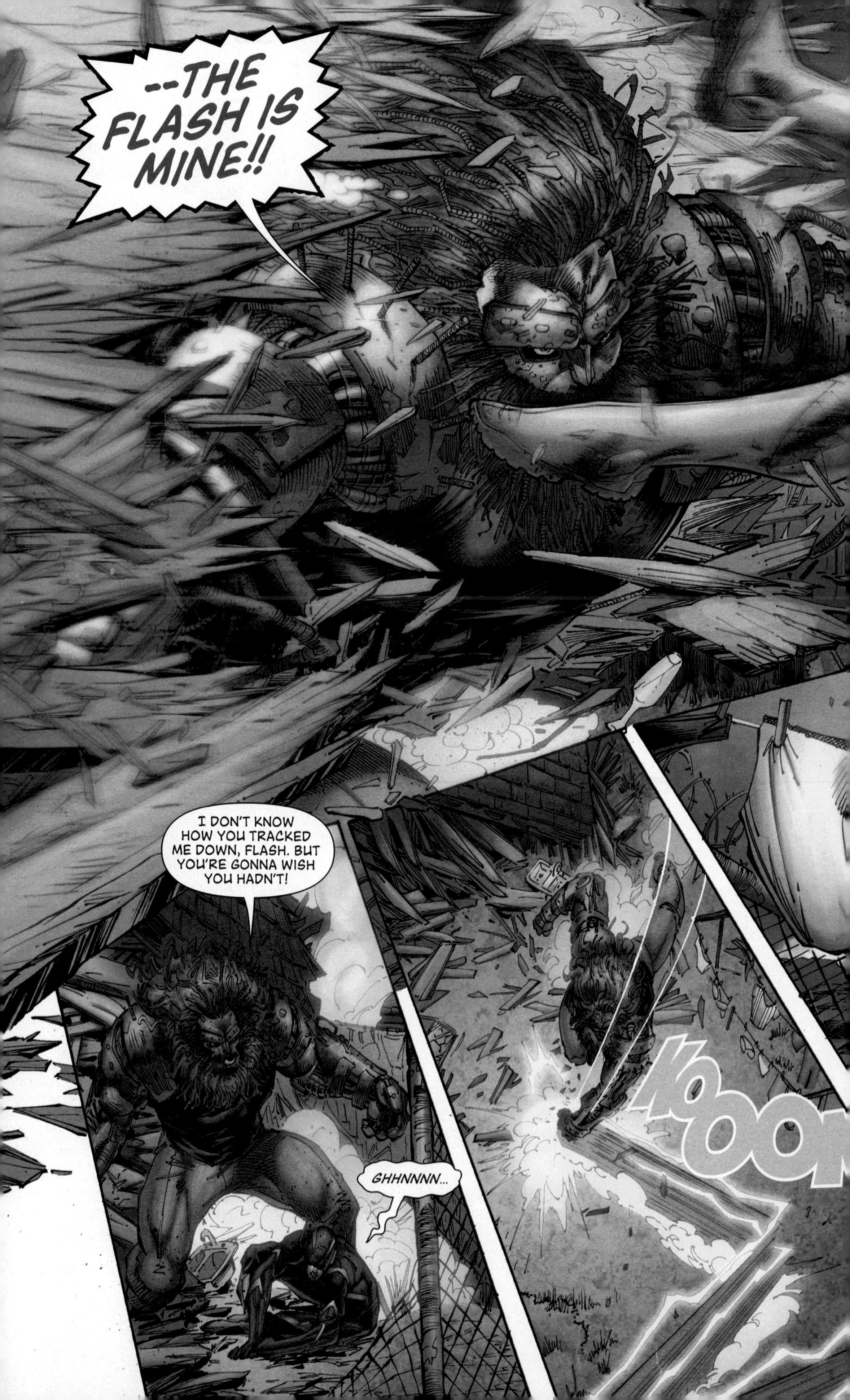
--THE FLASH IS MINE!!
I DON'T KNOW HOW YOU TRACKED ME DOWN, FLASH. BUT YOU'RE GONNA WISH YOU HADN'T!
GHHNNNN...
KOOOM

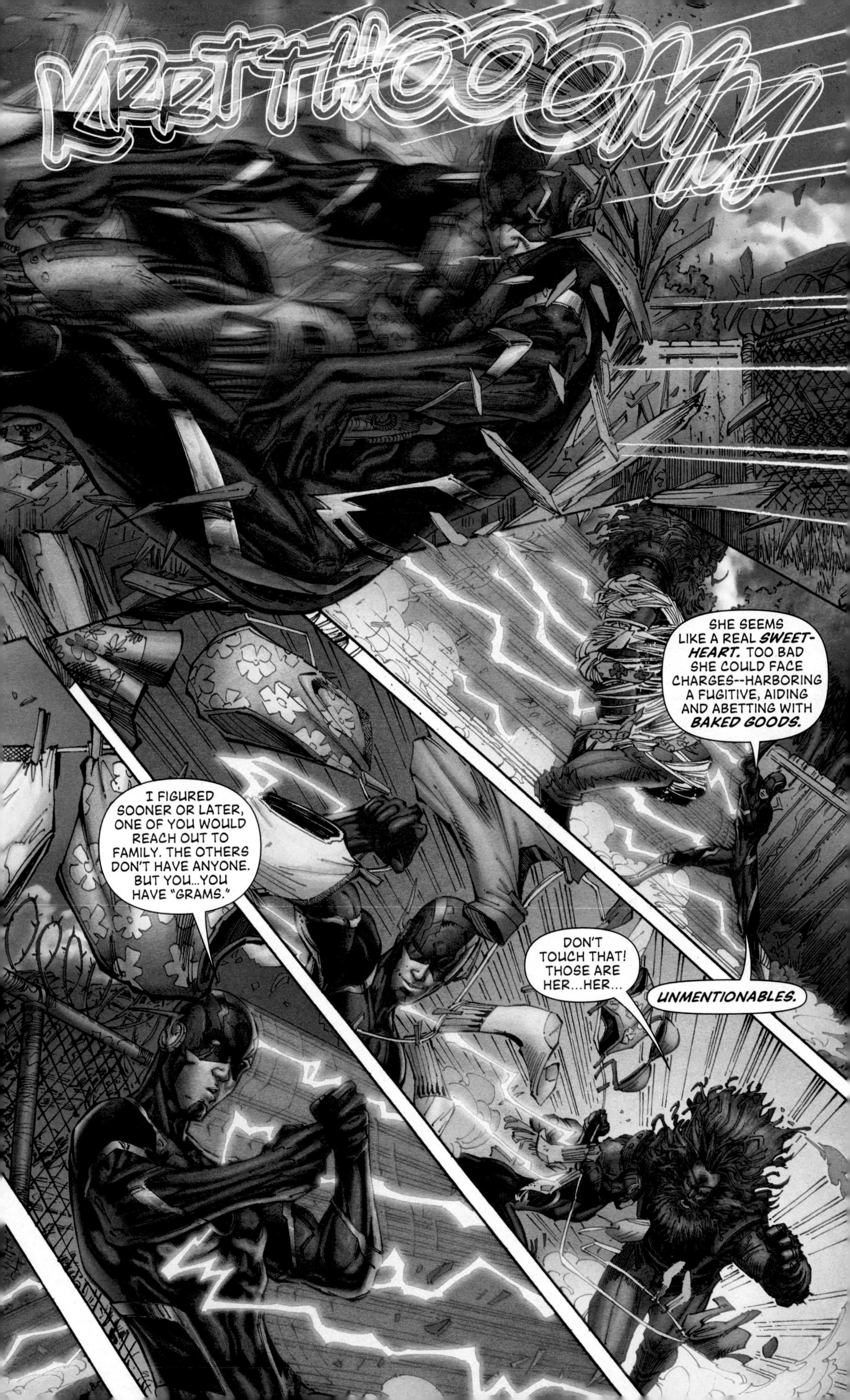
KRRTTHOOOOM
SHE SEEMS LIKE A REAL *SWEET-HEART.* TOO BAD SHE COULD FACE CHARGES--HARBORING A FUGITIVE, AIDING AND ABETTING WITH *BAKED GOODS.*
I FIGURED SOONER OR LATER, ONE OF YOU WOULD REACH OUT TO FAMILY. THE OTHERS DON'T HAVE ANYONE. BUT YOU...YOU HAVE "GRAMS."
DON'T TOUCH THAT! THOSE ARE HER...HER...
UNMENTIONABLES.

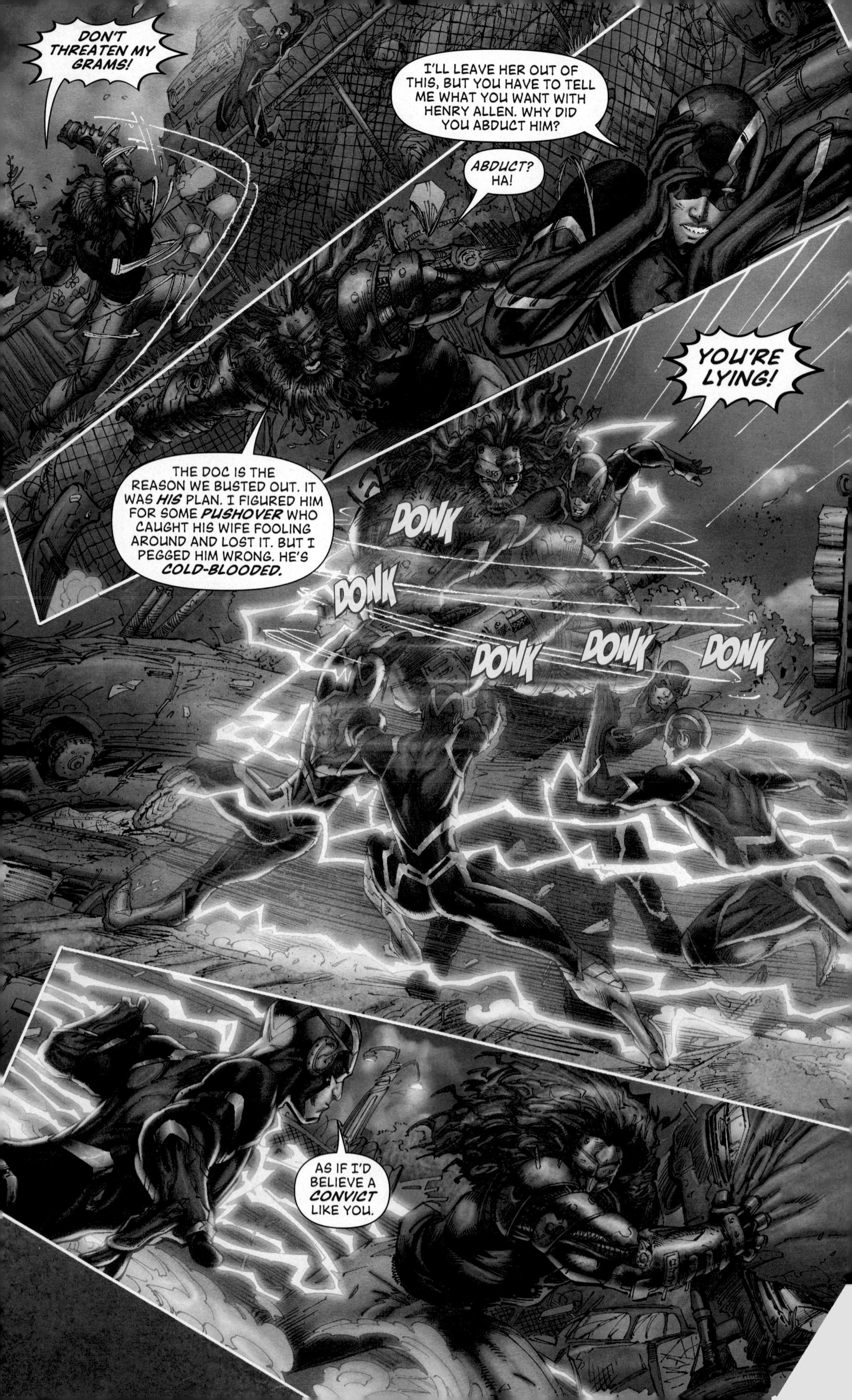
DON'T THREATEN MY GRAMS!
I'LL LEAVE HER OUT OF THIS, BUT YOU HAVE TO TELL ME WHAT YOU WANT WITH HENRY ALLEN. WHY DID YOU ABDUCT HIM?
ABDUCT? HA!
THE DOC IS THE REASON WE BUSTED OUT. IT WAS HIS PLAN. I FIGURED HIM FOR SOME PUSHOVER WHO CAUGHT HIS WIFE FOOLING AROUND AND LOST IT. BUT I PEGGED HIM WRONG. HE'S COLD-BLOODED.
YOU'RE LYING!
DONK
DONK
DONK
DONK
DONK
AS IF I'D BELIEVE A CONVICT LIKE YOU.

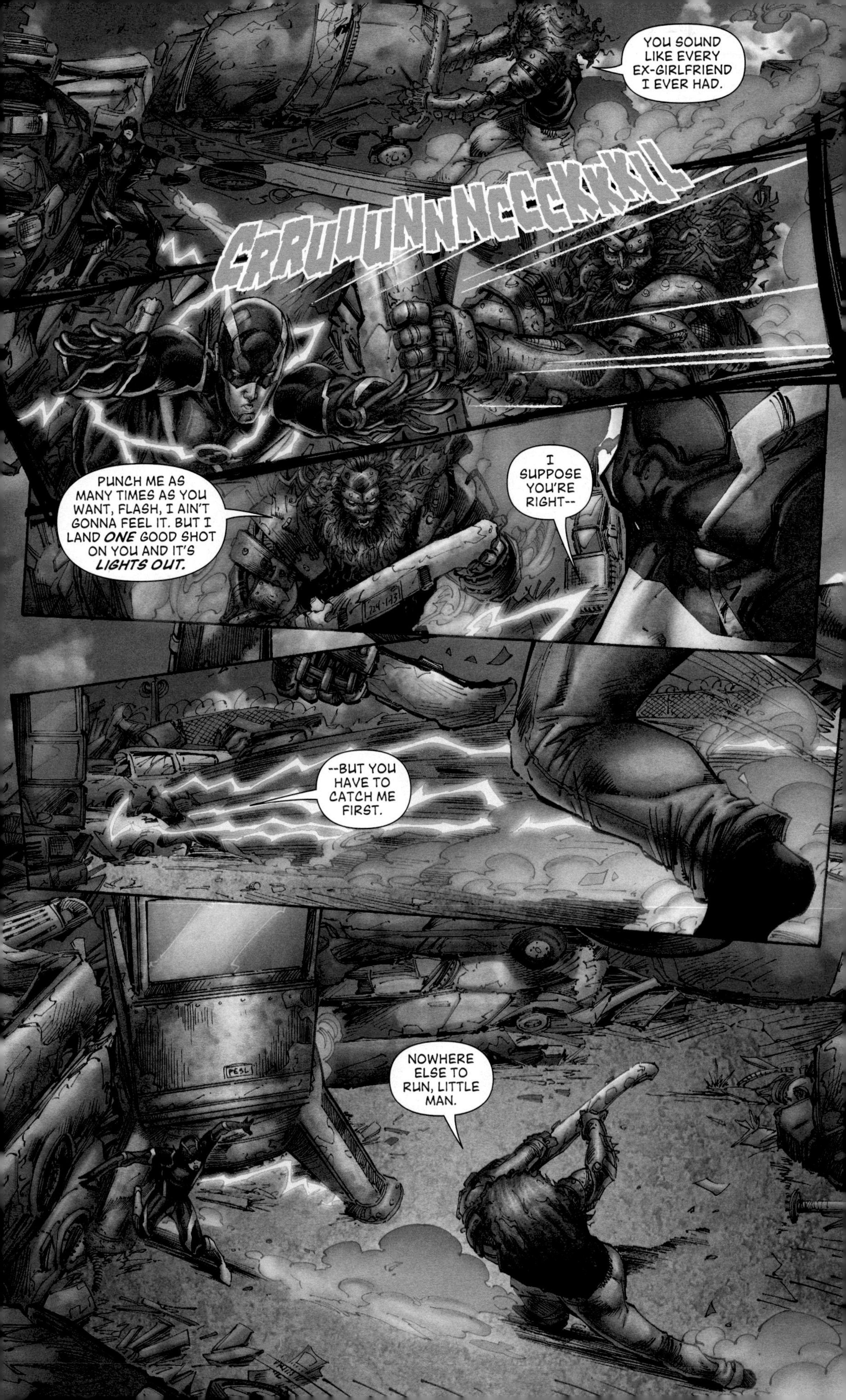
YOU SOUND LIKE EVERY EX-GIRLFRIEND I EVER HAD.
CRRUUUNNNCCCKKKLL
PUNCH ME AS MANY TIMES AS YOU WANT, FLASH, I AIN'T GONNA FEEL IT. BUT I LAND *ONE* GOOD SHOT ON YOU AND IT'S *LIGHTS OUT.*
I SUPPOSE YOU'RE RIGHT--
--BUT YOU HAVE TO CATCH ME FIRST.
NOWHERE ELSE TO RUN, LITTLE MAN.

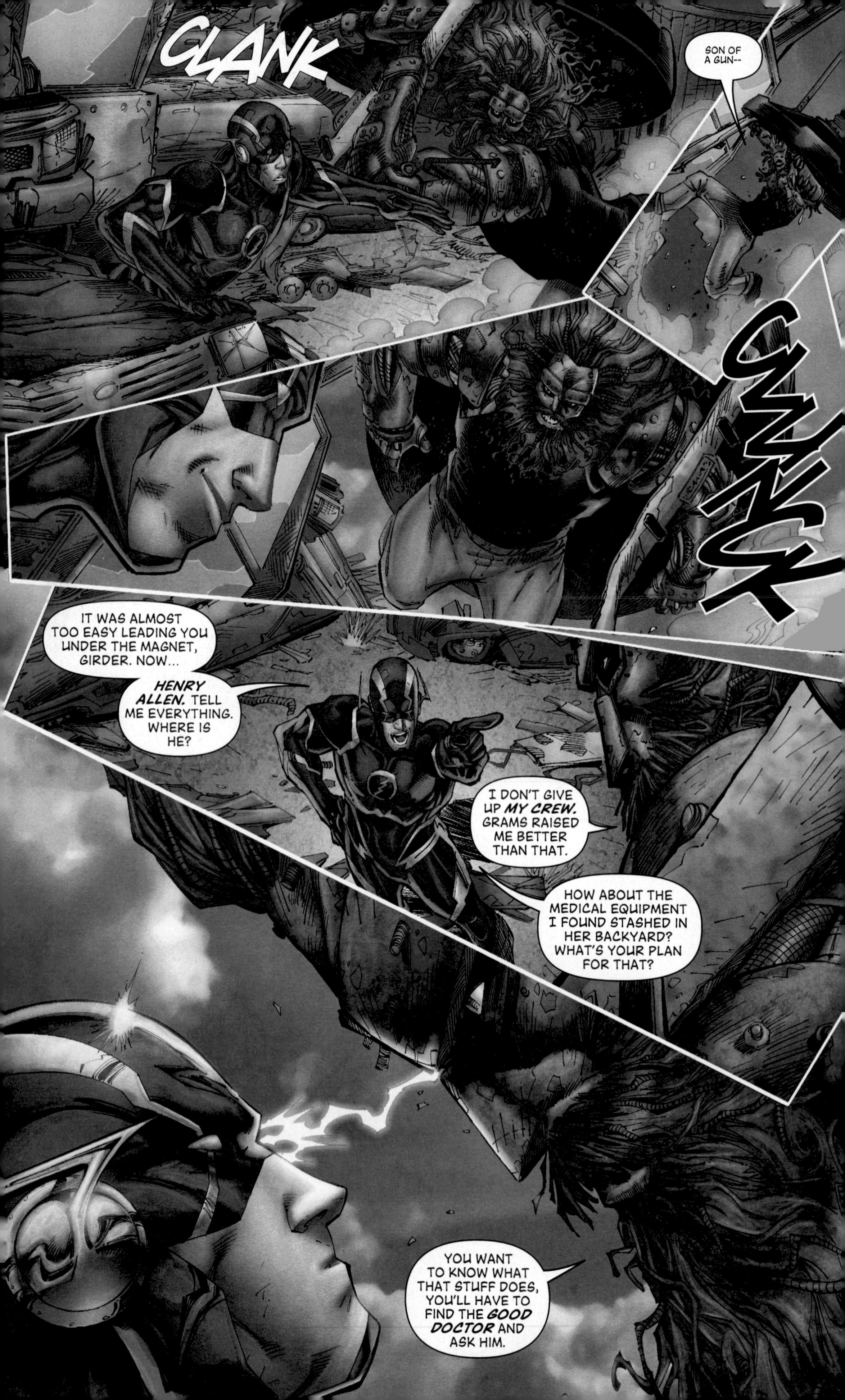
CLANK
SON OF A GUN--
CHUNK
IT WAS ALMOST TOO EASY LEADING YOU UNDER THE MAGNET, GIRDER. NOW...
HENRY ALLEN. TELL ME EVERYTHING. WHERE IS HE?
I DON'T GIVE UP MY CREW. GRAMS RAISED ME BETTER THAN THAT.
HOW ABOUT THE MEDICAL EQUIPMENT I FOUND STASHED IN HER BACKYARD? WHAT'S YOUR PLAN FOR THAT?
YOU WANT TO KNOW WHAT THAT STUFF DOES, YOU'LL HAVE TO FIND THE GOOD DOCTOR AND ASK HIM.

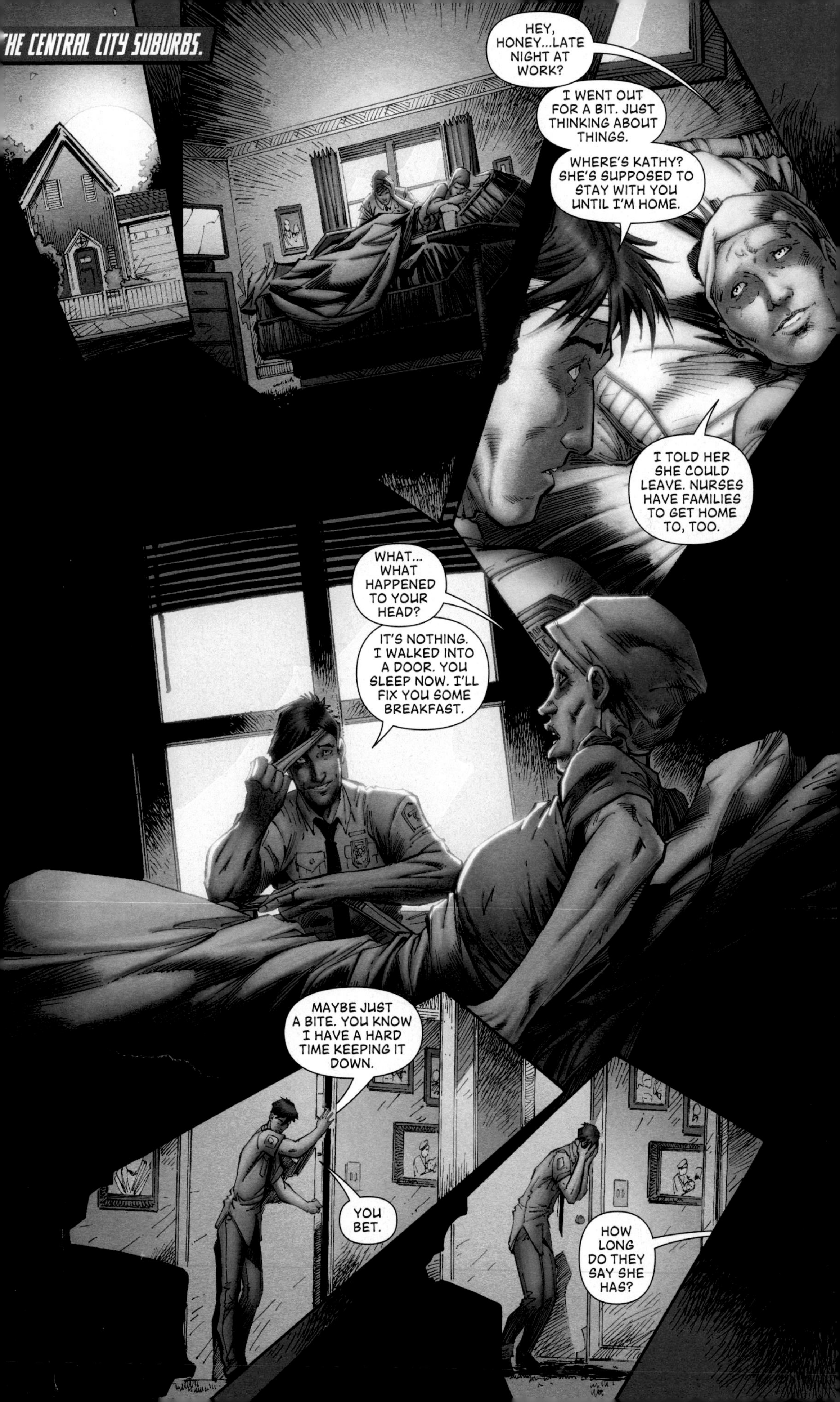
THE CENTRAL CITY SUBURBS.
HEY, HONEY...LATE NIGHT AT WORK?
I WENT OUT FOR A BIT. JUST THINKING ABOUT THINGS.
WHERE'S KATHY? SHE'S SUPPOSED TO STAY WITH YOU UNTIL I'M HOME.
I TOLD HER SHE COULD LEAVE. NURSES HAVE FAMILIES TO GET HOME TO, TOO.
WHAT... WHAT HAPPENED TO YOUR HEAD?
IT'S NOTHING. I WALKED INTO A DOOR. YOU SLEEP NOW. I'LL FIX YOU SOME BREAKFAST.
MAYBE JUST A BITE. YOU KNOW I HAVE A HARD TIME KEEPING IT DOWN.
YOU BET.
HOW LONG DO THEY SAY SHE HAS?

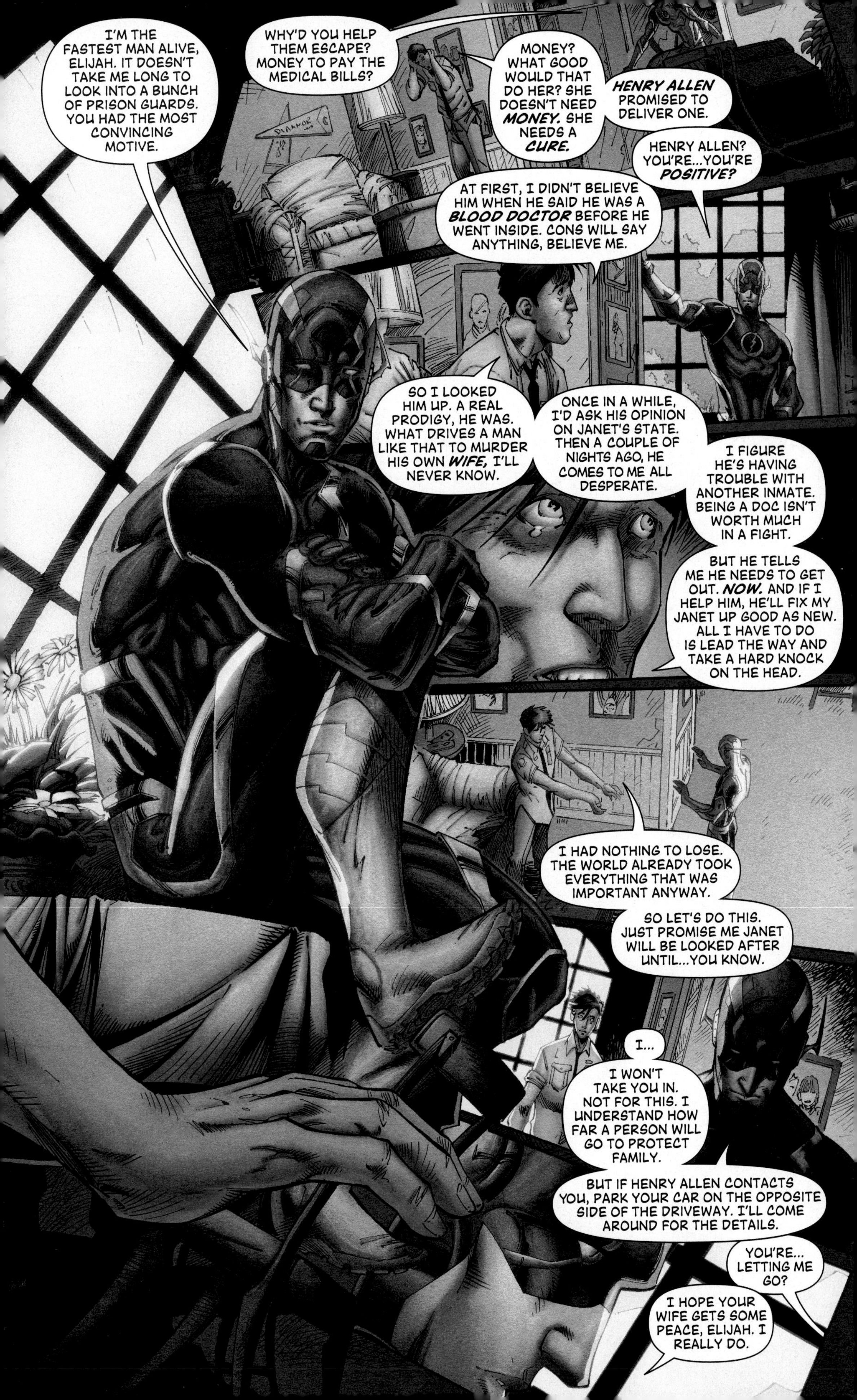
I'M THE FASTEST MAN ALIVE, ELIJAH. IT DOESN'T TAKE ME LONG TO LOOK INTO A BUNCH OF PRISON GUARDS. YOU HAD THE MOST CONVINCING MOTIVE.
WHY'D YOU HELP THEM ESCAPE? MONEY TO PAY THE MEDICAL BILLS?
MONEY? WHAT GOOD WOULD THAT DO HER? SHE DOESN'T NEED MONEY. SHE NEEDS A CURE.
HENRY ALLEN PROMISED TO DELIVER ONE.
HENRY ALLEN? YOU'RE...YOU'RE POSITIVE?
AT FIRST, I DIDN'T BELIEVE HIM WHEN HE SAID HE WAS A BLOOD DOCTOR BEFORE HE WENT INSIDE. CONS WILL SAY ANYTHING, BELIEVE ME.
SO I LOOKED HIM UP. A REAL PRODIGY, HE WAS. WHAT DRIVES A MAN LIKE THAT TO MURDER HIS OWN WIFE, I'LL NEVER KNOW.
ONCE IN A WHILE, I'D ASK HIS OPINION ON JANET'S STATE. THEN A COUPLE OF NIGHTS AGO, HE COMES TO ME ALL DESPERATE.
I FIGURE HE'S HAVING TROUBLE WITH ANOTHER INMATE. BEING A DOC ISN'T WORTH MUCH IN A FIGHT.
BUT HE TELLS ME HE NEEDS TO GET OUT. NOW. AND IF I HELP HIM, HE'LL FIX MY JANET UP GOOD AS NEW. ALL I HAVE TO DO IS LEAD THE WAY AND TAKE A HARD KNOCK ON THE HEAD.
I HAD NOTHING TO LOSE. THE WORLD ALREADY TOOK EVERYTHING THAT WAS IMPORTANT ANYWAY.
SO LET'S DO THIS. JUST PROMISE ME JANET WILL BE LOOKED AFTER UNTIL...YOU KNOW.
I...
I WON'T TAKE YOU IN. NOT FOR THIS. I UNDERSTAND HOW FAR A PERSON WILL GO TO PROTECT FAMILY.
BUT IF HENRY ALLEN CONTACTS YOU, PARK YOUR CAR ON THE OPPOSITE SIDE OF THE DRIVEWAY. I'LL COME AROUND FOR THE DETAILS.
YOU'RE... LETTING ME GO?
I HOPE YOUR WIFE GETS SOME PEACE, ELIJAH. I REALLY DO.

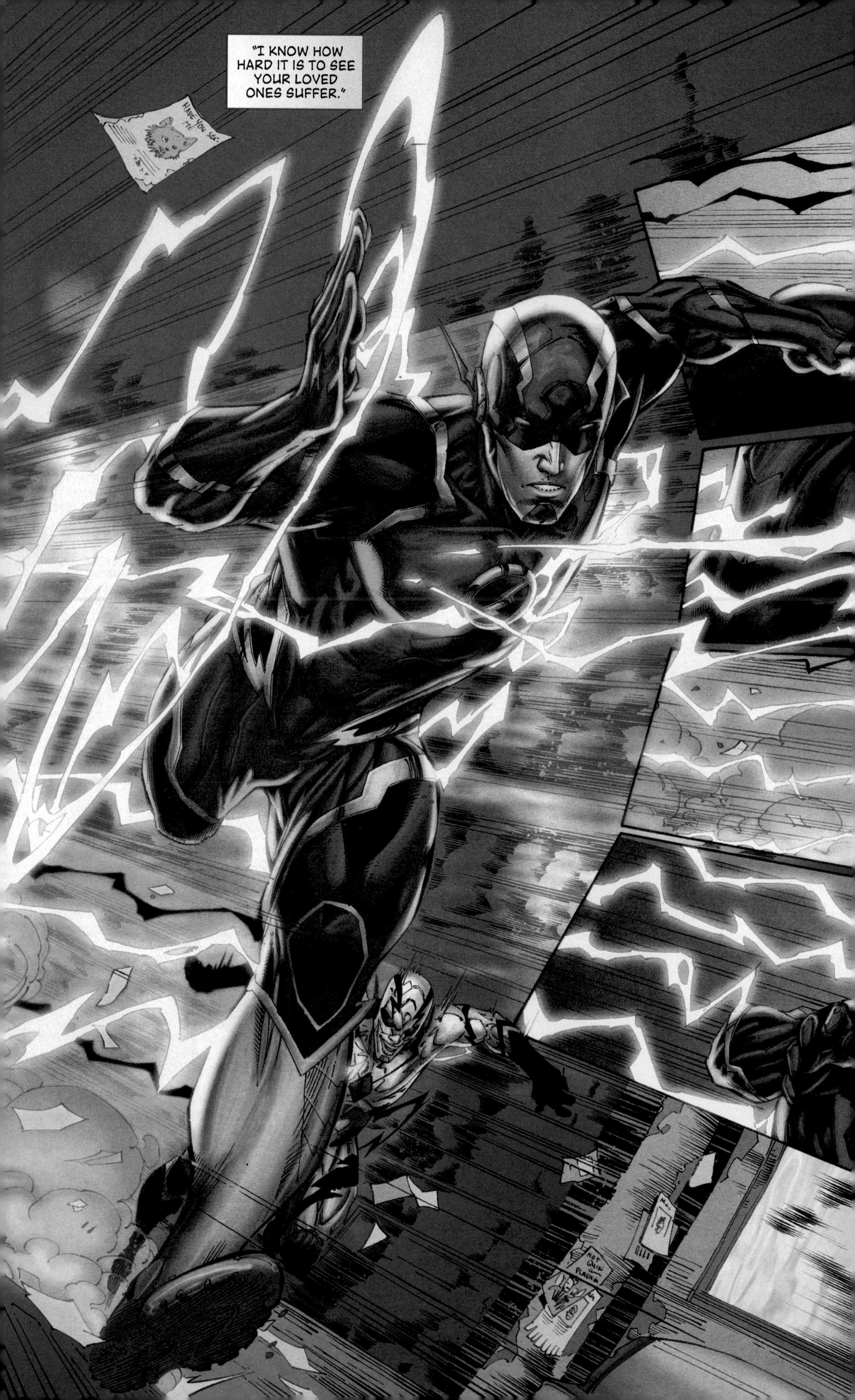
"I KNOW HOW HARD IT IS TO SEE YOUR LOVED ONES SUFFER."

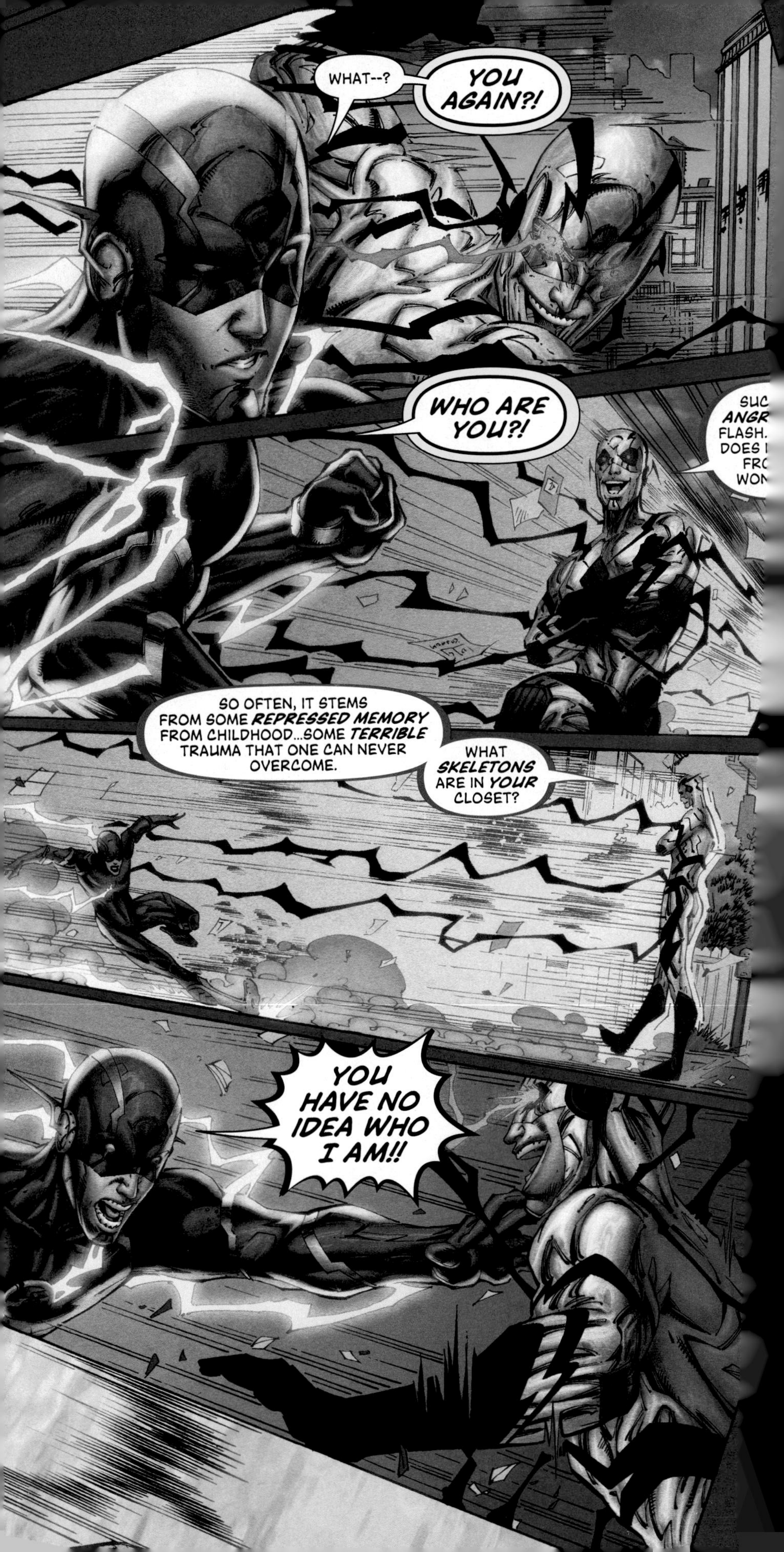
WHAT--?
YOU AGAIN?!
WHO ARE YOU?!
FLASH.
SO OFTEN, IT STEMS FROM SOME REPRESSED MEMORY FROM CHILDHOOD...SOME TERRIBLE TRAUMA THAT ONE CAN NEVER OVERCOME.
WHAT SKELETONS ARE IN YOUR CLOSET?
YOU HAVE NO IDEA WHO I AM!!

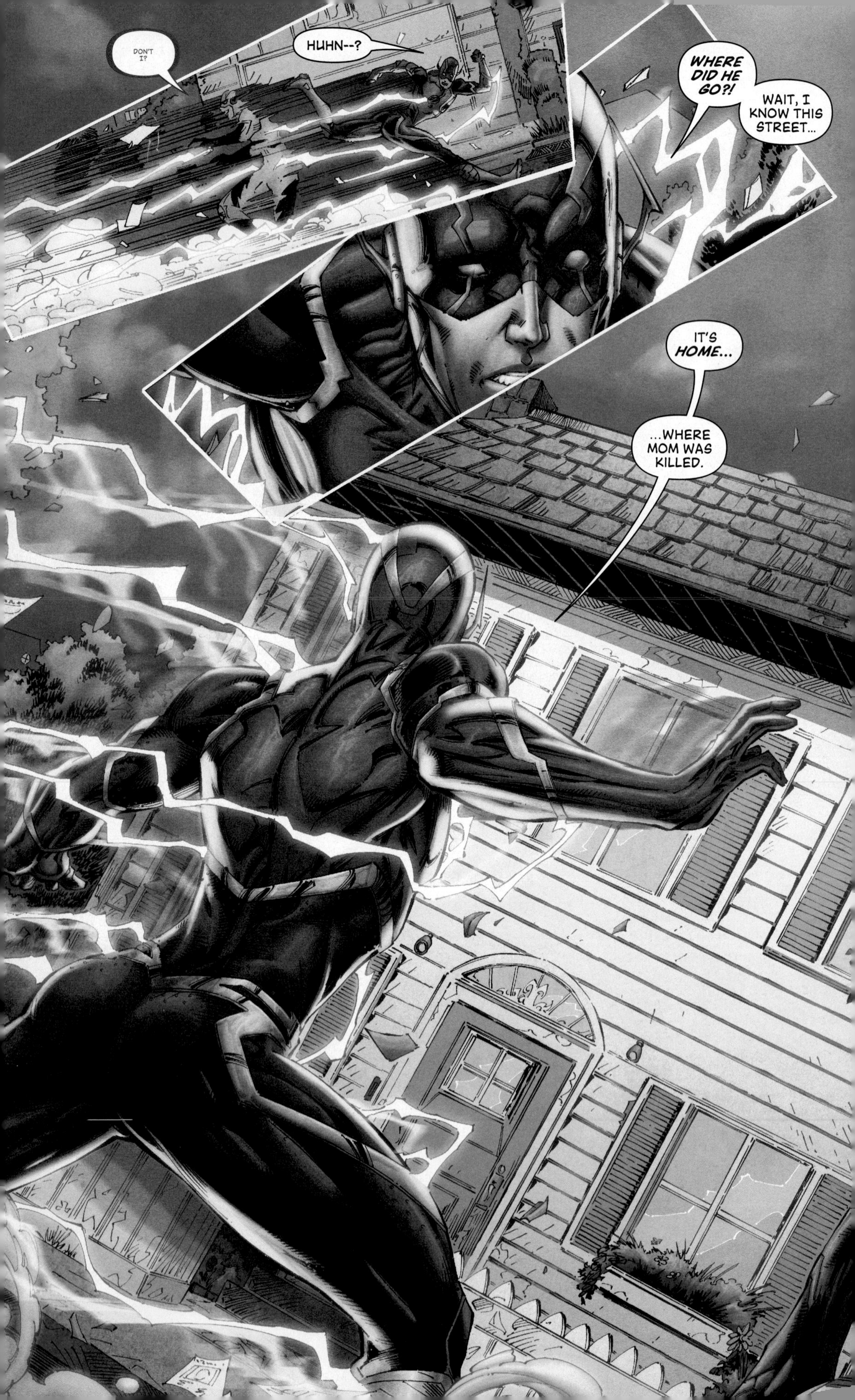
DON'T I?
HUHN--?
WHERE DID HE GO?!
WAIT, I KNOW THIS STREET...
IT'S HOME...
...WHERE MOM WAS KILLED.

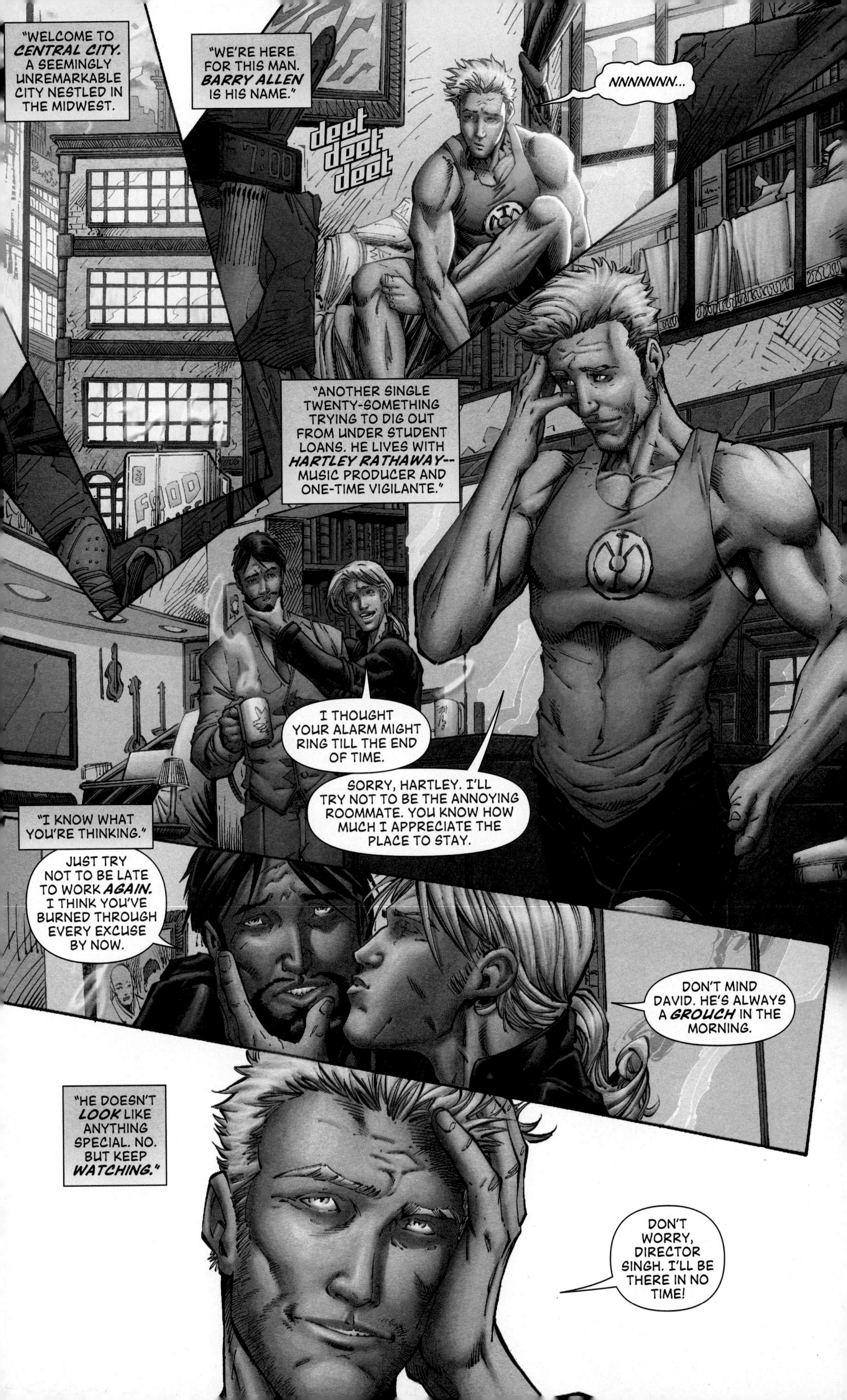
"WELCOME TO CENTRAL CITY. A SEEMINGLY UNREMARKABLE CITY NESTLED IN THE MIDWEST.
"WE'RE HERE FOR THIS MAN. BARRY ALLEN IS HIS NAME."
deet deet deet
NNNNNNN...
"ANOTHER SINGLE TWENTY-SOMETHING TRYING TO DIG OUT FROM UNDER STUDENT LOANS. HE LIVES WITH HARTLEY RATHAWAY--MUSIC PRODUCER AND ONE-TIME VIGILANTE."
I THOUGHT YOUR ALARM MIGHT RING TILL THE END OF TIME.
SORRY, HARTLEY. I'LL TRY NOT TO BE THE ANNOYING ROOMMATE. YOU KNOW HOW MUCH I APPRECIATE THE PLACE TO STAY.
"I KNOW WHAT YOU'RE THINKING."
JUST TRY NOT TO BE LATE TO WORK AGAIN. I THINK YOU'VE BURNED THROUGH EVERY EXCUSE BY NOW.
DON'T MIND DAVID. HE'S ALWAYS A GROUCH IN THE MORNING.
"HE DOESN'T LOOK LIKE ANYTHING SPECIAL. NO. BUT KEEP WATCHING."
DON'T WORRY, DIRECTOR SINGH. I'LL BE THERE IN NO TIME!

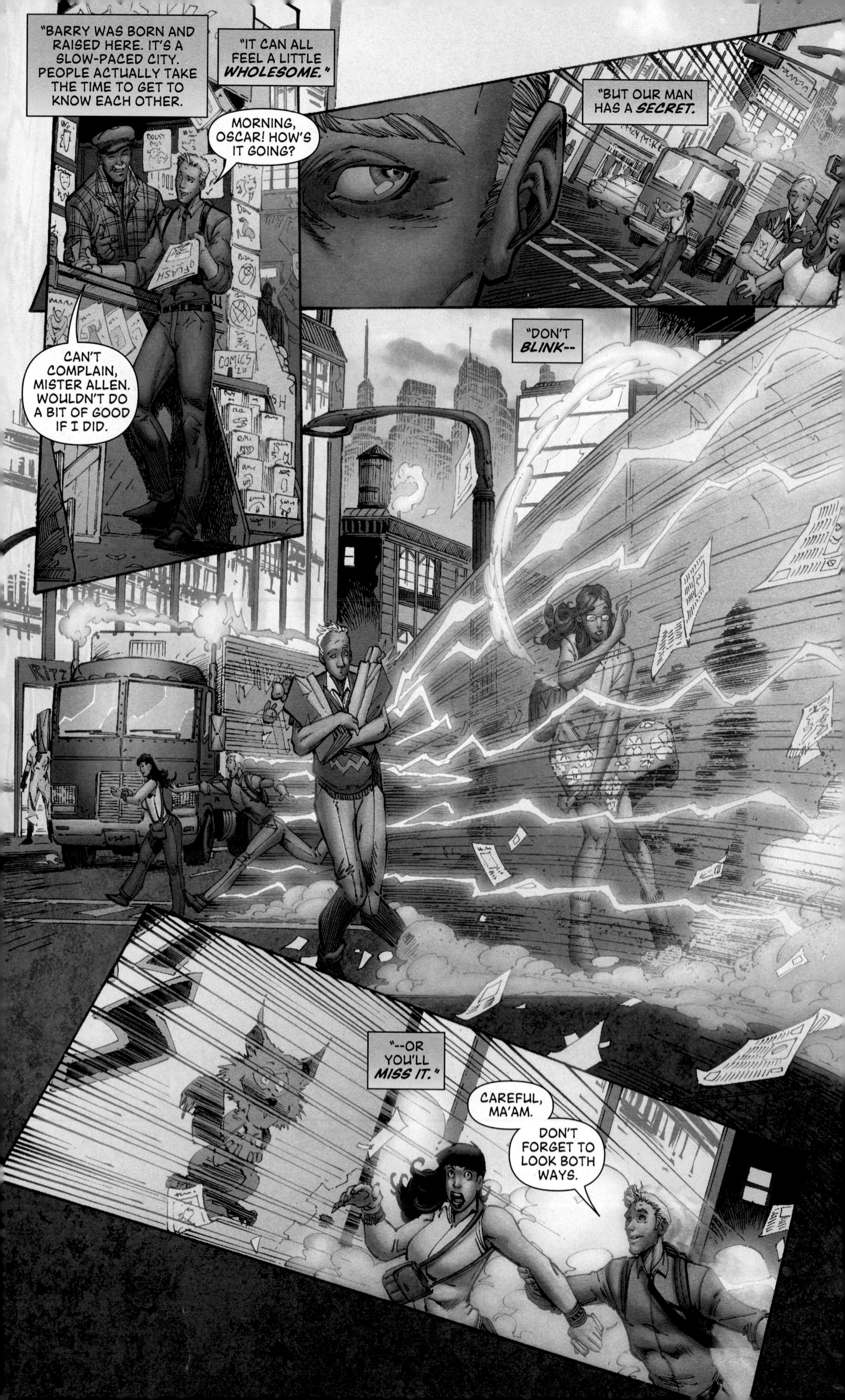
"BARRY WAS BORN AND RAISED HERE. IT'S A SLOW-PACED CITY. PEOPLE ACTUALLY TAKE THE TIME TO GET TO KNOW EACH OTHER.
"IT CAN ALL FEEL A LITTLE WHOLESOME."
MORNING, OSCAR! HOW'S IT GOING?
CAN'T COMPLAIN, MISTER ALLEN. WOULDN'T DO A BIT OF GOOD IF I DID.
"BUT OUR MAN HAS A SECRET.
"DON'T BLINK--
"--OR YOU'LL MISS IT."
CAREFUL, MA'AM.
DON'T FORGET TO LOOK BOTH WAYS.

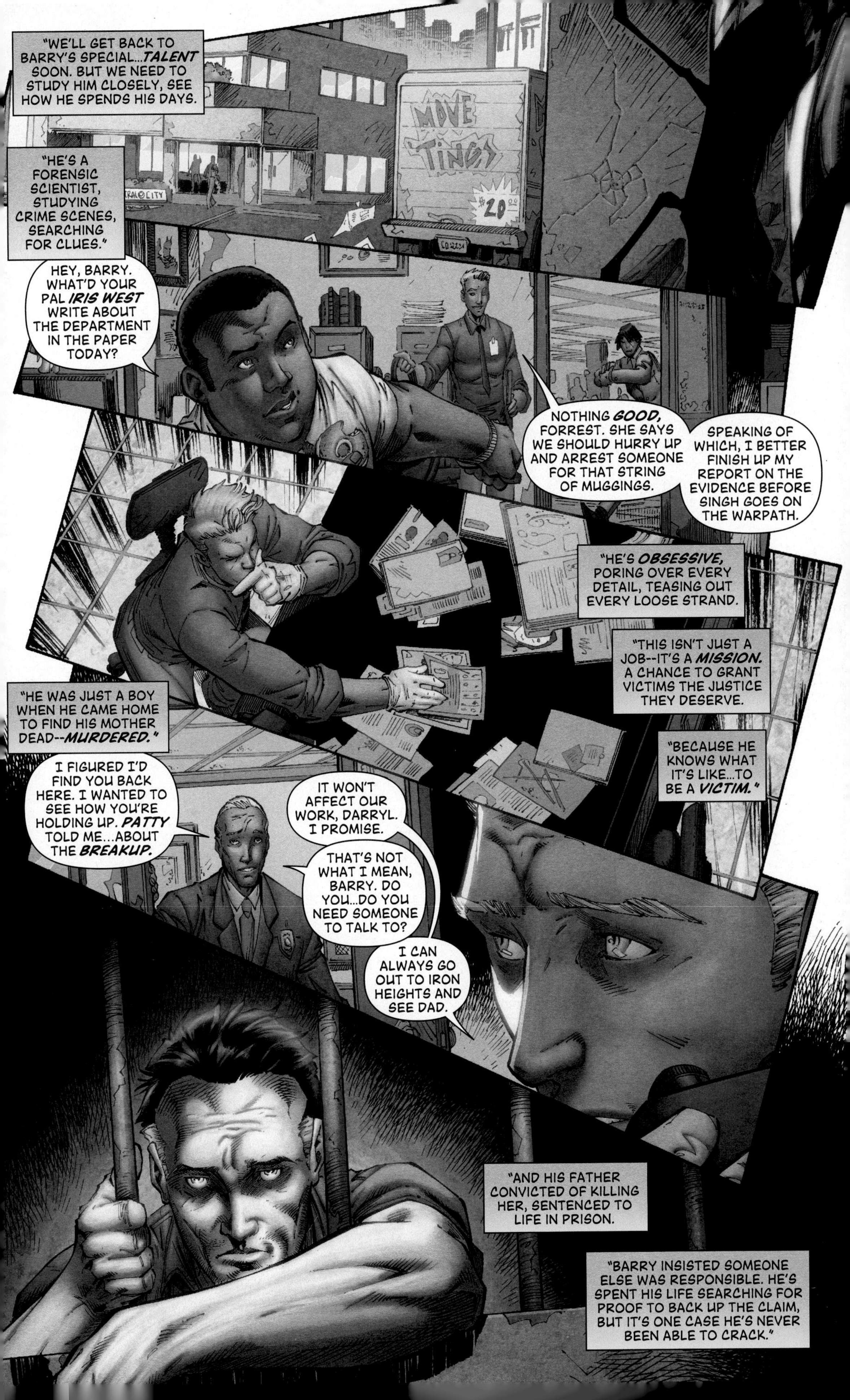

"WE'LL GET BACK TO BARRY'S SPECIAL...TALENT SOON. BUT WE NEED TO STUDY HIM CLOSELY, SEE HOW HE SPENDS HIS DAYS.
MOVE TINGS
$20
"HE'S A FORENSIC SCIENTIST, STUDYING CRIME SCENES, SEARCHING FOR CLUES."
HEY, BARRY. WHAT'D YOUR PAL IRIS WEST WRITE ABOUT THE DEPARTMENT IN THE PAPER TODAY?
NOTHING GOOD, FORREST. SHE SAYS WE SHOULD HURRY UP AND ARREST SOMEONE FOR THAT STRING OF MUGGINGS.
SPEAKING OF WHICH, I BETTER FINISH UP MY REPORT ON THE EVIDENCE BEFORE SINGH GOES ON THE WARPATH.
"HE'S OBSESSIVE, PORING OVER EVERY DETAIL, TEASING OUT EVERY LOOSE STRAND.
"THIS ISN'T JUST A JOB--IT'S A MISSION. A CHANCE TO GRANT VICTIMS THE JUSTICE THEY DESERVE.
"BECAUSE HE KNOWS WHAT IT'S LIKE...TO BE A VICTIM."
"HE WAS JUST A BOY WHEN HE CAME HOME TO FIND HIS MOTHER DEAD--MURDERED."
I FIGURED I'D FIND YOU BACK HERE. I WANTED TO SEE HOW YOU'RE HOLDING UP. PATTY TOLD ME...ABOUT THE BREAKUP.
IT WON'T AFFECT OUR WORK, DARRYL. I PROMISE.
THAT'S NOT WHAT I MEAN, BARRY. DO YOU...DO YOU NEED SOMEONE TO TALK TO?
I CAN ALWAYS GO OUT TO IRON HEIGHTS AND SEE DAD.
"AND HIS FATHER CONVICTED OF KILLING HER, SENTENCED TO LIFE IN PRISON.
"BARRY INSISTED SOMEONE ELSE WAS RESPONSIBLE. HE'S SPENT HIS LIFE SEARCHING FOR PROOF TO BACK UP THE CLAIM, BUT IT'S ONE CASE HE'S NEVER BEEN ABLE TO CRACK."

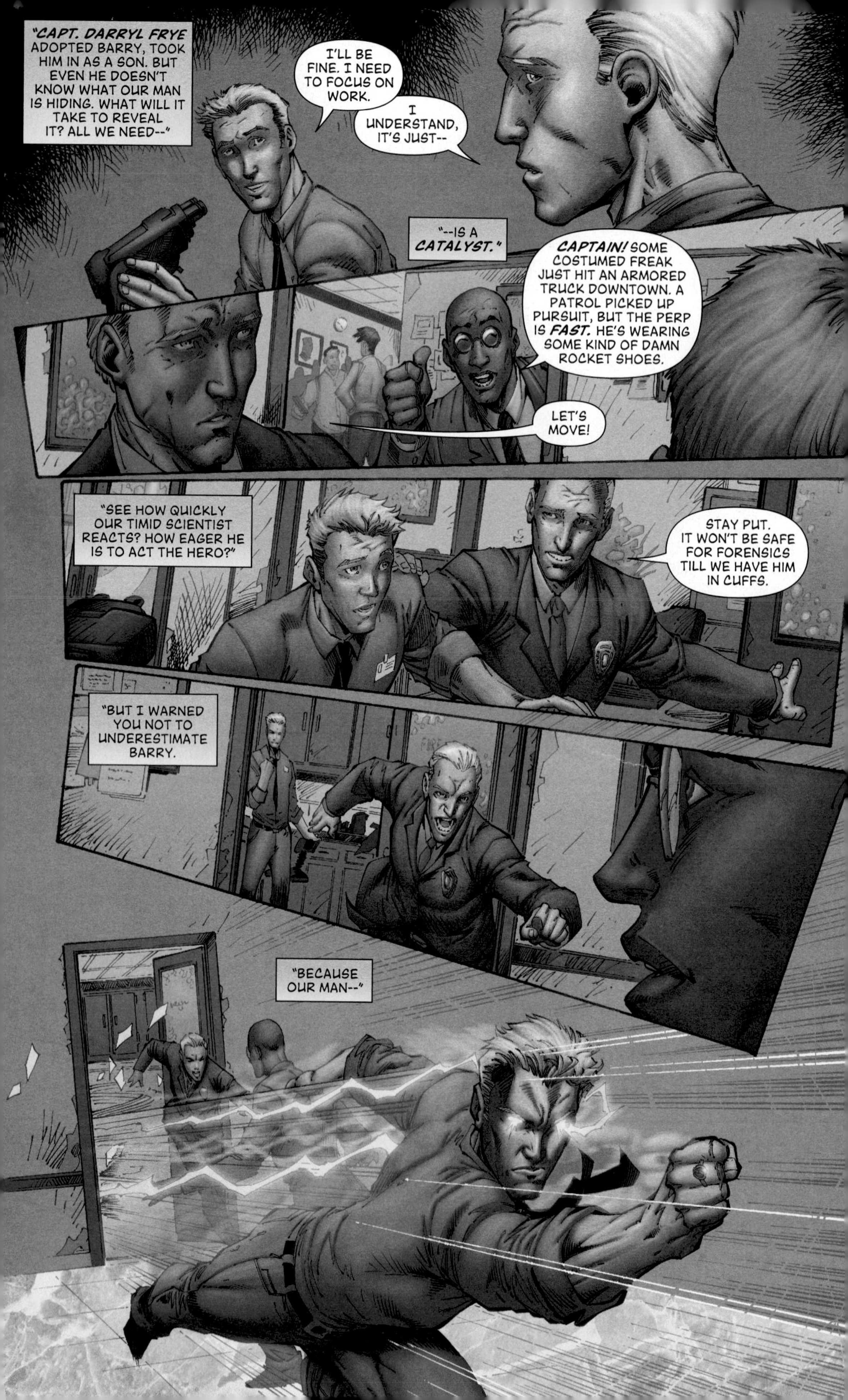
"CAPT. DARRYL FRYE ADOPTED BARRY, TOOK HIM IN AS A SON. BUT EVEN HE DOESN'T KNOW WHAT OUR MAN IS HIDING. WHAT WILL IT TAKE TO REVEAL IT? ALL WE NEED--"
I'LL BE FINE. I NEED TO FOCUS ON WORK.
I UNDERSTAND, IT'S JUST--
"--IS A CATALYST."
CAPTAIN! SOME COSTUMED FREAK JUST HIT AN ARMORED TRUCK DOWNTOWN. A PATROL PICKED UP PURSUIT, BUT THE PERP IS FAST. HE'S WEARING SOME KIND OF DAMN ROCKET SHOES.
LET'S MOVE!
"SEE HOW QUICKLY OUR TIMID SCIENTIST REACTS? HOW EAGER HE IS TO ACT THE HERO?"
STAY PUT. IT WON'T BE SAFE FOR FORENSICS TILL WE HAVE HIM IN CUFFS.
"BUT I WARNED YOU NOT TO UNDERESTIMATE BARRY.
"BECAUSE OUR MAN--"

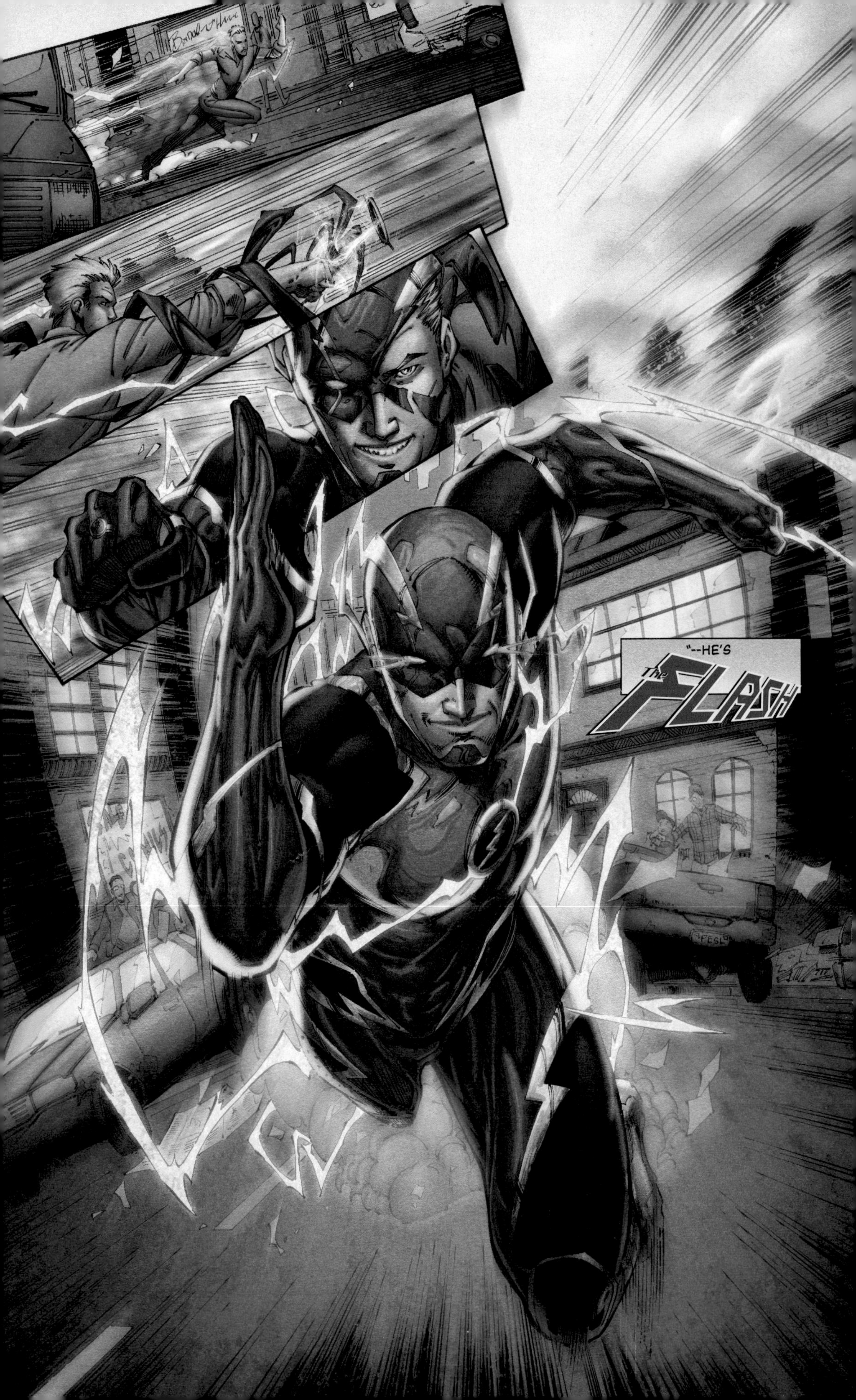
"--HE'S
The FLASH

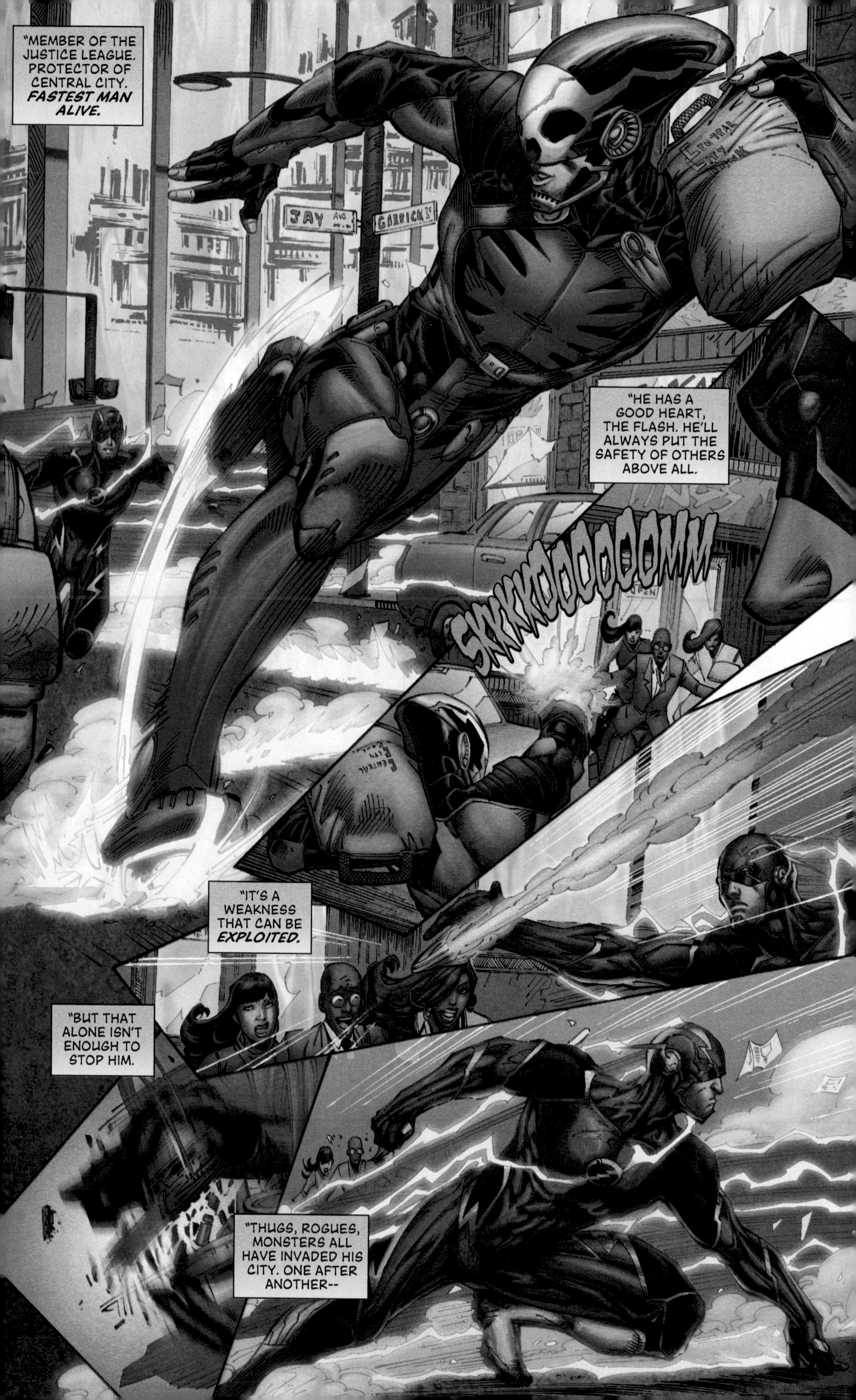
"MEMBER OF THE JUSTICE LEAGUE. PROTECTOR OF CENTRAL CITY. *FASTEST MAN ALIVE.*
JAY AVE
GARRICK ST
"HE HAS A GOOD HEART, THE FLASH. HE'LL ALWAYS PUT THE SAFETY OF OTHERS ABOVE ALL.
SKKKOOOOOOMM
OPEN
"IT'S A WEAKNESS THAT CAN BE *EXPLOITED.*
"BUT THAT ALONE ISN'T ENOUGH TO STOP HIM.
"THUGS, ROGUES, MONSTERS ALL HAVE INVADED HIS CITY. ONE AFTER ANOTHER--

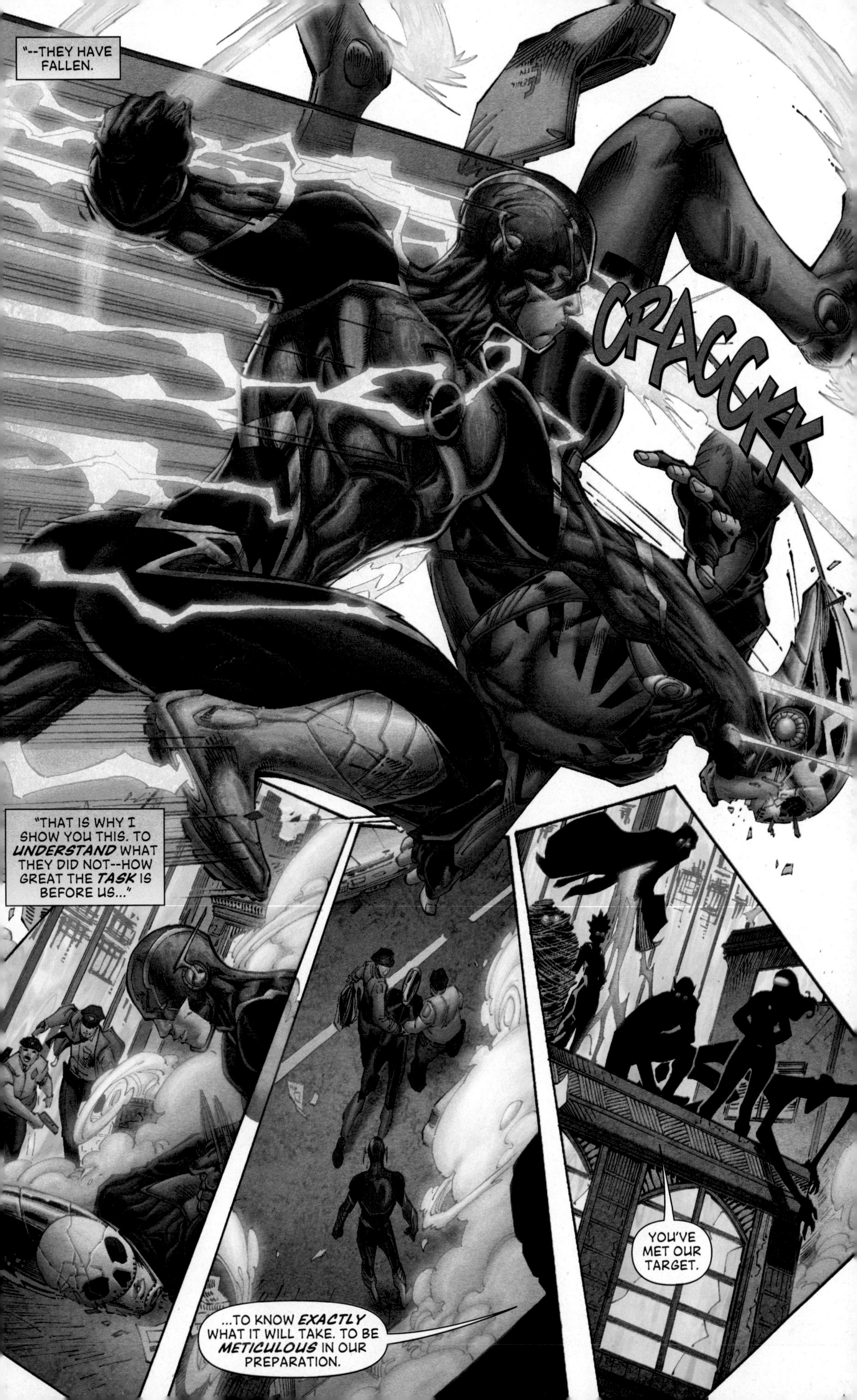
"--THEY HAVE FALLEN.
CRACCKK
"THAT IS WHY I SHOW YOU THIS. TO UNDERSTAND WHAT THEY DID NOT--HOW GREAT THE TASK IS BEFORE US..."
...TO KNOW EXACTLY WHAT IT WILL TAKE. TO BE METICULOUS IN OUR PREPARATION.
YOU'VE MET OUR TARGET.

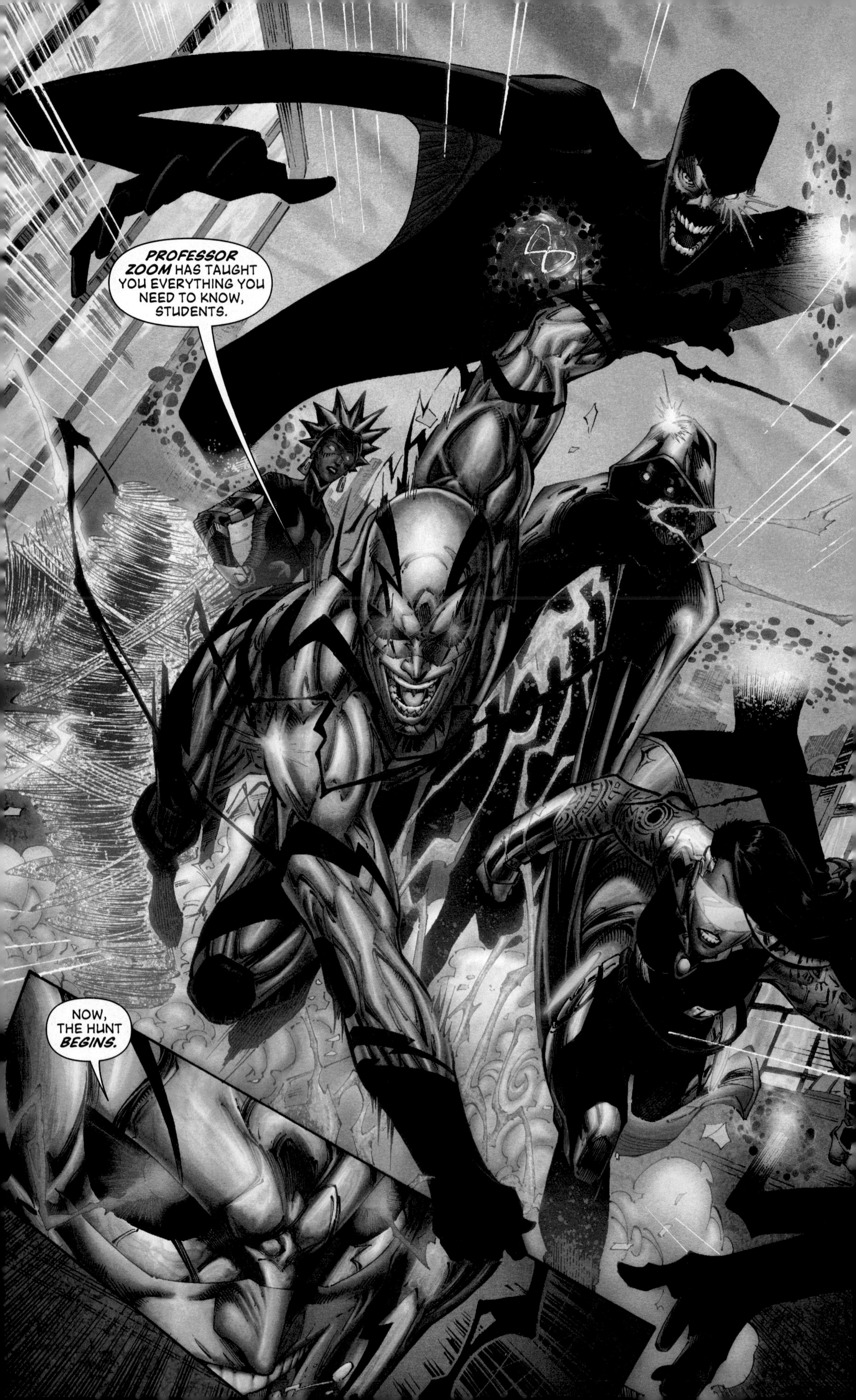
PROFESSOR ZOOM HAS TAUGHT YOU EVERYTHING YOU NEED TO KNOW, STUDENTS.
NOW, THE HUNT BEGINS.

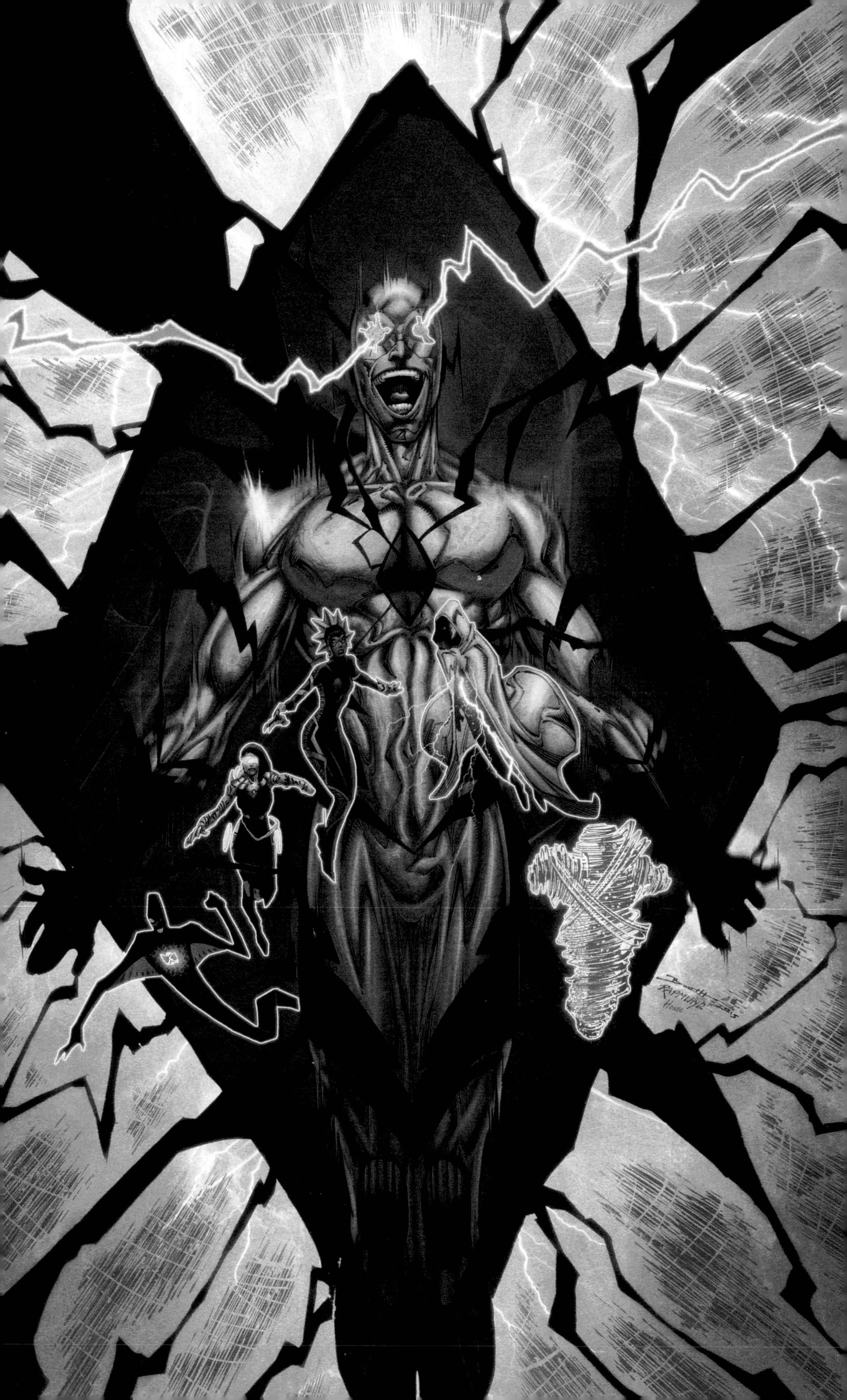

cover by **BRETT BOOTH, NORM RAPMUND, ANDREW DALHOUSE**

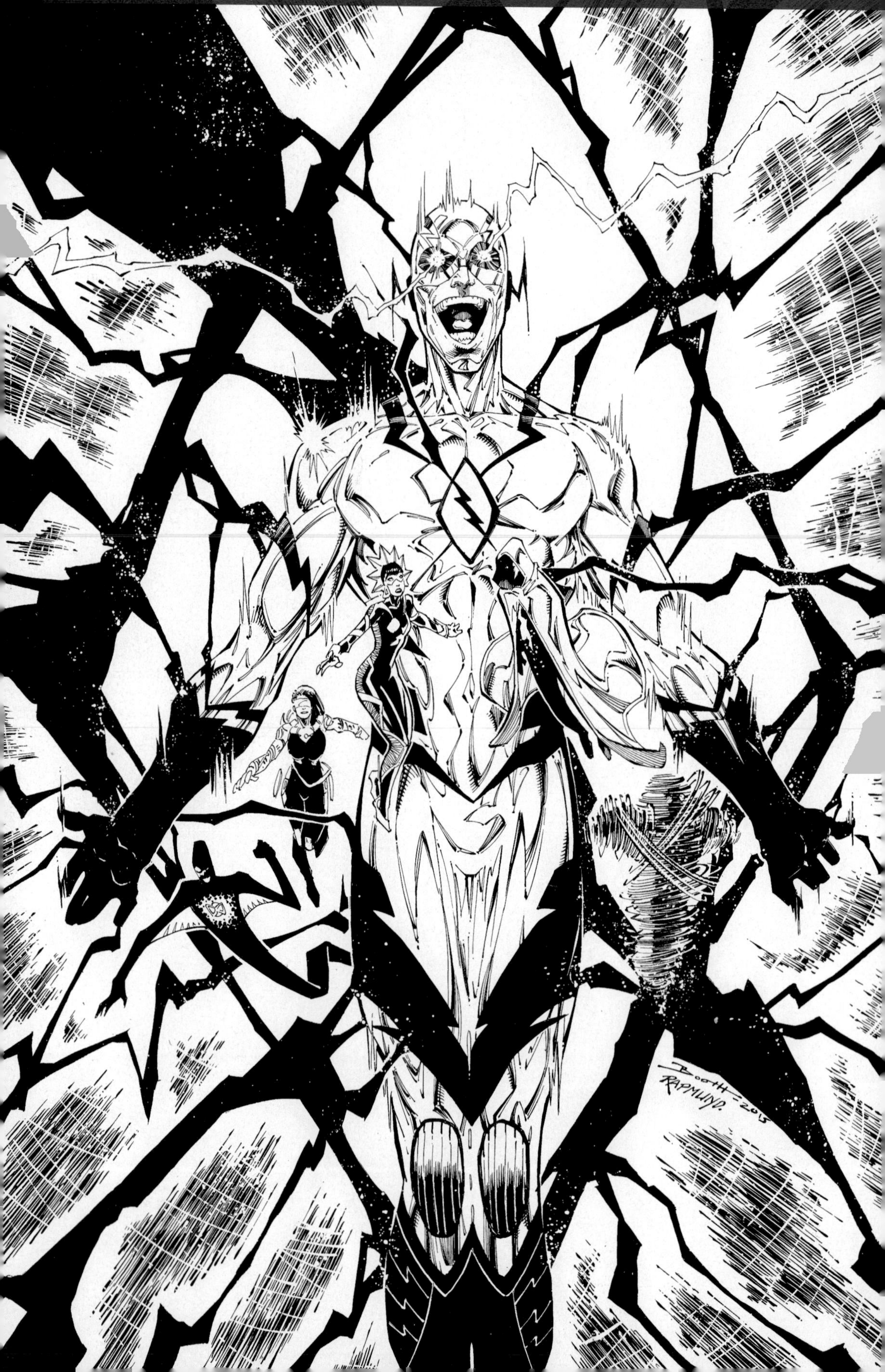
BOOTH 2015
RAPMUND

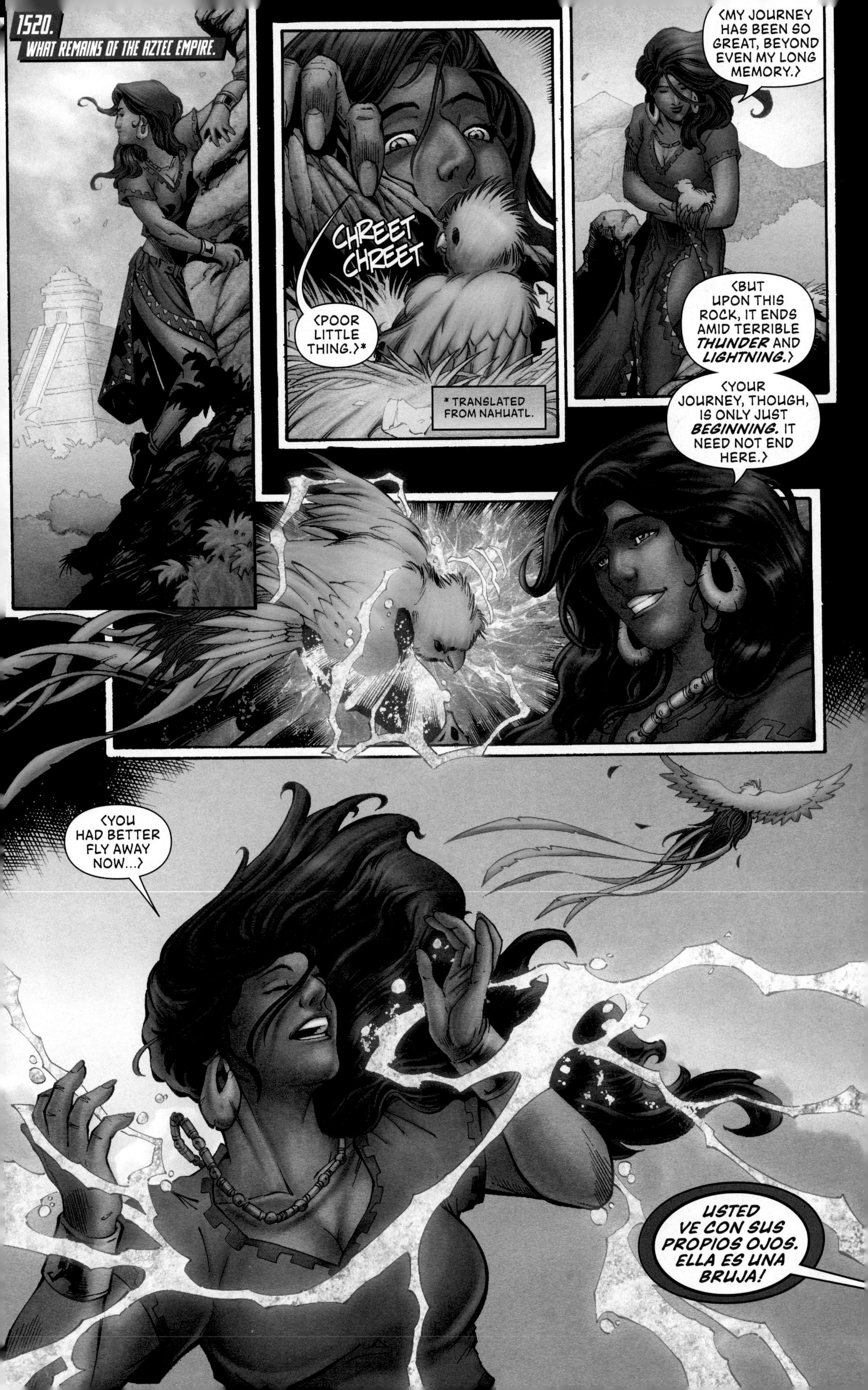
1520.
WHAT REMAINS OF THE AZTEC EMPIRE.
CHREET CHREET
<POOR LITTLE THING.>*
* TRANSLATED FROM NAHUATL.
<MY JOURNEY HAS BEEN SO GREAT, BEYOND EVEN MY LONG MEMORY.>
<BUT UPON THIS ROCK, IT ENDS AMID TERRIBLE THUNDER AND LIGHTNING.>
<YOUR JOURNEY, THOUGH, IS ONLY JUST BEGINNING. IT NEED NOT END HERE.>
<YOU HAD BETTER FLY AWAY NOW...>
USTED VE CON SUS PROPIOS OJOS. ELLA ES UNA BRUJA!

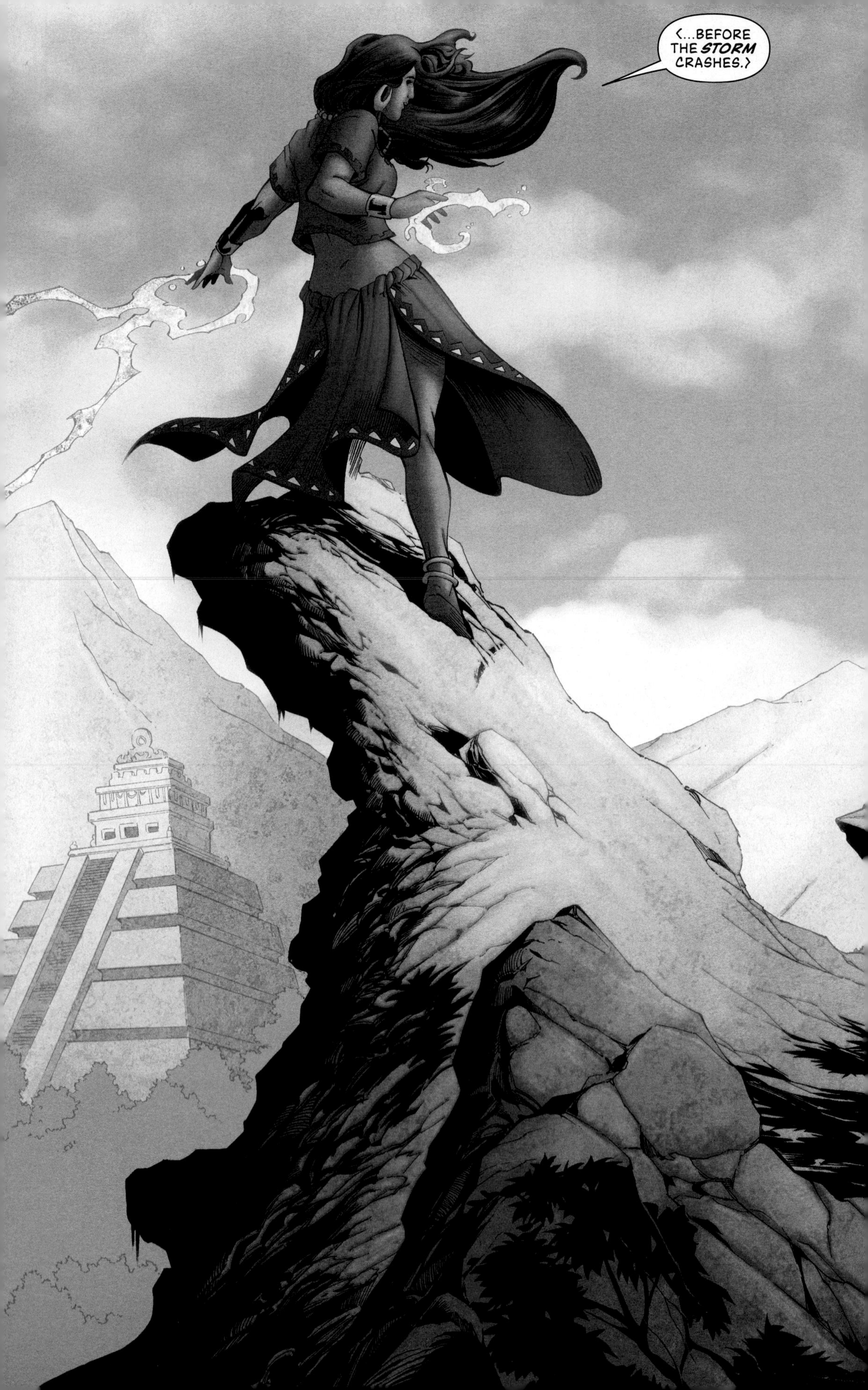
<...BEFORE THE STORM CRASHES.>

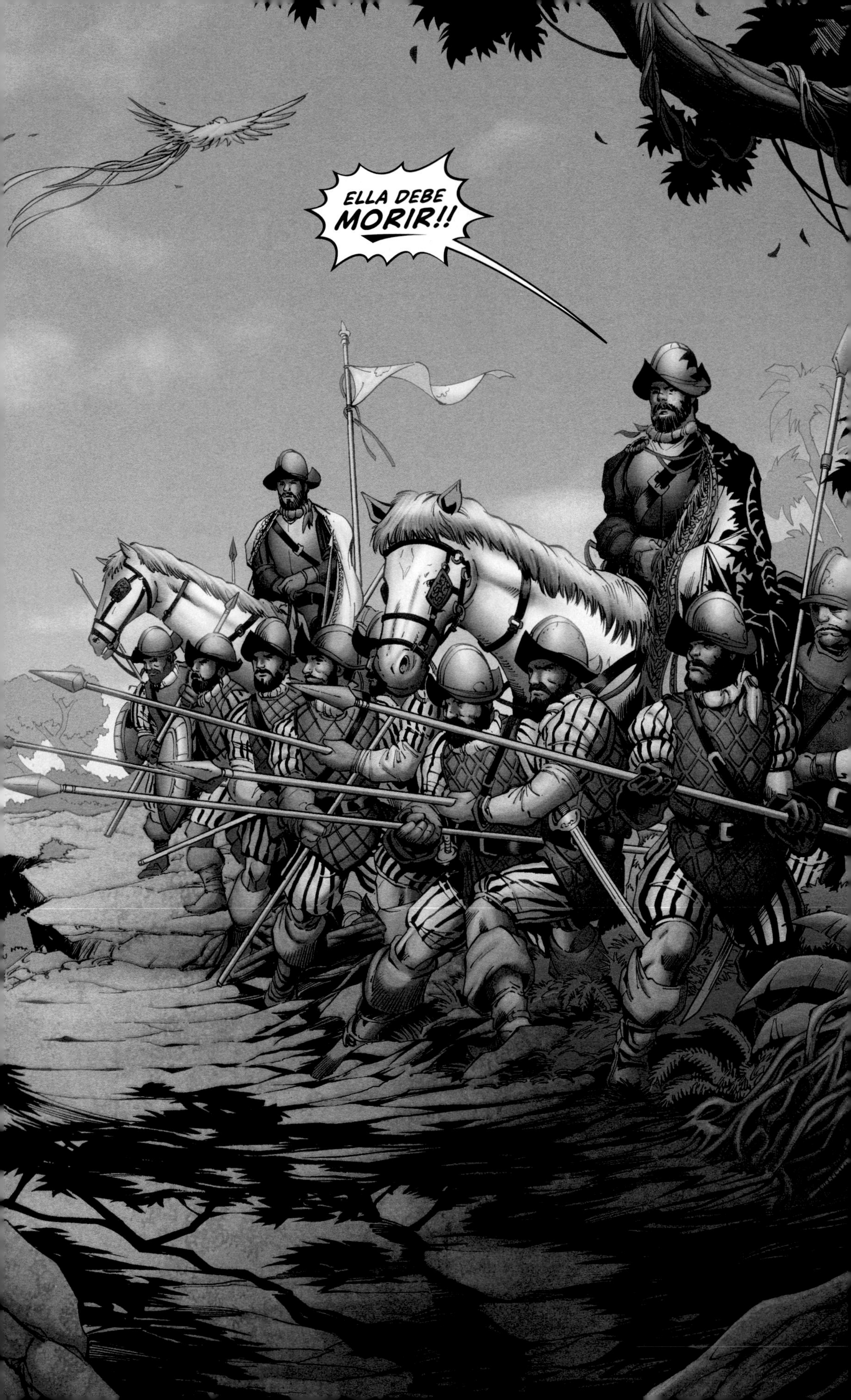
ELLA DEBE MORIR!!

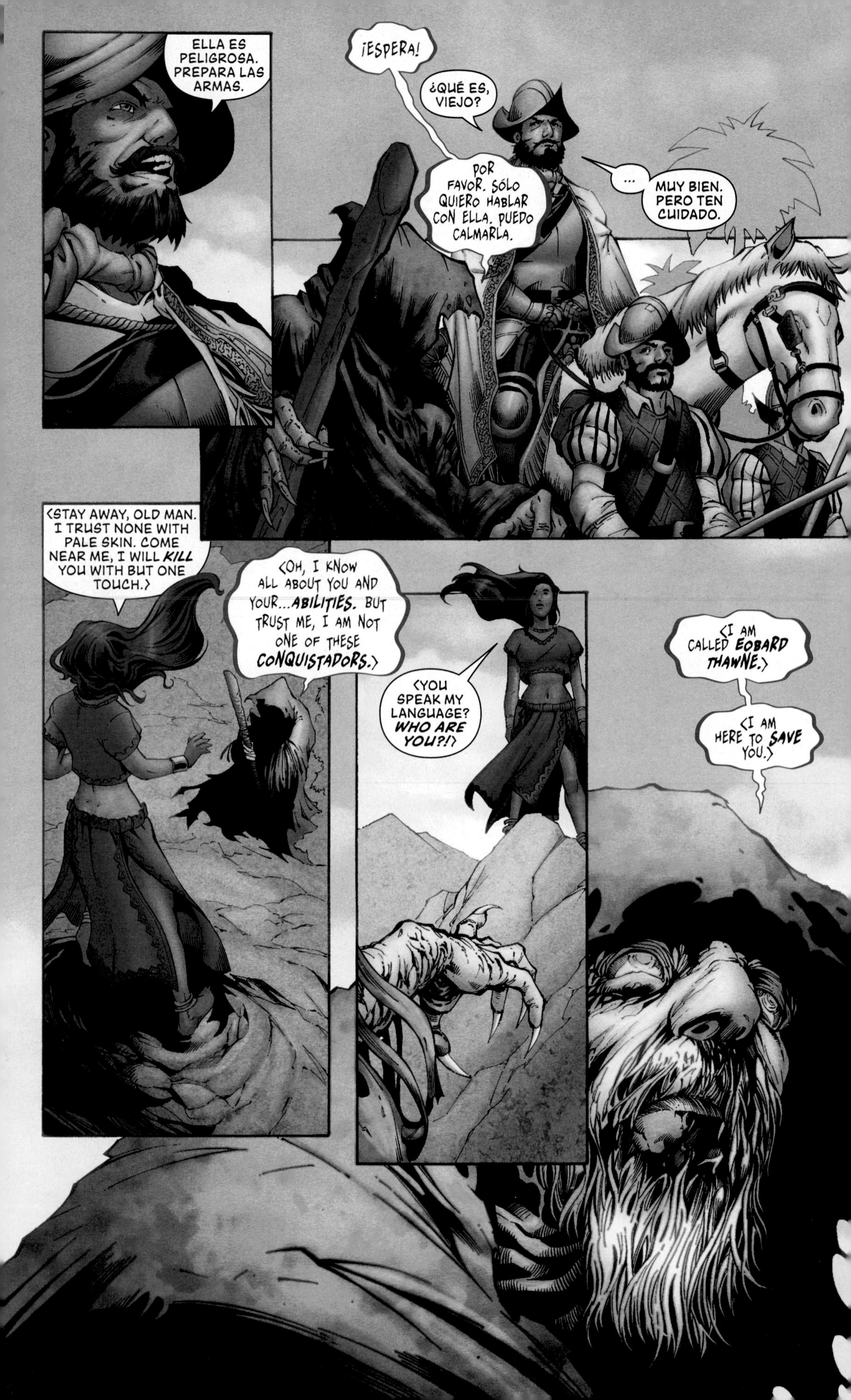
ELLA ES PELIGROSA. PREPARA LAS ARMAS.
¡ESPERA!
¿QUÉ ES, VIEJO?
POR FAVOR. SÓLO QUIERO HABLAR CON ELLA. PUEDO CALMARLA.
...
MUY BIEN. PERO TEN CUIDADO.
<STAY AWAY, OLD MAN. I TRUST NONE WITH PALE SKIN. COME NEAR ME, I WILL KILL YOU WITH BUT ONE TOUCH.>
<OH, I KNOW ALL ABOUT YOU AND YOUR...ABILITIES. BUT TRUST ME, I AM NOT ONE OF THESE CONQUISTADORS.>
<YOU SPEAK MY LANGUAGE? WHO ARE YOU?!>
<I AM CALLED EOBARD THAWNE.>
<I AM HERE TO SAVE YOU.>

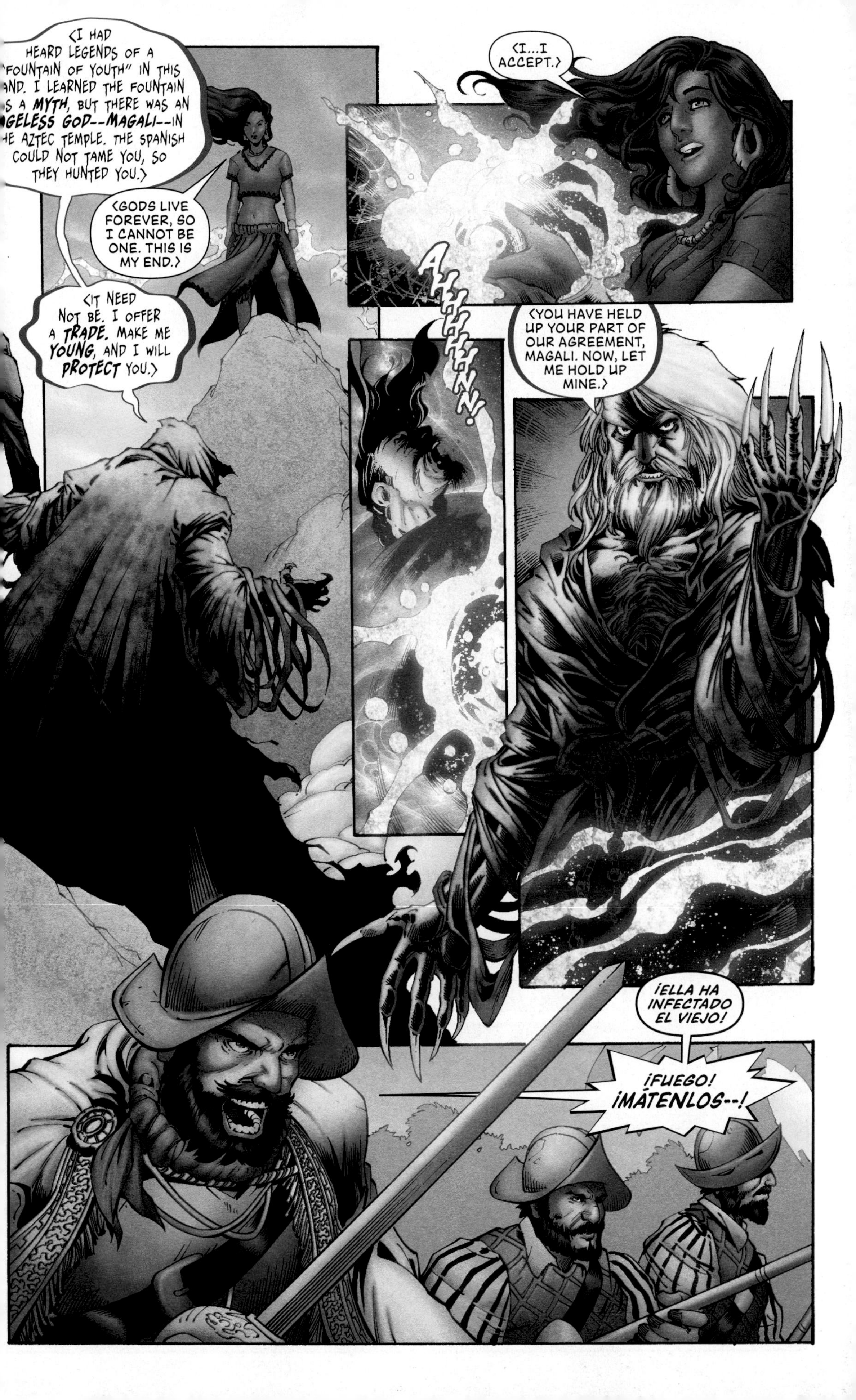
<I HAD HEARD LEGENDS OF A "FOUNTAIN OF YOUTH" IN THIS LAND. I LEARNED THE FOUNTAIN WAS A MYTH, BUT THERE WAS AN AGELESS GOD--MAGALI--IN THE AZTEC TEMPLE. THE SPANISH COULD NOT TAME YOU, SO THEY HUNTED YOU.>
<GODS LIVE FOREVER, SO I CANNOT BE ONE. THIS IS MY END.>
<IT NEED NOT BE. I OFFER A TRADE. MAKE ME YOUNG, AND I WILL PROTECT YOU.>
<I...I ACCEPT.>
AHHHHNN!
<YOU HAVE HELD UP YOUR PART OF OUR AGREEMENT, MAGALI. NOW, LET ME HOLD UP MINE.>
¡ELLA HA INFECTADO EL VIEJO!
¡FUEGO! ¡MÁTENLOS--!

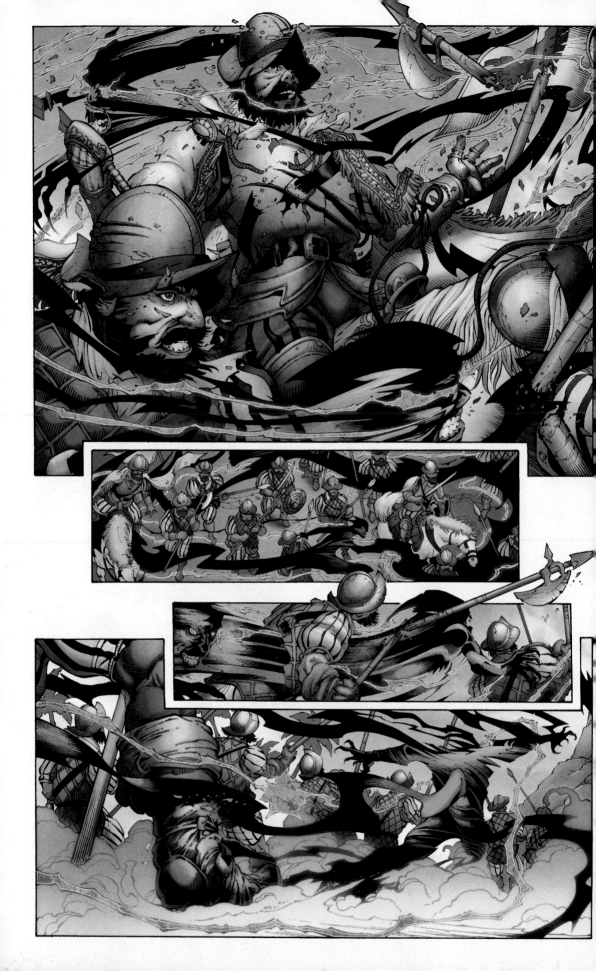

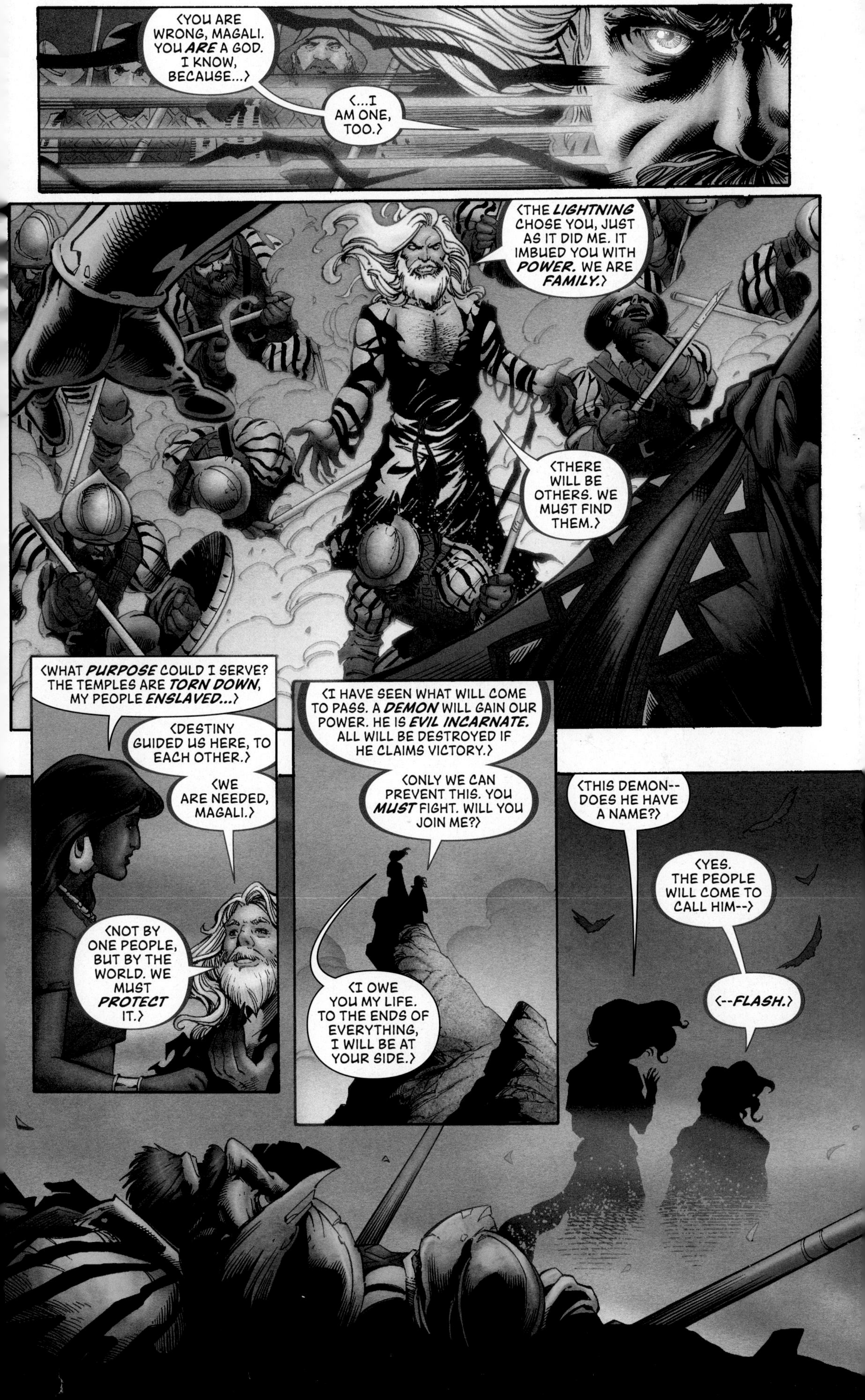

<YOU ARE WRONG, MAGALI. YOU *ARE* A GOD. I KNOW, BECAUSE...>
<...I AM ONE, TOO.>
<THE *LIGHTNING* CHOSE YOU, JUST AS IT DID ME. IT IMBUED YOU WITH *POWER.* WE ARE *FAMILY.*>
<THERE WILL BE OTHERS. WE MUST FIND THEM.>
<WHAT *PURPOSE* COULD I SERVE? THE TEMPLES ARE *TORN DOWN*, MY PEOPLE *ENSLAVED...*>
<DESTINY GUIDED US HERE, TO EACH OTHER.>
<WE ARE NEEDED, MAGALI.>
<NOT BY ONE PEOPLE, BUT BY THE WORLD. WE MUST *PROTECT* IT.>
<I HAVE SEEN WHAT WILL COME TO PASS. A *DEMON* WILL GAIN OUR POWER. HE IS *EVIL INCARNATE.* ALL WILL BE DESTROYED IF HE CLAIMS VICTORY.>
<ONLY WE CAN PREVENT THIS. YOU *MUST* FIGHT. WILL YOU JOIN ME?>
<I OWE YOU MY LIFE. TO THE ENDS OF EVERYTHING, I WILL BE AT YOUR SIDE.>
<THIS DEMON-- DOES HE HAVE A NAME?>
<YES. THE PEOPLE WILL COME TO CALL HIM-->
<--*FLASH.*>

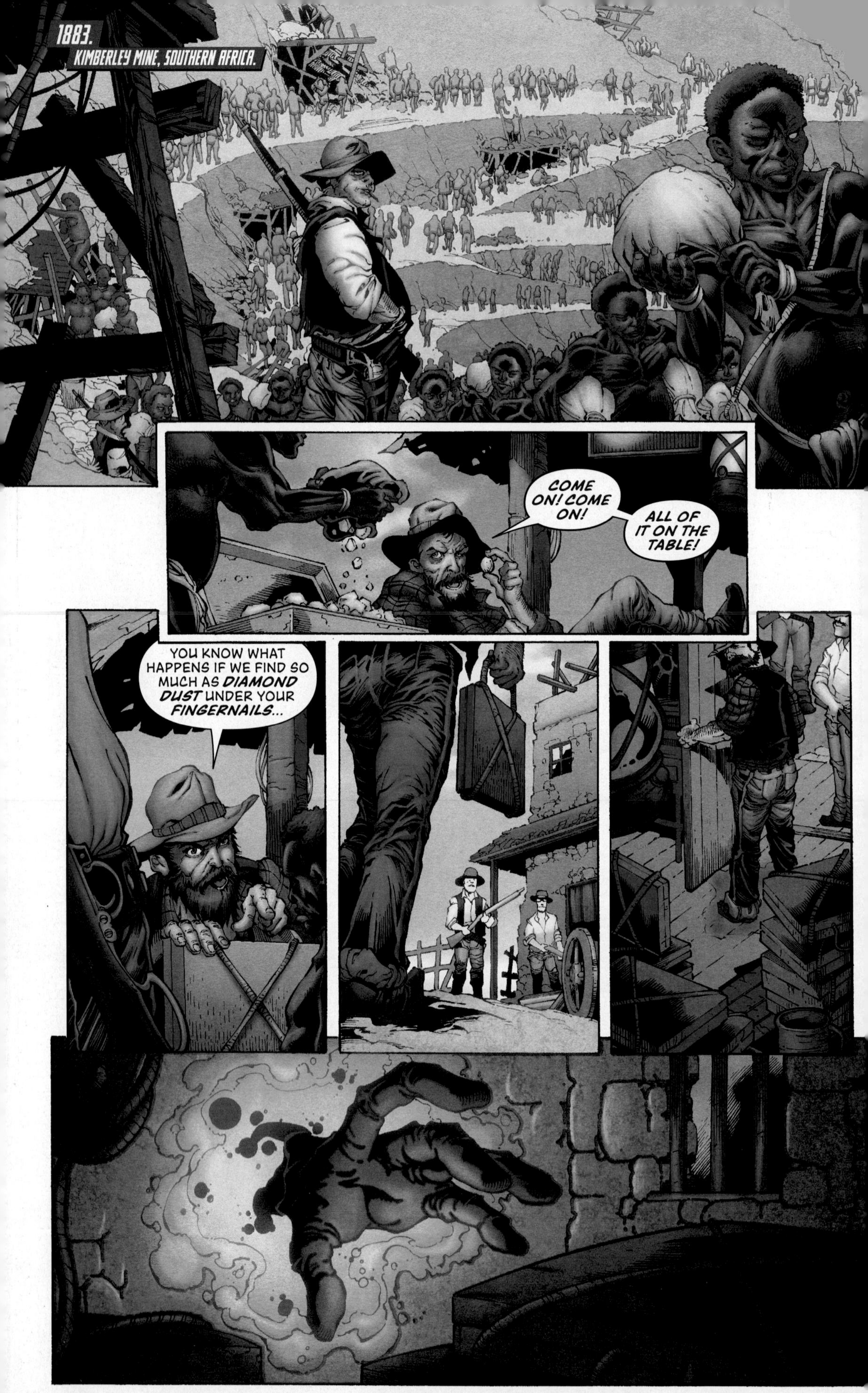
1883.
KIMBERLEY MINE, SOUTHERN AFRICA.
COME ON! COME ON!
ALL OF IT ON THE TABLE!
YOU KNOW WHAT HAPPENS IF WE FIND SO MUCH AS DIAMOND DUST UNDER YOUR FINGERNAILS...

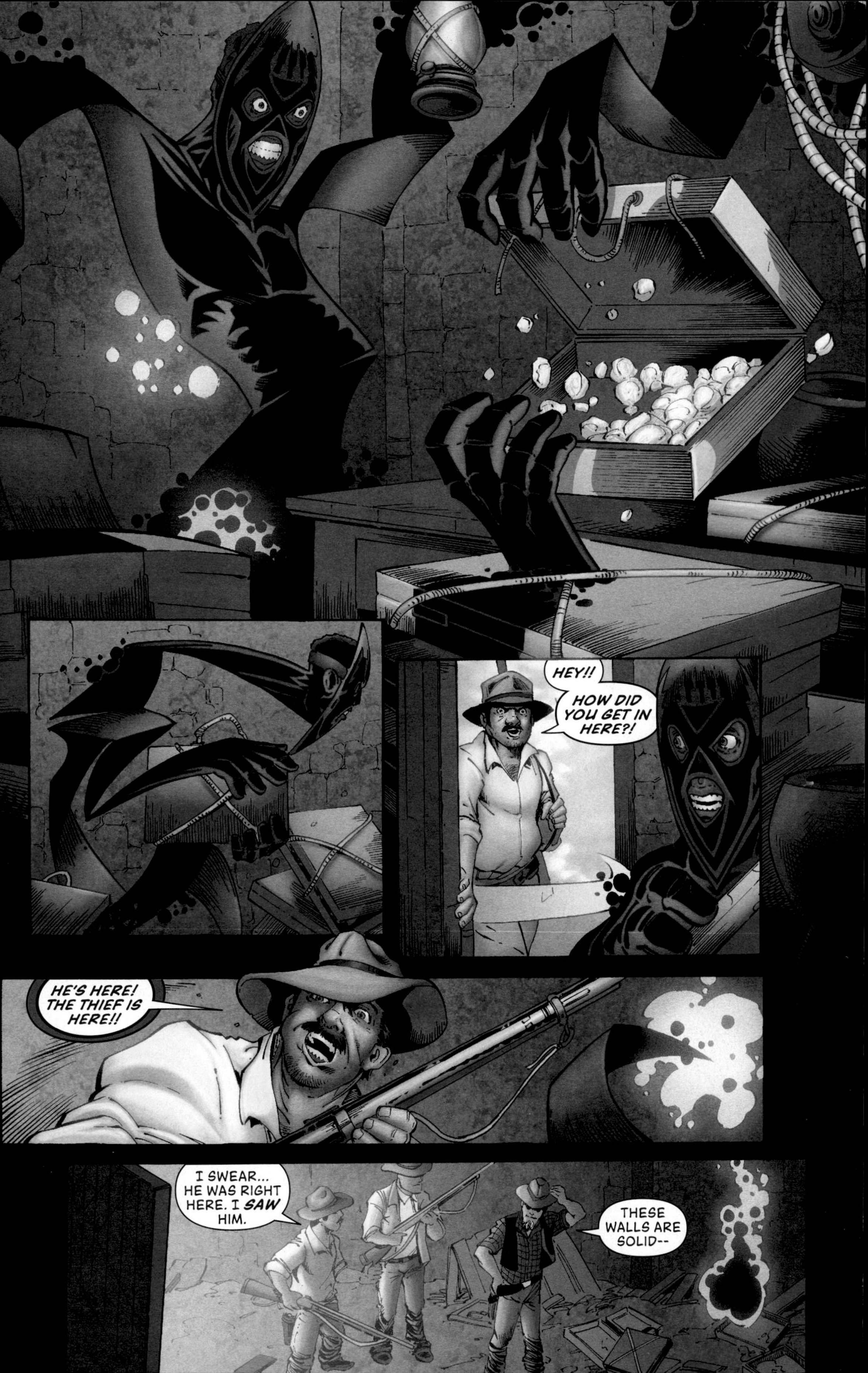
HEY!!
HOW DID YOU GET IN HERE?!
HE'S HERE! THE THIEF IS HERE!!
I SWEAR... HE WAS RIGHT HERE. I SAW HIM.
THESE WALLS ARE SOLID--

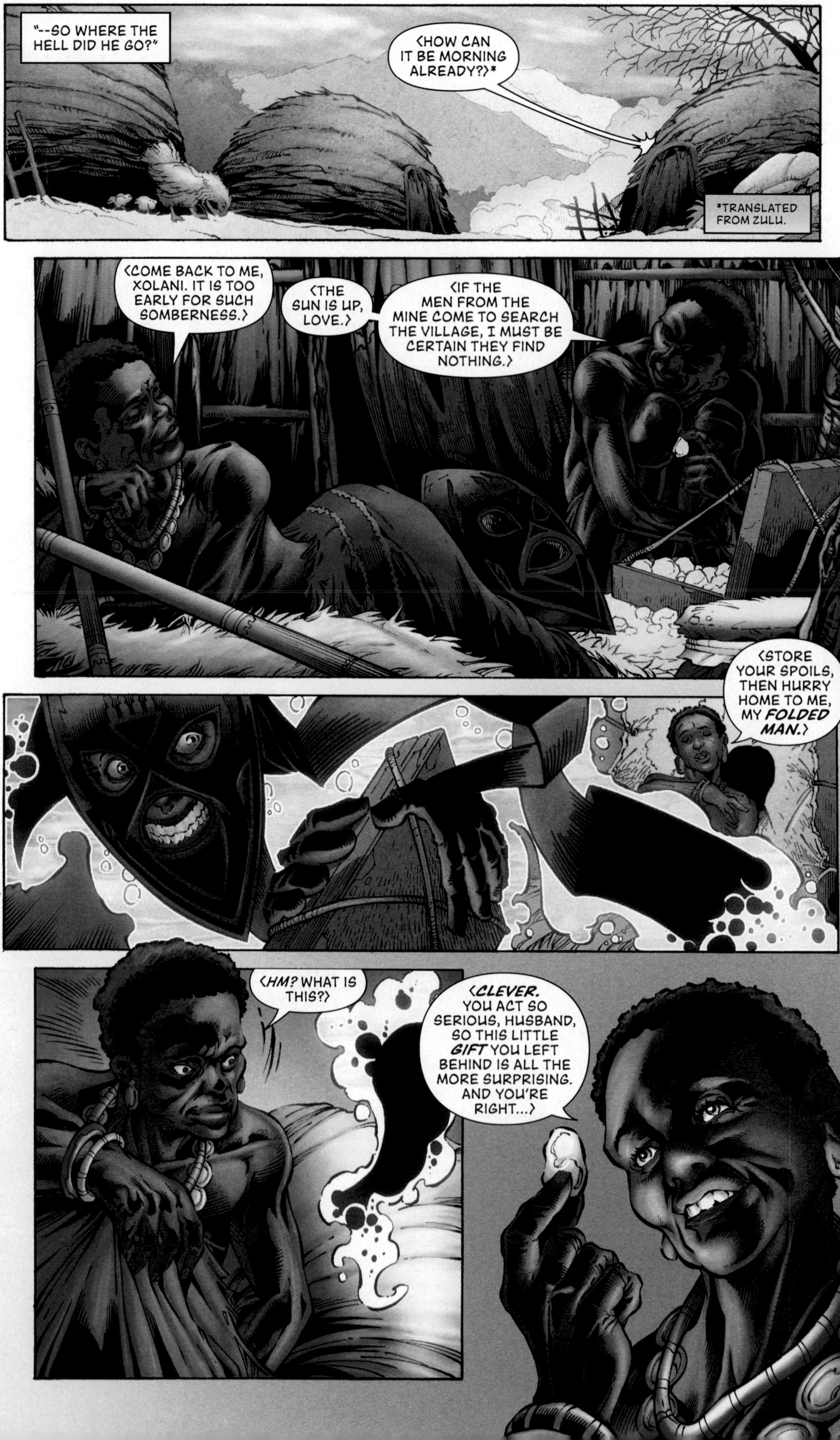
"--SO WHERE THE HELL DID HE GO?"
<HOW CAN IT BE MORNING ALREADY?>*
*TRANSLATED FROM ZULU.
<COME BACK TO ME, XOLANI. IT IS TOO EARLY FOR SUCH SOMBERNESS.>
<THE SUN IS UP, LOVE.>
<IF THE MEN FROM THE MINE COME TO SEARCH THE VILLAGE, I MUST BE CERTAIN THEY FIND NOTHING.>
<STORE YOUR SPOILS, THEN HURRY HOME TO ME, MY *FOLDED MAN.*>
<*HM?* WHAT IS THIS?>
<*CLEVER.* YOU ACT SO SERIOUS, HUSBAND, SO THIS LITTLE *GIFT* YOU LEFT BEHIND IS ALL THE MORE SURPRISING. AND YOU'RE RIGHT...>

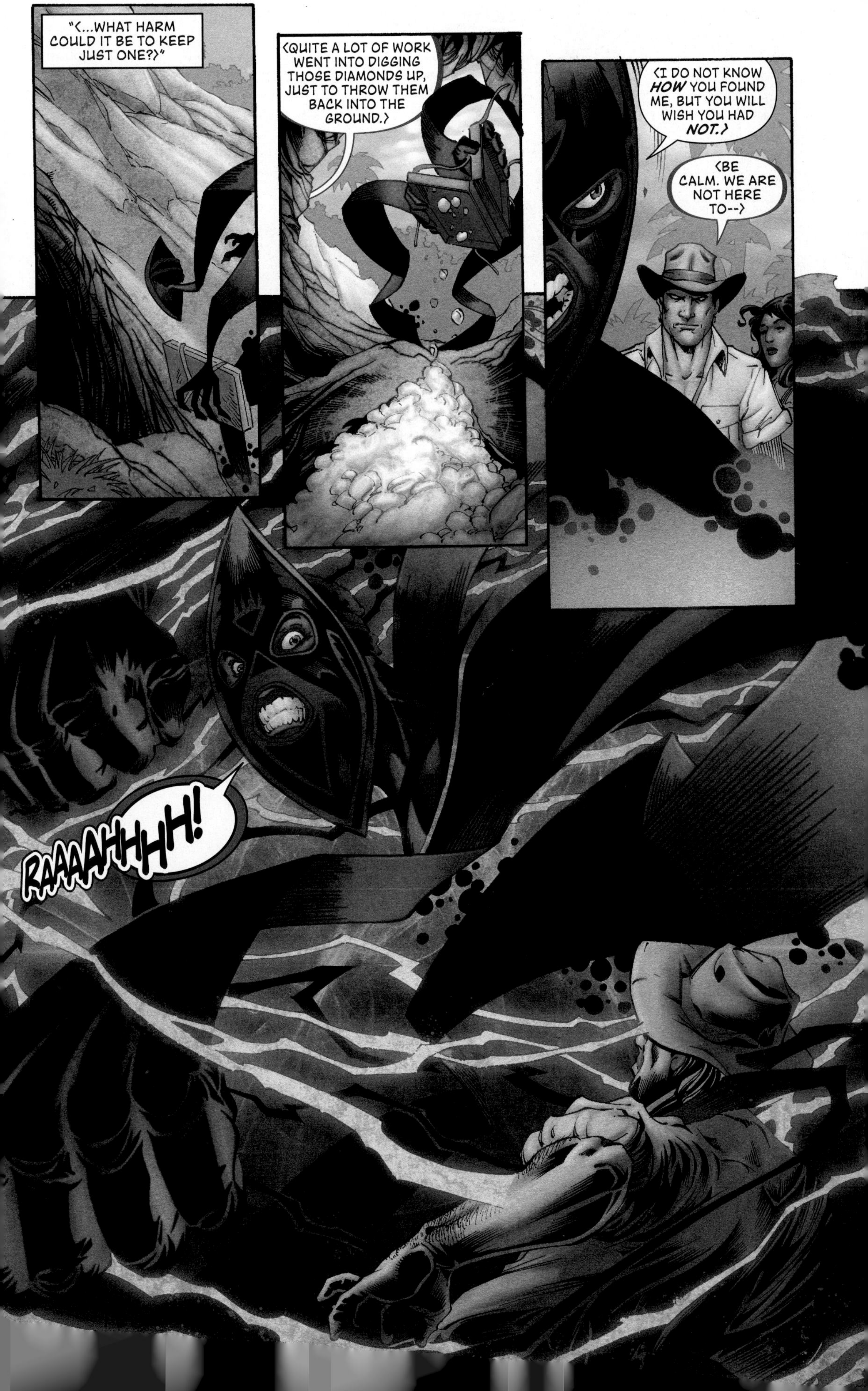
"<...WHAT HARM COULD IT BE TO KEEP JUST ONE?>"
<QUITE A LOT OF WORK WENT INTO DIGGING THOSE DIAMONDS UP, JUST TO THROW THEM BACK INTO THE GROUND.>
<I DO NOT KNOW *HOW* YOU FOUND ME, BUT YOU WILL WISH YOU HAD *NOT.*>
<BE CALM. WE ARE NOT HERE TO-->
RAAAHHHH!

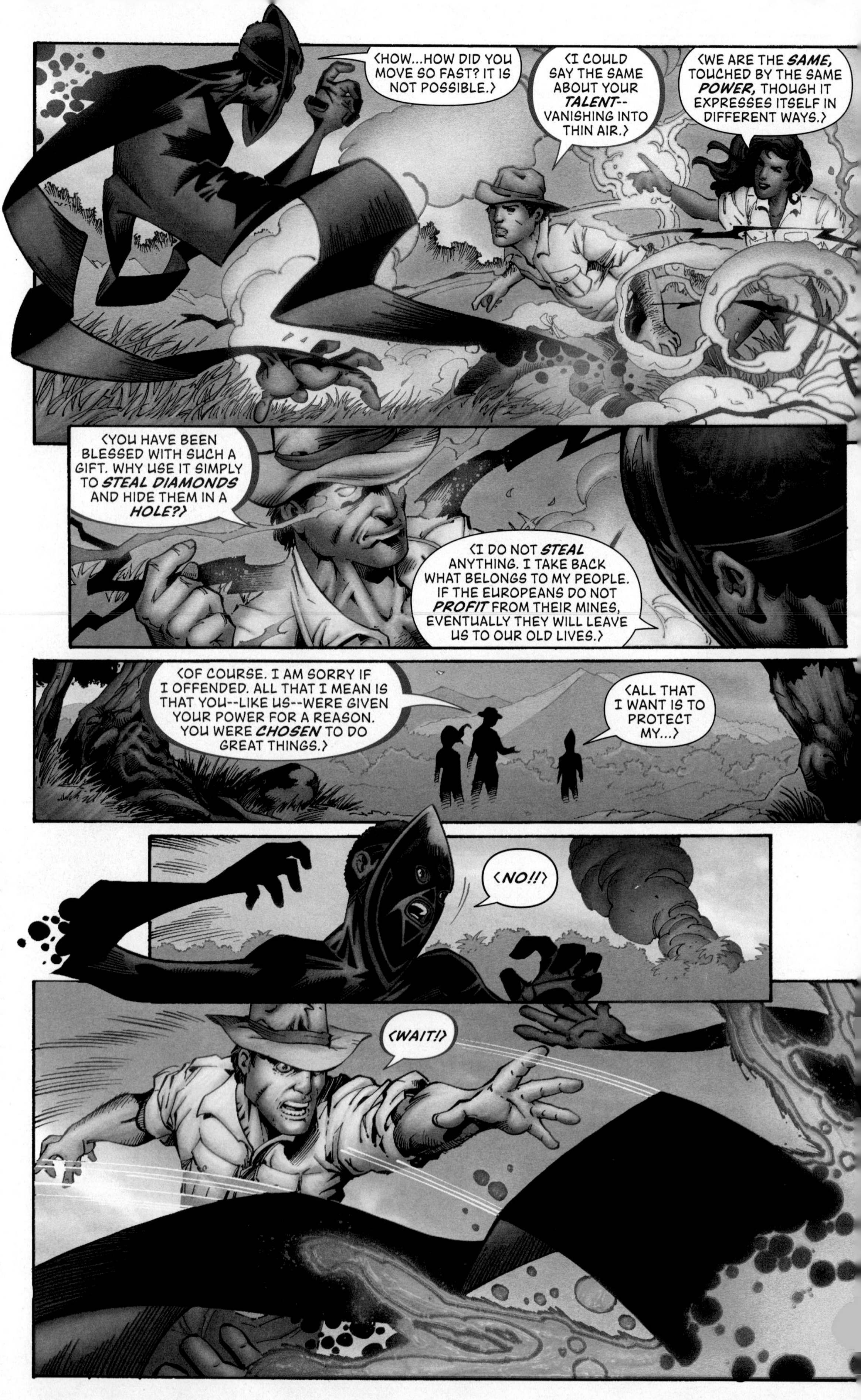
<HOW...HOW DID YOU MOVE SO FAST? IT IS NOT POSSIBLE.>
<I COULD SAY THE SAME ABOUT YOUR TALENT--VANISHING INTO THIN AIR.>
<WE ARE THE SAME, TOUCHED BY THE SAME POWER, THOUGH IT EXPRESSES ITSELF IN DIFFERENT WAYS.>
<YOU HAVE BEEN BLESSED WITH SUCH A GIFT. WHY USE IT SIMPLY TO STEAL DIAMONDS AND HIDE THEM IN A HOLE?>
<I DO NOT STEAL ANYTHING. I TAKE BACK WHAT BELONGS TO MY PEOPLE. IF THE EUROPEANS DO NOT PROFIT FROM THEIR MINES, EVENTUALLY THEY WILL LEAVE US TO OUR OLD LIVES.>
<OF COURSE. I AM SORRY IF I OFFENDED. ALL THAT I MEAN IS THAT YOU--LIKE US--WERE GIVEN YOUR POWER FOR A REASON. YOU WERE CHOSEN TO DO GREAT THINGS.>
<ALL THAT I WANT IS TO PROTECT MY...>
<NO!!>
<WAIT!>

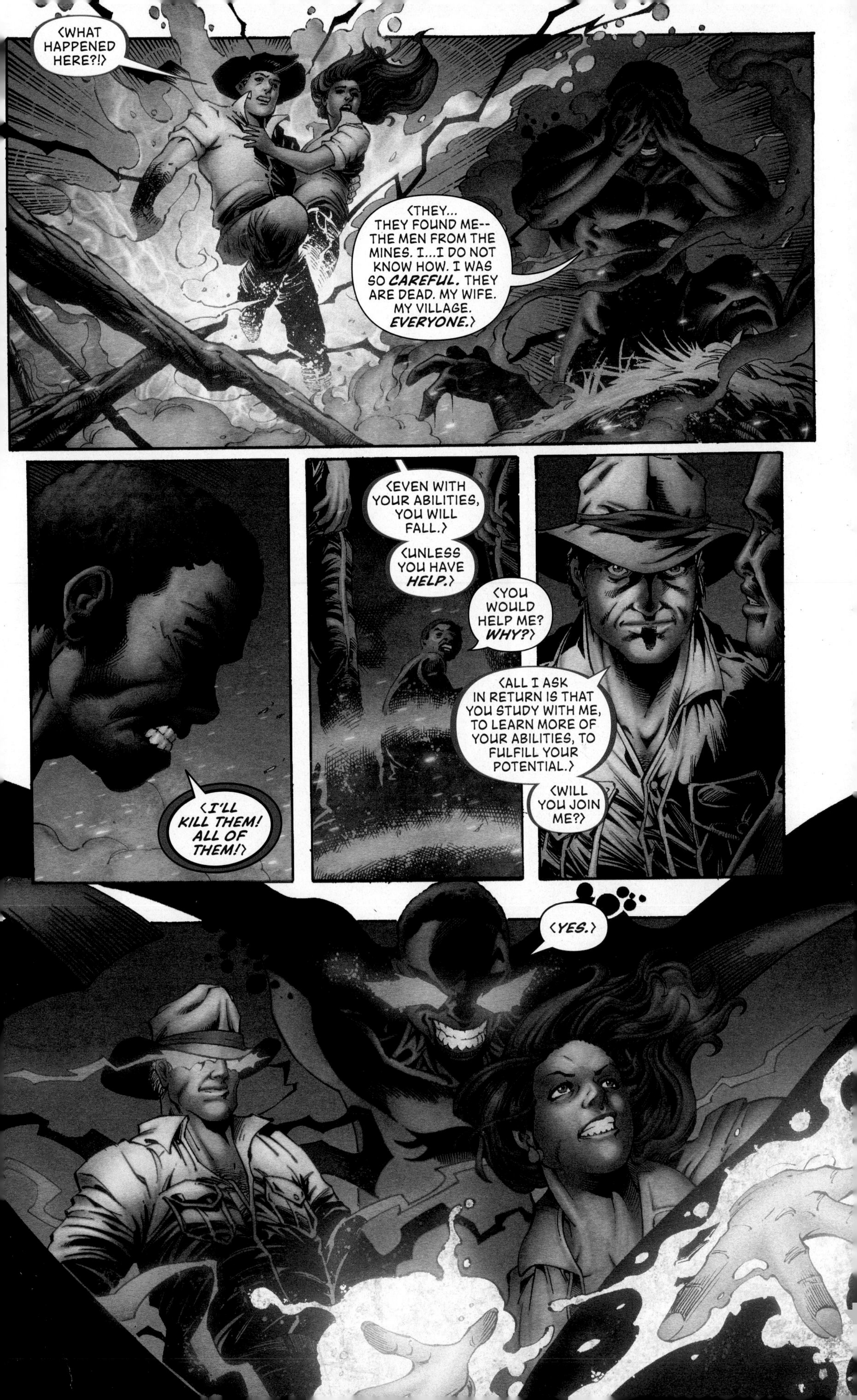
<WHAT HAPPENED HERE?!>
<THEY... THEY FOUND ME-- THE MEN FROM THE MINES. I...I DO NOT KNOW HOW. I WAS SO CAREFUL. THEY ARE DEAD. MY WIFE. MY VILLAGE. EVERYONE.>
<I'LL KILL THEM! ALL OF THEM!>
<EVEN WITH YOUR ABILITIES, YOU WILL FALL.>
<UNLESS YOU HAVE HELP.>
<YOU WOULD HELP ME? WHY?>
<ALL I ASK IN RETURN IS THAT YOU STUDY WITH ME, TO LEARN MORE OF YOUR ABILITIES, TO FULFILL YOUR POTENTIAL.>
<WILL YOU JOIN ME?>
<YES.>

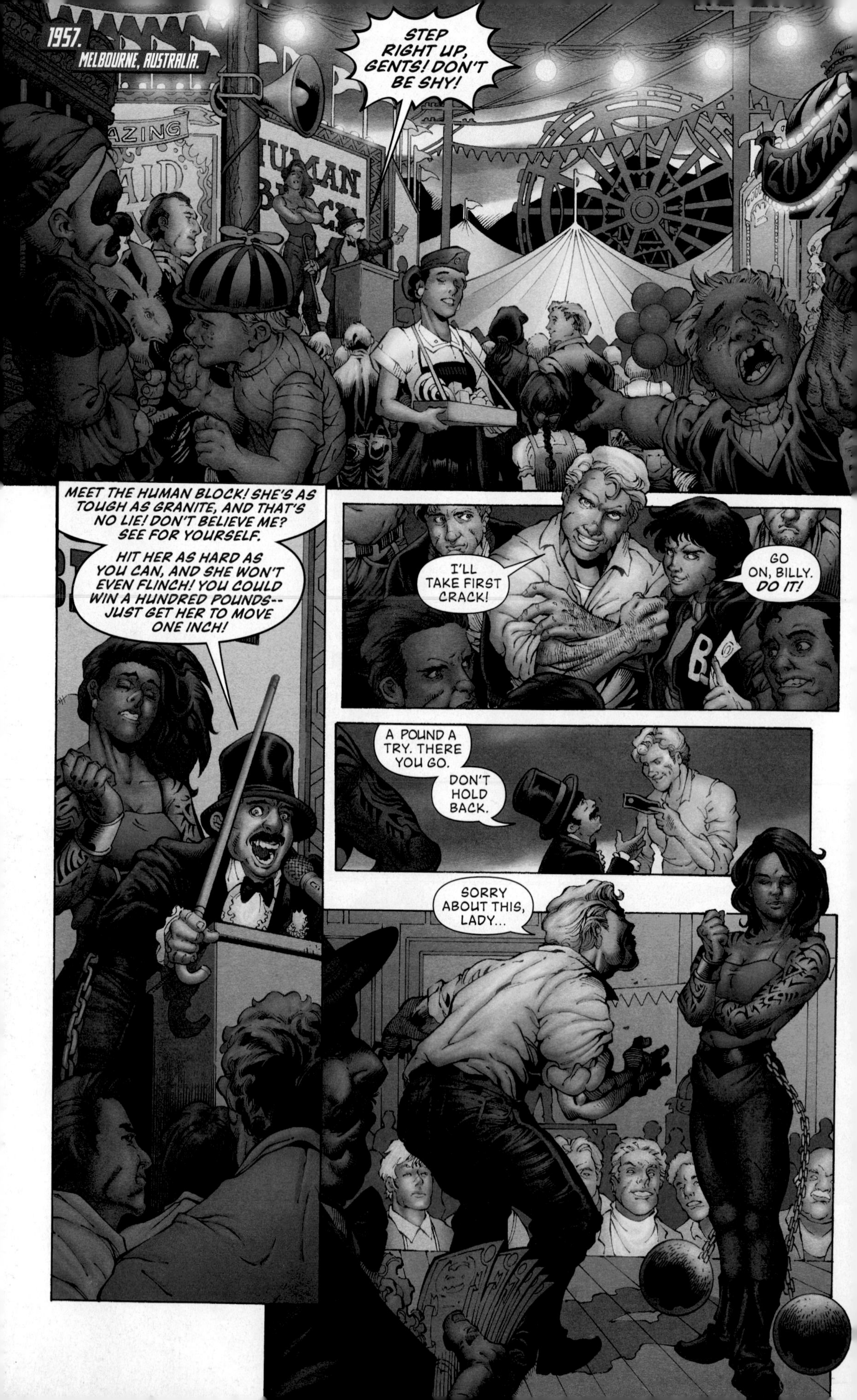
1957.
MELBOURNE, AUSTRALIA.
STEP RIGHT UP, GENTS! DON'T BE SHY!
MEET THE HUMAN BLOCK! SHE'S AS TOUGH AS GRANITE, AND THAT'S NO LIE! DON'T BELIEVE ME? SEE FOR YOURSELF.
HIT HER AS HARD AS YOU CAN, AND SHE WON'T EVEN FLINCH! YOU COULD WIN A HUNDRED POUNDS-- JUST GET HER TO MOVE ONE INCH!
I'LL TAKE FIRST CRACK!
GO ON, BILLY. DO IT!
A POUND A TRY. THERE YOU GO.
DON'T HOLD BACK.
SORRY ABOUT THIS, LADY...

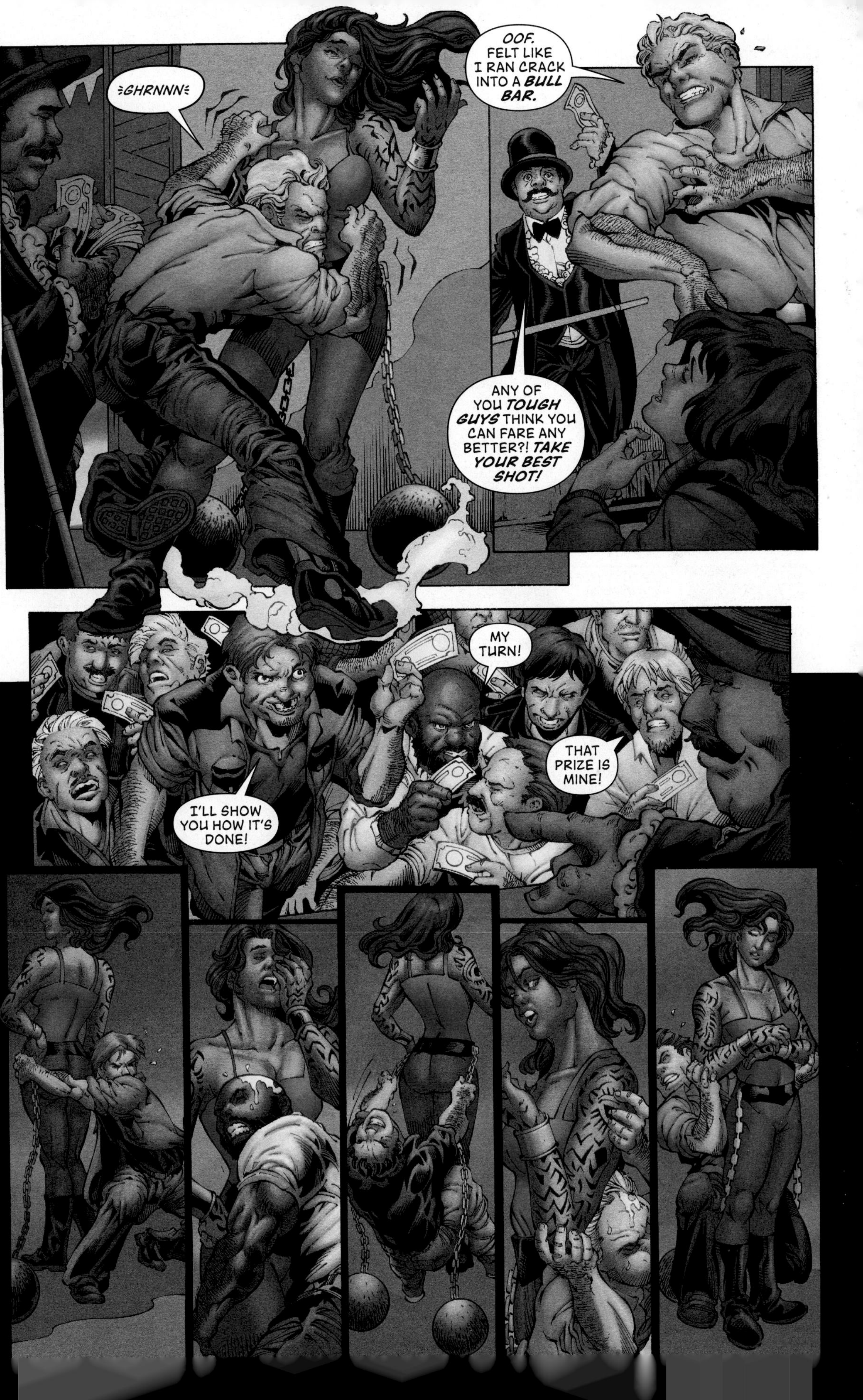

GHRNNN
OOF. FELT LIKE I RAN CRACK INTO A BULL BAR.
ANY OF YOU TOUGH GUYS THINK YOU CAN FARE ANY BETTER?! TAKE YOUR BEST SHOT!
MY TURN!
THAT PRIZE IS MINE!
I'LL SHOW YOU HOW IT'S DONE!

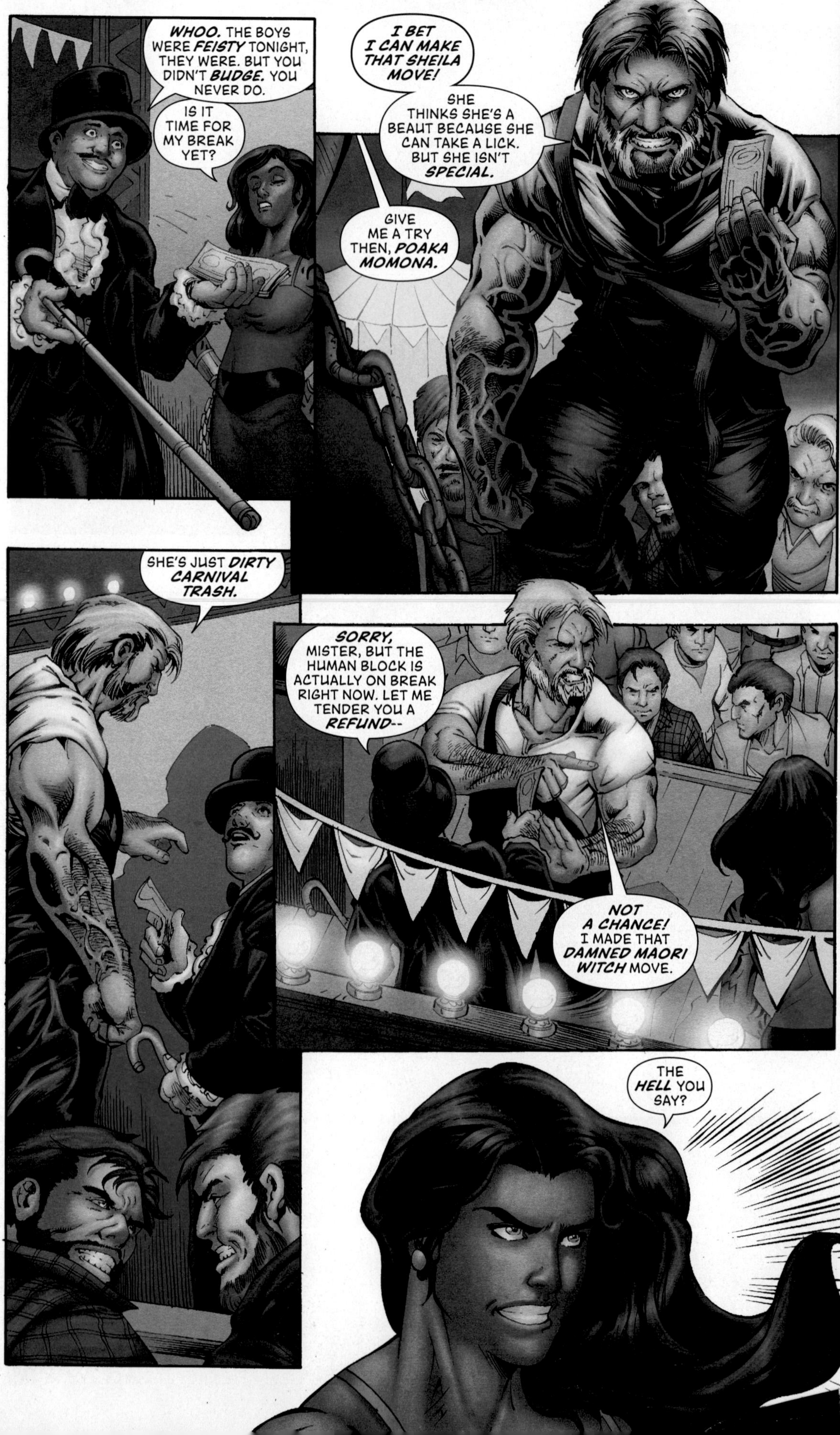
WHOO. THE BOYS WERE FEISTY TONIGHT, THEY WERE. BUT YOU DIDN'T BUDGE. YOU NEVER DO.
IS IT TIME FOR MY BREAK YET?
I BET I CAN MAKE THAT SHEILA MOVE!
SHE THINKS SHE'S A BEAUT BECAUSE SHE CAN TAKE A LICK. BUT SHE ISN'T SPECIAL.
GIVE ME A TRY THEN, POAKA MOMONA.
SHE'S JUST DIRTY CARNIVAL TRASH.
SORRY, MISTER, BUT THE HUMAN BLOCK IS ACTUALLY ON BREAK RIGHT NOW. LET ME TENDER YOU A REFUND--
NOT A CHANCE! I MADE THAT DAMNED MAORI WITCH MOVE.
THE HELL YOU SAY?

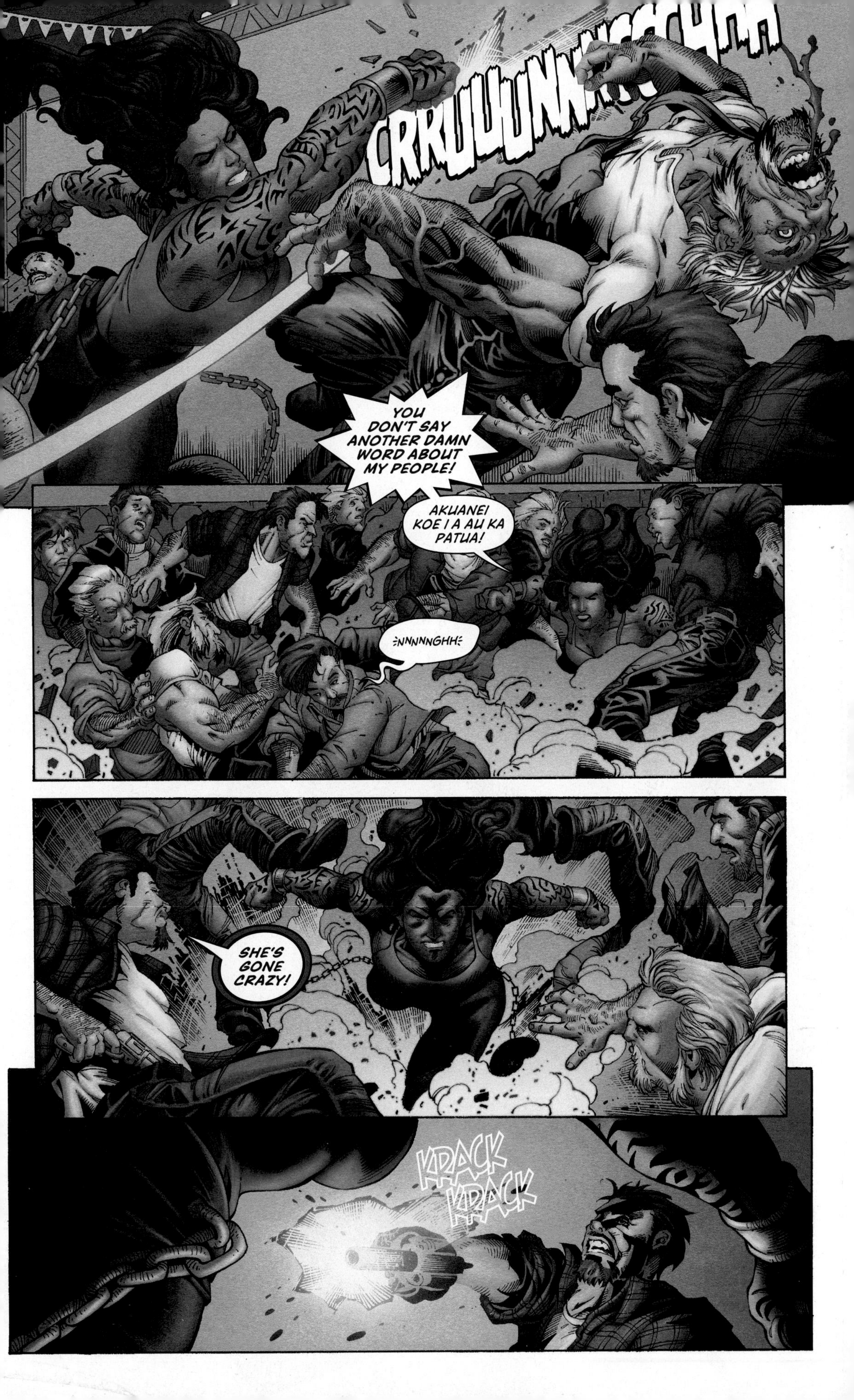
CRRUUUNNGGCHHH
YOU DON'T SAY ANOTHER DAMN WORD ABOUT MY PEOPLE!
AKUANE! KOE I A AU KA PATUA!
NNNNNGHH
SHE'S GONE CRAZY!
KRACK KRACK

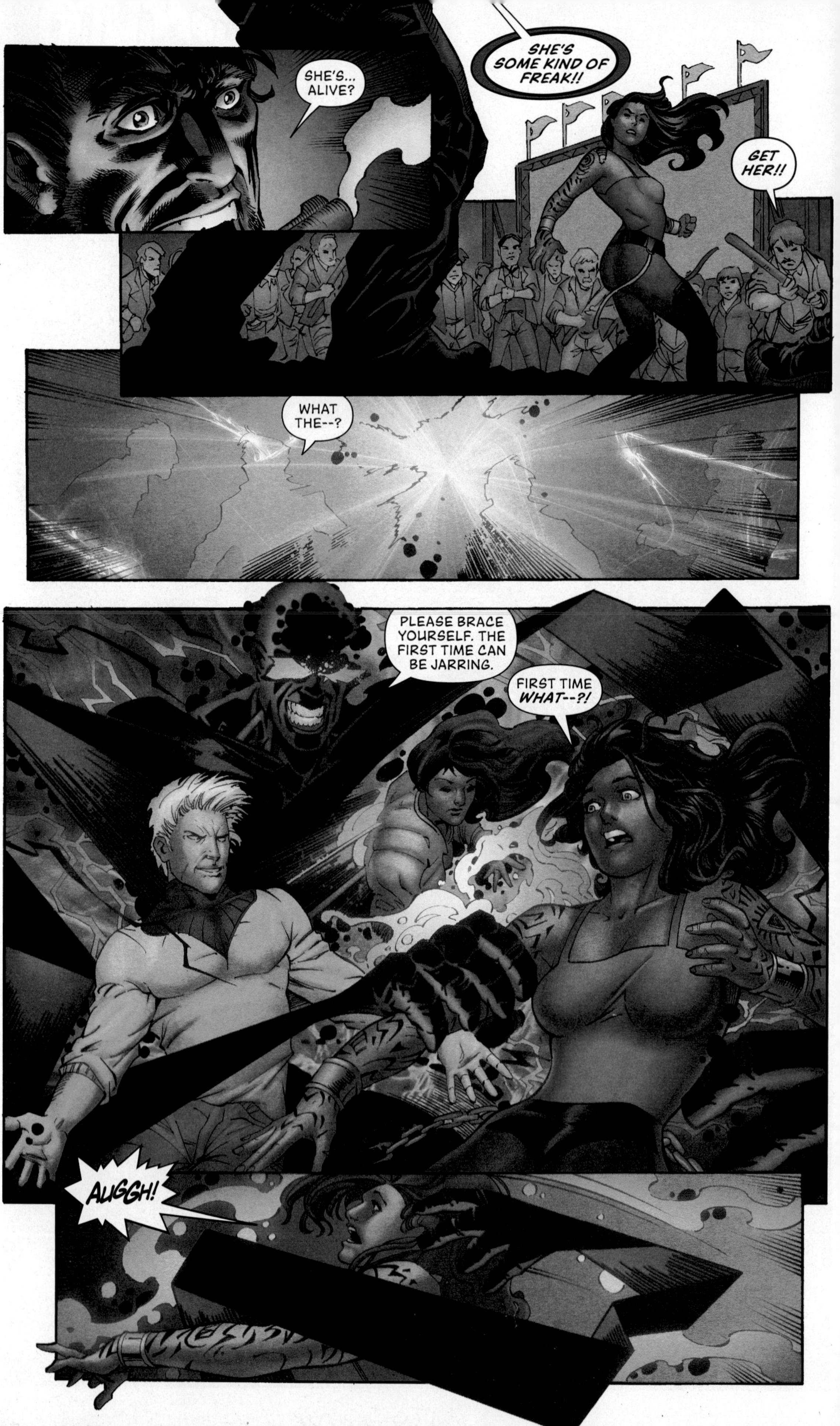
SHE'S... ALIVE?
SHE'S SOME KIND OF FREAK!!
GET HER!!
WHAT THE--?
PLEASE BRACE YOURSELF. THE FIRST TIME CAN BE JARRING.
FIRST TIME WHAT--?!
AUGGH!

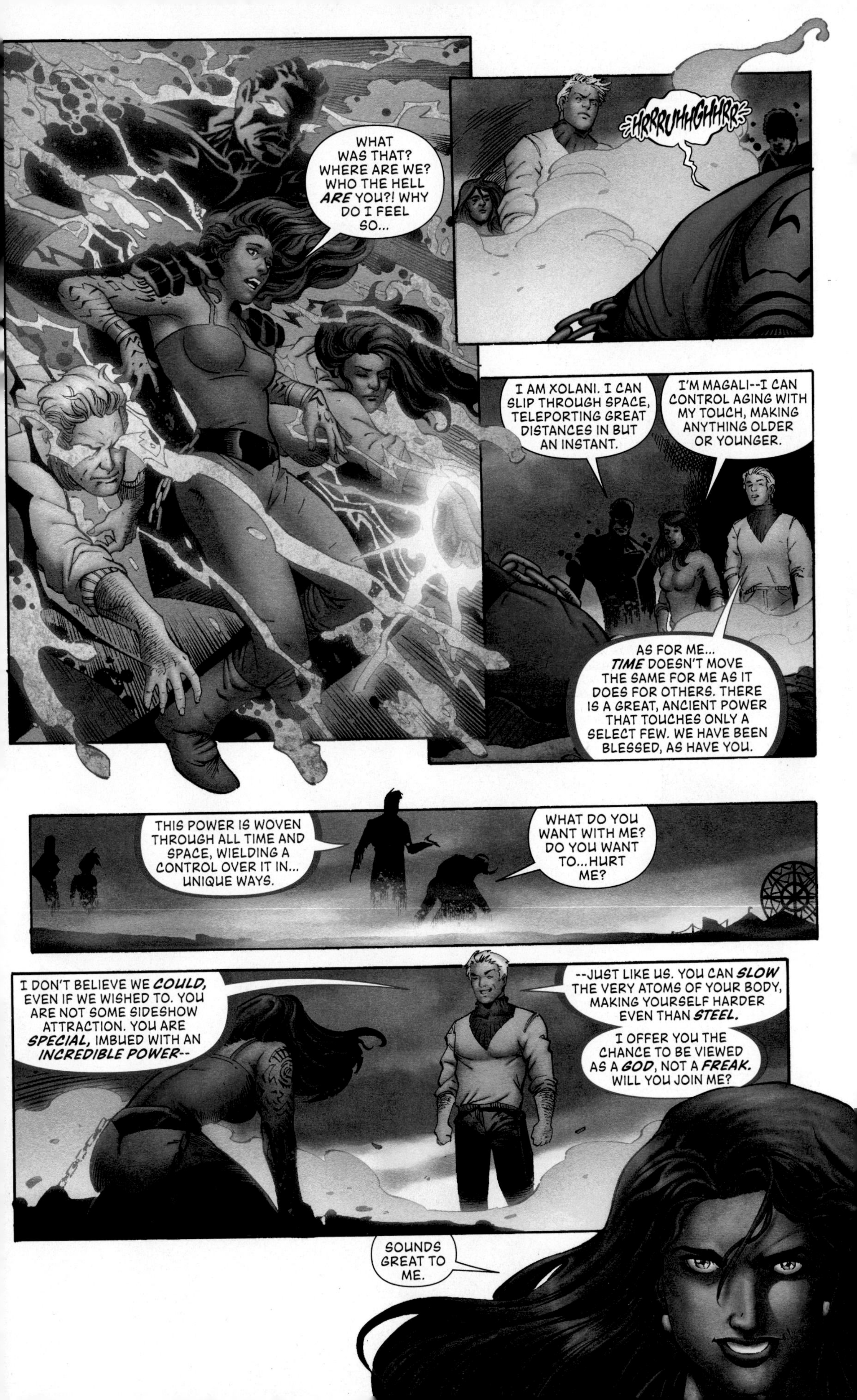
WHAT WAS THAT? WHERE ARE WE? WHO THE HELL *ARE* YOU?! WHY DO I FEEL SO...
HRRRUHHGHHRR
I AM XOLANI. I CAN SLIP THROUGH SPACE, TELEPORTING GREAT DISTANCES IN BUT AN INSTANT.
I'M MAGALI--I CAN CONTROL AGING WITH MY TOUCH, MAKING ANYTHING OLDER OR YOUNGER.
AS FOR ME... *TIME* DOESN'T MOVE THE SAME FOR ME AS IT DOES FOR OTHERS. THERE IS A GREAT, ANCIENT POWER THAT TOUCHES ONLY A SELECT FEW. WE HAVE BEEN BLESSED, AS HAVE YOU.
THIS POWER IS WOVEN THROUGH ALL TIME AND SPACE, WIELDING A CONTROL OVER IT IN... UNIQUE WAYS.
WHAT DO YOU WANT WITH ME? DO YOU WANT TO...HURT ME?
I DON'T BELIEVE WE *COULD*, EVEN IF WE WISHED TO. YOU ARE NOT SOME SIDESHOW ATTRACTION. YOU ARE *SPECIAL*, IMBUED WITH AN *INCREDIBLE POWER*--
--JUST LIKE US. YOU CAN *SLOW* THE VERY ATOMS OF YOUR BODY, MAKING YOURSELF HARDER EVEN THAN *STEEL*.
I OFFER YOU THE CHANCE TO BE VIEWED AS A *GOD*, NOT A *FREAK*. WILL YOU JOIN ME?
SOUNDS GREAT TO ME.

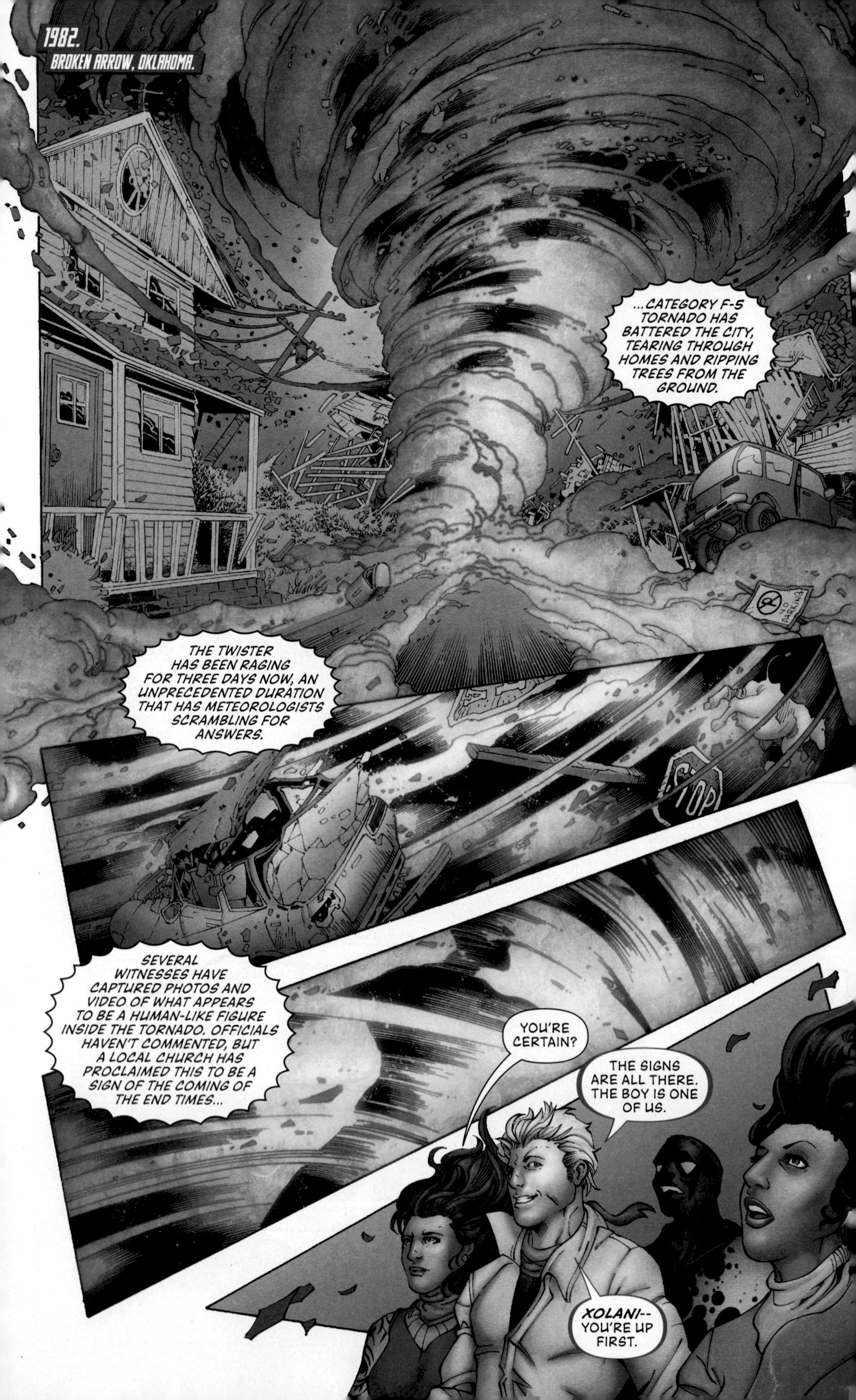
1982.
BROKEN ARROW, OKLAHOMA.
...CATEGORY F-5 TORNADO HAS BATTERED THE CITY, TEARING THROUGH HOMES AND RIPPING TREES FROM THE GROUND.
NO PARKING
THE TWISTER HAS BEEN RAGING FOR THREE DAYS NOW, AN UNPRECEDENTED DURATION THAT HAS METEOROLOGISTS SCRAMBLING FOR ANSWERS.
STOP
SEVERAL WITNESSES HAVE CAPTURED PHOTOS AND VIDEO OF WHAT APPEARS TO BE A HUMAN-LIKE FIGURE INSIDE THE TORNADO. OFFICIALS HAVEN'T COMMENTED, BUT A LOCAL CHURCH HAS PROCLAIMED THIS TO BE A SIGN OF THE COMING OF THE END TIMES...
YOU'RE CERTAIN?
THE SIGNS ARE ALL THERE. THE BOY IS ONE OF US.
XOLANI-- YOU'RE UP FIRST.

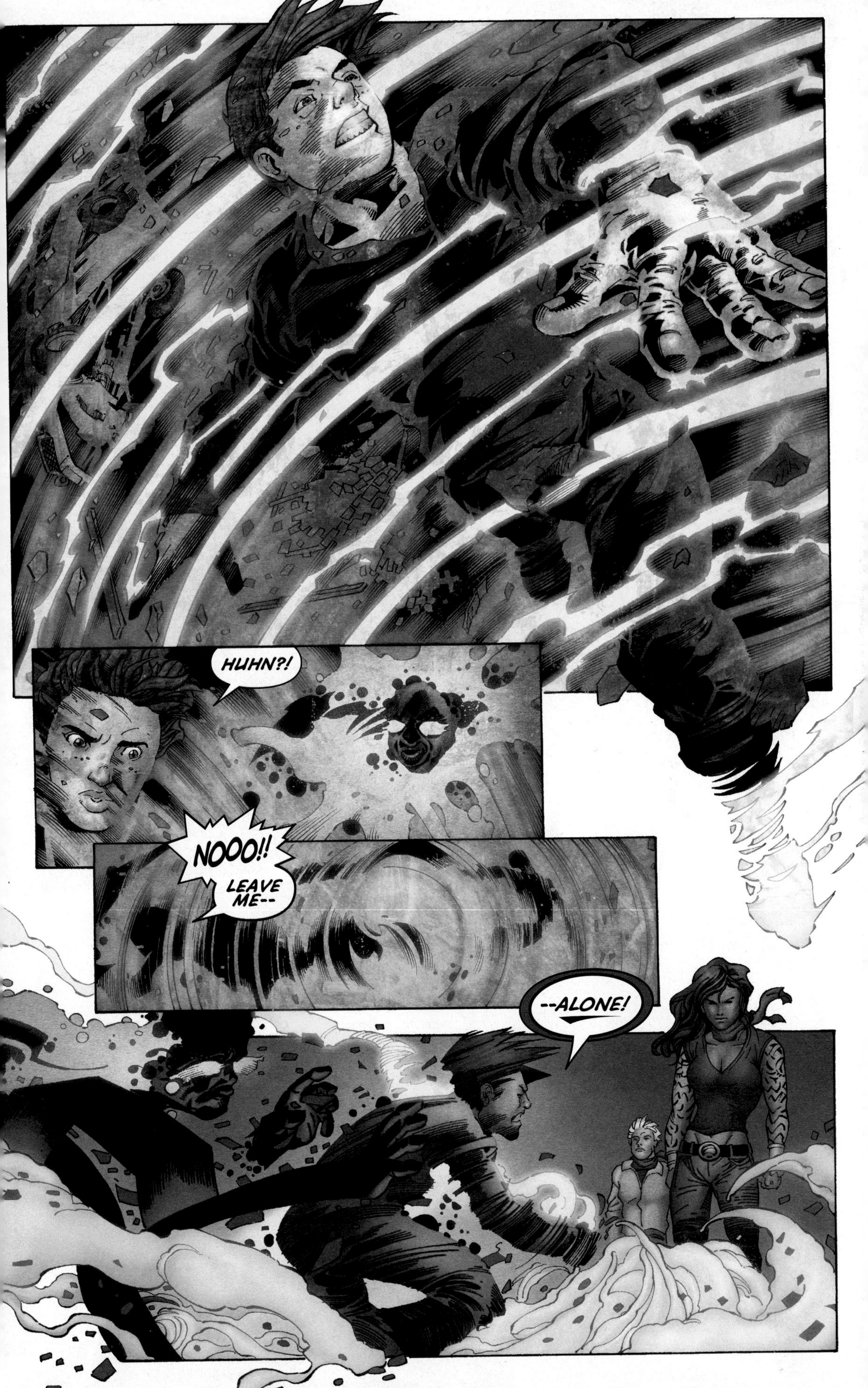
HUHN?!
NOOO!!
LEAVE ME--
--ALONE!

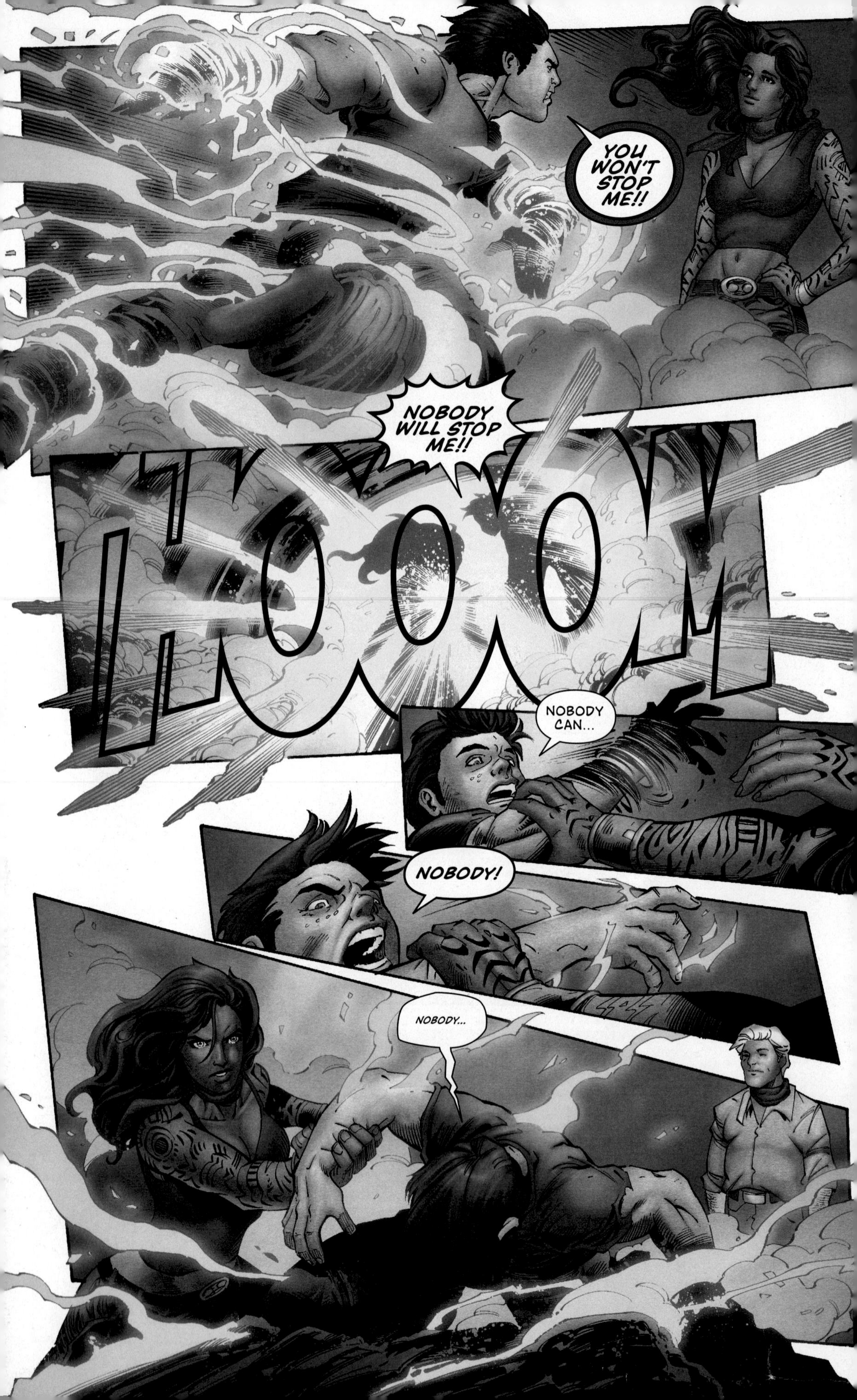
YOU WON'T STOP ME!!
NOBODY WILL STOP ME!!
HOOOM
NOBODY CAN...
NOBODY!
NOBODY...

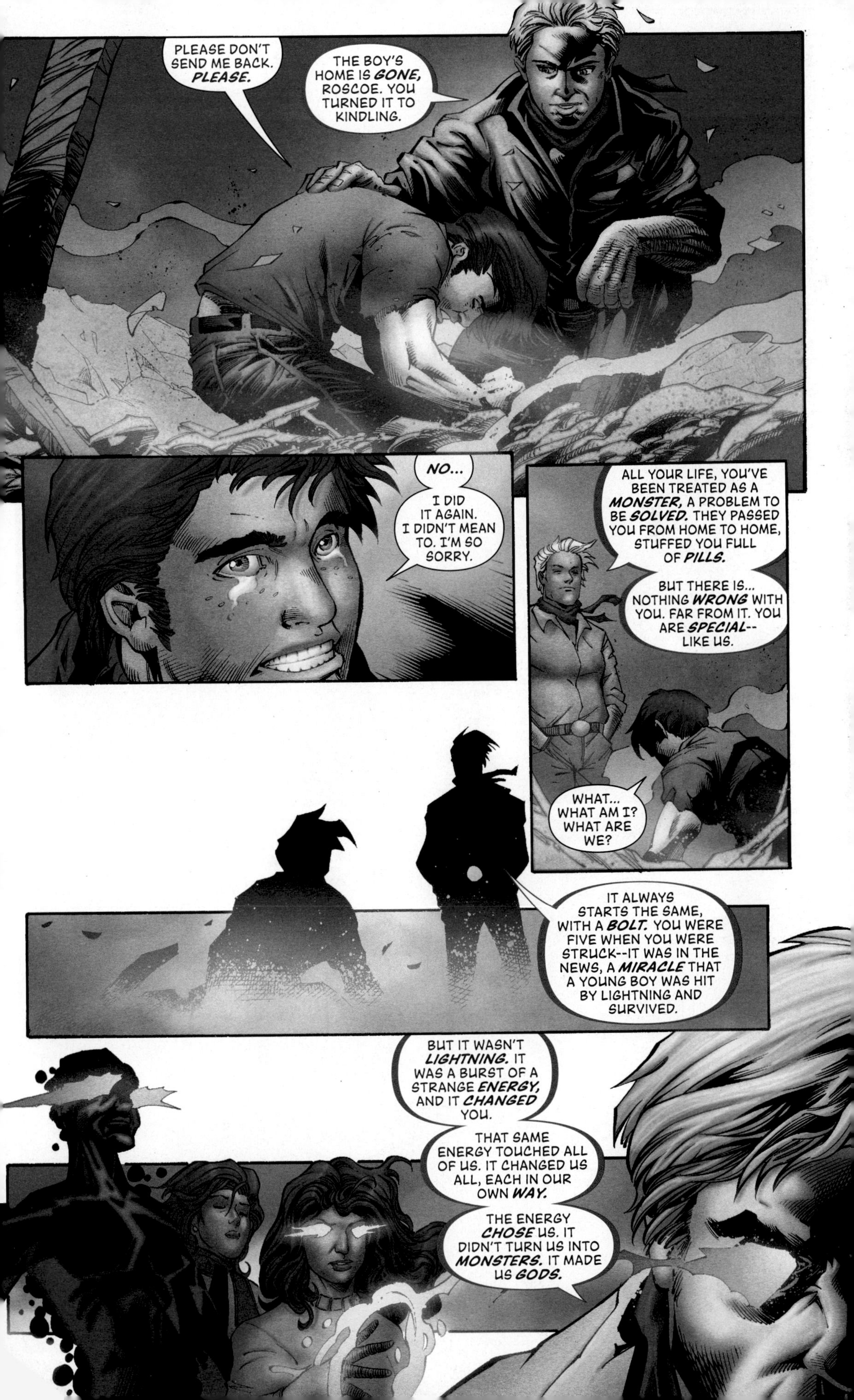
PLEASE DON'T SEND ME BACK. *PLEASE.*
THE BOY'S HOME IS *GONE,* ROSCOE. YOU TURNED IT TO KINDLING.
NO...
I DID IT AGAIN. I DIDN'T MEAN TO. I'M SO SORRY.
ALL YOUR LIFE, YOU'VE BEEN TREATED AS A *MONSTER,* A PROBLEM TO BE *SOLVED.* THEY PASSED YOU FROM HOME TO HOME, STUFFED YOU FULL OF *PILLS.*
BUT THERE IS... NOTHING *WRONG* WITH YOU. FAR FROM IT. YOU ARE *SPECIAL*-- LIKE US.
WHAT... WHAT AM I? WHAT ARE WE?
IT ALWAYS STARTS THE SAME, WITH A *BOLT.* YOU WERE FIVE WHEN YOU WERE STRUCK--IT WAS IN THE NEWS, A *MIRACLE* THAT A YOUNG BOY WAS HIT BY LIGHTNING AND SURVIVED.
BUT IT WASN'T *LIGHTNING.* IT WAS A BURST OF A STRANGE *ENERGY,* AND IT *CHANGED* YOU.
THAT SAME ENERGY TOUCHED ALL OF US. IT CHANGED US ALL, EACH IN OUR OWN *WAY.*
THE ENERGY *CHOSE* US. IT DIDN'T TURN US INTO *MONSTERS.* IT MADE US *GODS.*

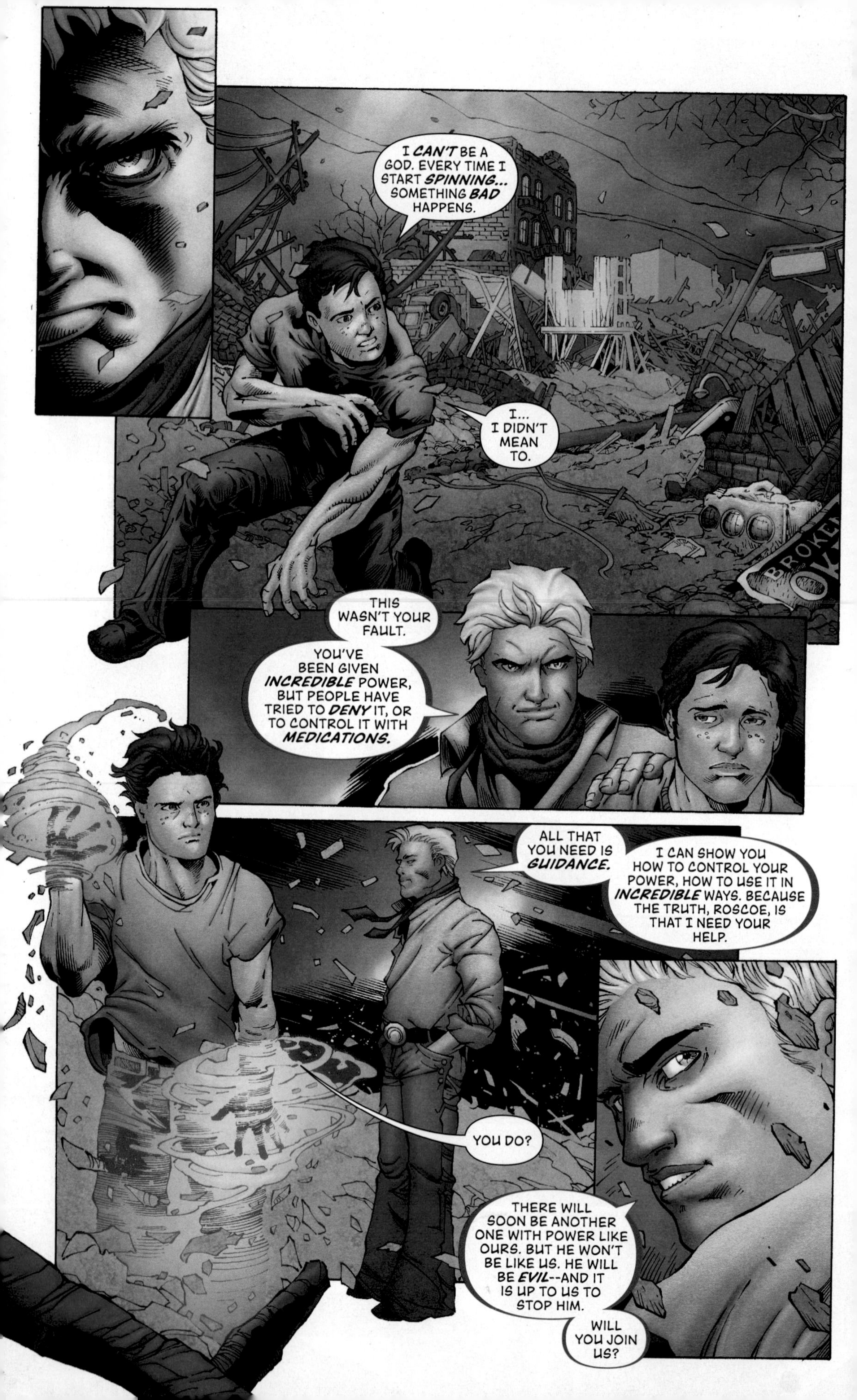
I CAN'T BE A GOD. EVERY TIME I START SPINNING... SOMETHING BAD HAPPENS.
I... I DIDN'T MEAN TO.
BROKEN
THIS WASN'T YOUR FAULT.
YOU'VE BEEN GIVEN INCREDIBLE POWER, BUT PEOPLE HAVE TRIED TO DENY IT, OR TO CONTROL IT WITH MEDICATIONS.
ALL THAT YOU NEED IS GUIDANCE.
I CAN SHOW YOU HOW TO CONTROL YOUR POWER, HOW TO USE IT IN INCREDIBLE WAYS. BECAUSE THE TRUTH, ROSCOE, IS THAT I NEED YOUR HELP.
YOU DO?
THERE WILL SOON BE ANOTHER ONE WITH POWER LIKE OURS. BUT HE WON'T BE LIKE US. HE WILL BE EVIL--AND IT IS UP TO US TO STOP HIM.
WILL YOU JOIN US?

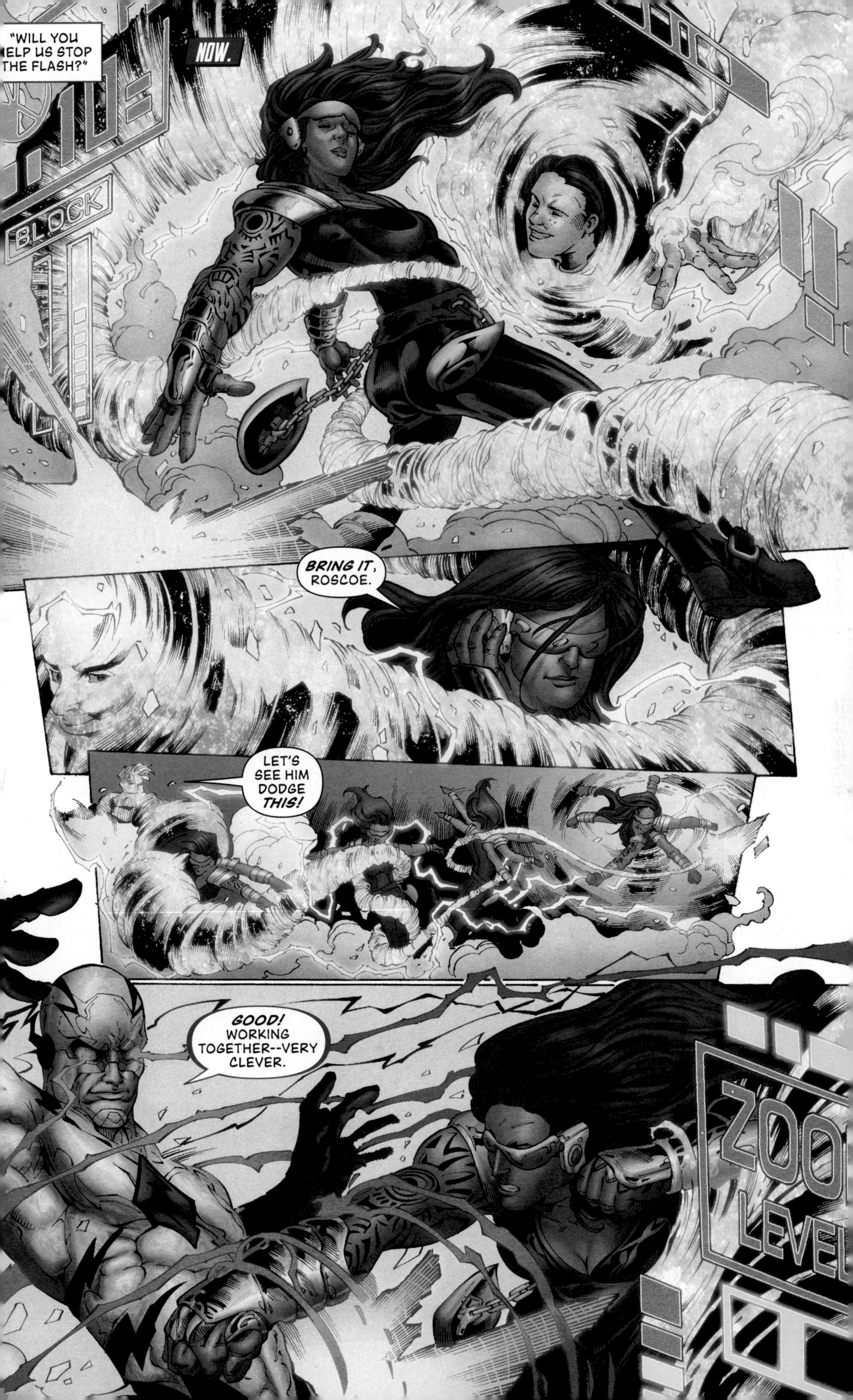
"WILL YOU
ELP US STOP
THE FLASH?"
NOW.
BLOCK
BRING IT, ROSCOE.
LET'S SEE HIM DODGE THIS!
GOOD! WORKING TOGETHER--VERY CLEVER.
ZOO
LEVEL

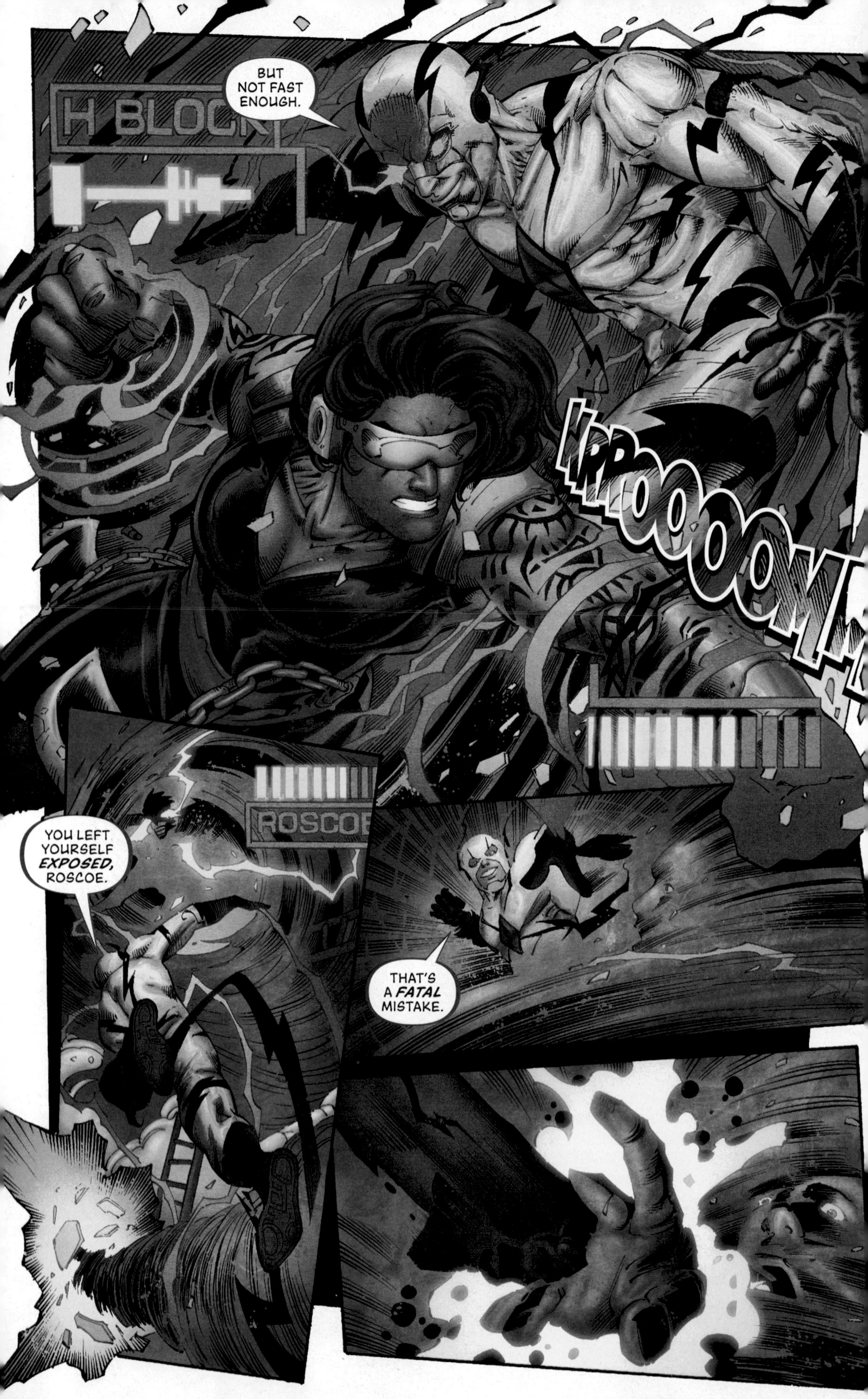
H BLOCK
BUT NOT FAST ENOUGH.
KRROOOOOM!
ROSCOE
YOU LEFT YOURSELF *EXPOSED,* ROSCOE.
THAT'S A *FATAL* MISTAKE.

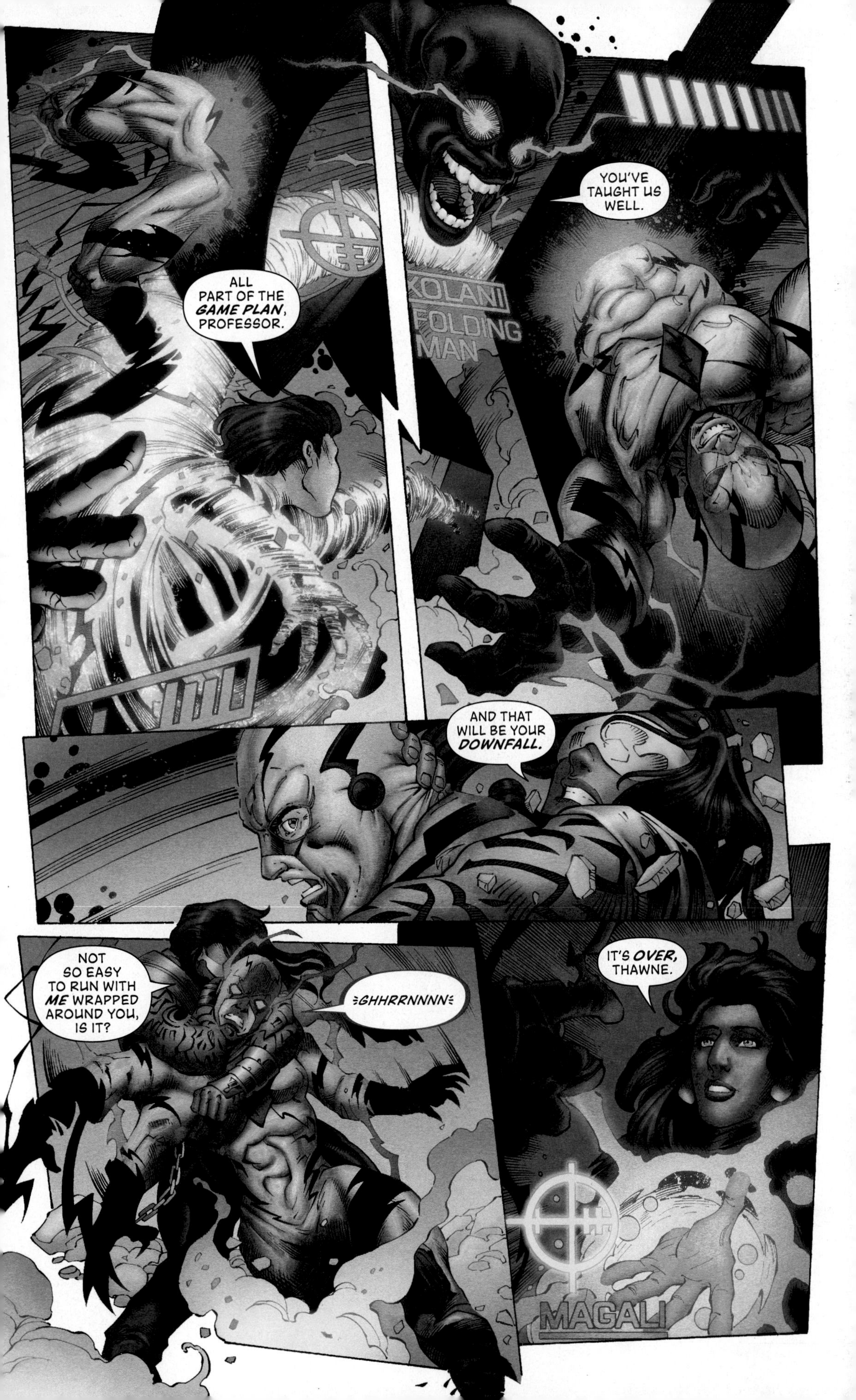
ALL PART OF THE GAME PLAN, PROFESSOR.
KOLANI FOLDING MAN
YOU'VE TAUGHT US WELL.
AND THAT WILL BE YOUR DOWNFALL.
NOT SO EASY TO RUN WITH ME WRAPPED AROUND YOU, IS IT?
GHHRRNNNN
IT'S OVER, THAWNE.
MAGALI

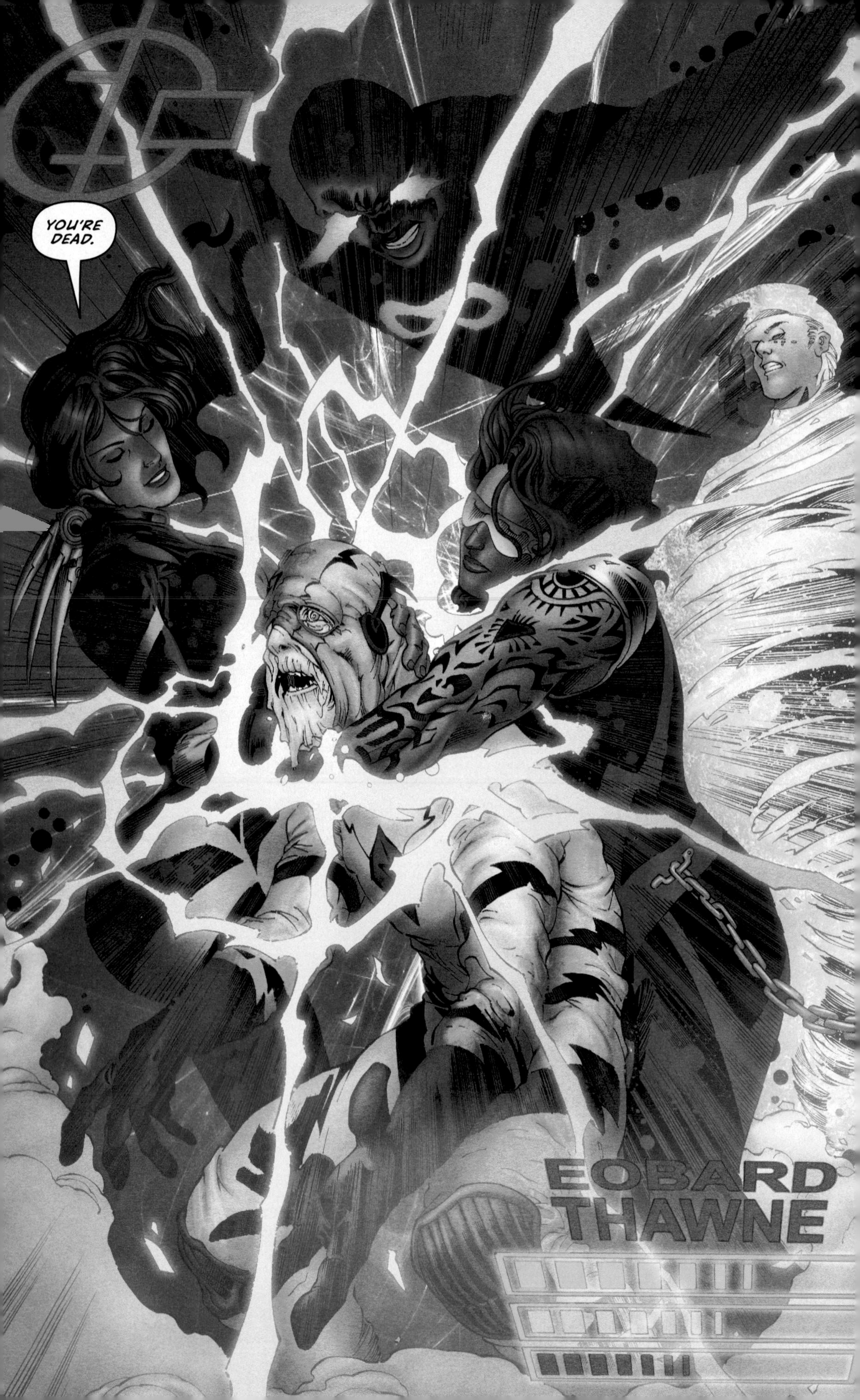
YOU'RE DEAD.
EOBARD THAWNE

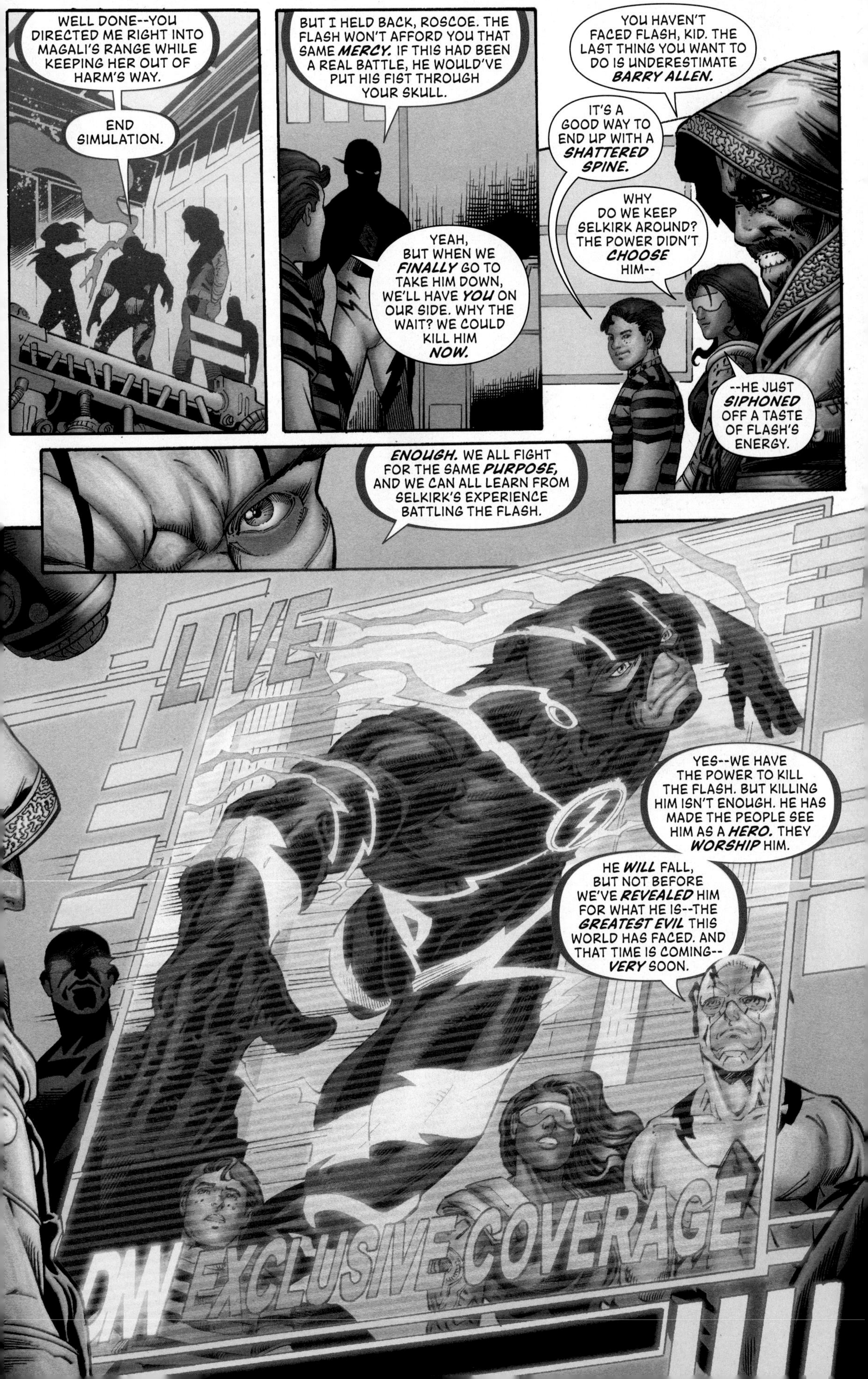
WELL DONE--YOU DIRECTED ME RIGHT INTO MAGALI'S RANGE WHILE KEEPING HER OUT OF HARM'S WAY.
END SIMULATION.
BUT I HELD BACK, ROSCOE. THE FLASH WON'T AFFORD YOU THAT SAME MERCY. IF THIS HAD BEEN A REAL BATTLE, HE WOULD'VE PUT HIS FIST THROUGH YOUR SKULL.
YEAH, BUT WHEN WE FINALLY GO TO TAKE HIM DOWN, WE'LL HAVE YOU ON OUR SIDE. WHY THE WAIT? WE COULD KILL HIM NOW.
YOU HAVEN'T FACED FLASH, KID. THE LAST THING YOU WANT TO DO IS UNDERESTIMATE BARRY ALLEN.
IT'S A GOOD WAY TO END UP WITH A SHATTERED SPINE.
WHY DO WE KEEP SELKIRK AROUND? THE POWER DIDN'T CHOOSE HIM--
--HE JUST SIPHONED OFF A TASTE OF FLASH'S ENERGY.
ENOUGH. WE ALL FIGHT FOR THE SAME PURPOSE, AND WE CAN ALL LEARN FROM SELKIRK'S EXPERIENCE BATTLING THE FLASH.
LIVE
YES--WE HAVE THE POWER TO KILL THE FLASH. BUT KILLING HIM ISN'T ENOUGH. HE HAS MADE THE PEOPLE SEE HIM AS A HERO. THEY WORSHIP HIM.
HE WILL FALL, BUT NOT BEFORE WE'VE REVEALED HIM FOR WHAT HE IS--THE GREATEST EVIL THIS WORLD HAS FACED. AND THAT TIME IS COMING--VERY SOON.
EXCLUSIVE COVERAGE

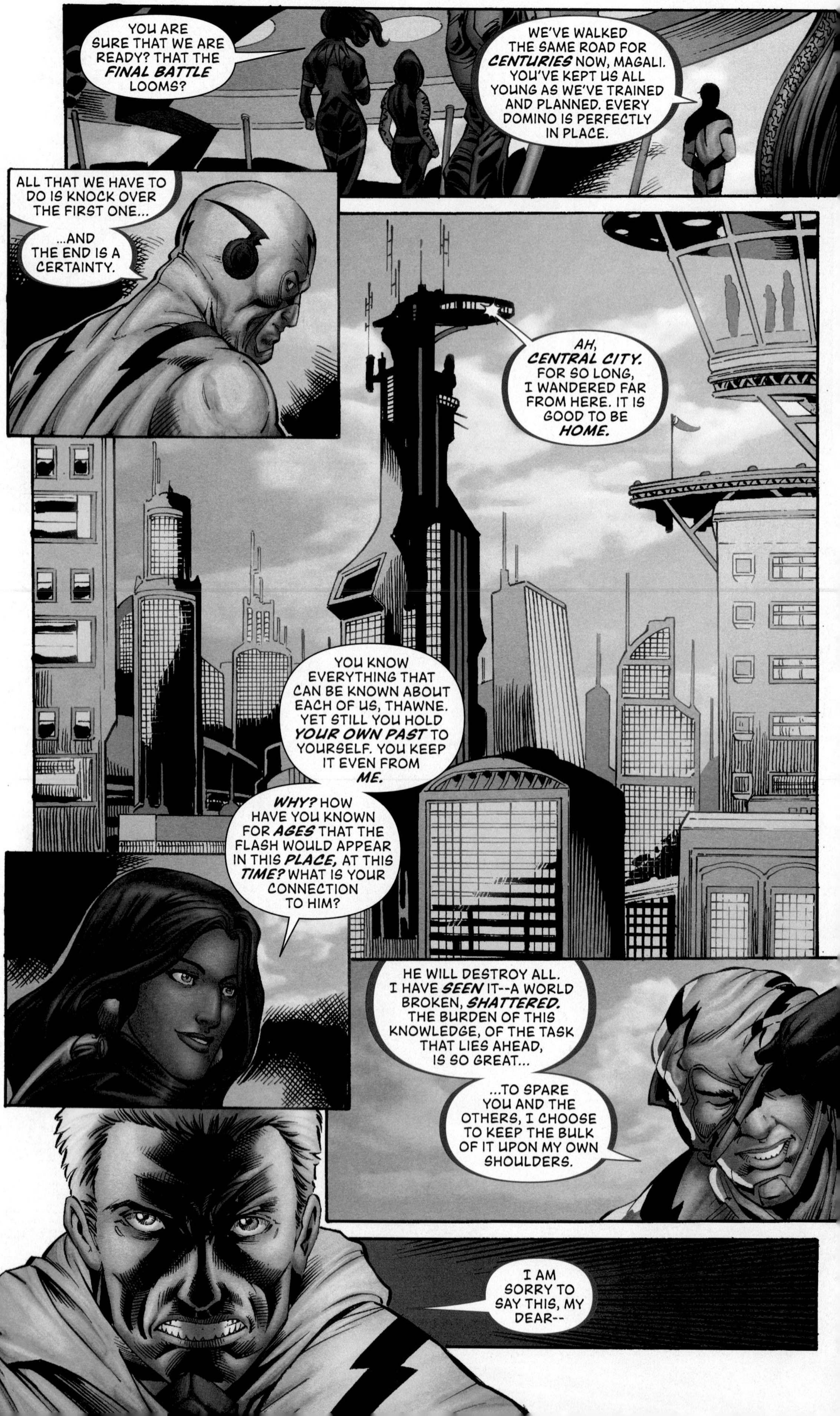
YOU ARE SURE THAT WE ARE READY? THAT THE FINAL BATTLE LOOMS?
WE'VE WALKED THE SAME ROAD FOR CENTURIES NOW, MAGALI. YOU'VE KEPT US ALL YOUNG AS WE'VE TRAINED AND PLANNED. EVERY DOMINO IS PERFECTLY IN PLACE.
ALL THAT WE HAVE TO DO IS KNOCK OVER THE FIRST ONE...
...AND THE END IS A CERTAINTY.
AH, CENTRAL CITY. FOR SO LONG, I WANDERED FAR FROM HERE. IT IS GOOD TO BE HOME.
YOU KNOW EVERYTHING THAT CAN BE KNOWN ABOUT EACH OF US, THAWNE. YET STILL YOU HOLD YOUR OWN PAST TO YOURSELF. YOU KEEP IT EVEN FROM ME.
WHY? HOW HAVE YOU KNOWN FOR AGES THAT THE FLASH WOULD APPEAR IN THIS PLACE, AT THIS TIME? WHAT IS YOUR CONNECTION TO HIM?
HE WILL DESTROY ALL. I HAVE SEEN IT--A WORLD BROKEN, SHATTERED. THE BURDEN OF THIS KNOWLEDGE, OF THE TASK THAT LIES AHEAD, IS SO GREAT...
...TO SPARE YOU AND THE OTHERS, I CHOOSE TO KEEP THE BULK OF IT UPON MY OWN SHOULDERS.
I AM SORRY TO SAY THIS, MY DEAR--

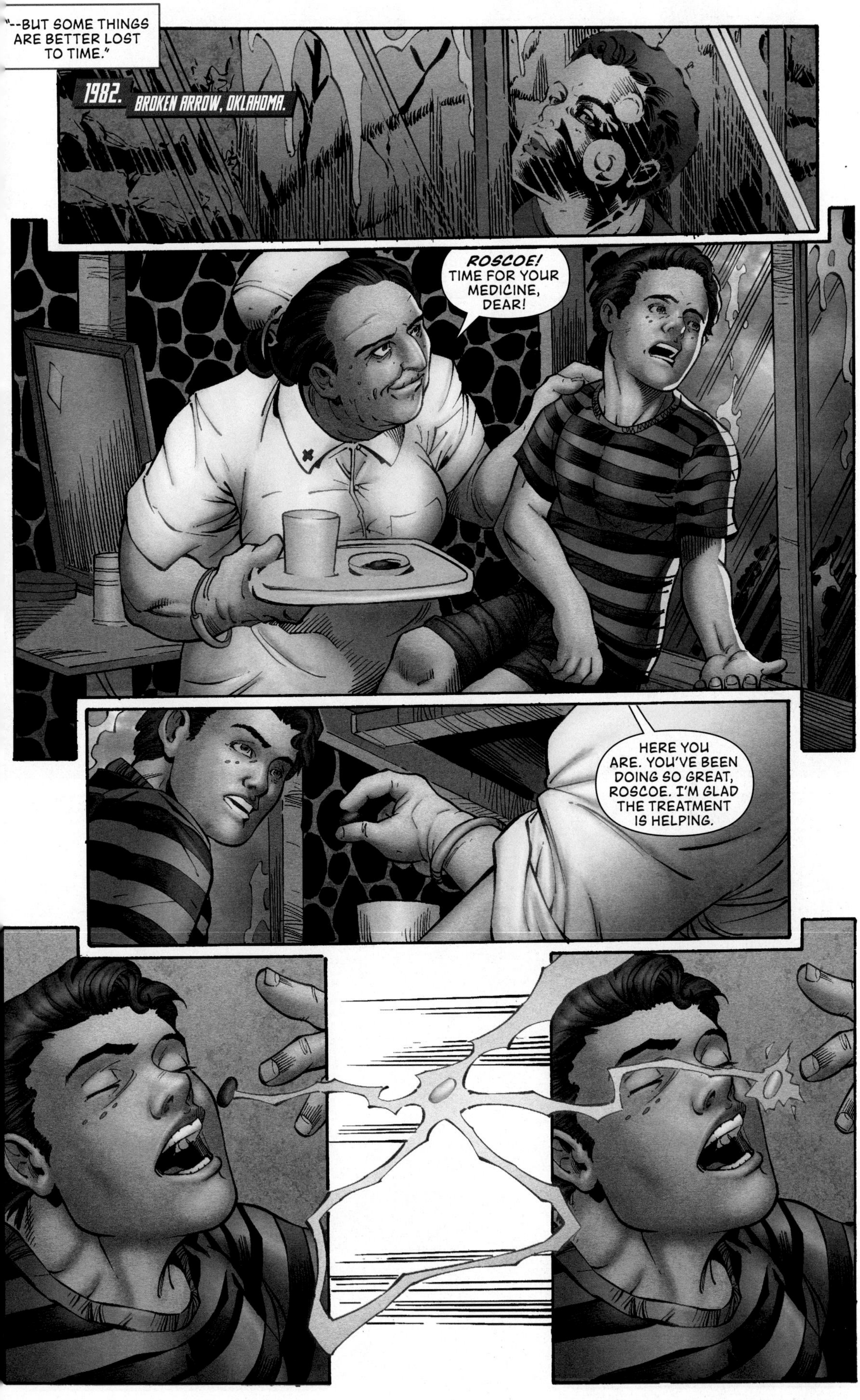

"--BUT SOME THINGS ARE BETTER LOST TO TIME."
1982. BROKEN ARROW, OKLAHOMA.
ROSCOE! TIME FOR YOUR MEDICINE, DEAR!
HERE YOU ARE. YOU'VE BEEN DOING SO GREAT, ROSCOE. I'M GLAD THE TREATMENT IS HELPING.

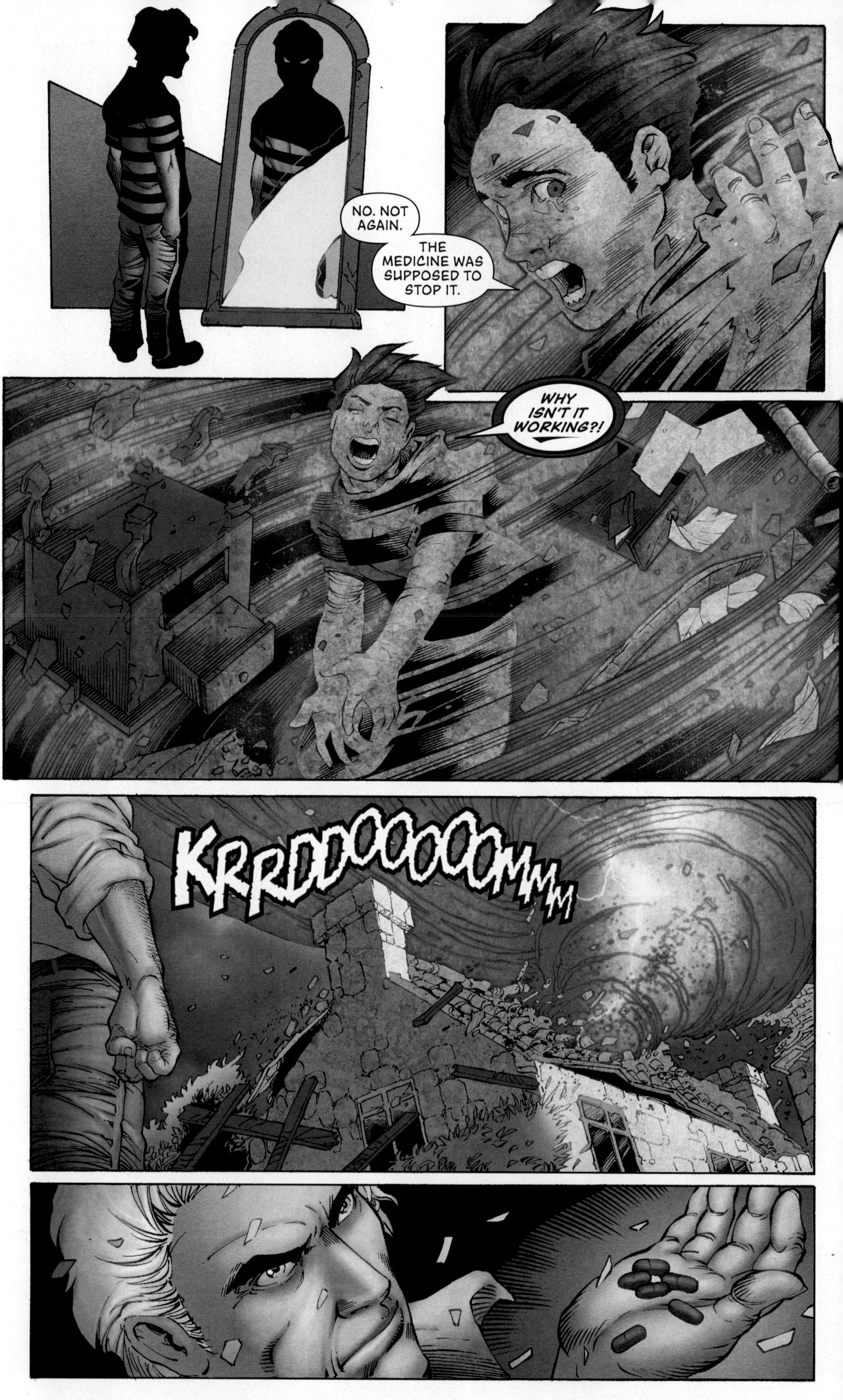
NO. NOT AGAIN.
THE MEDICINE WAS SUPPOSED TO STOP IT.
WHY ISN'T IT WORKING?!
KRRDDOOOOOOMMM

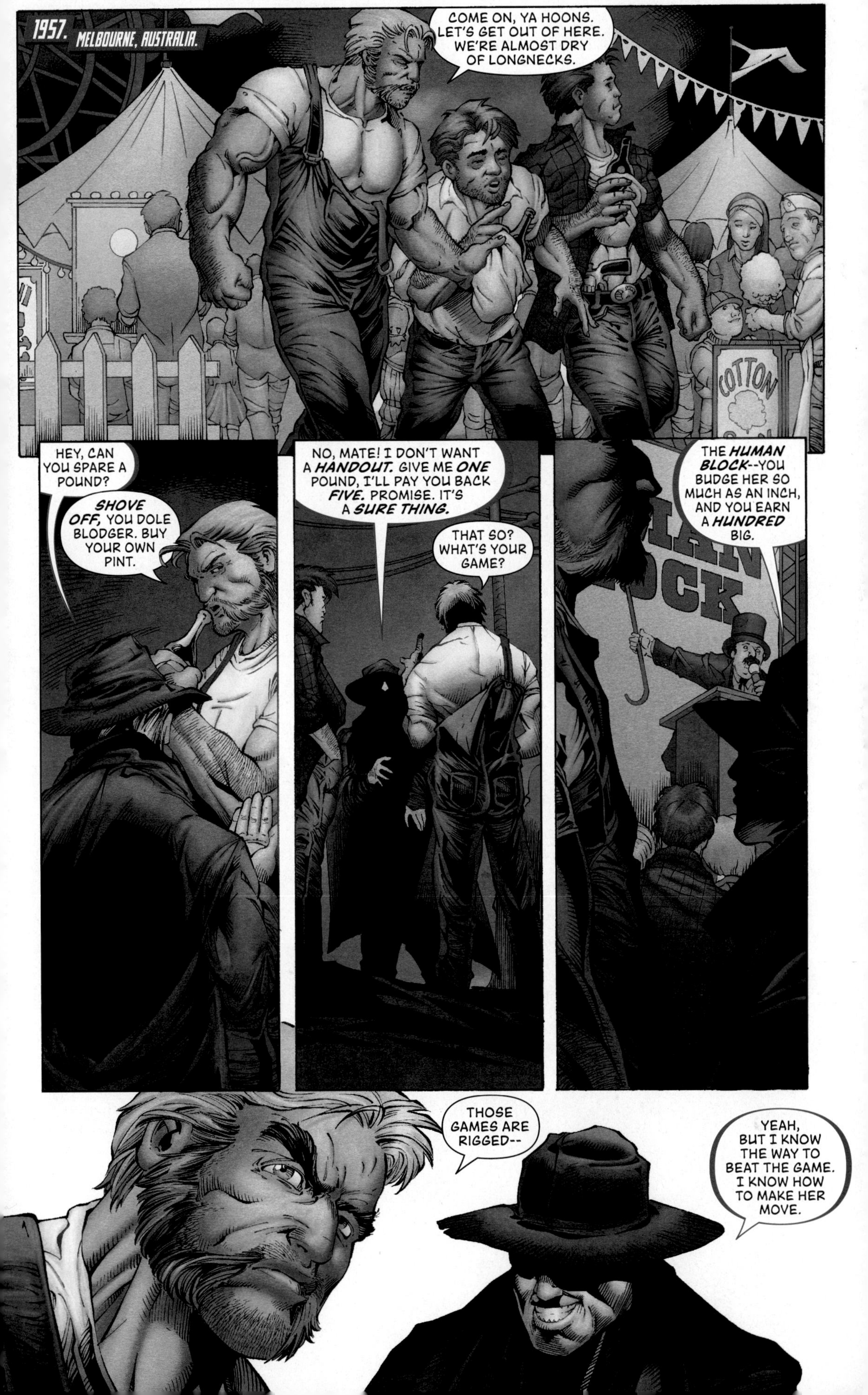
1957. MELBOURNE, AUSTRALIA.
COME ON, YA HOONS. LET'S GET OUT OF HERE. WE'RE ALMOST DRY OF LONGNECKS.
COTTON
HEY, CAN YOU SPARE A POUND?
SHOVE OFF, YOU DOLE BLODGER. BUY YOUR OWN PINT.
NO, MATE! I DON'T WANT A HANDOUT. GIVE ME ONE POUND, I'LL PAY YOU BACK FIVE. PROMISE. IT'S A SURE THING.
THAT SO? WHAT'S YOUR GAME?
THE HUMAN BLOCK--YOU BUDGE HER SO MUCH AS AN INCH, AND YOU EARN A HUNDRED BIG.
THOSE GAMES ARE RIGGED--
YEAH, BUT I KNOW THE WAY TO BEAT THE GAME. I KNOW HOW TO MAKE HER MOVE.

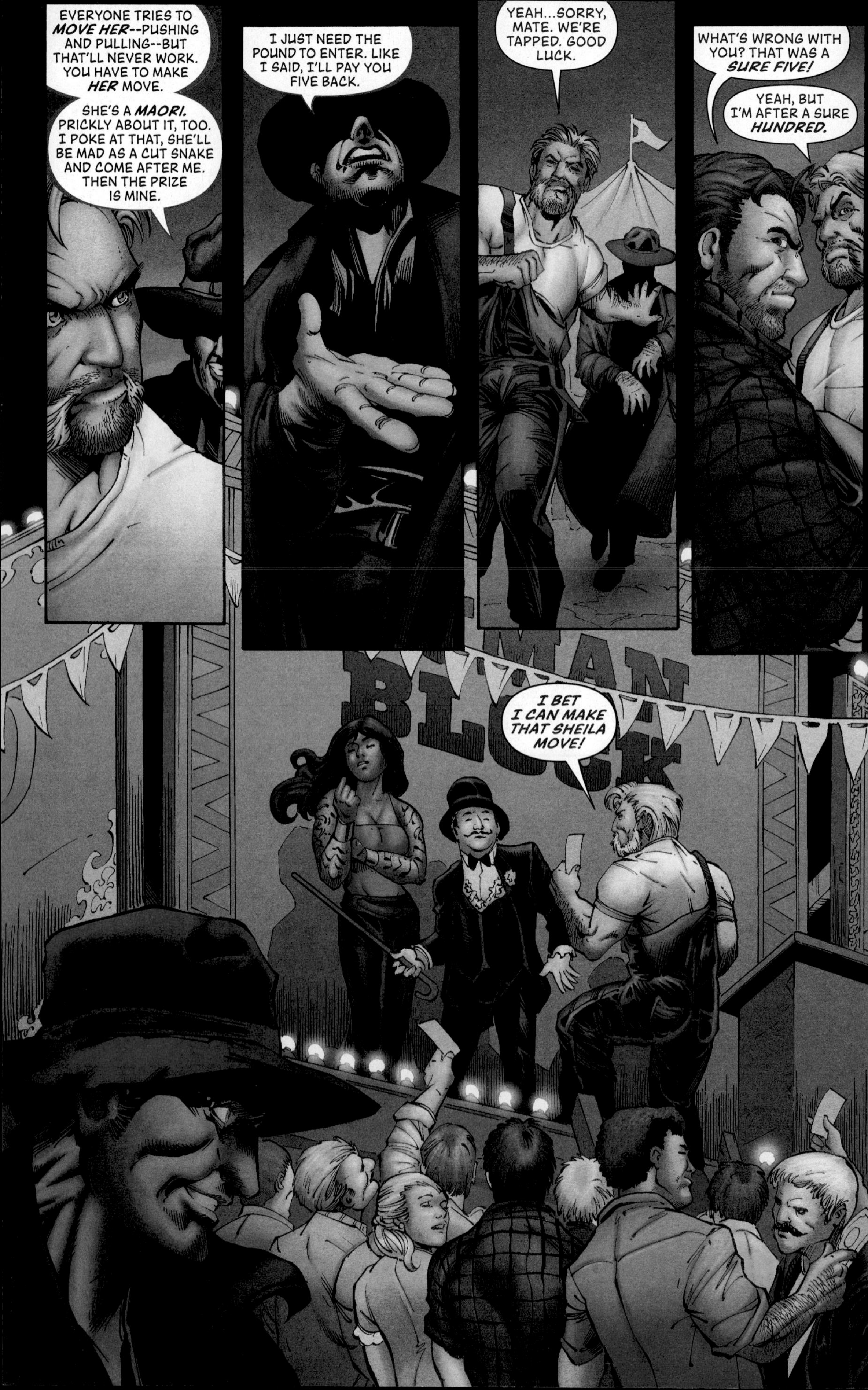
EVERYONE TRIES TO MOVE HER--PUSHING AND PULLING--BUT THAT'LL NEVER WORK. YOU HAVE TO MAKE HER MOVE.
SHE'S A MAORI. PRICKLY ABOUT IT, TOO. I POKE AT THAT, SHE'LL BE MAD AS A CUT SNAKE AND COME AFTER ME. THEN THE PRIZE IS MINE.
I JUST NEED THE POUND TO ENTER. LIKE I SAID, I'LL PAY YOU FIVE BACK.
YEAH...SORRY, MATE. WE'RE TAPPED. GOOD LUCK.
WHAT'S WRONG WITH YOU? THAT WAS A SURE FIVE!
YEAH, BUT I'M AFTER A SURE HUNDRED.
I BET I CAN MAKE THAT SHEILA MOVE!

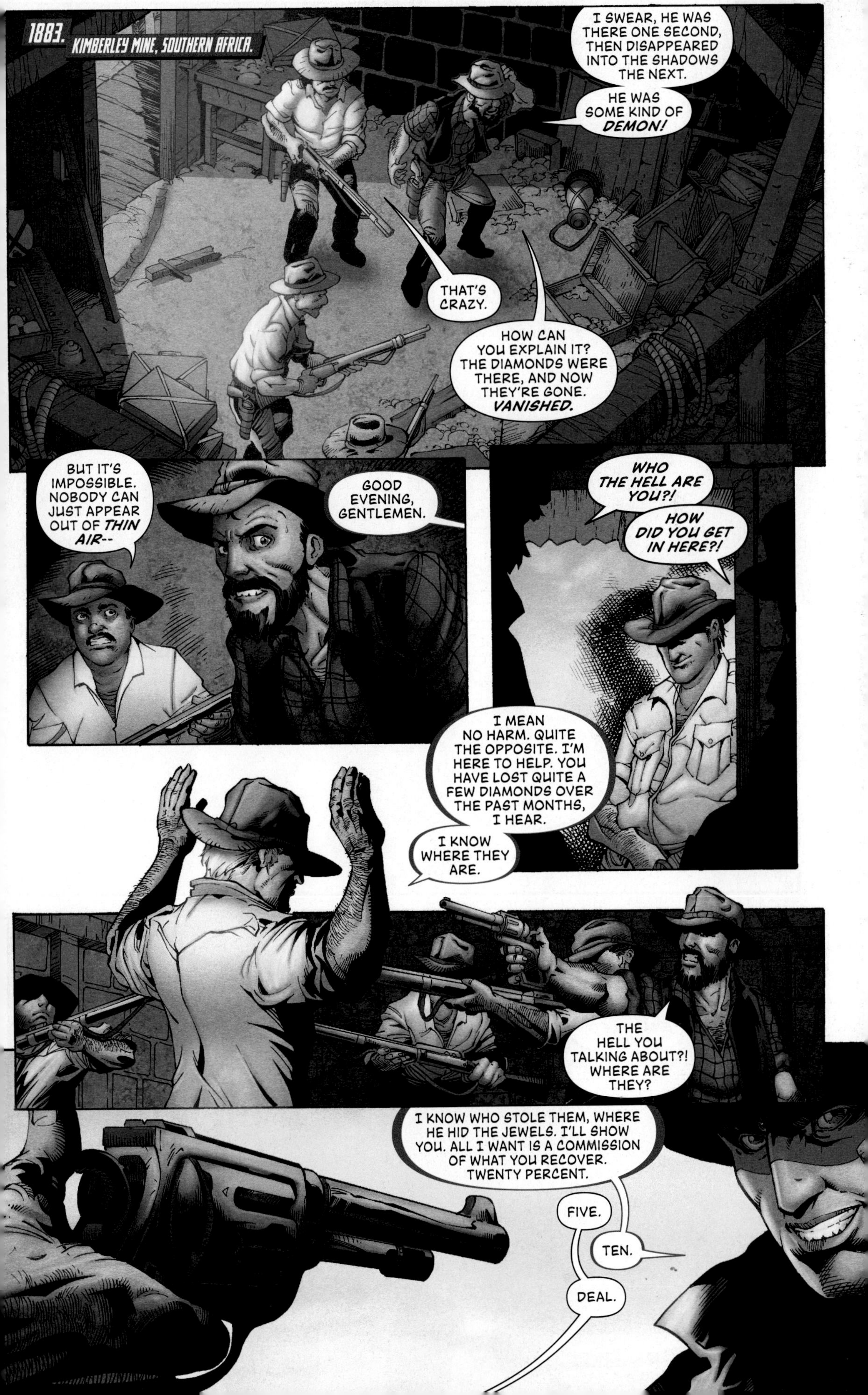

1883.
KIMBERLEY MINE, SOUTHERN AFRICA.
I SWEAR, HE WAS THERE ONE SECOND, THEN DISAPPEARED INTO THE SHADOWS THE NEXT.
HE WAS SOME KIND OF DEMON!
THAT'S CRAZY.
HOW CAN YOU EXPLAIN IT? THE DIAMONDS WERE THERE, AND NOW THEY'RE GONE. VANISHED.
BUT IT'S IMPOSSIBLE. NOBODY CAN JUST APPEAR OUT OF THIN AIR--
GOOD EVENING, GENTLEMEN.
WHO THE HELL ARE YOU?!
HOW DID YOU GET IN HERE?!
I MEAN NO HARM. QUITE THE OPPOSITE. I'M HERE TO HELP. YOU HAVE LOST QUITE A FEW DIAMONDS OVER THE PAST MONTHS, I HEAR.
I KNOW WHERE THEY ARE.
THE HELL YOU TALKING ABOUT?! WHERE ARE THEY?
I KNOW WHO STOLE THEM, WHERE HE HID THE JEWELS. I'LL SHOW YOU. ALL I WANT IS A COMMISSION OF WHAT YOU RECOVER. TWENTY PERCENT.
FIVE.
TEN.
DEAL.

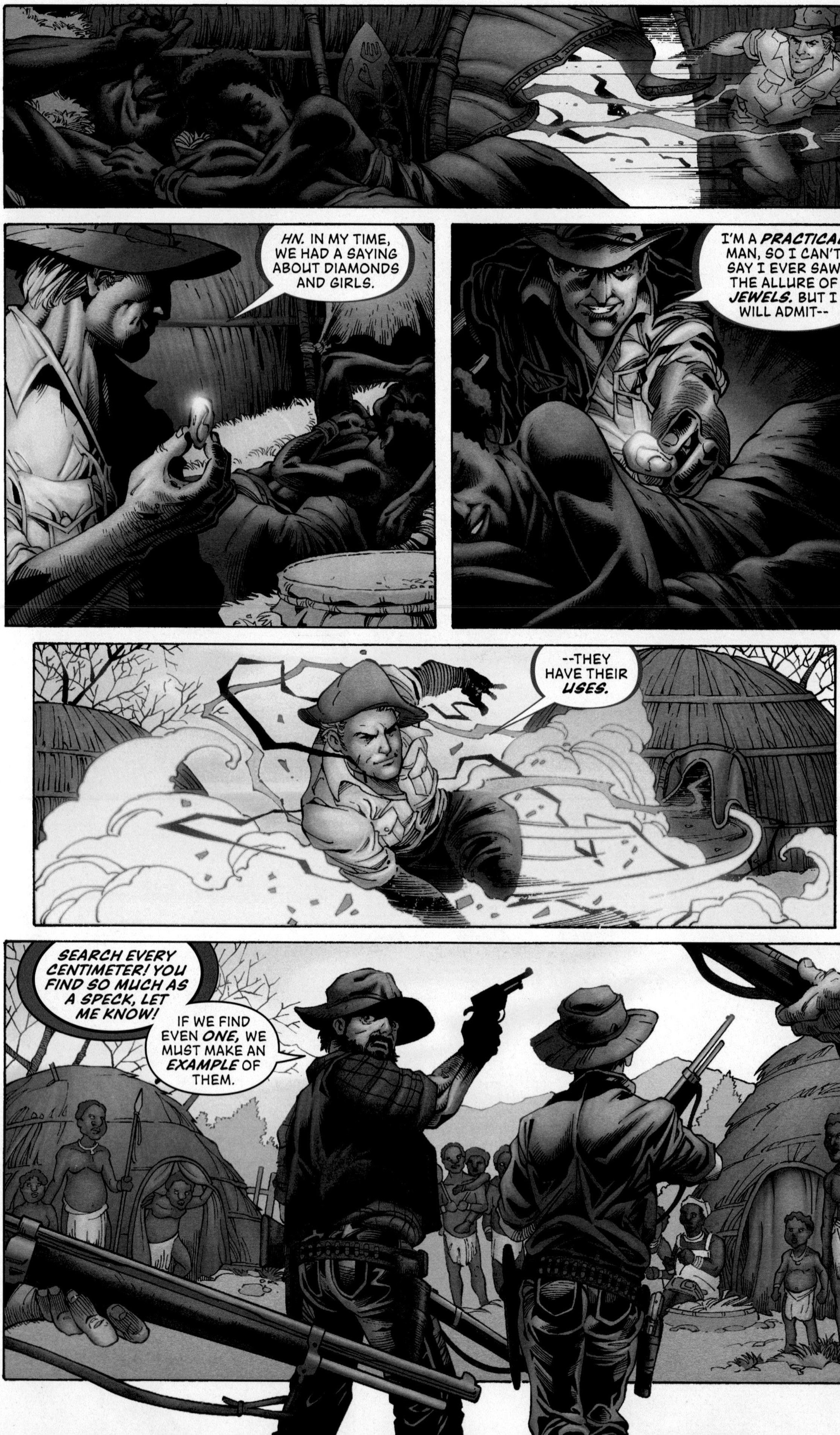
HN. IN MY TIME, WE HAD A SAYING ABOUT DIAMONDS AND GIRLS.
I'M A PRACTICAL MAN, SO I CAN'T SAY I EVER SAW THE ALLURE OF JEWELS. BUT I WILL ADMIT--
--THEY HAVE THEIR USES.
SEARCH EVERY CENTIMETER! YOU FIND SO MUCH AS A SPECK, LET ME KNOW!
IF WE FIND EVEN ONE, WE MUST MAKE AN EXAMPLE OF THEM.

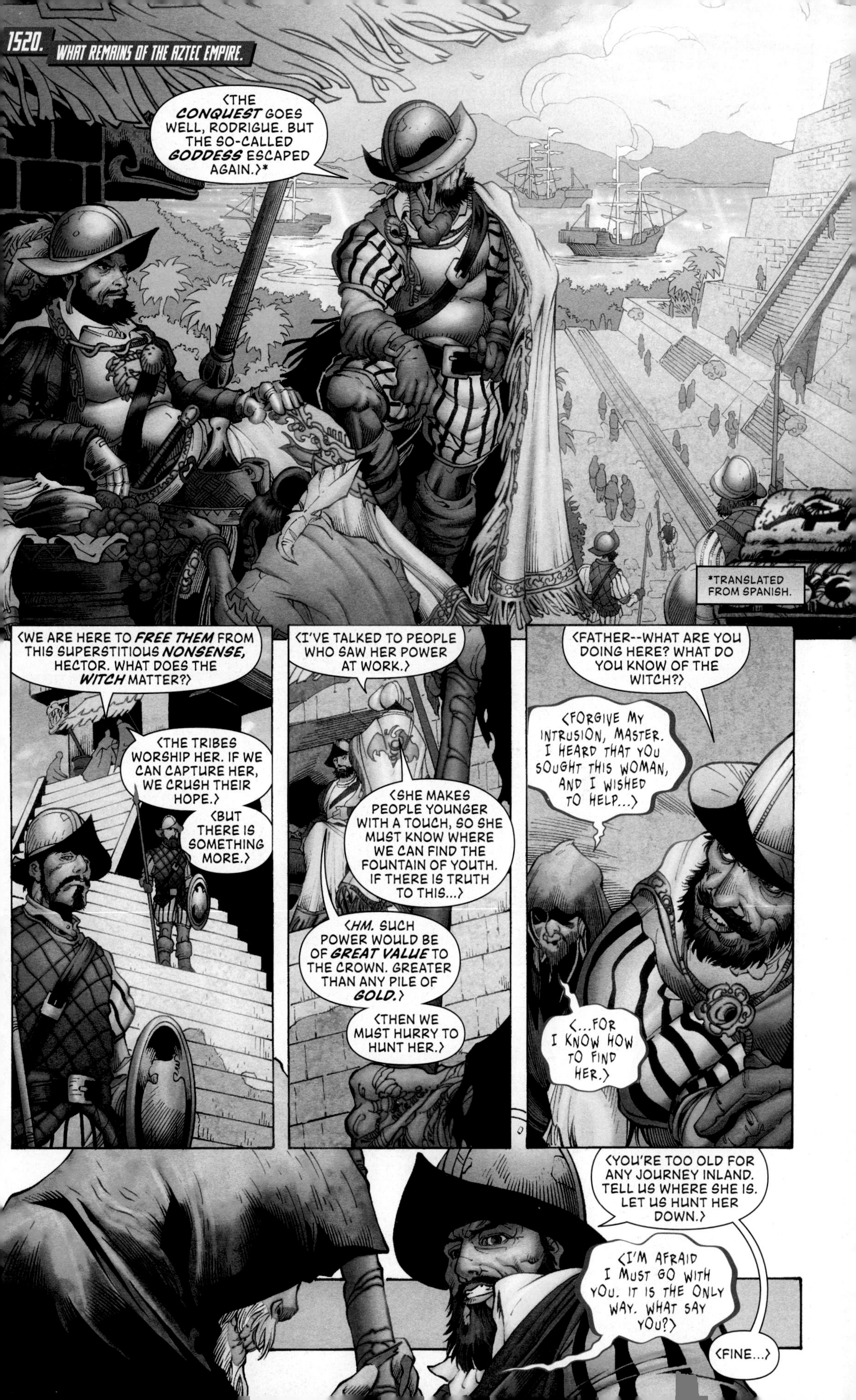
1520.
WHAT REMAINS OF THE AZTEC EMPIRE.
<THE CONQUEST GOES WELL, RODRIGUE. BUT THE SO-CALLED GODDESS ESCAPED AGAIN.>*
*TRANSLATED FROM SPANISH.
<WE ARE HERE TO FREE THEM FROM THIS SUPERSTITIOUS NONSENSE, HECTOR. WHAT DOES THE WITCH MATTER?>
<THE TRIBES WORSHIP HER. IF WE CAN CAPTURE HER, WE CRUSH THEIR HOPE.>
<BUT THERE IS SOMETHING MORE.>
<I'VE TALKED TO PEOPLE WHO SAW HER POWER AT WORK.>
<SHE MAKES PEOPLE YOUNGER WITH A TOUCH, SO SHE MUST KNOW WHERE WE CAN FIND THE FOUNTAIN OF YOUTH. IF THERE IS TRUTH TO THIS...>
<HM. SUCH POWER WOULD BE OF GREAT VALUE TO THE CROWN. GREATER THAN ANY PILE OF GOLD.>
<THEN WE MUST HURRY TO HUNT HER.>
<FATHER--WHAT ARE YOU DOING HERE? WHAT DO YOU KNOW OF THE WITCH?>
<FORGIVE MY INTRUSION, MASTER. I HEARD THAT YOU SOUGHT THIS WOMAN, AND I WISHED TO HELP...>
<...FOR I KNOW HOW TO FIND HER.>
<YOU'RE TOO OLD FOR ANY JOURNEY INLAND. TELL US WHERE SHE IS. LET US HUNT HER DOWN.>
<I'M AFRAID I MUST GO WITH YOU. IT IS THE ONLY WAY. WHAT SAY YOU?>
<FINE...>

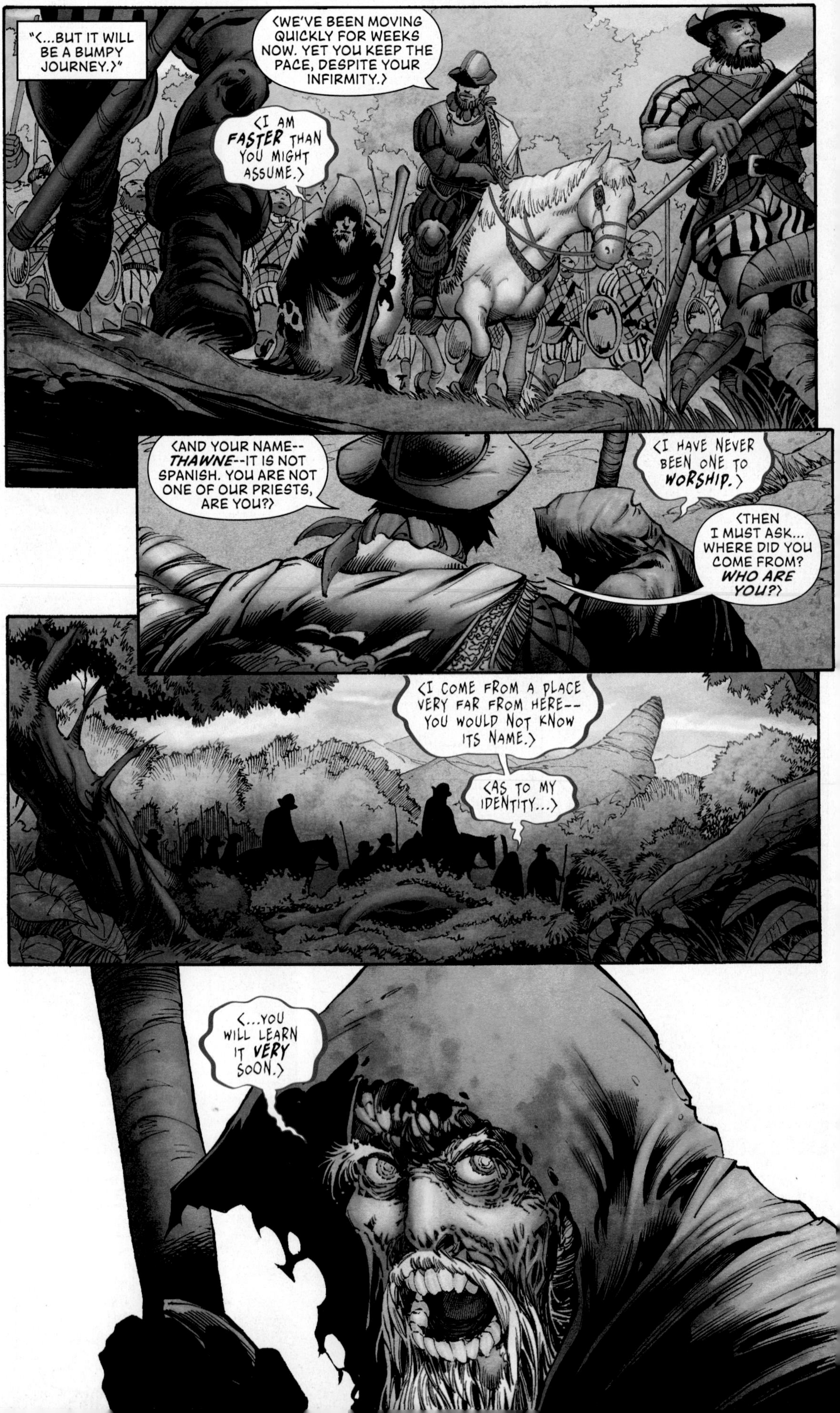
"<...BUT IT WILL BE A BUMPY JOURNEY.>"
<WE'VE BEEN MOVING QUICKLY FOR WEEKS NOW. YET YOU KEEP THE PACE, DESPITE YOUR INFIRMITY.>
<I AM FASTER THAN YOU MIGHT ASSUME.>
<AND YOUR NAME--THAWNE--IT IS NOT SPANISH. YOU ARE NOT ONE OF OUR PRIESTS, ARE YOU?>
<I HAVE NEVER BEEN ONE TO WORSHIP.>
<THEN I MUST ASK... WHERE DID YOU COME FROM? WHO ARE YOU?>
<I COME FROM A PLACE VERY FAR FROM HERE--YOU WOULD NOT KNOW ITS NAME.>
<AS TO MY IDENTITY...>
<...YOU WILL LEARN IT VERY SOON.>

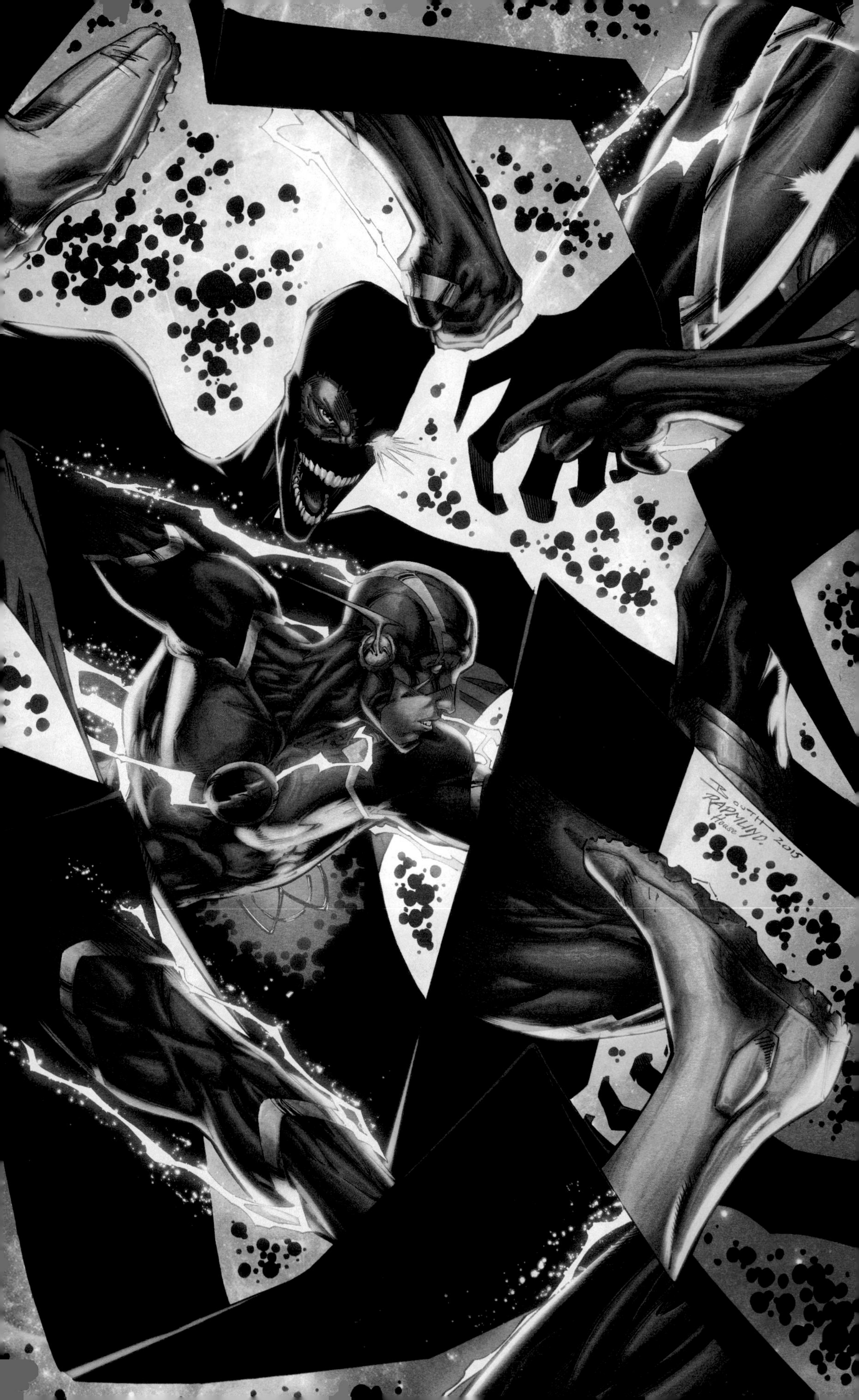
BOOTH
RAPMUND.
House
2015

ROBERT VENDITTI, VAN JENSEN writers BRETT BOOTH penciller NORM RAPMUND inker ANDREW DALHOUSE, WENDY BROOME colorists PAT BROSSEAU letterer
cover by BRETT BOOTH, NORM RAPMUND, ANDREW DALHOUSE

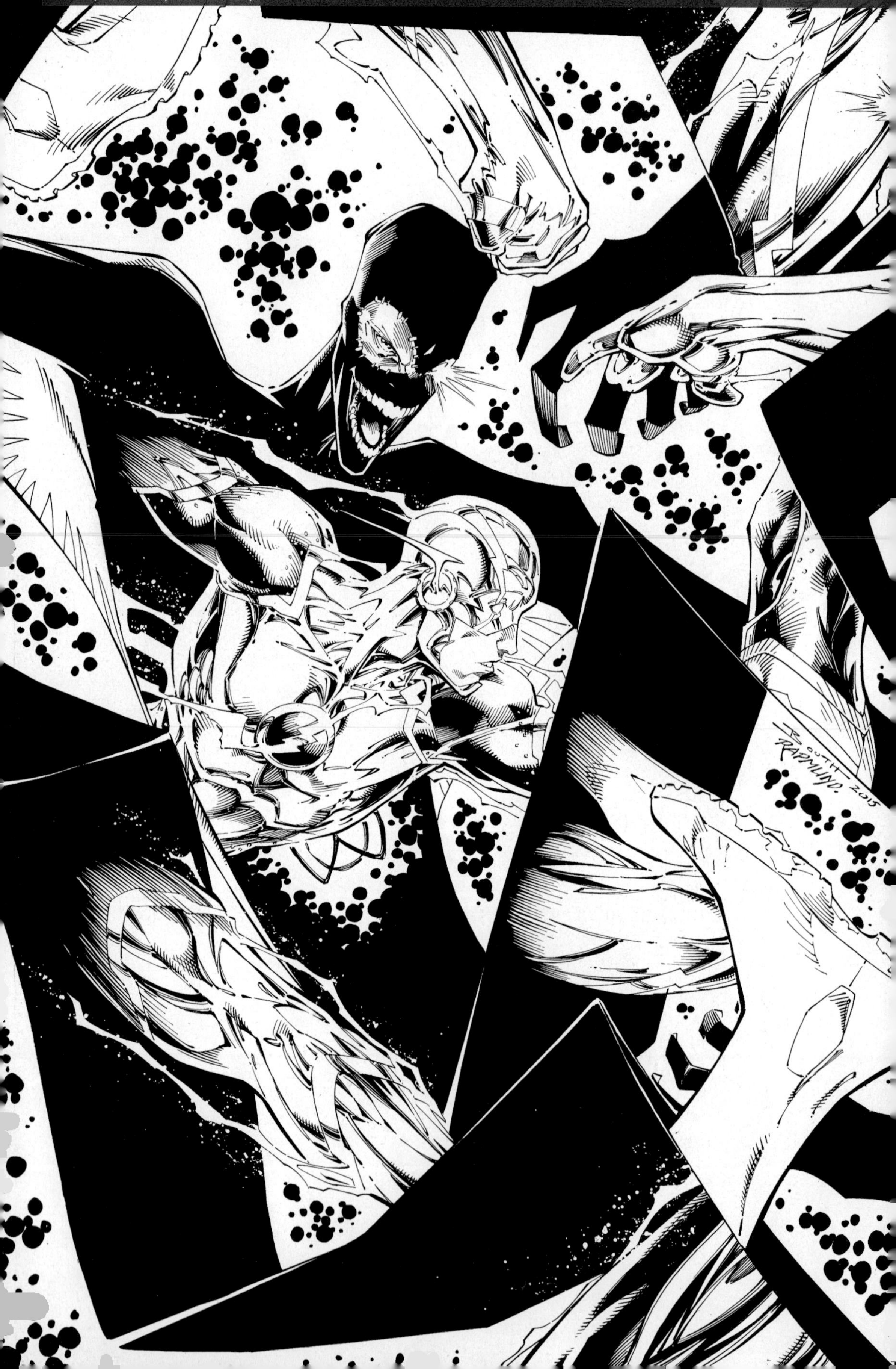

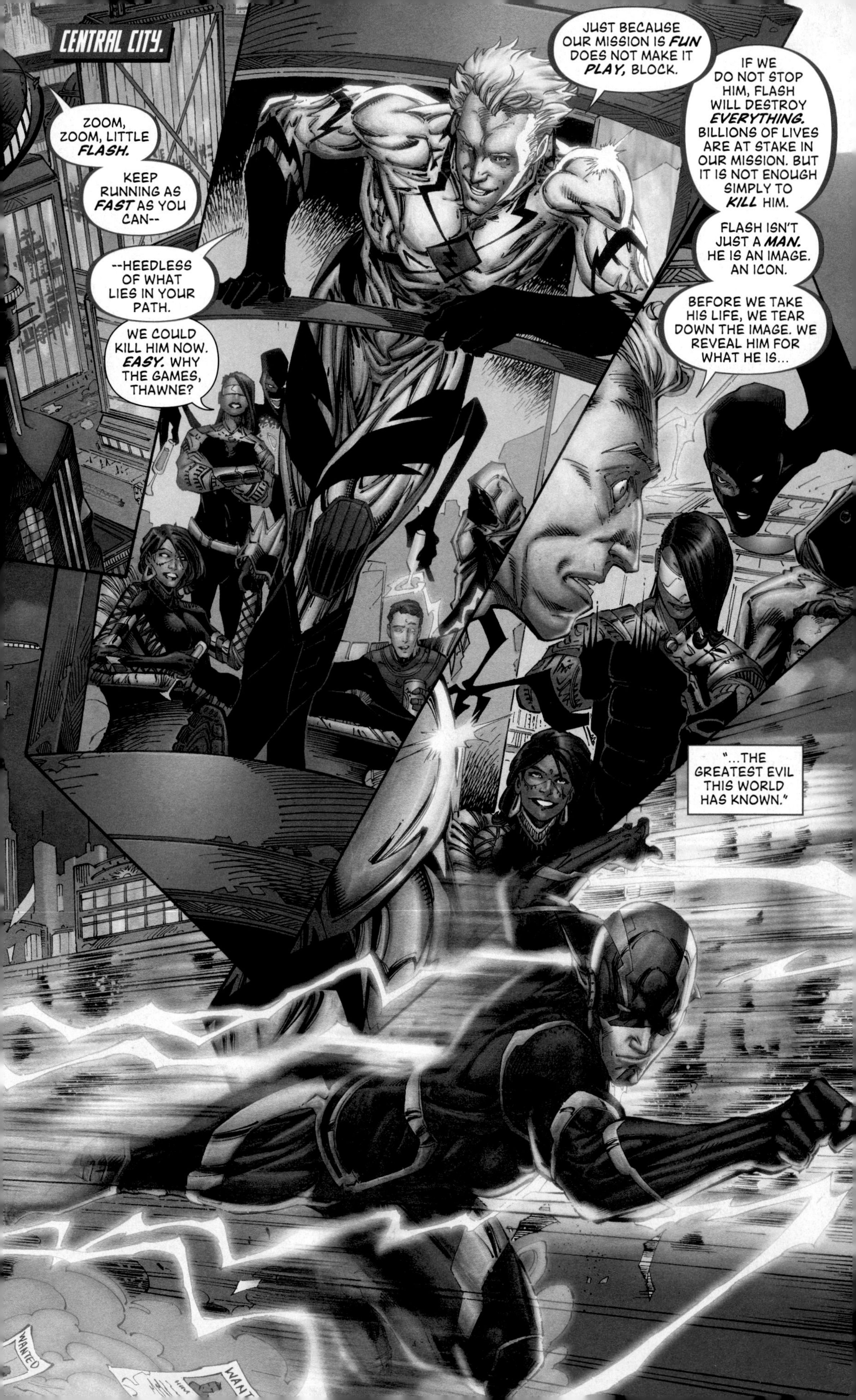
CENTRAL CITY.
ZOOM, ZOOM, LITTLE FLASH.
KEEP RUNNING AS FAST AS YOU CAN--
--HEEDLESS OF WHAT LIES IN YOUR PATH.
WE COULD KILL HIM NOW. EASY. WHY THE GAMES, THAWNE?
JUST BECAUSE OUR MISSION IS FUN DOES NOT MAKE IT PLAY, BLOCK.
IF WE DO NOT STOP HIM, FLASH WILL DESTROY EVERYTHING. BILLIONS OF LIVES ARE AT STAKE IN OUR MISSION. BUT IT IS NOT ENOUGH SIMPLY TO KILL HIM.
FLASH ISN'T JUST A MAN. HE IS AN IMAGE. AN ICON.
BEFORE WE TAKE HIS LIFE, WE TEAR DOWN THE IMAGE. WE REVEAL HIM FOR WHAT HE IS...
"...THE GREATEST EVIL THIS WORLD HAS KNOWN."
WANTED

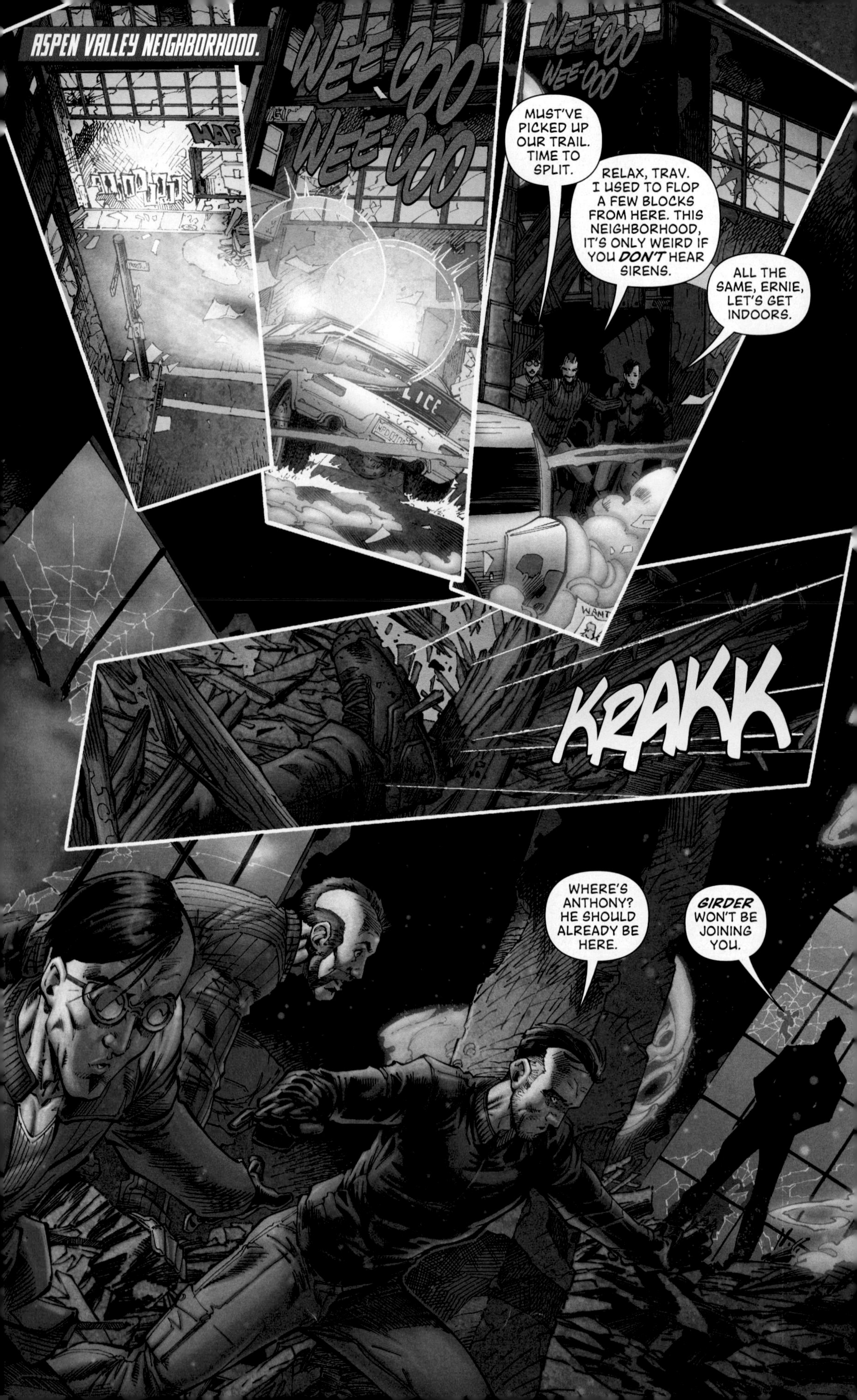
ASPEN VALLEY NEIGHBORHOOD.
WEE-OOO WEE-OOO
WEE-OOO WEE-OOO
MUST'VE PICKED UP OUR TRAIL. TIME TO SPLIT.
RELAX, TRAV. I USED TO FLOP A FEW BLOCKS FROM HERE. THIS NEIGHBORHOOD, IT'S ONLY WEIRD IF YOU DON'T HEAR SIRENS.
ALL THE SAME, ERNIE, LET'S GET INDOORS.
KRAKK
WHERE'S ANTHONY? HE SHOULD ALREADY BE HERE.
GIRDER WON'T BE JOINING YOU.

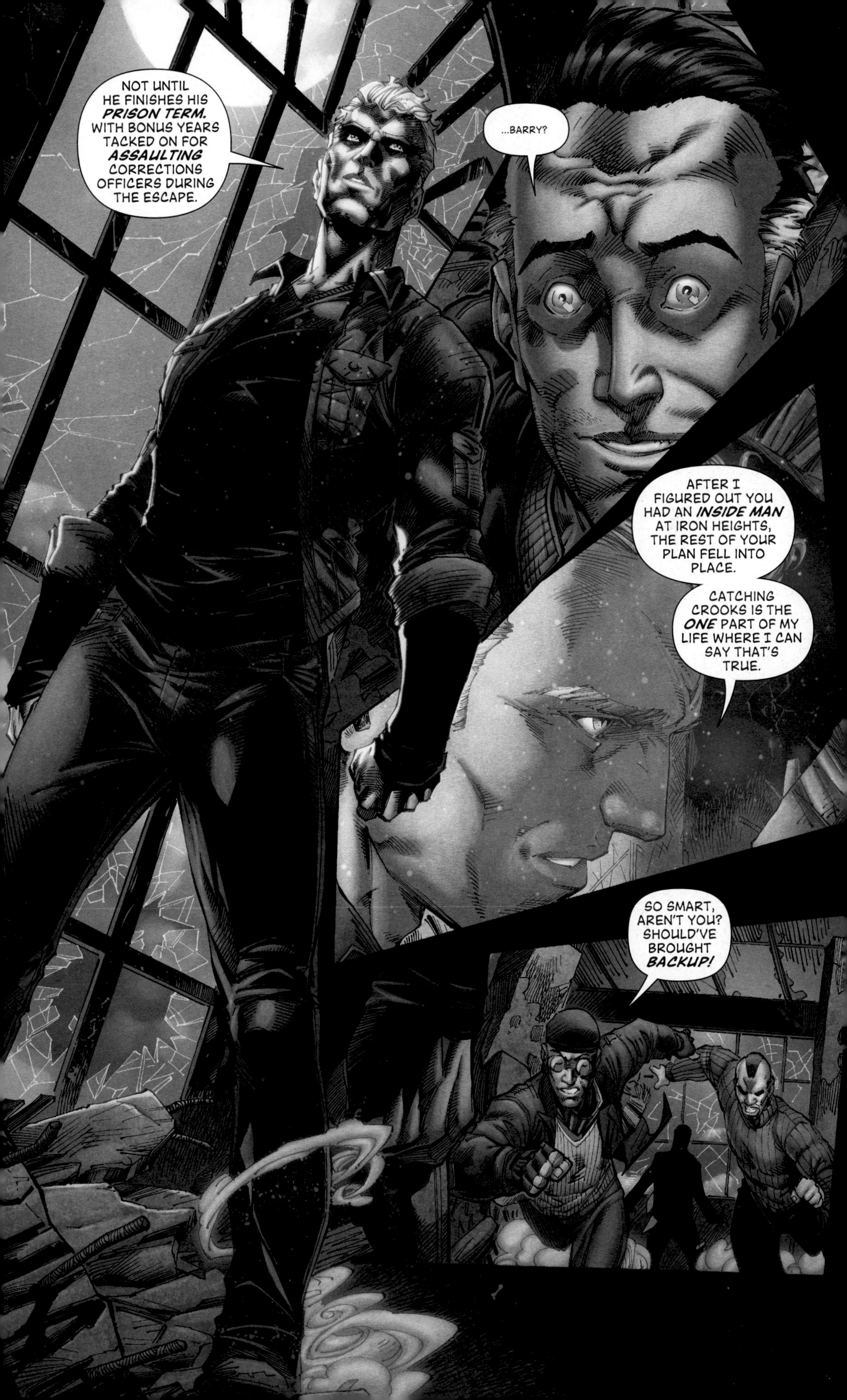

NOT UNTIL HE FINISHES HIS *PRISON TERM.* WITH BONUS YEARS TACKED ON FOR *ASSAULTING* CORRECTIONS OFFICERS DURING THE ESCAPE.
...BARRY?
AFTER I FIGURED OUT YOU HAD AN *INSIDE MAN* AT IRON HEIGHTS, THE REST OF YOUR PLAN FELL INTO PLACE.
CATCHING CROOKS IS THE *ONE* PART OF MY LIFE WHERE I CAN SAY THAT'S TRUE.
SO SMART, AREN'T YOU? SHOULD'VE BROUGHT *BACKUP!*

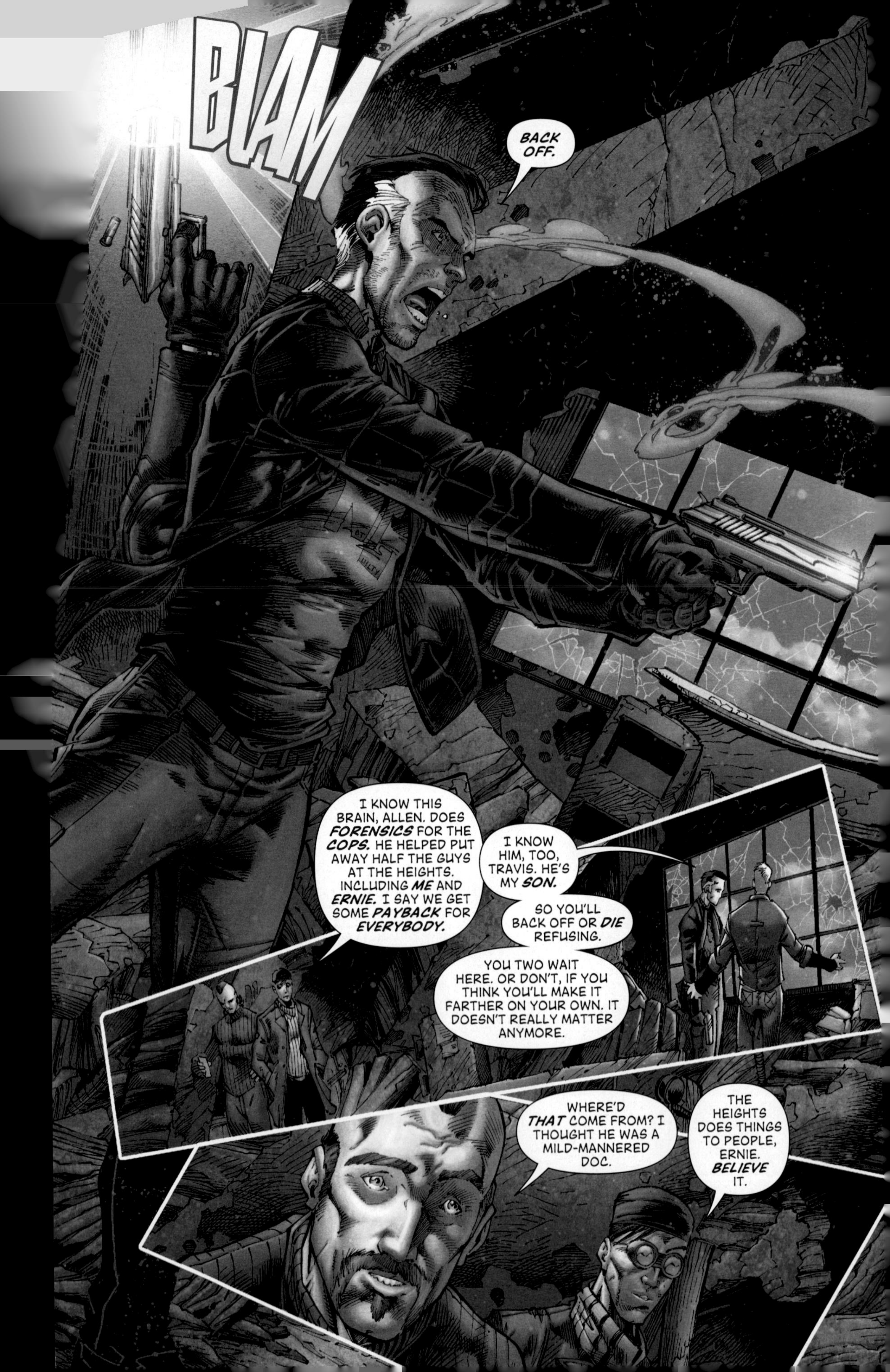
BLAM
BACK OFF.
I KNOW THIS BRAIN, ALLEN. DOES FORENSICS FOR THE COPS. HE HELPED PUT AWAY HALF THE GUYS AT THE HEIGHTS. INCLUDING ME AND ERNIE. I SAY WE GET SOME PAYBACK FOR EVERYBODY.
I KNOW HIM, TOO, TRAVIS. HE'S MY SON.
SO YOU'LL BACK OFF OR DIE REFUSING.
YOU TWO WAIT HERE. OR DON'T, IF YOU THINK YOU'LL MAKE IT FARTHER ON YOUR OWN. IT DOESN'T REALLY MATTER ANYMORE.
WHERE'D THAT COME FROM? I THOUGHT HE WAS A MILD-MANNERED DOC.
THE HEIGHTS DOES THINGS TO PEOPLE, ERNIE. BELIEVE IT.

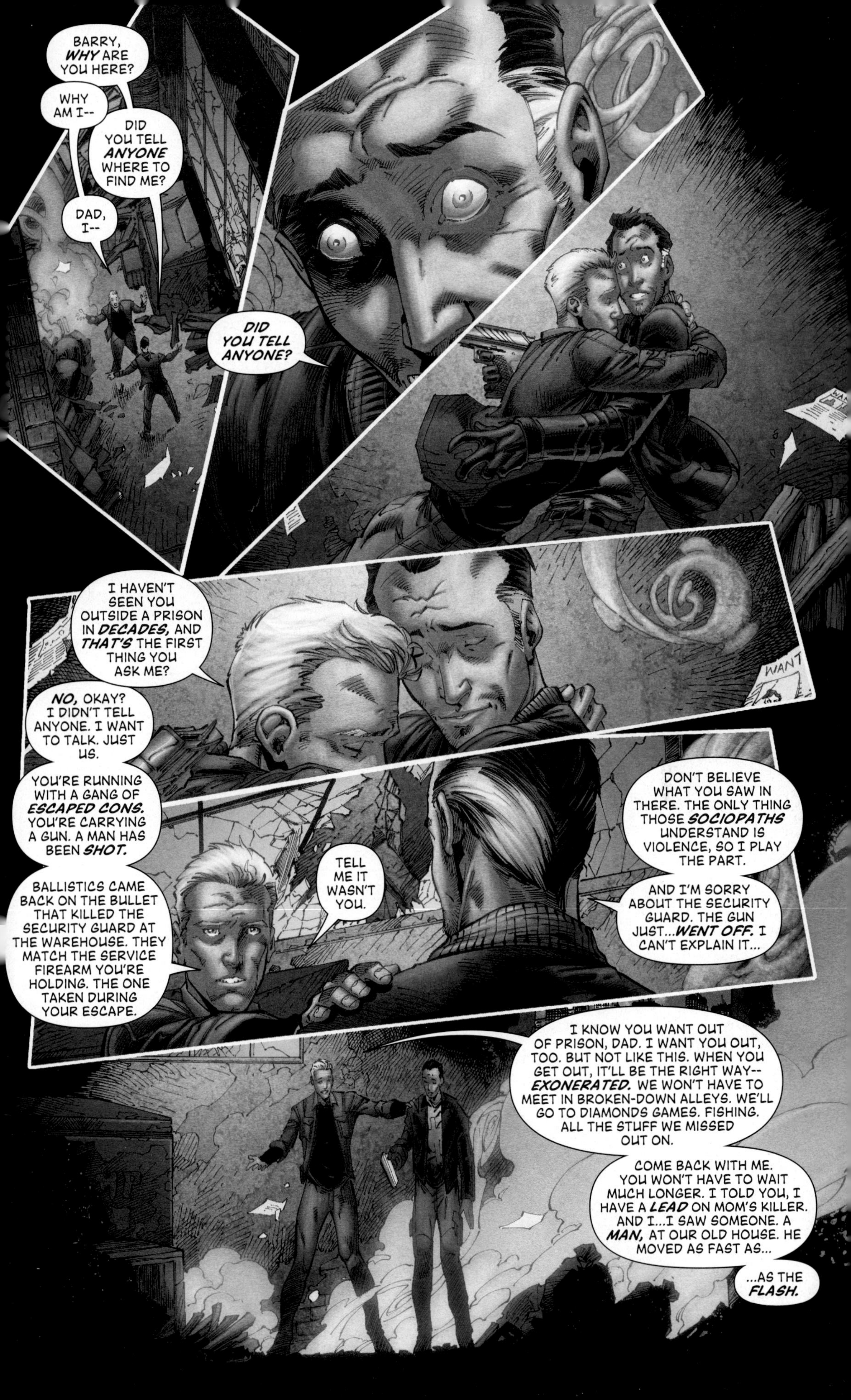
BARRY, *WHY* ARE YOU HERE?
WHY AM I--
DID YOU TELL *ANYONE* WHERE TO FIND ME?
DAD, I--
DID YOU TELL ANYONE?
I HAVEN'T SEEN YOU OUTSIDE A PRISON IN *DECADES,* AND *THAT'S* THE FIRST THING YOU ASK ME?
NO, OKAY? I DIDN'T TELL ANYONE. I WANT TO TALK. JUST US.
YOU'RE RUNNING WITH A GANG OF *ESCAPED CONS.* YOU'RE CARRYING A GUN. A MAN HAS BEEN *SHOT.*
BALLISTICS CAME BACK ON THE BULLET THAT KILLED THE SECURITY GUARD AT THE WAREHOUSE. THEY MATCH THE SERVICE FIREARM YOU'RE HOLDING. THE ONE TAKEN DURING YOUR ESCAPE.
TELL ME IT WASN'T YOU.
DON'T BELIEVE WHAT YOU SAW IN THERE. THE ONLY THING THOSE *SOCIOPATHS* UNDERSTAND IS VIOLENCE, SO I PLAY THE PART.
AND I'M SORRY ABOUT THE SECURITY GUARD. THE GUN JUST...*WENT OFF.* I CAN'T EXPLAIN IT...
I KNOW YOU WANT OUT OF PRISON, DAD. I WANT YOU OUT, TOO. BUT NOT LIKE THIS. WHEN YOU GET OUT, IT'LL BE THE RIGHT WAY-- *EXONERATED.* WE WON'T HAVE TO MEET IN BROKEN-DOWN ALLEYS. WE'LL GO TO DIAMONDS GAMES. FISHING. ALL THE STUFF WE MISSED OUT ON.
COME BACK WITH ME. YOU WON'T HAVE TO WAIT MUCH LONGER. I TOLD YOU, I HAVE A *LEAD* ON MOM'S KILLER. AND I...I SAW SOMEONE. A *MAN,* AT OUR OLD HOUSE. HE MOVED AS FAST AS...
...AS THE *FLASH.*

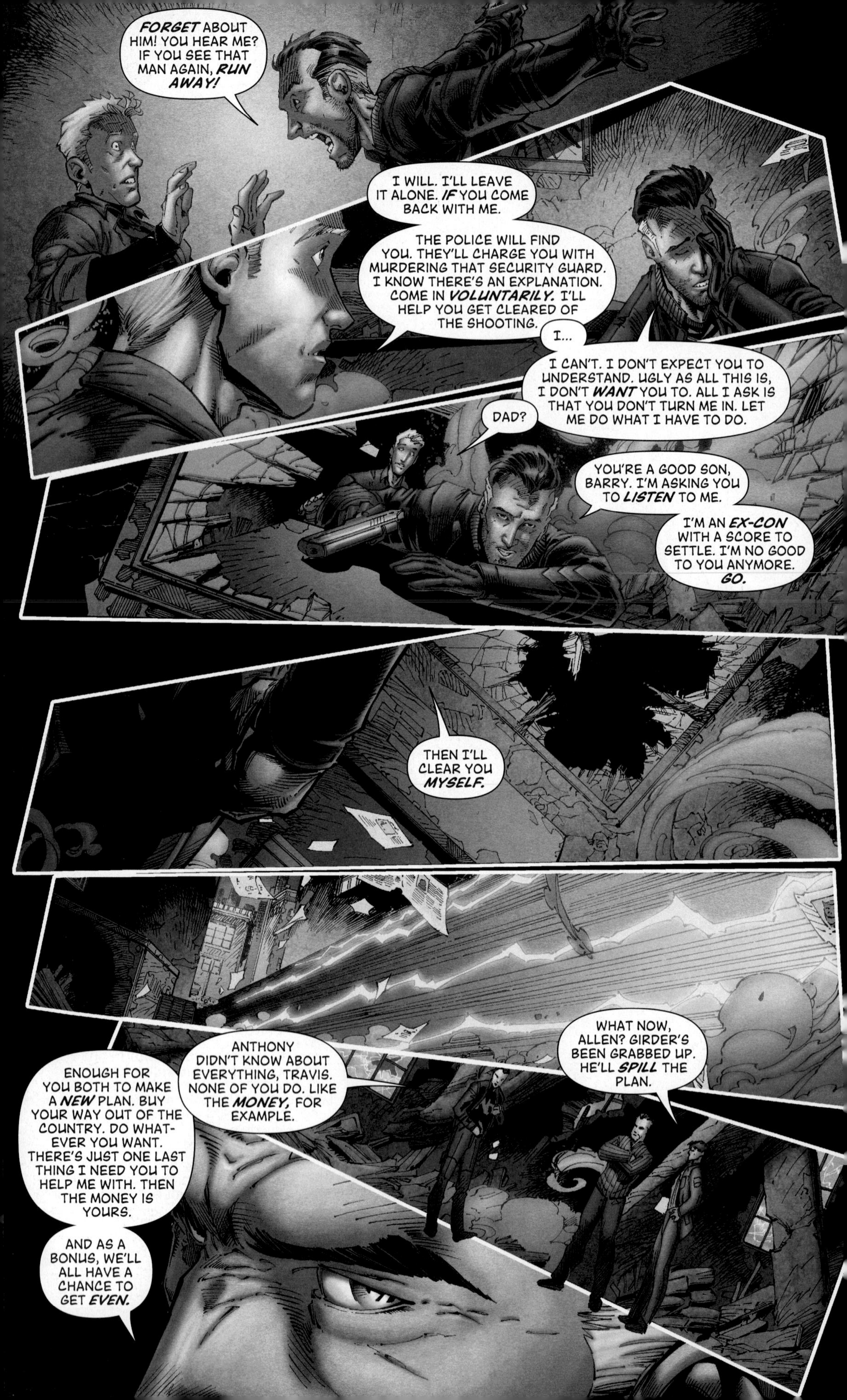
FORGET ABOUT HIM! YOU HEAR ME? IF YOU SEE THAT MAN AGAIN, RUN AWAY!
I WILL. I'LL LEAVE IT ALONE. IF YOU COME BACK WITH ME.
THE POLICE WILL FIND YOU. THEY'LL CHARGE YOU WITH MURDERING THAT SECURITY GUARD. I KNOW THERE'S AN EXPLANATION. COME IN VOLUNTARILY. I'LL HELP YOU GET CLEARED OF THE SHOOTING.
I...
I CAN'T. I DON'T EXPECT YOU TO UNDERSTAND. UGLY AS ALL THIS IS, I DON'T WANT YOU TO. ALL I ASK IS THAT YOU DON'T TURN ME IN. LET ME DO WHAT I HAVE TO DO.
DAD?
YOU'RE A GOOD SON, BARRY. I'M ASKING YOU TO LISTEN TO ME.
I'M AN EX-CON WITH A SCORE TO SETTLE. I'M NO GOOD TO YOU ANYMORE. GO.
THEN I'LL CLEAR YOU MYSELF.
WHAT NOW, ALLEN? GIRDER'S BEEN GRABBED UP. HE'LL SPILL THE PLAN.
ANTHONY DIDN'T KNOW ABOUT EVERYTHING, TRAVIS. NONE OF YOU DO. LIKE THE MONEY, FOR EXAMPLE.
ENOUGH FOR YOU BOTH TO MAKE A NEW PLAN. BUY YOUR WAY OUT OF THE COUNTRY. DO WHAT-EVER YOU WANT. THERE'S JUST ONE LAST THING I NEED YOU TO HELP ME WITH. THEN THE MONEY IS YOURS.
AND AS A BONUS, WE'LL ALL HAVE A CHANCE TO GET EVEN.

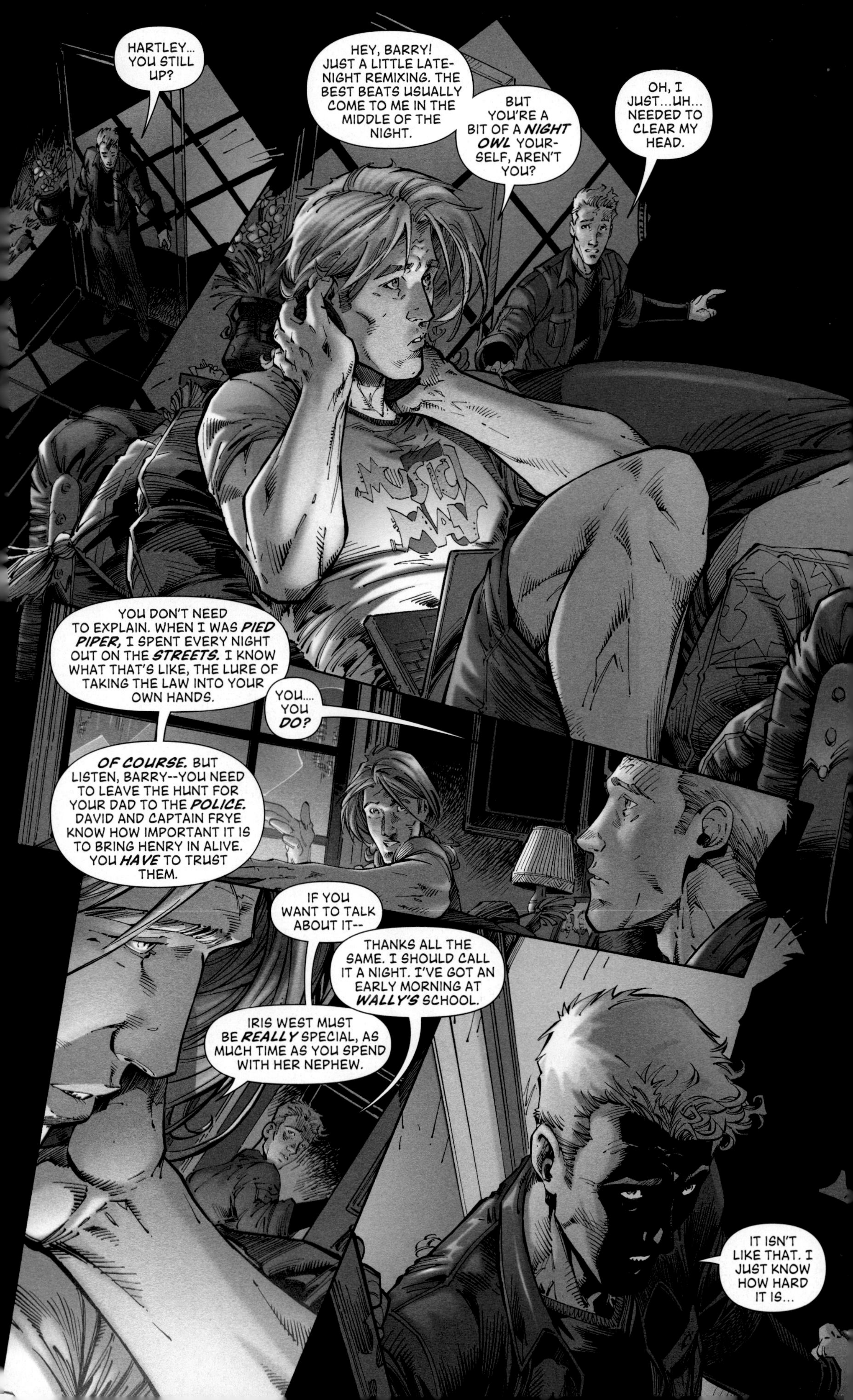
HARTLEY... YOU STILL UP?
HEY, BARRY! JUST A LITTLE LATE-NIGHT REMIXING. THE BEST BEATS USUALLY COME TO ME IN THE MIDDLE OF THE NIGHT.
BUT YOU'RE A BIT OF A NIGHT OWL YOURSELF, AREN'T YOU?
OH, I JUST...UH... NEEDED TO CLEAR MY HEAD.
YOU DON'T NEED TO EXPLAIN. WHEN I WAS PIED PIPER, I SPENT EVERY NIGHT OUT ON THE STREETS. I KNOW WHAT THAT'S LIKE, THE LURE OF TAKING THE LAW INTO YOUR OWN HANDS.
YOU.... YOU DO?
OF COURSE. BUT LISTEN, BARRY--YOU NEED TO LEAVE THE HUNT FOR YOUR DAD TO THE POLICE. DAVID AND CAPTAIN FRYE KNOW HOW IMPORTANT IT IS TO BRING HENRY IN ALIVE. YOU HAVE TO TRUST THEM.
IF YOU WANT TO TALK ABOUT IT--
THANKS ALL THE SAME. I SHOULD CALL IT A NIGHT. I'VE GOT AN EARLY MORNING AT WALLY'S SCHOOL.
IRIS WEST MUST BE REALLY SPECIAL, AS MUCH TIME AS YOU SPEND WITH HER NEPHEW.
IT ISN'T LIKE THAT. I JUST KNOW HOW HARD IT IS...

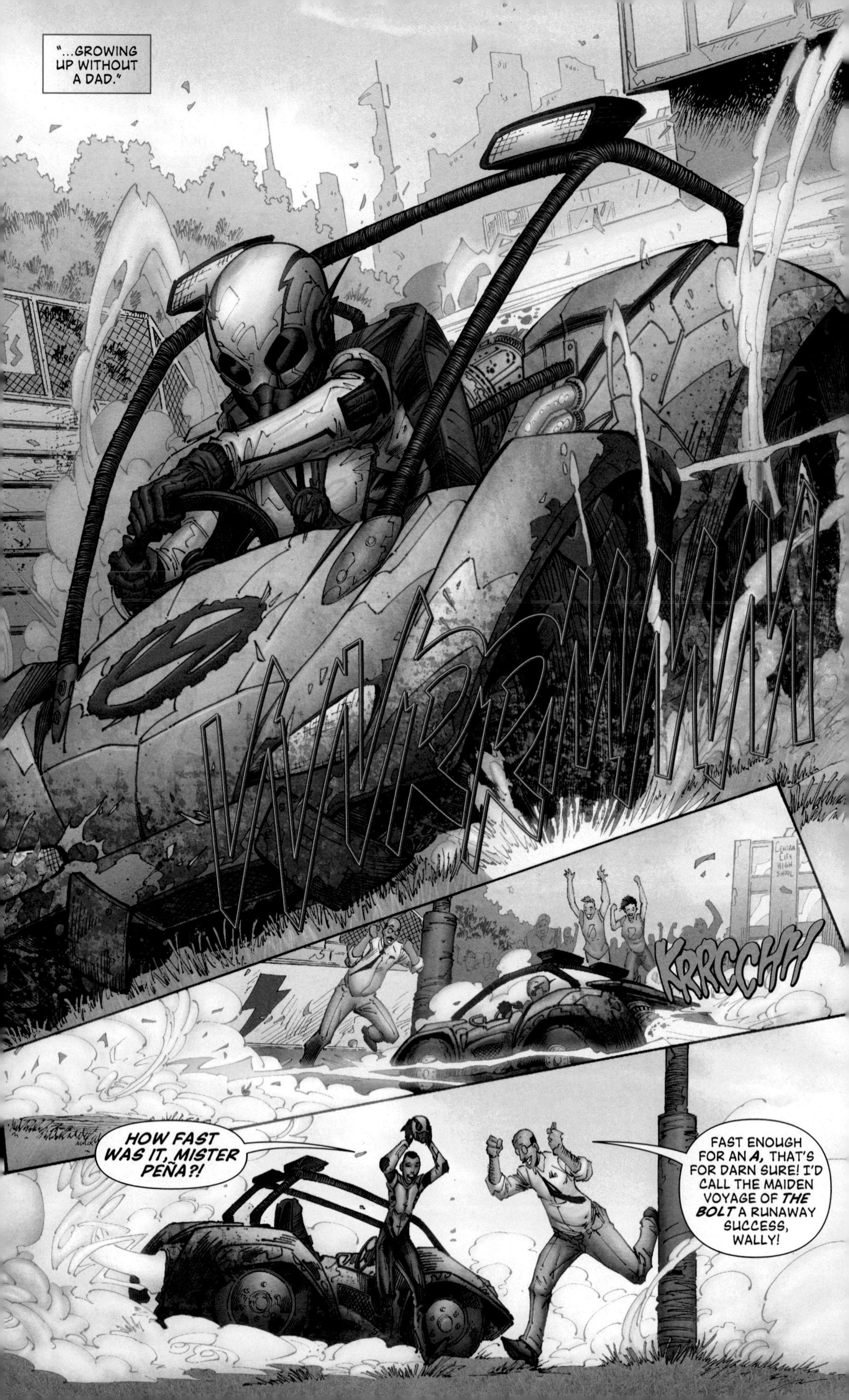
"...GROWING UP WITHOUT A DAD."
WWRRMMMMM
KRRCCHH
HOW FAST WAS IT, MISTER PEÑA?!
FAST ENOUGH FOR AN *A*, THAT'S FOR DARN SURE! I'D CALL THE MAIDEN VOYAGE OF *THE BOLT* A RUNAWAY SUCCESS, WALLY!

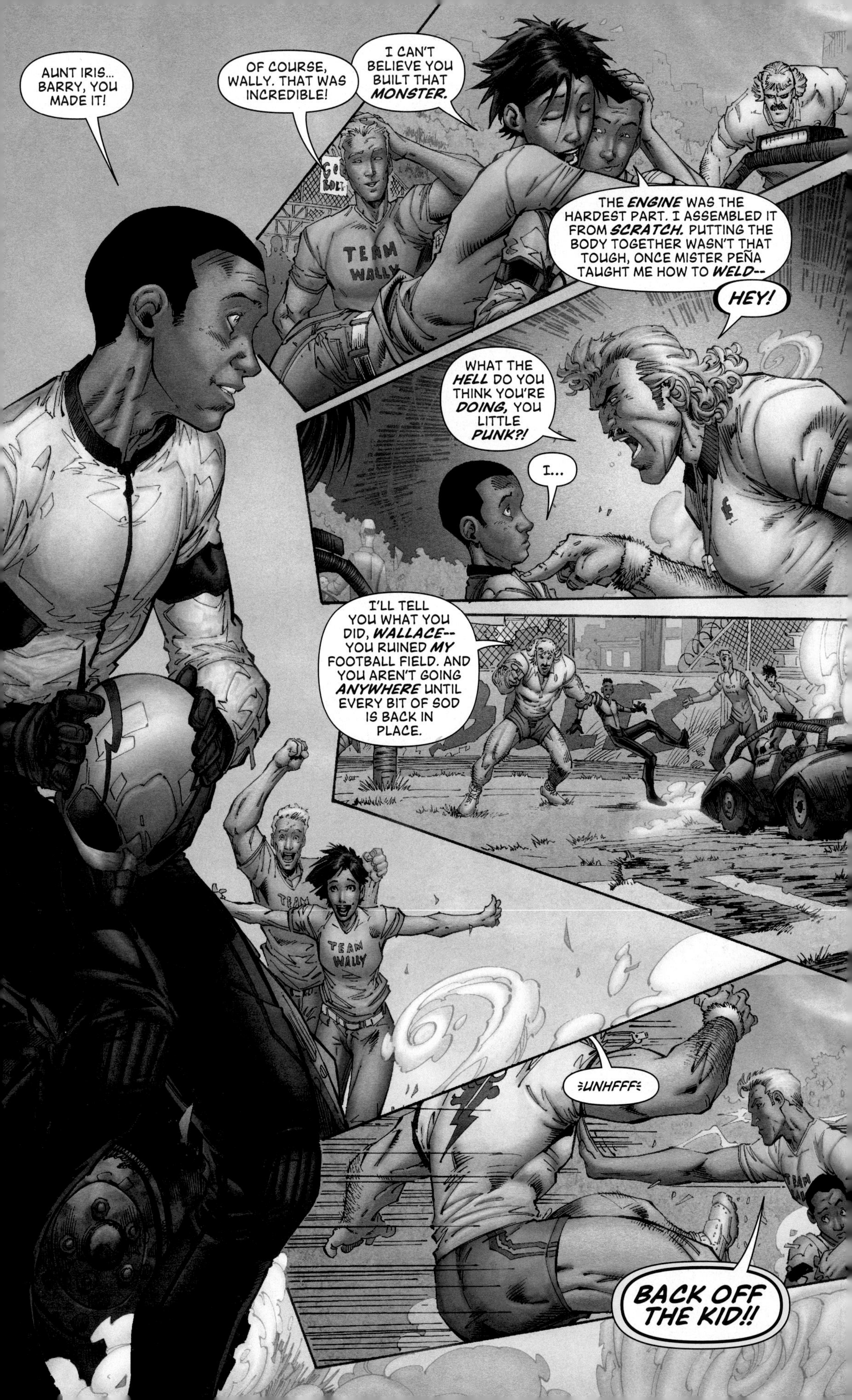
AUNT IRIS... BARRY, YOU MADE IT!
OF COURSE, WALLY. THAT WAS INCREDIBLE!
I CAN'T BELIEVE YOU BUILT THAT MONSTER.
THE ENGINE WAS THE HARDEST PART. I ASSEMBLED IT FROM SCRATCH. PUTTING THE BODY TOGETHER WASN'T THAT TOUGH, ONCE MISTER PEÑA TAUGHT ME HOW TO WELD--
HEY!
WHAT THE HELL DO YOU THINK YOU'RE DOING, YOU LITTLE PUNK?!
I...
I'LL TELL YOU WHAT YOU DID, WALLACE-- YOU RUINED MY FOOTBALL FIELD. AND YOU AREN'T GOING ANYWHERE UNTIL EVERY BIT OF SOD IS BACK IN PLACE.
UNHFFF
BACK OFF THE KID!!
TEAM WALLY

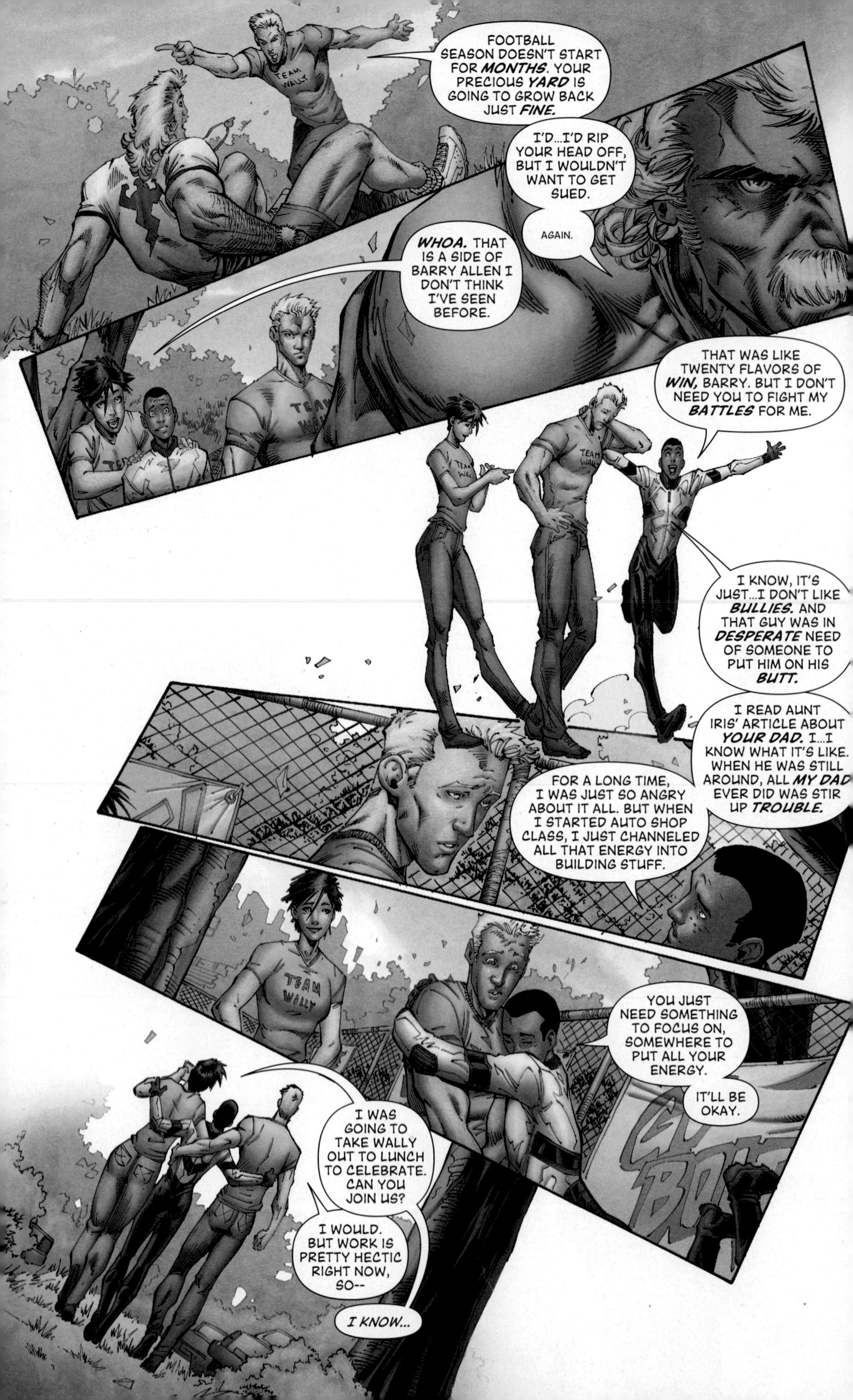
FOOTBALL SEASON DOESN'T START FOR MONTHS. YOUR PRECIOUS YARD IS GOING TO GROW BACK JUST FINE.
I'D...I'D RIP YOUR HEAD OFF, BUT I WOULDN'T WANT TO GET SUED.
AGAIN.
WHOA. THAT IS A SIDE OF BARRY ALLEN I DON'T THINK I'VE SEEN BEFORE.
THAT WAS LIKE TWENTY FLAVORS OF WIN, BARRY. BUT I DON'T NEED YOU TO FIGHT MY BATTLES FOR ME.
I KNOW, IT'S JUST...I DON'T LIKE BULLIES. AND THAT GUY WAS IN DESPERATE NEED OF SOMEONE TO PUT HIM ON HIS BUTT.
I READ AUNT IRIS' ARTICLE ABOUT YOUR DAD. I...I KNOW WHAT IT'S LIKE. WHEN HE WAS STILL AROUND, ALL MY DAD EVER DID WAS STIR UP TROUBLE.
FOR A LONG TIME, I WAS JUST SO ANGRY ABOUT IT ALL. BUT WHEN I STARTED AUTO SHOP CLASS, I JUST CHANNELED ALL THAT ENERGY INTO BUILDING STUFF.
YOU JUST NEED SOMETHING TO FOCUS ON, SOMEWHERE TO PUT ALL YOUR ENERGY.
IT'LL BE OKAY.
I WAS GOING TO TAKE WALLY OUT TO LUNCH TO CELEBRATE. CAN YOU JOIN US?
I WOULD. BUT WORK IS PRETTY HECTIC RIGHT NOW, SO--
I KNOW...

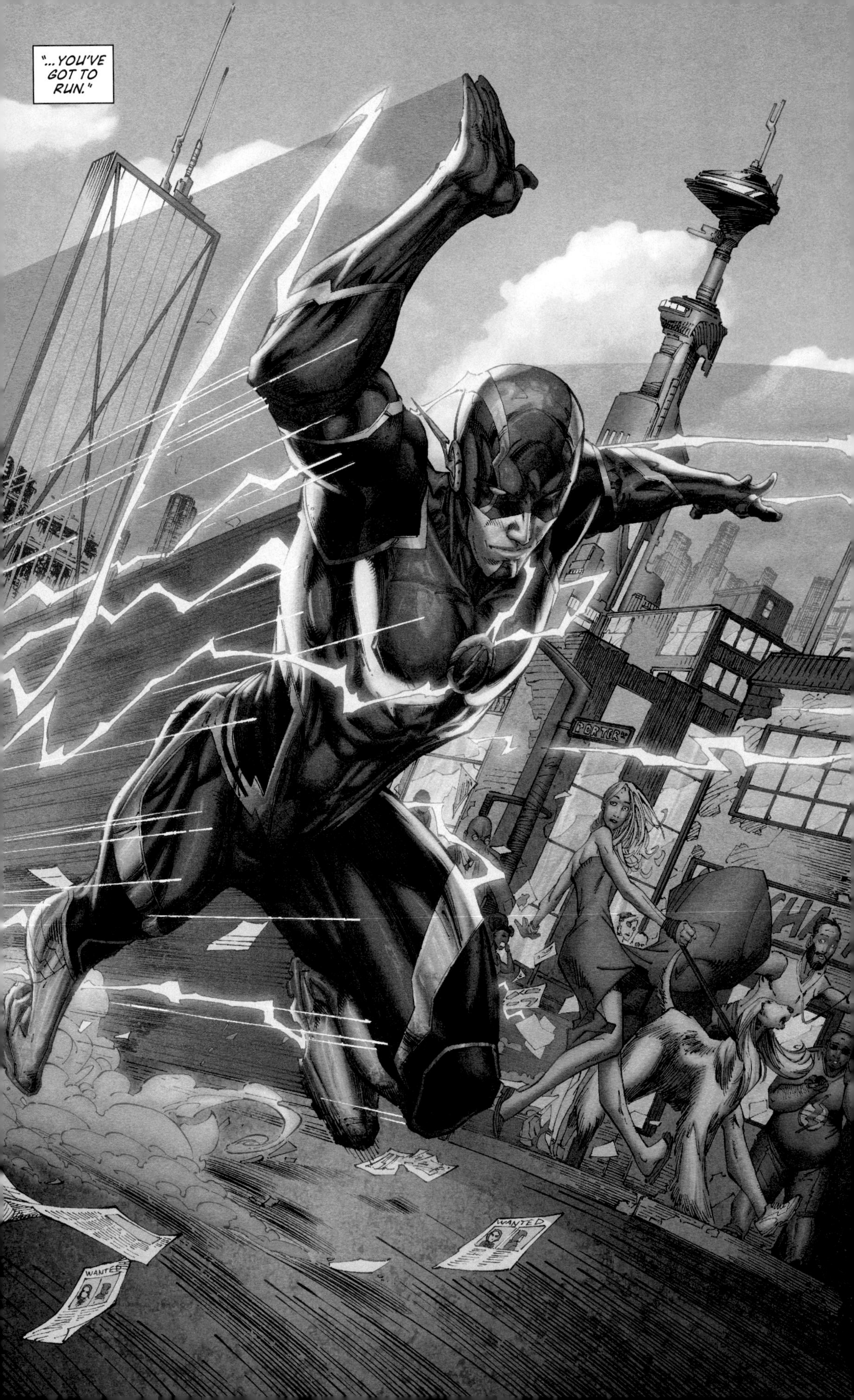
"...YOU'VE GOT TO RUN."
PORTER
WANTED
WANTED

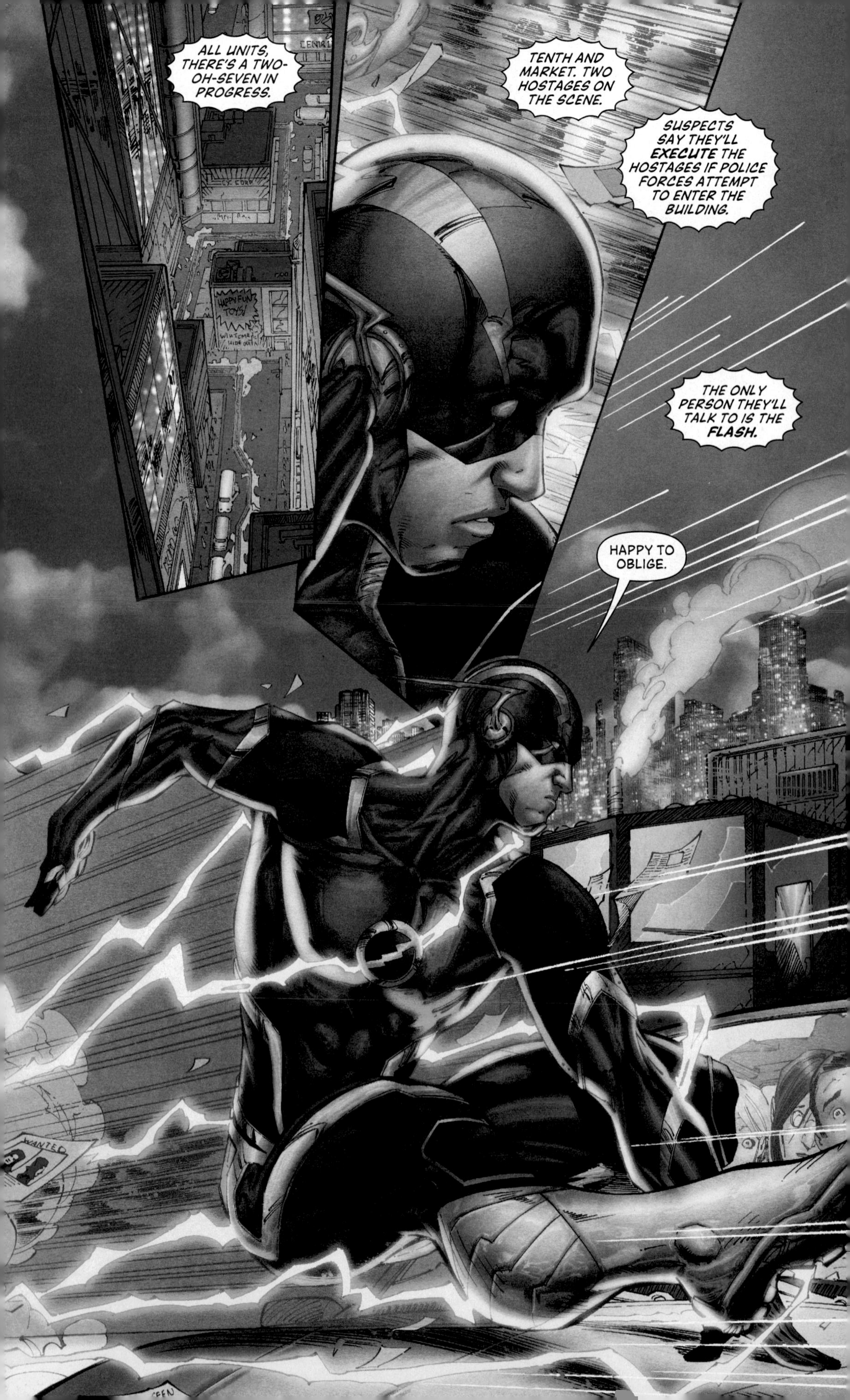
ALL UNITS, THERE'S A TWO-OH-SEVEN IN PROGRESS.
TENTH AND MARKET. TWO HOSTAGES ON THE SCENE.
SUSPECTS SAY THEY'LL **EXECUTE** THE HOSTAGES IF POLICE FORCES ATTEMPT TO ENTER THE BUILDING.
THE ONLY PERSON THEY'LL TALK TO IS THE **FLASH.**
HAPPY TO OBLIGE.
HAPPY FUN TOYS!
WANTED

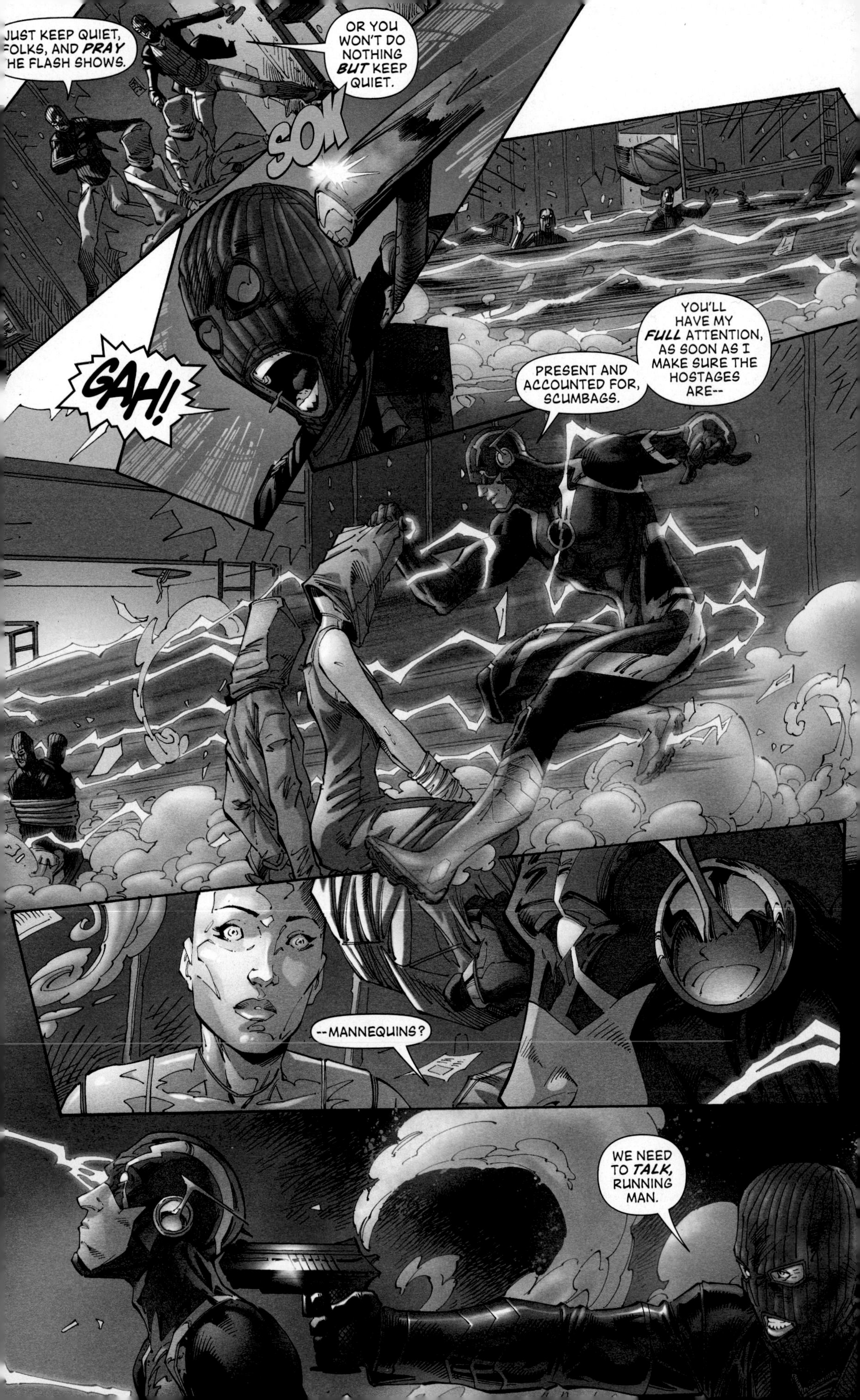
JUST KEEP QUIET, FOLKS, AND PRAY THE FLASH SHOWS.
OR YOU WON'T DO NOTHING BUT KEEP QUIET.
SOK
GAH!
PRESENT AND ACCOUNTED FOR, SCUMBAGS.
YOU'LL HAVE MY FULL ATTENTION, AS SOON AS I MAKE SURE THE HOSTAGES ARE--
--MANNEQUINS?
WE NEED TO TALK, RUNNING MAN.

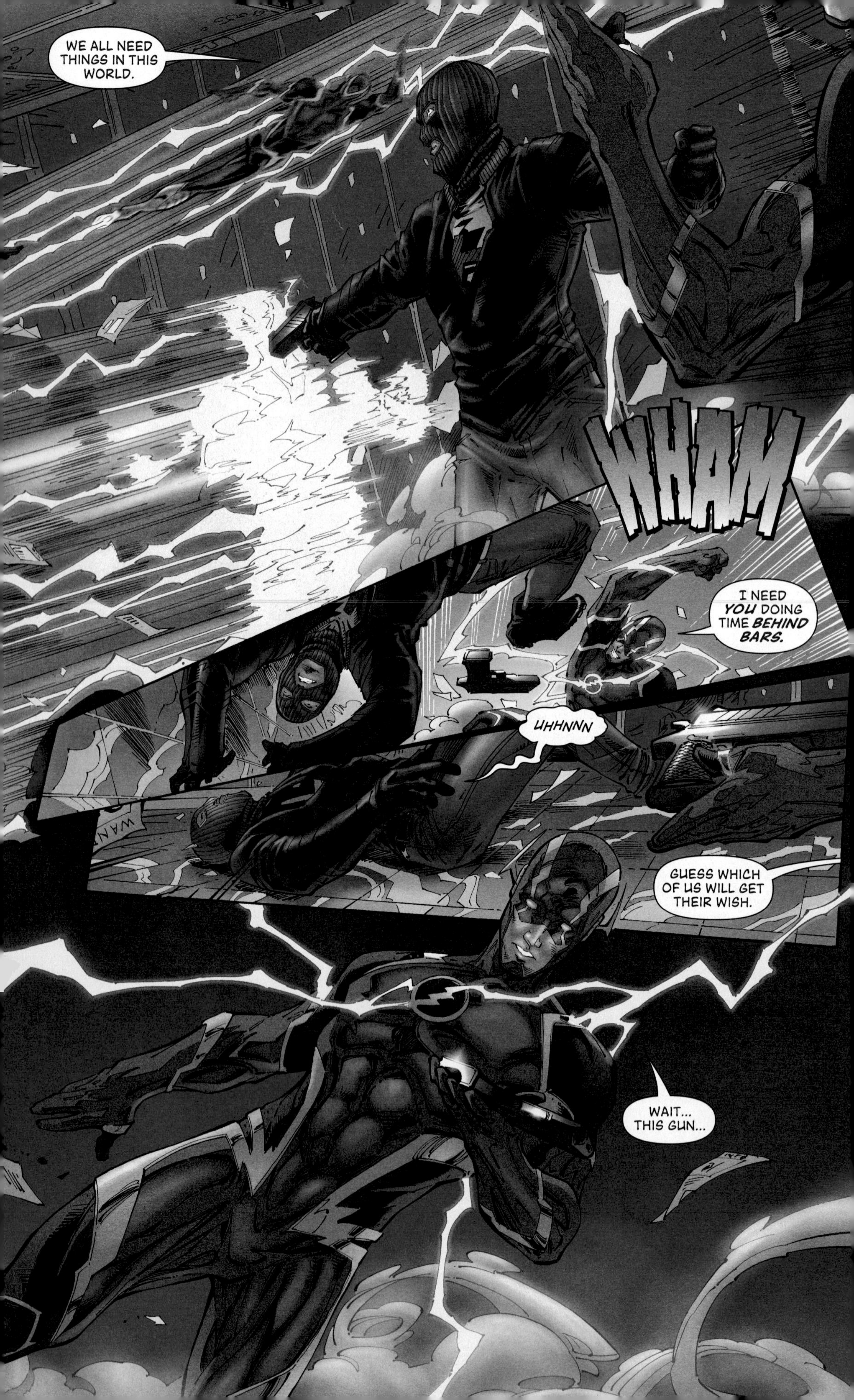
WE ALL NEED THINGS IN THIS WORLD.
WHAM
I NEED YOU DOING TIME BEHIND BARS.
UHHNNN
GUESS WHICH OF US WILL GET THEIR WISH.
WAIT... THIS GUN...

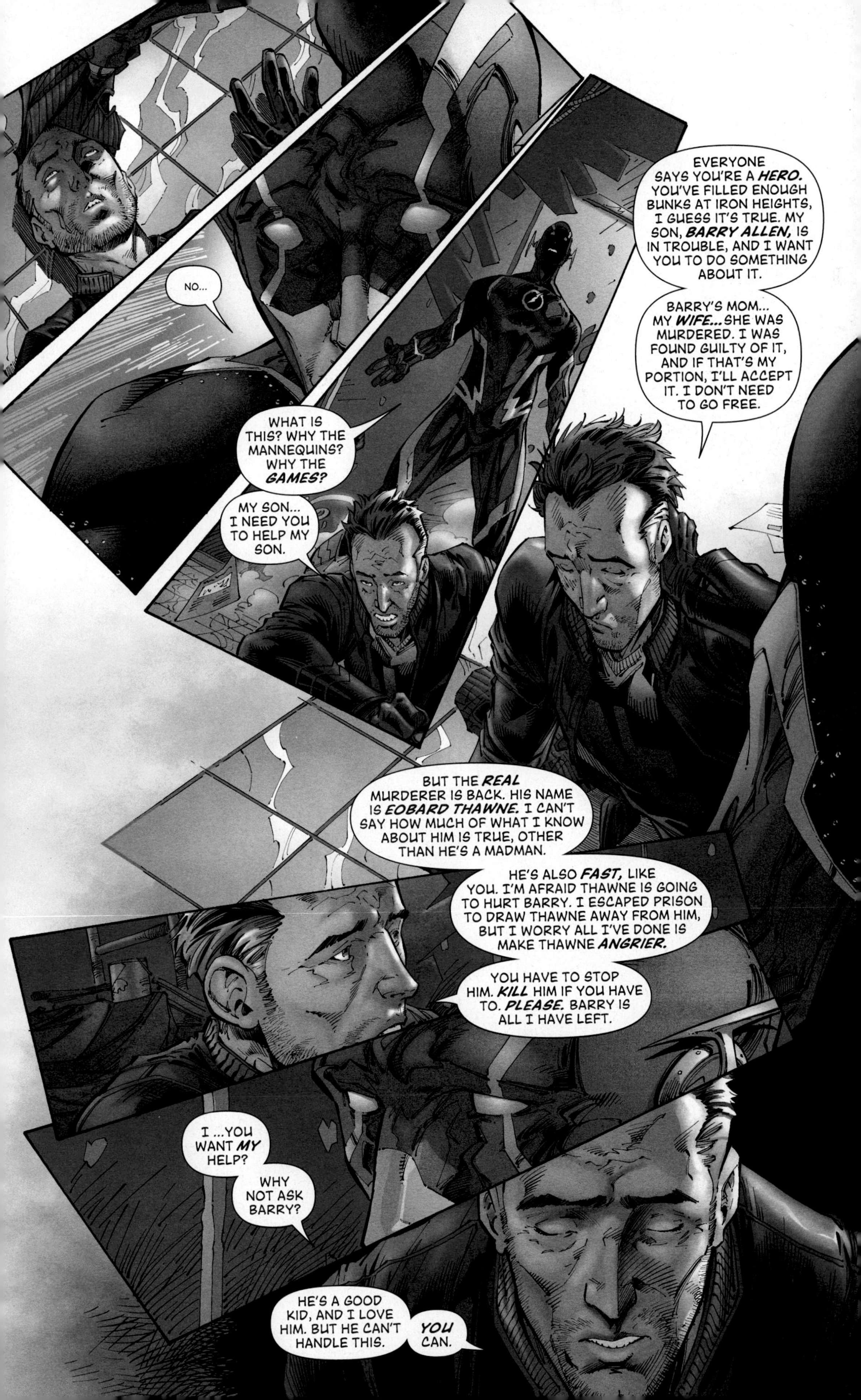
EVERYONE SAYS YOU'RE A HERO. YOU'VE FILLED ENOUGH BUNKS AT IRON HEIGHTS, I GUESS IT'S TRUE. MY SON, BARRY ALLEN, IS IN TROUBLE, AND I WANT YOU TO DO SOMETHING ABOUT IT.
BARRY'S MOM... MY WIFE... SHE WAS MURDERED. I WAS FOUND GUILTY OF IT, AND IF THAT'S MY PORTION, I'LL ACCEPT IT. I DON'T NEED TO GO FREE.
NO...
WHAT IS THIS? WHY THE MANNEQUINS? WHY THE GAMES?
MY SON... I NEED YOU TO HELP MY SON.
BUT THE REAL MURDERER IS BACK. HIS NAME IS EOBARD THAWNE. I CAN'T SAY HOW MUCH OF WHAT I KNOW ABOUT HIM IS TRUE, OTHER THAN HE'S A MADMAN.
HE'S ALSO FAST, LIKE YOU. I'M AFRAID THAWNE IS GOING TO HURT BARRY. I ESCAPED PRISON TO DRAW THAWNE AWAY FROM HIM, BUT I WORRY ALL I'VE DONE IS MAKE THAWNE ANGRIER.
YOU HAVE TO STOP HIM. KILL HIM IF YOU HAVE TO. PLEASE. BARRY IS ALL I HAVE LEFT.
I ...YOU WANT MY HELP?
WHY NOT ASK BARRY?
HE'S A GOOD KID, AND I LOVE HIM. BUT HE CAN'T HANDLE THIS.
YOU CAN.

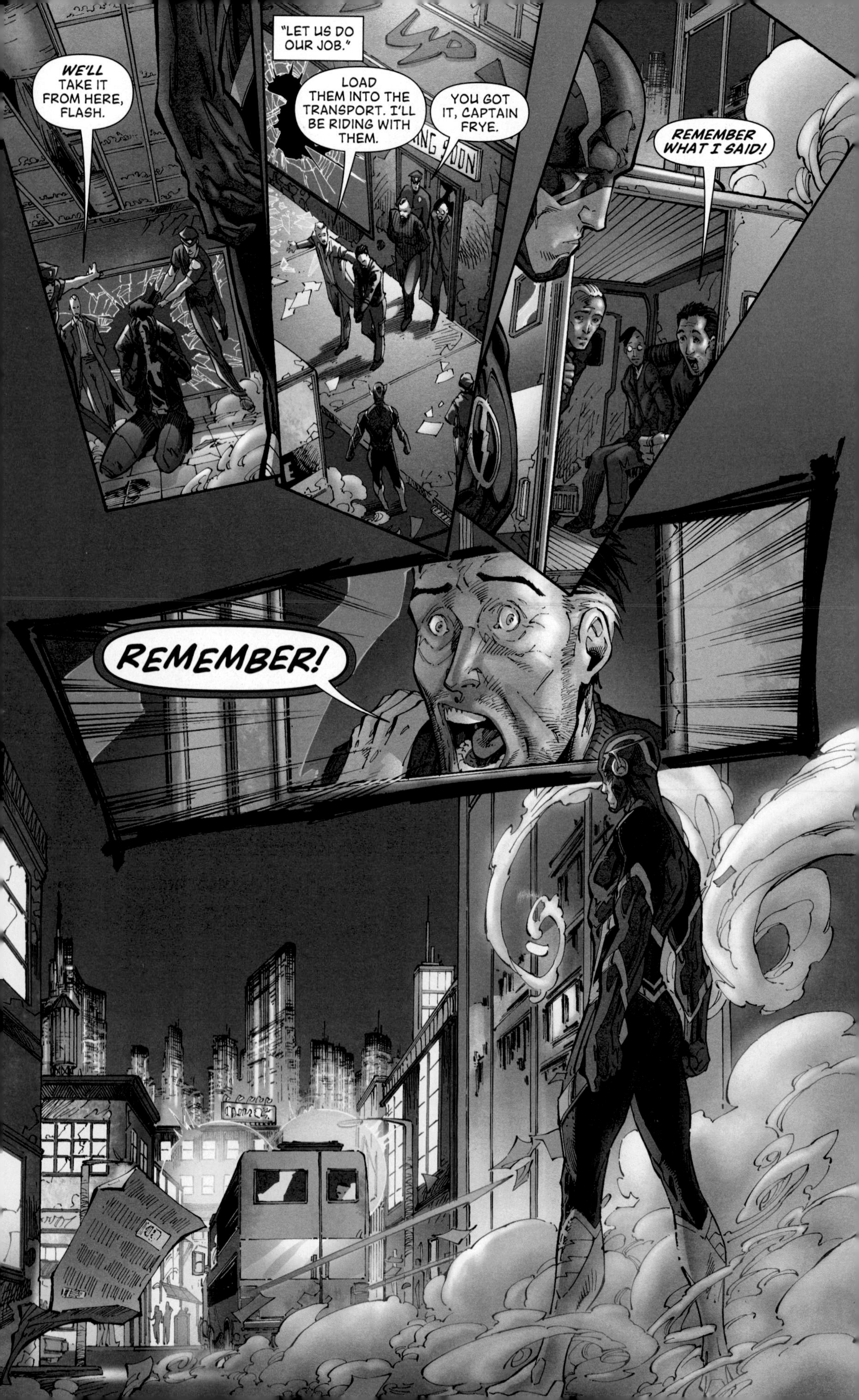
WE'LL TAKE IT FROM HERE, FLASH.
"LET US DO OUR JOB."
LOAD THEM INTO THE TRANSPORT. I'LL BE RIDING WITH THEM.
YOU GOT IT, CAPTAIN FRYE.
REMEMBER WHAT I SAID!
REMEMBER!

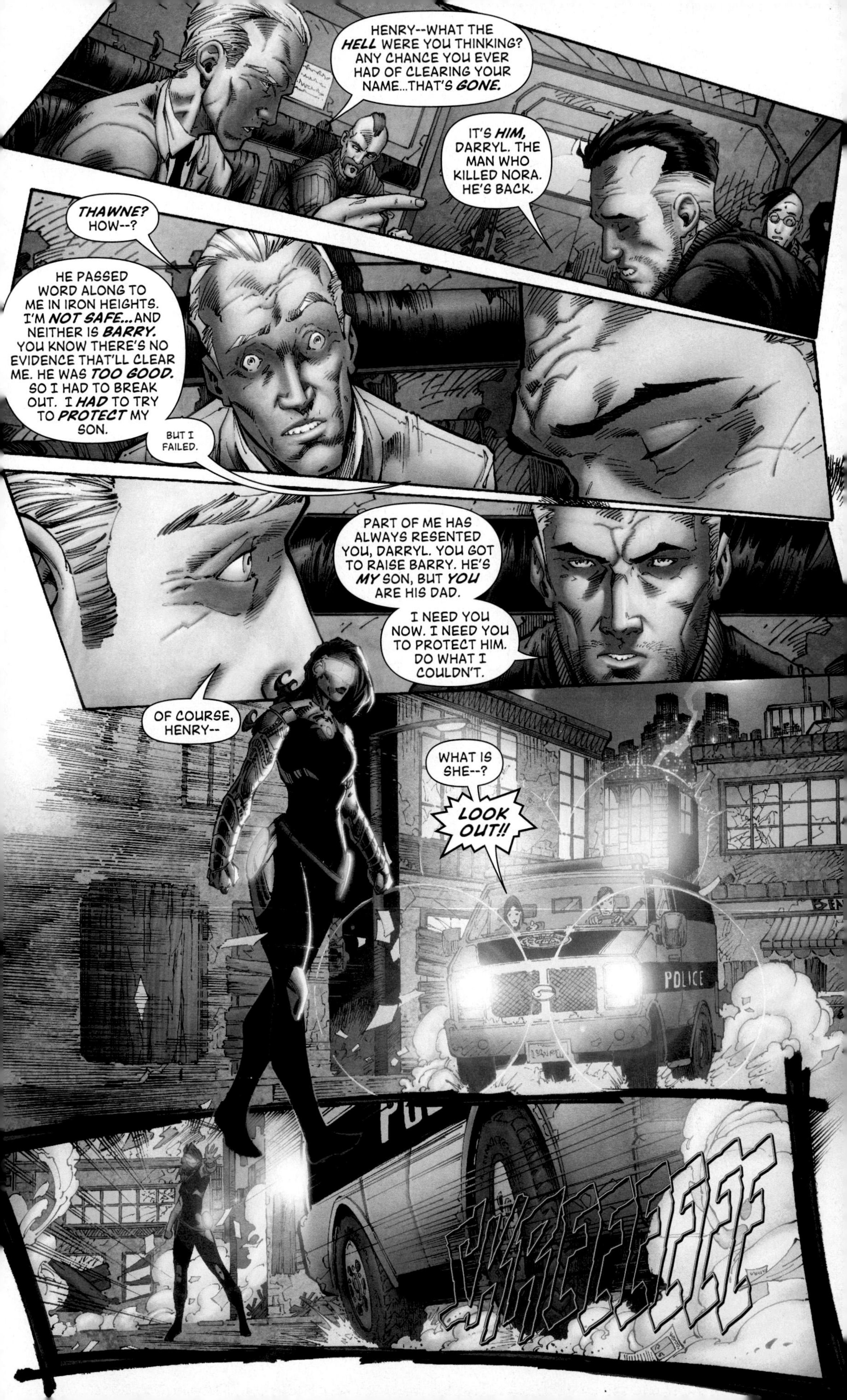
HENRY--WHAT THE *HELL* WERE YOU THINKING? ANY CHANCE YOU EVER HAD OF CLEARING YOUR NAME...THAT'S *GONE.*
IT'S *HIM,* DARRYL. THE MAN WHO KILLED NORA. HE'S BACK.
THAWNE? HOW--?
HE PASSED WORD ALONG TO ME IN IRON HEIGHTS. I'M *NOT SAFE...*AND NEITHER IS *BARRY.* YOU KNOW THERE'S NO EVIDENCE THAT'LL CLEAR ME. HE WAS *TOO GOOD.* SO I HAD TO BREAK OUT. I *HAD* TO TRY TO *PROTECT* MY SON.
BUT I FAILED.
PART OF ME HAS ALWAYS RESENTED YOU, DARRYL. YOU GOT TO RAISE BARRY. HE'S *MY* SON, BUT *YOU* ARE HIS DAD.
I NEED YOU NOW. I NEED YOU TO PROTECT HIM. DO WHAT I COULDN'T.
OF COURSE, HENRY--
WHAT IS SHE--?
LOOK OUT!!
POLICE

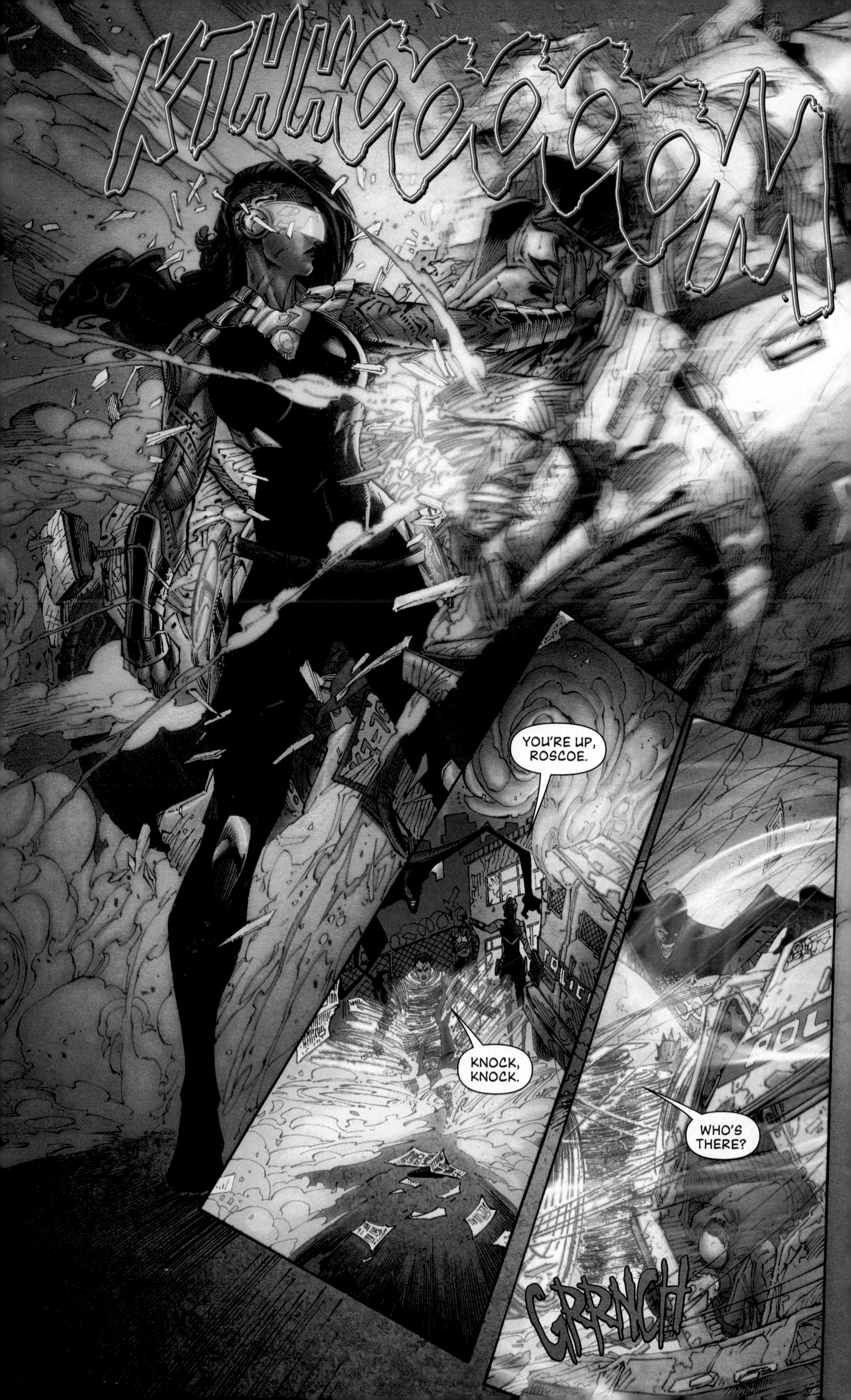
KTHHOOOOOOM
YOU'RE UP, ROSCOE.
KNOCK, KNOCK.
WHO'S THERE?
GRRNCH

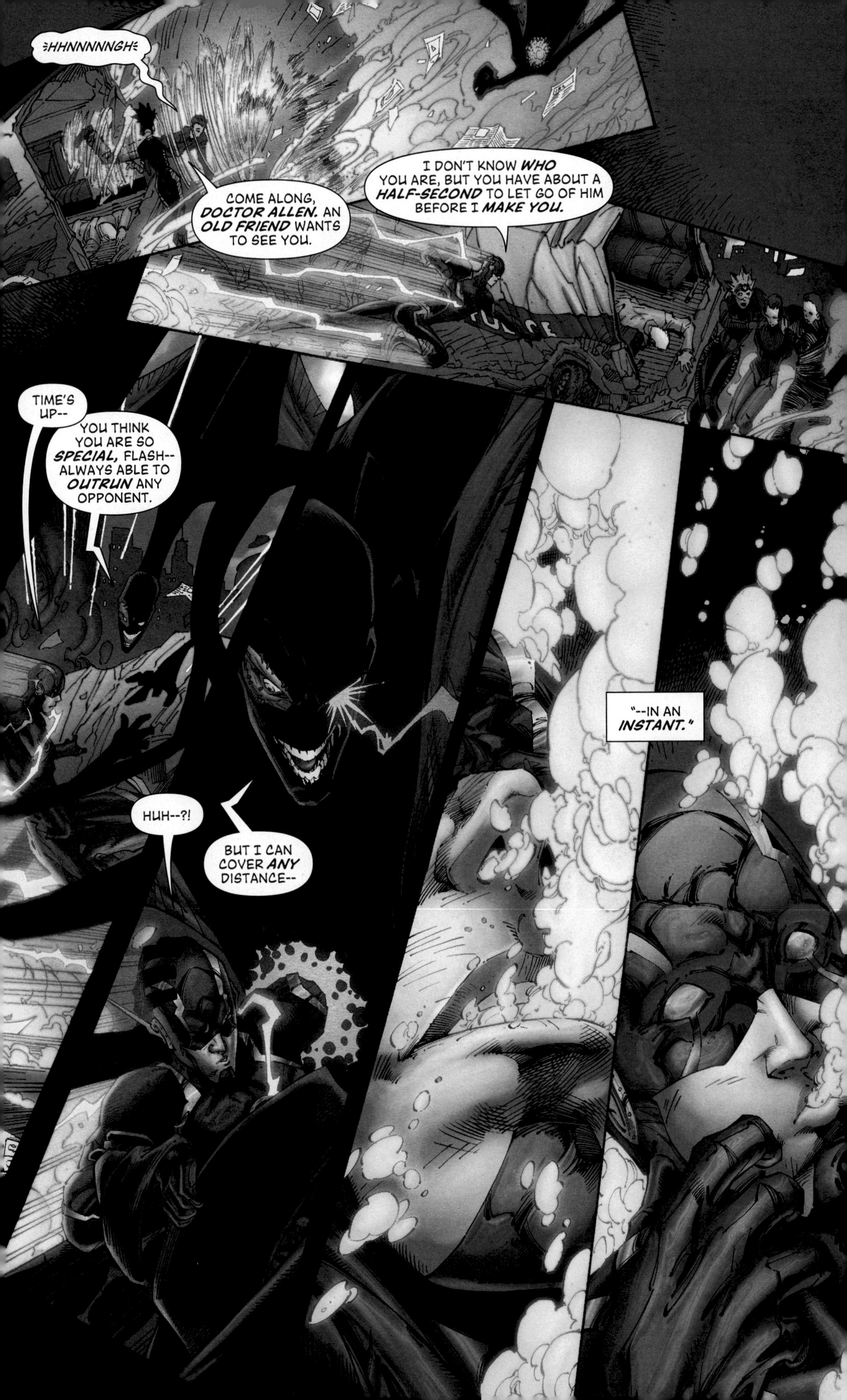

HHNNNNNGH
COME ALONG, DOCTOR ALLEN. AN OLD FRIEND WANTS TO SEE YOU.
I DON'T KNOW WHO YOU ARE, BUT YOU HAVE ABOUT A HALF-SECOND TO LET GO OF HIM BEFORE I MAKE YOU.
TIME'S UP--
YOU THINK YOU ARE SO SPECIAL, FLASH-- ALWAYS ABLE TO OUTRUN ANY OPPONENT.
HUH--?!
BUT I CAN COVER ANY DISTANCE--
"--IN AN INSTANT."

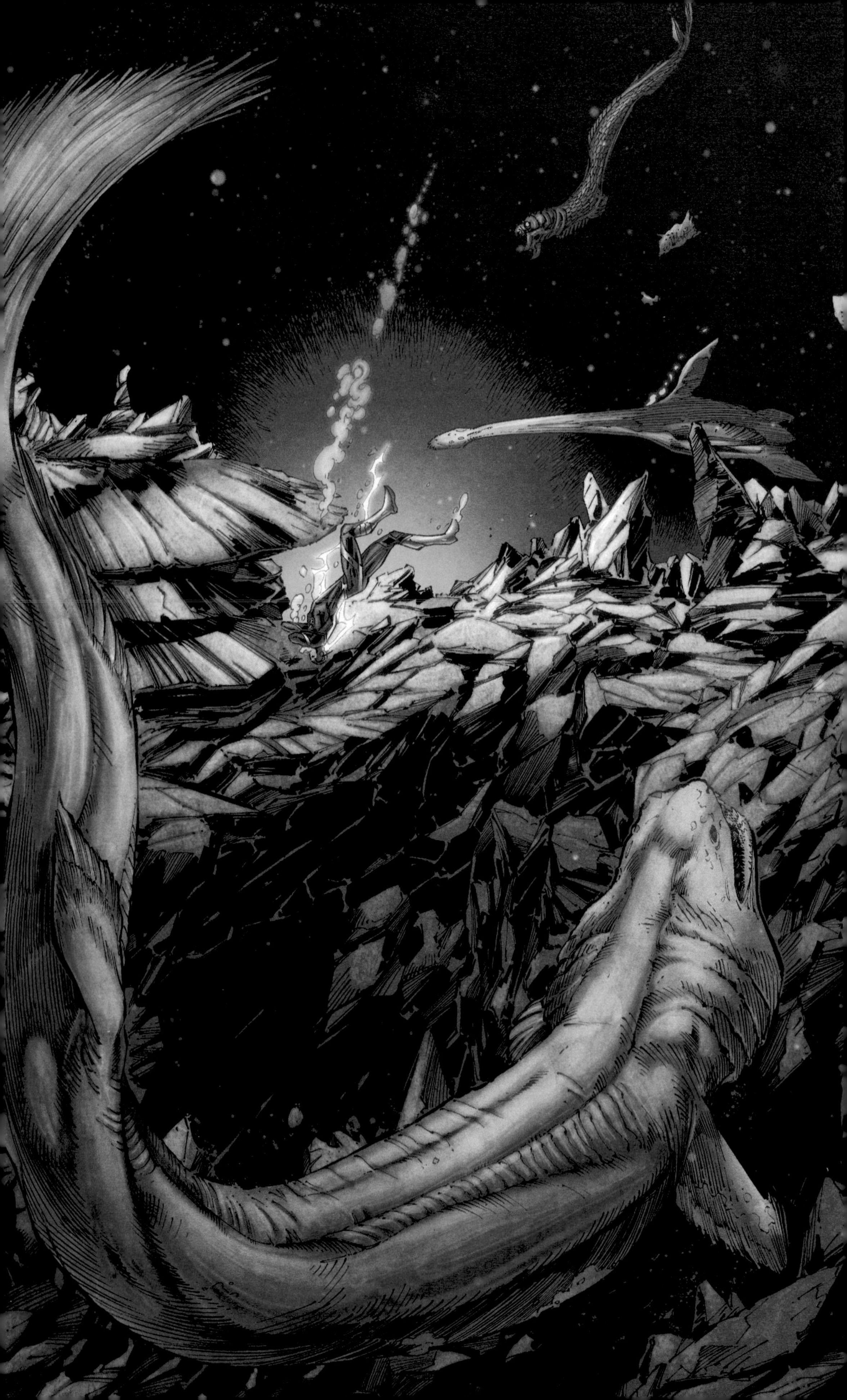

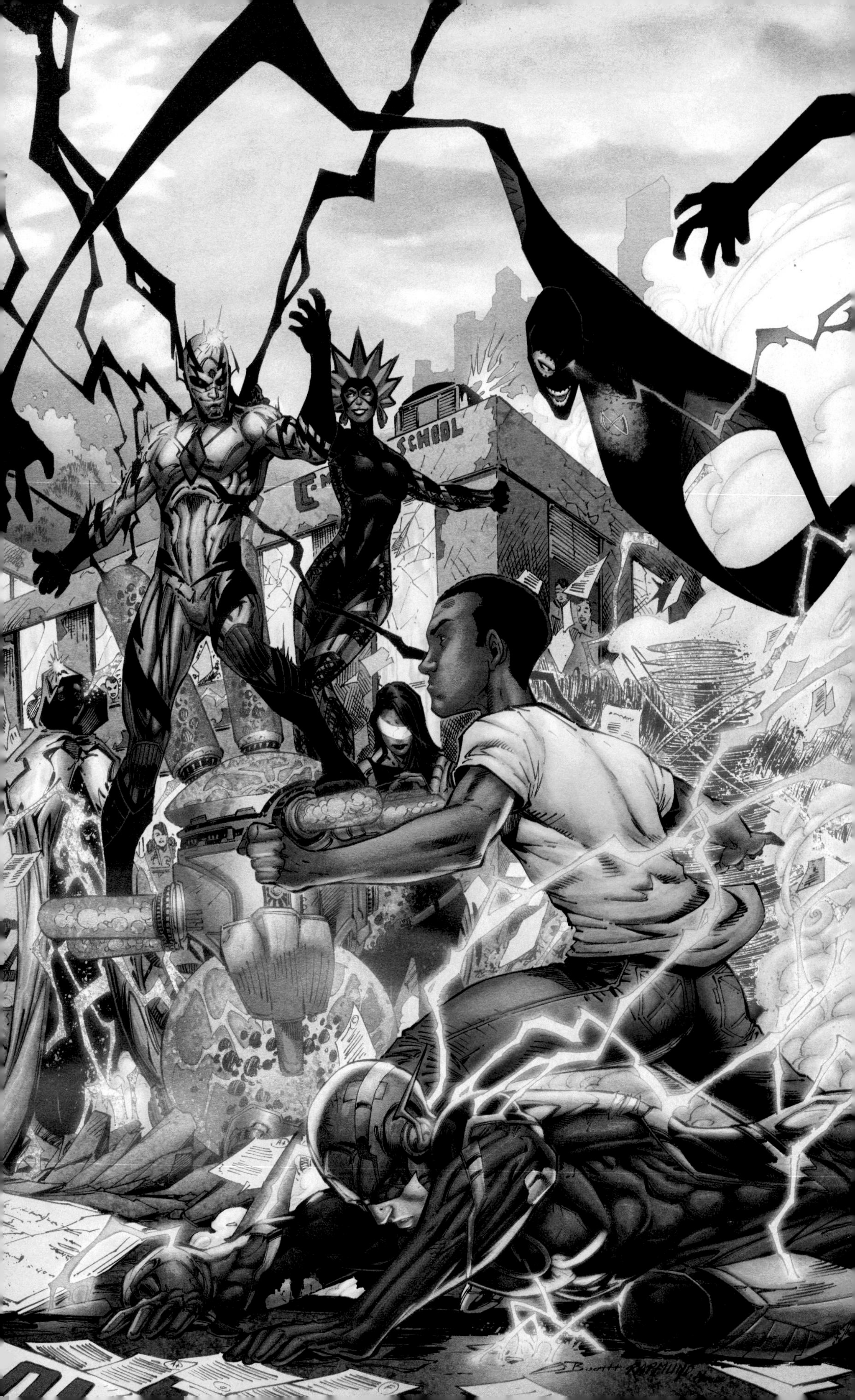
SCHOOL

ROBERT VENDITTI, VAN JENSEN writers BRETT BOOTH penciller NORM RAPMUND inker ANDREW DALHOUSE colorist PAT BROSSEAU letterer
cover by BRETT BOOTH, NORM RAPMUND, ANDREW DALHOUSE

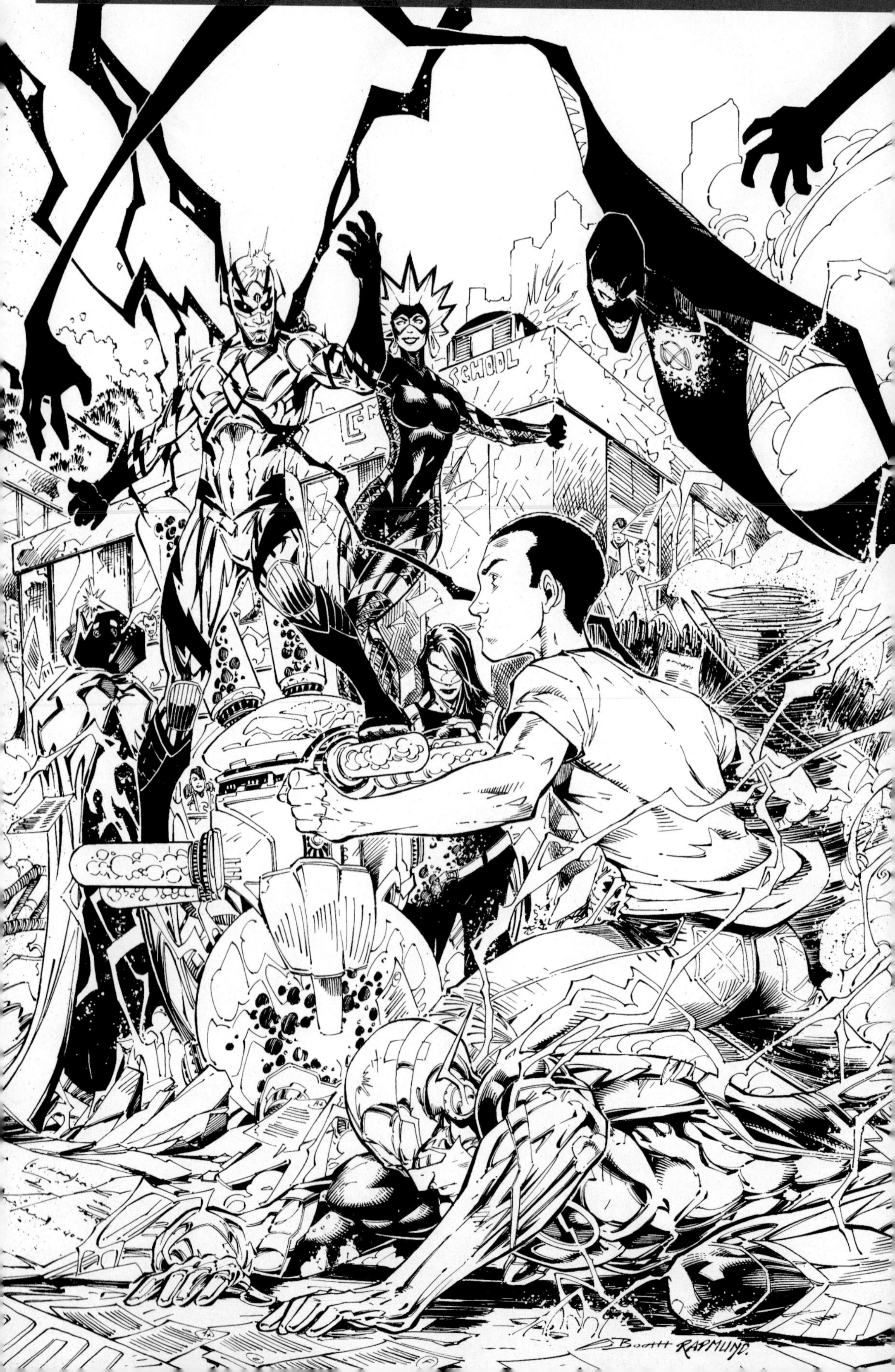
SCHOOL
BOOTH RAPMUND

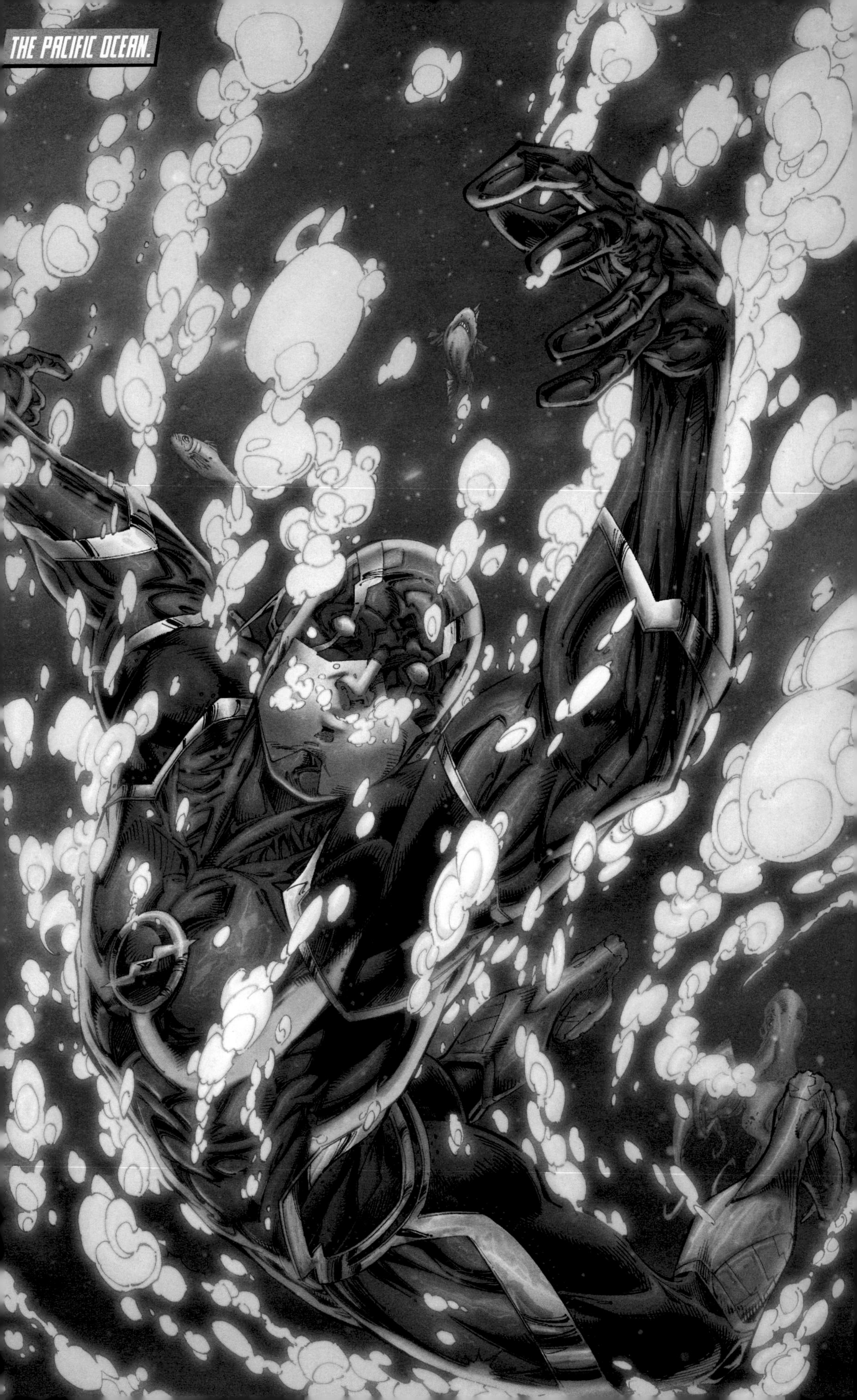
THE PACIFIC OCEAN.

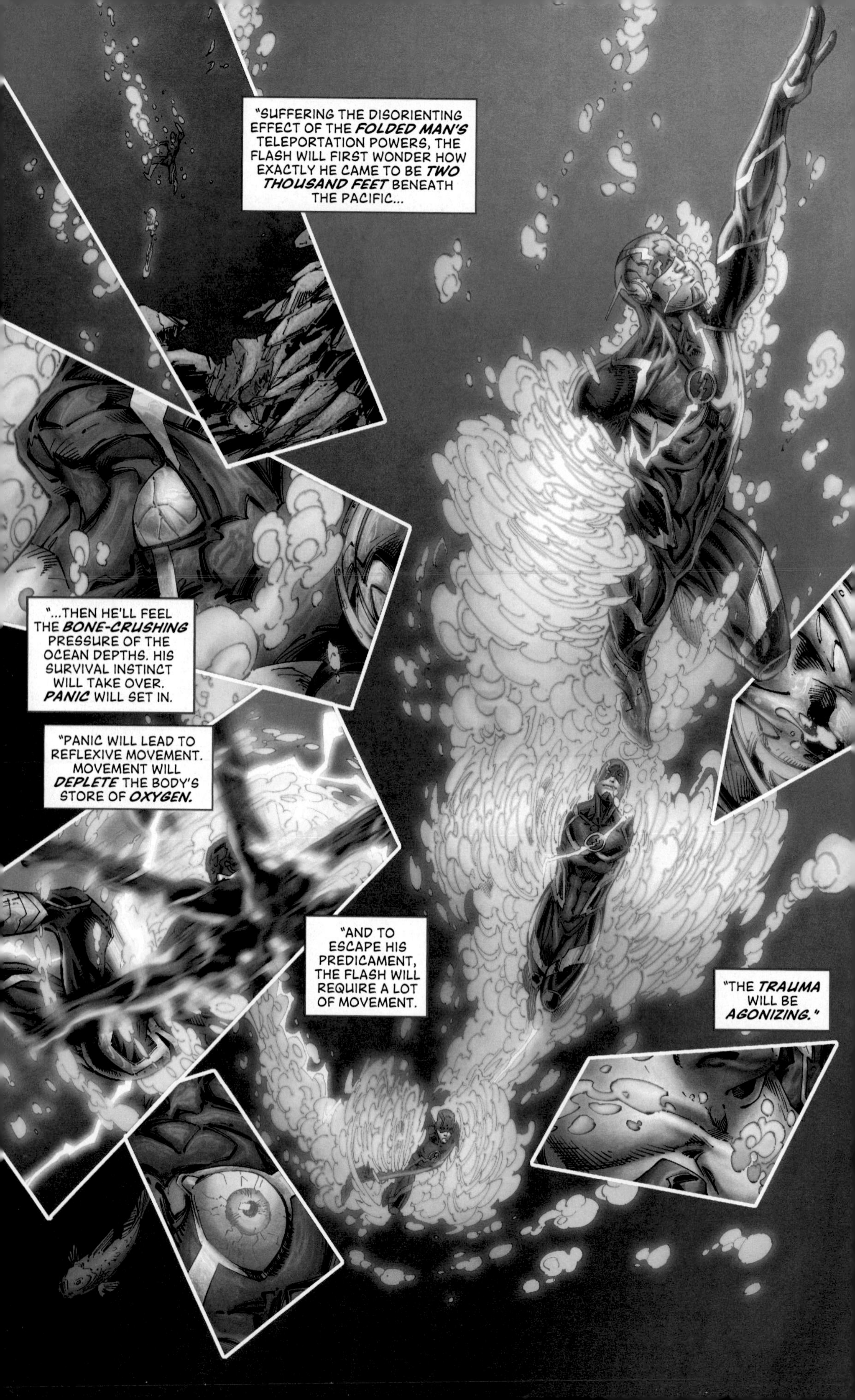
"SUFFERING THE DISORIENTING EFFECT OF THE *FOLDED MAN'S* TELEPORTATION POWERS, THE FLASH WILL FIRST WONDER HOW EXACTLY HE CAME TO BE *TWO THOUSAND FEET* BENEATH THE PACIFIC...
"...THEN HE'LL FEEL THE *BONE-CRUSHING* PRESSURE OF THE OCEAN DEPTHS. HIS SURVIVAL INSTINCT WILL TAKE OVER. *PANIC* WILL SET IN.
"PANIC WILL LEAD TO REFLEXIVE MOVEMENT. MOVEMENT WILL *DEPLETE* THE BODY'S STORE OF *OXYGEN.*
"AND TO ESCAPE HIS PREDICAMENT, THE FLASH WILL REQUIRE A LOT OF MOVEMENT.
"THE *TRAUMA* WILL BE *AGONIZING.*"

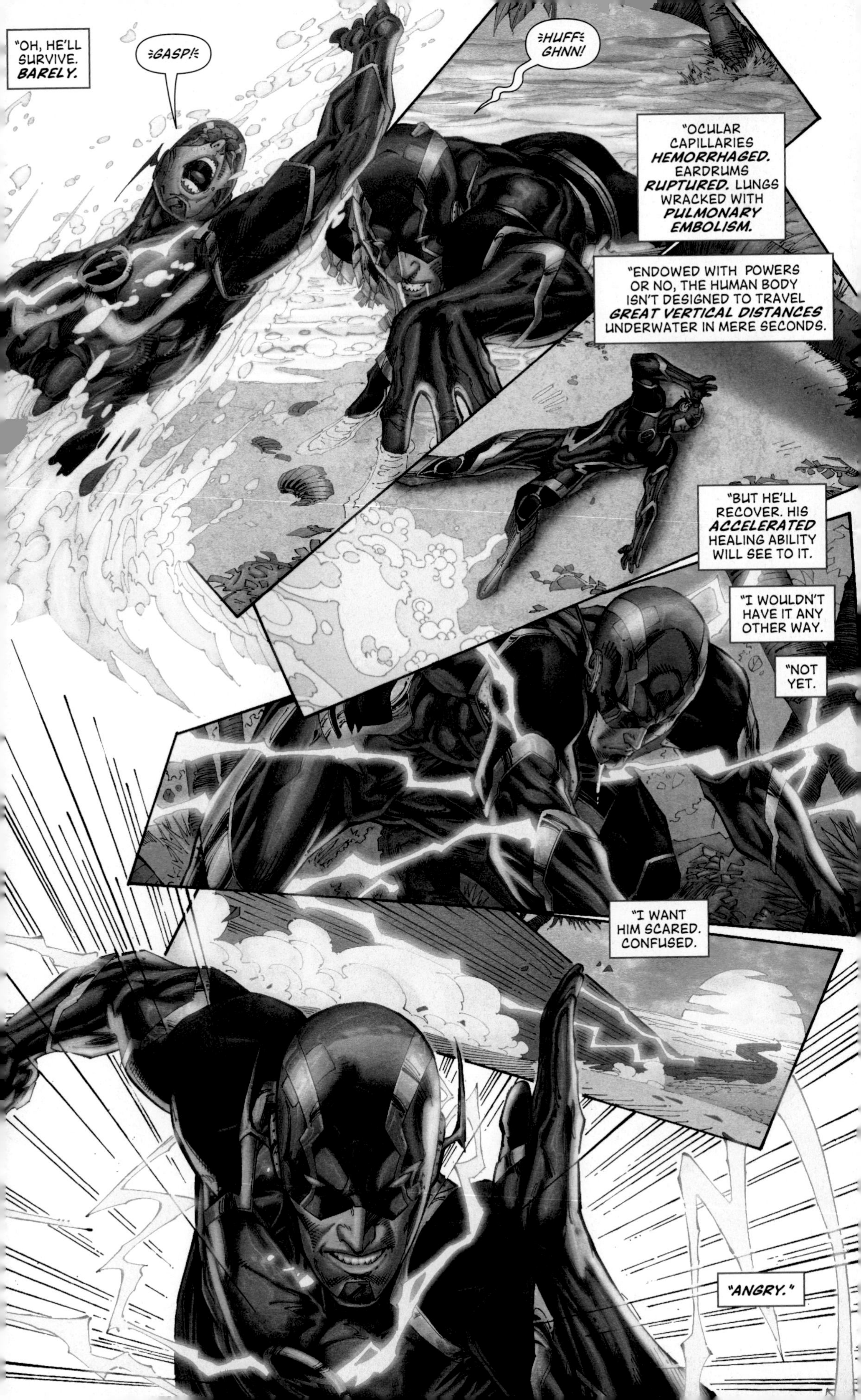
"OH, HE'LL SURVIVE. BARELY.
GASP!
HUFF GHNN!
"OCULAR CAPILLARIES HEMORRHAGED. EARDRUMS RUPTURED. LUNGS WRACKED WITH PULMONARY EMBOLISM.
"ENDOWED WITH POWERS OR NO, THE HUMAN BODY ISN'T DESIGNED TO TRAVEL GREAT VERTICAL DISTANCES UNDERWATER IN MERE SECONDS.
"BUT HE'LL RECOVER. HIS ACCELERATED HEALING ABILITY WILL SEE TO IT.
"I WOULDN'T HAVE IT ANY OTHER WAY.
"NOT YET.
"I WANT HIM SCARED. CONFUSED.
"ANGRY."

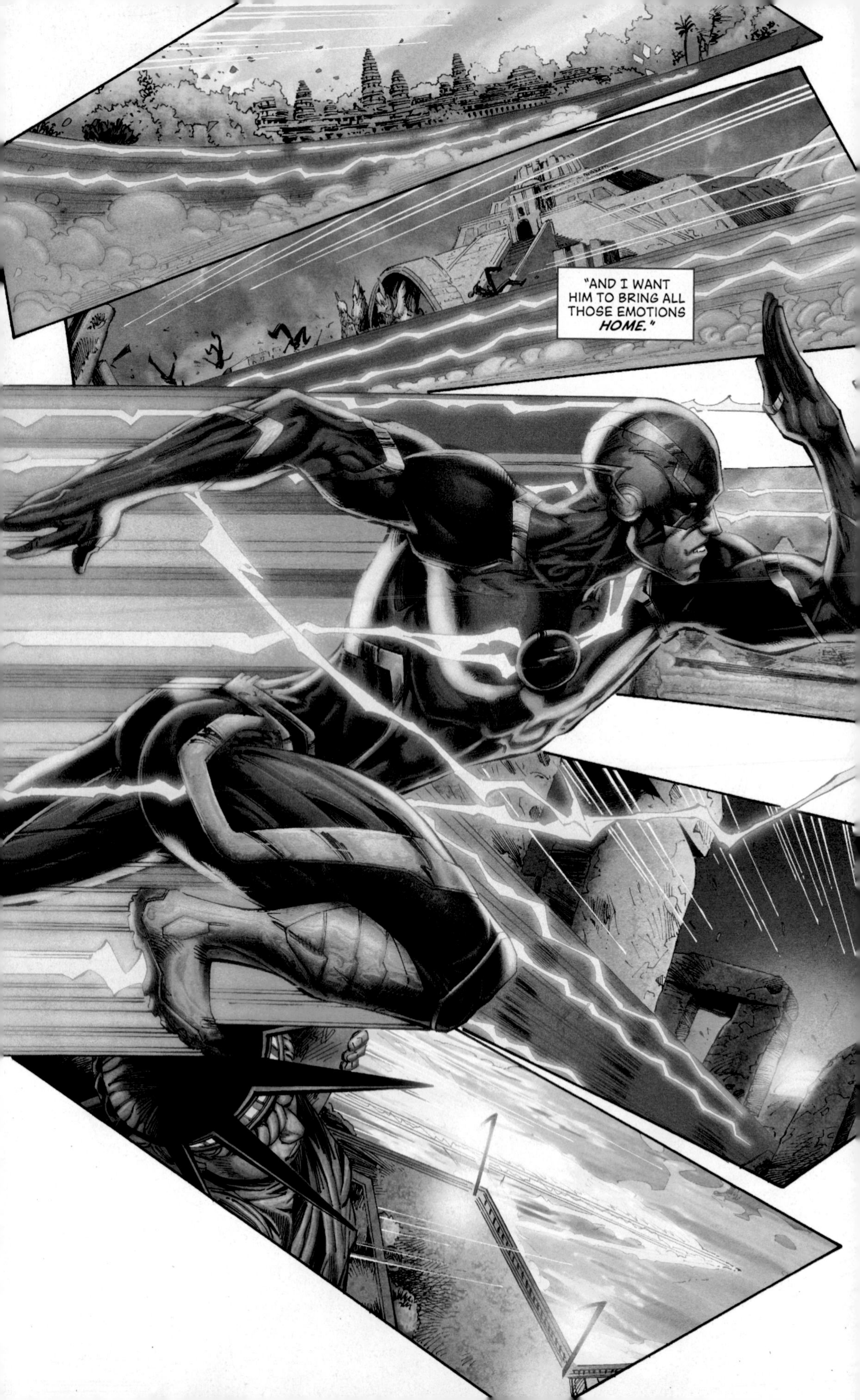
"AND I WANT HIM TO BRING ALL THOSE EMOTIONS HOME."

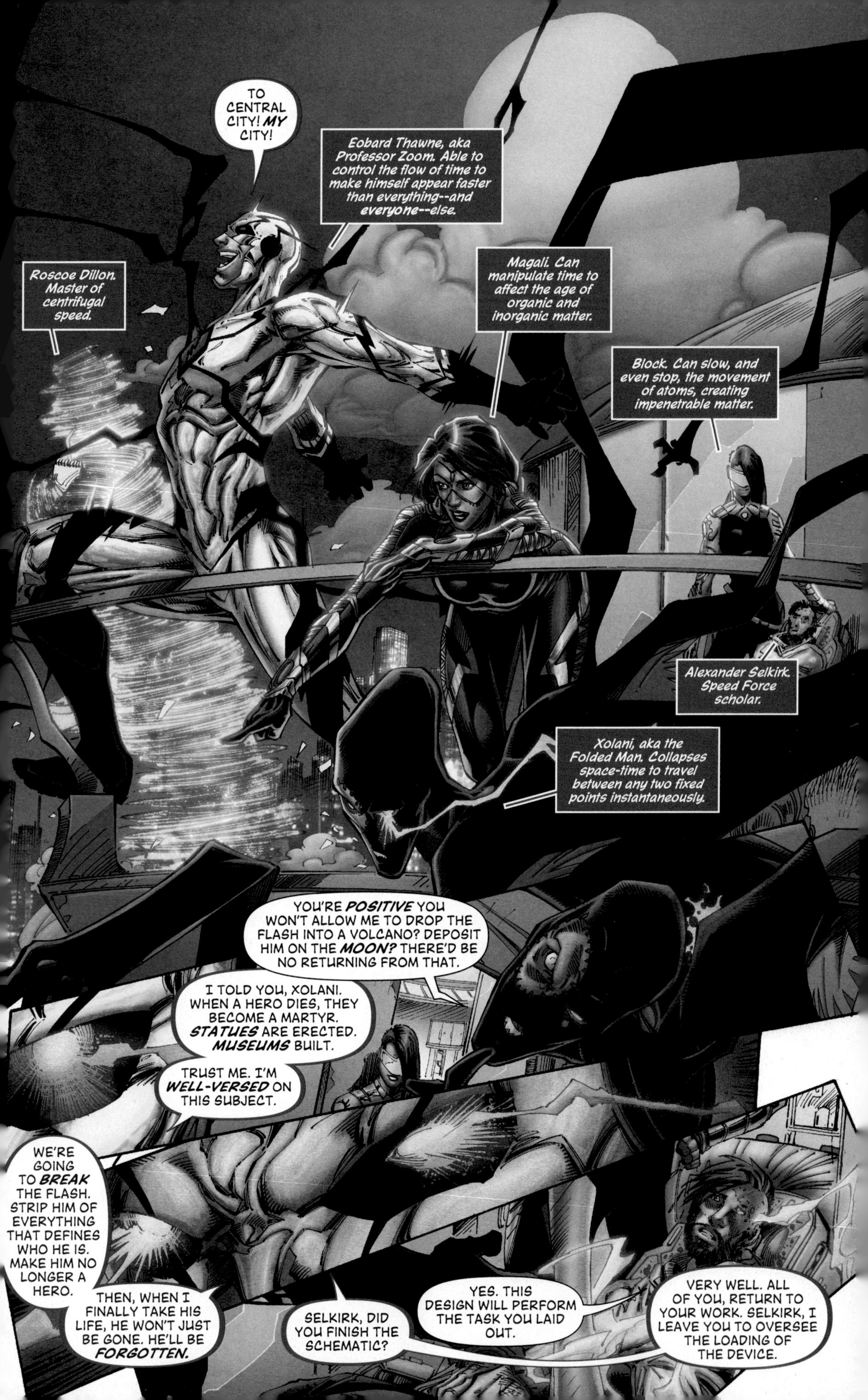
TO CENTRAL CITY! MY CITY!
Eobard Thawne, aka Professor Zoom. Able to control the flow of time to make himself appear faster than everything--and everyone--else.
Roscoe Dillon. Master of centrifugal speed.
Magali. Can manipulate time to affect the age of organic and inorganic matter.
Block. Can slow, and even stop, the movement of atoms, creating impenetrable matter.
Alexander Selkirk. Speed Force scholar.
Xolani, aka the Folded Man. Collapses space-time to travel between any two fixed points instantaneously.
YOU'RE POSITIVE YOU WON'T ALLOW ME TO DROP THE FLASH INTO A VOLCANO? DEPOSIT HIM ON THE MOON? THERE'D BE NO RETURNING FROM THAT.
I TOLD YOU, XOLANI. WHEN A HERO DIES, THEY BECOME A MARTYR. STATUES ARE ERECTED. MUSEUMS BUILT.
TRUST ME. I'M WELL-VERSED ON THIS SUBJECT.
WE'RE GOING TO BREAK THE FLASH. STRIP HIM OF EVERYTHING THAT DEFINES WHO HE IS. MAKE HIM NO LONGER A HERO.
THEN, WHEN I FINALLY TAKE HIS LIFE, HE WON'T JUST BE GONE. HE'LL BE FORGOTTEN.
SELKIRK, DID YOU FINISH THE SCHEMATIC?
YES. THIS DESIGN WILL PERFORM THE TASK YOU LAID OUT.
VERY WELL. ALL OF YOU, RETURN TO YOUR WORK. SELKIRK, I LEAVE YOU TO OVERSEE THE LOADING OF THE DEVICE.

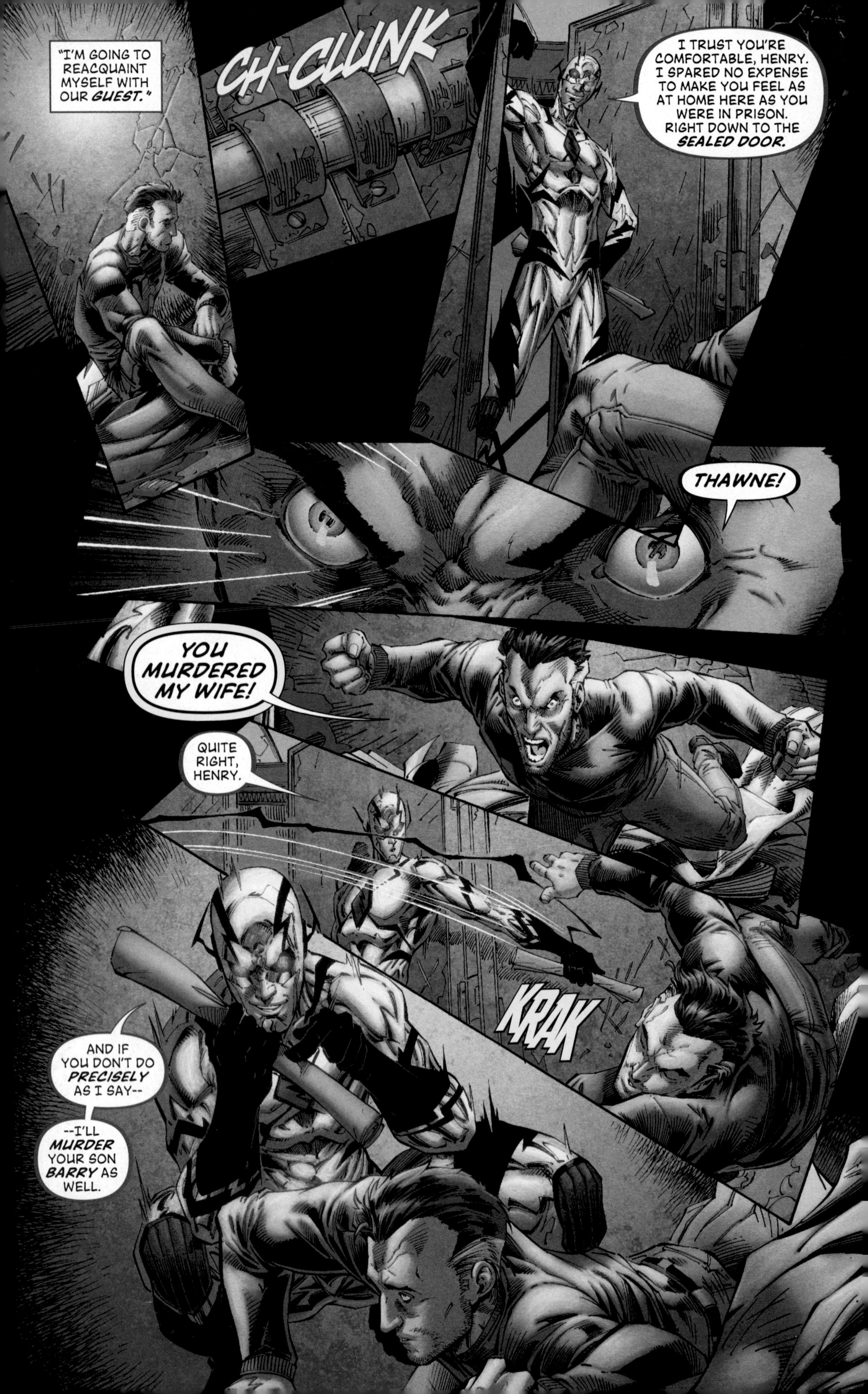
"I'M GOING TO REACQUAINT MYSELF WITH OUR GUEST."
CH-CLUNK
I TRUST YOU'RE COMFORTABLE, HENRY. I SPARED NO EXPENSE TO MAKE YOU FEEL AS AT HOME HERE AS YOU WERE IN PRISON. RIGHT DOWN TO THE SEALED DOOR.
THAWNE!
YOU MURDERED MY WIFE!
QUITE RIGHT, HENRY.
KRAK
AND IF YOU DON'T DO PRECISELY AS I SAY--
--I'LL MURDER YOUR SON BARRY AS WELL.

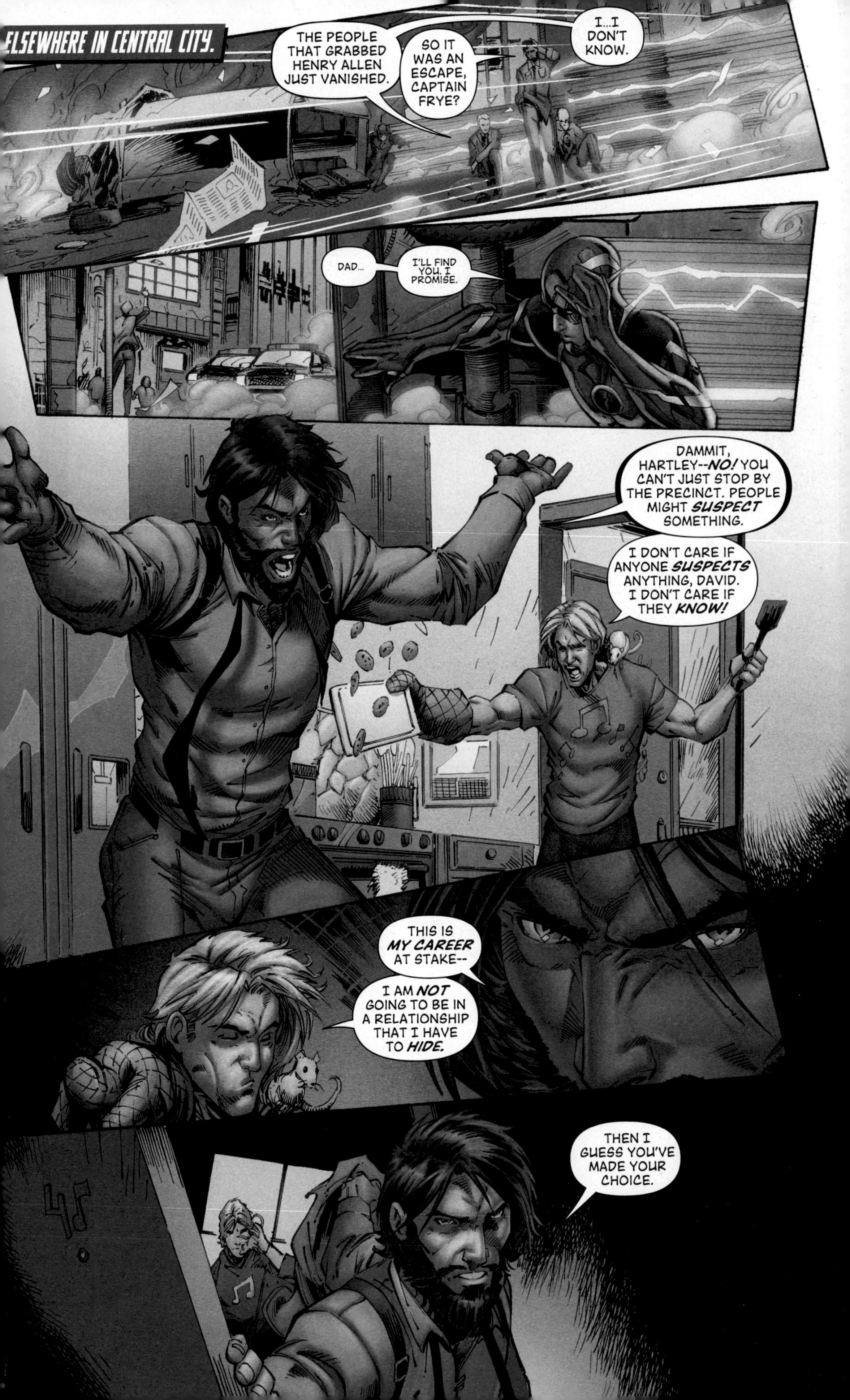
ELSEWHERE IN CENTRAL CITY.
THE PEOPLE THAT GRABBED HENRY ALLEN JUST VANISHED.
SO IT WAS AN ESCAPE, CAPTAIN FRYE?
I...I DON'T KNOW.
DAD...
I'LL FIND YOU. I PROMISE.
DAMMIT, HARTLEY--NO! YOU CAN'T JUST STOP BY THE PRECINCT. PEOPLE MIGHT SUSPECT SOMETHING.
I DON'T CARE IF ANYONE SUSPECTS ANYTHING, DAVID. I DON'T CARE IF THEY KNOW!
THIS IS MY CAREER AT STAKE--
I AM NOT GOING TO BE IN A RELATIONSHIP THAT I HAVE TO HIDE.
THEN I GUESS YOU'VE MADE YOUR CHOICE.

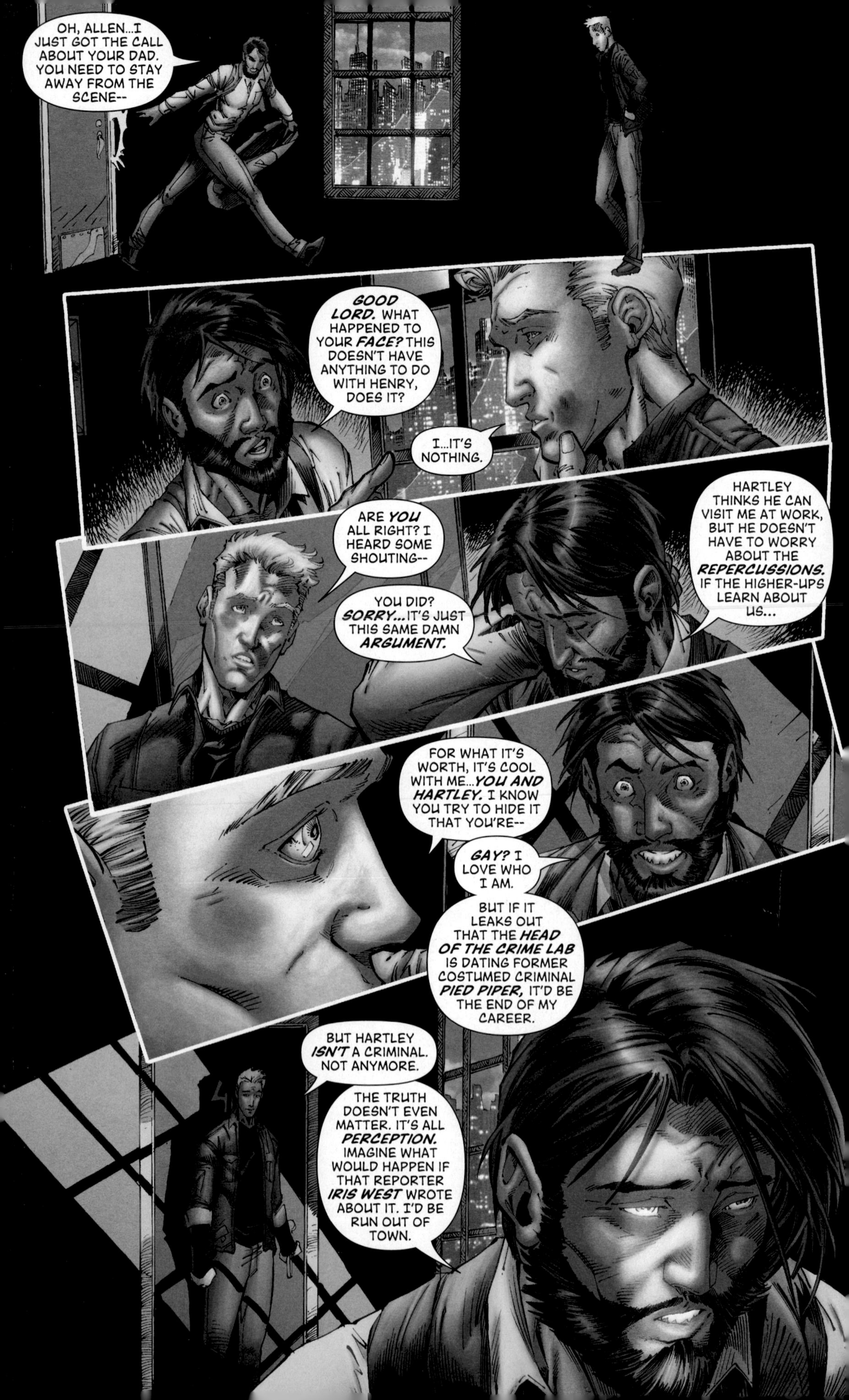
OH, ALLEN...I JUST GOT THE CALL ABOUT YOUR DAD. YOU NEED TO STAY AWAY FROM THE SCENE--
GOOD LORD. WHAT HAPPENED TO YOUR FACE? THIS DOESN'T HAVE ANYTHING TO DO WITH HENRY, DOES IT?
I...IT'S NOTHING.
ARE YOU ALL RIGHT? I HEARD SOME SHOUTING--
YOU DID? SORRY...IT'S JUST THIS SAME DAMN ARGUMENT.
HARTLEY THINKS HE CAN VISIT ME AT WORK, BUT HE DOESN'T HAVE TO WORRY ABOUT THE REPERCUSSIONS. IF THE HIGHER-UPS LEARN ABOUT US...
FOR WHAT IT'S WORTH, IT'S COOL WITH ME...YOU AND HARTLEY. I KNOW YOU TRY TO HIDE IT THAT YOU'RE--
GAY? I LOVE WHO I AM.
BUT IF IT LEAKS OUT THAT THE HEAD OF THE CRIME LAB IS DATING FORMER COSTUMED CRIMINAL PIED PIPER, IT'D BE THE END OF MY CAREER.
BUT HARTLEY ISN'T A CRIMINAL. NOT ANYMORE.
THE TRUTH DOESN'T EVEN MATTER. IT'S ALL PERCEPTION. IMAGINE WHAT WOULD HAPPEN IF THAT REPORTER IRIS WEST WROTE ABOUT IT. I'D BE RUN OUT OF TOWN.

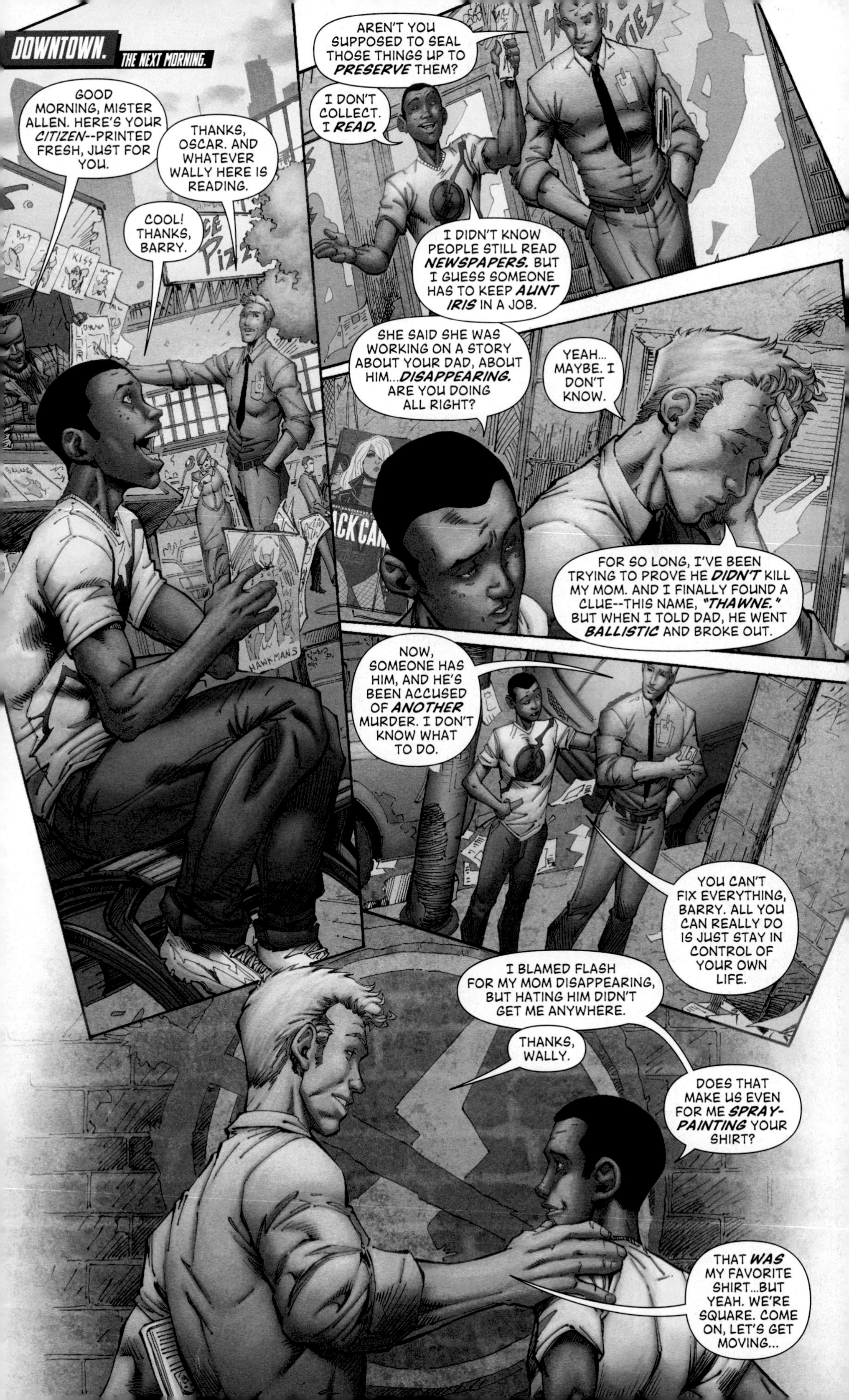
DOWNTOWN. THE NEXT MORNING.
GOOD MORNING, MISTER ALLEN. HERE'S YOUR CITIZEN--PRINTED FRESH, JUST FOR YOU.
THANKS, OSCAR. AND WHATEVER WALLY HERE IS READING.
COOL! THANKS, BARRY.
AREN'T YOU SUPPOSED TO SEAL THOSE THINGS UP TO PRESERVE THEM?
I DON'T COLLECT. I READ.
I DIDN'T KNOW PEOPLE STILL READ NEWSPAPERS. BUT I GUESS SOMEONE HAS TO KEEP AUNT IRIS IN A JOB.
SHE SAID SHE WAS WORKING ON A STORY ABOUT YOUR DAD, ABOUT HIM...DISAPPEARING. ARE YOU DOING ALL RIGHT?
YEAH... MAYBE. I DON'T KNOW.
FOR SO LONG, I'VE BEEN TRYING TO PROVE HE DIDN'T KILL MY MOM. AND I FINALLY FOUND A CLUE--THIS NAME, "THAWNE." BUT WHEN I TOLD DAD, HE WENT BALLISTIC AND BROKE OUT.
NOW, SOMEONE HAS HIM, AND HE'S BEEN ACCUSED OF ANOTHER MURDER. I DON'T KNOW WHAT TO DO.
YOU CAN'T FIX EVERYTHING, BARRY. ALL YOU CAN REALLY DO IS JUST STAY IN CONTROL OF YOUR OWN LIFE.
I BLAMED FLASH FOR MY MOM DISAPPEARING, BUT HATING HIM DIDN'T GET ME ANYWHERE.
THANKS, WALLY.
DOES THAT MAKE US EVEN FOR ME SPRAY-PAINTING YOUR SHIRT?
THAT WAS MY FAVORITE SHIRT...BUT YEAH. WE'RE SQUARE. COME ON, LET'S GET MOVING...

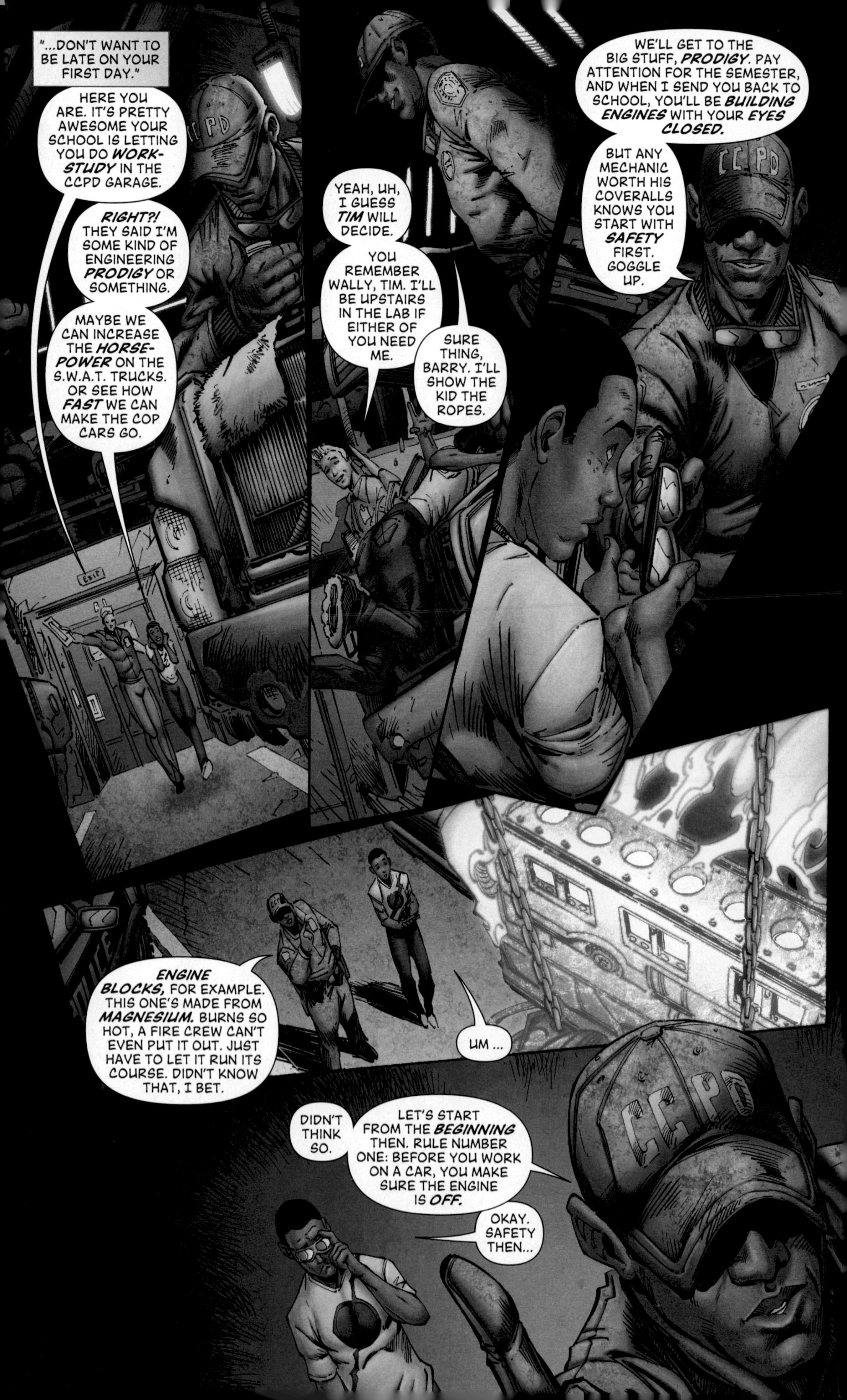
"...DON'T WANT TO BE LATE ON YOUR FIRST DAY."
HERE YOU ARE. IT'S PRETTY AWESOME YOUR SCHOOL IS LETTING YOU DO WORK-STUDY IN THE CCPD GARAGE.
RIGHT?! THEY SAID I'M SOME KIND OF ENGINEERING PRODIGY OR SOMETHING.
MAYBE WE CAN INCREASE THE HORSE-POWER ON THE S.W.A.T. TRUCKS. OR SEE HOW FAST WE CAN MAKE THE COP CARS GO.
YEAH, UH, I GUESS TIM WILL DECIDE.
YOU REMEMBER WALLY, TIM. I'LL BE UPSTAIRS IN THE LAB IF EITHER OF YOU NEED ME.
SURE THING, BARRY. I'LL SHOW THE KID THE ROPES.
WE'LL GET TO THE BIG STUFF, PRODIGY. PAY ATTENTION FOR THE SEMESTER, AND WHEN I SEND YOU BACK TO SCHOOL, YOU'LL BE BUILDING ENGINES WITH YOUR EYES CLOSED.
BUT ANY MECHANIC WORTH HIS COVERALLS KNOWS YOU START WITH SAFETY FIRST. GOGGLE UP.
ENGINE BLOCKS, FOR EXAMPLE. THIS ONE'S MADE FROM MAGNESIUM. BURNS SO HOT, A FIRE CREW CAN'T EVEN PUT IT OUT. JUST HAVE TO LET IT RUN ITS COURSE. DIDN'T KNOW THAT, I BET.
UM ...
DIDN'T THINK SO.
LET'S START FROM THE BEGINNING THEN. RULE NUMBER ONE: BEFORE YOU WORK ON A CAR, YOU MAKE SURE THE ENGINE IS OFF.
OKAY. SAFETY THEN...

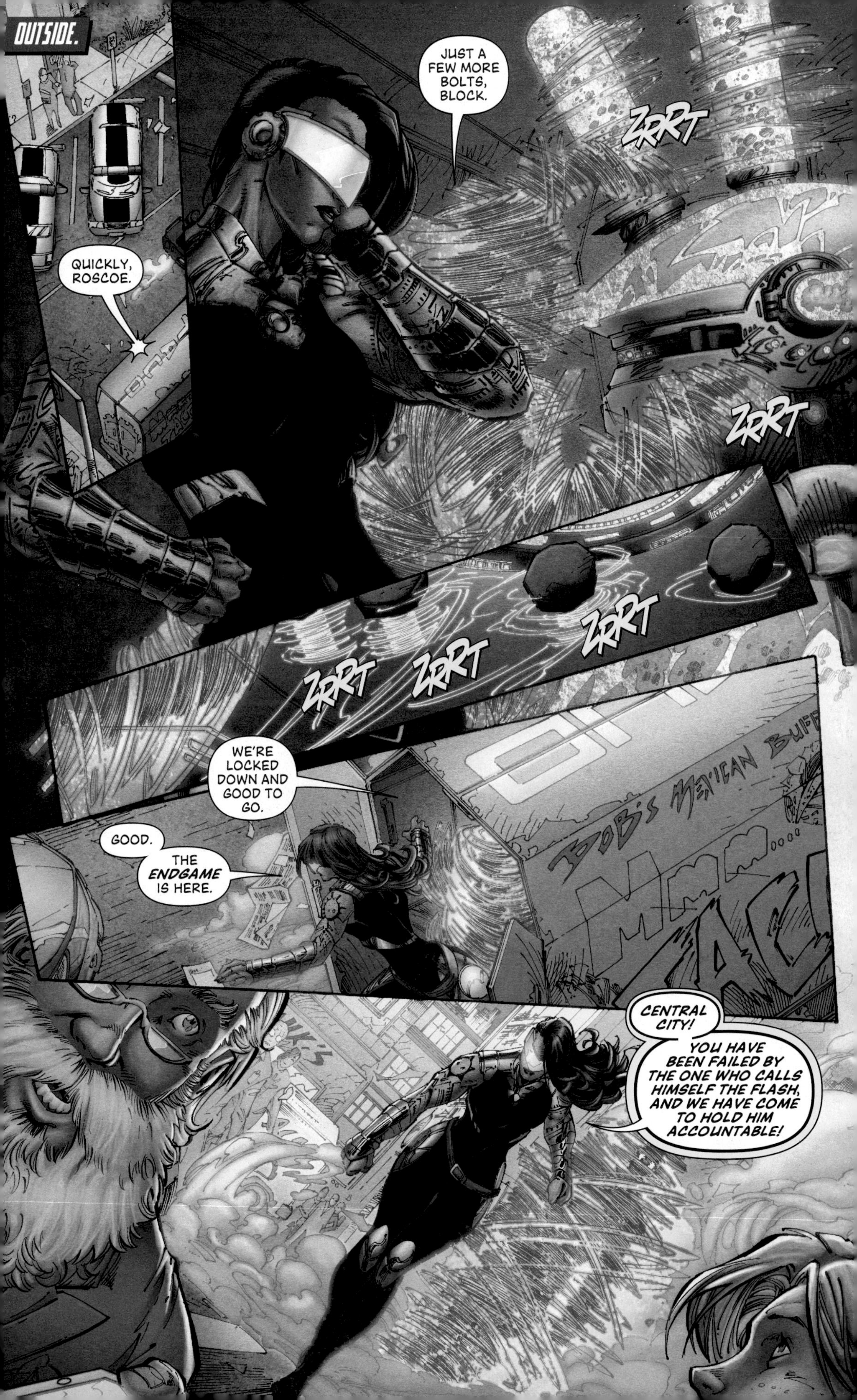
OUTSIDE.
JUST A FEW MORE BOLTS, BLOCK.
ZRRT
QUICKLY, ROSCOE.
ZRRT
ZRRT
ZRRT
ZRRT
WE'RE LOCKED DOWN AND GOOD TO GO.
GOOD.
THE *ENDGAME* IS HERE.
BOB'S MEXICAN BUFF
CENTRAL CITY!
YOU HAVE BEEN FAILED BY THE ONE WHO CALLS HIMSELF THE FLASH, AND WE HAVE COME TO HOLD HIM ACCOUNTABLE!

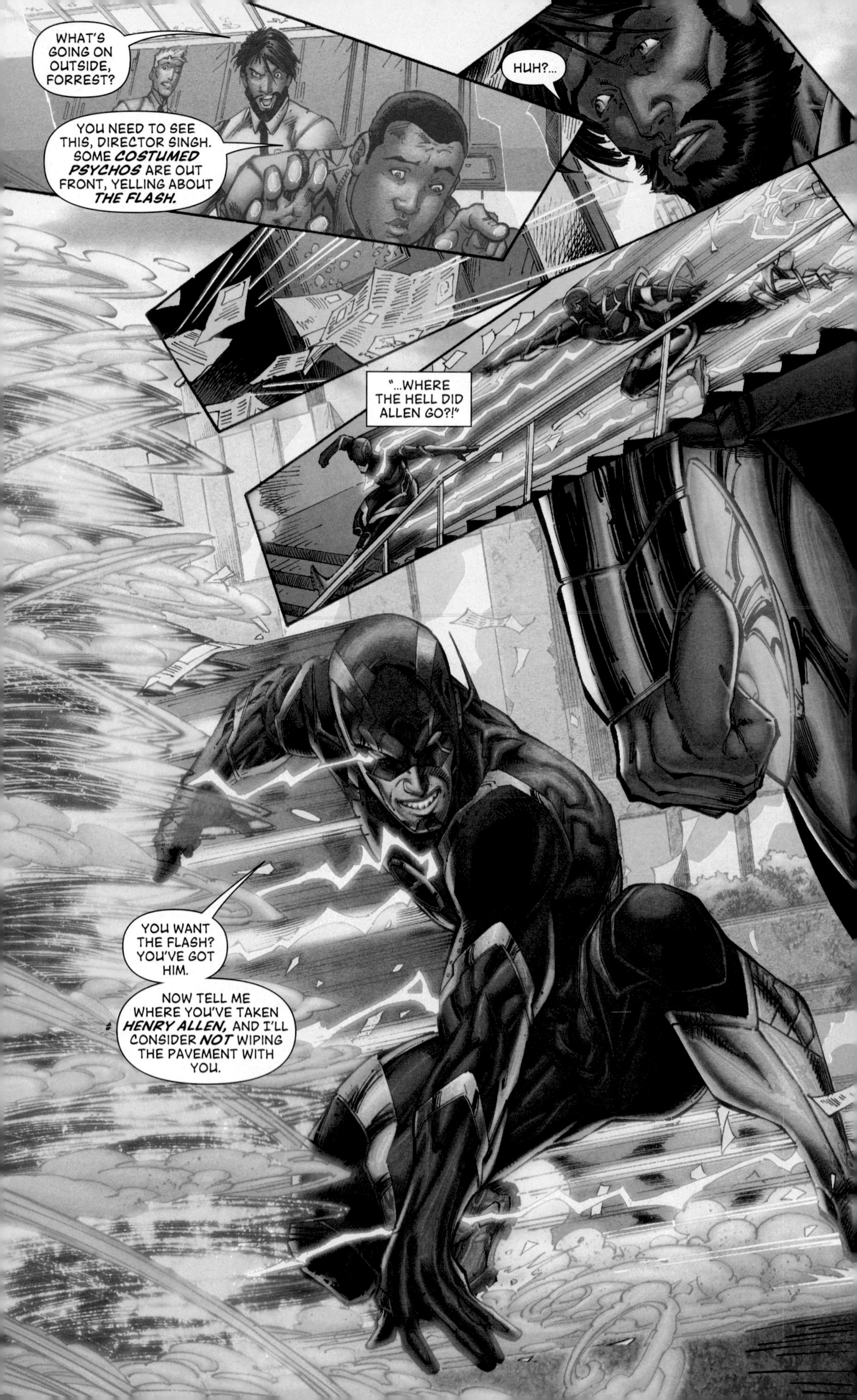
WHAT'S GOING ON OUTSIDE, FORREST?
HUH?...
YOU NEED TO SEE THIS, DIRECTOR SINGH. SOME COSTUMED PSYCHOS ARE OUT FRONT, YELLING ABOUT THE FLASH.
"...WHERE THE HELL DID ALLEN GO?!"
YOU WANT THE FLASH? YOU'VE GOT HIM.
NOW TELL ME WHERE YOU'VE TAKEN HENRY ALLEN, AND I'LL CONSIDER NOT WIPING THE PAVEMENT WITH YOU.

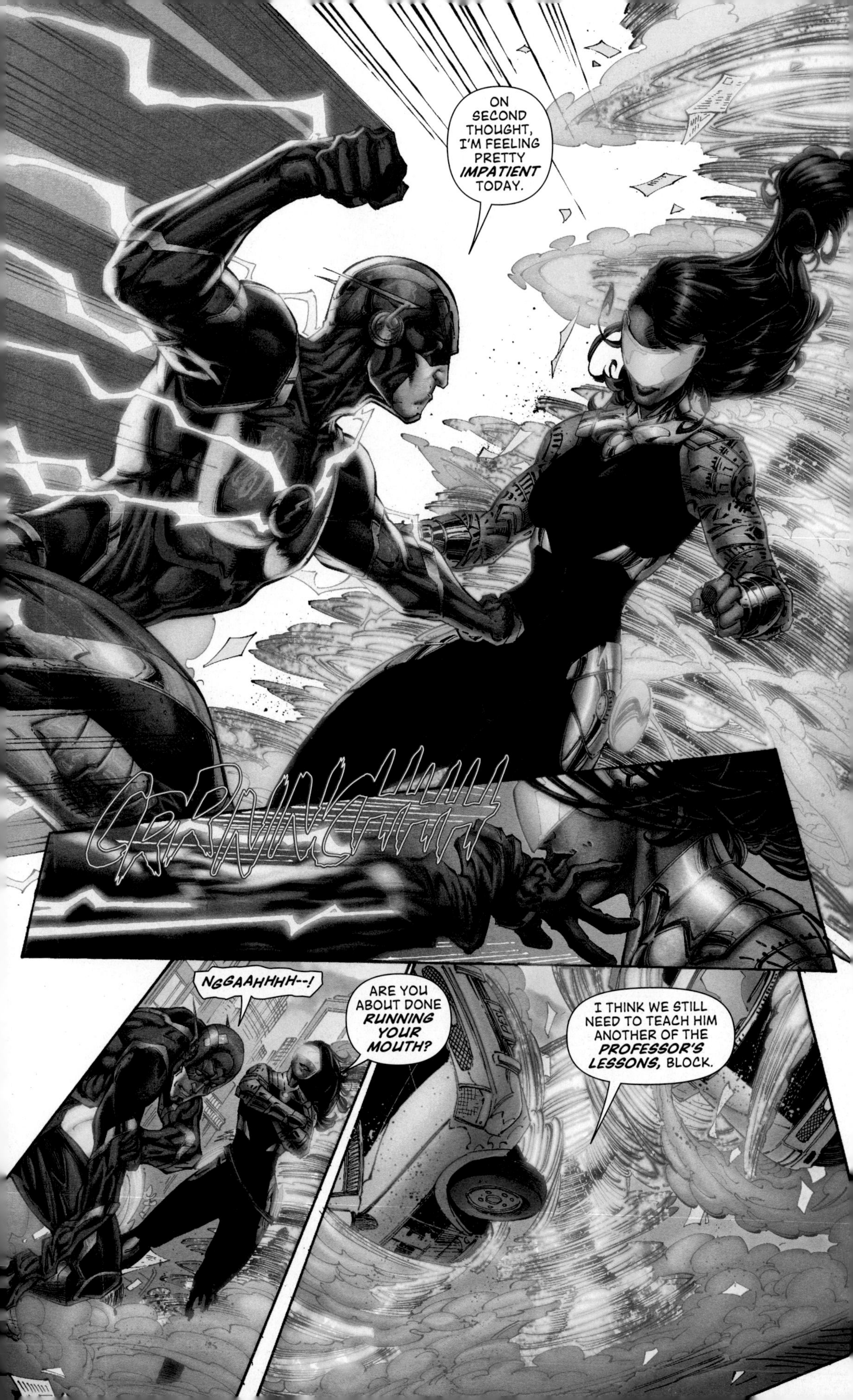
ON SECOND THOUGHT, I'M FEELING PRETTY IMPATIENT TODAY.
NGGAAHHHH--!
ARE YOU ABOUT DONE RUNNING YOUR MOUTH?
I THINK WE STILL NEED TO TEACH HIM ANOTHER OF THE PROFESSOR'S LESSONS, BLOCK.

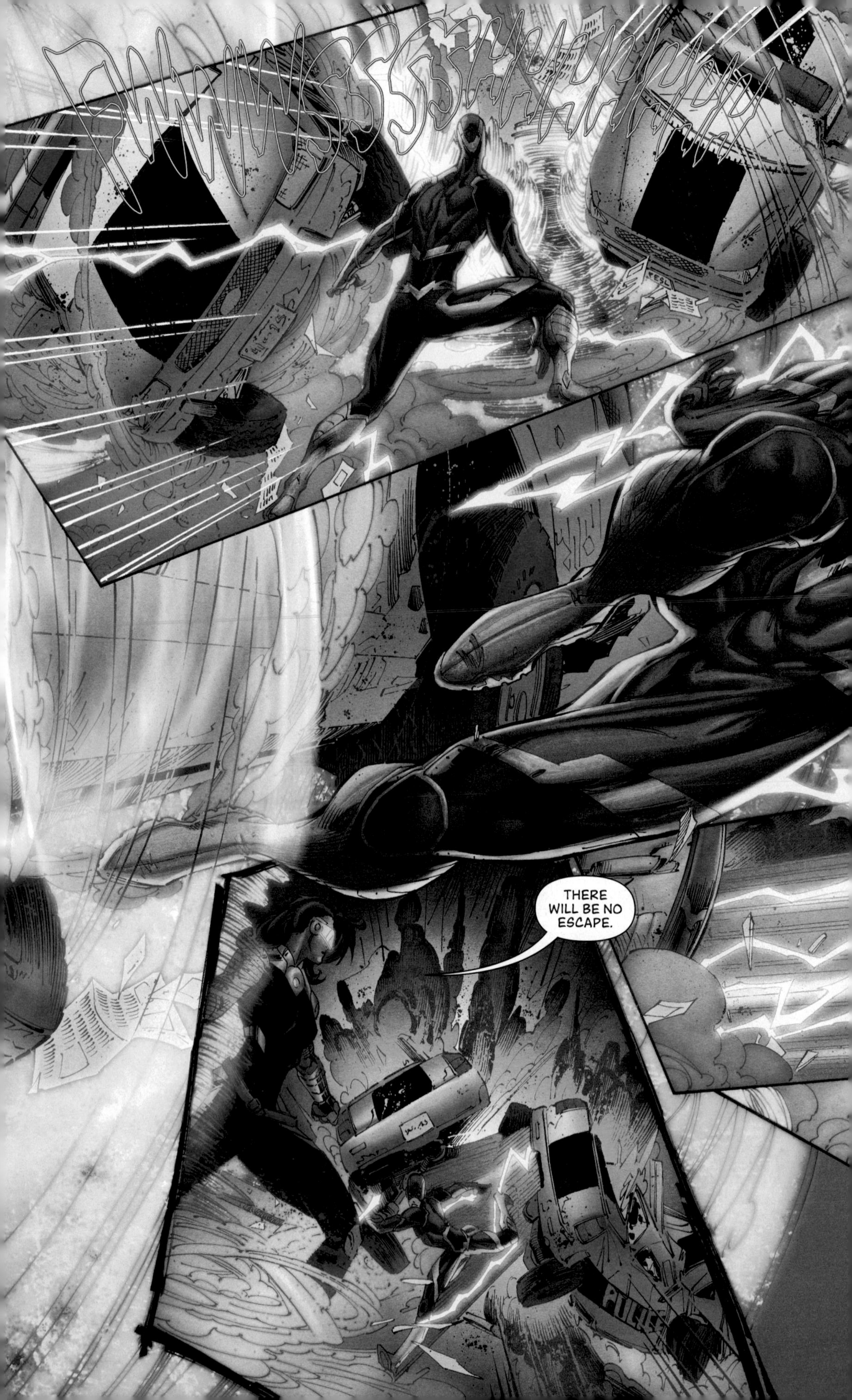
THERE WILL BE NO ESCAPE.

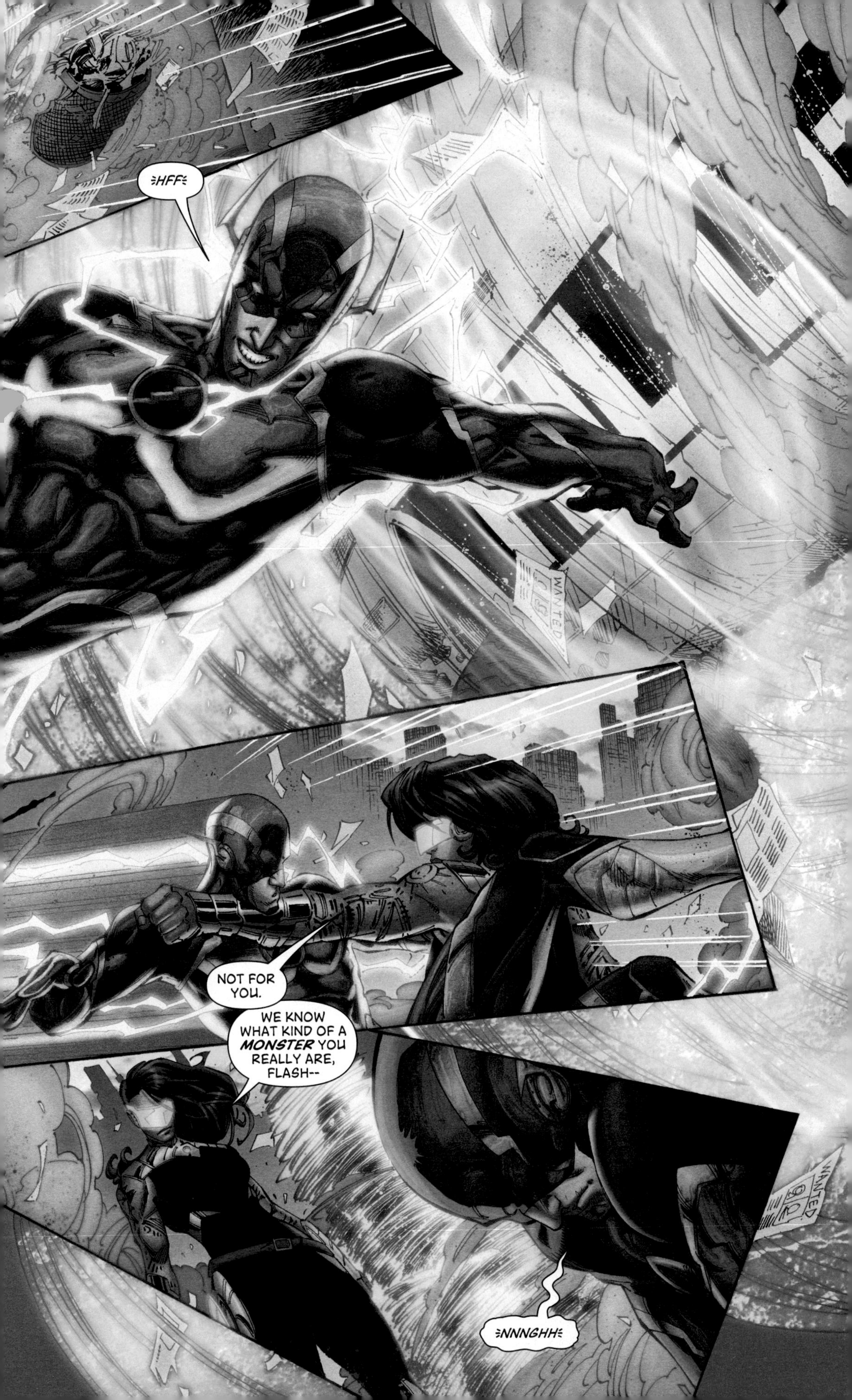
HFF
WANTED
NOT FOR YOU.
WE KNOW WHAT KIND OF A MONSTER YOU REALLY ARE, FLASH--
WANTED
NNNGHH

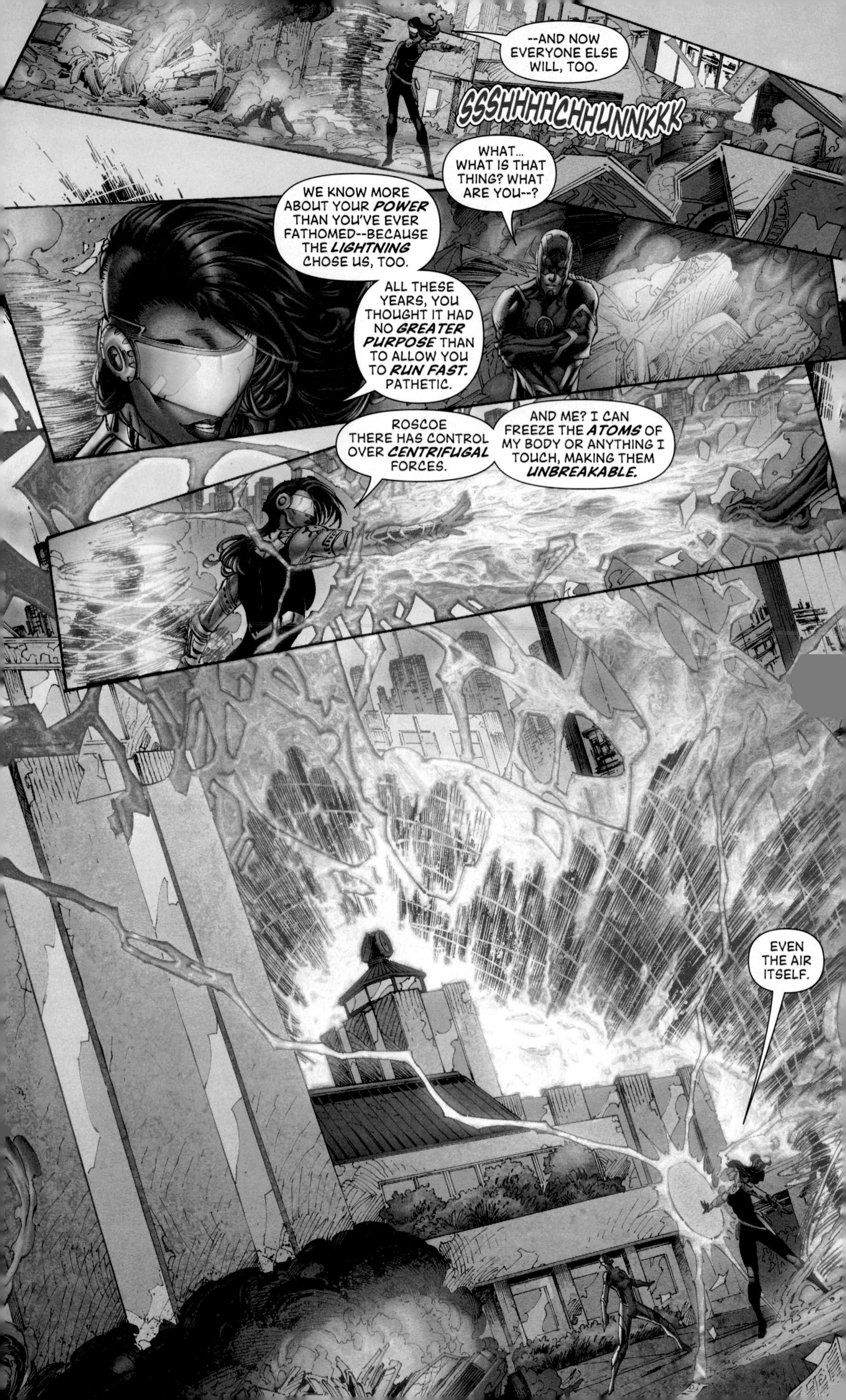
--AND NOW EVERYONE ELSE WILL, TOO.
SSSHHHHCHHUNNKKK
WHAT... WHAT IS THAT THING? WHAT ARE YOU--?
WE KNOW MORE ABOUT YOUR POWER THAN YOU'VE EVER FATHOMED--BECAUSE THE LIGHTNING CHOSE US, TOO.
ALL THESE YEARS, YOU THOUGHT IT HAD NO GREATER PURPOSE THAN TO ALLOW YOU TO RUN FAST. PATHETIC.
ROSCOE THERE HAS CONTROL OVER CENTRIFUGAL FORCES.
AND ME? I CAN FREEZE THE ATOMS OF MY BODY OR ANYTHING I TOUCH, MAKING THEM UNBREAKABLE.
EVEN THE AIR ITSELF.

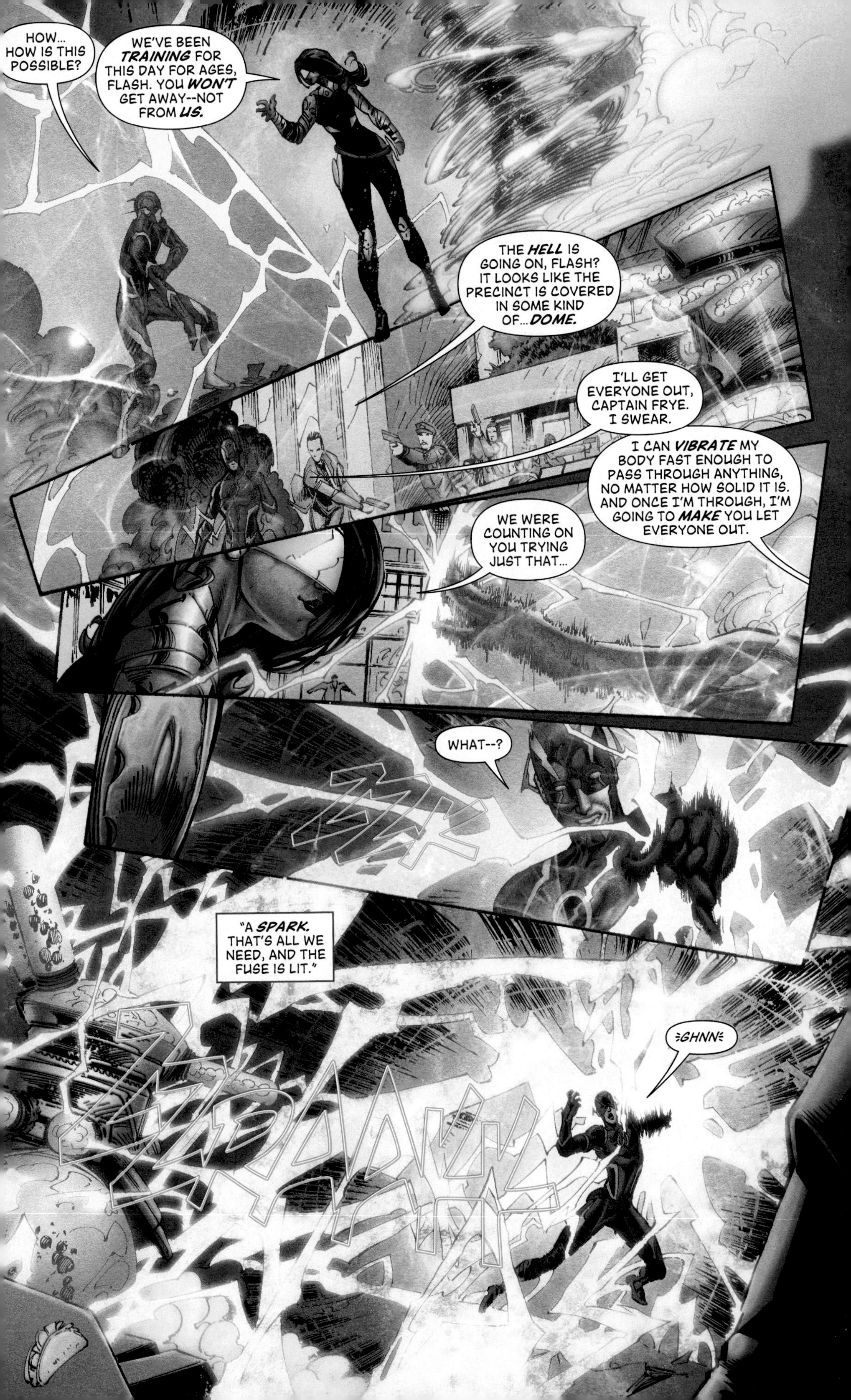
HOW... HOW IS THIS POSSIBLE?
WE'VE BEEN TRAINING FOR THIS DAY FOR AGES, FLASH. YOU WON'T GET AWAY--NOT FROM US.
THE HELL IS GOING ON, FLASH? IT LOOKS LIKE THE PRECINCT IS COVERED IN SOME KIND OF...DOME.
I'LL GET EVERYONE OUT, CAPTAIN FRYE. I SWEAR.
I CAN VIBRATE MY BODY FAST ENOUGH TO PASS THROUGH ANYTHING, NO MATTER HOW SOLID IT IS. AND ONCE I'M THROUGH, I'M GOING TO MAKE YOU LET EVERYONE OUT.
WE WERE COUNTING ON YOU TRYING JUST THAT...
WHAT--?
"A SPARK. THAT'S ALL WE NEED, AND THE FUSE IS LIT."
GHNN

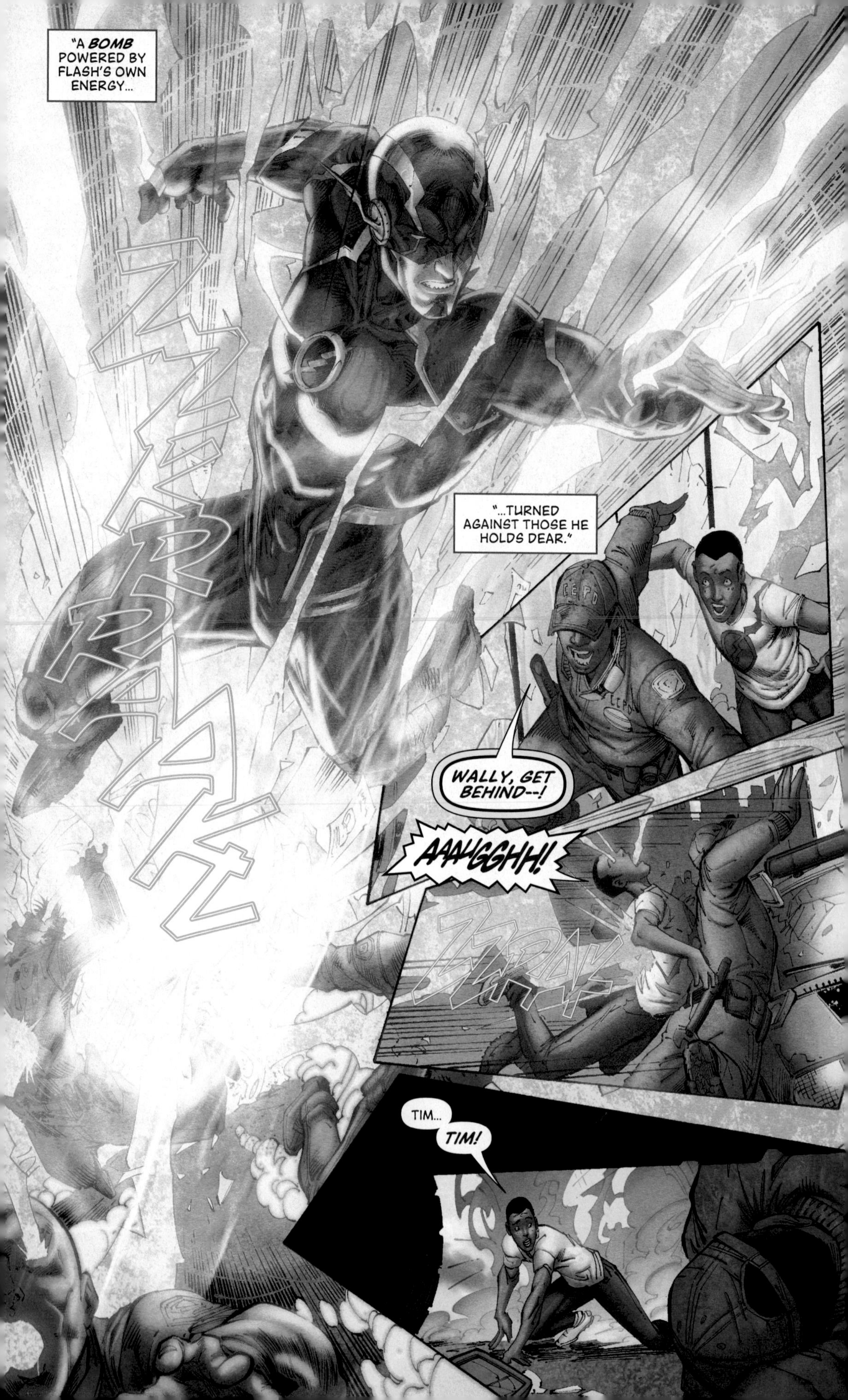

"A *BOMB* POWERED BY FLASH'S OWN ENERGY...
"...TURNED AGAINST THOSE HE HOLDS DEAR."
WALLY, GET BEHIND--!
AAAUGGHH!
TIM...
TIM!

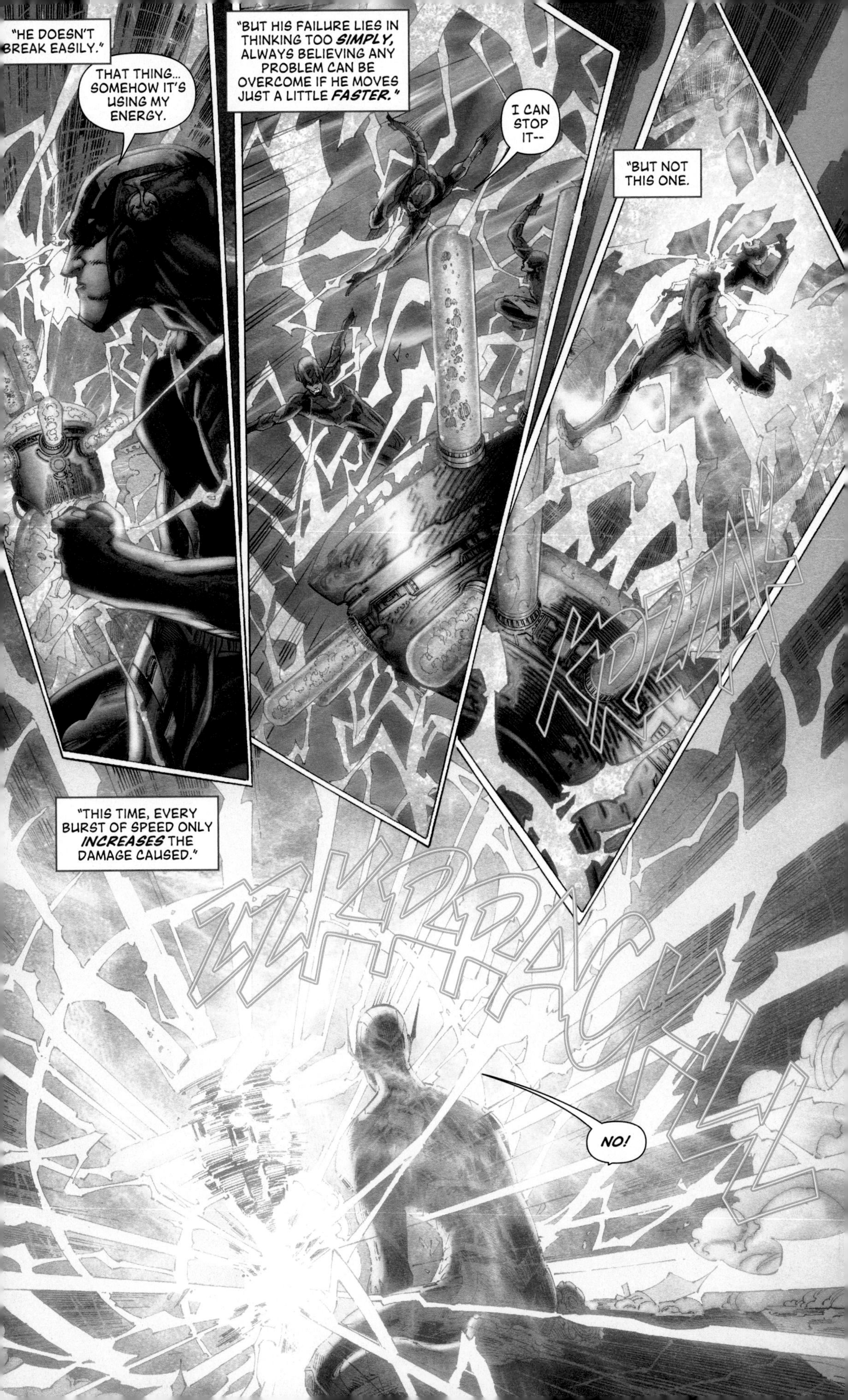
"HE DOESN'T BREAK EASILY."
THAT THING... SOMEHOW IT'S USING MY ENERGY.
"BUT HIS FAILURE LIES IN THINKING TOO SIMPLY, ALWAYS BELIEVING ANY PROBLEM CAN BE OVERCOME IF HE MOVES JUST A LITTLE FASTER."
I CAN STOP IT--
"BUT NOT THIS ONE.
KZZZAK
"THIS TIME, EVERY BURST OF SPEED ONLY INCREASES THE DAMAGE CAUSED."
ZZKRRACKKL
NO!

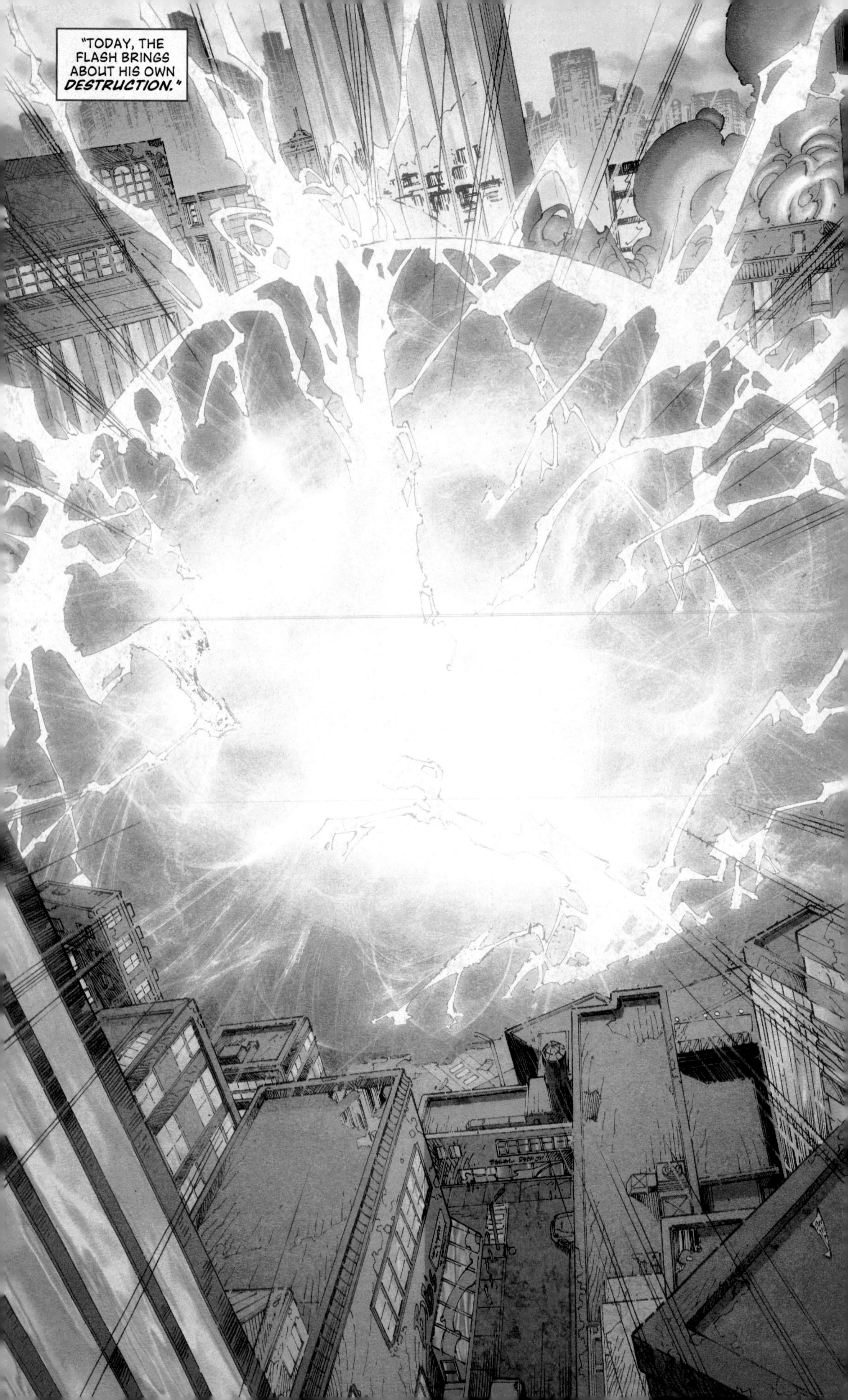
"TODAY, THE FLASH BRINGS ABOUT HIS OWN DESTRUCTION."

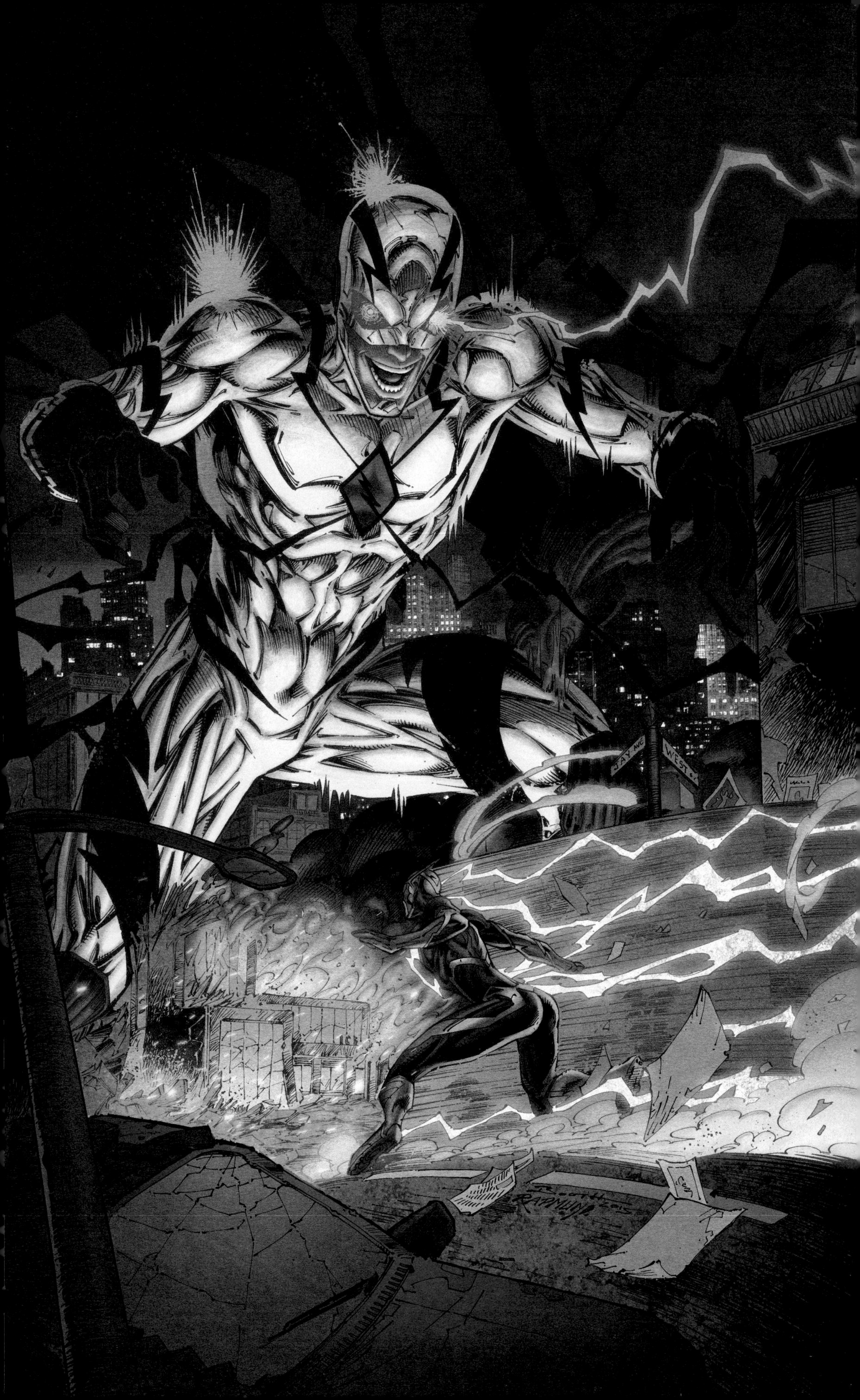

JAY AVE
WEST St

ROBERT VENDITTI, VAN JENSEN writers BRETT BOOTH, VICENTE CIFUENTES, ALE GARZA pencillers NORM RAPMUND inker ANDREW DALHOUSE colorist PAT BROSSEAU letterer
cover by BRETT BOOTH, NORM RAPMUND, ANDREW DALHOUSE

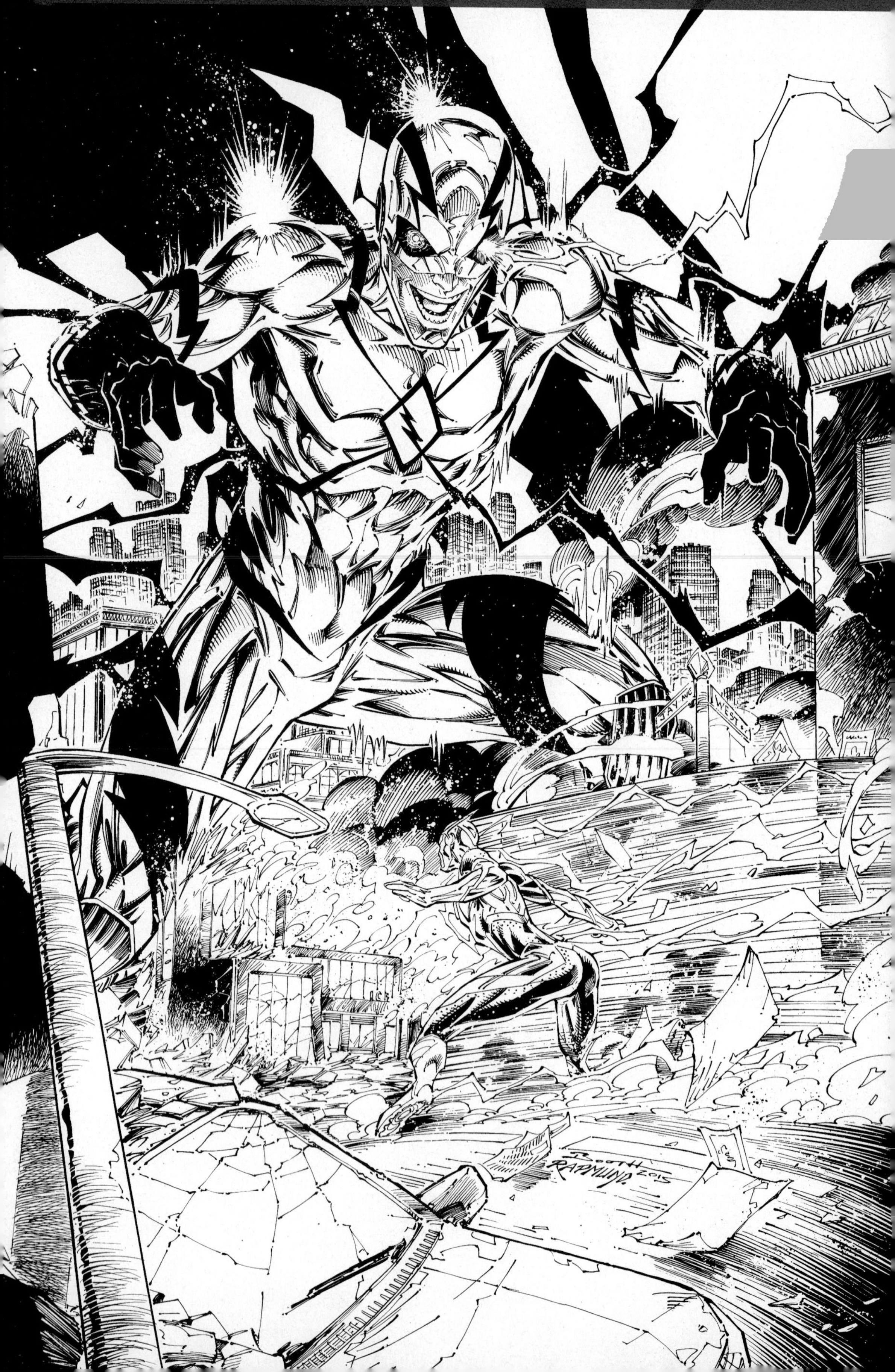
JAY AVE
WEST
BOOTH
RAPMUND 2015

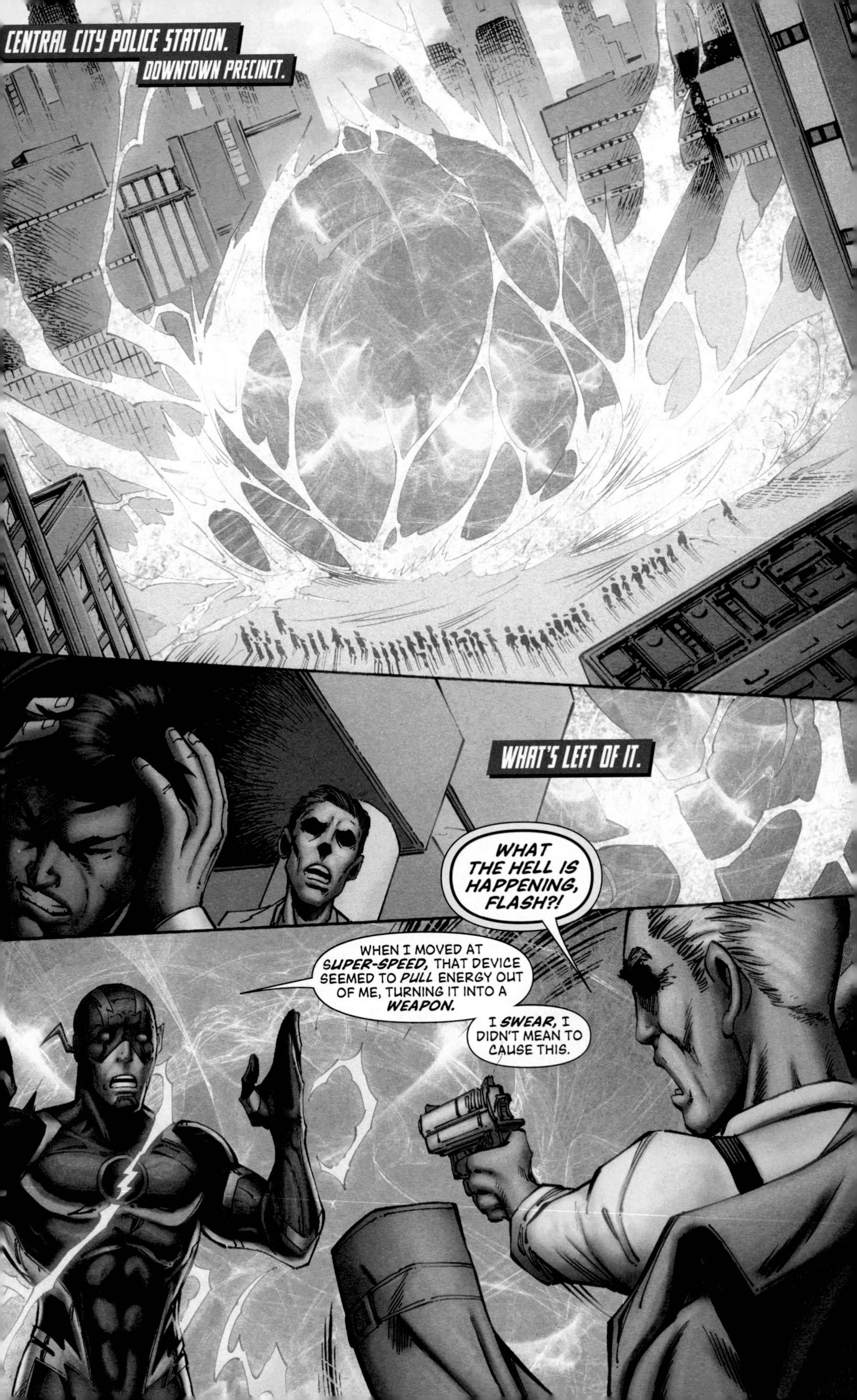

CENTRAL CITY POLICE STATION.
DOWNTOWN PRECINCT.
WHAT'S LEFT OF IT.
WHAT THE HELL IS HAPPENING, FLASH?!
WHEN I MOVED AT SUPER-SPEED, THAT DEVICE SEEMED TO PULL ENERGY OUT OF ME, TURNING IT INTO A WEAPON.
I SWEAR, I DIDN'T MEAN TO CAUSE THIS.

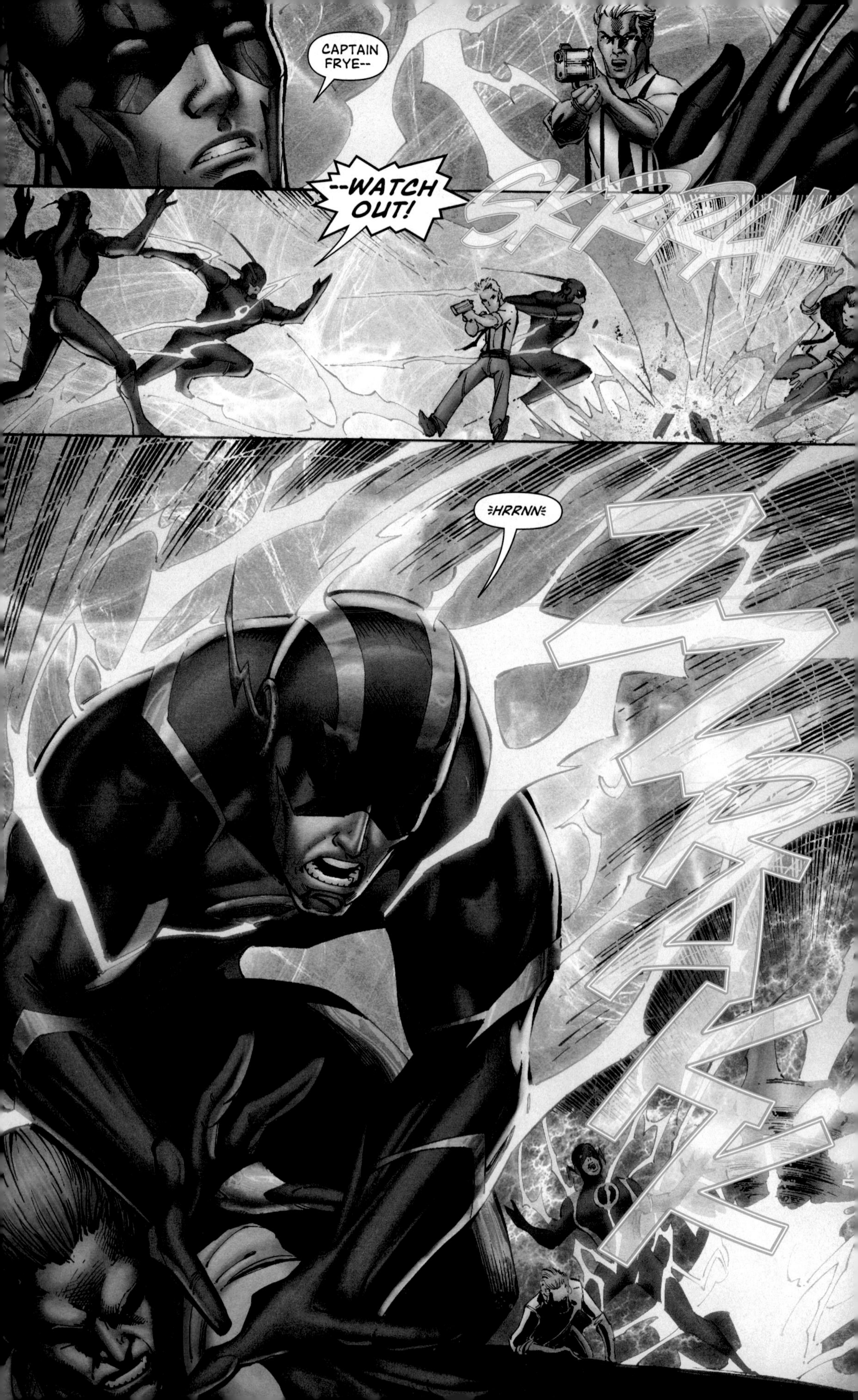
CAPTAIN FRYE--
--WATCH OUT!
SKRRDAK
HRRNN
ZZRRAKK

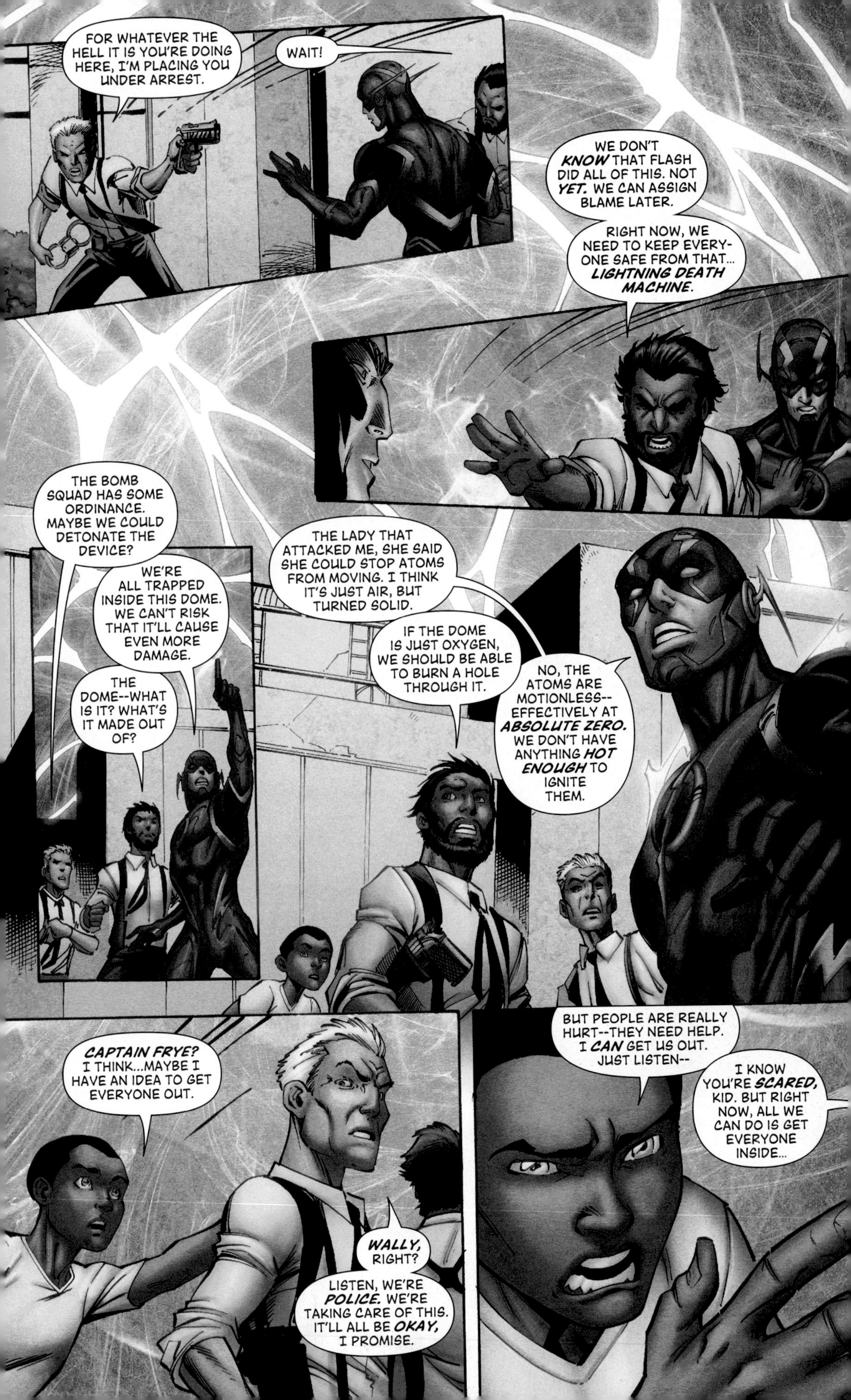
FOR WHATEVER THE HELL IT IS YOU'RE DOING HERE, I'M PLACING YOU UNDER ARREST.
WAIT!
WE DON'T KNOW THAT FLASH DID ALL OF THIS. NOT YET. WE CAN ASSIGN BLAME LATER.
RIGHT NOW, WE NEED TO KEEP EVERY-ONE SAFE FROM THAT... LIGHTNING DEATH MACHINE.
THE BOMB SQUAD HAS SOME ORDINANCE. MAYBE WE COULD DETONATE THE DEVICE?
WE'RE ALL TRAPPED INSIDE THIS DOME. WE CAN'T RISK THAT IT'LL CAUSE EVEN MORE DAMAGE.
THE DOME--WHAT IS IT? WHAT'S IT MADE OUT OF?
THE LADY THAT ATTACKED ME, SHE SAID SHE COULD STOP ATOMS FROM MOVING. I THINK IT'S JUST AIR, BUT TURNED SOLID.
IF THE DOME IS JUST OXYGEN, WE SHOULD BE ABLE TO BURN A HOLE THROUGH IT.
NO, THE ATOMS ARE MOTIONLESS--EFFECTIVELY AT ABSOLUTE ZERO. WE DON'T HAVE ANYTHING HOT ENOUGH TO IGNITE THEM.
CAPTAIN FRYE? I THINK...MAYBE I HAVE AN IDEA TO GET EVERYONE OUT.
WALLY, RIGHT?
LISTEN, WE'RE POLICE. WE'RE TAKING CARE OF THIS. IT'LL ALL BE OKAY, I PROMISE.
BUT PEOPLE ARE REALLY HURT--THEY NEED HELP. I CAN GET US OUT. JUST LISTEN--
I KNOW YOU'RE SCARED, KID. BUT RIGHT NOW, ALL WE CAN DO IS GET EVERYONE INSIDE...

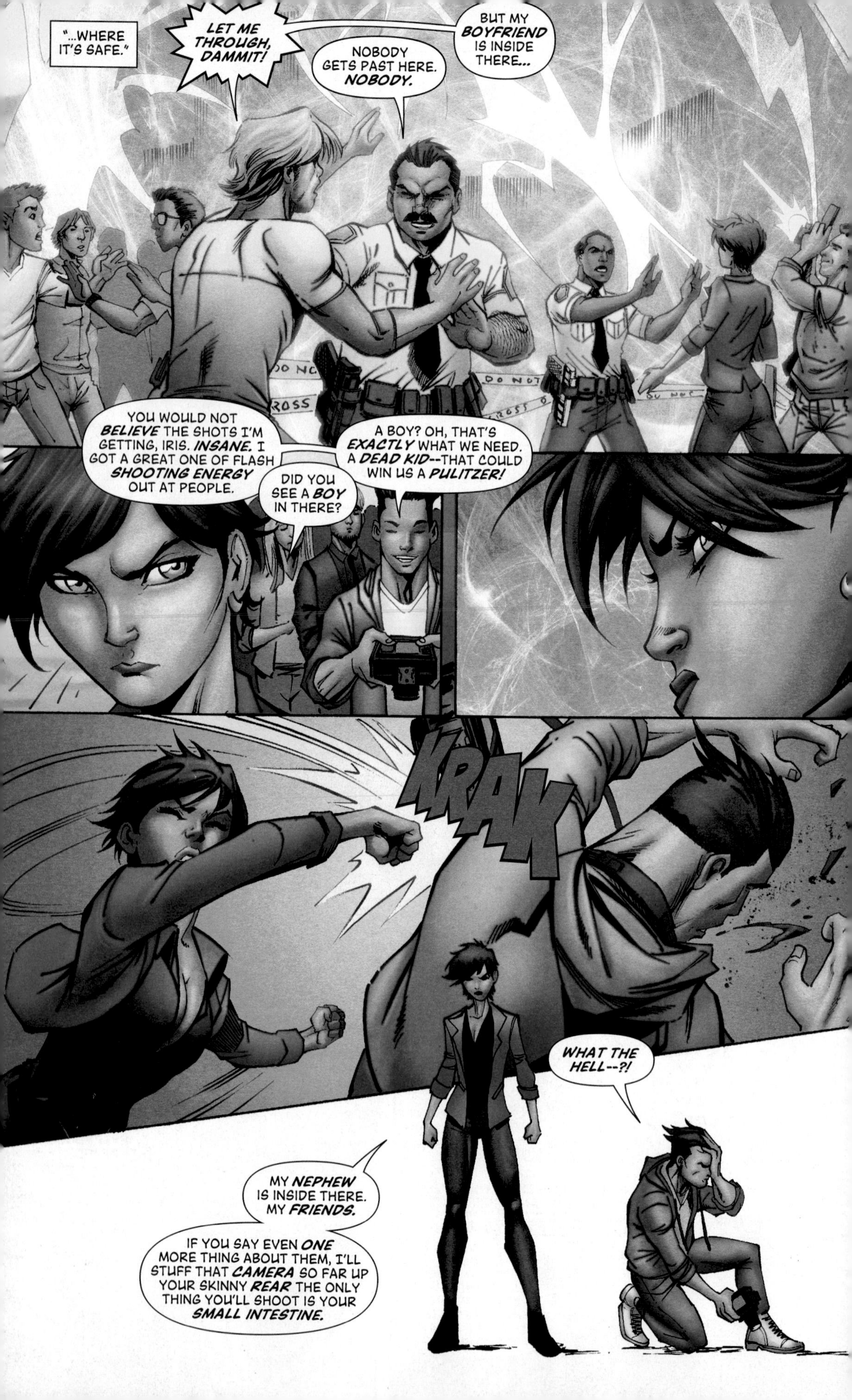

"...WHERE IT'S SAFE."
LET ME THROUGH, DAMMIT!
BUT MY BOYFRIEND IS INSIDE THERE...
NOBODY GETS PAST HERE. NOBODY.
YOU WOULD NOT BELIEVE THE SHOTS I'M GETTING, IRIS. INSANE. I GOT A GREAT ONE OF FLASH SHOOTING ENERGY OUT AT PEOPLE.
DID YOU SEE A BOY IN THERE?
A BOY? OH, THAT'S EXACTLY WHAT WE NEED. A DEAD KID--THAT COULD WIN US A PULITZER!
KRAK
WHAT THE HELL--?!
MY NEPHEW IS INSIDE THERE. MY FRIENDS.
IF YOU SAY EVEN ONE MORE THING ABOUT THEM, I'LL STUFF THAT CAMERA SO FAR UP YOUR SKINNY REAR THE ONLY THING YOU'LL SHOOT IS YOUR SMALL INTESTINE.

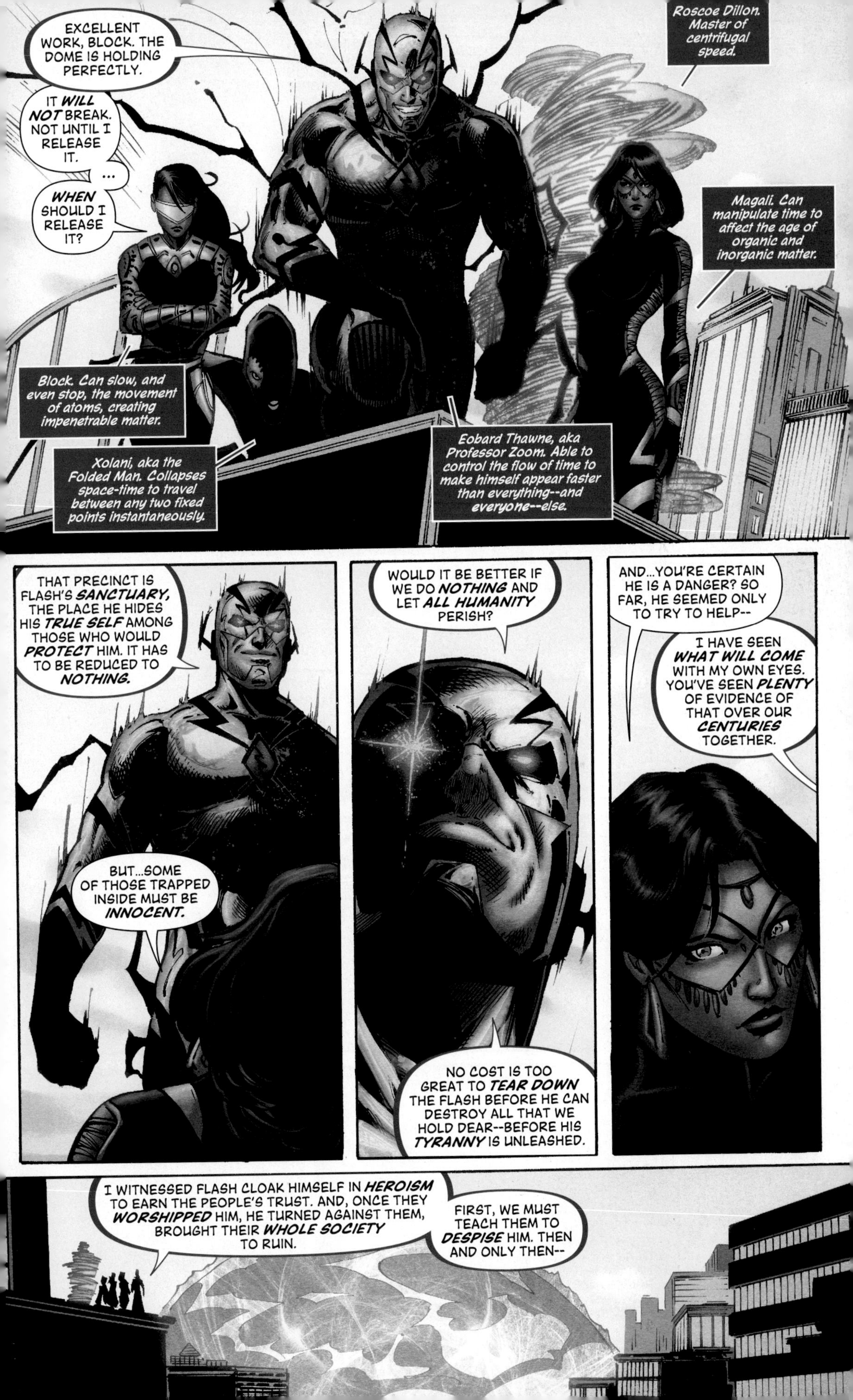

EXCELLENT WORK, BLOCK. THE DOME IS HOLDING PERFECTLY.
IT WILL NOT BREAK. NOT UNTIL I RELEASE IT.
...
WHEN SHOULD I RELEASE IT?
Roscoe Dillon. Master of centrifugal speed.
Magali. Can manipulate time to affect the age of organic and inorganic matter.
Block. Can slow, and even stop, the movement of atoms, creating impenetrable matter.
Xolani, aka the Folded Man. Collapses space-time to travel between any two fixed points instantaneously.
Eobard Thawne, aka Professor Zoom. Able to control the flow of time to make himself appear faster than everything--and everyone--else.
THAT PRECINCT IS FLASH'S SANCTUARY, THE PLACE HE HIDES HIS TRUE SELF AMONG THOSE WHO WOULD PROTECT HIM. IT HAS TO BE REDUCED TO NOTHING.
BUT...SOME OF THOSE TRAPPED INSIDE MUST BE INNOCENT.
WOULD IT BE BETTER IF WE DO NOTHING AND LET ALL HUMANITY PERISH?
NO COST IS TOO GREAT TO TEAR DOWN THE FLASH BEFORE HE CAN DESTROY ALL THAT WE HOLD DEAR--BEFORE HIS TYRANNY IS UNLEASHED.
AND...YOU'RE CERTAIN HE IS A DANGER? SO FAR, HE SEEMED ONLY TO TRY TO HELP--
I HAVE SEEN WHAT WILL COME WITH MY OWN EYES. YOU'VE SEEN PLENTY OF EVIDENCE OF THAT OVER OUR CENTURIES TOGETHER.
I WITNESSED FLASH CLOAK HIMSELF IN HEROISM TO EARN THE PEOPLE'S TRUST. AND, ONCE THEY WORSHIPPED HIM, HE TURNED AGAINST THEM, BROUGHT THEIR WHOLE SOCIETY TO RUIN.
FIRST, WE MUST TEACH THEM TO DESPISE HIM. THEN AND ONLY THEN--

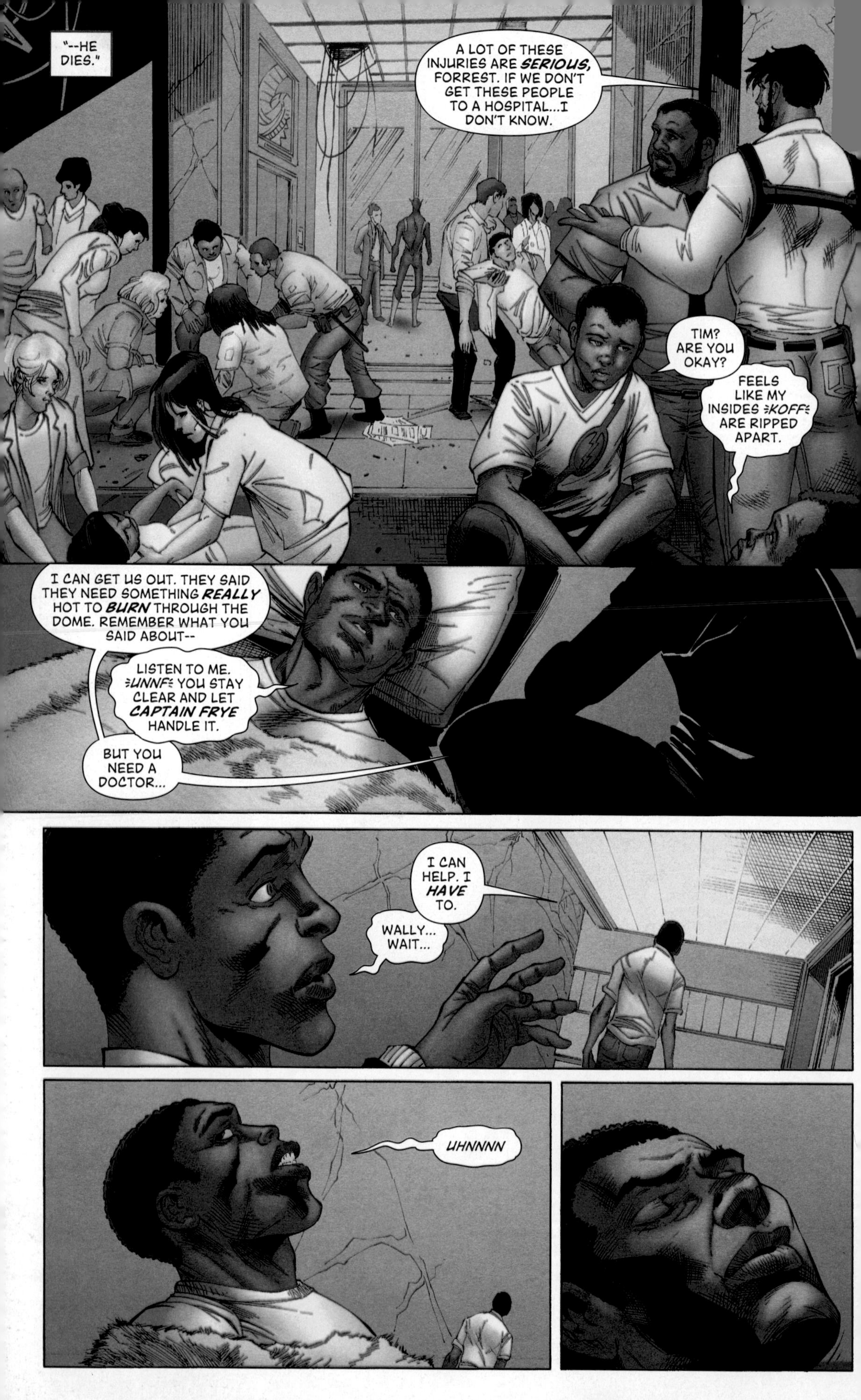
"--HE DIES."
A LOT OF THESE INJURIES ARE SERIOUS, FORREST. IF WE DON'T GET THESE PEOPLE TO A HOSPITAL...I DON'T KNOW.
TIM? ARE YOU OKAY?
FEELS LIKE MY INSIDES =KOFF= ARE RIPPED APART.
I CAN GET US OUT. THEY SAID THEY NEED SOMETHING REALLY HOT TO BURN THROUGH THE DOME. REMEMBER WHAT YOU SAID ABOUT--
LISTEN TO ME. =UNNF= YOU STAY CLEAR AND LET CAPTAIN FRYE HANDLE IT.
BUT YOU NEED A DOCTOR...
I CAN HELP. I HAVE TO.
WALLY... WAIT...
UHNNNN

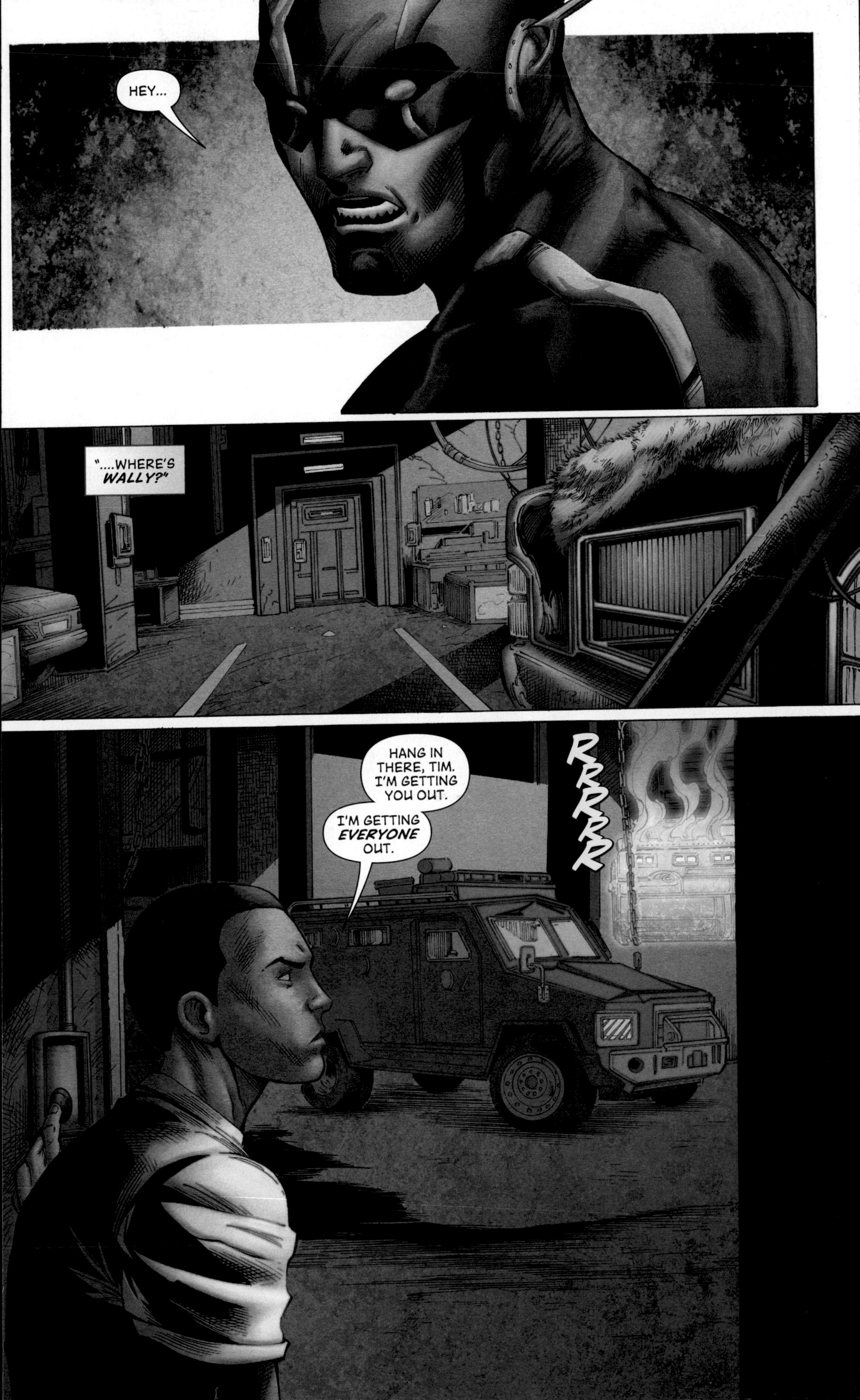
HEY...
"....WHERE'S *WALLY?*"
HANG IN THERE, TIM. I'M GETTING YOU OUT.
I'M GETTING *EVERYONE* OUT.
RRRRR

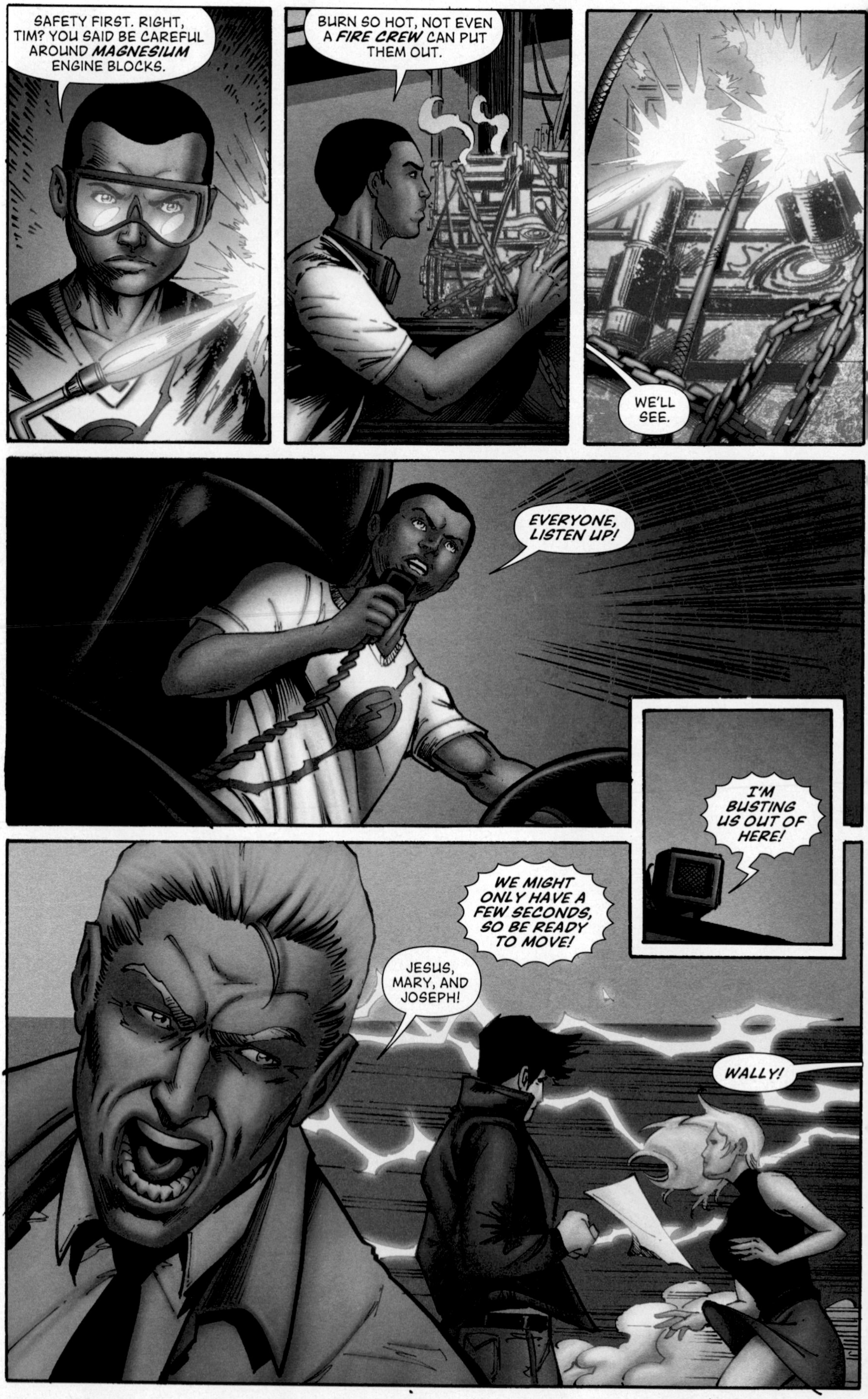
SAFETY FIRST. RIGHT, TIM? YOU SAID BE CAREFUL AROUND MAGNESIUM ENGINE BLOCKS.
BURN SO HOT, NOT EVEN A FIRE CREW CAN PUT THEM OUT.
WE'LL SEE.
EVERYONE, LISTEN UP!
I'M BUSTING US OUT OF HERE!
WE MIGHT ONLY HAVE A FEW SECONDS, SO BE READY TO MOVE!
JESUS, MARY, AND JOSEPH!
WALLY!

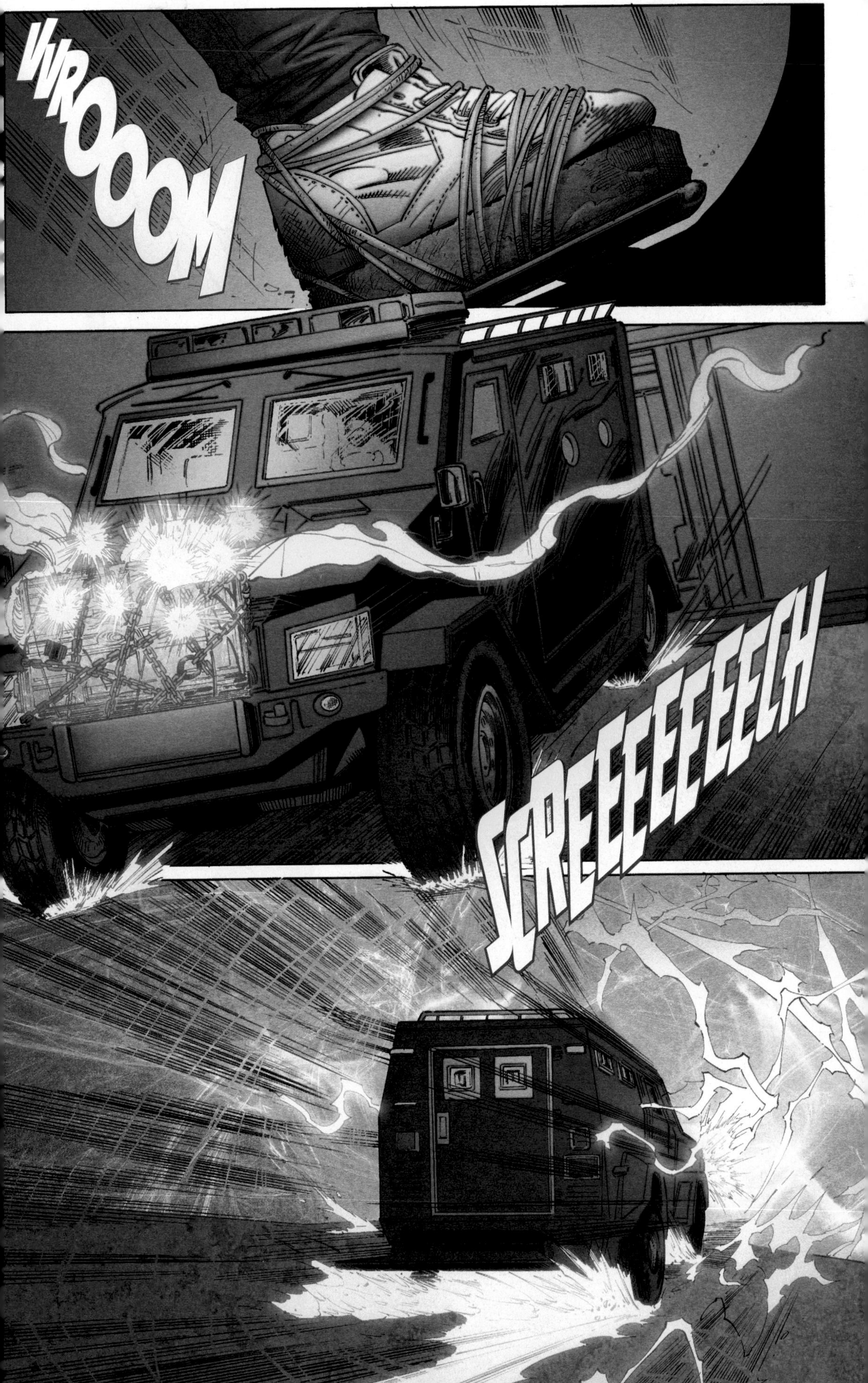
VVROOOM
SCREEEEEEECH

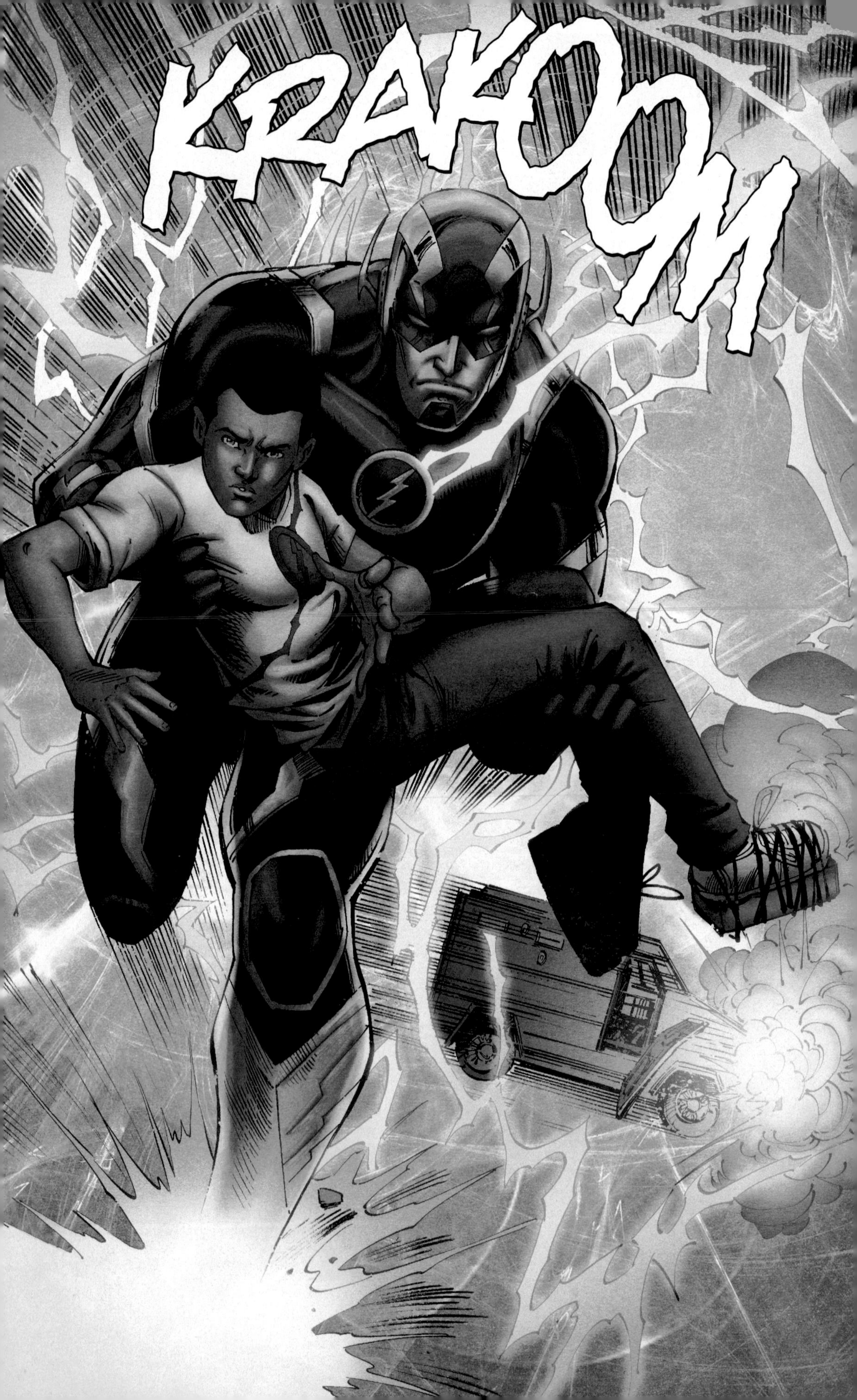
KRAKOOM

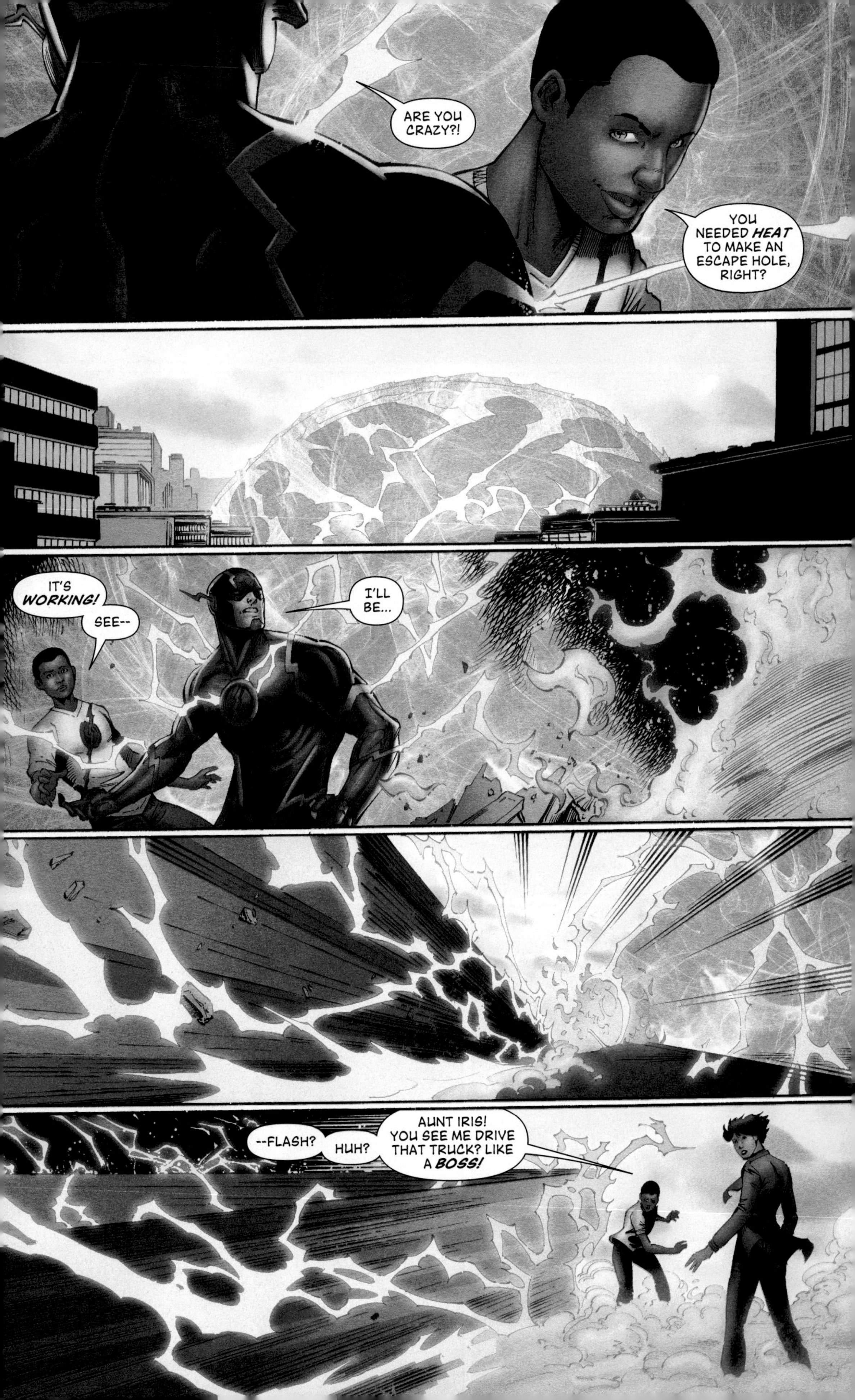
ARE YOU CRAZY?!
YOU NEEDED *HEAT* TO MAKE AN ESCAPE HOLE, RIGHT?
IT'S *WORKING!*
SEE--
I'LL BE...
--FLASH?
HUH?
AUNT IRIS! YOU SEE ME DRIVE THAT TRUCK? LIKE A *BOSS!*

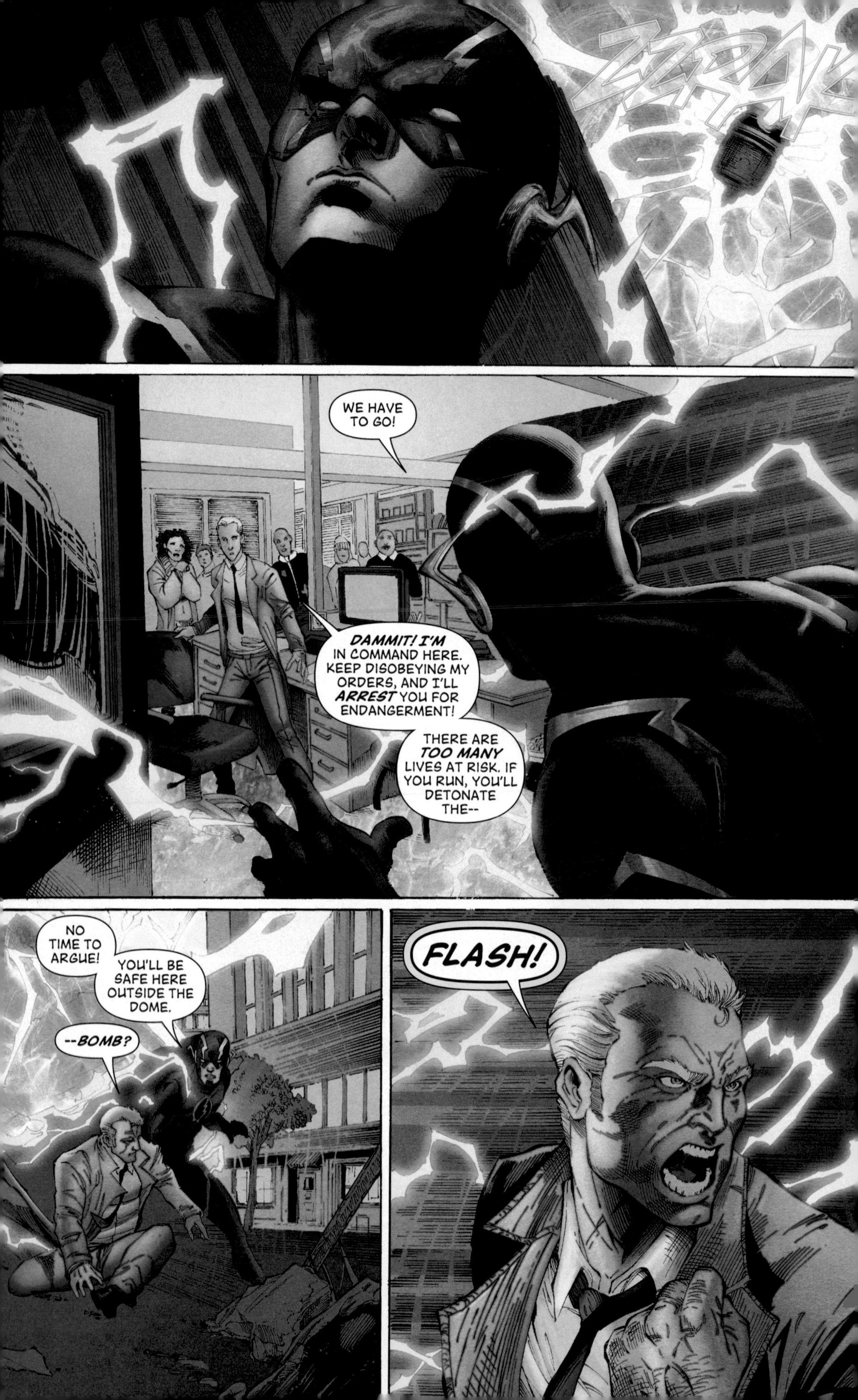
WE HAVE TO GO!
DAMMIT! I'M IN COMMAND HERE. KEEP DISOBEYING MY ORDERS, AND I'LL ARREST YOU FOR ENDANGERMENT!
THERE ARE TOO MANY LIVES AT RISK. IF YOU RUN, YOU'LL DETONATE THE--
NO TIME TO ARGUE!
YOU'LL BE SAFE HERE OUTSIDE THE DOME.
--BOMB?
FLASH!

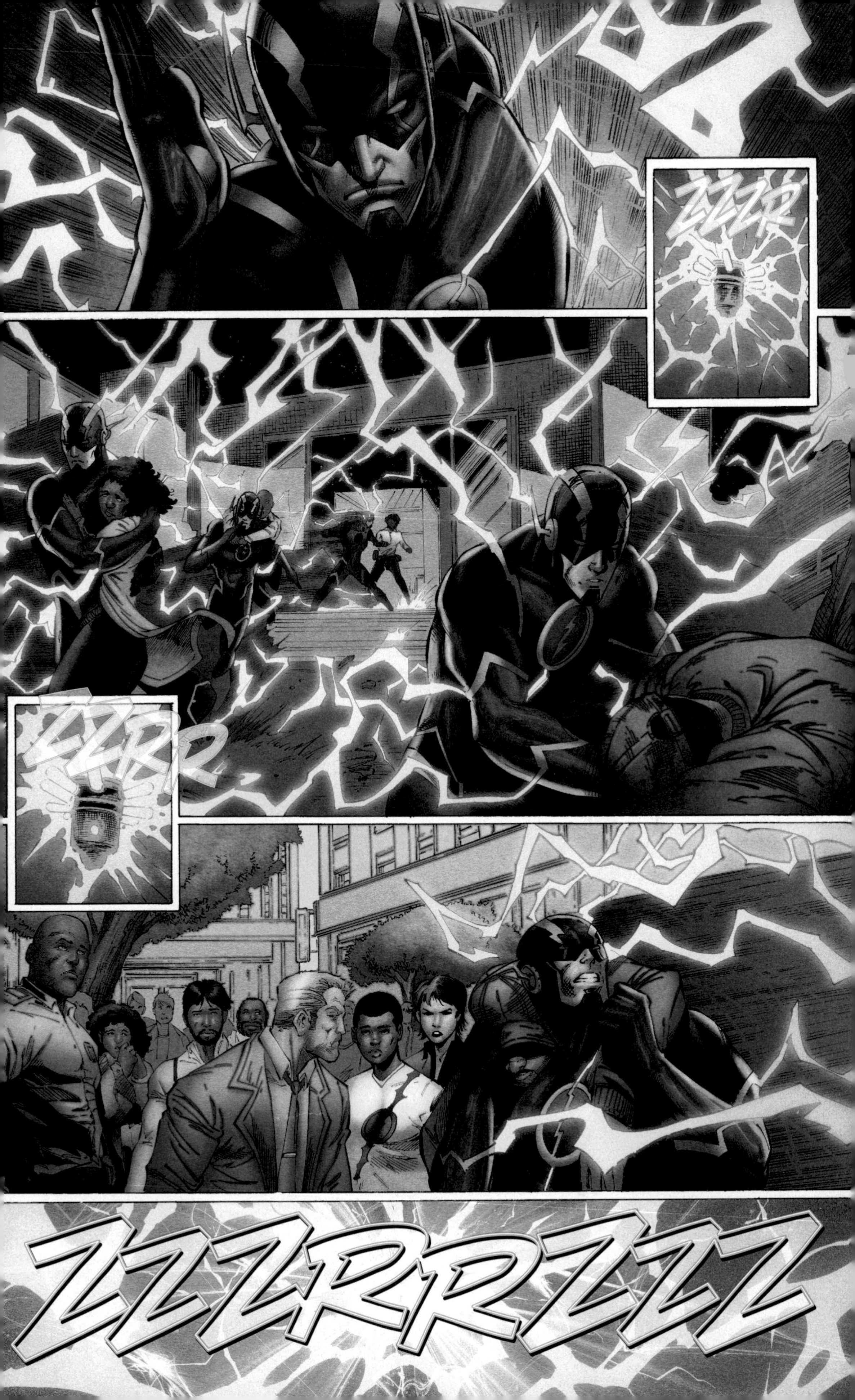
ZZZR
ZZRR
ZZZRRZZZ

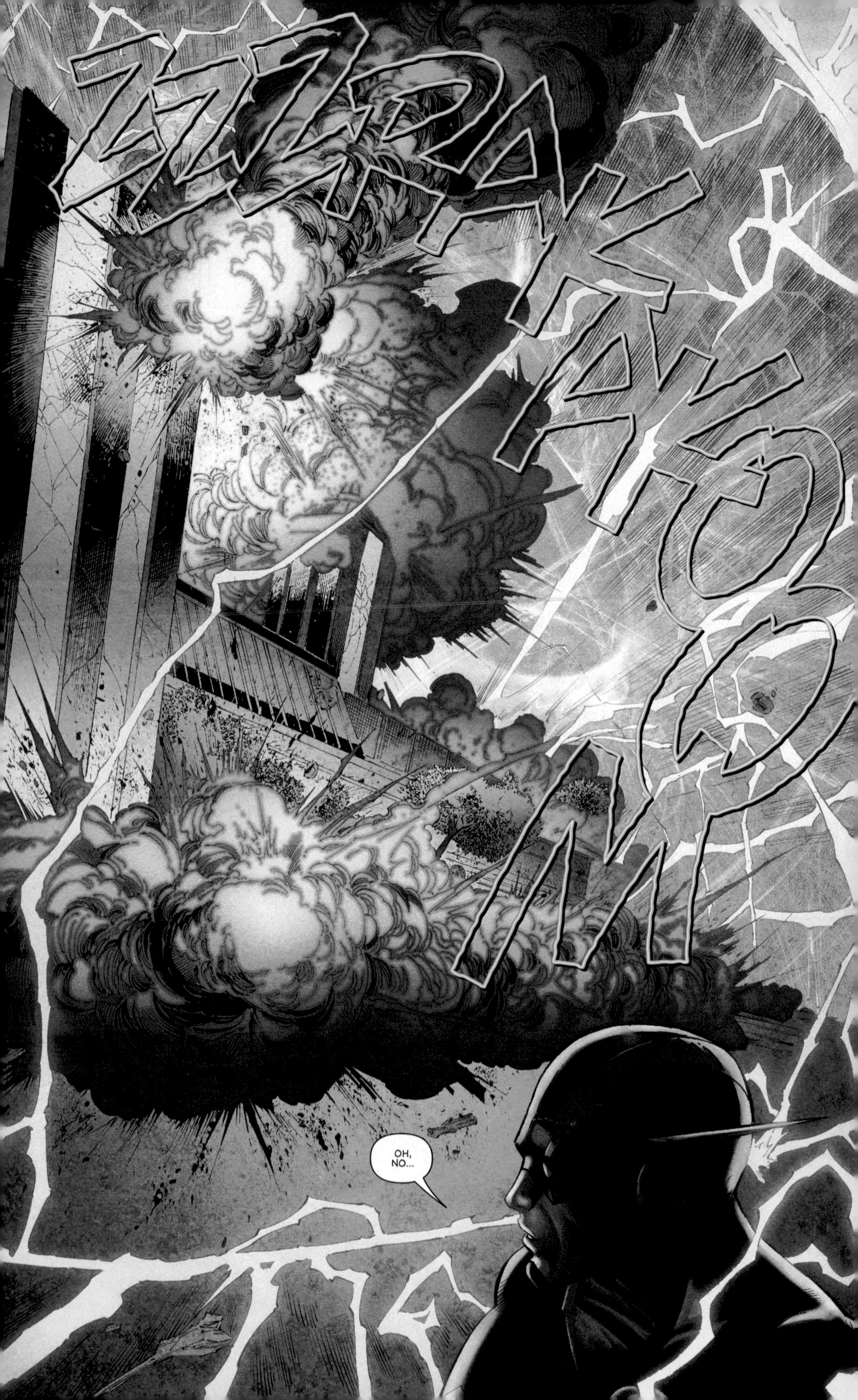
OH, NO...

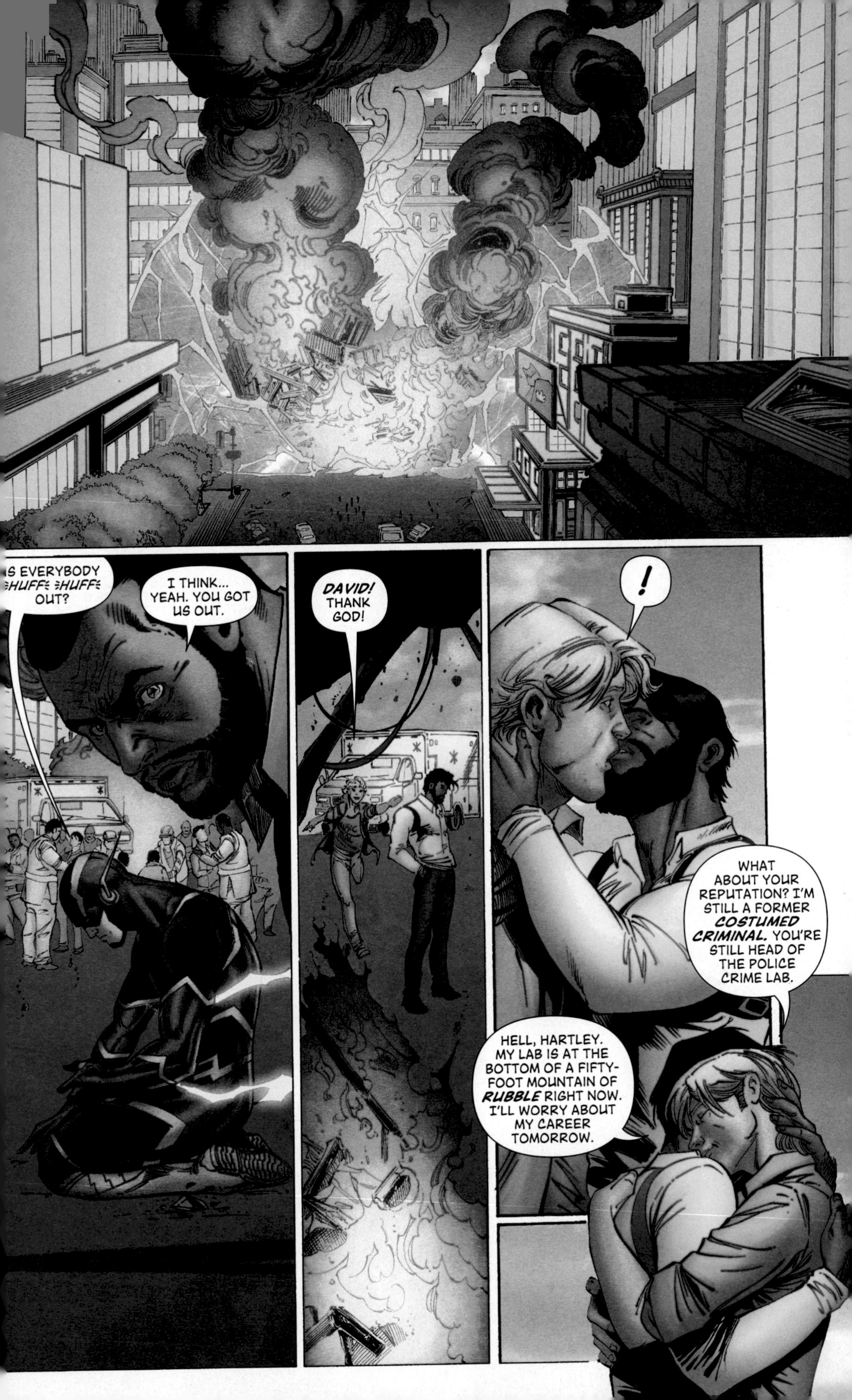

IS EVERYBODY *HUFF* *HUFF* OUT?
I THINK... YEAH. YOU GOT US OUT.
DAVID! THANK GOD!
!
WHAT ABOUT YOUR REPUTATION? I'M STILL A FORMER COSTUMED CRIMINAL. YOU'RE STILL HEAD OF THE POLICE CRIME LAB.
HELL, HARTLEY. MY LAB IS AT THE BOTTOM OF A FIFTY-FOOT MOUNTAIN OF RUBBLE RIGHT NOW. I'LL WORRY ABOUT MY CAREER TOMORROW.

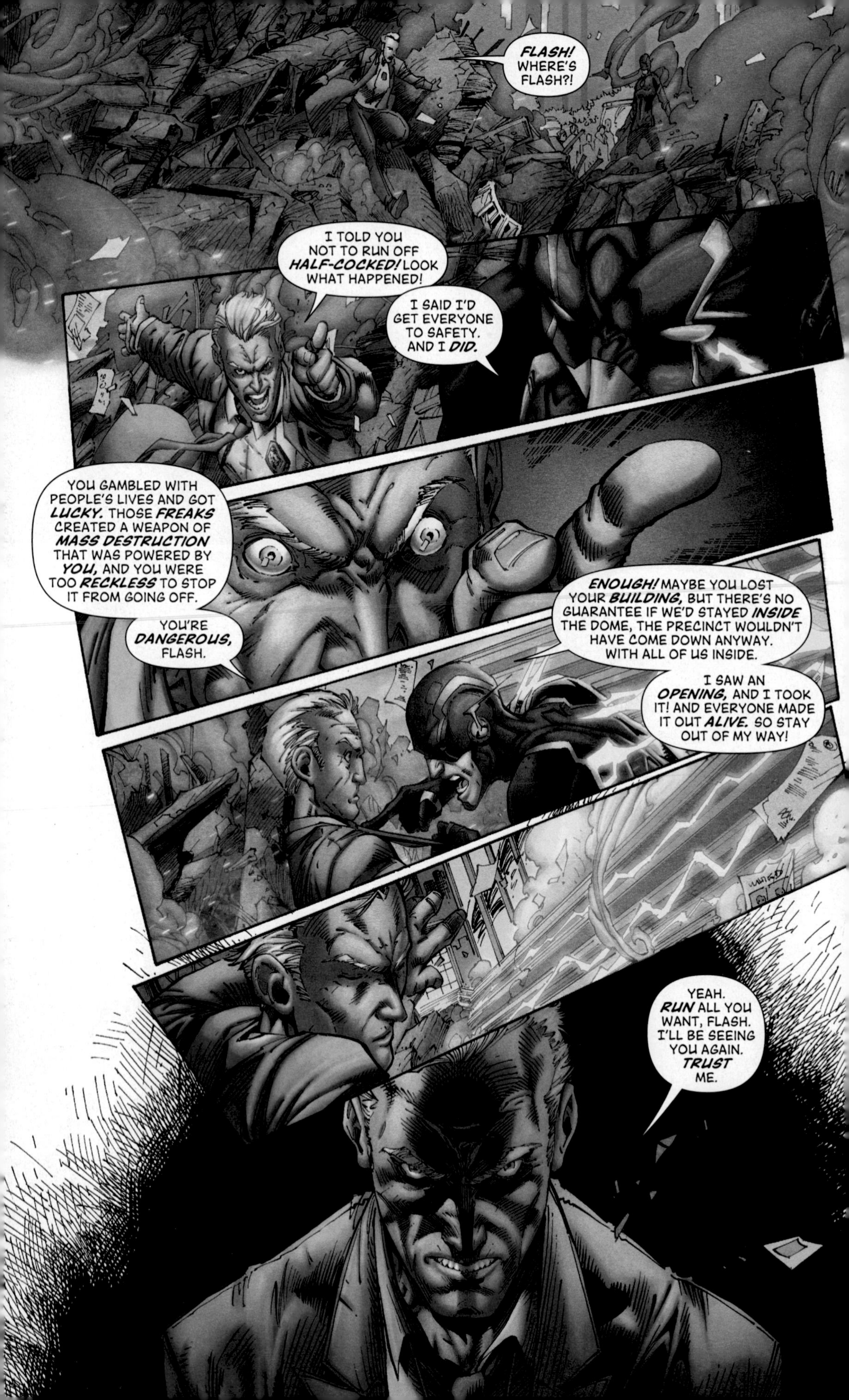
FLASH! WHERE'S FLASH?!
I TOLD YOU NOT TO RUN OFF HALF-COCKED! LOOK WHAT HAPPENED!
I SAID I'D GET EVERYONE TO SAFETY. AND I DID.
YOU GAMBLED WITH PEOPLE'S LIVES AND GOT LUCKY. THOSE FREAKS CREATED A WEAPON OF MASS DESTRUCTION THAT WAS POWERED BY YOU, AND YOU WERE TOO RECKLESS TO STOP IT FROM GOING OFF.
YOU'RE DANGEROUS, FLASH.
ENOUGH! MAYBE YOU LOST YOUR BUILDING, BUT THERE'S NO GUARANTEE IF WE'D STAYED INSIDE THE DOME, THE PRECINCT WOULDN'T HAVE COME DOWN ANYWAY. WITH ALL OF US INSIDE.
I SAW AN OPENING, AND I TOOK IT! AND EVERYONE MADE IT OUT ALIVE. SO STAY OUT OF MY WAY!
YEAH. RUN ALL YOU WANT, FLASH. I'LL BE SEEING YOU AGAIN. TRUST ME.

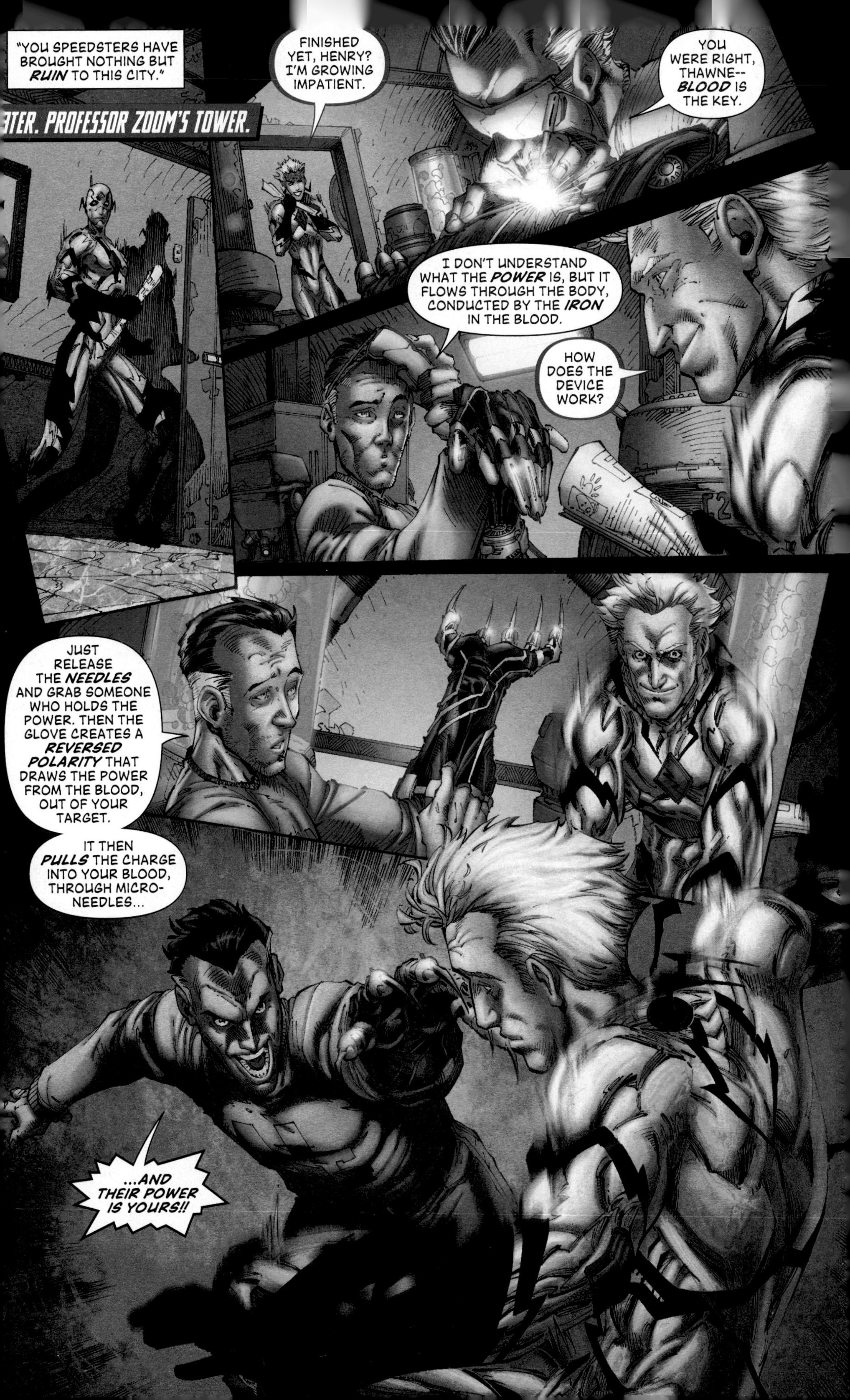
"YOU SPEEDSTERS HAVE BROUGHT NOTHING BUT RUIN TO THIS CITY."
FINISHED YET, HENRY? I'M GROWING IMPATIENT.
YOU WERE RIGHT, THAWNE-- BLOOD IS THE KEY.
...TER. PROFESSOR ZOOM'S TOWER.
I DON'T UNDERSTAND WHAT THE POWER IS, BUT IT FLOWS THROUGH THE BODY, CONDUCTED BY THE IRON IN THE BLOOD.
HOW DOES THE DEVICE WORK?
JUST RELEASE THE NEEDLES AND GRAB SOMEONE WHO HOLDS THE POWER. THEN THE GLOVE CREATES A REVERSED POLARITY THAT DRAWS THE POWER FROM THE BLOOD, OUT OF YOUR TARGET.
IT THEN PULLS THE CHARGE INTO YOUR BLOOD, THROUGH MICRO-NEEDLES...
...AND THEIR POWER IS YOURS!!

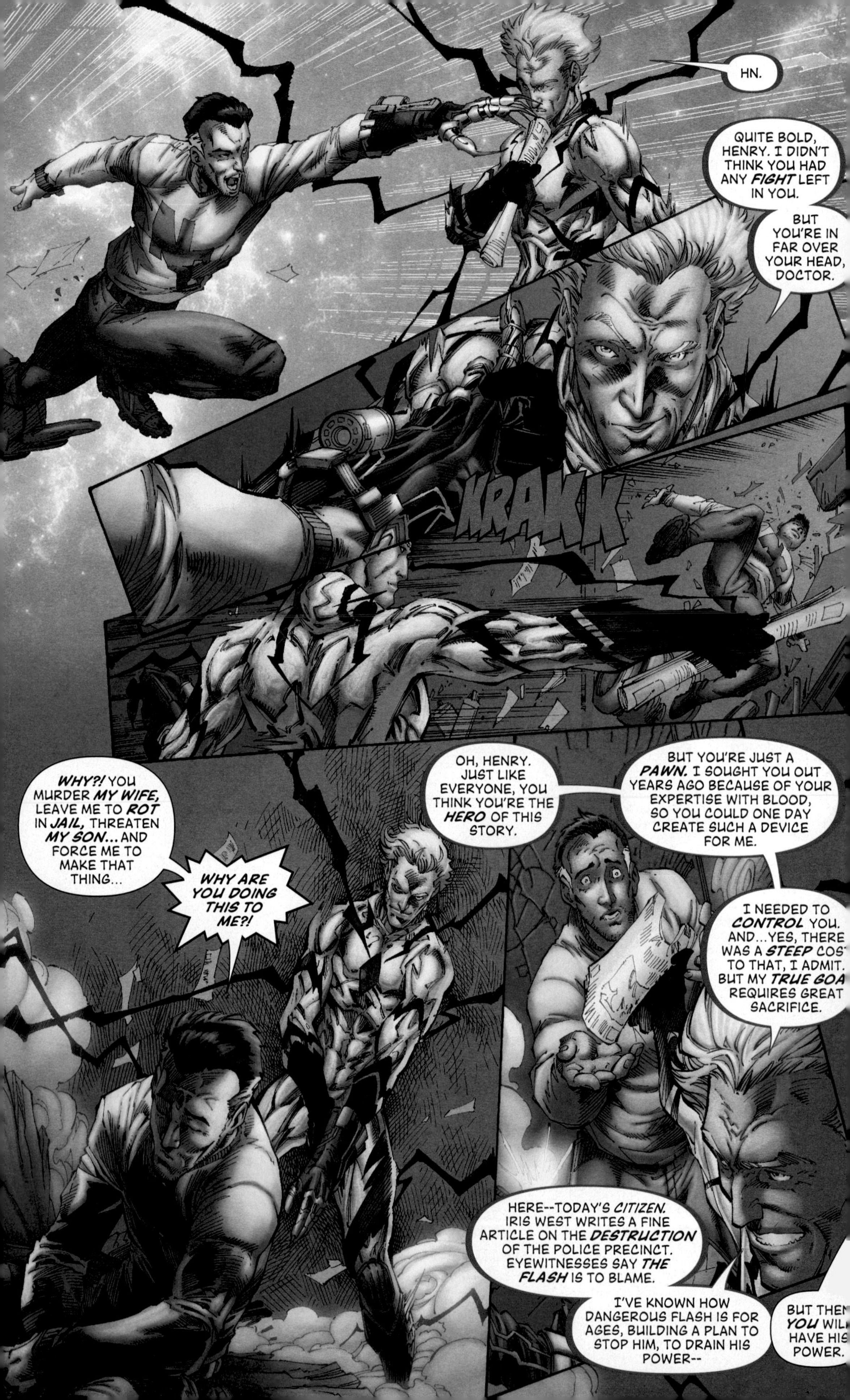
HN.
QUITE BOLD, HENRY. I DIDN'T THINK YOU HAD ANY FIGHT LEFT IN YOU.
BUT YOU'RE IN FAR OVER YOUR HEAD, DOCTOR.
KRAKK
WHY?! YOU MURDER MY WIFE, LEAVE ME TO ROT IN JAIL, THREATEN MY SON... AND FORCE ME TO MAKE THAT THING...
WHY ARE YOU DOING THIS TO ME?!
OH, HENRY. JUST LIKE EVERYONE, YOU THINK YOU'RE THE HERO OF THIS STORY.
BUT YOU'RE JUST A PAWN. I SOUGHT YOU OUT YEARS AGO BECAUSE OF YOUR EXPERTISE WITH BLOOD, SO YOU COULD ONE DAY CREATE SUCH A DEVICE FOR ME.
I NEEDED TO CONTROL YOU. AND...YES, THERE WAS A STEEP COS TO THAT, I ADMIT. BUT MY TRUE GOA REQUIRES GREAT SACRIFICE.
HERE--TODAY'S CITIZEN. IRIS WEST WRITES A FINE ARTICLE ON THE DESTRUCTION OF THE POLICE PRECINCT. EYEWITNESSES SAY THE FLASH IS TO BLAME.
I'VE KNOWN HOW DANGEROUS FLASH IS FOR AGES, BUILDING A PLAN TO STOP HIM, TO DRAIN HIS POWER--
BUT THEN YOU WIL HAVE HIS POWER.

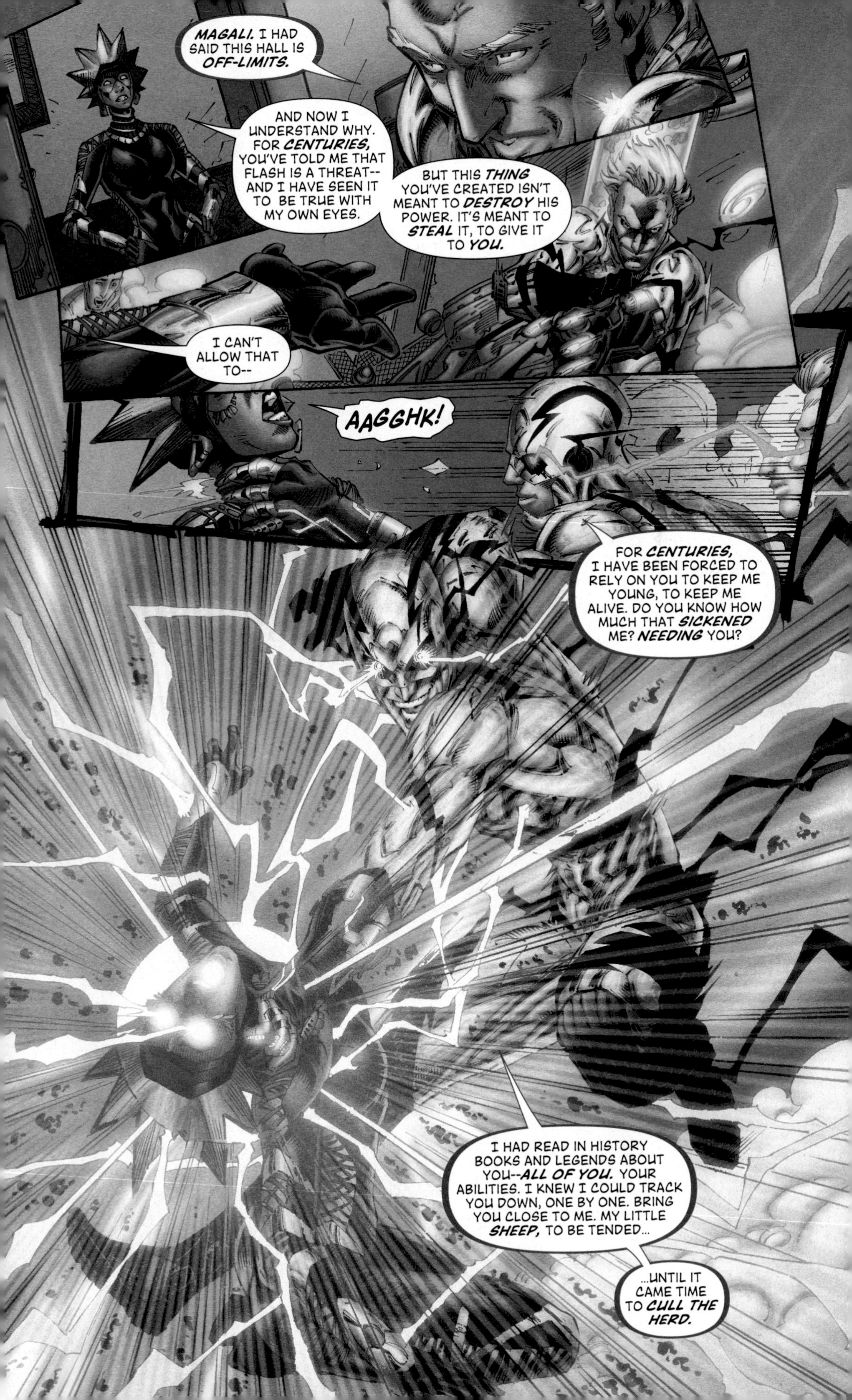
MAGALI. I HAD SAID THIS HALL IS OFF-LIMITS.
AND NOW I UNDERSTAND WHY. FOR CENTURIES, YOU'VE TOLD ME THAT FLASH IS A THREAT-- AND I HAVE SEEN IT TO BE TRUE WITH MY OWN EYES.
BUT THIS THING YOU'VE CREATED ISN'T MEANT TO DESTROY HIS POWER. IT'S MEANT TO STEAL IT, TO GIVE IT TO YOU.
I CAN'T ALLOW THAT TO--
AAGGHK!
FOR CENTURIES, I HAVE BEEN FORCED TO RELY ON YOU TO KEEP ME YOUNG, TO KEEP ME ALIVE. DO YOU KNOW HOW MUCH THAT SICKENED ME? NEEDING YOU?
I HAD READ IN HISTORY BOOKS AND LEGENDS ABOUT YOU--ALL OF YOU. YOUR ABILITIES. I KNEW I COULD TRACK YOU DOWN, ONE BY ONE. BRING YOU CLOSE TO ME. MY LITTLE SHEEP, TO BE TENDED...
...UNTIL IT CAME TIME TO CULL THE HERD.

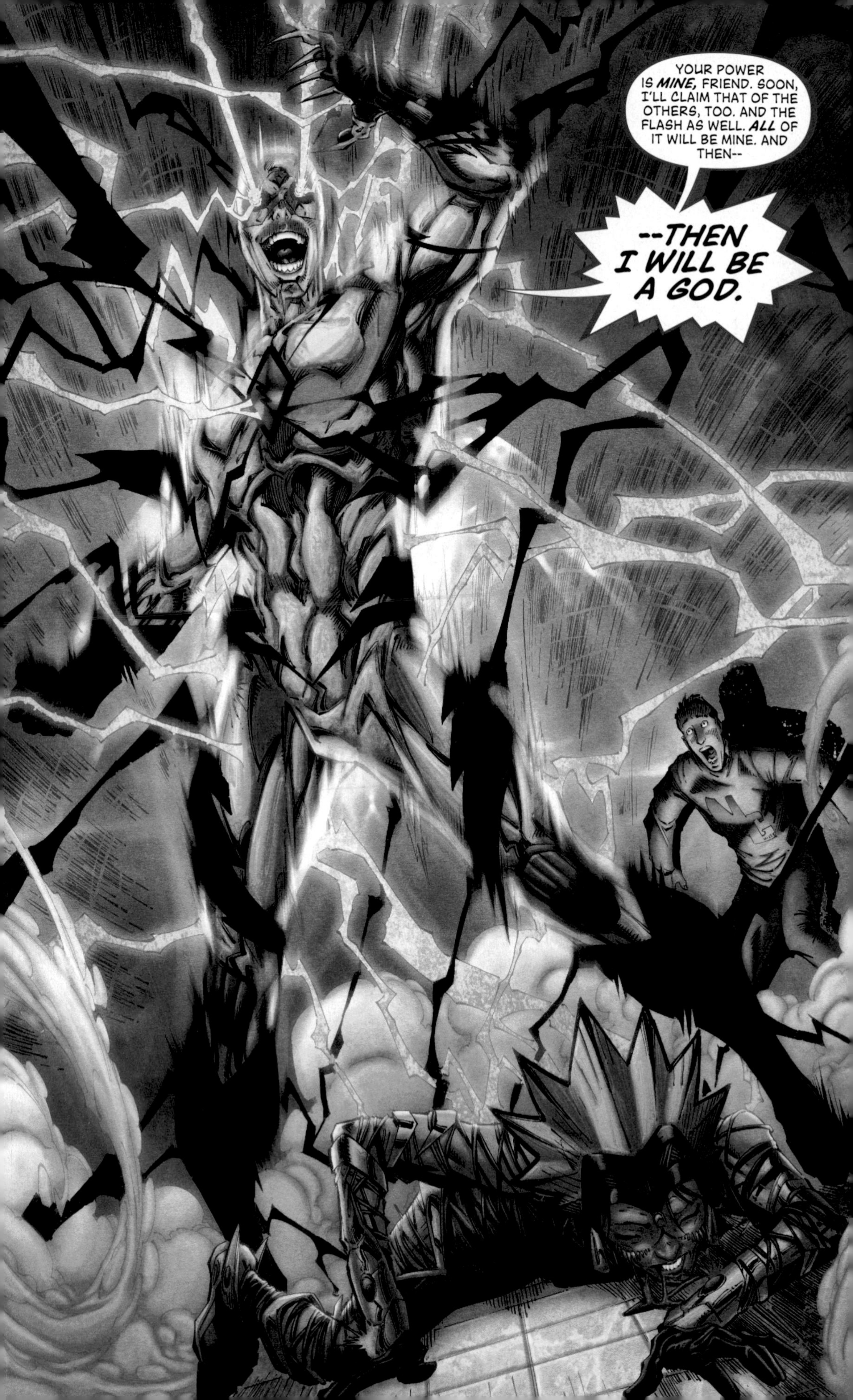
YOUR POWER IS MINE, FRIEND. SOON, I'LL CLAIM THAT OF THE OTHERS, TOO. AND THE FLASH AS WELL. ALL OF IT WILL BE MINE. AND THEN--
--THEN I WILL BE A GOD.

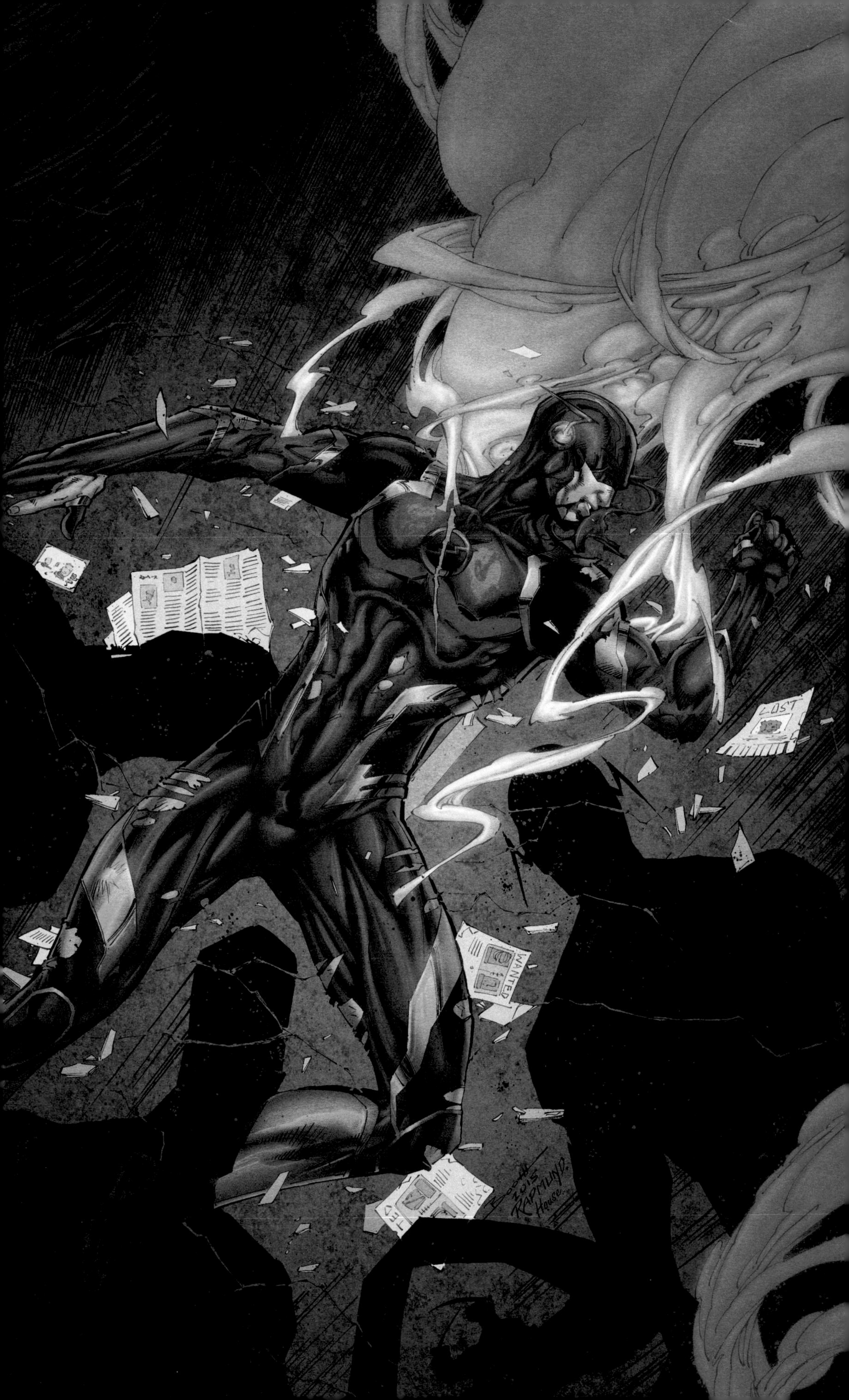
LOST
WANTED

END OF THE HUNT

ROBERT VENDITTI, VAN JENSEN writers BRETT BOOTH penciller NORM RAPMUND inker ANDREW DALHOUSE colorist PAT BROSSEAU letterer
cover by BRETT BOOTH, NORM RAPMUND, ANDREW DALHOUSE

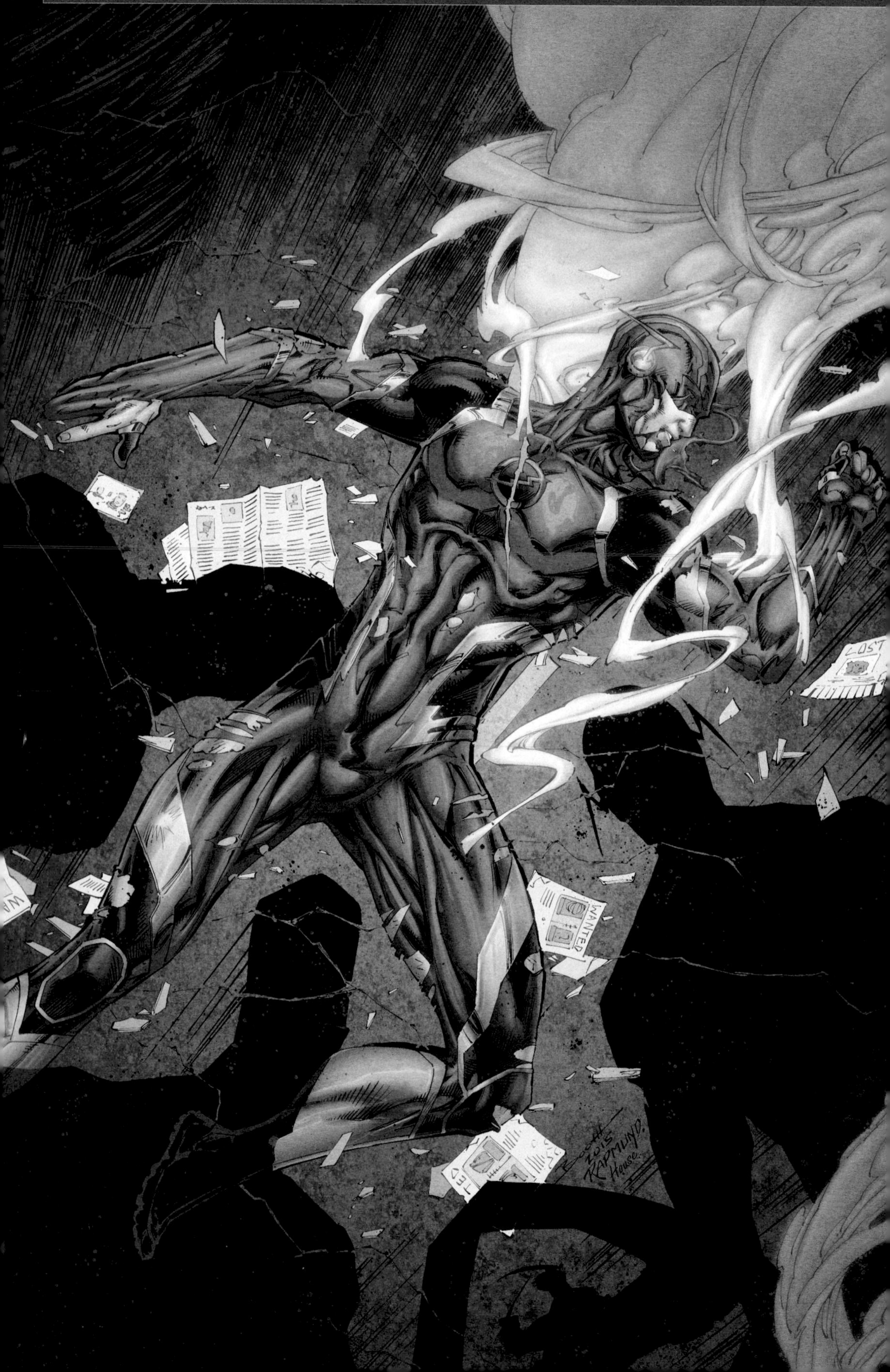
LOST
WANTED

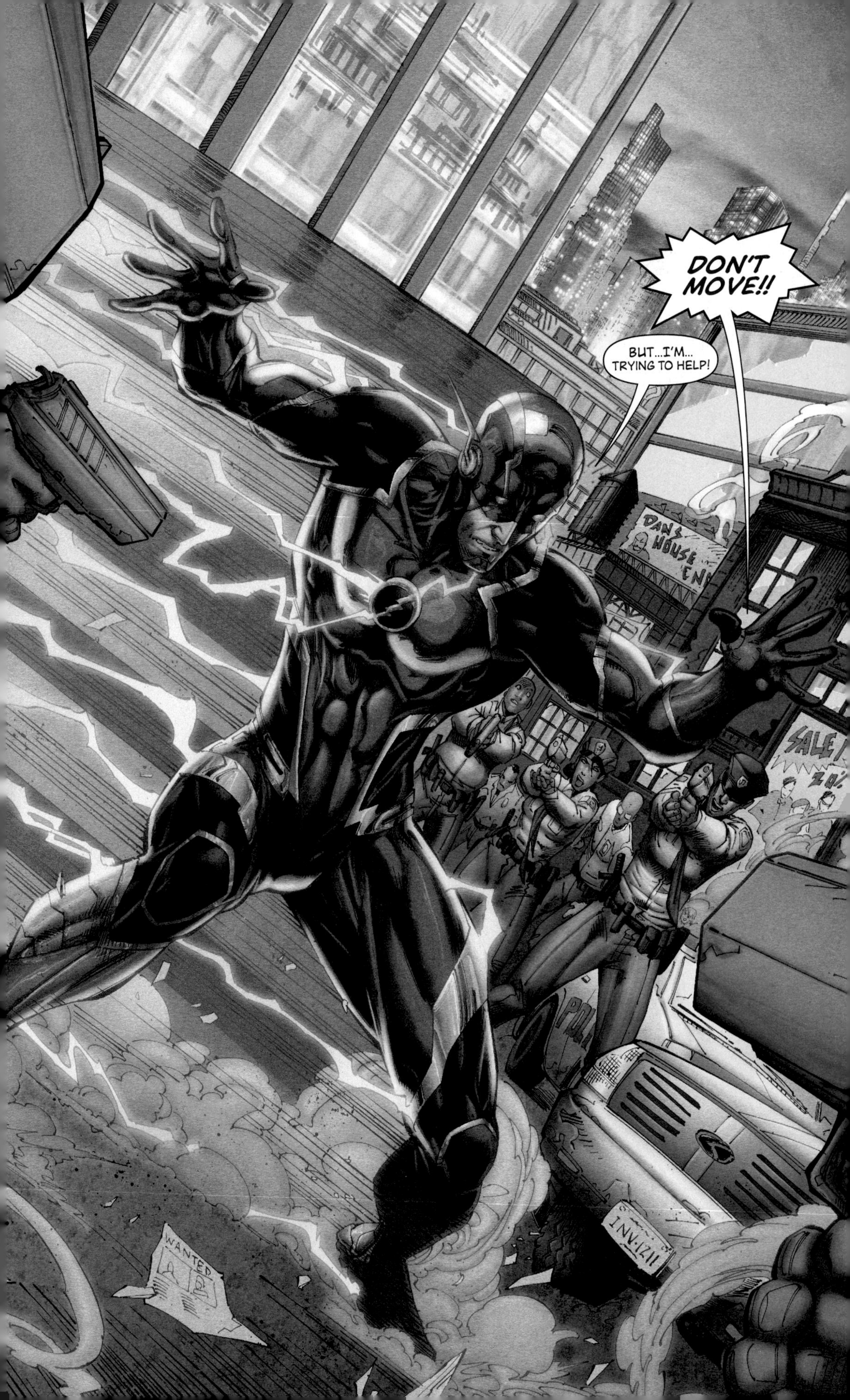
DON'T MOVE!!
BUT...I'M... TRYING TO HELP!
WANTED

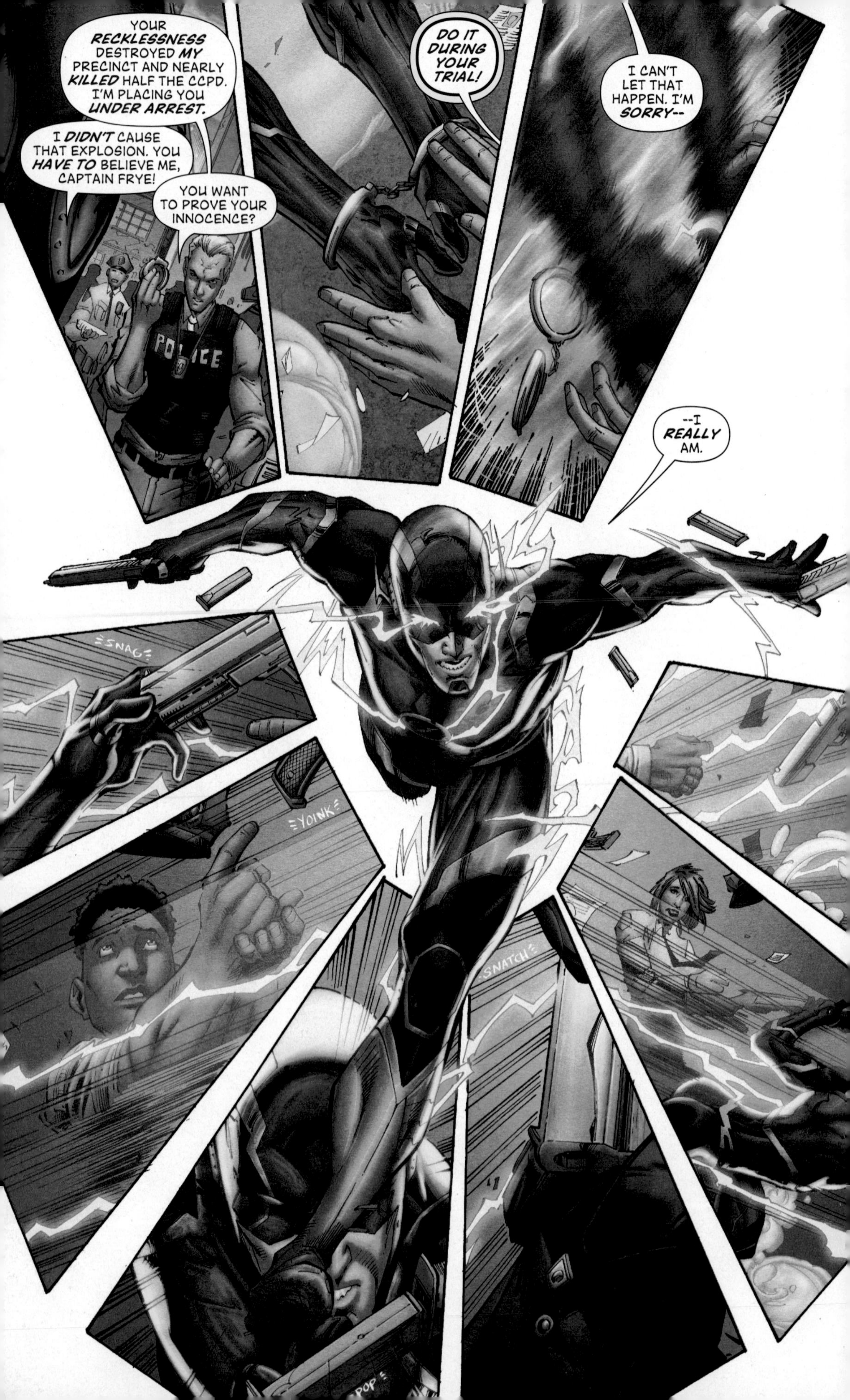
YOUR RECKLESSNESS DESTROYED MY PRECINCT AND NEARLY KILLED HALF THE CCPD. I'M PLACING YOU UNDER ARREST.
I DIDN'T CAUSE THAT EXPLOSION. YOU HAVE TO BELIEVE ME, CAPTAIN FRYE!
YOU WANT TO PROVE YOUR INNOCENCE?
POLICE
DO IT DURING YOUR TRIAL!
I CAN'T LET THAT HAPPEN. I'M SORRY--
--I REALLY AM.
SNAG
YOINK
SNATCH
POP

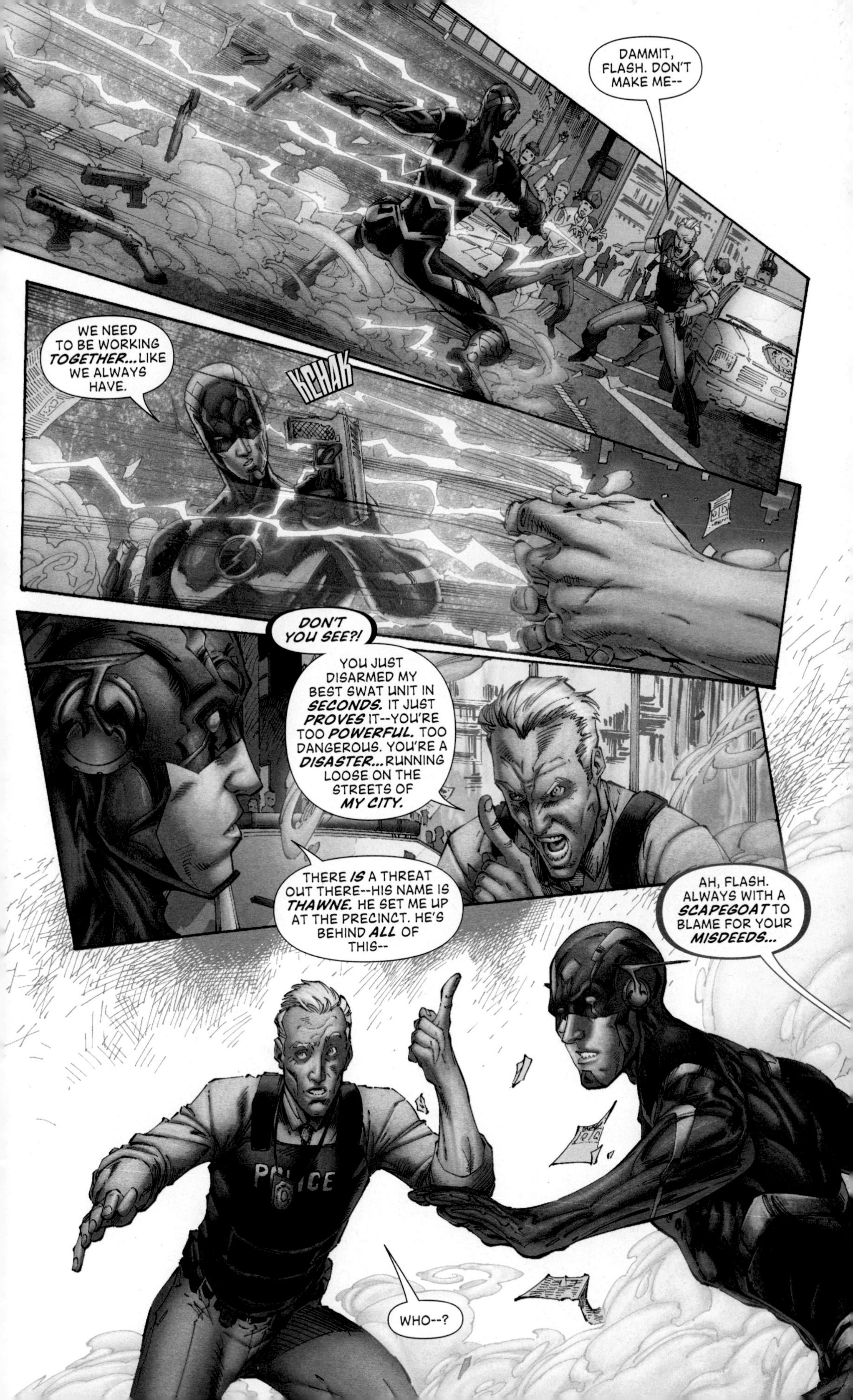

DAMMIT, FLASH. DON'T MAKE ME--
WE NEED TO BE WORKING TOGETHER...LIKE WE ALWAYS HAVE.
KCHAK
DON'T YOU SEE?!
YOU JUST DISARMED MY BEST SWAT UNIT IN SECONDS. IT JUST PROVES IT--YOU'RE TOO POWERFUL. TOO DANGEROUS. YOU'RE A DISASTER...RUNNING LOOSE ON THE STREETS OF MY CITY.
THERE IS A THREAT OUT THERE--HIS NAME IS THAWNE. HE SET ME UP AT THE PRECINCT. HE'S BEHIND ALL OF THIS--
AH, FLASH. ALWAYS WITH A SCAPEGOAT TO BLAME FOR YOUR MISDEEDS...
POLICE
WHO--?

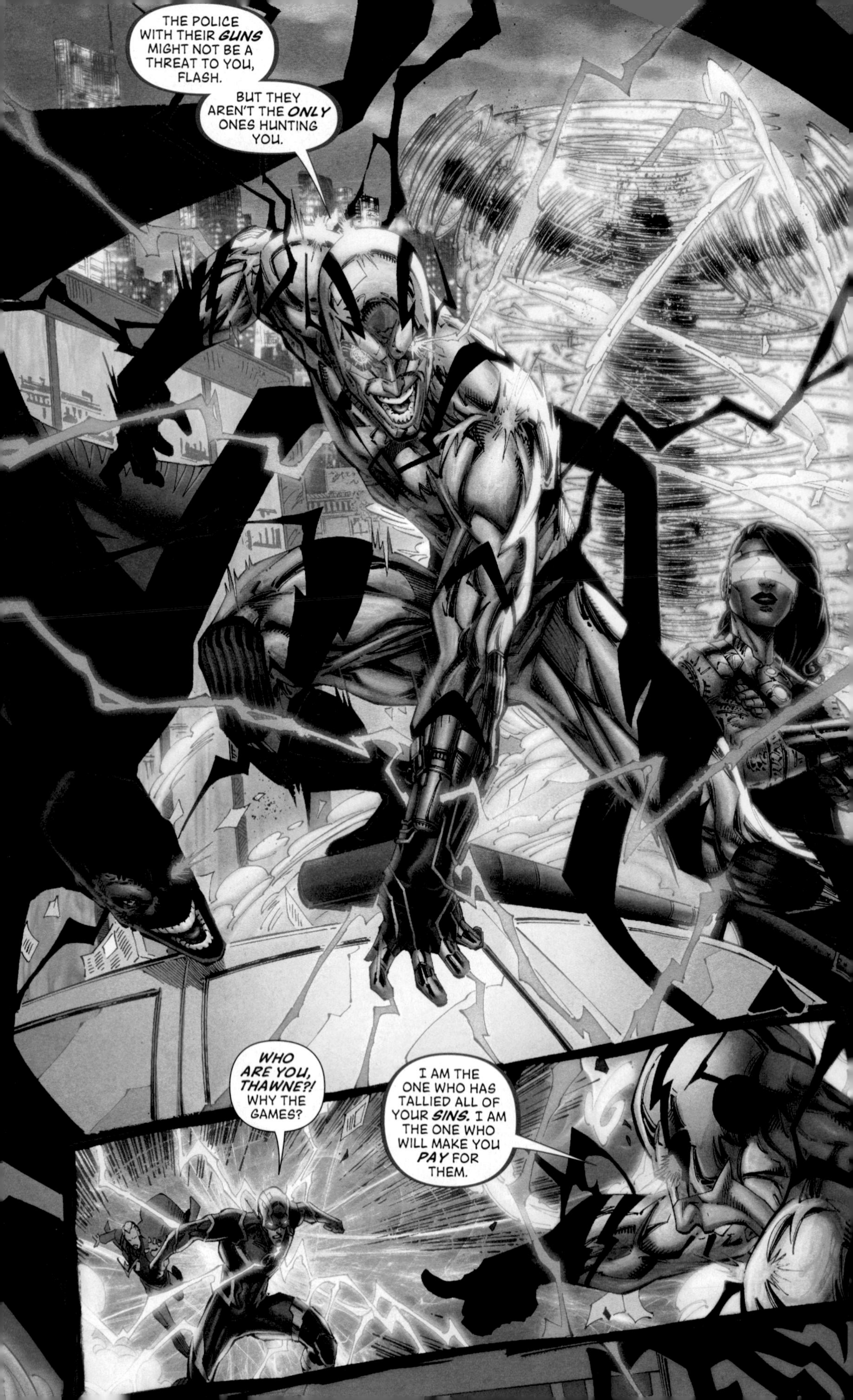
THE POLICE WITH THEIR GUNS MIGHT NOT BE A THREAT TO YOU, FLASH.
BUT THEY AREN'T THE ONLY ONES HUNTING YOU.
WHO ARE YOU, THAWNE?! WHY THE GAMES?
I AM THE ONE WHO HAS TALLIED ALL OF YOUR SINS. I AM THE ONE WHO WILL MAKE YOU PAY FOR THEM.

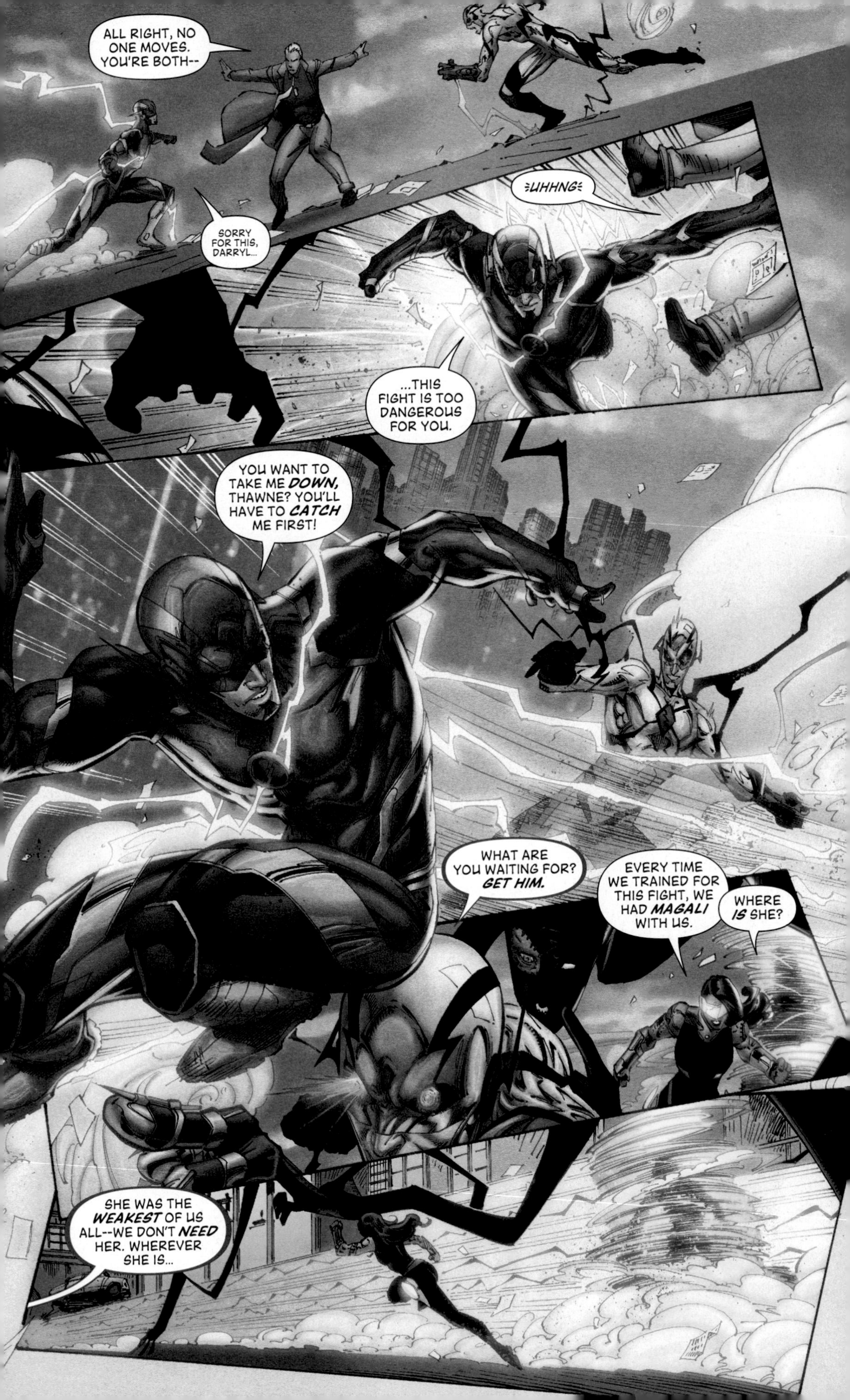
ALL RIGHT, NO ONE MOVES. YOU'RE BOTH--
SORRY FOR THIS, DARRYL...
UHHNG
...THIS FIGHT IS TOO DANGEROUS FOR YOU.
YOU WANT TO TAKE ME DOWN, THAWNE? YOU'LL HAVE TO CATCH ME FIRST!
WHAT ARE YOU WAITING FOR? GET HIM.
EVERY TIME WE TRAINED FOR THIS FIGHT, WE HAD MAGALI WITH US.
WHERE IS SHE?
SHE WAS THE WEAKEST OF US ALL--WE DON'T NEED HER. WHEREVER SHE IS...

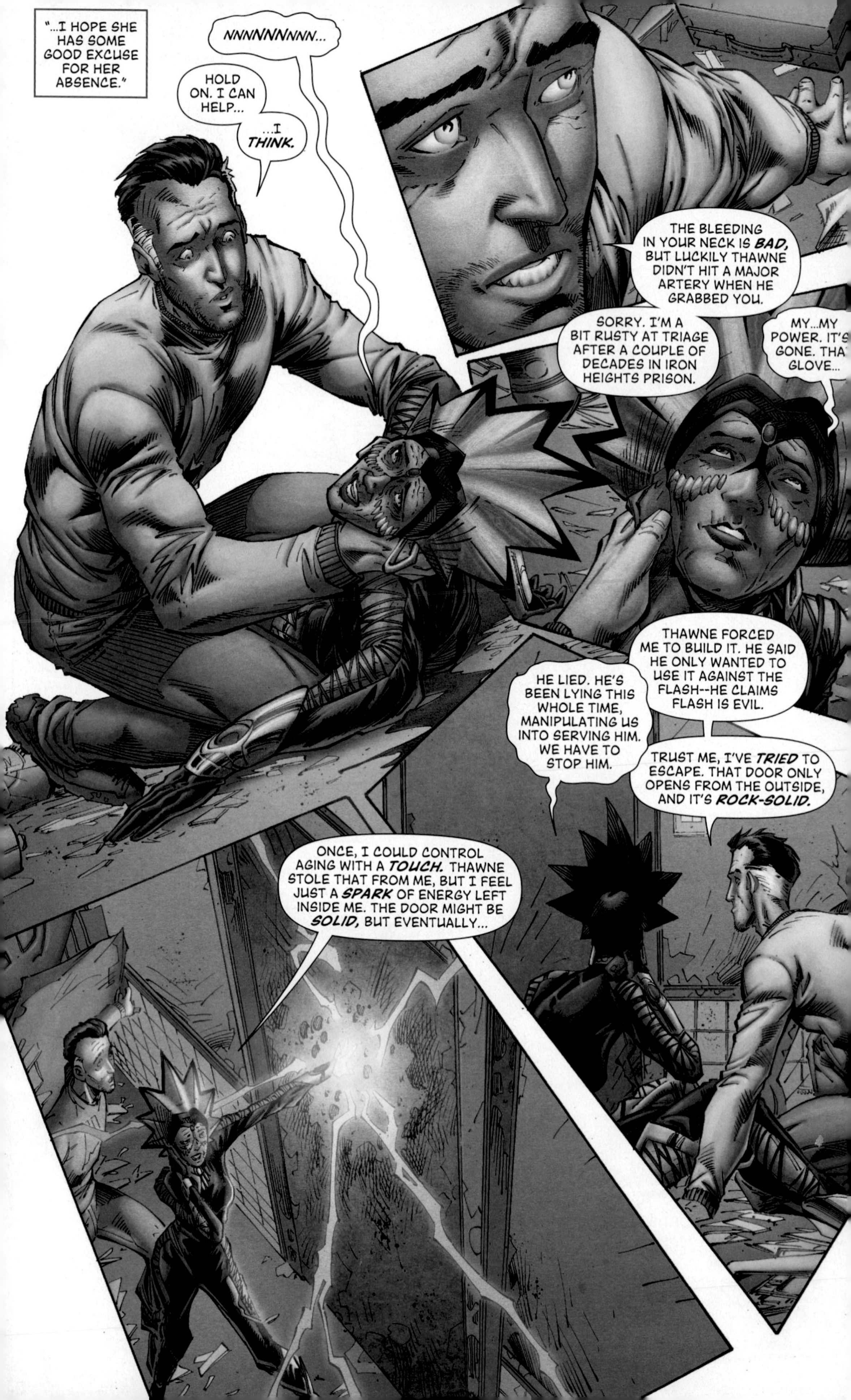
"...I HOPE SHE HAS SOME GOOD EXCUSE FOR HER ABSENCE."
NNNNNNNNN...
HOLD ON. I CAN HELP...
...I THINK.
THE BLEEDING IN YOUR NECK IS BAD, BUT LUCKILY THAWNE DIDN'T HIT A MAJOR ARTERY WHEN HE GRABBED YOU.
SORRY. I'M A BIT RUSTY AT TRIAGE AFTER A COUPLE OF DECADES IN IRON HEIGHTS PRISON.
MY...MY POWER. IT'S GONE. THAT GLOVE...
THAWNE FORCED ME TO BUILD IT. HE SAID HE ONLY WANTED TO USE IT AGAINST THE FLASH--HE CLAIMS FLASH IS EVIL.
HE LIED. HE'S BEEN LYING THIS WHOLE TIME, MANIPULATING US INTO SERVING HIM. WE HAVE TO STOP HIM.
TRUST ME, I'VE TRIED TO ESCAPE. THAT DOOR ONLY OPENS FROM THE OUTSIDE, AND IT'S ROCK-SOLID.
ONCE, I COULD CONTROL AGING WITH A TOUCH. THAWNE STOLE THAT FROM ME, BUT I FEEL JUST A SPARK OF ENERGY LEFT INSIDE ME. THE DOOR MIGHT BE SOLID, BUT EVENTUALLY...

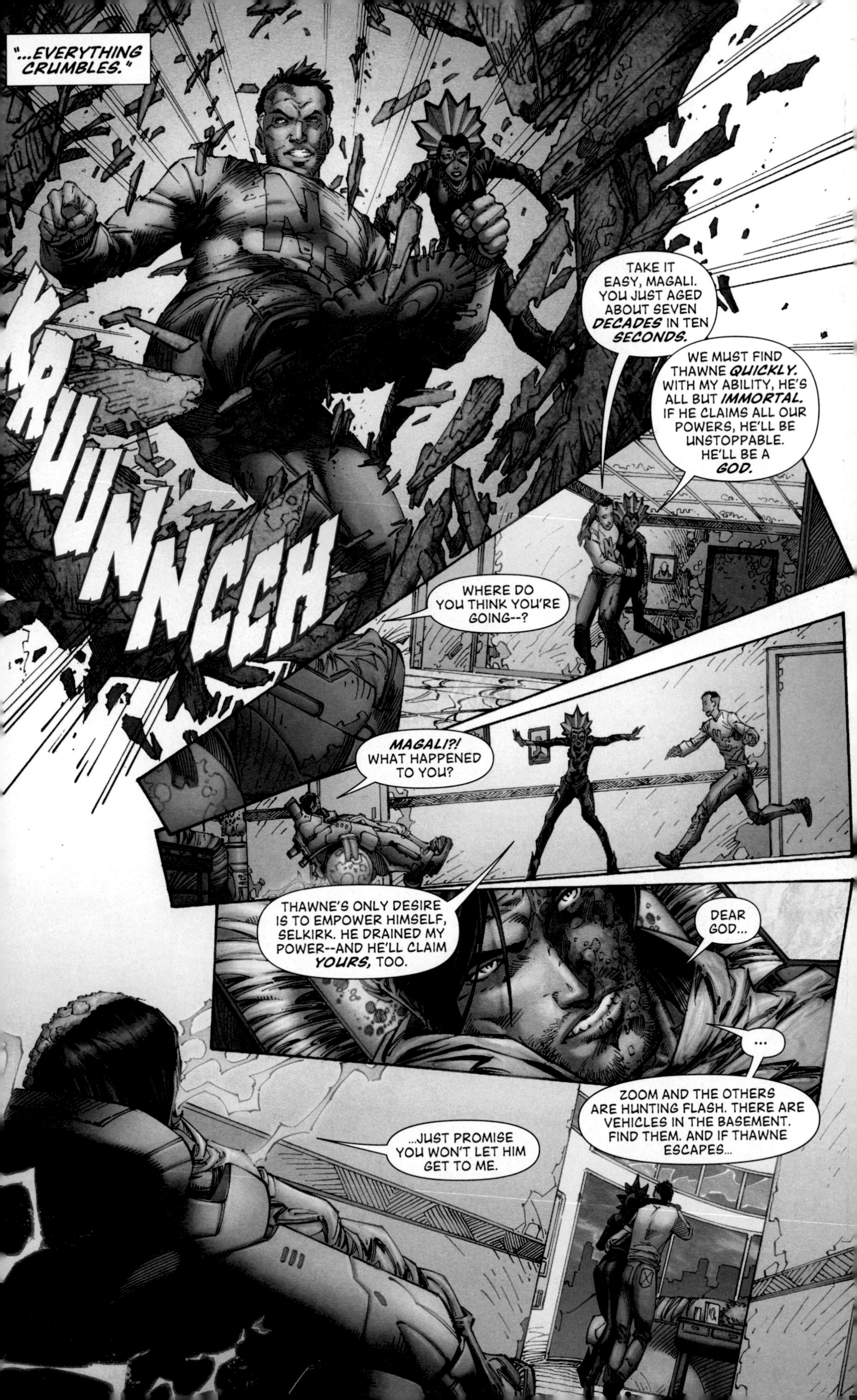
"...EVERYTHING CRUMBLES."
KRUUNNCCH
TAKE IT EASY, MAGALI. YOU JUST AGED ABOUT SEVEN DECADES IN TEN SECONDS.
WE MUST FIND THAWNE QUICKLY. WITH MY ABILITY, HE'S ALL BUT IMMORTAL. IF HE CLAIMS ALL OUR POWERS, HE'LL BE UNSTOPPABLE. HE'LL BE A GOD.
WHERE DO YOU THINK YOU'RE GOING--?
MAGALI?! WHAT HAPPENED TO YOU?
THAWNE'S ONLY DESIRE IS TO EMPOWER HIMSELF, SELKIRK. HE DRAINED MY POWER--AND HE'LL CLAIM YOURS, TOO.
DEAR GOD...
...
ZOOM AND THE OTHERS ARE HUNTING FLASH. THERE ARE VEHICLES IN THE BASEMENT. FIND THEM. AND IF THAWNE ESCAPES...
...JUST PROMISE YOU WON'T LET HIM GET TO ME.

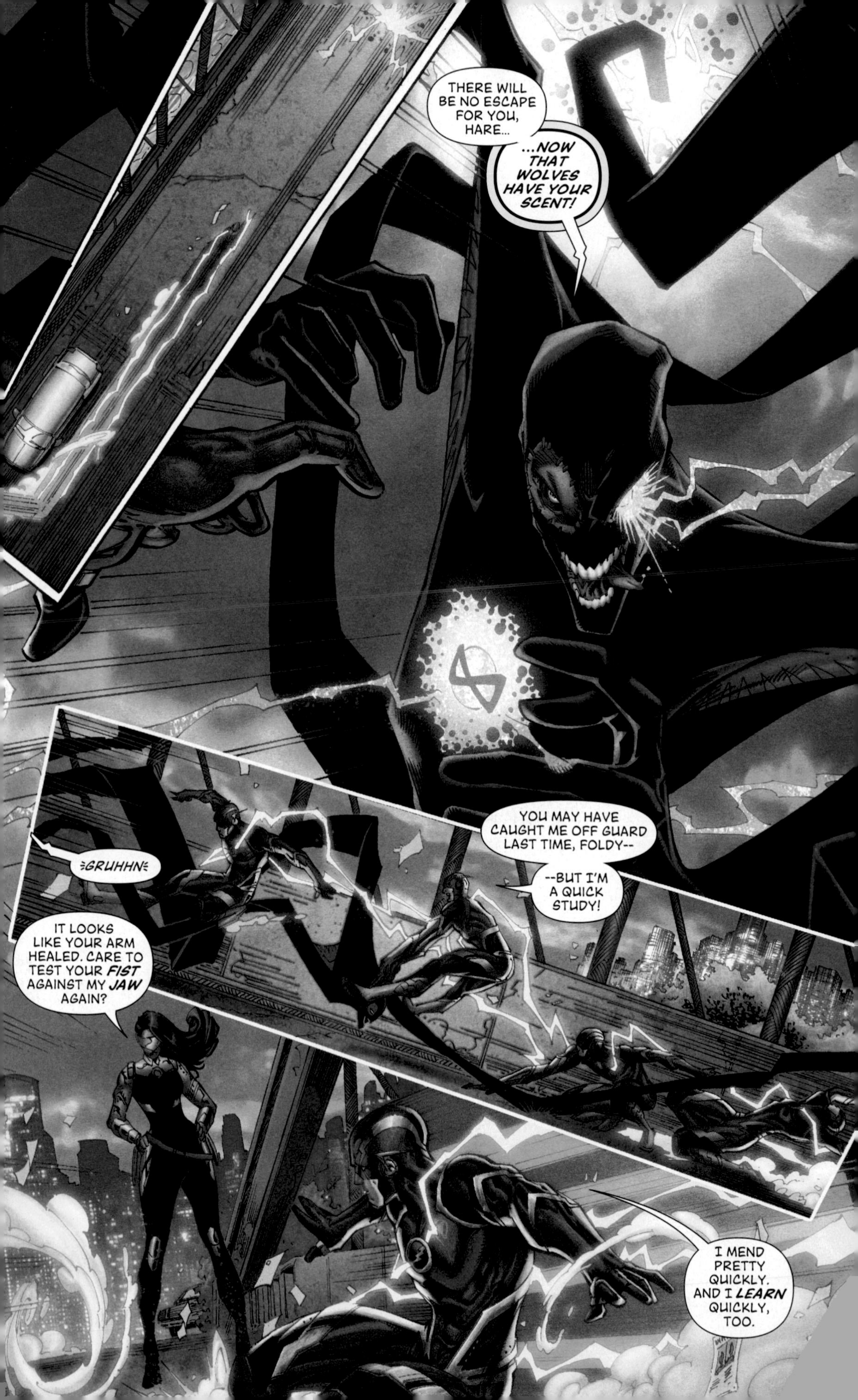
THERE WILL BE NO ESCAPE FOR YOU, HARE...
...NOW THAT WOLVES HAVE YOUR SCENT!
YOU MAY HAVE CAUGHT ME OFF GUARD LAST TIME, FOLDY--
--BUT I'M A QUICK STUDY!
GRUHHN
IT LOOKS LIKE YOUR ARM HEALED. CARE TO TEST YOUR FIST AGAINST MY JAW AGAIN?
I MEND PRETTY QUICKLY. AND I LEARN QUICKLY, TOO.

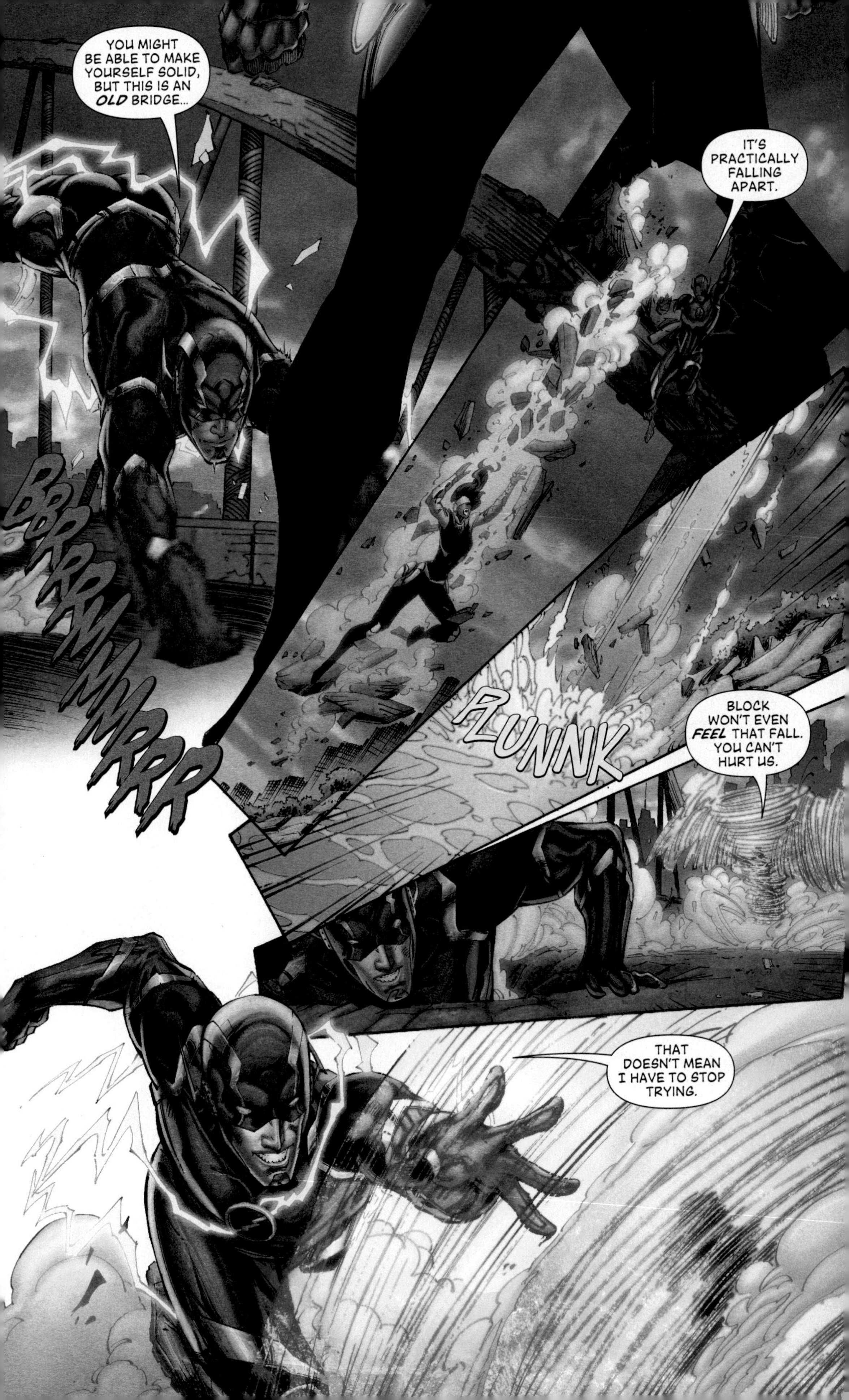
YOU MIGHT BE ABLE TO MAKE YOURSELF SOLID, BUT THIS IS AN OLD BRIDGE...
IT'S PRACTICALLY FALLING APART.
BBRRRMMMRRR
PLUNNK
BLOCK WON'T EVEN FEEL THAT FALL. YOU CAN'T HURT US.
THAT DOESN'T MEAN I HAVE TO STOP TRYING.

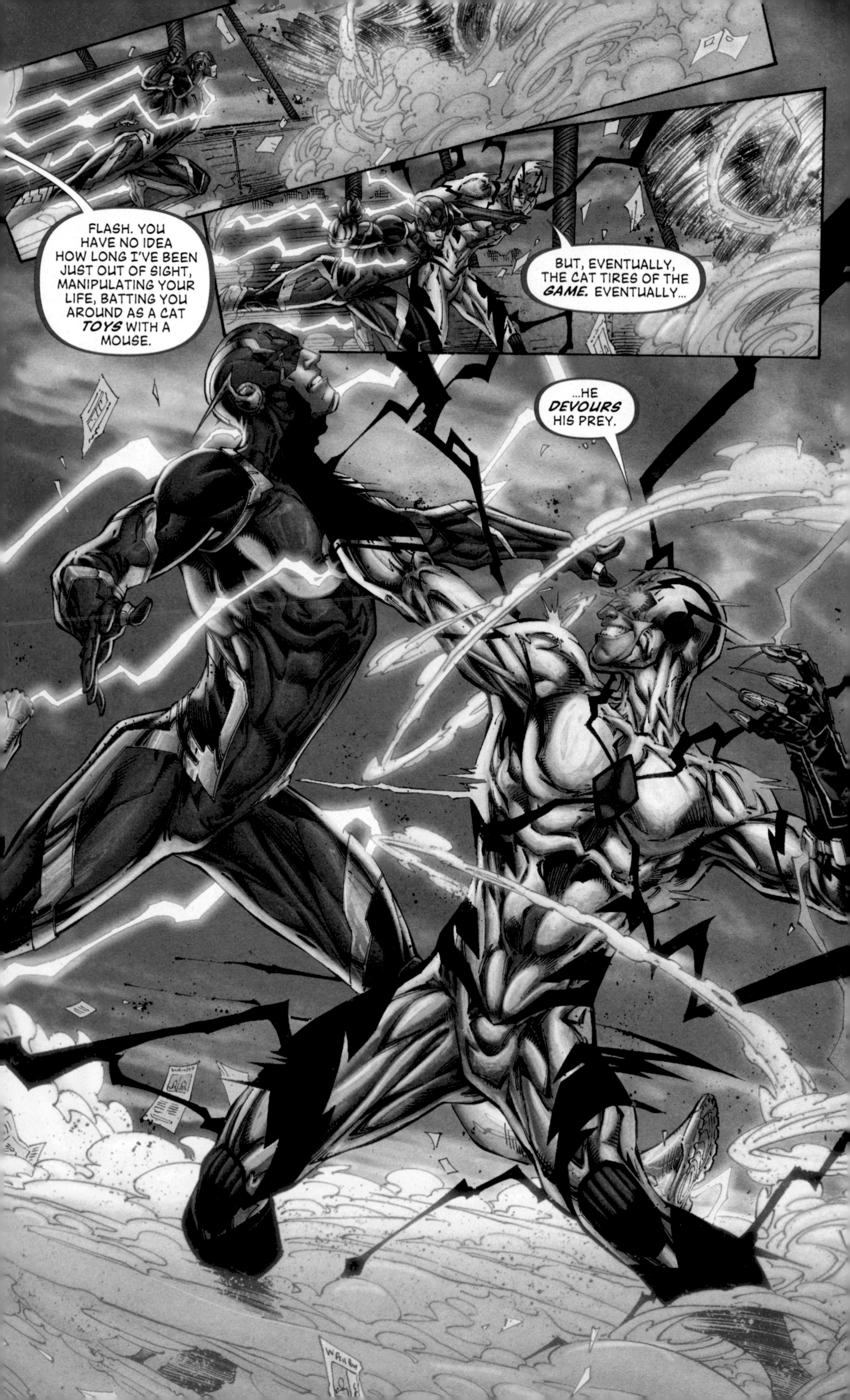
FLASH. YOU HAVE NO IDEA HOW LONG I'VE BEEN JUST OUT OF SIGHT, MANIPULATING YOUR LIFE, BATTING YOU AROUND AS A CAT *TOYS* WITH A MOUSE.
BUT, EVENTUALLY, THE CAT TIRES OF THE *GAME.* EVENTUALLY...
...HE *DEVOURS* HIS PREY.

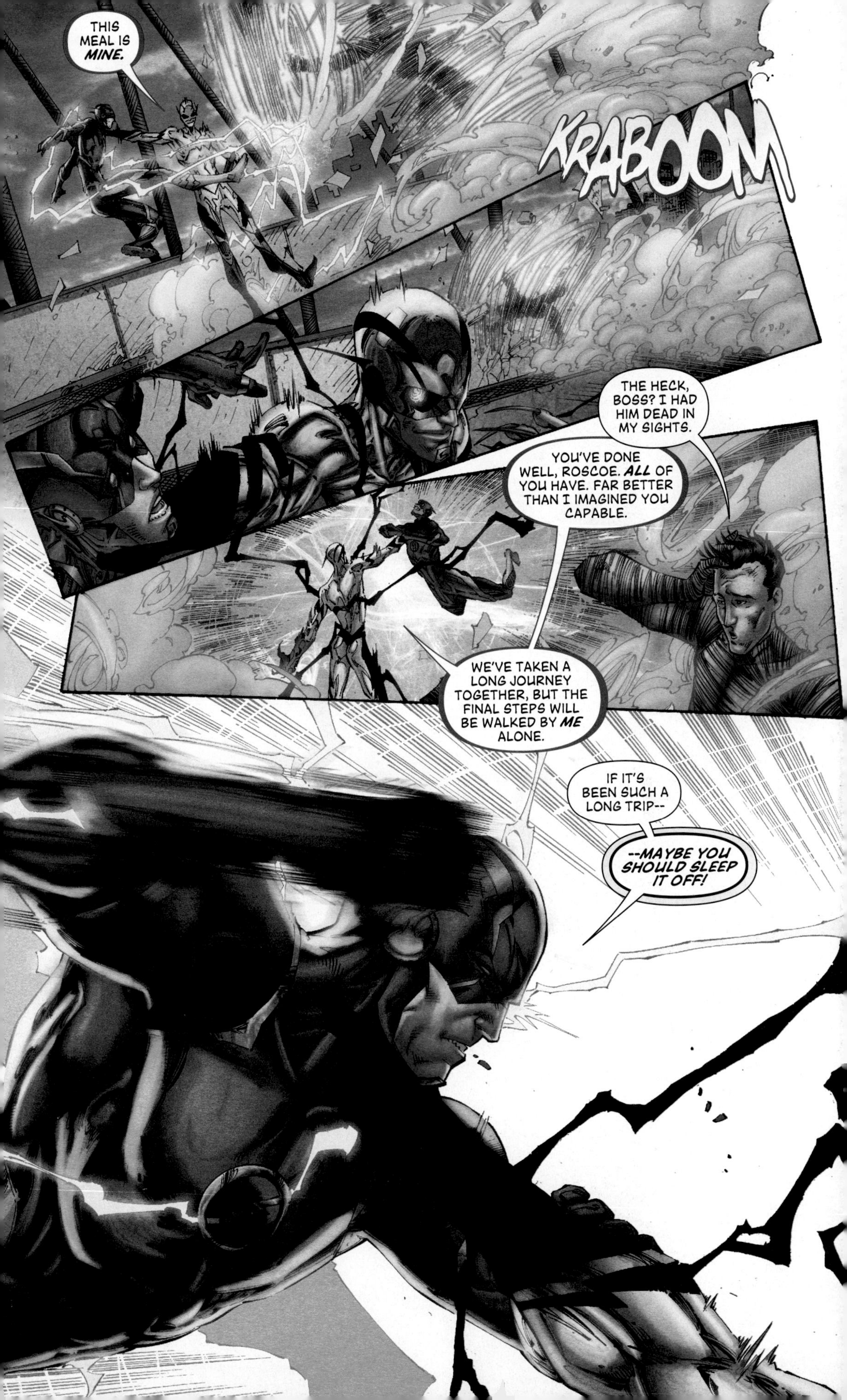
THIS MEAL IS *MINE.*
KRABOOM
THE HECK, BOSS? I HAD HIM DEAD IN MY SIGHTS.
YOU'VE DONE WELL, ROSCOE. *ALL* OF YOU HAVE. FAR BETTER THAN I IMAGINED YOU CAPABLE.
WE'VE TAKEN A LONG JOURNEY TOGETHER, BUT THE FINAL STEPS WILL BE WALKED BY *ME* ALONE.
IF IT'S BEEN SUCH A LONG TRIP--
--MAYBE YOU SHOULD SLEEP IT OFF!

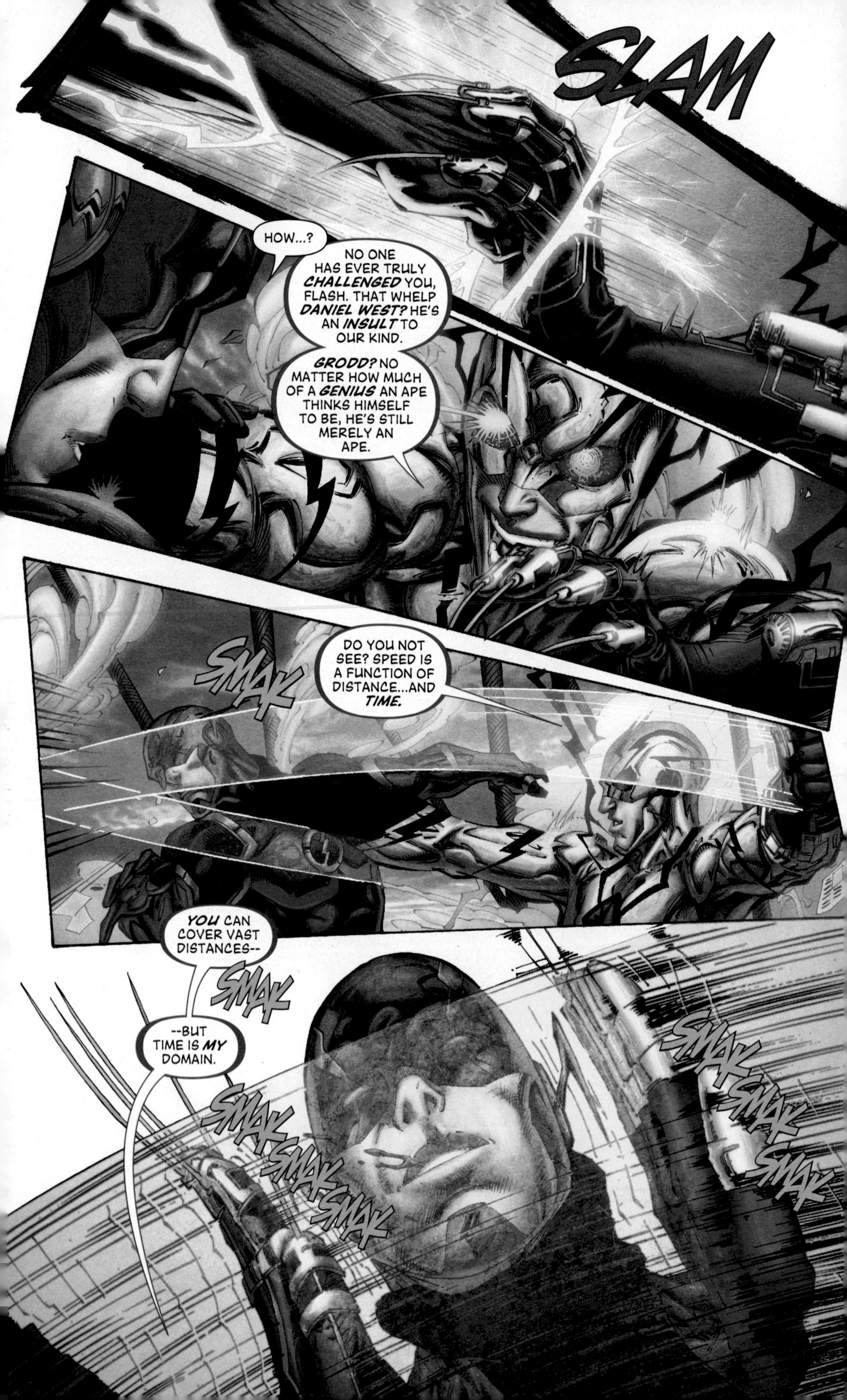
SLAM
HOW...?
NO ONE HAS EVER TRULY CHALLENGED YOU, FLASH. THAT WHELP DANIEL WEST? HE'S AN INSULT TO OUR KIND.
GRODD? NO MATTER HOW MUCH OF A GENIUS AN APE THINKS HIMSELF TO BE, HE'S STILL MERELY AN APE.
SMAK
DO YOU NOT SEE? SPEED IS A FUNCTION OF DISTANCE...AND TIME.
YOU CAN COVER VAST DISTANCES--
SMAK
--BUT TIME IS MY DOMAIN.
SMAK SMAK SMAK
SMAK SMAK SMAK

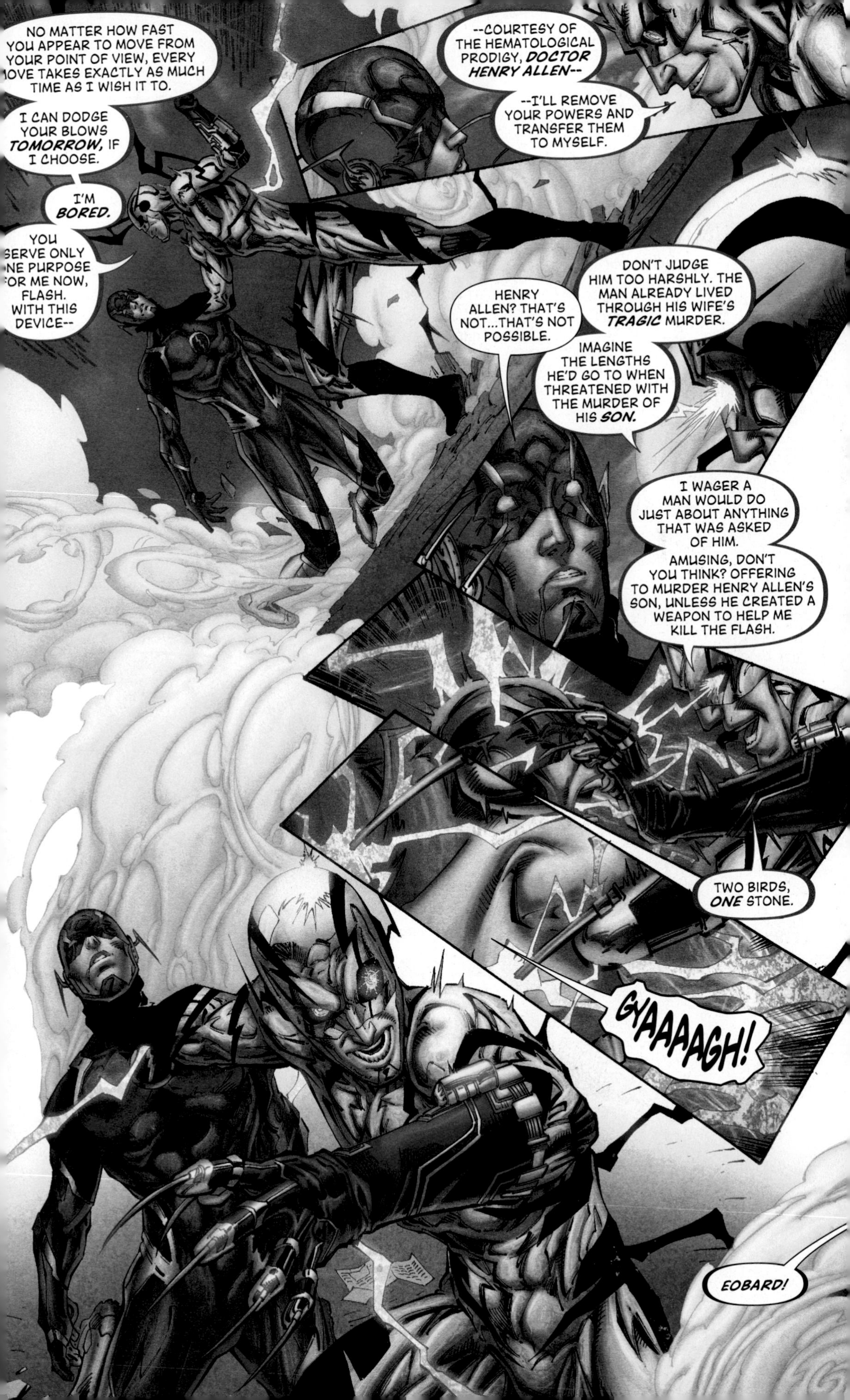

NO MATTER HOW FAST YOU APPEAR TO MOVE FROM YOUR POINT OF VIEW, EVERY MOVE TAKES EXACTLY AS MUCH TIME AS I WISH IT TO.
I CAN DODGE YOUR BLOWS TOMORROW, IF I CHOOSE.
I'M BORED.
YOU SERVE ONLY ONE PURPOSE FOR ME NOW, FLASH. WITH THIS DEVICE--
--COURTESY OF THE HEMATOLOGICAL PRODIGY, DOCTOR HENRY ALLEN--
--I'LL REMOVE YOUR POWERS AND TRANSFER THEM TO MYSELF.
HENRY ALLEN? THAT'S NOT...THAT'S NOT POSSIBLE.
DON'T JUDGE HIM TOO HARSHLY. THE MAN ALREADY LIVED THROUGH HIS WIFE'S TRAGIC MURDER.
IMAGINE THE LENGTHS HE'D GO TO WHEN THREATENED WITH THE MURDER OF HIS SON.
I WAGER A MAN WOULD DO JUST ABOUT ANYTHING THAT WAS ASKED OF HIM.
AMUSING, DON'T YOU THINK? OFFERING TO MURDER HENRY ALLEN'S SON, UNLESS HE CREATED A WEAPON TO HELP ME KILL THE FLASH.
TWO BIRDS, ONE STONE.
GYAAAAGH!
EOBARD!

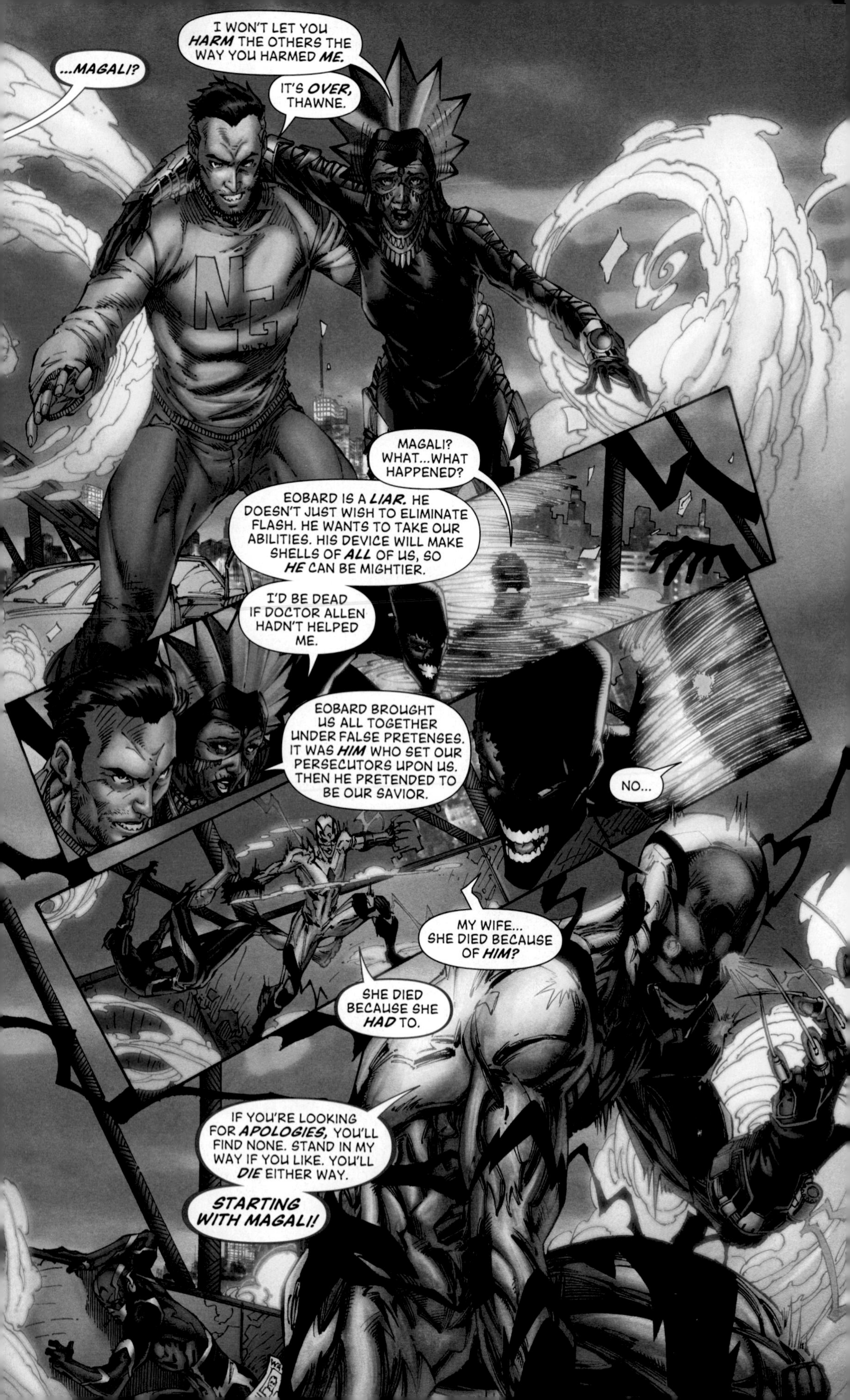
...MAGALI?
I WON'T LET YOU HARM THE OTHERS THE WAY YOU HARMED ME.
IT'S OVER, THAWNE.
MAGALI? WHAT...WHAT HAPPENED?
EOBARD IS A LIAR. HE DOESN'T JUST WISH TO ELIMINATE FLASH. HE WANTS TO TAKE OUR ABILITIES. HIS DEVICE WILL MAKE SHELLS OF ALL OF US, SO HE CAN BE MIGHTIER.
I'D BE DEAD IF DOCTOR ALLEN HADN'T HELPED ME.
EOBARD BROUGHT US ALL TOGETHER UNDER FALSE PRETENSES. IT WAS HIM WHO SET OUR PERSECUTORS UPON US. THEN HE PRETENDED TO BE OUR SAVIOR.
NO...
MY WIFE... SHE DIED BECAUSE OF HIM?
SHE DIED BECAUSE SHE HAD TO.
IF YOU'RE LOOKING FOR APOLOGIES, YOU'LL FIND NONE. STAND IN MY WAY IF YOU LIKE. YOU'LL DIE EITHER WAY.
STARTING WITH MAGALI!

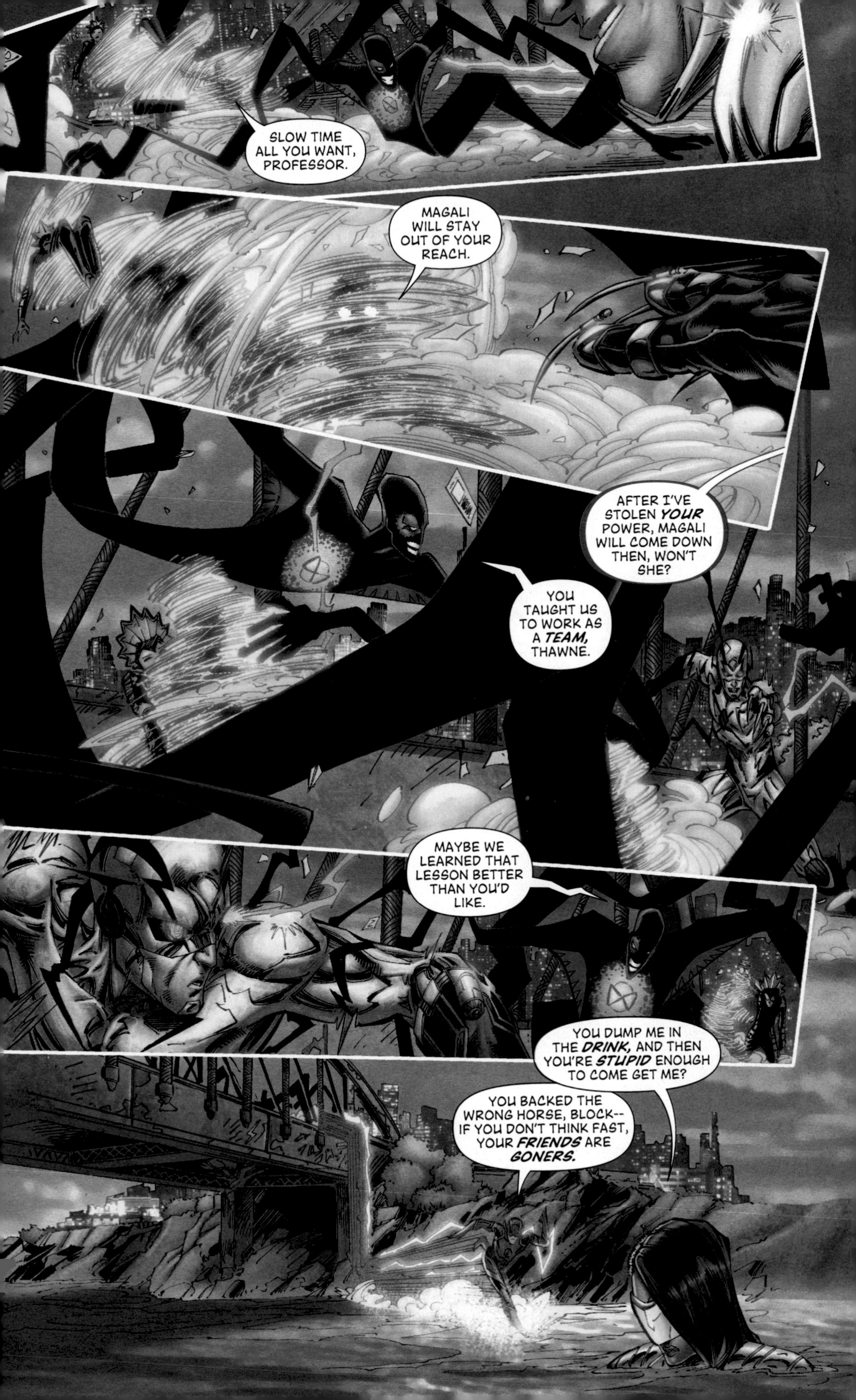

SLOW TIME ALL YOU WANT, PROFESSOR.
MAGALI WILL STAY OUT OF YOUR REACH.
AFTER I'VE STOLEN YOUR POWER, MAGALI WILL COME DOWN THEN, WON'T SHE?
YOU TAUGHT US TO WORK AS A TEAM, THAWNE.
MAYBE WE LEARNED THAT LESSON BETTER THAN YOU'D LIKE.
YOU DUMP ME IN THE DRINK, AND THEN YOU'RE STUPID ENOUGH TO COME GET ME?
YOU BACKED THE WRONG HORSE, BLOCK--IF YOU DON'T THINK FAST, YOUR FRIENDS ARE GONERS.

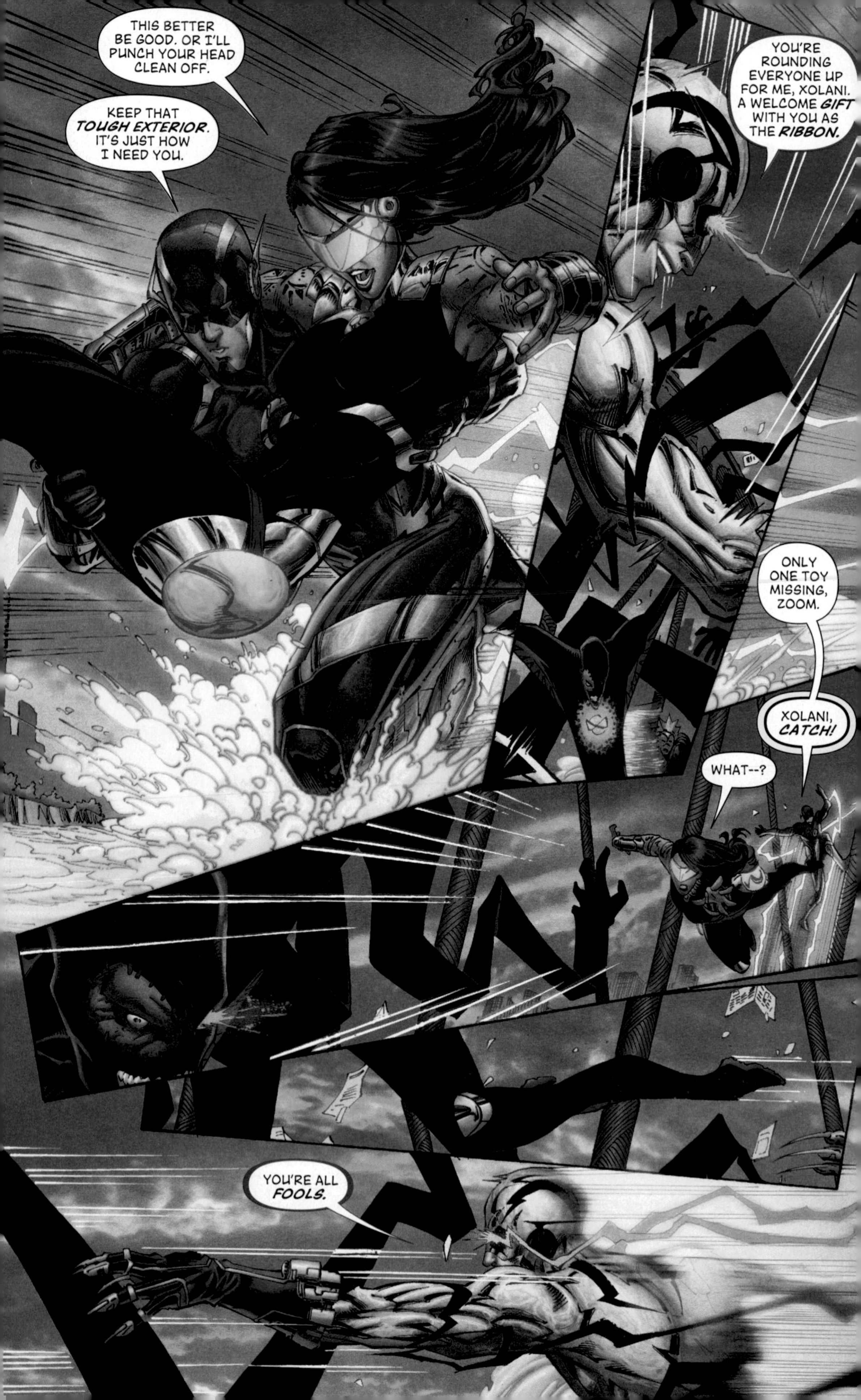
THIS BETTER BE GOOD. OR I'LL PUNCH YOUR HEAD CLEAN OFF.
KEEP THAT *TOUGH EXTERIOR*. IT'S JUST HOW I NEED YOU.
YOU'RE ROUNDING EVERYONE UP FOR ME, XOLANI. A WELCOME *GIFT* WITH YOU AS THE *RIBBON.*
ONLY ONE TOY MISSING, ZOOM.
XOLANI, *CATCH!*
WHAT--?
YOU'RE ALL *FOOLS.*

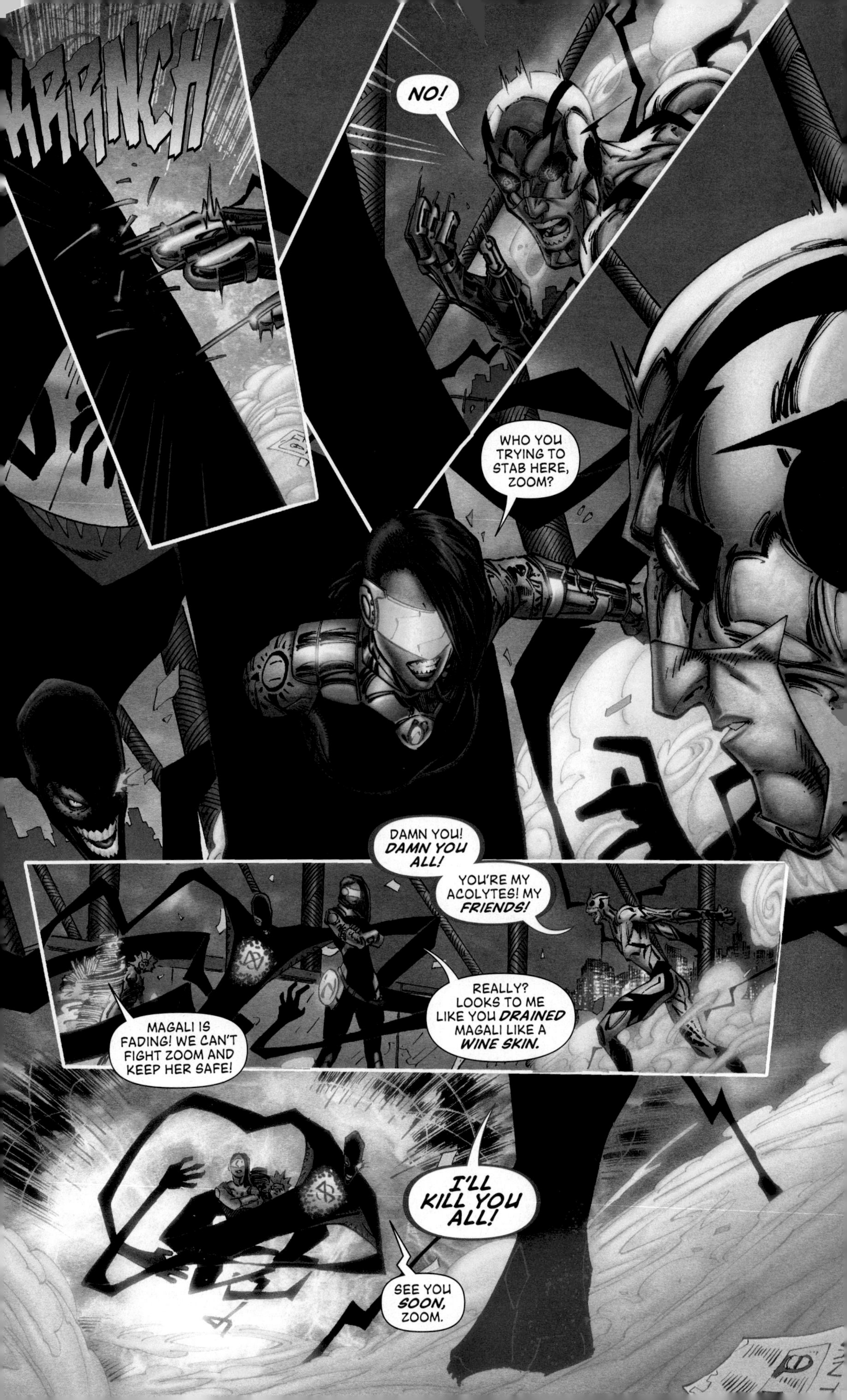

KRRNCH
NO!
WHO YOU TRYING TO STAB HERE, ZOOM?
DAMN YOU! DAMN YOU ALL!
YOU'RE MY ACOLYTES! MY FRIENDS!
MAGALI IS FADING! WE CAN'T FIGHT ZOOM AND KEEP HER SAFE!
REALLY? LOOKS TO ME LIKE YOU DRAINED MAGALI LIKE A WINE SKIN.
I'LL KILL YOU ALL!
SEE YOU SOON, ZOOM.

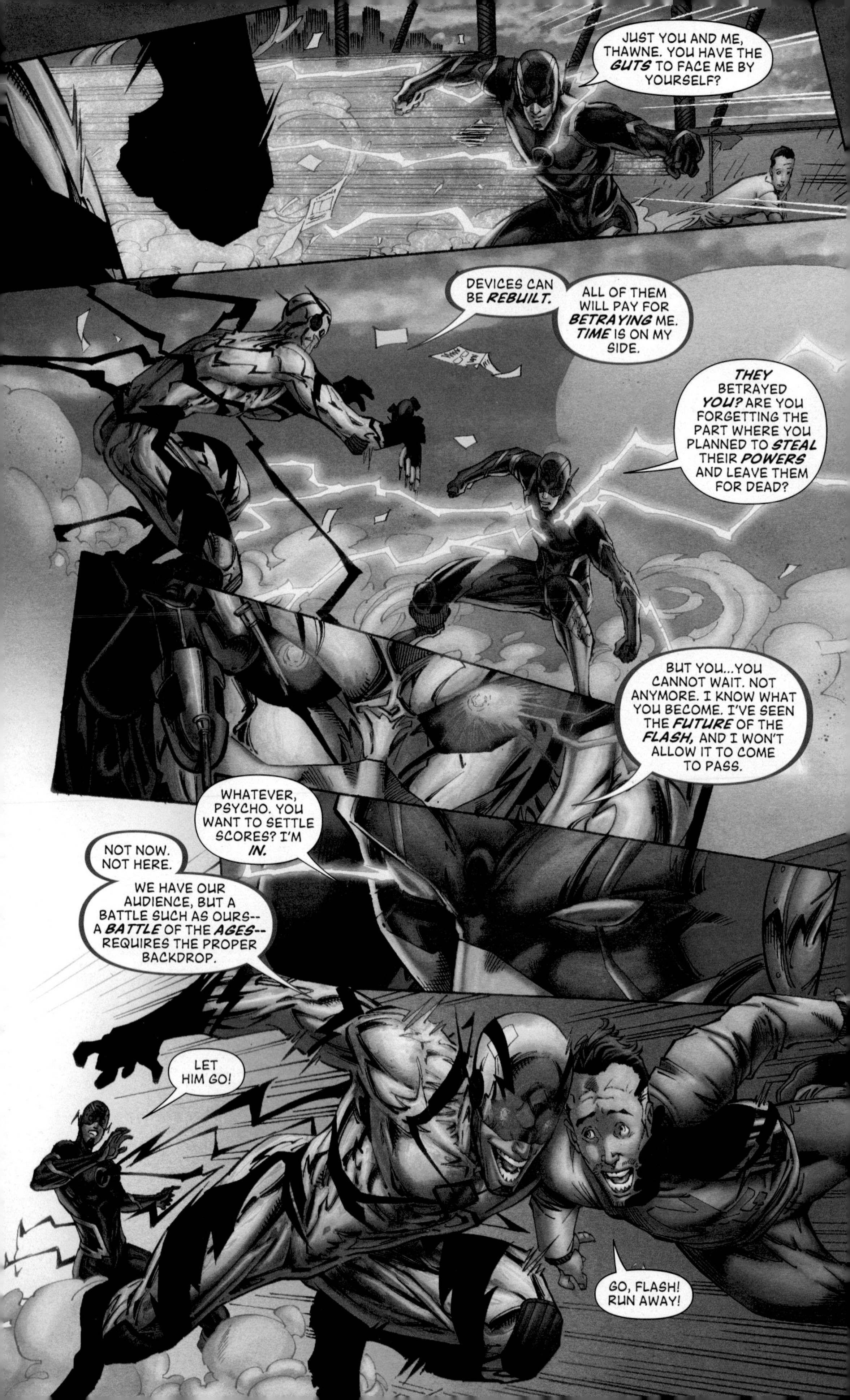
JUST YOU AND ME, THAWNE. YOU HAVE THE GUTS TO FACE ME BY YOURSELF?
DEVICES CAN BE REBUILT.
ALL OF THEM WILL PAY FOR BETRAYING ME. TIME IS ON MY SIDE.
THEY BETRAYED YOU? ARE YOU FORGETTING THE PART WHERE YOU PLANNED TO STEAL THEIR POWERS AND LEAVE THEM FOR DEAD?
BUT YOU...YOU CANNOT WAIT. NOT ANYMORE. I KNOW WHAT YOU BECOME. I'VE SEEN THE FUTURE OF THE FLASH, AND I WON'T ALLOW IT TO COME TO PASS.
WHATEVER, PSYCHO. YOU WANT TO SETTLE SCORES? I'M IN.
NOT NOW. NOT HERE.
WE HAVE OUR AUDIENCE, BUT A BATTLE SUCH AS OURS-- A BATTLE OF THE AGES-- REQUIRES THE PROPER BACKDROP.
LET HIM GO!
GO, FLASH! RUN AWAY!

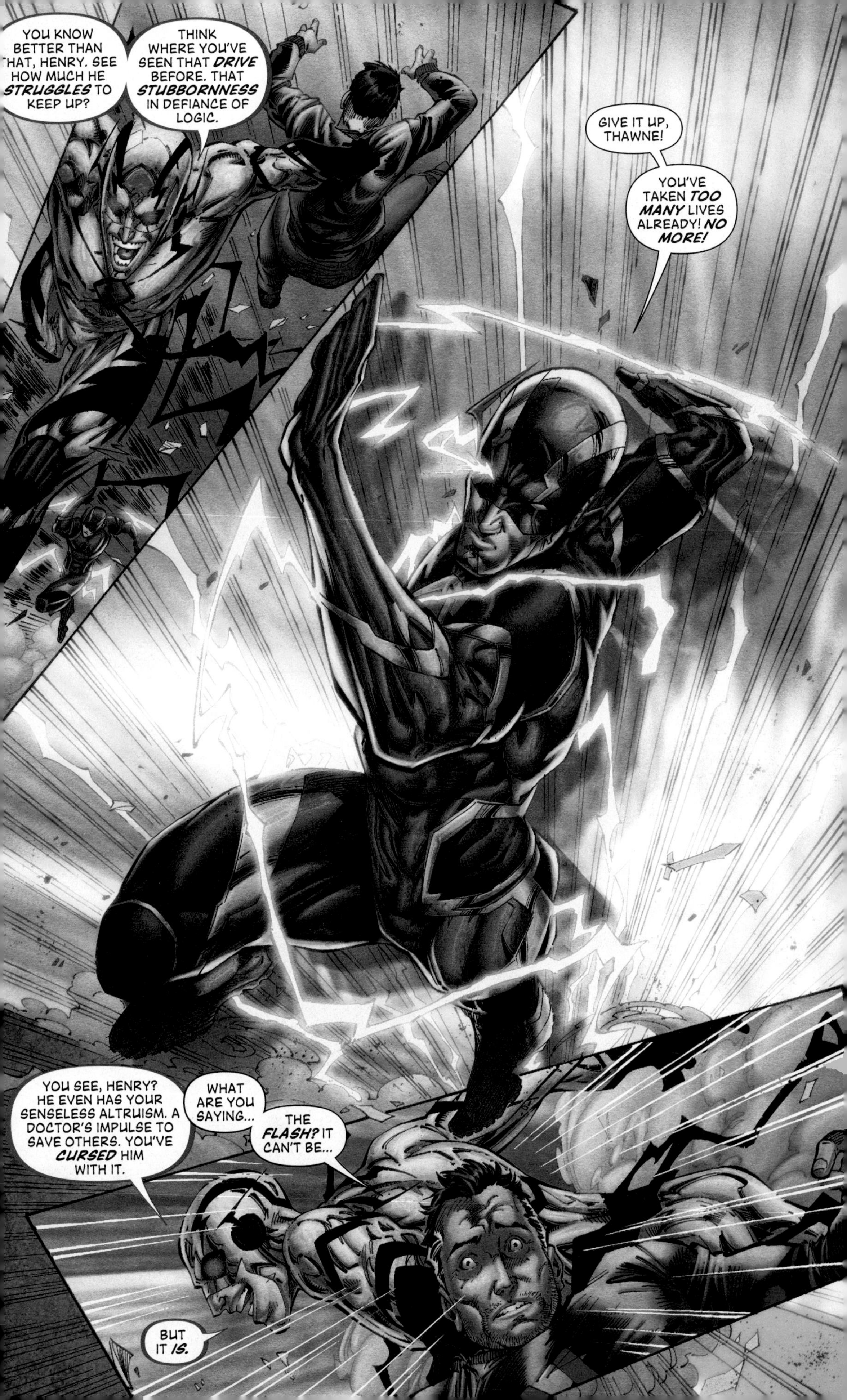
YOU KNOW BETTER THAN THAT, HENRY. SEE HOW MUCH HE STRUGGLES TO KEEP UP?
THINK WHERE YOU'VE SEEN THAT DRIVE BEFORE. THAT STUBBORNNESS IN DEFIANCE OF LOGIC.
GIVE IT UP, THAWNE!
YOU'VE TAKEN TOO MANY LIVES ALREADY! NO MORE!
YOU SEE, HENRY? HE EVEN HAS YOUR SENSELESS ALTRUISM. A DOCTOR'S IMPULSE TO SAVE OTHERS. YOU'VE CURSED HIM WITH IT.
WHAT ARE YOU SAYING...
THE FLASH? IT CAN'T BE...
BUT IT IS.

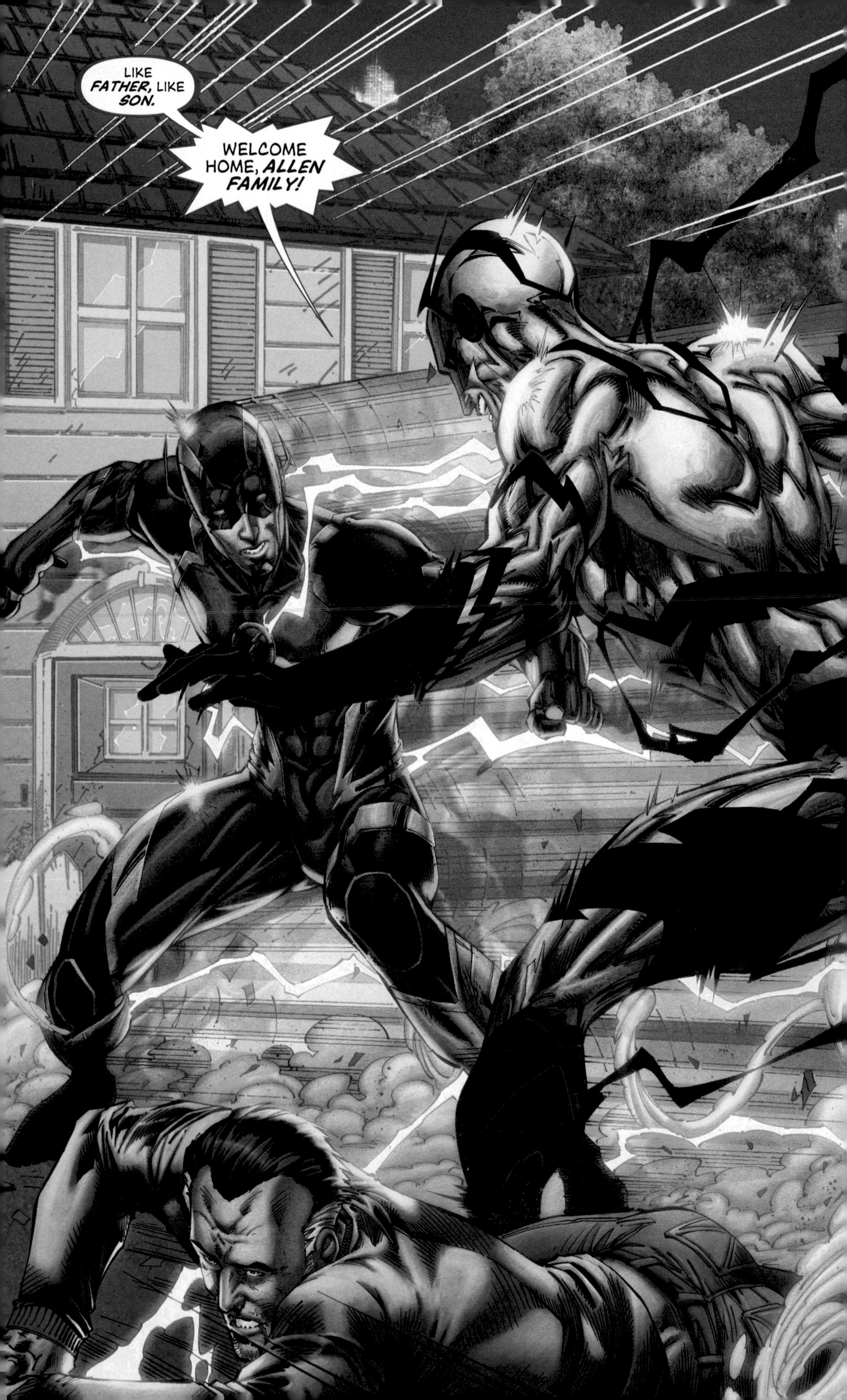
LIKE FATHER, LIKE SON.
WELCOME HOME, ALLEN FAMILY!

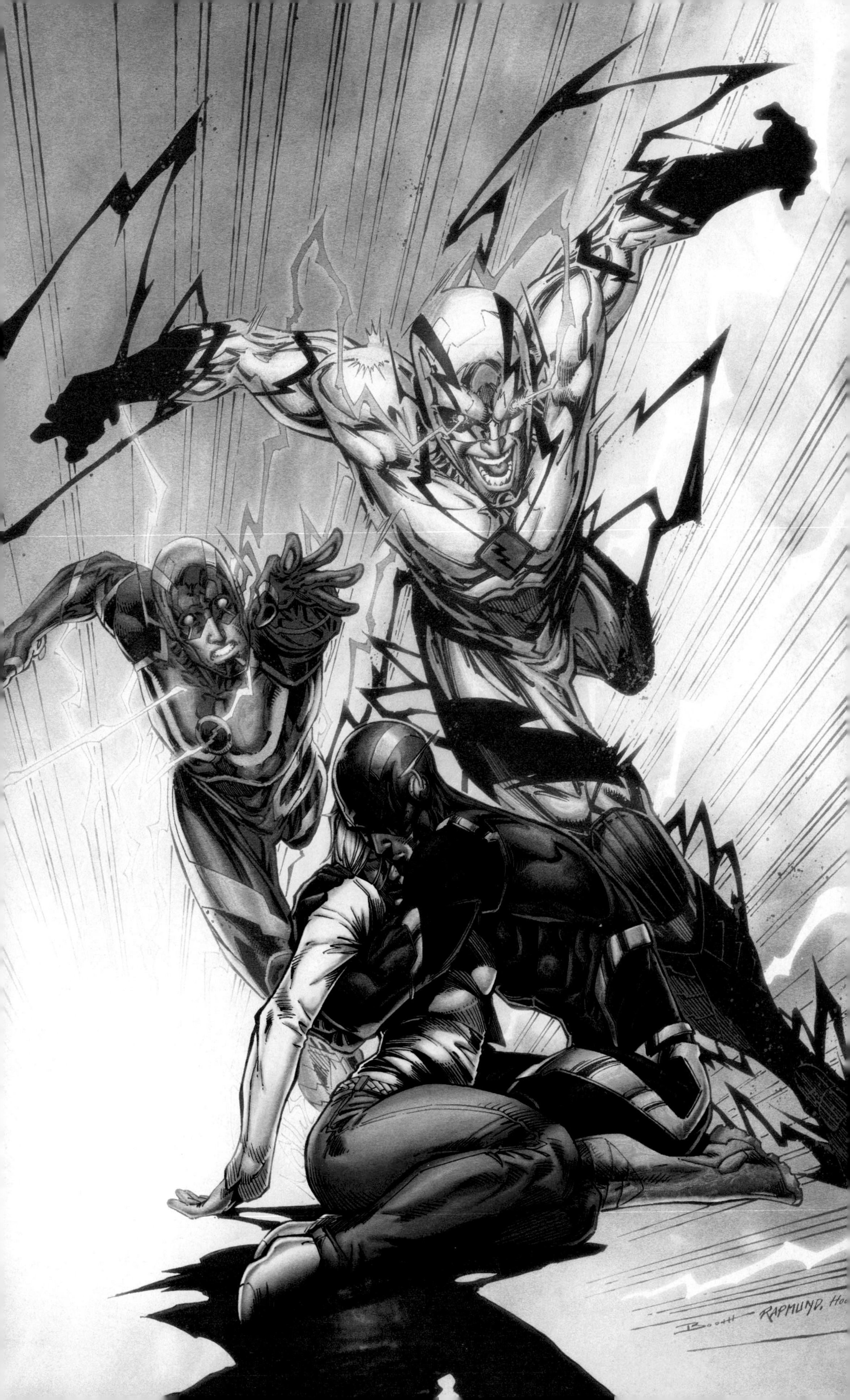
Booth
RAPMUND.

ROBERT VENDITTI, VAN JENSEN writers **BRETT BOOTH** penciller **NORM RAPMUND** inker **ANDREW DALHOUSE, JEROMY COX** colorists **PAT BROSSEAU** letterer
cover by **BRETT BOOTH, NORM RAPMUND, ANDREW DALHOUSE**

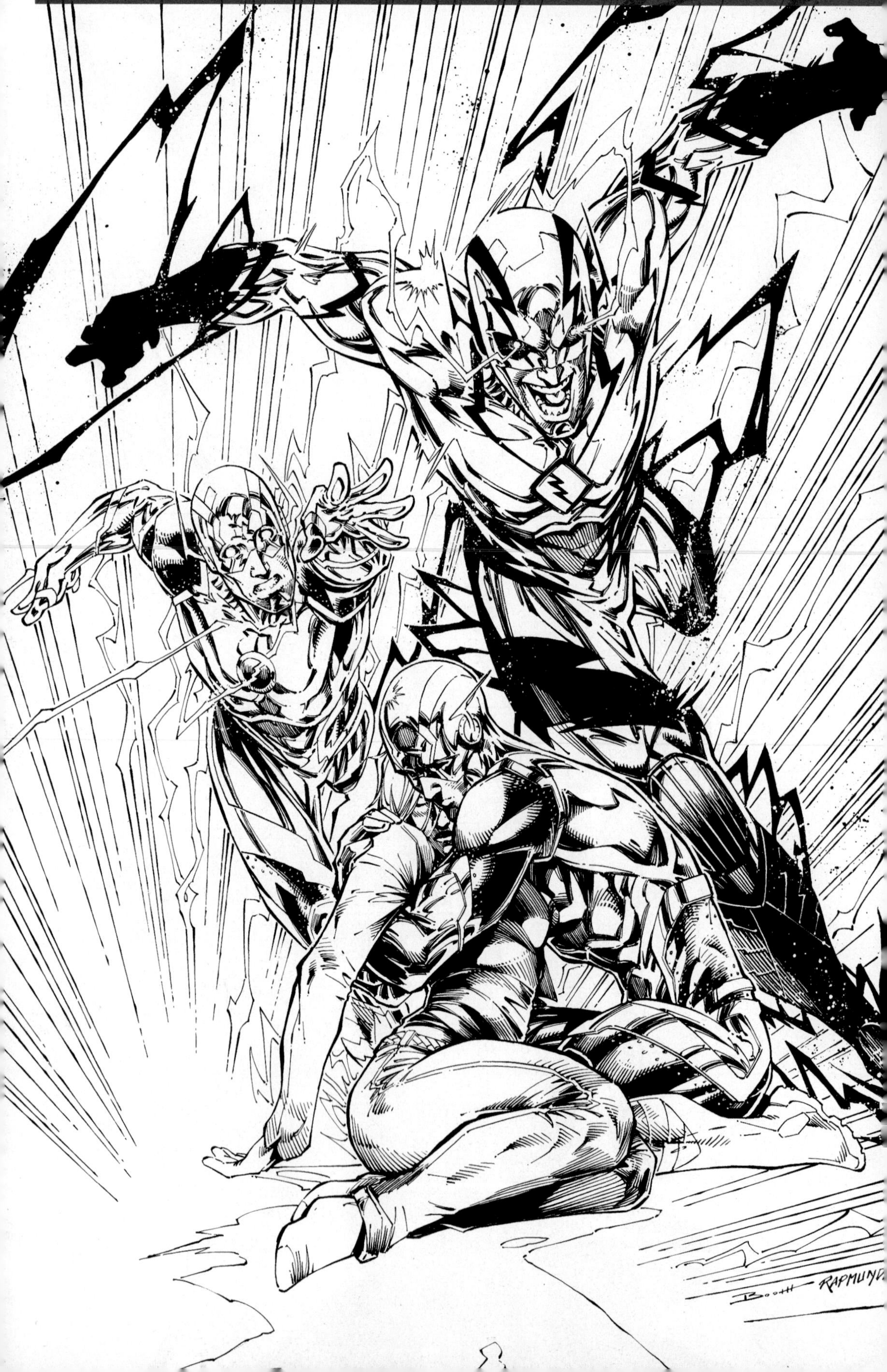

BOOTH
RAPMUND

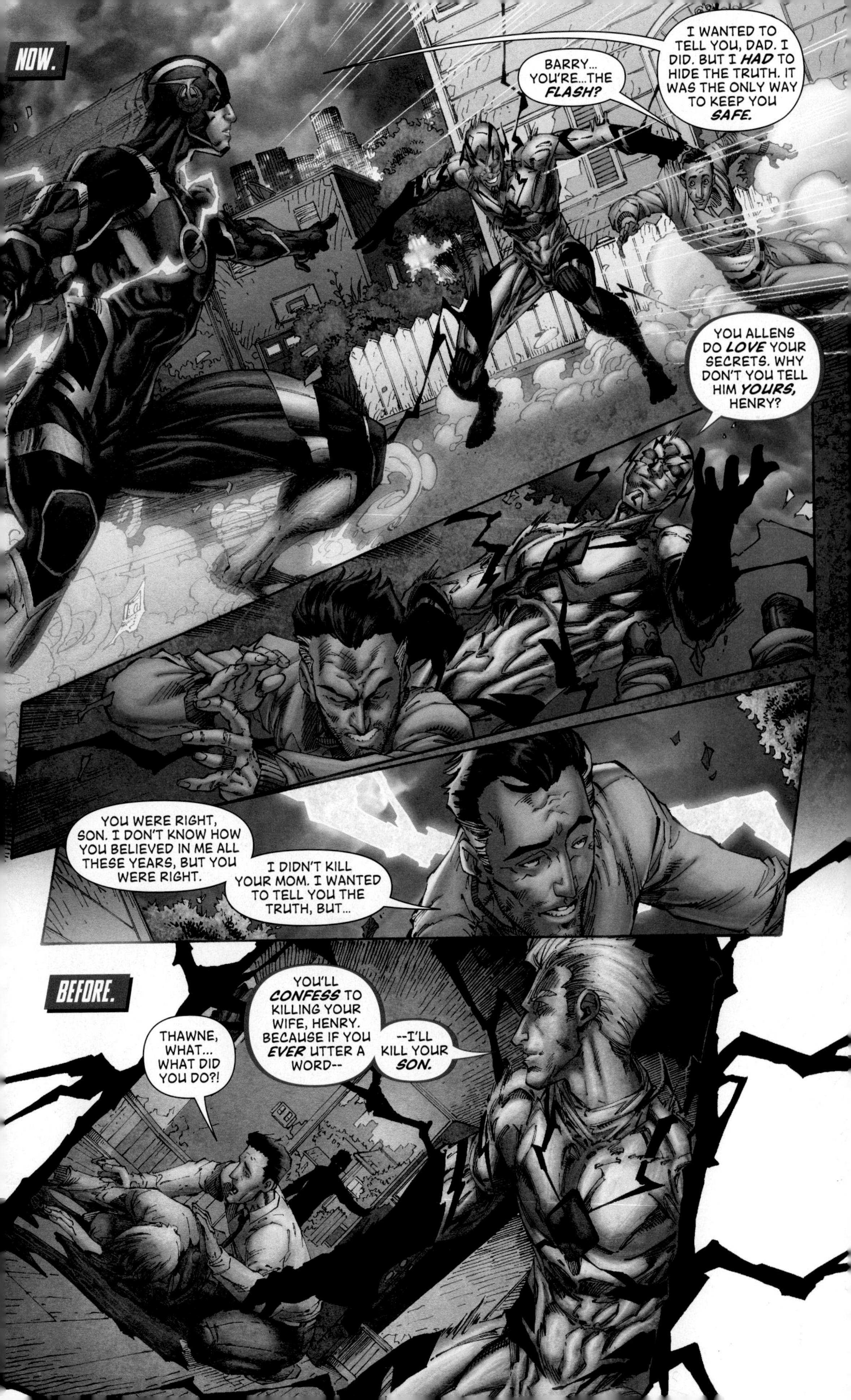
NOW.
BARRY... YOU'RE...THE FLASH?
I WANTED TO TELL YOU, DAD. I DID. BUT I HAD TO HIDE THE TRUTH. IT WAS THE ONLY WAY TO KEEP YOU SAFE.
YOU ALLENS DO LOVE YOUR SECRETS. WHY DON'T YOU TELL HIM YOURS, HENRY?
YOU WERE RIGHT, SON. I DON'T KNOW HOW YOU BELIEVED IN ME ALL THESE YEARS, BUT YOU WERE RIGHT.
I DIDN'T KILL YOUR MOM. I WANTED TO TELL YOU THE TRUTH, BUT...
BEFORE.
THAWNE, WHAT... WHAT DID YOU DO?!
YOU'LL CONFESS TO KILLING YOUR WIFE, HENRY. BECAUSE IF YOU EVER UTTER A WORD--
--I'LL KILL YOUR SON.

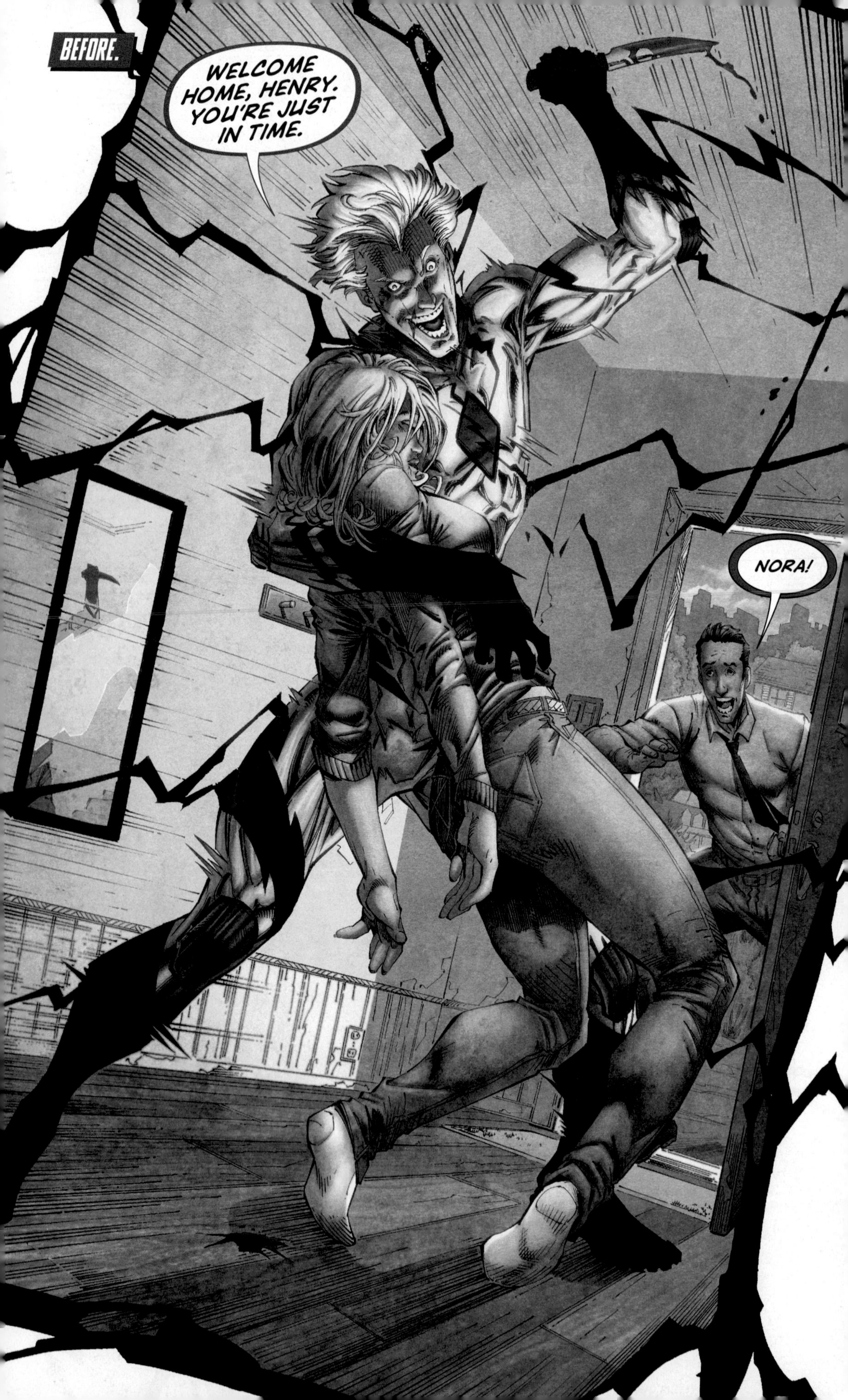
BEFORE.
WELCOME HOME, HENRY. YOU'RE JUST IN TIME.
NORA!

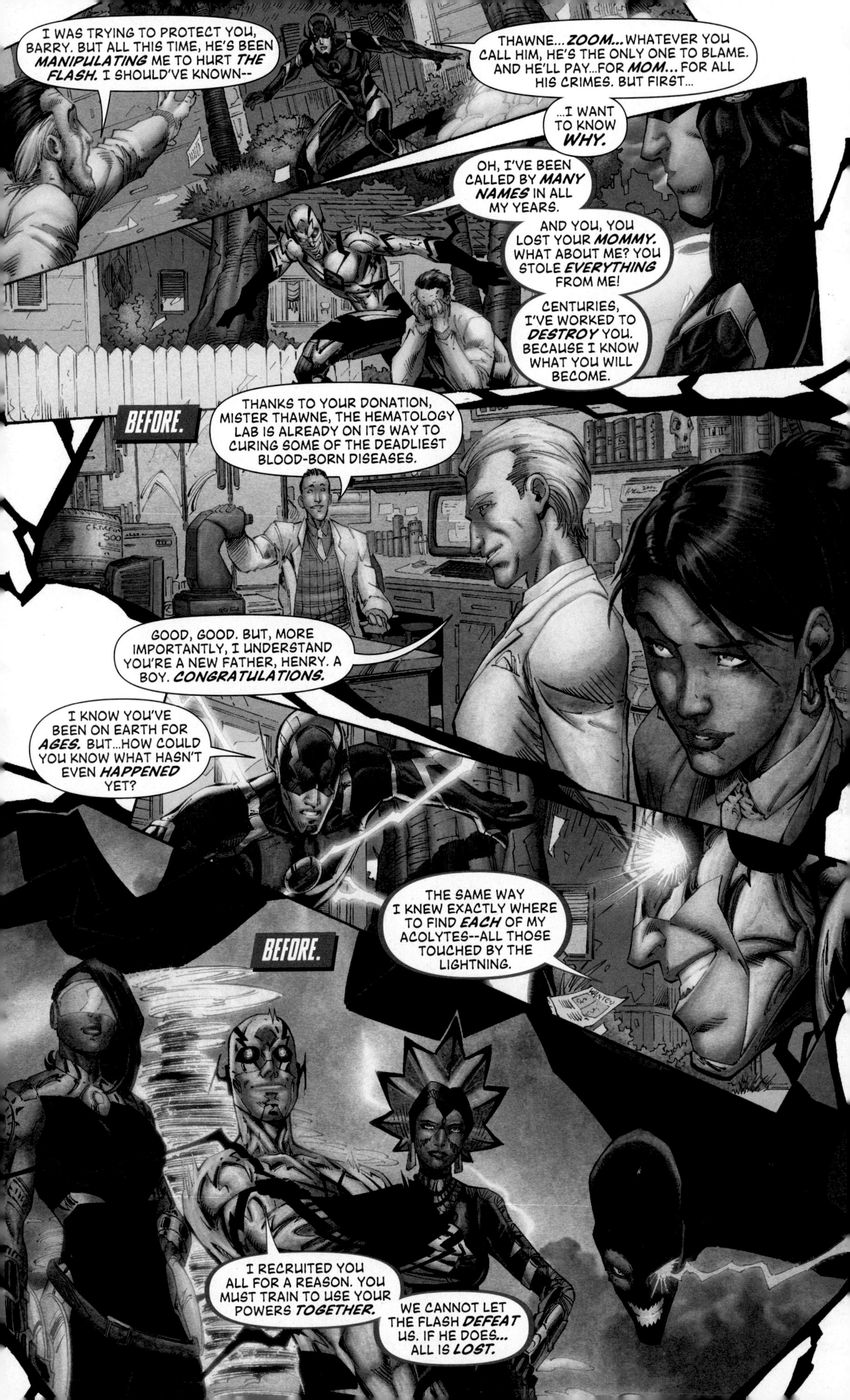
I WAS TRYING TO PROTECT YOU, BARRY. BUT ALL THIS TIME, HE'S BEEN MANIPULATING ME TO HURT THE FLASH. I SHOULD'VE KNOWN--
THAWNE... ZOOM... WHATEVER YOU CALL HIM, HE'S THE ONLY ONE TO BLAME. AND HE'LL PAY...FOR MOM... FOR ALL HIS CRIMES. BUT FIRST...
...I WANT TO KNOW WHY.
OH, I'VE BEEN CALLED BY MANY NAMES IN ALL MY YEARS.
AND YOU, YOU LOST YOUR MOMMY. WHAT ABOUT ME? YOU STOLE EVERYTHING FROM ME!
CENTURIES, I'VE WORKED TO DESTROY YOU. BECAUSE I KNOW WHAT YOU WILL BECOME.
BEFORE.
THANKS TO YOUR DONATION, MISTER THAWNE, THE HEMATOLOGY LAB IS ALREADY ON ITS WAY TO CURING SOME OF THE DEADLIEST BLOOD-BORN DISEASES.
GOOD, GOOD. BUT, MORE IMPORTANTLY, I UNDERSTAND YOU'RE A NEW FATHER, HENRY. A BOY. CONGRATULATIONS.
I KNOW YOU'VE BEEN ON EARTH FOR AGES. BUT...HOW COULD YOU KNOW WHAT HASN'T EVEN HAPPENED YET?
THE SAME WAY I KNEW EXACTLY WHERE TO FIND EACH OF MY ACOLYTES--ALL THOSE TOUCHED BY THE LIGHTNING.
BEFORE.
I RECRUITED YOU ALL FOR A REASON. YOU MUST TRAIN TO USE YOUR POWERS TOGETHER.
WE CANNOT LET THE FLASH DEFEAT US. IF HE DOES... ALL IS LOST.

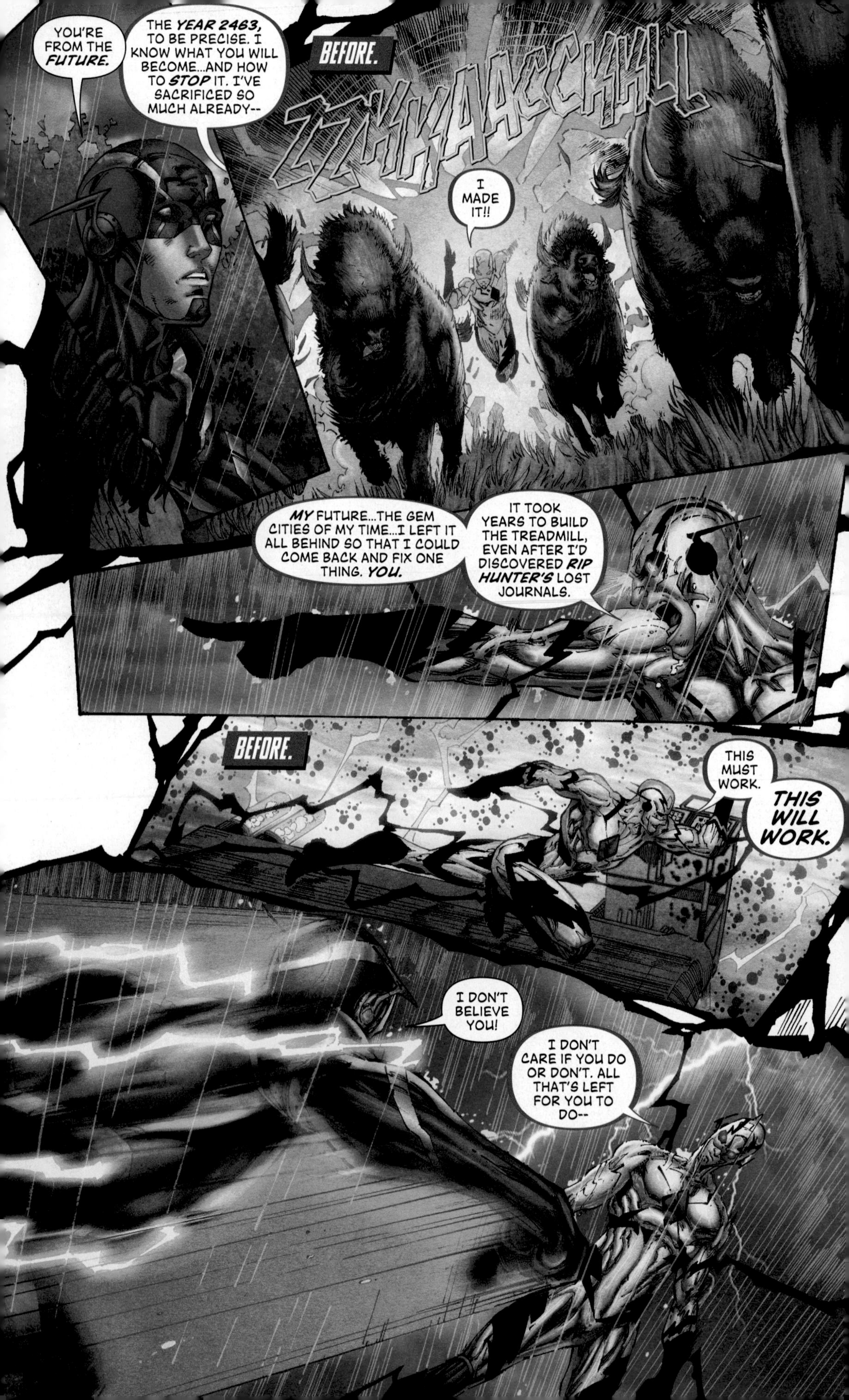
YOU'RE FROM THE FUTURE.
THE YEAR 2463, TO BE PRECISE. I KNOW WHAT YOU WILL BECOME...AND HOW TO STOP IT. I'VE SACRIFICED SO MUCH ALREADY--
BEFORE.
ZZKKAACCKKLL
I MADE IT!!
MY FUTURE...THE GEM CITIES OF MY TIME...I LEFT IT ALL BEHIND SO THAT I COULD COME BACK AND FIX ONE THING. YOU.
IT TOOK YEARS TO BUILD THE TREADMILL, EVEN AFTER I'D DISCOVERED RIP HUNTER'S LOST JOURNALS.
BEFORE.
THIS MUST WORK.
THIS WILL WORK.
I DON'T BELIEVE YOU!
I DON'T CARE IF YOU DO OR DON'T. ALL THAT'S LEFT FOR YOU TO DO--

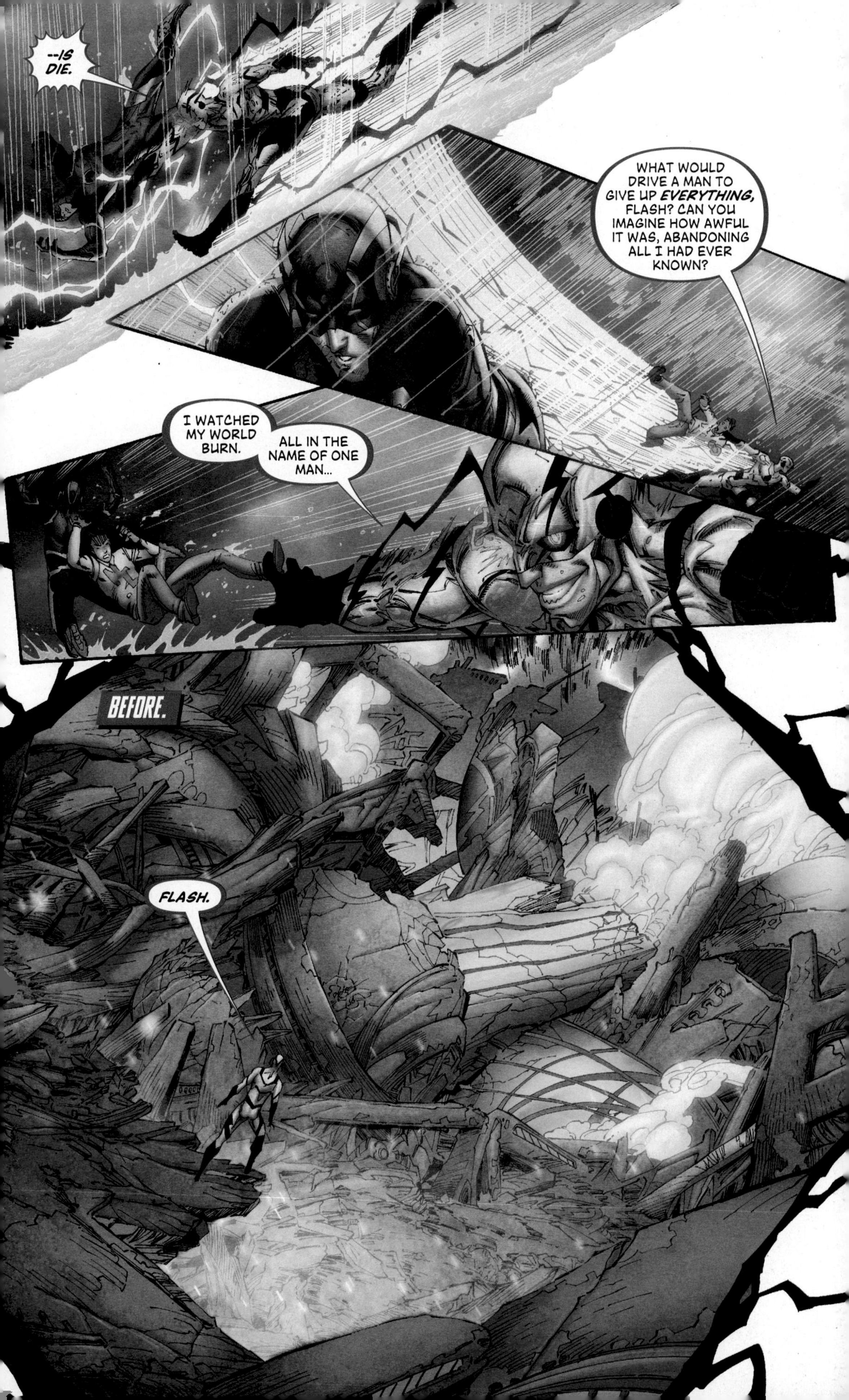
--IS DIE.
WHAT WOULD DRIVE A MAN TO GIVE UP EVERYTHING, FLASH? CAN YOU IMAGINE HOW AWFUL IT WAS, ABANDONING ALL I HAD EVER KNOWN?
I WATCHED MY WORLD BURN.
ALL IN THE NAME OF ONE MAN...
BEFORE.
FLASH.

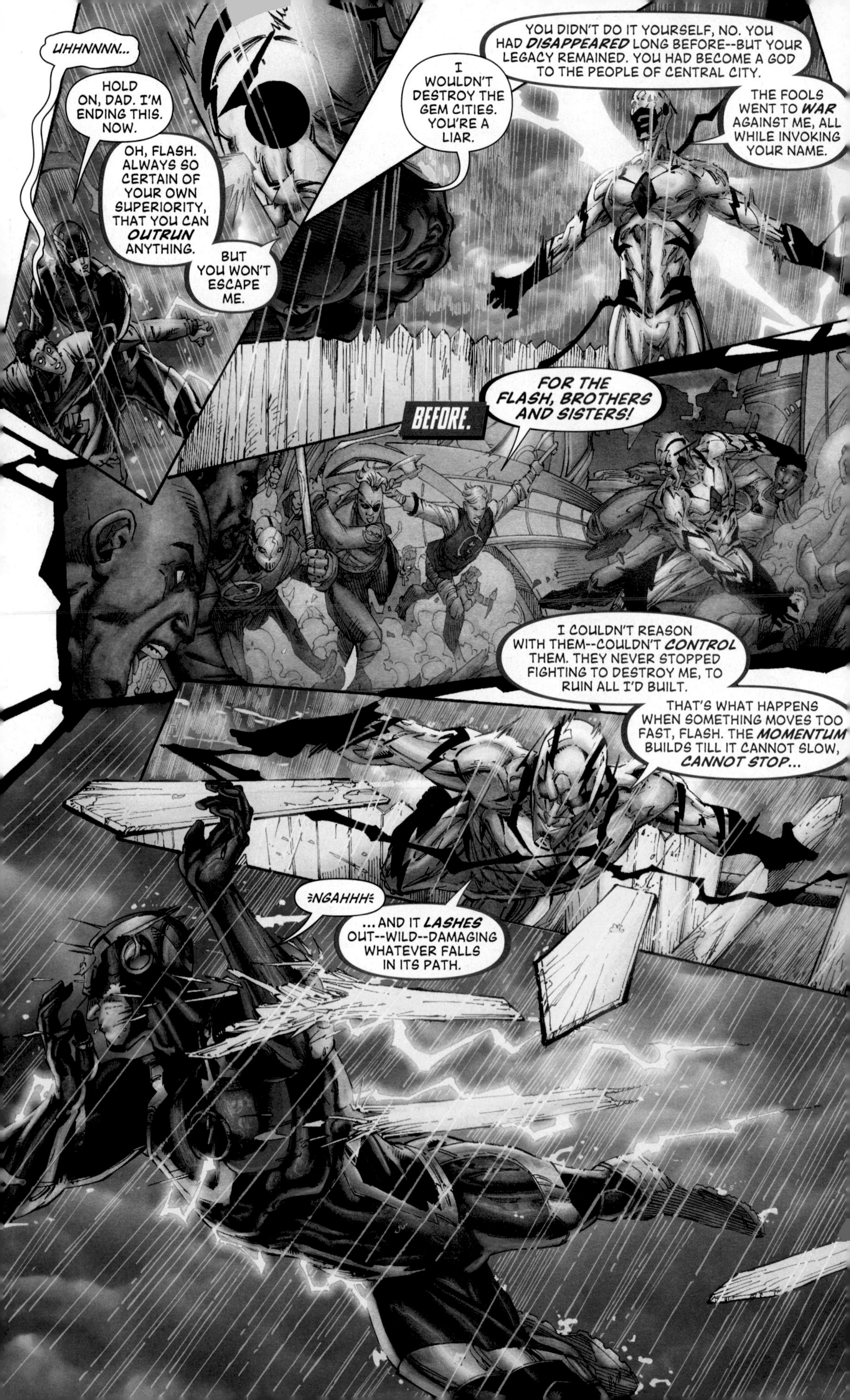
UHHNNNN...
HOLD ON, DAD. I'M ENDING THIS. NOW.
OH, FLASH. ALWAYS SO CERTAIN OF YOUR OWN SUPERIORITY, THAT YOU CAN OUTRUN ANYTHING.
BUT YOU WON'T ESCAPE ME.
I WOULDN'T DESTROY THE GEM CITIES. YOU'RE A LIAR.
YOU DIDN'T DO IT YOURSELF, NO. YOU HAD DISAPPEARED LONG BEFORE--BUT YOUR LEGACY REMAINED. YOU HAD BECOME A GOD TO THE PEOPLE OF CENTRAL CITY.
THE FOOLS WENT TO WAR AGAINST ME, ALL WHILE INVOKING YOUR NAME.
BEFORE.
FOR THE FLASH, BROTHERS AND SISTERS!
I COULDN'T REASON WITH THEM--COULDN'T CONTROL THEM. THEY NEVER STOPPED FIGHTING TO DESTROY ME, TO RUIN ALL I'D BUILT.
THAT'S WHAT HAPPENS WHEN SOMETHING MOVES TOO FAST, FLASH. THE MOMENTUM BUILDS TILL IT CANNOT SLOW, CANNOT STOP...
NGAHHH
...AND IT LASHES OUT--WILD--DAMAGING WHATEVER FALLS IN ITS PATH.

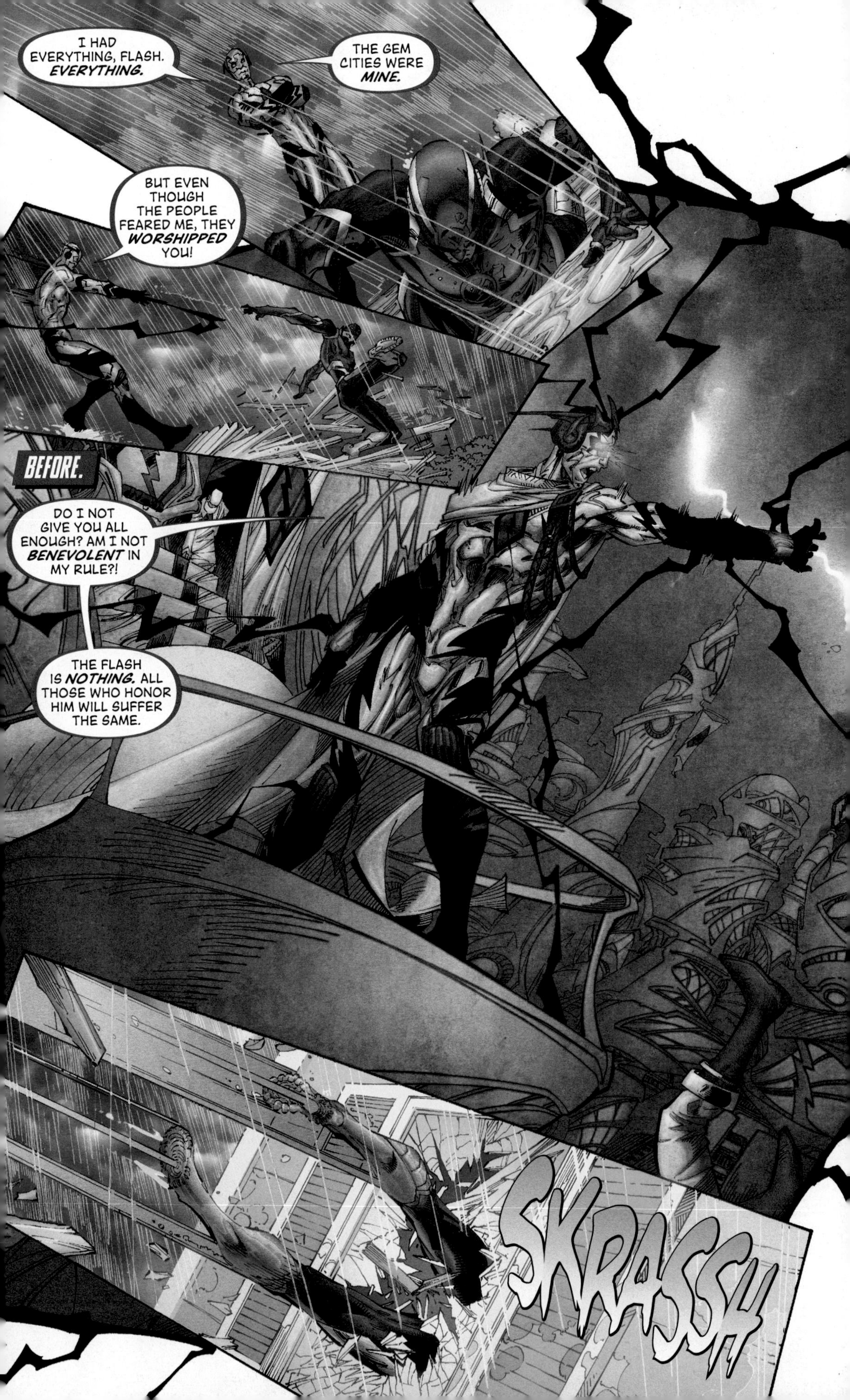
I HAD EVERYTHING, FLASH. ***EVERYTHING.***
THE GEM CITIES WERE ***MINE.***
BUT EVEN THOUGH THE PEOPLE FEARED ME, THEY ***WORSHIPPED*** YOU!
BEFORE.
DO I NOT GIVE YOU ALL ENOUGH? AM I NOT ***BENEVOLENT*** IN MY RULE?!
THE FLASH IS ***NOTHING.*** ALL THOSE WHO HONOR HIM WILL SUFFER THE SAME.
SKRASSH

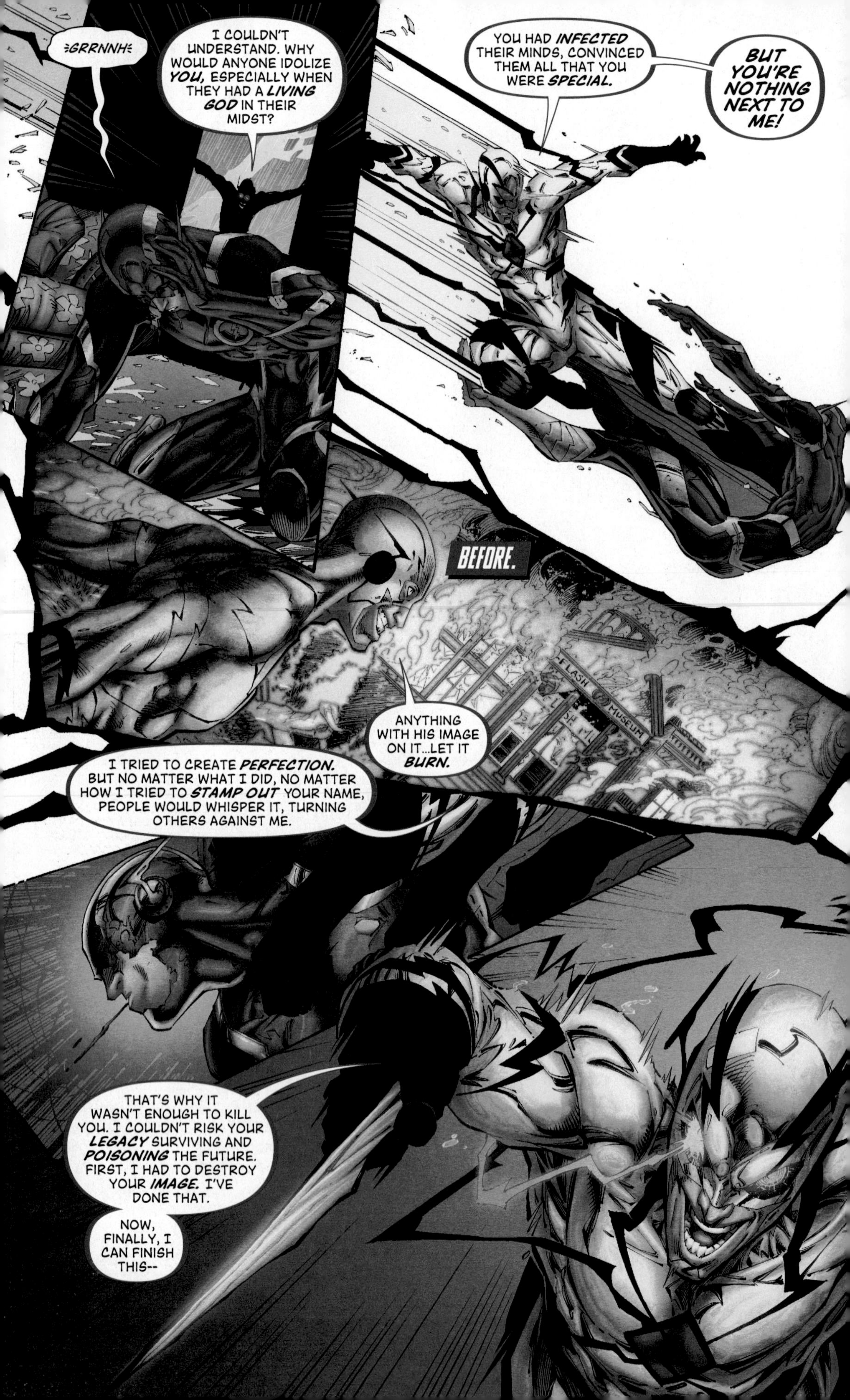

GRRNNH
I COULDN'T UNDERSTAND. WHY WOULD ANYONE IDOLIZE YOU, ESPECIALLY WHEN THEY HAD A LIVING GOD IN THEIR MIDST?
YOU HAD INFECTED THEIR MINDS, CONVINCED THEM ALL THAT YOU WERE SPECIAL.
BUT YOU'RE NOTHING NEXT TO ME!
BEFORE.
FLASH MUSEUM
ANYTHING WITH HIS IMAGE ON IT...LET IT BURN.
I TRIED TO CREATE PERFECTION. BUT NO MATTER WHAT I DID, NO MATTER HOW I TRIED TO STAMP OUT YOUR NAME, PEOPLE WOULD WHISPER IT, TURNING OTHERS AGAINST ME.
THAT'S WHY IT WASN'T ENOUGH TO KILL YOU. I COULDN'T RISK YOUR LEGACY SURVIVING AND POISONING THE FUTURE. FIRST, I HAD TO DESTROY YOUR IMAGE. I'VE DONE THAT.
NOW, FINALLY, I CAN FINISH THIS--

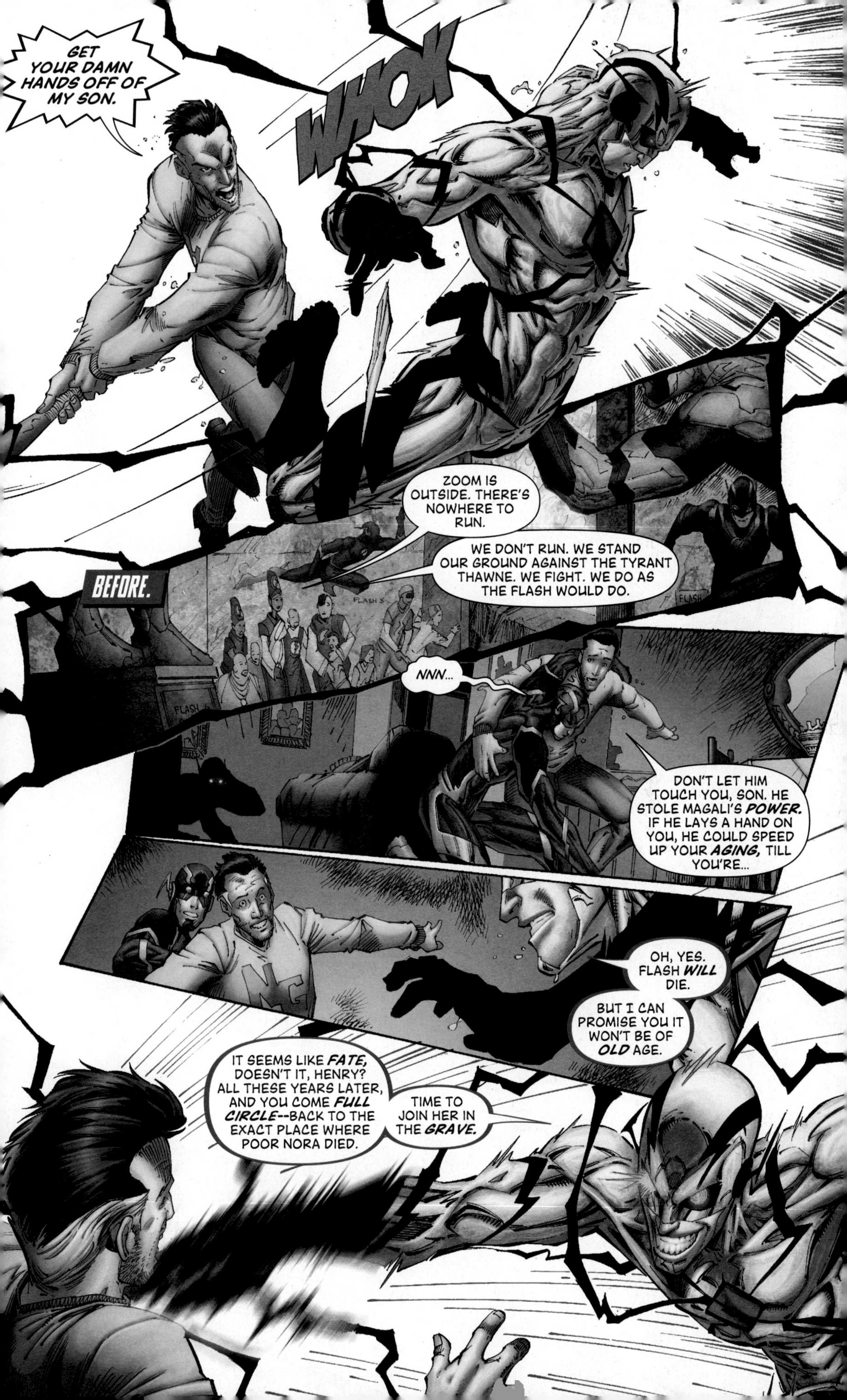
GET YOUR DAMN HANDS OFF OF MY SON.
WHOK
ZOOM IS OUTSIDE. THERE'S NOWHERE TO RUN.
BEFORE.
WE DON'T RUN. WE STAND OUR GROUND AGAINST THE TYRANT THAWNE. WE FIGHT. WE DO AS THE FLASH WOULD DO.
NNN...
DON'T LET HIM TOUCH YOU, SON. HE STOLE MAGALI'S POWER. IF HE LAYS A HAND ON YOU, HE COULD SPEED UP YOUR AGING, TILL YOU'RE...
OH, YES. FLASH WILL DIE.
BUT I CAN PROMISE YOU IT WON'T BE OF OLD AGE.
IT SEEMS LIKE FATE, DOESN'T IT, HENRY? ALL THESE YEARS LATER, AND YOU COME FULL CIRCLE--BACK TO THE EXACT PLACE WHERE POOR NORA DIED.
TIME TO JOIN HER IN THE GRAVE.

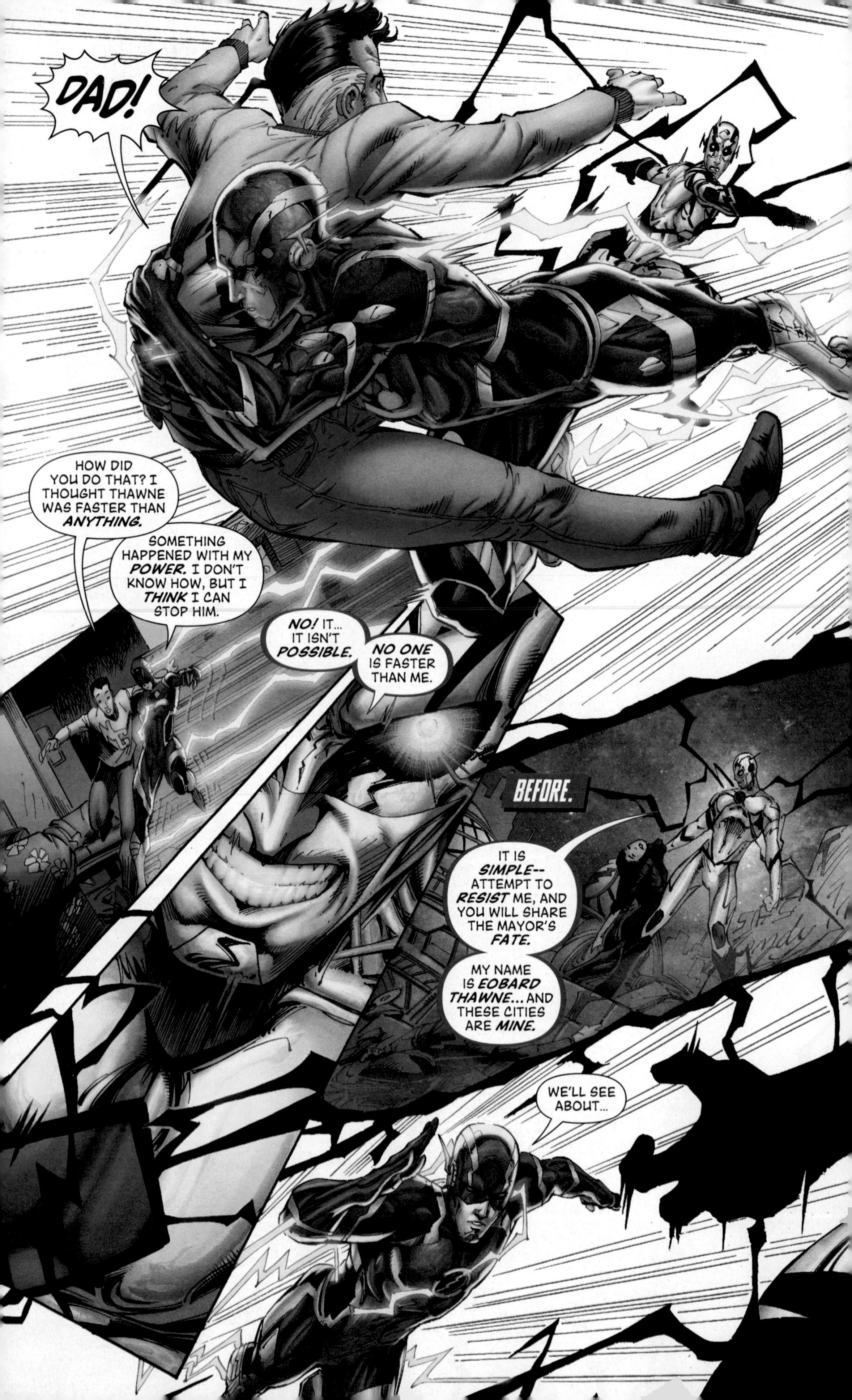
DAD!
HOW DID YOU DO THAT? I THOUGHT THAWNE WAS FASTER THAN ANYTHING.
SOMETHING HAPPENED WITH MY POWER. I DON'T KNOW HOW, BUT I THINK I CAN STOP HIM.
NO! IT... IT ISN'T POSSIBLE.
NO ONE IS FASTER THAN ME.
BEFORE.
IT IS SIMPLE-- ATTEMPT TO RESIST ME, AND YOU WILL SHARE THE MAYOR'S FATE.
MY NAME IS EOBARD THAWNE... AND THESE CITIES ARE MINE.
WE'LL SEE ABOUT...

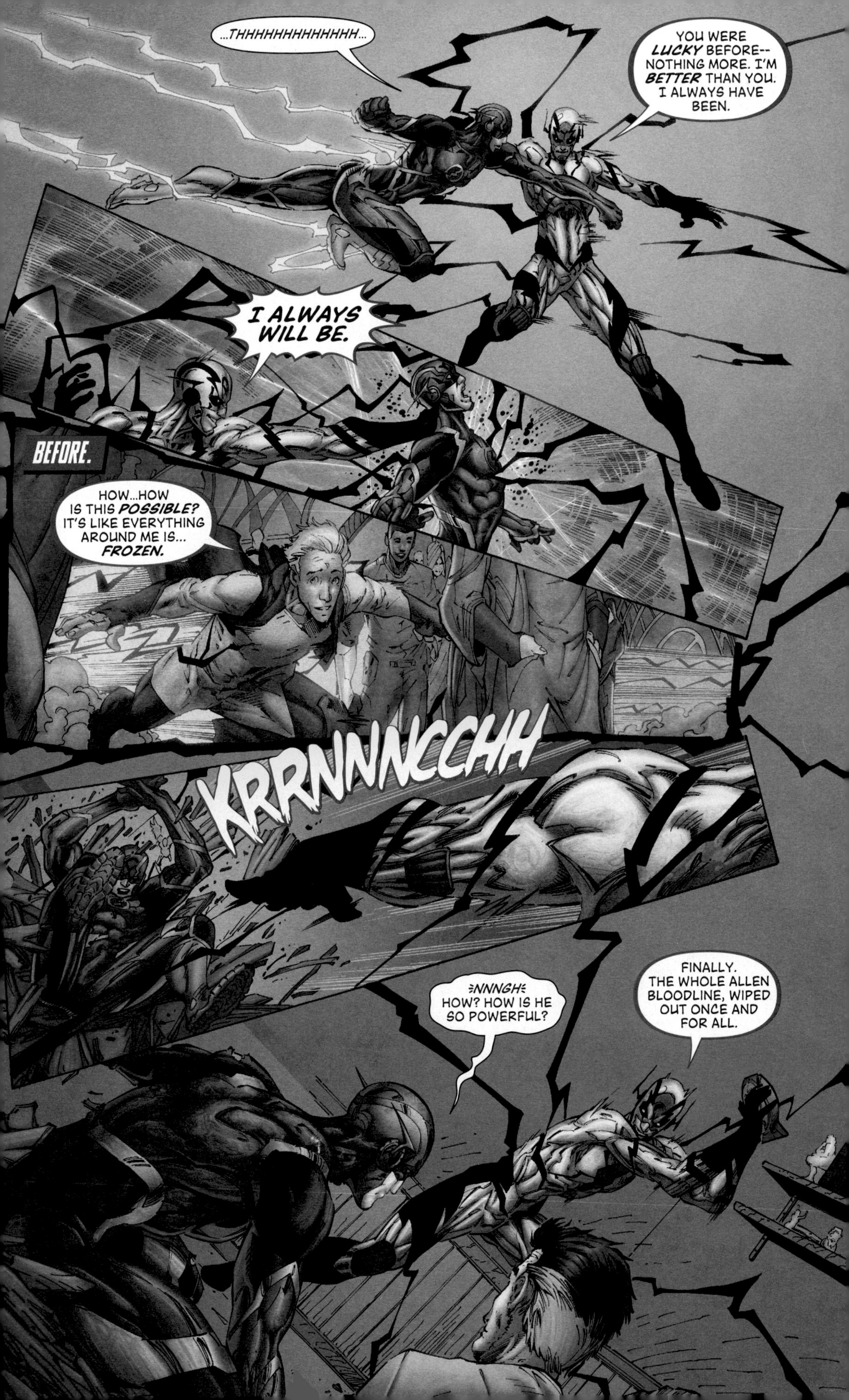
...THHHHHHHHHHHHH...
YOU WERE LUCKY BEFORE-- NOTHING MORE. I'M BETTER THAN YOU. I ALWAYS HAVE BEEN.
I ALWAYS WILL BE.
BEFORE.
HOW...HOW IS THIS POSSIBLE? IT'S LIKE EVERYTHING AROUND ME IS... FROZEN.
KRRNNNCCHH
NNNGH HOW? HOW IS HE SO POWERFUL?
FINALLY. THE WHOLE ALLEN BLOODLINE, WIPED OUT ONCE AND FOR ALL.

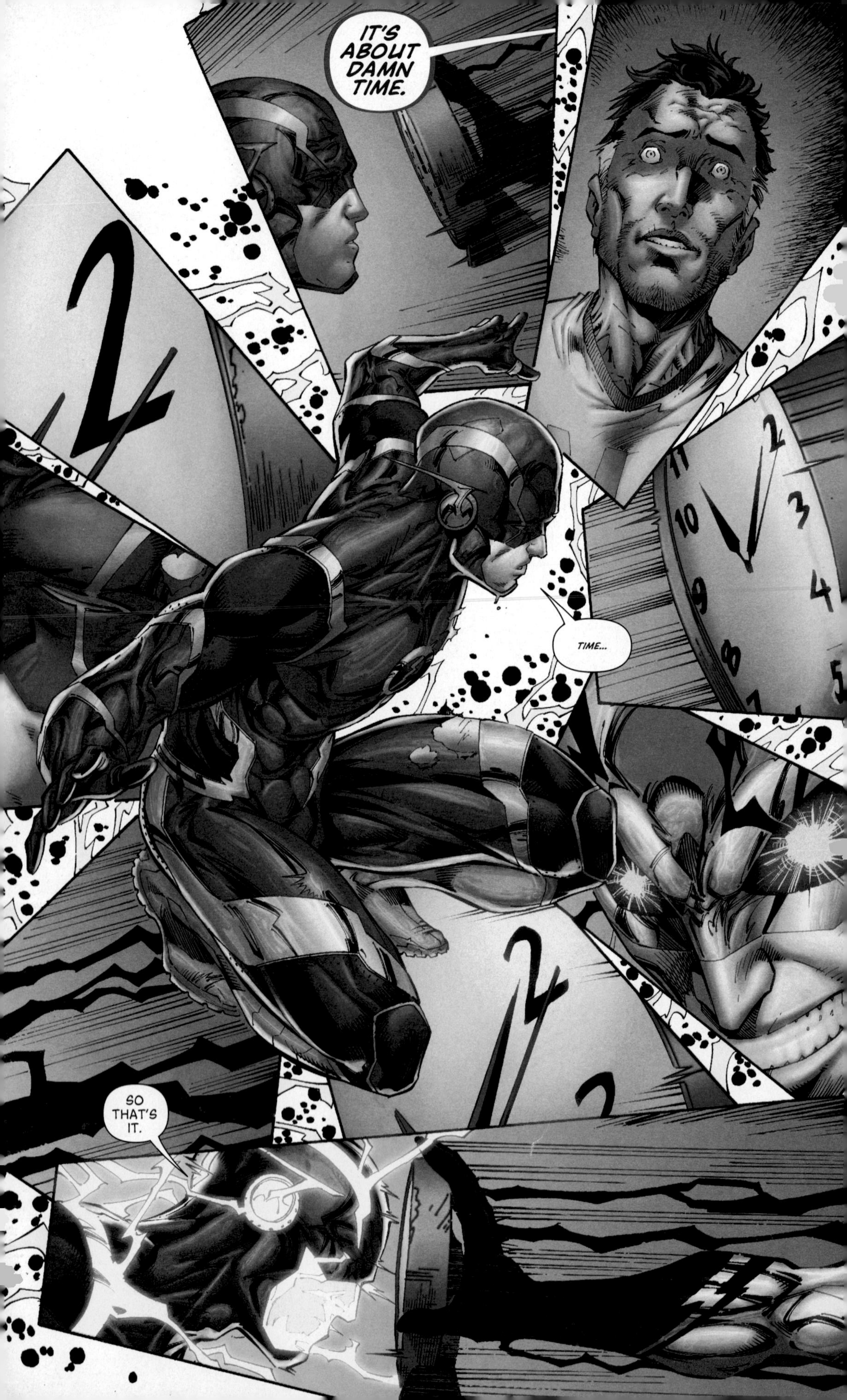
IT'S ABOUT DAMN TIME.
TIME...
SO THAT'S IT.

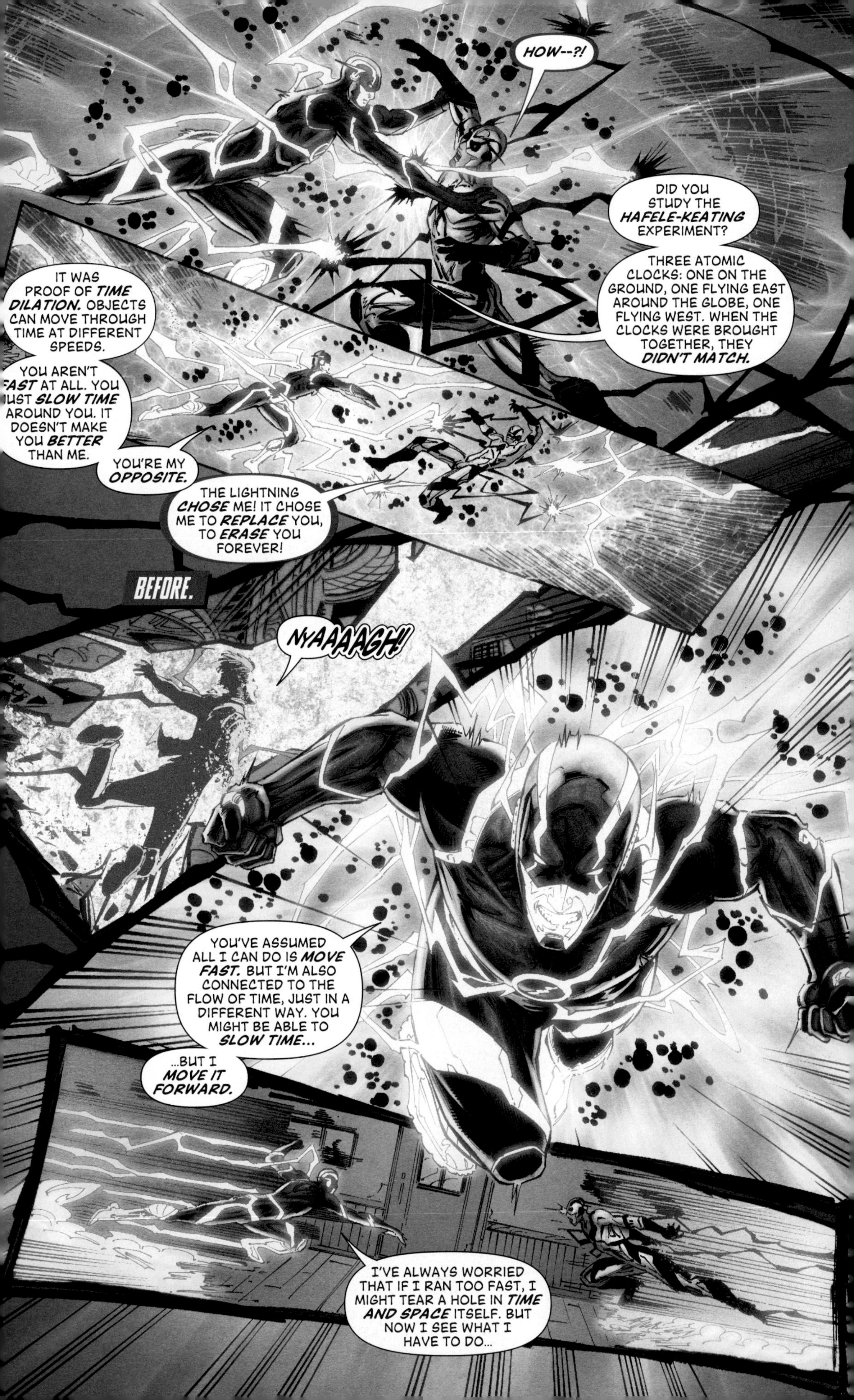
HOW--?!
DID YOU STUDY THE HAFELE-KEATING EXPERIMENT?
THREE ATOMIC CLOCKS: ONE ON THE GROUND, ONE FLYING EAST AROUND THE GLOBE, ONE FLYING WEST. WHEN THE CLOCKS WERE BROUGHT TOGETHER, THEY DIDN'T MATCH.
IT WAS PROOF OF TIME DILATION. OBJECTS CAN MOVE THROUGH TIME AT DIFFERENT SPEEDS.
YOU AREN'T FAST AT ALL. YOU JUST SLOW TIME AROUND YOU. IT DOESN'T MAKE YOU BETTER THAN ME.
YOU'RE MY OPPOSITE.
THE LIGHTNING CHOSE ME! IT CHOSE ME TO REPLACE YOU, TO ERASE YOU FOREVER!
BEFORE.
NYAAAAGH!
YOU'VE ASSUMED ALL I CAN DO IS MOVE FAST. BUT I'M ALSO CONNECTED TO THE FLOW OF TIME, JUST IN A DIFFERENT WAY. YOU MIGHT BE ABLE TO SLOW TIME...
...BUT I MOVE IT FORWARD.
I'VE ALWAYS WORRIED THAT IF I RAN TOO FAST, I MIGHT TEAR A HOLE IN TIME AND SPACE ITSELF. BUT NOW I SEE WHAT I HAVE TO DO...

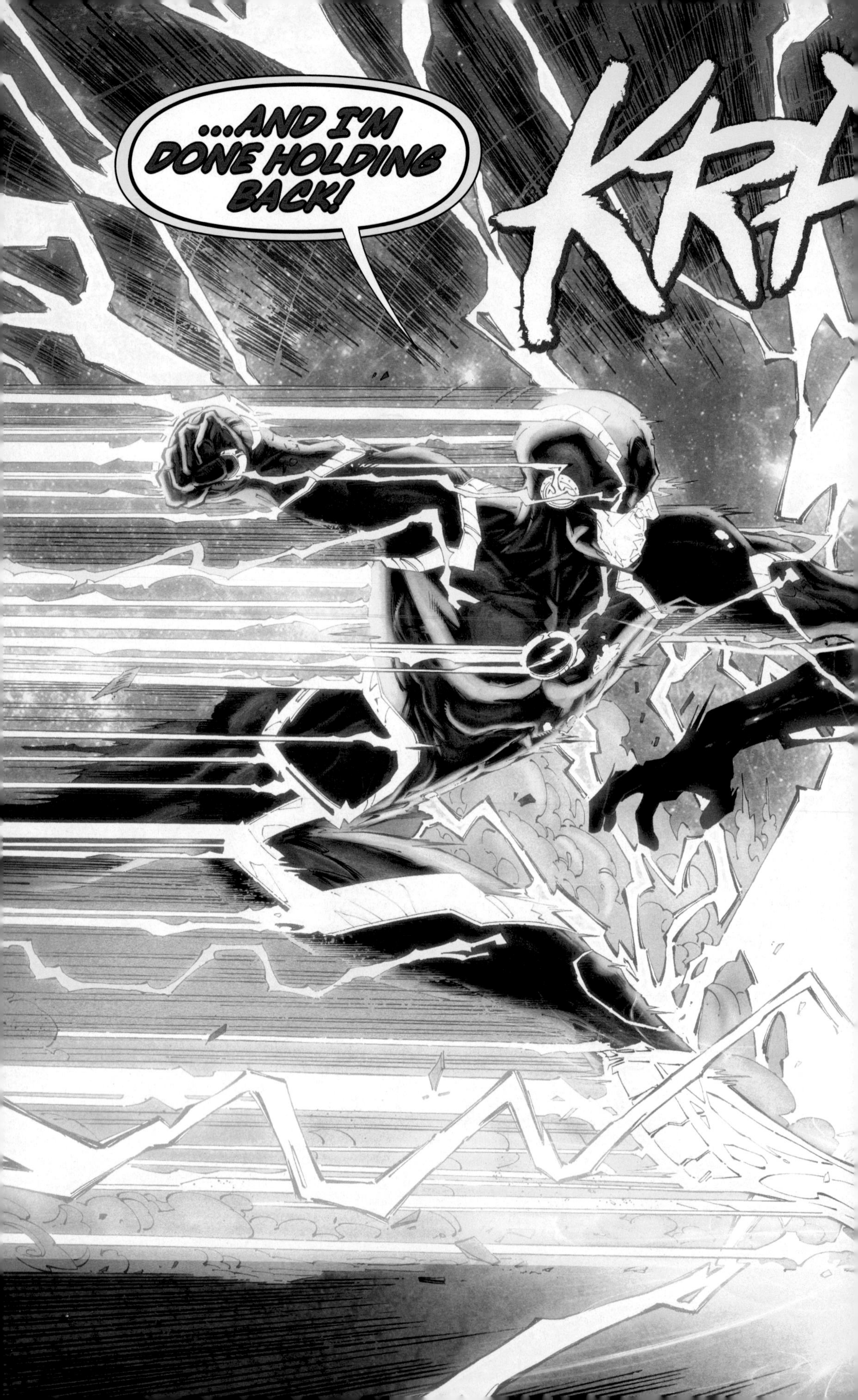
...AND I'M DONE HOLDING BACK!
KRA

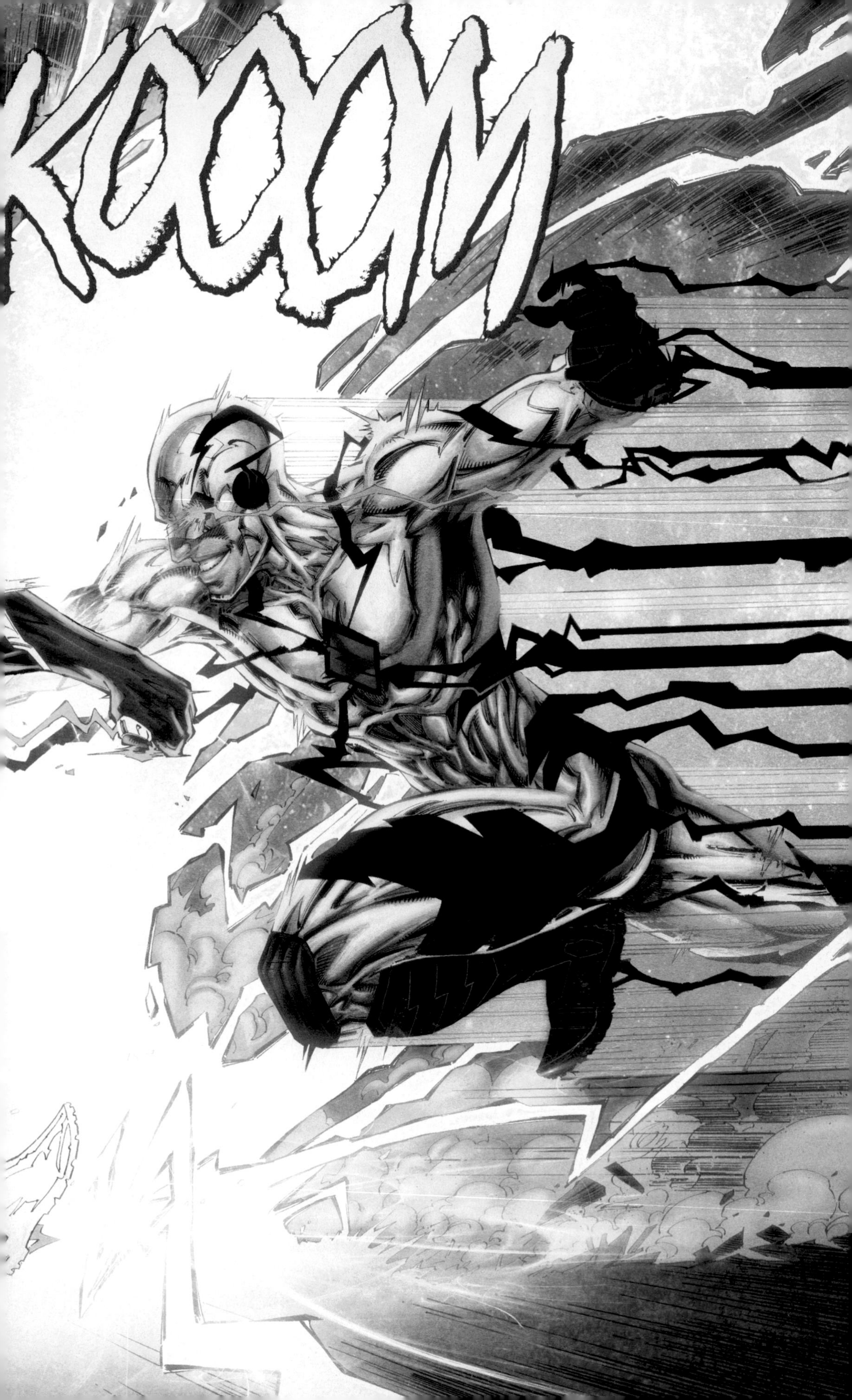
KOOOM

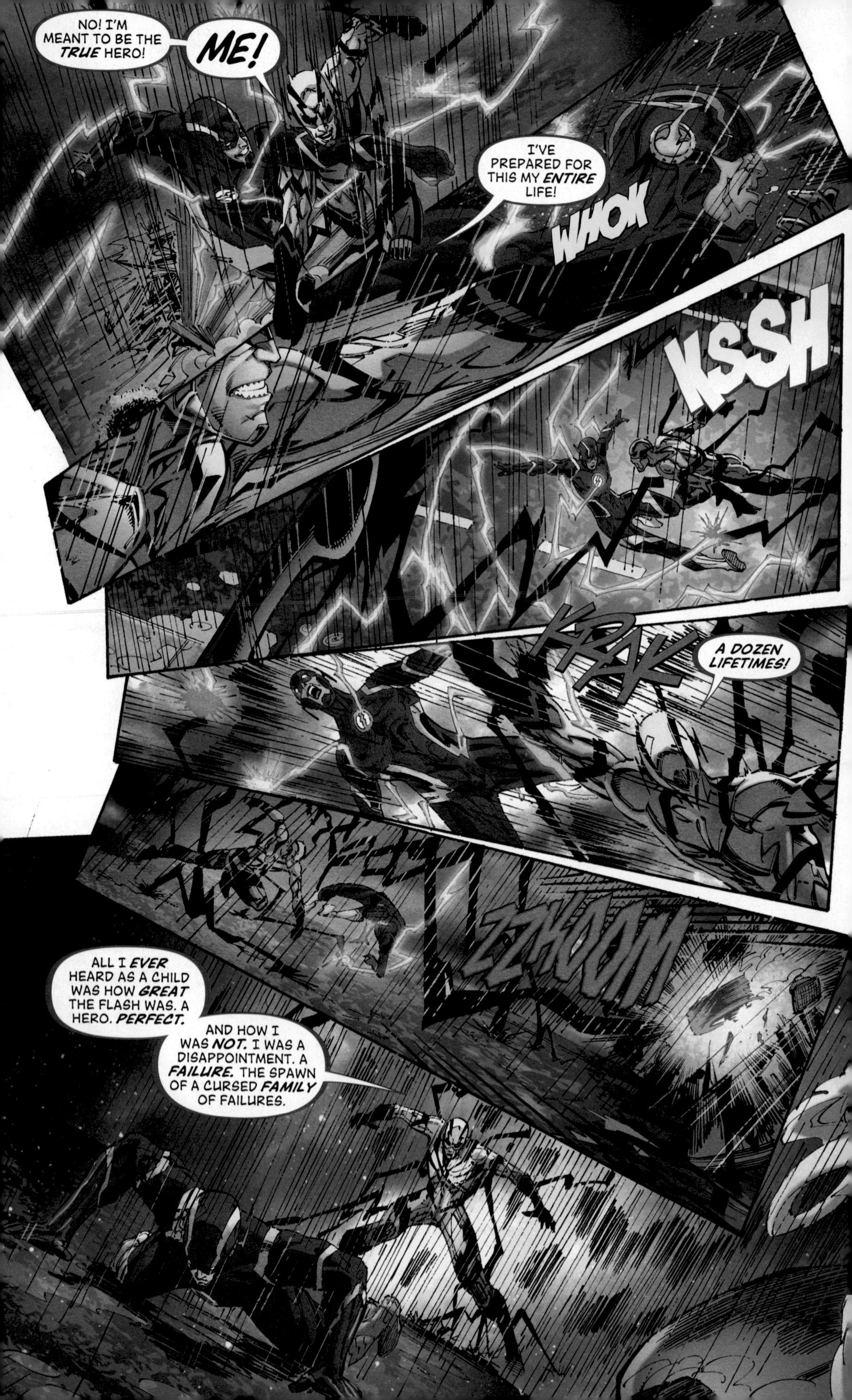
NO! I'M MEANT TO BE THE TRUE HERO!
ME!
I'VE PREPARED FOR THIS MY ENTIRE LIFE!
WHOK
KSSH
KRAK
A DOZEN LIFETIMES!
ZZHOOM
ALL I EVER HEARD AS A CHILD WAS HOW GREAT THE FLASH WAS. A HERO. PERFECT.
AND HOW I WAS NOT. I WAS A DISAPPOINTMENT. A FAILURE. THE SPAWN OF A CURSED FAMILY OF FAILURES.

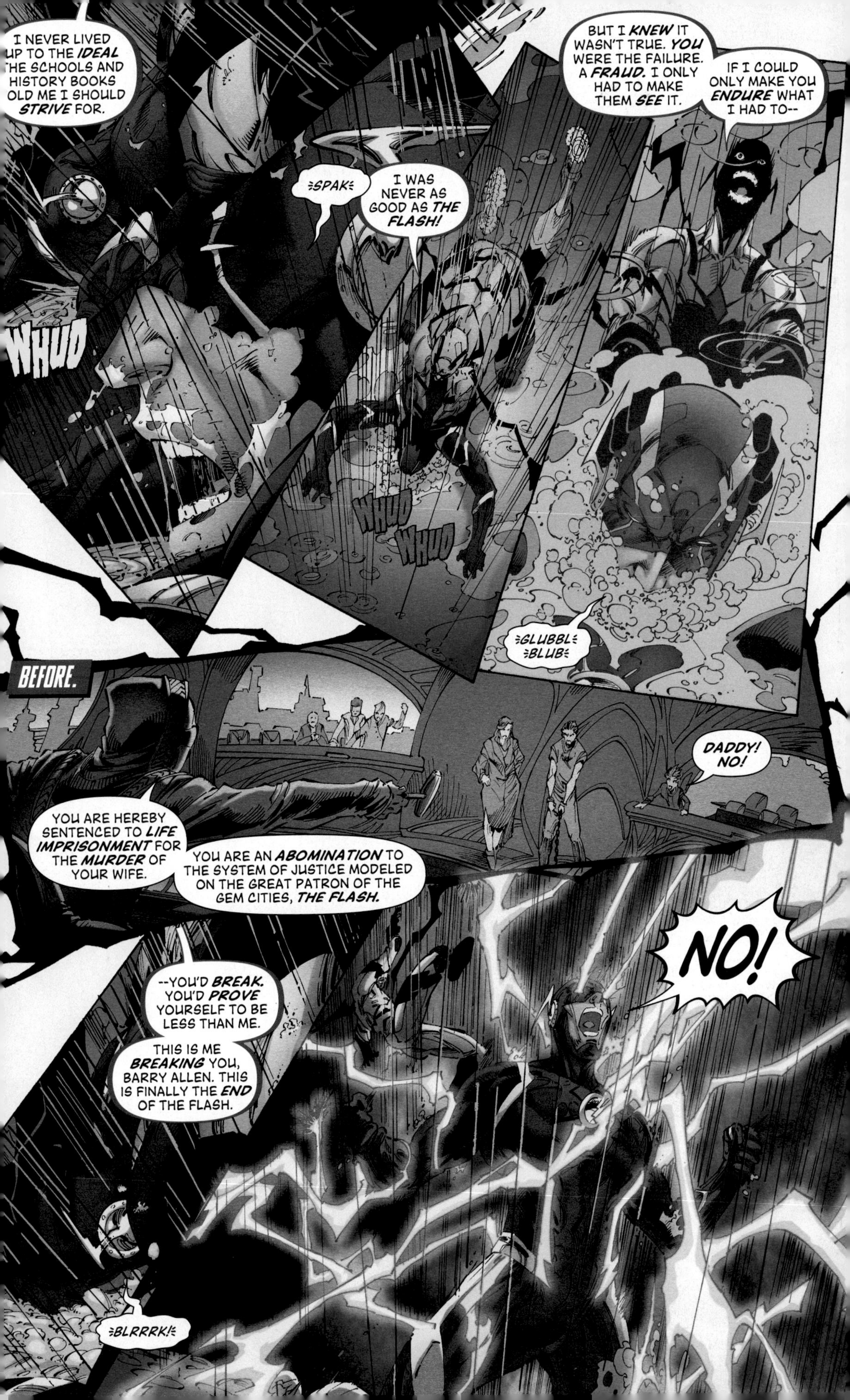

I NEVER LIVED UP TO THE IDEAL THE SCHOOLS AND HISTORY BOOKS OLD ME I SHOULD STRIVE FOR.
WHUD
SPAK
I WAS NEVER AS GOOD AS THE FLASH!
WHUD
WHUD
BUT I KNEW IT WASN'T TRUE. YOU WERE THE FAILURE. A FRAUD. I ONLY HAD TO MAKE THEM SEE IT.
IF I COULD ONLY MAKE YOU ENDURE WHAT I HAD TO--
GLUBBL BLUB
BEFORE.
YOU ARE HEREBY SENTENCED TO LIFE IMPRISONMENT FOR THE MURDER OF YOUR WIFE.
YOU ARE AN ABOMINATION TO THE SYSTEM OF JUSTICE MODELED ON THE GREAT PATRON OF THE GEM CITIES, THE FLASH.
DADDY! NO!
--YOU'D BREAK. YOU'D PROVE YOURSELF TO BE LESS THAN ME.
THIS IS ME BREAKING YOU, BARRY ALLEN. THIS IS FINALLY THE END OF THE FLASH.
NO!
BLRRRK!

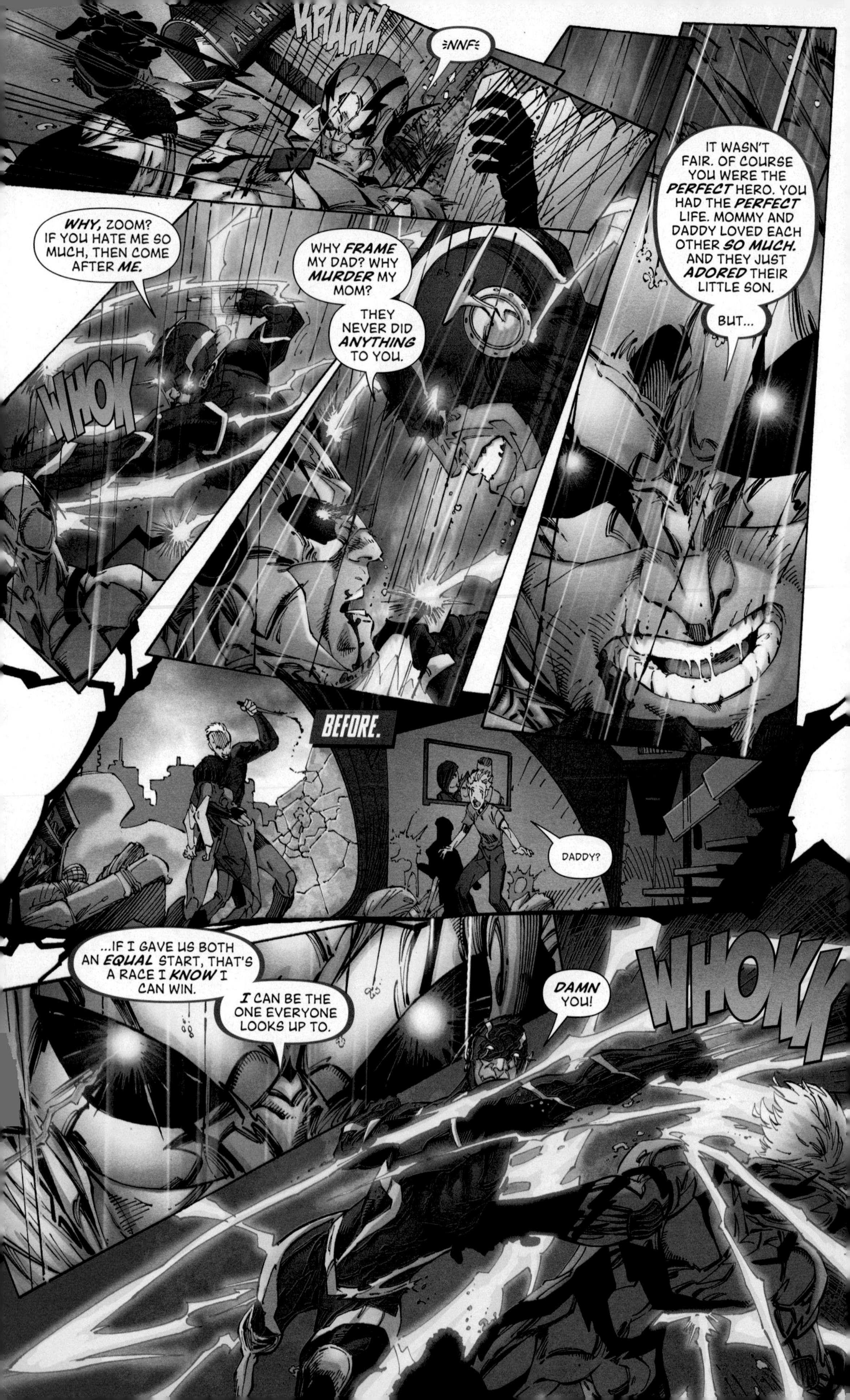
KRAKK
NNF
WHY, ZOOM? IF YOU HATE ME SO MUCH, THEN COME AFTER ME.
WHOK
WHY FRAME MY DAD? WHY MURDER MY MOM?
THEY NEVER DID ANYTHING TO YOU.
IT WASN'T FAIR. OF COURSE YOU WERE THE PERFECT HERO. YOU HAD THE PERFECT LIFE. MOMMY AND DADDY LOVED EACH OTHER SO MUCH. AND THEY JUST ADORED THEIR LITTLE SON.
BUT...
BEFORE.
DADDY?
...IF I GAVE US BOTH AN EQUAL START, THAT'S A RACE I KNOW I CAN WIN.
I CAN BE THE ONE EVERYONE LOOKS UP TO.
DAMN YOU!
WHOKK

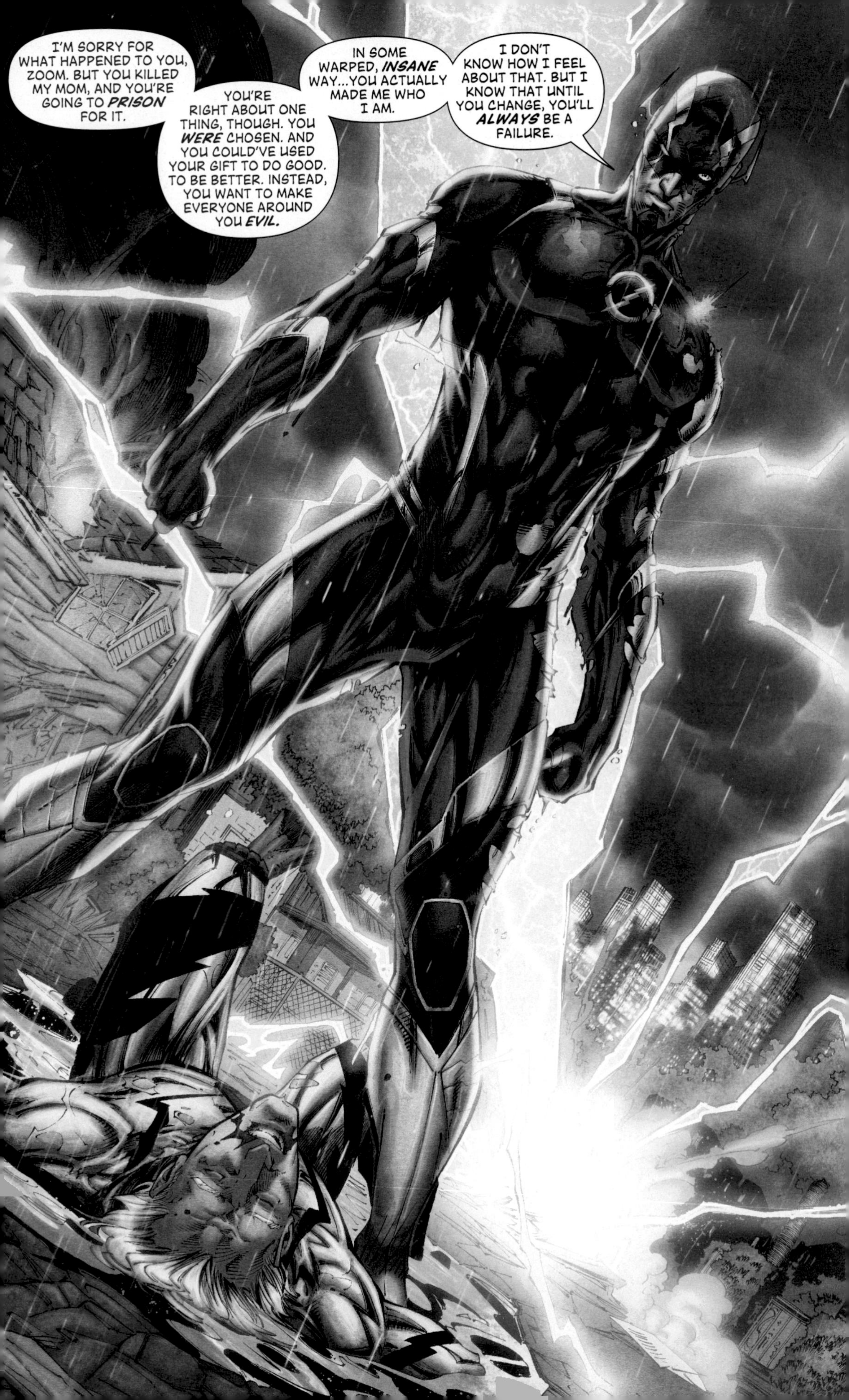
I'M SORRY FOR WHAT HAPPENED TO YOU, ZOOM. BUT YOU KILLED MY MOM, AND YOU'RE GOING TO *PRISON* FOR IT.
YOU'RE RIGHT ABOUT ONE THING, THOUGH. YOU *WERE* CHOSEN. AND YOU COULD'VE USED YOUR GIFT TO DO GOOD. TO BE BETTER. INSTEAD, YOU WANT TO MAKE EVERYONE AROUND YOU *EVIL.*
IN SOME WARPED, *INSANE* WAY...YOU ACTUALLY MADE ME WHO I AM.
I DON'T KNOW HOW I FEEL ABOUT THAT. BUT I KNOW THAT UNTIL YOU CHANGE, YOU'LL *ALWAYS* BE A FAILURE.

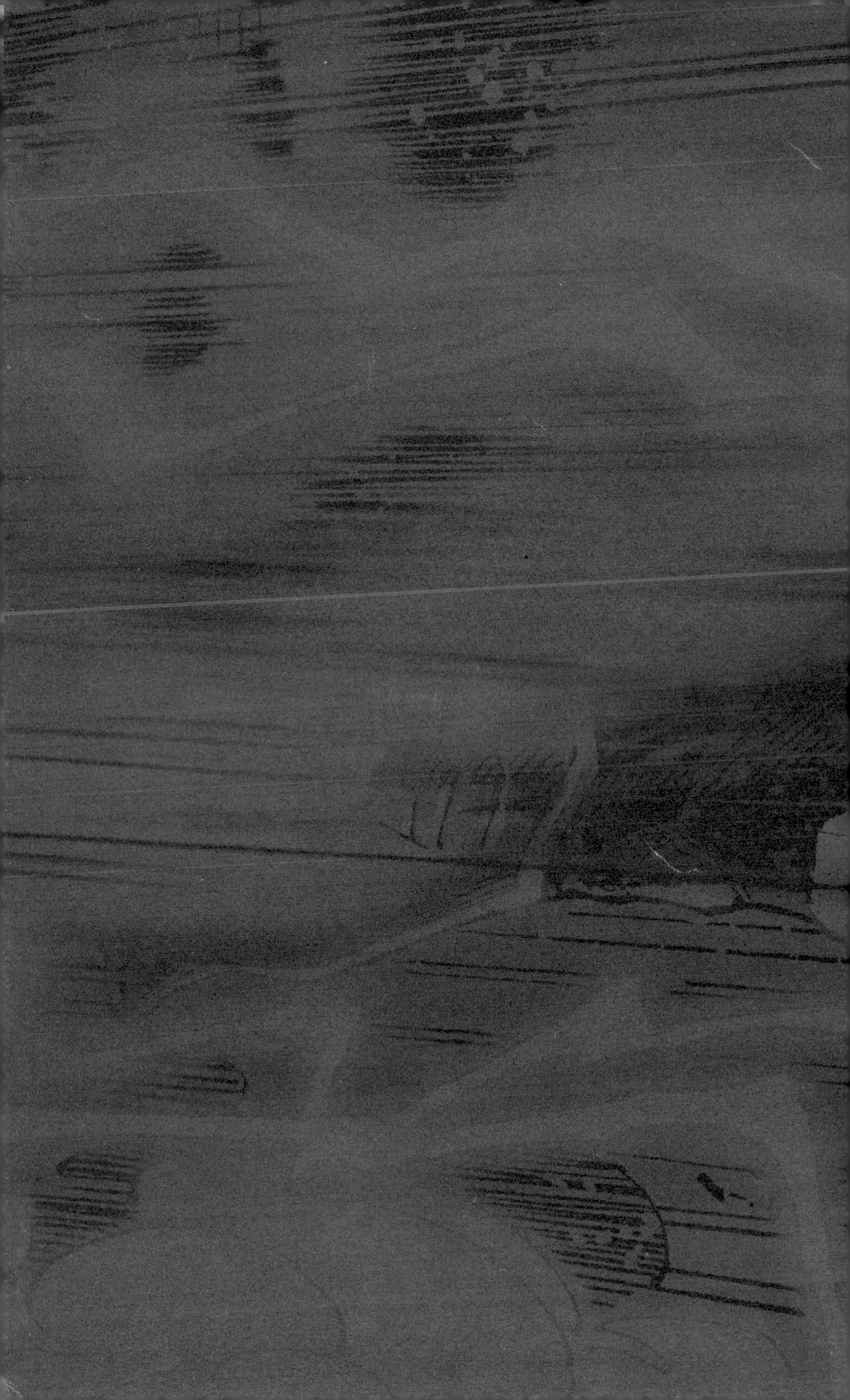

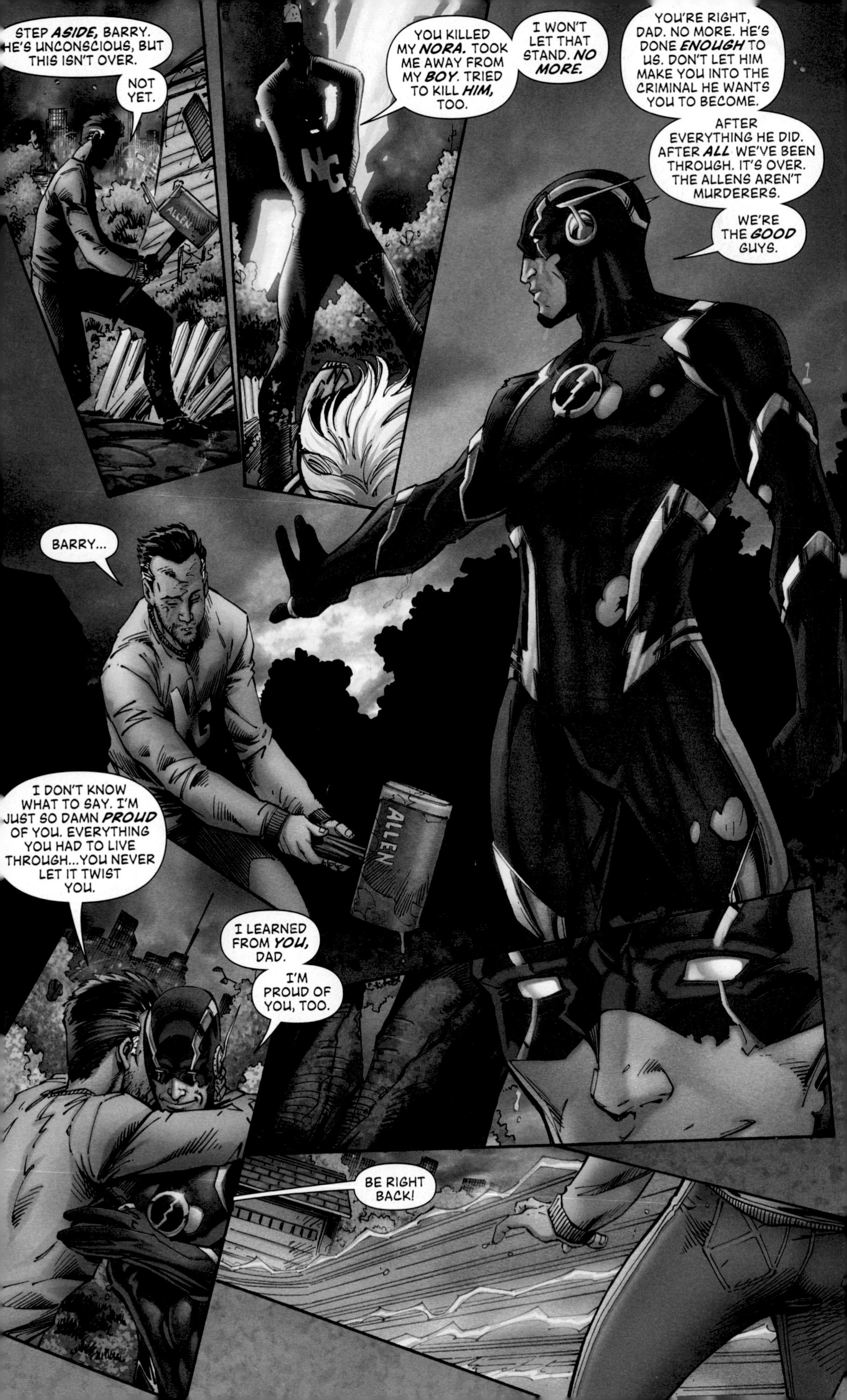
STEP ASIDE, BARRY. HE'S UNCONSCIOUS, BUT THIS ISN'T OVER.
NOT YET.
YOU KILLED MY NORA. TOOK ME AWAY FROM MY BOY. TRIED TO KILL HIM, TOO.
I WON'T LET THAT STAND. NO MORE.
YOU'RE RIGHT, DAD. NO MORE. HE'S DONE ENOUGH TO US. DON'T LET HIM MAKE YOU INTO THE CRIMINAL HE WANTS YOU TO BECOME.
AFTER EVERYTHING HE DID. AFTER ALL WE'VE BEEN THROUGH. IT'S OVER. THE ALLENS AREN'T MURDERERS.
WE'RE THE GOOD GUYS.
ALLEN
BARRY...
I DON'T KNOW WHAT TO SAY. I'M JUST SO DAMN PROUD OF YOU. EVERYTHING YOU HAD TO LIVE THROUGH...YOU NEVER LET IT TWIST YOU.
ALLEN
I LEARNED FROM YOU, DAD.
I'M PROUD OF YOU, TOO.
BE RIGHT BACK!

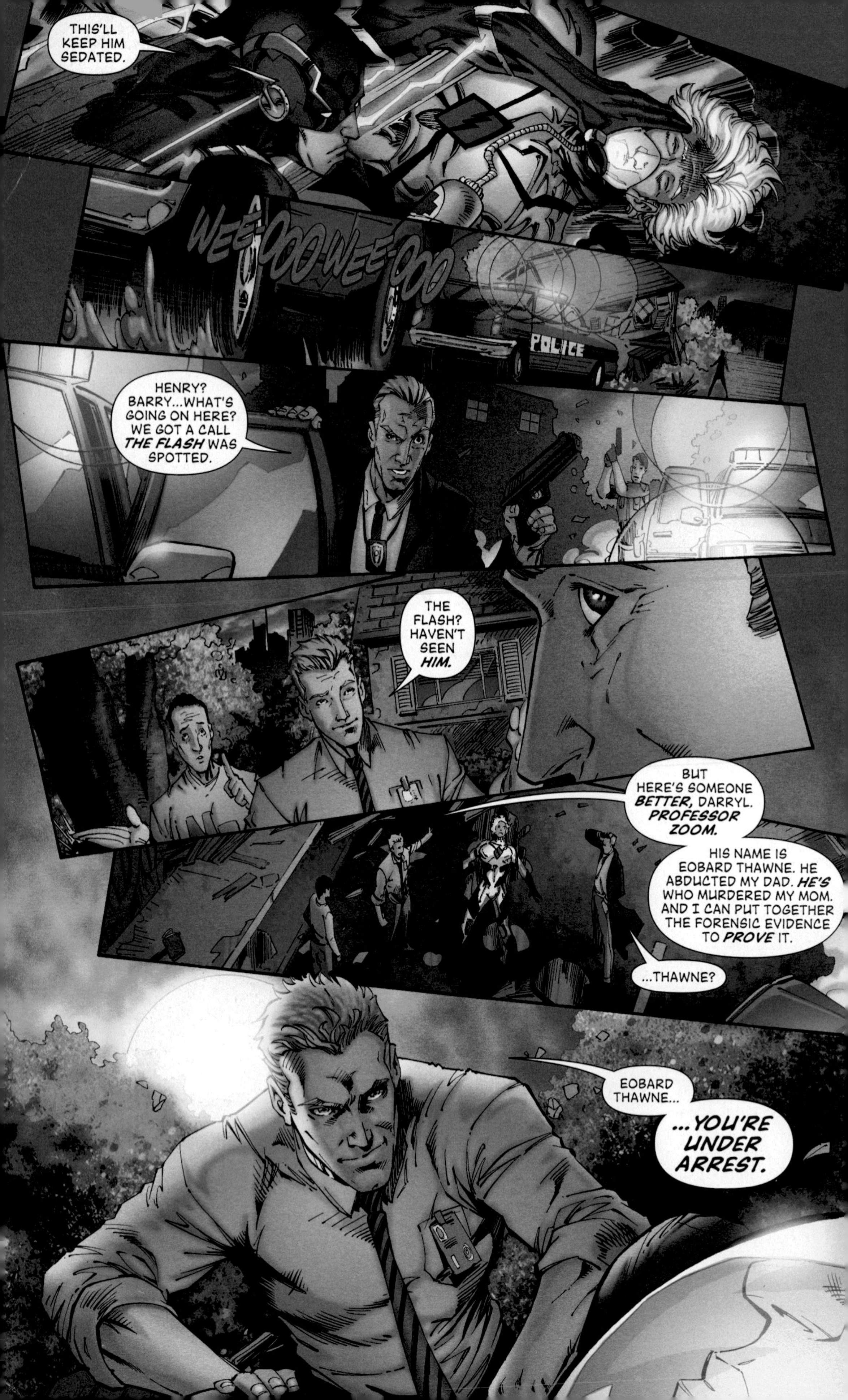

THIS'LL KEEP HIM SEDATED.
WEE-OOO-WEE-OOO
POLICE
HENRY? BARRY...WHAT'S GOING ON HERE? WE GOT A CALL THE FLASH WAS SPOTTED.
THE FLASH? HAVEN'T SEEN HIM.
BUT HERE'S SOMEONE BETTER, DARRYL. PROFESSOR ZOOM.
HIS NAME IS EOBARD THAWNE. HE ABDUCTED MY DAD. HE'S WHO MURDERED MY MOM. AND I CAN PUT TOGETHER THE FORENSIC EVIDENCE TO PROVE IT.
...THAWNE?
EOBARD THAWNE...
...YOU'RE UNDER ARREST.

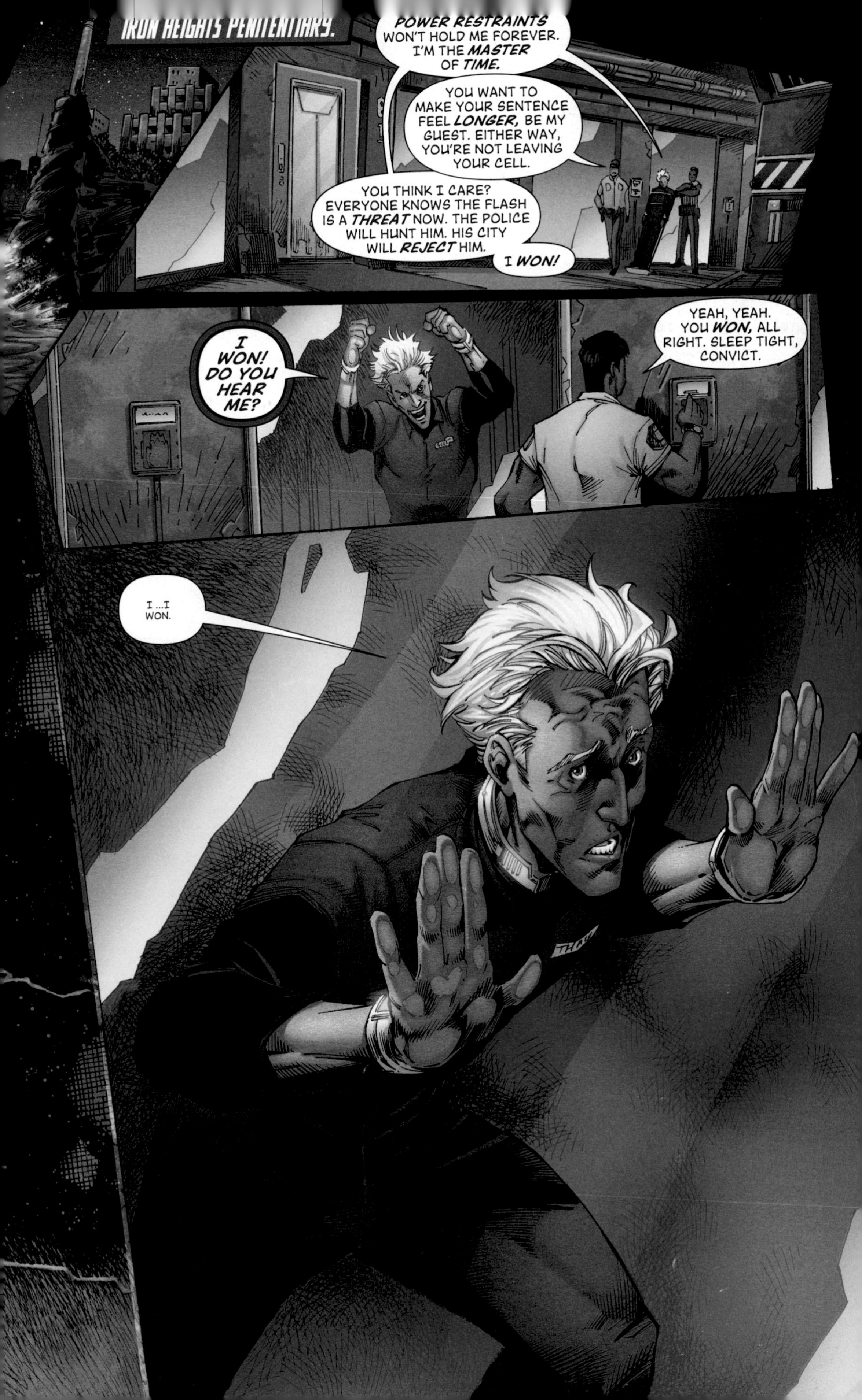
IRON HEIGHTS PENITENTIARY.
POWER RESTRAINTS WON'T HOLD ME FOREVER. I'M THE MASTER OF TIME.
YOU WANT TO MAKE YOUR SENTENCE FEEL LONGER, BE MY GUEST. EITHER WAY, YOU'RE NOT LEAVING YOUR CELL.
YOU THINK I CARE? EVERYONE KNOWS THE FLASH IS A THREAT NOW. THE POLICE WILL HUNT HIM. HIS CITY WILL REJECT HIM.
I WON!
I WON! DO YOU HEAR ME?
YEAH, YEAH. YOU WON, ALL RIGHT. SLEEP TIGHT, CONVICT.
I ...I WON.

VARIANT COVER GALLERY

THE FLASH #41
JOKER 75TH ANNIVERSARY
VARIANT BY EDDY BARROWS &
MARCELO MAIOLO

THE FLASH #42
TEEN TITANS GO!
VARIANT BY JORGE CORONA

THE FLASH #43
BOMBSHELLS
VARIANT BY ANT LUCIA

THE FLASH #44
GREEN LANTERN
75TH ANNIVERSARY
VARIANT BY WES CRAIG &
NATHAN FAIRBAIRN

THE FLASH #45
MONSTER VARIANT BY
GUSTAVO DUARTE

THE FLASH #46
LOONEY TUNES VARIANT BY
FRANCIS MANAPUL &
SPIKE BRANDT

THE FLASH #47
HARLEY'S LITTLE BLACK BOOK
VARIANT BY TERRY DODSON &
RACHEL DODSON

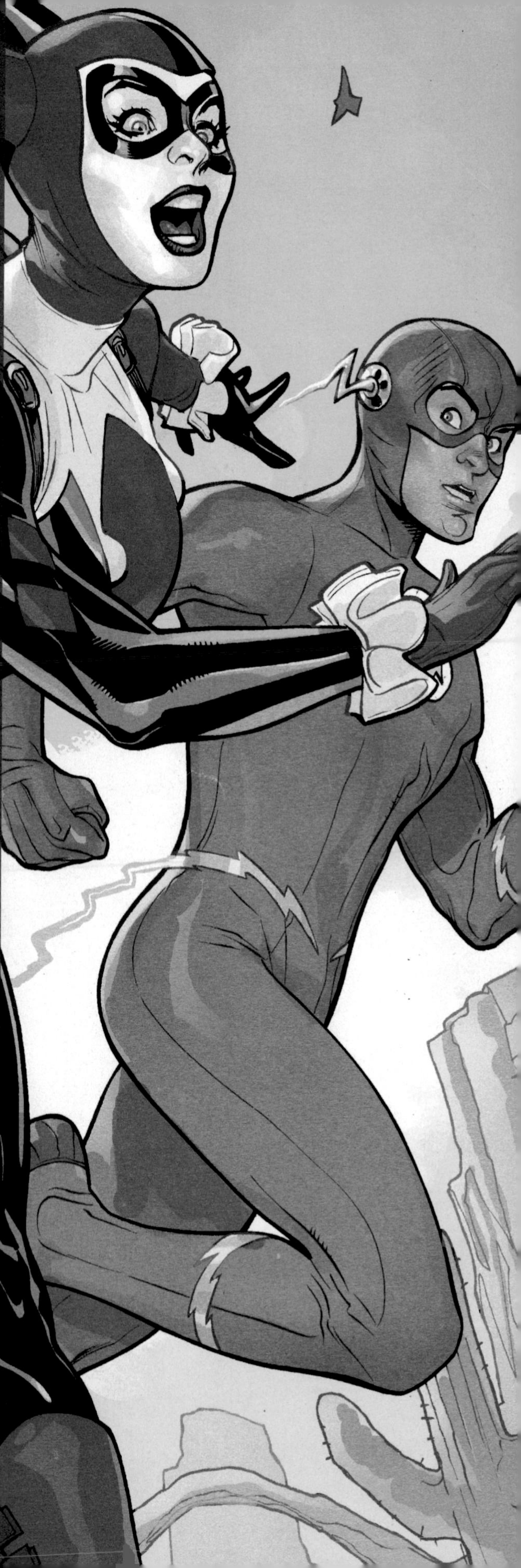

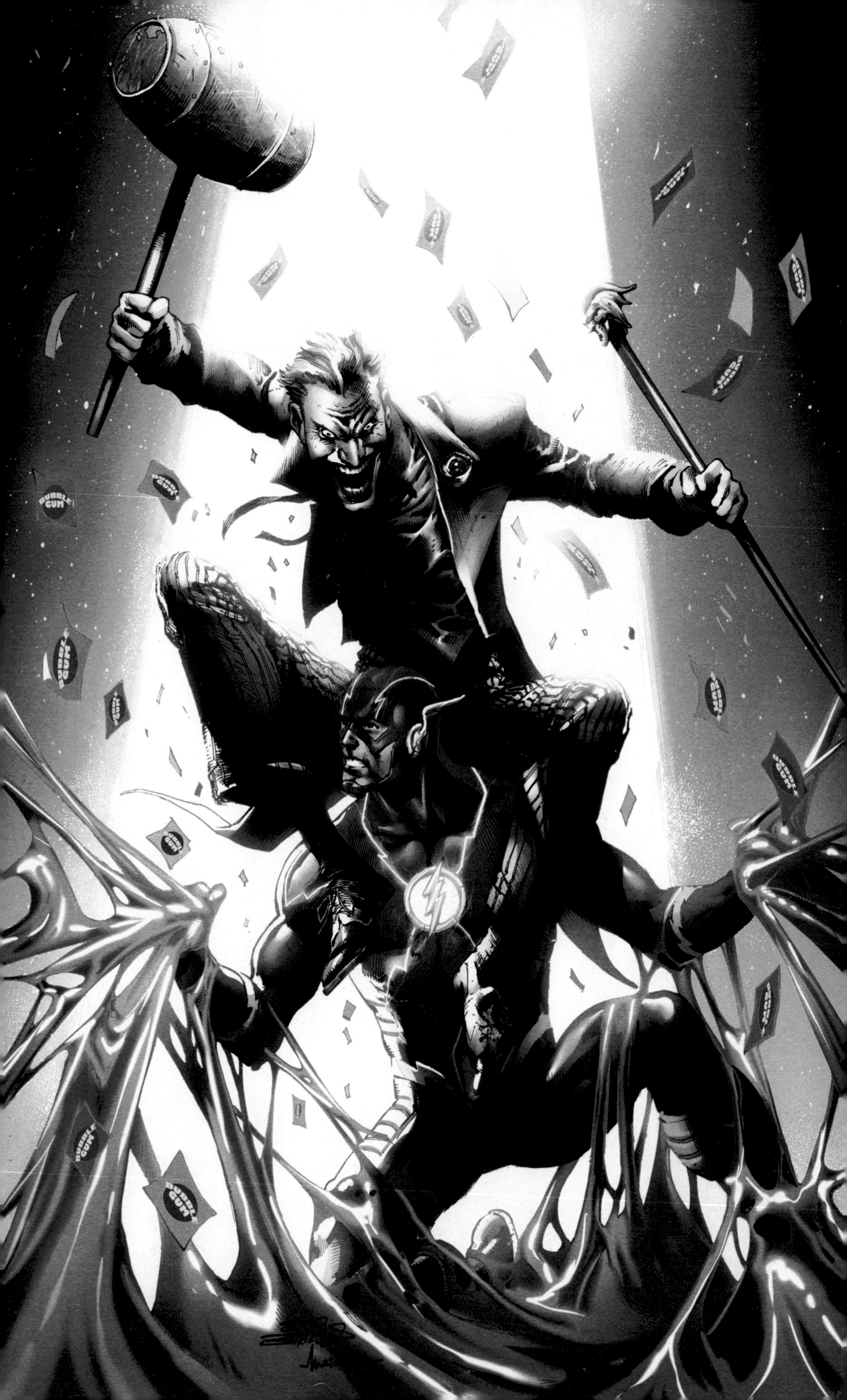
BUBBLE GUM
BUBBLE GUM
BUBBLE GUM
BUBBLE GUM

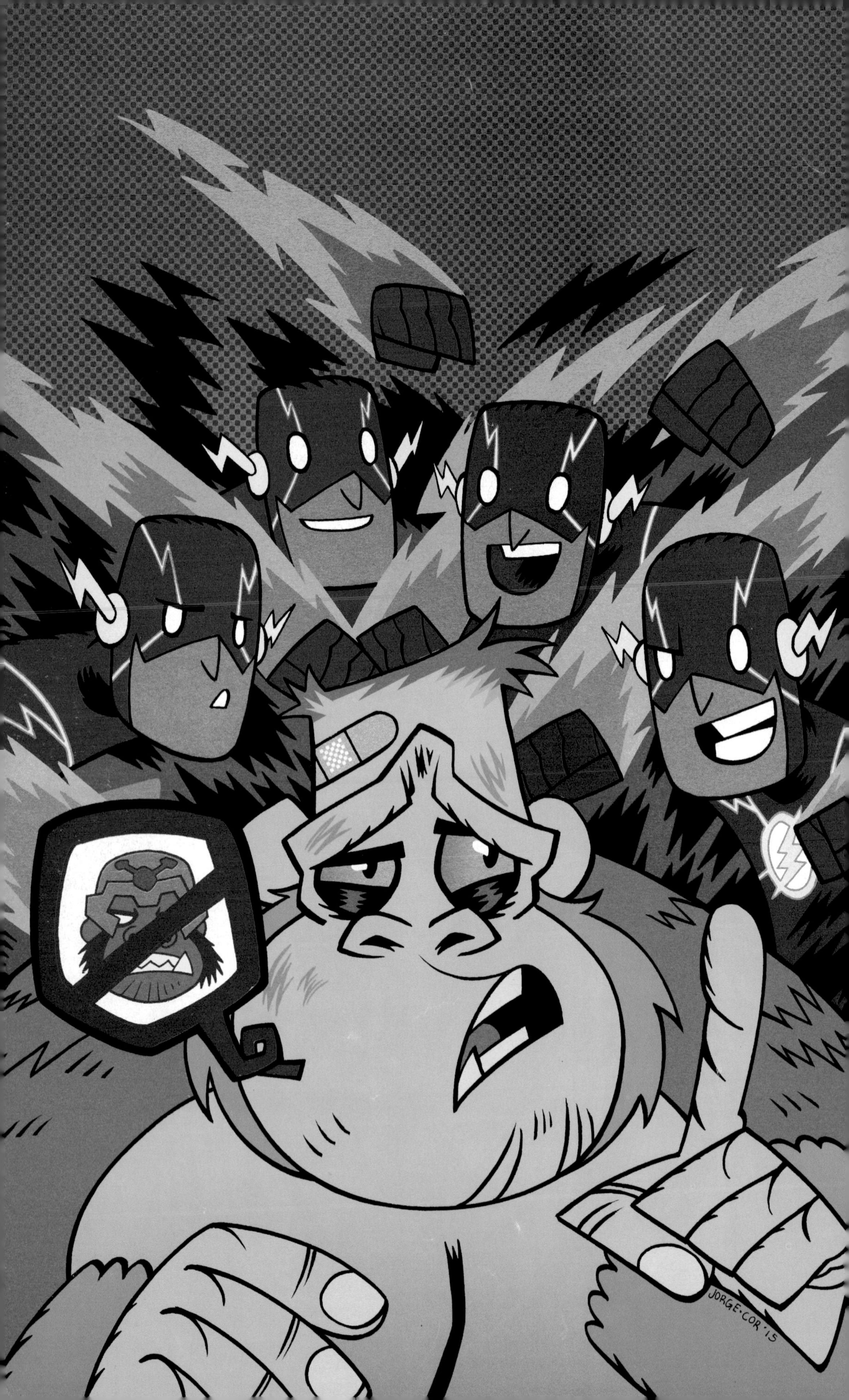
JORGE·COR '15

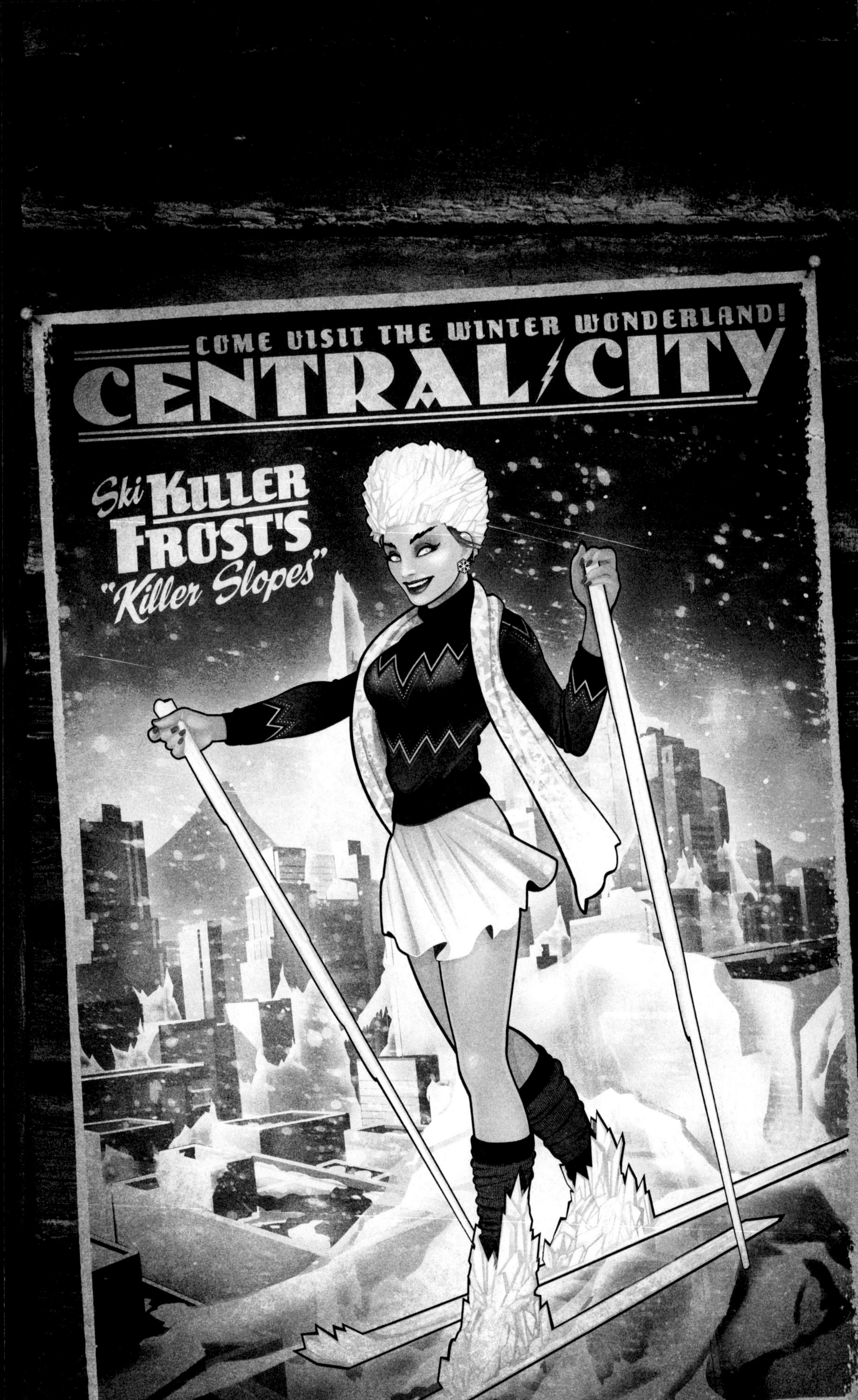
COME VISIT THE WINTER WONDERLAND!
CENTRAL CITY
Ski KILLER FROST'S
"Killer Slopes"

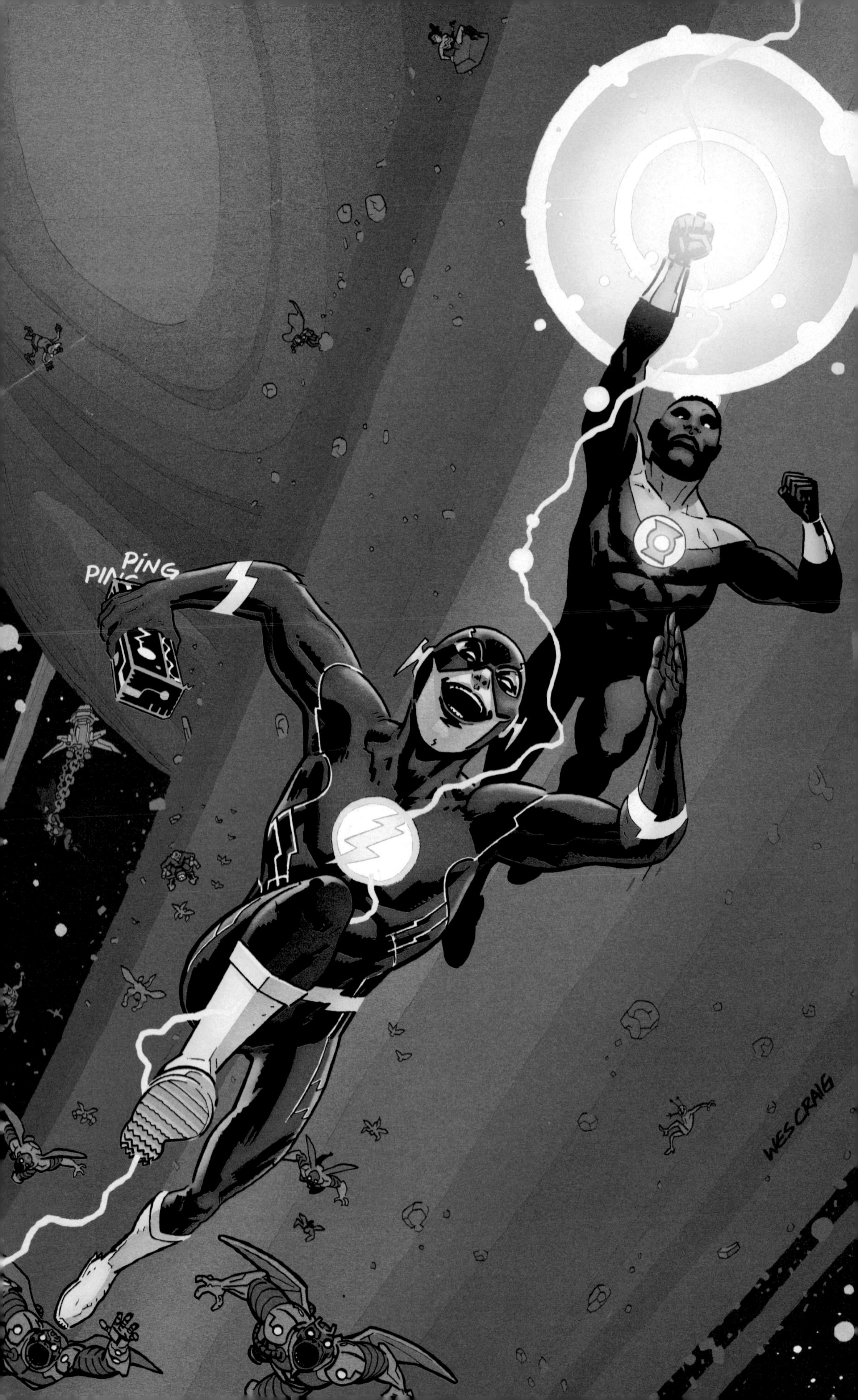
PING
PING
WES CRAIG

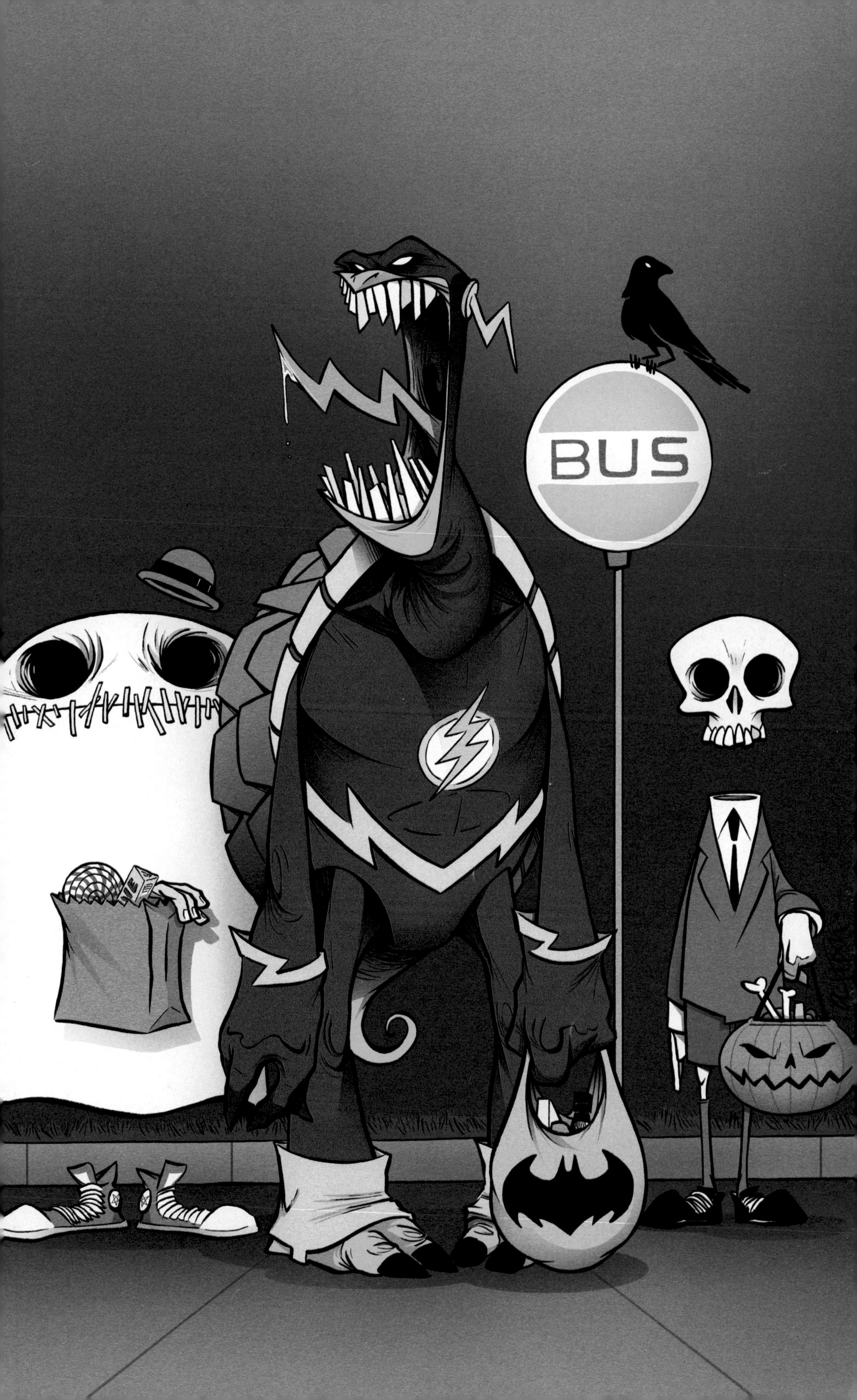
BUS

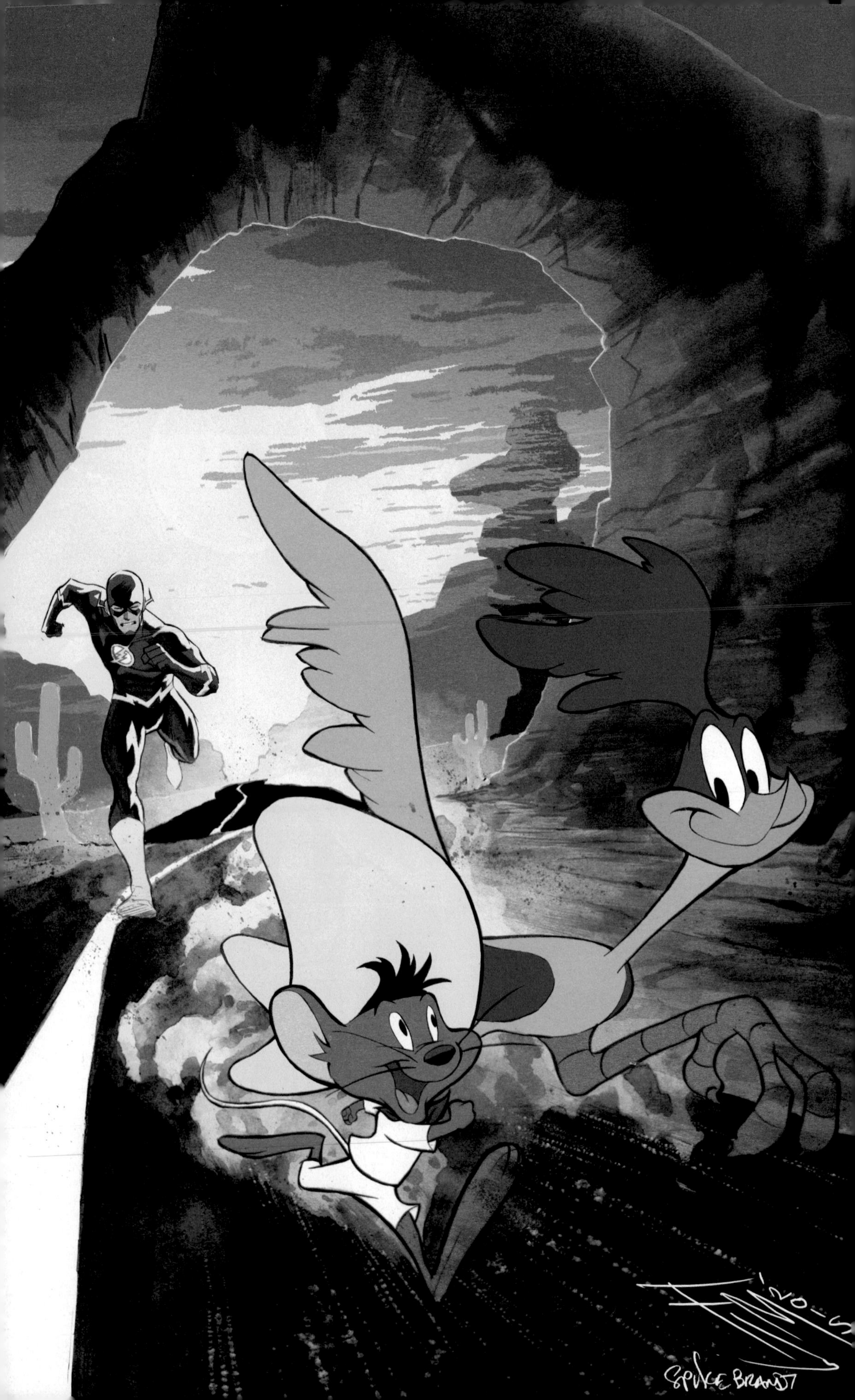
SPIKE BRANDT

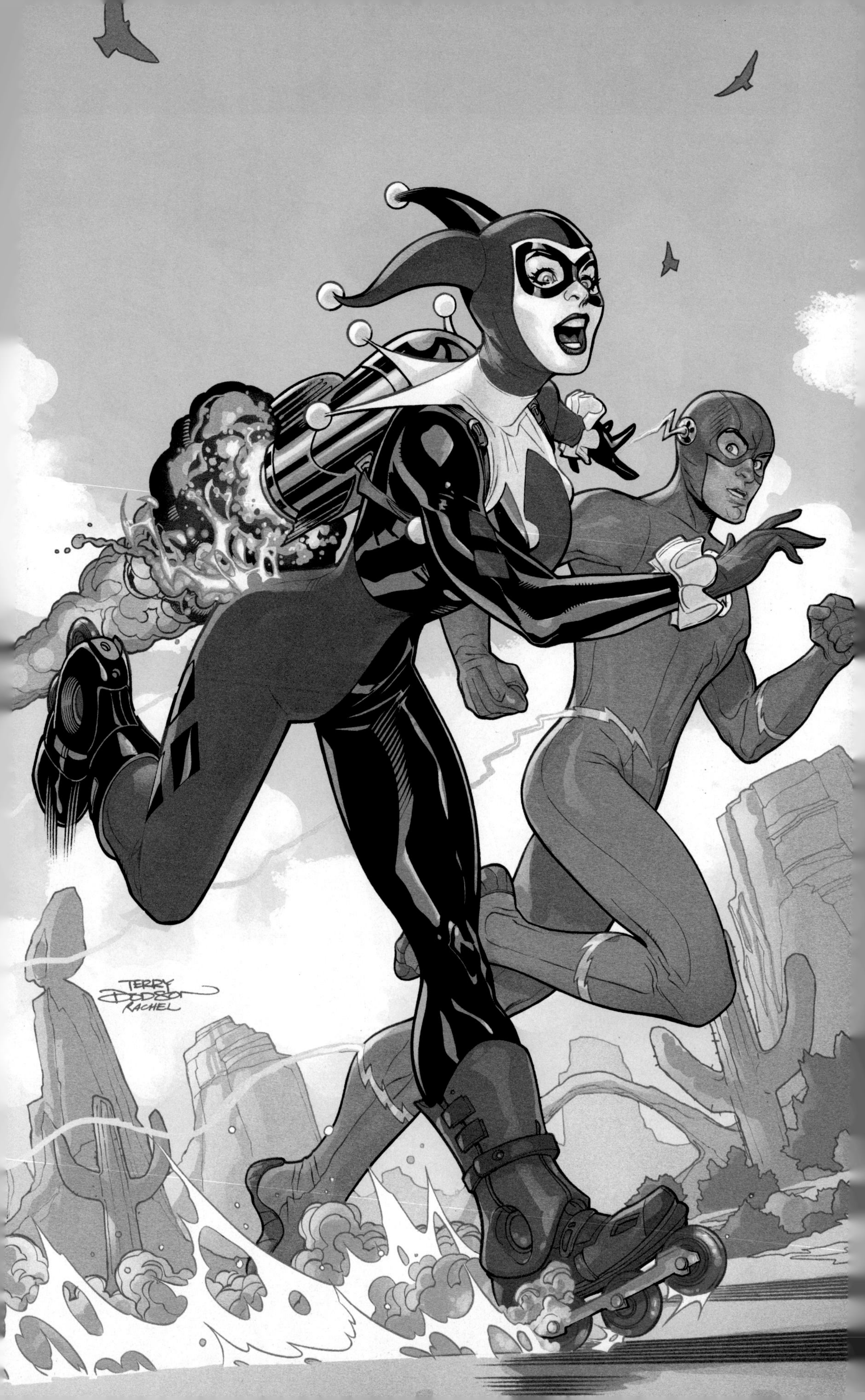
TERRY DODSON RACHEL

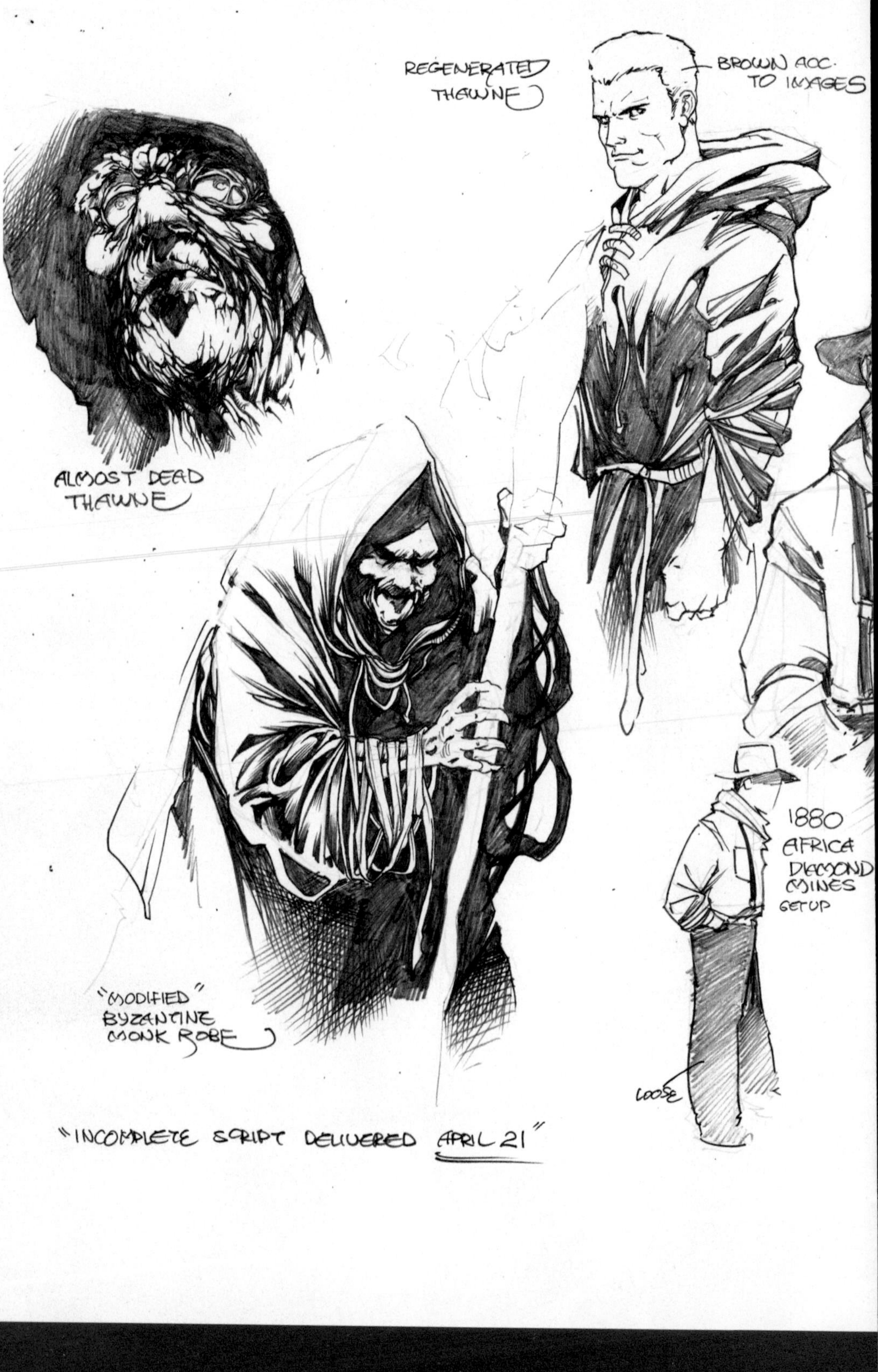

REGENERATED THAWNE
BROWN ACC. TO IMAGES
ALMOST DEAD THAWNE
"MODIFIED" BYZANTINE MONK ROBE
1880 AFRICA DIAMOND MINES GETUP
LOOSE
"INCOMPLETE SCRIPT DELIVERED APRIL 21"

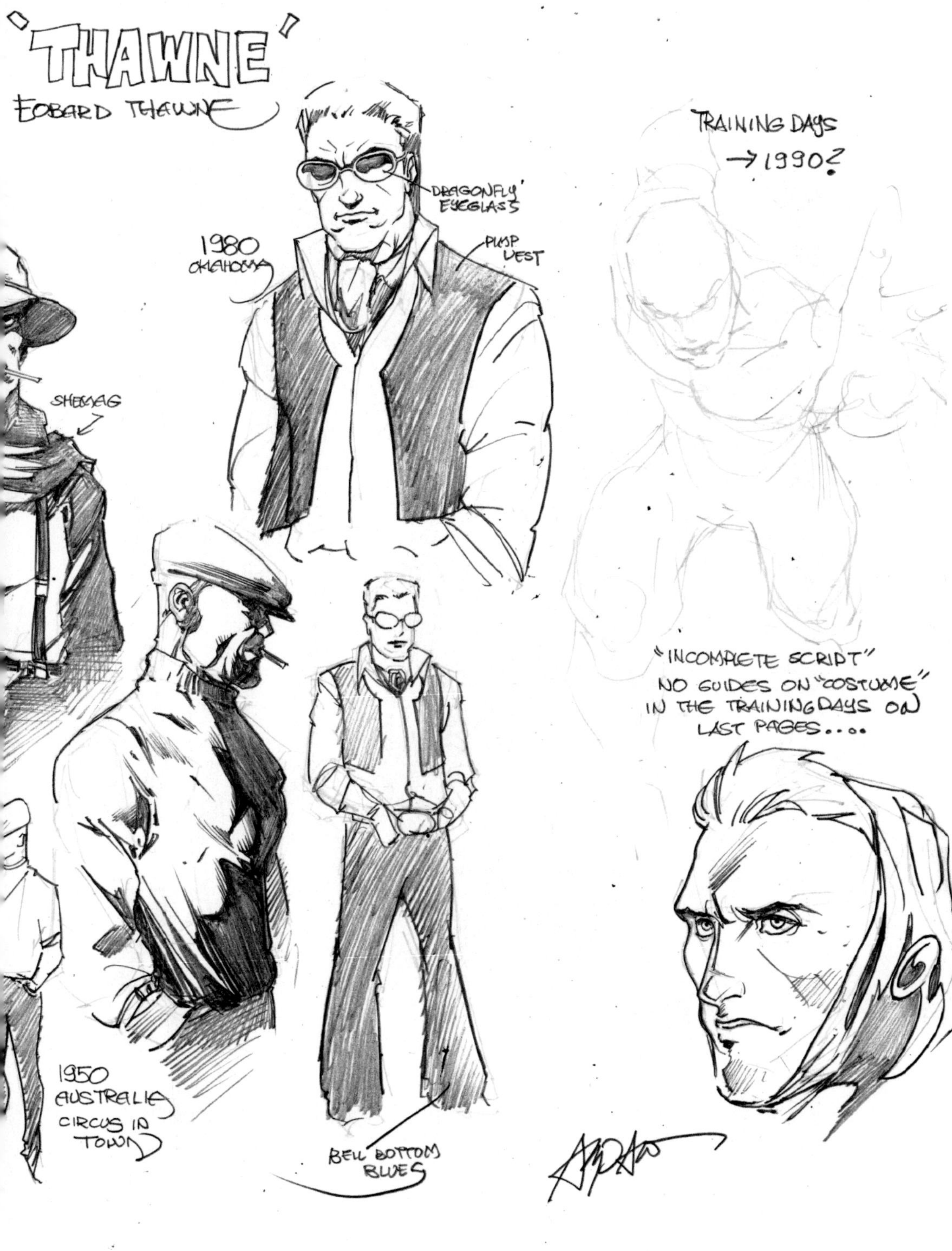

'THAWNE'
EOBARD THAWNE
DRAGONFLY' EYEGLASS
1980 OKLAHOMA
PIMP VEST
TRAINING DAYS
→1990?
SHEMAG
"INCOMPLETE SCRIPT"
NO GUIDES ON "COSTUME"
IN THE TRAININGDAYS ON
LAST PAGES....
1950
AUSTRALIA
CIRCUS IN
TOWN
BELL BOTTOM
BLUES

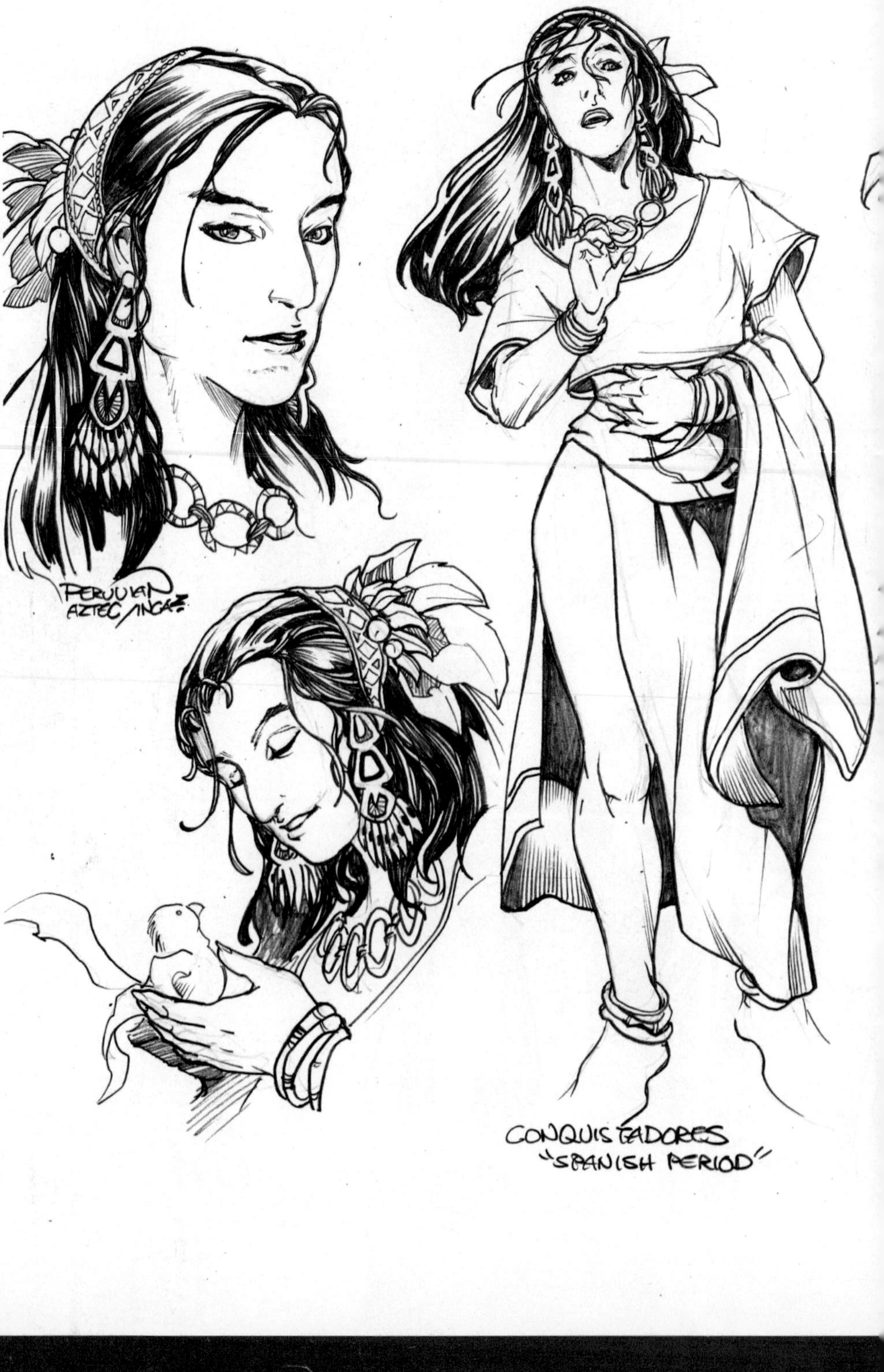
PERUVIAN
AZTEC/INCA
CONQUISTADORES
"SPANISH PERIOD"

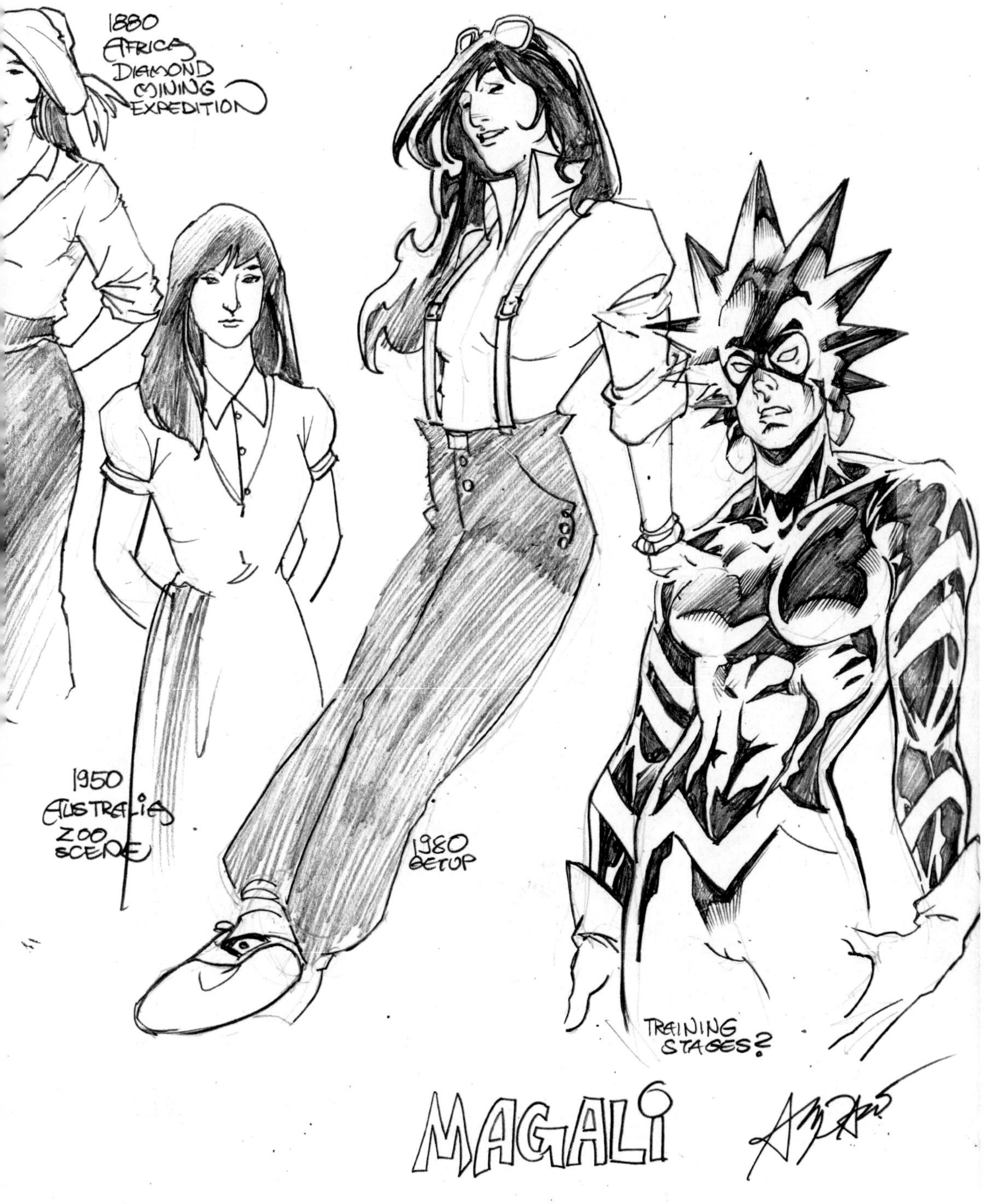
1880
AFRICA
DIAMOND
MINING
EXPEDITION
1950
AUSTRALIA
ZOO
SCENE
1980
GETUP
TRAINING
STAGES?
MAGALI

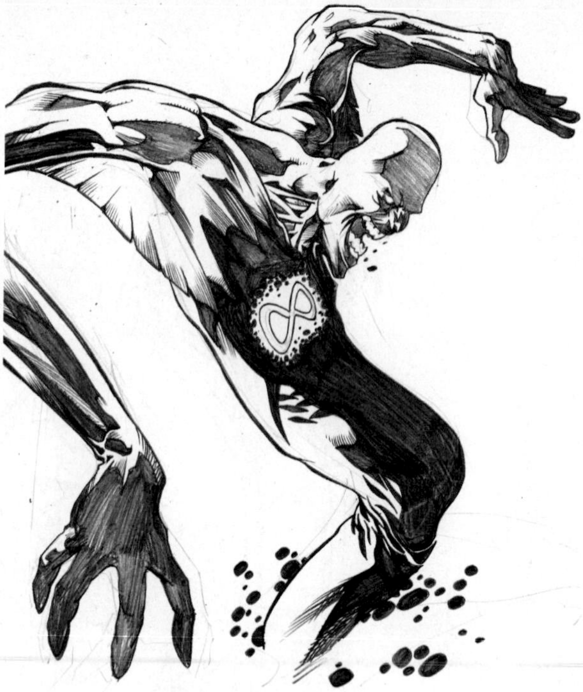

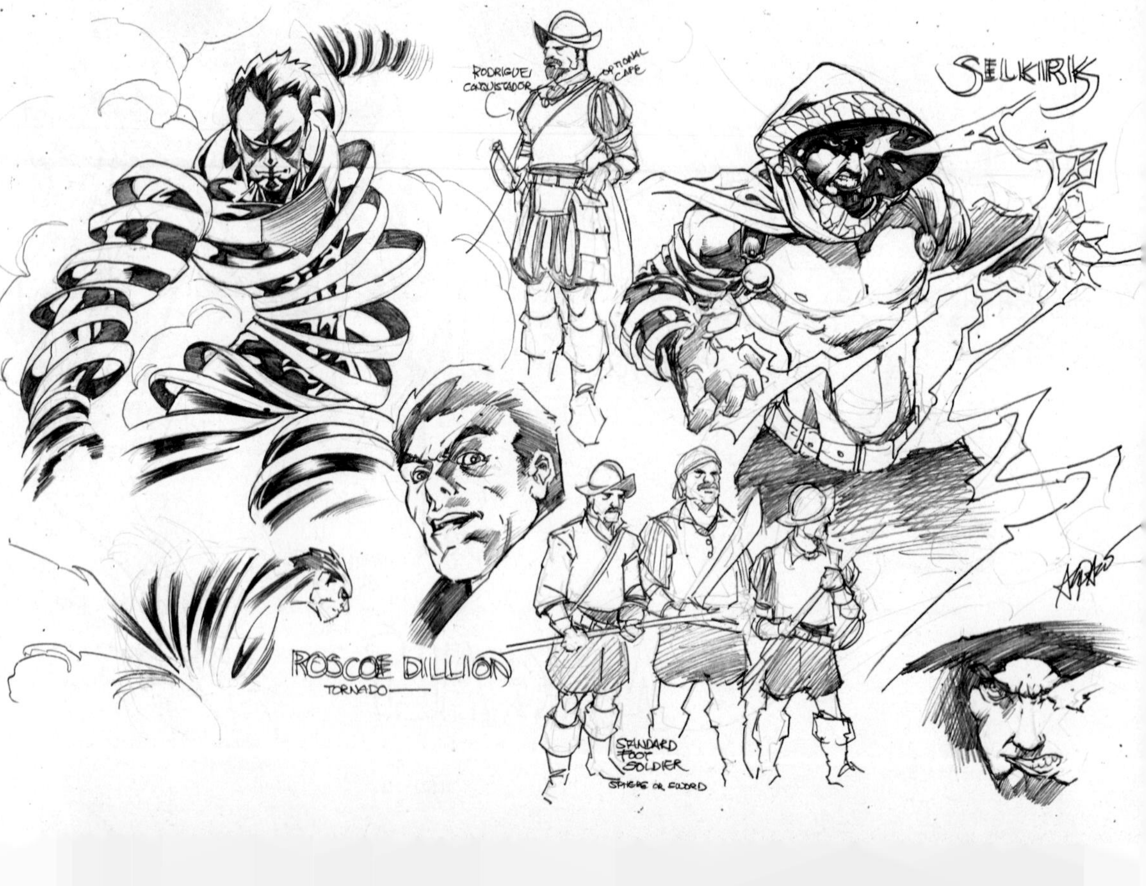
RODRIGUEZ
CONQUISTADOR
OPTIONAL CAPE
SELKIRK
ROSCOE DILLION
TORNADO
STANDARD FOOT SOLDIER